Memoirs of a Dutch Mudsill

~

Memoirs of a Dutch Mudsill

THE "WAR MEMORIES" OF

JOHN HENRY OTTO,

CAPTAIN, COMPANY D,

21ST REGIMENT

WISCONSIN VOLUNTEER

INFANTRY

Edited by David Gould

and James B. Kennedy

THE KENT STATE UNIVERSITY PRESS
Kent and London

Frontispiece: Head and shoulders portrait believed to be that of
John Henry Otto of the 21st Wisconsin Infantry, Company D.
(Courtesy State Historical Society of Wisconsin)

© 2004 by The Kent State University Press, Kent, Ohio 44242
All rights reserved
Library of Congress Catalog Card Number 2004001312
ISBN 0-87338-799-6
Manufactured in the United States of America

08   07   06   05   04   5   4   3   2   1

Library of Congress Cataloging-in-Publication Data
Otto, John Henry, 1822–1908.
Memoirs of a Dutch mudsill : the "war memories" of John Henry Otto, Captain, Company D,
21st Regiment Wisconsin Volunteer Infantry / edited by David Gould and James B. Kennedy.
p.   cm.
Includes bibliographical references and index.
ISBN 0-87338-799-6 (alk. paper) ∞
1. Otto, John Henry, 1822–1908.
2. United States. Army. Wisconsin Infantry Regiment, 21st (1862–1865)
3. Wisconsin—History—Civil War, 1861–1865—Personal narratives.
4. United States—History—Civil War, 1861–1865—Personal narratives.
5. United States—History—Civil War, 1861–1865—Campaigns.
6. United States—History—Civil War, 1861–1865—Participation, German American.
7. Soldiers—Wisconsin—Biography.
8. German Americans—Wisconsin—Biography.
I. Gould, David, 1952– II. Kennedy, James B., 1932– III. Title.
E537.521st .O88   2004
973.7'475'092—dc22   2004001312

British Library Cataloging-in-Publication data are available.

Contents

❧

Acknowledgments   vii

Introduction   ix

1. The Organization of Company D, 21st Regiment
of Wisconsin Volunteer Infantry   1

2. Preparing for Actual Warfare   14

3. Progress and Incidents of Our First Campaign   29

4. The Battle of Perryville, or Chaplin Hills   42

5. In Which We Chase Bragg Again,
Which Amounts to Nothing   53

6. The Battle of Stone River, or Murfreesboro   76

7. About Our "Coozie" Winter Quarters, Light Duty,
and Our Bully Picnic in General   100

8. Expedition into East Tennessee   117

9. The Tullahoma Campaign   134

10. The Chickamauga Campaign   153

11. The Battle of Chickamauga, Georgia   168

12. Chattanooga: Battles of Lookout Mountain
and Missionary Ridge   189

13. Preparation for the Atlanta Campaign   224

14. The Battle of Resaca: Tedious Skirmishing
and Final Advance   240

15. Advance on Atlanta   261

16. The Army Found Again. Savannah.
A Valuable Christmas Present   285

17. Facing Northward: Averysboro.
The Battle at Bentonville   323

18. Washington. The Great Parade   362

Notes   378

Bibliography   411

Index   417

Acknowledgments

~

~ It is not unusual for an undertaking of this magnitude to be carried out collaboratively; however, this collaboration was unusual in that two individuals, thousands of miles apart, who had both undertaken the same project independently, agreed to cooperate and combine their efforts in a joint project. This collaboration endured through nine years, two publishers, six revisions, and three moves. The editors would like to publicly thank each other for the patience and forbearance that made this possible. We are also deeply indebted to numerous individuals and organizations that provided their time, resources, and able assistance. Without their help and encouragement this project would have been an impossible task.

We are greatly obligated to the staff at the State Historical Society of Wisconsin. Attempting to investigate the enormous amount of materials held at the society was a daunting prospect. The archivists' helpful manner, expertise, and repeated guidance are deeply appreciated. We would like to thank the following individuals: Harold L. Miller, archives division, for his personal interest and encouragement and for allowing access to the society's collections; Gerry Strey, archives division, for her expertise regarding Wisconsin and Civil War maps; James Hansen, genealogy division, whose guidance through the genealogical maze was invaluable; Paul Hass, editorial division, for his helpful suggestions in reviewing original materials; Andy Kraushaar, visual materials archive, for his assistance and expertise in photographic materials; Richard L. Pifer, collections and development division, for making us aware of newly acquired materials; Joel W. Heiman, division viii

of public history, for his expertise in cartography; and Lisa Hinzman, image reproduction business manager, for her assistance with pictures and permissions. We are also deeply grateful for the assistance of many unnamed society members.

We would like to thank Carol J. Butts, Lawrence University, Appleton, Wisconsin, for her help in identifying individual soldiers; and Richard H. Sewell, University of Wisconsin, for his valuable time, suggestions, and advice on publication. We would like to express a special thank you to Brett Barker, University of Wisconsin. His encouragement, expertise, and enthusiasm for Civil War history helped make this all possible.

No manuscript of this nature can be completed without the able assistance of other institutions. Thanks must be extended to Michael Musick, Stuart L. Butler, Gary L. Morgan, and the staff at the National Archives Military Reference Branch. Their help with soldiers' records and court-martial records was invaluable. Richard Sommers and the staff at the U. S. Army Military History Institute were most helpful in assisting with the identification of individual soldiers and soldiers' photographs. Linda Middlestadt and Scott Cross, archivists at the Oshkosh Public Museum, provided valuable help with and information about visual images. James Ogden, National Parks Service, Fort Oglethorpe, Chickamauga National Battlefield Park, provided helpful insights on the Battle of Chickamauga. Sue Fuller at the National Park Service Andersonville Historic Site provided valuable help with identifying soldiers imprisoned there. Stuart W. Sanders, director of the Perryville Battlefield Preservation Association, provided help in understanding the fighting at Perryville. The assistance of Mary Devitt, Henry Geitz, and the staff at the Max Kade Institute for German-American Studies in interpreting original German language documents was invaluable.

Introduction

⮑

⮑ John Henry Otto was my great-grandfather. He was born September 12, 1822, in Westphalia, Germany, and enrolled in the Prussian army in the fortress of Luxembourg sometime around 1845. According to his own account he served in the war between Prussia and Denmark in 1848, and in 1849 in the suppression of the revolution in southern Germany, he fought as a sergeant under the command of Prince William of Prussia (later emperor of Germany). After the revolution he applied for admission into the Cadet's College to prepare for the examination for commissioning as an officer, was accepted, and ultimately passed the examinations. After the examinations his three-year term of service expired, and he took his discharge with the rank of first lieutenant in the reserve. Shortly afterward, in 1850, Prussia declared war against Austria, Bavaria, and Hesse, and Lieutenant Otto was called into the service for another two years. Although by this time he was in command of a company, he had no desire to spend his life as a soldier, and being unable to ascertain when he would be discharged, he deserted the Prussian army. He went first to Holland, then across the North Sea to England, and finally to New York in 1853, "glad," he says, "to find a country where the Army is subject to the Civil Authority." He moved to Wisconsin the following year and settled in Appleton, where he engaged in the cabinetmaking business. Family tradition has it that he first met his wife when he saw her working barefoot in a field and gave her his boots.

By the time the Civil War broke out he was married, had five small children, and was almost forty years old. Nevertheless, in August 1862 he enlisted in the Union army and served until the close of the war, starting as third sergeant and ending as a captain, commanding his company. He led his company from the Battle of Chickamauga, September 19–20, 1863, until it was disbanded on June 8, 1865. He was engaged in many of the major battles and campaigns in the West, including the battles of Perryville and Stone's River; the Tullahoma campaign; the battles of Chickamauga, Lookout Mountain, and Missionary Ridge; and Sherman's march through Georgia and the Carolinas.

After the war John Henry and his wife had three more children, making a total of eight, of whom my grandfather George Myers Otto, born in 1871, was the last. From his pension records and an autobiographical fragment found among my grandfather's papers, I have been able to piece together something of John Henry's history after his discharge. According to my grandfather he returned from the war to find that his partner had sold their cabinet business and spent the proceeds; as the partner was now without resources John Henry was unable to recover anything from him. He bought a half-interest in a hardware store with a tin shop connected to it that manufactured pans; pails; coffeepots; tea kettles; cake, pie, and bread tins; sheet iron stoves and stovepipes; bathtubs; and tin roofing squares. This business prospered, but John Henry felt out of his element; he sold out to his partner and went back into the cabinetmaking business.

Before the war cabinetmaking in Appleton had all been handwork, but by this time it was being done by machine. John Henry located a sash, door, and blind factory that had gone out of business, and in partnership with several friends he opened a firm to manufacture furniture, window sashes, doors, and blinds, as well as to supply all sorts of lumber required for building. His friends, who were expert woodworkers, were to have charge of the manufacturing, and John Henry, who was already partly disabled by rheumatism, was to be in charge of the office and all business matters. However, John Henry was once again unfortunate in his choice of partners, who failed to keep their end of the bargain; the business failed after he had sunk all his capital into it.

In 1868 John Henry obtained the job of assistant postmaster at Appleton from his friend George Meyers, a county court judge who had been given the postmastership as a political favor. Unable because of his responsibilities as a judge to perform the duties of postmaster, he appointed John Henry as his assistant and left him in charge. John Henry held this job until 1874. In gratitude he named my grandfather after George Meyers.

At this point my grandfather's account breaks off, and the only further information I have about John Henry's postwar career is a "Claimant's Statement" attached to his pension application, dated July 30, 1884:

> From discharge until 1867 I worked in a hardware store at Appleton Wis. Then I went into the sash door and blind business at Appleton Wis. Sold out spring of 1868. Worked at carpenter business that summer. In the fall was appointed Asst. Post Master at Appleton Wis. Geo. H. Meyers now Circuit Judge was Post Master. I was in the Post Office until 1874—then I was Notary Public and Insurance agent at Appleton until the fall of 1877 when I moved here to Vesper where I have since resided. I have been engaged in farming and carpentering since I have been here.[1]

John Henry applied for an invalid's pension on April 20, 1881, for the rheumatism he contracted during the march from Savannah, Georgia, to Washington, D.C., January–June 1865. His claim was rejected on August 8, 1883, but after obtaining statements from more than twenty-five friends and neighbors, many of whom had been soldiers in his company during the war, he finally on March 1, 1885, was granted a pension of fifteen dollars a month for "rheumatism in legs and small of back." Several times he filed for an increase in his pension, due to "rheumatism and resultant disease of the heart," to which was later added "general debility."[2] In 1889 he moved to Grand Rapids, now Wisconsin Rapids, where he died January 20, 1908, at the age of eighty-six, of "congestion of the lungs." He is buried in Forrest Hill Cemetery in Wisconsin Rapids.[3]

John Henry kept a journal throughout the war. After the war he arranged his reminiscences in the form of a book, which he completed around 1890. He made two copies of his manuscript, one for each of his two sons, August C. Otto and my grandfather, George Myers Otto—writing it out twice in longhand so that neither son would have to settle for a carbon copy (but making no provision for his six daughters). My grandfather's copy of the manuscript was burned in a house fire in 1932. The other manuscript still survives; it was donated to the State Historical Society of Wisconsin in 1953 by Carl Otto and can be found in the archives division. The thirty-one exercise books, each measuring six and three-quarters by eight inches and containing one hundred pages, are in the autograph of the author, which is very clear and legible. The manuscript is written on the right-hand pages only, with occasional notes on the left-hand pages. The notebooks are still in good condition, although the paper is brittle, and the ink has faded in places.

While preparing this text for publication I discovered that James B. Kennedy of the Wisconsin Historical Society had already devoted several years to research on the manuscript; we agreed to collaborate on the project, and this volume is the result of our collaboration. I have taken responsibility for the editing of the manuscript, and Kennedy has provided most of the notes.

This edition of John Henry Otto's memoirs has been prepared from the original manuscript; however, the memoirs are not presented in their entirety. The best parts of his memoir are stories of his own experiences as a line officer in some of the decisive battles of the Civil War, as well as in many lesser conflicts—some of them, as Captain Otto notes, "not mentioned in history." These we have preserved. We have deleted anecdotal material that, however interesting in itself, would make the book too long. Much of this omitted material has to do with the experiences of other people as told to Captain Otto, who loved a good story. We have also deleted the account of his journey home on leave during the autumn of 1864 to rebuild his house, which had burned, and various stories of life in camp between campaigns, where much of a soldier's time was spent. Altogether we have omitted a little more than half the manuscript, producing a much more readable book. Scholars desiring access to the complete text will, of course, wish to consult the original manuscript.

The transcription of the manuscript has been conservative: crossed *l*s, uncrossed *t*s, and inadvertently repeated words have been corrected silently, and superscriptions and interlineations have been dropped to the line; in all other respects we have reproduced what John Henry wrote exactly as he wrote it, without altering spelling, grammar, or punctuation except where necessary to facilitate understanding. In a few cases, mostly misplaced quotation marks, punctuation has been silently corrected. Alterations and omissions are indicated by the usual editorial apparatus of brackets and ellipses; editorial additions and corrections have been kept to a minimum, resorted to only when necessary to prevent confusion. For the most part, John Henry's English is quite easy to understand, although it is clear at times that English is not his native language. He often uses the word "as" for "than," and "moreover" for "however." His orthography is sometimes idiosyncratic, but it is easy enough to decipher: he uses *j* for *y* and sometimes *y* for *j;* he substitutes *k* for *c* and *ck;* and his spelling is sometimes phonetic. He attempts to reproduce dialect at times and is fairly successful at it, according to the standards of the day. Although his sentences do not always parse, they are always understandable.

The 21st Wisconsin Volunteer Infantry was organized in August 1862 in the counties of Calumet, Fond du Lac, Manitowoc, Outagamie, Waupaca, and Winnebago. Company D was raised in Outagamie County. Its members were mostly farmers, tradesmen, and mechanics from the city of Appleton and the surrounding villages of Bovina, Dale, Ellington, Freedom, Grand Chute, Greenville, and Hortonia; a minority were students from Lawrence College in Appleton, the sons of prominent local families or white-collar workers of various sorts. Its commanding officer, Capt. John Jewett Jr., was a lawyer from Appleton. The regiment included a sizeable minority of Germans, who were recruited by John Henry Otto and were referred to as the "Dutch squad"—a nickname originally intended as a slur but that soon came to indicate "good fellowship," as Otto notes. Many of the members of the company and regiment—especially but not exclusively those of the "Dutch squad"—we come to know as individuals over the course of the memoir.

Captain Otto presents a candid picture of the men he served with—he does not hesitate to name the names of those soldiers who deserted before their first battle, feigned illness to get into the Invalid Corps, or embezzled company funds. He tells how the men cut up the colonel's horse and ate it half-raw when it was killed by a cannonball, and how they ran away at Perryville, as well as how they stood their ground at Chickamauga. Although his loyalty to his commanding officers is strong, even when they make mistakes he paints them, warts and all. Of Gen. Jefferson C. Davis, for example, he recounts that when he first encountered land mines in Georgia, Davis made Confederate prisoners march in front of his army so they would get blown up, if anyone did. He also records that when bushwhackers were taking potshots at trains between Chattanooga and Atlanta, Gen. William T. Sherman ordered Confederate civilians tied to the locomotives. He is not shy about telling tales that reflect on himself, either—such as his invention of recycled chewing tobacco at Chattanooga or his taking the boots of a dead Confederate officer on the field of Stone's River because he needed them desperately for winter marching.

Like many Civil War regiments, the 21st Wisconsin Volunteer Infantry left no official history. John Henry Otto's memoirs are as close to a history of the regiment as anything that has yet been written. There are, however, many sources of information about the regiment. In the Wisconsin adjutant general's *Records of Civil War Regiments, 1861–1900* (series 1200) in the archives division of the State Historical Society of Wisconsin, there is a short sketch, a bare fifteen-hundred-word outline, of the history of the 21st Wisconsin up until the siege of Atlanta; it was probably written by Col. Michael Fitch, who at that time was commander of the regiment. Colonel Fitch also wrote a memoir of his Civil War experiences, *Echoes of the Civil War as I Hear Them,* which was published in 1905 and which covers much of the same ground that Otto's memoir does—though in considerably less detail. There is also a posthumously published memoir of Mead Holmes Jr., a sergeant in Company K of the 21st; the memoir, *A Soldier of the Cumberland,* was published by his father in 1864. The papers and letters of the chaplain of the regiment, Orson P. Clinton, are available at the State Historical Society of Wisconsin, as are the letters, papers, and diaries of the regimental surgeon, James T. Reeve.

As Colonel Fitch notes in his memoir, no regimental reports were filed for the 21st Wisconsin before the Atlanta campaign.[4] The actions of the regiment are, of course, included in the official reports of officers at the brigade and division level, but these reports do not always reflect accurately the experiences of the regiment; there were also many engagements and smaller actions for which no official reports are to be found. There is a large body of other official records of various sorts, however, the most valuable of which are the *Regimental Muster Rolls,* which are available in the archives division of the historical society. These documents are listed in the bibliography.

These records alone cannot tell the entire story of the 21st Wisconsin Volunteers. They do, however, provide a wealth of information against which to check the accuracy of Captain Otto's memoirs. There are many valuable secondary sources available today as well that provide us with much more accurate and detailed information about many aspects of the Civil War than Captain Otto could have. Wherever possible we have attempted to check Otto's statements against these other sources and in the notes report to the reader what we have found.

Otto emerges as a remarkably accurate reporter. Sometimes he mentions by name people who cannot be located in the official records, and many of his anecdotes by their very nature cannot be verified. Still, much of what he tells us, especially about the experiences of his own company and regiment, can be independently confirmed. That he was for a large part of the war either the orderly sergeant or commander of his company—

both positions that required him to keep records and make reports—adds to the reliability of his narrative, as does his reliance on a detailed diary written at the time. His previous military experience adds further to the value of his observations.

Nonetheless, there are many instances, especially with events outside his own personal experience, in which Captain Otto makes mistakes in his facts or figures. In filling in the background to put his own experiences in perspective he obviously used many sources other than his own diaries—books, newspaper articles, and conversations with other soldiers—and in some cases may have uncritically accepted information that was unreliable. We have pointed out as many of these mistakes as possible in the notes and provided the correct information. Where his facts are accurate, however, we have generally passed over them in silence to avoid overburdening the book with notes.

Although we have not been able to identify all of Captain Otto's sources for background information, we know two of them with certainty because he cites and quotes them on several occasions. These are Sherman's *Memoirs* and S. M. Bowman's and R. B. Irwin's *Sherman and His Campaigns* (1865). He was clearly quite familiar with Sherman's *Memoirs* and sometimes used statistics from them without acknowledgment. In two instances he took a short passage verbatim from Bowman and Irwin without enclosing it in quotation marks or acknowledging the source—probably a matter of carelessness rather than plagiarism since he cites the book elsewhere. (The reader will find these passages identified in the notes.) Otto also took some statistics and letters from this source without acknowledgment. Wherever this has happened, we have indicated the source in the notes and given some indication of how closely Otto followed it.

At times Captain Otto may have indulged in the universal human tendency to exaggerate or improve upon often-told anecdotes. Further, some of what he tells us undoubtedly was reconstructed from memory or even more or less fictionalized—as when he reports in detail conversations that he was unlikely to have recorded at length in his diary. Our conclusion, however, is that he was a trained and accurate observer who told the truth about what he himself experienced. He may have stretched the truth a little at times to make himself look good, but he was not a liar; he was a storyteller and a good one.

The manuscript is untitled, although some of the notebooks are labeled "War Memories." We decided to call it *Memoirs of a Dutch Mudsill* because it evokes a term that, although unfamiliar to many readers today, is central to the social conflict that, in John Henry Otto's view at least, brought about the Civil War. The word *mudsill* has two meanings in American English. In builder's jargon it refers to the lowest timber, or sill, in a timber-frame structure; this timber comes in direct contact with the earth—affectionately known as "mud." The second meaning, invented around the time the Civil War was brewing, is derived from the first: a mudsill is a person of the very lowest class of society. This metaphorical use of the term was coined by Senator James Hammond of South Carolina in 1858 when he said in a speech to the Senate, "In all social systems there must be a class to perform the drudgery of life. . . . It constitutes the mudsills of society."[5]

When the Civil War broke out the aristocratic Southerners soon adopted this term to refer to the soldiers in the Northern army; according to the Southern newspapers of the time, the Union army was composed of "Hessians," "Lincoln hirelings," and "northern mudsills." The word *Dutch*, of course, is not traditionally reserved for natives of Holland but is a slang term for all people of German origin, otherwise known as "sauerkrauts." There were many of these sauerkrauts in the Union army, because the German states were prime sources at the time of trained and experienced soldiers; John Henry paints a vivid picture of the prejudice they often encountered in the army. As a former officer in the Prussian army, Captain Otto probably would not have thought of himself as a mudsill, but he was well aware that many people on both sides of the conflict considered all immigrants to be members of the very lowest class. I would not call my own great-grandfather a Dutch mudsill had he not himself proudly claimed the title in an argument with a Rebel prisoner after the battle of Resaca, Georgia. He told him, "Do not dream any more of a Confederacy; the Lincoln hirelings and the Dutch mudsills will take care of your Confederacy." Indeed the Union victory in the Civil War was seen by Captain Otto as the victory of the "northern mudsills" over the "southern chevaliers."

David Gould

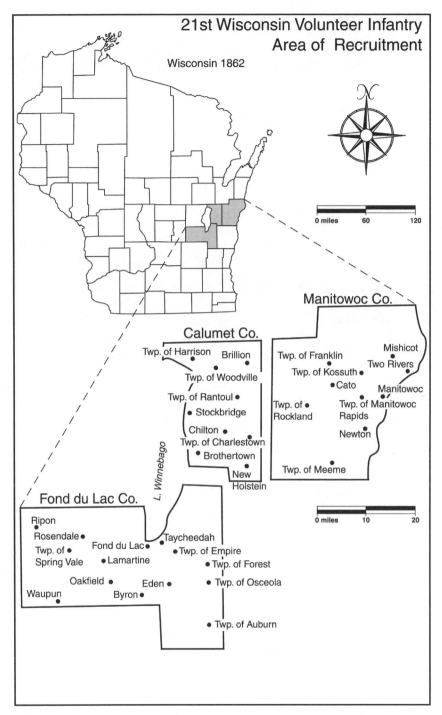

21st Wisconsin Volunteer Infantry Area of Recruitment: Fond du Lac, Calumet, and Manitowoc Counties (Map by Joel Heiman)

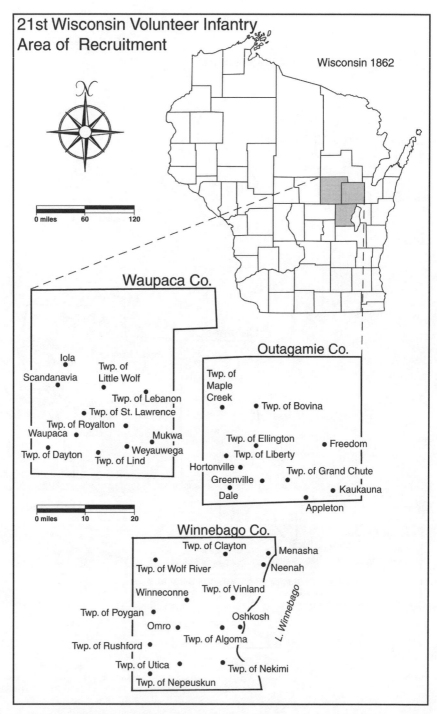

21st Wisconsin Volunteer Infantry Area of Recruitment: Waupaca, Outagamie, and Winnebago Counties (Map by Joel Heiman)

~

CHAPTER ONE

The Organization of Company D, 21st Regiment of Wisconsin Volunteer Infantry

~ In the early part of August 1862 a certain Major Schumacher[1] was ordered by Governeur S[a]lomon of Wis. to proceed to Appleton to organize the Volunteers there into a Company which was afterwards to be attached to the 21st Regiment Wis. Vols. The Counties Manitowoc, Calumet, Fond Du Lac, Winnebago, Waupacca and Outagamie had to furnish two Regiments (2000 men) of ten Companies (100 men) each. A certain George Kreis, an Alsacian Frenchm[a]n who could not speak french, kept a tavern which was considered and taken as the democratic Headquarters of the City. There every evening the leading democrats and Ward politicians would gather and gossip about the late news in politics and war. I used to go there every night after supper to hear and see what was going on etc. Stopping in one evening I found an Officer in Uncle Sams Uniform standing at the bar speaking with George Kreis. No sooner had Geo. Kreiss seen me he exclaimed: "There, Major, is your man!" "Mr. Otto; Major Schumacher. Mr. Otto is an old soldier from Europe and as he is well acquainted here can probably be of some service to you."

After the usual handshaking the Major led me aside to an unoccupied table wher we took a seat. He then explained his Mission here, that he had been detailed to organize a Regiment in this vicinity and was looking for a person suitable to fill the Office as Captain and popular enough to raise a Company. He inquired about my military carier in the prussian army. It did not take long to disclose the fact to our mutual surprise that we were old comrades, allthough strangers, we had ser[v]ed in the same Army Corps,

Maj. F[rederick] Schumacher and Capt. John Jewett Jr. From a lithograph, "Col. B. J. Sweet's 21st Wis. Vol Regt. Located at Oshkosh, Wis. 1862." (Courtesy Oshkosh Public Museum)

in the same wars from 1848 to 1857, he as a Captain, I as a Sergeant and first Lieutenant. Here he had served in the Potomac army as a Captain, promoted to Major and sent on this mission. He wanted me to raise a Company and go along with it as its Captain. I convinced him that my circumstances did not allow such a scheme.

There were but few persons in the room at the time and I espied in the farther corner behind a table a certain John Jewett, a lawyer, reading a newspaper.[2] More out of a sudden desire for fun and at the same time to get rid of the Major I said, "Major! yonder sits your man; Mr. Jewett, I think he is the man you want." The Major took it serious and wished me to introduce him to Mr. Jewett. I did so and stepped back but kept in hearing distance. Jewett seemed at first greatly surprised at the Majors proposal, but after some scirmishing I heard Jewett say to the Major he would think over the matter, speak with his wife and give his final decision the next day.... As was my custom, I went early in the shop next morning and to my great surprise shortly after who should step in, but Mr. John Jewett. In a few words he informed me that he had concluded to accept Major Schumachers proposal, that he was going to try to raise a Company and that he wished me to enlist in his Company and assist him in enlisting Recruits among the Germans. If I would do so he would give me a Commission as recruiting Officer and at muster in would appoint me first (Orderly) Sergeant. . . . I promised him to inform him of my decision at night at Kreiss Tavern which satisfied him.

During the day I made up my mind to enlist but did not cherish to enlist in Jewett's Company as I most certainly knew he would make a poor commander. I thought to go to Milwaukee where just then a german Regiment (The 26th called "Sigels Regt.") was raised and enlist in the same. But during the afternoon I read in a Milwaukee paper that so many Germans from all over the state had made application for enlistment there that not all could be accepted.[3] Besides a certain Henry Turner,[4] a great friend of mine, who kept a livery stable, met me that afternoon and informed me that he intended to go into Jewett's Compagnie and urged me to do the same. He held the same opinion about Jewett as I, but did not think it of so much consequence as I did. Of course he did not know anything about soldiering and therefore no competent Judge. But after all I concluded to take the risk let come what may. I informed Jewett of my decision, which he accepted very gracefully; he repeated the promise given before and so the matter was settled.

At 11. A.M. August 12th 1862 I stepped into the recruiting Office and entered my name on the list of defenders of the Country.[5] There was something about this act which struck me as remarkable; this is why: Twelve years ago I had deserted the prussian Flag in order to get rid of military rule. I had served five years faithfully from the pike and Private upward to first Lieutenant, commanding a Company the last year. I took part in the first prussian war against Danemark 1848. Again in the war against the South german revolution in 1849. Again in the War against Austria and Hesse 1850–1851. Being unable to ascertain when I would be discharged and having no desire to spend my life as a soldier, I deserted to Holland from thence across the North Sea to England and finally to New York, glad to find a country where the Army is subject to the Civil Authority. Now I was to face the same music again, to brave the same hardships and dangers; but of one thing I was sure; Let come what may, I never would desert again. . . .

When I returned to town it had become known I had enlisted as I was one of the first who had signed the name on the list and taken the oath. I met several of my friends who thought if such an old chap (I was then 40 years within a month) as I could undertake the job, they certainly could. Before night 8 stought german boys had responded to the call. . . .

The Monday following Capt. Jewett went hunting recruits in the County. The recruiting Office in the City was on the first floor of a large empty store. A certain Amos Lawrence who had also enlisted was detailed by Captain Jewett as Enrolling Clerk.[6] He had been bookeeper for a Mr. Turner who run a sawmill. He was a joung, tall fellow, proud and conceited. . . .

THE ORGANIZATION OF COMPANY D

I had by this time enlisted 13 germans and 10 americans. I should have succeeded in enlisting more, but a certain Jim McGillen had undertaken to raise the other Compagny, and in order to gain Volunteers, he made the most absurd promises, which I knew he never could fulfill; but good many trusted his buncomb speeches and got caught. He did not succeed however to complete the Comp. and withdrew in favor of a certain Wood, then sheriff of the County who, long after we left, filled the Comp. which was afterward assigned to the 32nd Regt. Wis. Vols. Saturday evening Capt Jewett returned from his recruiting trip in the County. Looking over the lists we found we had 10 men more [than] we needed. But at muster into the United States service the examining Surgeons certainly would throw out some. . . .

The first of Sept. the Co. was to leave Appleton for Camp Bragg at Oshkosh. There 10. Companies were to be organized into one Regiment; be examined by the Doctors and mustered into the service of the United States. As there were nine days to spare [y]et Major Schumac[h]er ordered Capt. Jewett to drill the men two hours morning and afternoon. That was easyly said, but who was to drill the m[e]n? None of the men had ever been a soldier; Jewett himself did not know the difference between right and left face. So one evening Jewett ordered me to be next morning at 9. o.clock on the College grounds to drill the Comp. that is so much of it as was present. Most of the men who had enlisted in the County were busy work- ing on the farms and would not come in until the day before we had to leave. I explained to him I could not drill all the men alone and needed some help. Well, there were two soldiers in town, on sick leave they said, although they looked very hale and hearty, who had served several months in the army of the Potomac. Capt. Jewett got them to help me. It turned out however those chaps did not know much more about drill as the re- cruits themselves. One of them, Quimby, had been in hospital most of the time and the other; Bill Frazur, had driven a mule team.

It was a very unpleasant business. None of the men had the least Idea of military discipline and obeying of orders. Others thought and said they had not enlisted to while away the time with trying to keep step, or to step off with the right foot, and keep the proper distance, or to face right or left and right about face; to learn to wheel right or left in Company, platoon or section front. That would not scare the rebels they said and laughed at the whole proceeding. All what was necessary they said, was to go down south, give the rebs a good, sound drumming and come home again. I undertook to explain to them that, although the drumming Idea was an exellent one, there always were two parties in the game, and that the party who were prepared best and know to obey orders would do the drumming part. But to no purpose. Of cour[s]e, not all were of the same opinion. The best men always were mechanics and farmers and laborers. But there were about a dozen students who had enlisted from Lawrence University, some clercs or bookeepers, some sons or relatives of real or petit politicians, some sons or relatives of families of real or immaginary influence, who on the strenght of such conceited pride immagined they stood far above all order and discipline. And this class it was who made all the trouble. But few of them made good soldiers, or earned honestly the hard tack and bacon furnish by Uncle Sam. And again they had an Idea that it was an insult to their native dignity to be instructed and drilled by a souerkraut dutchman who only kept a cabinet shop and wareroom in town. And many of them appeared in my book as debtors for articles I had made for, or sold to them; nor were they by any means backward in ventlating their disgust and contempt.

One afternoon I had a squad of twelfe of this sort, trying to march them by the right and left flank in line. They were more obstinate than ever and tried every kind of foolery to show their contemt. For a while I did as if I did not notice their pranks. They probably took this on my part for timidity or cowardice and increased their laudable efforts. Just then Capt. Jewett came up to look on. They did not mind the Captains presence but kept right along in the same way. Finally I halted the squad and ordered a rest. I turned to the Captain and told him loud enough for the boys to hear it, that I would not drill these Monkeys another minute until we were mustered into the United States service; he might do so if he had a mind to. I then informed them in plain English what I thought of them and what would become of them If they went on in that way and then left the grounds. . . . I expected Capt. Jewett would give me a rousing lecture that evening, but contrary to my expectation he approoved of my Course and said he had noted the boys and would remember them.

The germans I had enlisted I drilled alone and as they all were willing to learn they soon became experts in a small way. That raised to some extent the envy of the before mentioned conceits. They called them the "dutch squad" in a way that indicated inferiority and contempt. It did not take very long and that very expression indicated respect and good fellowship in the Compagnie. . . .

The 28 of August was quite an ex[c]ited day for the members of the Comp. We had to elect a first Lieutenant. According to the laws then in operation regarding Volunteer Comps. the Gouvernor of the State apointed the Capt. as soon as the Comp. was completed, the War Department appointed the 2d Lieut. from among worthy soldiers of the older Regts. but the first Lieut. was elected by the Comp. There were several Candidates in the field who were willing to wear the shoulderstraps. A little Tailor, foreman in Chs. Fays clothing store, Wm. H. Wood was electioneering for all he was worth. There was John Dey, a burly farmer from town Hortonia;[7] Also Amos Lawrence, bookeeper and enrolling clerk; last, but not least was Hank Turner, my friend of the livery stable. But it was by no means his own doings. It were his friends who urged him to take the position. He was very popular and a gentlemen in every respect. The night before the election he came to me and said: "So here Otto. A lot of my friends are pressing me to accept the first Lieutenancy. Now I am convinced that will put me in a wrong position. I am an ignorant recruit like all the others and would pile one blunder on top of the other. Now I tell you my scheme. You run for the position[.] You have been a soldier and know all about it. I will instruct my friends and you will be sure to be elected. What do you say?"—"I say 'No' Turner. That can not be done just now, and if it could be done I would not take it. You accept the position and I will find lots of chance to help you along and you in turn can help me along."—"Why" he said "will you not take the place?"—"Wait" I replied "in five or six Months from now, If I live, I will tell you all about it." That settled the mater and Turner was elected next day with a handsome majority. So I was sure to have one staunch friend.

The 3 days remaining before our departure were spent in arrainging business and home affairs; in taking leave of friends and neighbors etc. On Monday morning Sept. 1st the Compagnie in a body marched to the North Western Depot, accompanied by a music band and the Citizens of Appleton in general. Although there was noise enough, it seemed the majority of the Comp. felt somewhat melancholy. One could not help but to put the question to himself. Will I ever see this place and home again? Or if so, in what condition? Certainly one of the wisest and best arraingements in nature in regard to men is the total ignorance of the events which future has in store for us. . . . O, if those 100 healthy, stalwart man had known that nearly half of them never would see home again, and others maimed or cripled for lifetime?—

Arrived at the depot, hurried embraces and kisses were hastily exchanged and: "All aboard" shouted the conductor and the snorting, puffing Iron horse whirled us towards our destination. To drive away sad reflections I, as soon as the carrs were in fair motion, began a german war song in which many of the others heartily joined. The comrades approved of the course taken

Col. Benjamin J. Sweet. From an engraving in Michael J. Fitch, *Echoes of the Civil War as I Hear Them* (New York: R. F. Reno, 1905). (Courtesy State Historical Society of Wisconsin)

and when the verses were ended they asked us for more until almost exhausted we had to quit. Thus singing advanced the "dutch squad" a great step in the esteem of our native Comrades. Many a time afterwards did we cheer up the footsore and tired men with a lively song untill finally we became so broken up and scattered that no choir could be brought together.

Camp Bragg at Oshkosh was established within the fair grounds, one mile east of the city on the west shore of Lake Winnebago. Temporary barracks had been erected for the accommodation of a thousand men. There we landed at half past nine A.M. In the southwest corner of the ground stood a large, barn like building; there Colonel Sweet, Major Schumacher, Adjutant Fitch and Quartermaster Hamilton[8] had their quarters. The Captains of the Comp. were provided with Wall tents. Our Comp. was the first to arrive there but in the course of a few days the other nine Companies arrived successivly. Here for the first time the boys got a little test of military discipline and had ample chance to consider the serious fact, that not everything can be done according ones own will and with full personal liberty. As soon as the Companies were in, the Colonel ordered the Regiment to "fall in." (the command to assemble), and the Adjutant read the first regimental Orders. The men were strictly confined within the enclosure of the camp grounds. No one was to leave the grounds without a pass from his Captain or the Colonel. . . .

The demand for passe[s] was so enormous that, if every demand had been granted, not a man would have remained in Camp. Colonel Sweet therefore issued an Order that not more than ten percent of the same Comp. should receive passes on the same day, unless there were very urgent reasons for it. The Captains were to designate the men who should have passes. That created considerable dissatisfaction among the men, because it was left to the whims of the Captains who should have passes or not. Some fellows succeeded in scaling the fence after roll call unseen by the sentinels, or perhaps the sentinel would not seem to see them. The Colonel somehow got wind of it and in Co. with the Major and Adjutant watched one night and caught 4 of them. He had them shut up together with the sentinel who had suffered them to scale the fence, in a small smokehouse for 24. hours with only one meal during the time, and when they were released they had to go on extra guard duty. That stopped fence jumping somewhat. . . .

When we arrived in Camp the Quartermaster came with a load of victuals for dinner. He issued beans, pork, some beef, bread, pepper, salt, coffee and tea. We had to manage the cooking ourselfes. Potts, kettles, dishes,

Quartermaster Henry C. Hamilton and Adjutant Michael H. Fitch. From a lithograph, "Col. B. J. Sweet's 21st Wis. Vol Regt. Located at Oshkosh, Wis. 1862." (Courtesy Oshkosh Public Museum)

forks and spoons were furnished. The men had an Idea the cooking department could be handled on the plan as is adopted in the pinery camps. Therefore they engaged a certain Bill Allen as Comp. cook before we left Appleton. Every man was taxed a certain amount per month to secure the Cooks pay. I was strongly opposed to it, because the scheme was totally impractical. It might have worked well enough, had we always remained in camp, but in the field and during campains it was useless. I gave that much to understand to the boys and Mr. Allen, but of course they knew better and I thought experience would be the best teacher and kept quiet. Accordingly as soon as the victuals arrived Allen donned a white Cap, ditto apron. There was no arangement for a kitchen or cooking place, so the boys got up a contrivance which reminded one much of a soft soap making concern. Jack Gilbert, a carpenter from New London, and I put up a number of shelves and built a 64 foot long table and seats of common lumber. At 2. P.M. dinner was served but it prooved Allens culinary skill not to advantage. The beans were rather more burned then cooked and not done after all. The boys indulged in some strong language, but as Allen promised to do better after he had things in proper shape, peace and content was soon restored. . . .

Sept. 3d we were furnished with a part of a soldiers outfit. We drew Overcoat, dresscoat and hat, the latter with a broad brim, the left side of the brim turned upward and held in position by a shining brass clasp; a long, black rooster feather, held by the clasp, pointing proudly upward. Whether that feather was given us as a symbol of fight and coming battles I cannot say, but that much I know that a fortnight after we left camp not a feather was to be seen. The first rain made them as limber as a slender twig of a weeping willow, and they dropped ingloriously down alongside the road. Pantaloons, we were told, we would draw later, as none were ready at present. We also received the accoutrements, that is: Cartridge box and waistbelt, cappouch and knapsack. The nex[t] day shoes were issued. The shoes were issued in bulk; so many men, so many pairs of shoes, without regard to size. Under such rule it was impossible that every man could procure a reasonable fit. The boys were swapping and trading all day untill late in the night, but all could not find the proper size. I did not take any as I had a pair of new boots, but felt sorry for it when later the marching began.

We received also our shooting sticks; Belgian rifles, they called them. It was nothing but rough made, clumsy, heavy percussion musket, weighing nearly 15 pounds. Oh! how I longed for the light handsome needlegun, which we used in Prussia. Weighing only 9 pounds, we could hit a mark at 1000 yards distance and fire 5 shots in a minute, whereas it took almost five minutes to load one of thus Clumsy pieces and then good only for a distance of 150 yards. After proper inspection they were condemned and returned.[9] We also got a Canteen or waterflask, capable of holding 3 pints of water. But as they were made of the poorest kind of tin without any covering they were not worth carrying along. The reflection of the sun on the tin would make the water almost boiling hot in a short time; besides the water would corode the tin in a short time and the canteen would leak. Further a haversack to carry the rations in; also a tin cup capable of hol[d]ing a pint. Such a tin cup was a marvelous in[s]trument. It was expected to serve as a drinking cup, as coffee and teapot; it had to serve as frying pan and soup kettel, in fact it was the only implement we had to prepare, serve and eat our meals with.

On the fifth we were examined by surgeons appointed for that purpose by the U.S. Government. After that we were mustered into the United States service by Major H. A. Tenney, U.S. Mustering Officer for the State of Wisconsin. Twenty five dollar advance Bounty was paid us, as also one months pay in advance ($13.00). The day after I took a pass, went to Oshkosh and had a good time with the Kohlman Brothers, editors and proprietors of a newspaper; also with Major Shumacher, altogether in the Basement of the printing building. Major Schumacher and the brothers Kohlman were exellent singers. Major Schumaker was the best sociable men I ever met with. The boys all loved him. Although he was a strict disciplinarian he had such a pleasing winning smile in giving orders, or when administering a rebuke, or correcting a fault that nobody could resist him. His funny, broken English added much to the charm and whenever he choose to crack a joke, there certainly was a handle on it (as the men used to say). Quite different was Colonel Sweet. Of tall stature, erect soldierly bearing, he always wore a stern, proud face, never spoke to any of the men unless it was something pertaining to do duty and then always in a stern official way. But for all that he was an exellent soldier and took well care of his men. By this time our second Lieut. had also arrived from the Army of the Potomac. His name was Fred. Borchert [Borcherdt].[10] He hailed from Manitowoc where his father was German Consul. Fred had served one year in the army of the Potomac. He was 24 years old, a kind good natured and able fellow, of good education, but the most slow, easy going, I don't care fellow I ever met with. Besides he was a remarkable sound sleeper and when he had settled once fairly in peacefull repose, it required a good sized, double charged cannon to wake him up. In fact, I have serious doubts [whether] old Gabriel will b[e] able to wake him up with his trumpet at dooms day. On account of this weakness he was the cause of some amusing as well, as ridiculous incidents, of wich later on.

Captain Jewett did not come up to [the] promise he had made me before elistment. He apointed to first Sergeant Charles Fay, a dry goods clerk; to second Sergeant, John Dey; the former Candidate for first Lieut. The third in the line was myself; fourth Sergeant Hamlin B. Williams, and fifth: Th[e]odore Clark, a farmer of Stephenville.[11] Of course I had to be satisfied as there was no recourse open for me. The eight Corporal[s] appointed I need not mention here exept Amos Lawrence, the proud enrolling clerk was appointed first Corporal and Wm H. Wood, the tailor and also ex-candidate for first Lieut., eight[h] corporal. It seems Jewett took pride in giving all the ex Lieut. Candidates an Office, allthough he might have done considerable better. All three of them; Dey, Lawrence and Wood were not worth a row of pins as soldiers. We will meet them again soon. As regards Lawrence, his pride was touched to the quick. He had expected a better situation and thought himself to[o] good to carry a musket. . . .

Sept. 11th was the day we were to leave the barraks for the field. In the afternoon a special train was to co[n]vey us to Chicago. The Ladies of Oshkosh had prepared a splendid dinner that day. The tables actually groaned under the weight of costly, inviting cooking luxuries. But the old raskall Pluvius seemed to be jealous of the proceedings and was bound to have a hand in the matter. Just when we were ready to take seats and attack the tempting morsils, a dashing shower came pouring down, spoiling everything. Not much praying was done just then and I must admit that the majority of the men ventilated their disappointment in some strong language. "He, hee Poys! dat's nothing," rang out the clear, jolly voice of Major Schumacher. "That means only starting our business in a fair way. We must become used to, and be prepared to meet and cooly endure disappointments and failures. A Soldiers life is full of them." And the Major kept on in his humorous way to read us a little sermon of which the boys spoke many and many a time, long after the jolly Major had met a brave soldiers death. Just four weeks after we consigned his bullet riddled remains in the rocky battle ground at Perryville, Kentucky moistened with tears of his loving comrades.

The rain having stopped we swallowed such things as had not wholly dissolved and next the bugle reminded us to pack our military rumpus and fall in line. We were a funny looking lot of soldier[s] at best. We had no muskets or rifles, nor had we received pantaloons. The haversacks were empty, nor did we receive anything in the shape of rations to fall back on in case our stomachs should become rebellious. Good many of the boys wondered where, and in what Shape our nex[t] meal would turn up. We were ordered to fill the canteens with water, that was some consolation. Afterwards I learned that a goodly number of the boys had managed to have their Canteens filled in Oshkosh where the water was of a remarkable stronger quality [than] the stuff we pumped out of the old well in camp. The Regt. was formed in line, the Compagnies taking their places acording the seniority of the Captains. . . .

The dress parade, or review, from a military stand point, was a decided failure, but nevertheles it was an imposing show for all the people who had gathered from far and near to witness our departure. A thousand men in two ranks, standing shoulder to shoulder, each a waving a big feather on a big hat, an tremendous bundle on his back, is a great sight for one not accustomed to it. Several strangers made farewell speeches, and finally Old Major Ryan Menasha an 80 year old war horse of 1812 was lifted on a big box. He was dressed in full, old style military uniform and in loud, but trembling voice gave the boys some account of the rigors and hardships of field life and finally cautioned them to keep good comradeship and always obey their Officers under all circumstances.

Mounted officers of the 21st Wisconsin. From a lithograph, "Col. B. J. Sweet's 21st Wis. Vol Regt. Located at Oshkosh, Wis. 1862." (Courtesy Oshkosh Public Museum)

~

CHAPTER TWO

Preparing for Actual Warfare

~ During the afternoon we were marched to the railroad where a long train stood ready to take us aboard. A music band played: Hail Columbia, the Star spangled Banner and other patriotic effusions until we had boarded the cars. At this time the Government was compelled to make heavy demands on the railroad Companies for the transportation of soldiers and war materials. There was not enough rolling stock on hand to supply the demand. Consequently we were packed in the cars like herring in a barrel. A seat usually intended for two persons had to serve for three, and the passage way was filled with standing men. A hundred men in one coach will give an Idea of what Elbow room we had; But as the proverb has it: "It takes a good many patient sheep to fill a stable." We had to turn necessity into virtue and therefore divided the crowd into reliefs so that everyone had a chance to have a seat awhile. It was a tedious and tiresome journey.

When we reached Minnesota Junction it was just suppertime. Here is a so called Railroad Hotel where passenger trains stop for 20 minutes for supper. We thought that Uncle Sam would invite us to supper but "Rats." It seemed the Engine made special Efforts to carry us quik and safe past this dangerous place. "Put on half rations" shouted on[e] of the boys; "Training us for fighting," an other. "Charge 50 cents to bankrupt Uncle Sam" a third; and finally, a hissing, and roaring and howling and tooting ensued which almost lifted the roof from the coaches. But that did not fill the stomachs. Finally one fellow hit the right Idea. "Boys" he shouted, "We have to fall back on our canteens." As we could not do any better, that had

to be done. . . . Not long after it became singularly noisy and lively in the
coach. That peculiar Oshkosh water seemed to be drugged as it apparently
induced the boys to all sorts of funny tricks and doings; but after a while,
one by one would squat down [t]o indulge in a short nap if possible.

The following morning some where near 8. o.clock we arrived in Chicago. We had to march through the city in order to reach the Michigan
Central Depot. Contrary to our expectation, Chicago was very quiet. It
seemed allmost a deserted City. Now and then a flag would wave out of a
window, but besides that nobody took any notice of us. The citizens had
seen enough of that sort of things during the year and did pay no more
attention to it. At the depot we were hurried in the cars and no one was
allowed to go out and look for breakfast. Policemen guarded the train that
no one might escape. The men were hungry and became very boisterous.
After waiting about an hour each one was handed about half a pound of
coal black baloony sausage, hard as a brick; about a half pound of bread
and a mug of black stuf which they said was coffee. After the poor supper
of the night previous it all went down well enough, although good many
entered a solemn protest against such disgusting treatment of the becoming defenders of the Union. The poor fellows did not know then how delicate such a breakfast would have been one month hence.

At 10. A.M. we were moving again. We were not so close packed now and
everyone had a seat. At Michigan City we had to change cars for Indianapolis. . . . As it was nearing noon we hoped that some kind of dinner would
be given us. But it seemed Uncle Sam could not afford the expenses and
just when the whistle of some factory anounced dinner time, we were whirled
away again. Without stopping, exept for taking in wood and water, the
Engine dashed on until we reached Indianapolis at 10. P.M.

The citizens of Indianapolis understood the rules or customs of hospitality better than Chicago and Michigan City. A supstantial supper was
served in the large freight ro[o]ms of the depot. The waiting ladies must
have been astonished at the ravenous appetite the Wisconsin boys developed but after being informed that we were reduced to two meals a day
they pitied us and went for fresh supplies, which seemed to be inexhaustable.
Past experience had t[au]ght the boys a lesson. "Look out for to morrow"
and they acted accordingly, for no sooner were the sharp pangs of hunger
appeased they began to fill their second stomach, the haversack, with every
kind of eatable stuff, such as would not leak out. And well it was we had
done so. We had hardly swallowed the last bite when we were hurried to
the carrs again. With angry snorting the impaticnt firehorse darted in the

pitch dark night again. We had no Idea w[h]ere we were going. Of course the Colonel knew but he kept "mum." There was a rumor we were going to join the Army of the Potomac, but it seemed to me we would have taken an other road for that purpose. I for my part hated the Idea to belong to the Potomac Army, because of its notable and persistent bad luck; whereas the armies of the midle and western Departments, although greatly inferior in numbers, had a most splendid record. It seemed the commanders of the western Army had more pluck, or more militairy grit [than] the generals in the Eastern army. Be that as it may I hoped quietly we would be assigned to the western armies. . . .

The next morning no breakfast was forthcoming and lucky for us we could fall back on our haversacks. We had passed during the night through Indiana and were now in Ohio. . . .

At noon we arrived at Cincinnaty Ohio. We were marched to the market Hall where dinner was served in the shape of sandwiches, cheese, cold meats, and coffee. Dinner over we were marched into a big square to await further orders. . . .

Cincinnaty was at this time in a state of feverish ex[c]itement; in fact the entyre state was. The Confederate General Braxton Bragg had broken loose from Chattanooga Tenn. where he had been watched by the Union Genl. Don Carlos Buel [Buell]. Bragg's army was about 40,000 strong. Buel[l']s about the same.[1] Bragg had in quiet and forced marches moved around Buel[l']s left flank and marched toward midle Kentuky in the direction of Louisville Ky. His main object was enlisting recruits for his army, gathering fourage for beast and men, as also horses and mules for his cavalry and teams. If by chance Louisville or Cincinnaty could be surprised, an immense amount of military stores such as: Clothing, Boots, shoes, rations, amunitions, army wagons, cannons and artillerie implements etc, would fall in his hands if not previously removed or destroyed. It must be borne in mind that at that time Louisville as well as Cincinnaty were nearly bare of troops. All the troops the Government had then were needed at the front.

Bragg['s] first direction of march was for Louisville, but Genl Buel[l], finding that Bragg had flanked him and was actually two days marches in his rear, hastily faced about and tried by forced marches to he[a]d him off. Buel[l] succeeded in heading off Bragg from Louisville but he could not prevent him from striking for Cincinnaty. In that direction Bragg now turned his army. That was the reason the good people of Ohio in general, but Cincinnaty specially, expected the rebels every minute. New Regts, as fast as they could be raised and equipped, were forwarded to the threatened places and ours was one of them. The governor of Ohio called on all able men to arm themselves and hasten to Cincinnaty for the defense of the City. The peopl were willing enough and in a few days the city was brimfull of country people who offered help. The greatest evil was there were to[o] many of them. They could not be properly organized in so short a time and besides they had to be fed; they had not come to starve. The streets and public places were blokaded by this motley crew. All possible kinds of weapons for defensive, or offensive warfare were represented. From the old-fashioned, singlebarrel rifle and shotgun down to twelve foot long pike, manure and pitchforks, sythes, ugly looking clubs the list was made up. Some felt proud by parading an old rusty flintlock musket, an heirloom from great-grandfather of revolutionary fame; others were proud of some oldfashioned pistol or Colts Revolver first patent and some had nothing at all, trusting to pick up something somewhere. There were gray haired old man and boys from ten years and upward. Strange rumors were afloat how near the rebel army was already; how cruel they were, how they would ransack and burn the City, how they did delight in murder and rapine. Some vere looking for hiding places for their valuables, others were bent on leaving the City and fly[ing] northward and moved in crowds to the depots and got half crazy because they could get no transportation; Couriers and messengers flew this way and that way in hot haste, with very important air[s] which plainly said: "I know something but I must not tell you."

In the west part of the City some scared cranks were busy constructing barrikades. The scare seemed to be contagious. Good many of our boys became infected with it and said that for once we had got in a tight place, especially as we had no weapons at all. (A marked exeption of thus feeling was exibited by Philip Rose[2][—]the tallest fellow so he marched at the head of the Company. "Give me a rifle" he would shout, "and I will take care of a dozen of those rebel gray hounds." It is but natural that most of the boys considered this as mere bombastic bragging. (By and by we will have a chance to admire his cool, heroic bravery. . . .) And while all this wild turmoil was going on Genl. Bragg was 150 miles away in Kentuky quietly gathering recruits, horses, mules and other plunder; nor did he come much nearer. But of that later on.

After a couple hours delay the order to fall in was given and the Regt. marched on a floating bridge across the Ohio, through Covington Ky. on the south of which we went in camp; that is to say: we went in an open field along side the road, halted and were informed that we were to remain here until we got our rifles. We threw our knapsacks on the ground and ourselfes

PREPARING FOR ACTUAL WARFARE

on the knapsacks and waited for the next thing to turn up. We had no tents to put up, no rations to cook, no muskets to take care of. After a little while the prospect changed. A number of wagons with a number of long and short boxes arrived and halted in front of us. The long boxes contained Austrian rifles, the short boxes the cartridges. In a little while every men was provided with a rifle 60 rounds of cartridges and a corresponding number of caps. Of course it were muzzle loading rifles and their appearance and finish did not speak in their favor, they seemed to be of very inferior workmanship. In fact they seemed to be not a whit better than the belgian rifle we had seen at Oshkosh; but they were not so heavy and clumsy buil[t] and that goes a great ways with a man who has to lug the thing around all day. But in course of time a great surprise was in store for us. Those innocent, plain looking shooting irons prooved to be fully equal to the demands made of them. They were very dangerous weapons in cool and steady hands.

Hardly had we disposed of rifle and cartridges and caps, when another wagon loaded with big boxes came rattling up the pike. They brought us the regular army blue pantaloons. Each men received on[e] without regard to size; they might swap afterward in order to have the proper fit. That was the cause of considerable trouble. There were plenty short, but not enough long ones. But that was not the fault of Uncle Sam though. It were the shysters who took the Contracts from the Government to furnish so many pair of pants. I was lucky in getting a good fit on the start, but our brave giant Philip Rose was in a bad fix. He had to run through the whole Regt. in order to hunt up the longest pair, and even they were full 4 inches short. He presented a funny picture indeed. The uniform coat he had drawn in Oshkosh ended a hands breadth above the point where the spinal column ends; his trousers reached down only a little ways below the calfs and he wore shoes and cotton socks which would persist in settling down on the shoes, there was allways a rim of native territory to be seen. . . . Van Stratum[3] advised him to have that uncovered territory painted blue, that would an[s]wer all purposes. The boys teased him without mercy about his funny figure and that induced him to tear a strip off the flaps of his overcoat and add it to the extremities of his trousers. After that he went under the name of "addition, or two storied Phil."

Night was coming on and no sign whatever of rations or supper. The boys began to grumble in quite plain expressions. "Poys! Poys!" shouted Major Schumacher, "try to get used to it. As soon a[s] Uncle sam getts his pig hotel retty we will haf a pig Oyster supper." That raised a big laugh but did not fill the stomach. We were informed however that the Quartermaster was in town loading rations for the Regt. That prooved to be the fact because at about 9. P.M. several wagons loaded with craker boxes and barrels made their appearance. It took an hour before crakers, bacon coffee, sugar and salt was all distributed. Thus were the first field rations we ever had seen or received. But now for the cooking process. It was night now. The sky was clear but there was no moon. But the worst was to come [y]et. There was not the least material to make fire with. A detail of a Corporal and 12 men of each Comp. was sent to the woods a mile off to gather such material. The team which had brought in the rations went along to haul in the wood. The empty boxes which had contained the rifles, pants, crakers etc. served as Kindling wood. Mr. Allen, our hired Comp. cook had got tired of the business at Oskosh and gone back to Appleton. So every men had to be his own cook. As our entire cooking apparatus consisted of a tin cup, to make the coffee in it did not take long to go through the operation. The coffee was furnished in roasted beans, and it was left to our choice whether to boil the beans whole or smash them. No Coffeemill was at hand so I adopted the plan we had in Europe; put the beans in the cup[;] hold the cup solid on a board, flat stone, or any other hard level substance in order to save the bottom of the cup; then took the bajonet and with the tube end of it stamp the beans to powder. The entire Regt. adopted that plan and stoo[d] to it to the end of the war. Sometimes it would happen that the beans had become damp or wet and would not break readily. In that case they had to be dried first either in the sun or at the fire.

The bacon we had received was finely cured and could readily be eaten raw with crakers, but good many put a slice of it on a stick, or on the bajonet and roasted it over the fire. But the greatest problem to be solved was represented in the Craker; the renowned and million fold cursed hard tak, the unchangeable, ironclad, dairrhea and scurvy producing craker. True they looked innocent and very inviting when put edgeways in rows into a box, or spread onto a blanket, but as one sets to work to develop their promising fine qualities, they in turn would devellop a most determined percistence to remain forever an undivided quantity of mixed flour and water dried up to the concistency of common granite. Hundreds of experiments were tried by the boys to coax thos innocent looking fellows into a reasonable digestive condition, but all in vain. Some fellows even tried to invent a kind of a hand mill to reduce the fellows to flour again but on account of time and the scarcity of proper tools the laudable enterprise never came to a focus. That was a pity indeed. A wag said: (and he was not much out of the way neither.) the government, in order to secure good and able soldiers, ought to give every recruit at enlistment a solid craker to eat and if he could grind the same in a proper manner, without his jaws giving out to accept him at once. The men tried different methods to overcome the obstinacy of Mr. Craker and to entice him to devellop a more tender disposition but generally with indifferent success. Some would soak them for hours (if time allowed) in warm or cold water, to succeed only in rasing smal blisters on both sides, the balance being as perverse as ever; some would fry them in bacon gries [grease], and compel them to split asunder in two flat disks, but that was all they gained in the operation; Again others would pound them untill they assumed a shape somewhat like course corn-meal and make a sort of cake or biscuit of it which they gave the honorable name of: "Grandmothers porridge." But the greater part, being provided with sound grinders, and a laudable desire to save time and trouble, reso-lutely attacked them in the shape they were received. In fact, if the army was moving, or during campain, it was the only way to handle them, as there was no time for experiments. But all this was not the worst about the "craker." As they merely consisted of flour and water, without salt, or shorting of any kind, the[y] would readily produce an innumerable number of mag-gots or larvae, much like those found in rotten timber; big, fat, cylinder formed white bodies with black, or dark brown heads. I have seen the bot-tom of craker boxes, after the last row was taken out, covered inch high with these wigling, crowding parasites. Although some smart fellows as-serted they contained the very essence of the nourishing quality of the craker, they were not very inducive to a good appetite. At least I came to this conclusion by observing how carefull the boys would examine each morsel before it was delivered to the mill, and if one was found, sent it flying to his neighbor. Walker Fish,[4] who was of a speculative turn of mind, very soberly observed the Government ought to improve such a Chance and combine a poultry yard with each Regt.

Having disposed of the luxurious supper, it was but natural that all of us felt a keen desire to lay down and indulge in sweet dreams of home or "the girl I left behind me." Since we left Oshkosh we had not been, properly speaking, off our legs. Consequently, after pickets and camp guards had been detailed and posted we all squatted down on mother earth bosom. . . . I was ready to enter the realm of dreams when I plainly heard the clatter of horse hoofs on the pike coming from the direction of Covington. I came to a sitting posture and: "Ha[l]t! who comes there!?" again echoed through the night. A minute after the long roll was beaten by the drummer of the guard and: "Fall in! Fall in"! it sounded in clear voices all over camp; the voices of the Major and Adjutant. It took me hardly a minute to be in fighting trim, but to describe the confusion, the cussing and swearing among the boys defies description. And very natural it was to be so. Having always been accustomed to a regular nights rest, and having missed that the two nights previous the men were, so to speak, drunk with sleep.

"Poys! do not forget your cattridgeboxes," warned Majors [Schumacher] in his funny way. "we shall need them very much; the Reps are alreatty south of the Licking riffer and maypee dey want some of your blue pills." . . . After this short allusion to a probable engagement at short distance with the rebels, the boys became remarkabl quiet; even the brave Phill Rose forgot his usual challenges to an invisible foe and patiently pocketed the sneering remarks of more sensible and cooler comrades. I must remark here that many of the boys, especially the younger ones, never had taken the trouble to consider their actual condition, or position. They imagined the rebellion so far away that by the time we reached there the rebellion would have busted. Hence the Majors remarks acted like a bombshell among a flock of geese. "If it only was daylight it would not be so bad," some one remarked; "The Officers dont know anything or they would have started before this" remarked an other. "I say, Phill," drawled Walker Fish, "here is your chance; you keep at the head of the company and the tail end will be safe."—"Damn the rebels," Phill growled. "but why don't they sent that crowd from Cincinnaty over to scare the rebs? they know the country better than we do," and swinging his Austrian rifle around he was proceeding to load the same, when Capt. Jewett informed him that no rifle was to be loaded without orders [y]et.

"Attention Regiment!" broke in at this moment the sonorous voice of Col. Sweet. "Shoulder arms! . . . right shoulder shift arms! Right face! Foward march! Keep well closed up; file closers will see that the men keep proper distance. No noise! No smoking!" And with those cautionary rules we started forward. The right of the Regt. had marched near half a mile when the left started; so much for keeping distances. . . . All pickets and camp guards had to go along.

Well, we marched on. Nothing was said. I suppose every one had his head full enough of thoughts to take care of. The pike was very dusty and the light stuff stirred up by a thousand pair of feet rose up in thick clouds high over the mens head. That started considerable sneezing which prompted the Major to the timely remark that if we did not stop sneezing we soon would scare away all the Reps. "Never mind Major," Fish remarked, "let's save powder and bullet." We reached Licking river but did not cross it; instead of that were herded to the right, marching up stream on the north side about 2 miles, always through a dense growth of brush and briar. Anxious looks peered through the darkness across the river in quest of some sign of the dreaded rebels but nothing could be seen. Finally we were halted in an open spot some 200 yards from the river and ordered to stake [stack] arms. As the men never had gone through the operation it took qu[i]te a while before the stacks would stand alone. Pickets were posted along the river bank with instructions to keep a sharp lookout across the river and report any noise they should hear. The rest of the men were allowed to lay down behind the stacks but not take of[f] the accoutrements. Nobody thought of sleep. The Majors assurance that the rebels were the other side the river prevented that. Half an hour later a fellow from the picket line came hurrying up and reported they had heard a lot of roosters Crow and dogs bark. "Brave Poys," the Major replied shuckling, "always observe and mind effory thing. You know it was a lot of geese who with their cackling saved Rome." This incident gave rise to much amusement but after all there was sound morale in it.

A little while after the pickets were called in and the Regt. marched back to the place we had left. Here we staked arms and laid down again to have, if possible a little sleep [y]et. The first faint streak of day glimmered in the East when I bedded my head on my knapsack but I was not to enjoy any sleep. From every direction of the Compass roosters loudly proclaimed the approaching day; in an adjoining field several hundred mules were coralled awaiting the breaking in for field service, and who now, as if by order, started their informal "gee-gawing" concert. Army and market wagons, milk carts and drays came rattling along the pike. Bells began to toll here and there in Covington; Factories and steamboat whistles aranged a concert from the highest tenor down to the deepest bass. Railroad trains were coming and going and switching and so I did not feel sorry at all when at 5 o.clock Reveillee was sounded, warning us to be up, prepare our Coffee and be ready for the duties of the day.

During breakfast much speculation was going on what for we had to make that tramp during the night. Many different opinions were put forward, but only those hit the nail straight who argued that it merely was done for exercise; as an experiment to see how quick the men could get ready on short notice and make them used to such untimely calls. Phil Rose, who had been remarkably quiet during the scout, succumbed again to his bragging habit and swore he felt sorry that no rebs had been there. Breakfast over we were ordered to fall in without knapsack. The Colonel marched us into a field a mile from camp and drilled the Regt. until 11. A.M. in a manner which drove the perspiration through pantaloons and coat. It certainly was the reason that the boys found the hardtack and bacon more palatable than before. The afternoon was passed in the same manner and when at night the boys took their frugal meal they agreed that the Colonel understood [how] to entertain the Regt. But it was begun at the wrong end; like building a house and begin with the roof. The Commissioned Officers as well as the non commissioned Officers were as ignorant as the men. These should have been thoroughly drilled first. They in turn could have drilled the men in the manual of arms and company drill. Then the Colonel would have been able to make a decent Regiments drill; as it was, it was merely a bungling business, to me at least absurd to look at. I spoke to Major Schumacher that night about that matter and he informed me that this was the only course left for the Colonel to adopt, as we might at any moment be called to the field. There was no time to drill in detail. . . .

Meanwhile Genl. Bragg had not been idle. Heretofore his movements had indicated that Cincinaty would be his objective point; but while [y]et in the midle of the State he took his direction towards Louisville. To prevent this an other shift had to be made by the Union troops. Accordingly we recived orders to be ready to move at a moments notice. At five A.M. we started back through Covington and halted at the Ohio river. Quite a number of big river steamers were busy taking troops on board, to be transferred down the river to Louisville. We too expected to get a boatride but in this were sorely disappointed. At about 10. A.M. we were marched through Cincinnaty to the western Depot. A long train of box Cars stood ready for us and we had to bord them through the gaping side doors. We had to stand up and were crowded so close as to be hardly able to move. The floor of the Carr was handsomly carpeted by about 6 inches of cattle droppings. As soon as a Carr was filled, the heavy sliding doors were shut and locked and we were actually prisoners in a pitch dark stable. I could not help thinking that if a smash up should happen, what an immense heap of hash would be secured from so many human bodies. The boys did not take it very quietly and became very noisy.

The air in the crowded box soon became thick and sickening. In vain did we try to knock of[f] some bords to admit pure air. James Orr[5] broke the stock of his rifle in the attempt. Of course it was charged against him on the payrol and 13 dollars were deducted from his pay. I finally succeeded in forcing open a bord window about two foot square in the End of the Carr where I had taken my stand. It is extremely tiring to stand for a long time on the same spot without being able to move around. We finally agreed [on a method] whereby we were enabled to find some relief. The men in one half of the car had to squeeze together as close as possible which would give the other a chance to unsling their knapsacks and sit down on them. Every quarter of an hour relief was called and the squatters in their turn had to go through the squeezing process, while the others took the squatting turn. It was past noon when the concern began to move. . . .

At sundown we arrived at Jeffersonville Indiana opposite Louisville on the north side of the Ohio. We were marched in a large enc[l]osed pasture which seemed to be a sort of fairground, judging by the building and stalls put up there. It rained lustily, the first time since we had left Appleton. We had a hard time of it to make a cup of coffee. There was no firewood and only a few old boards were furnished for that purpose. The boys would have attacked the fence and stalls but guards posted there prevented that. But that was not the worst part of it. It kept on raining steadily until near daylight. We had no tents nor rubber blankets. In the old buildings and sheds it was even worse than out doors as the roof were in the worst of repairs. So we went through a regular soaking process and in spite of overcoat and blanket we were wet to the bones. The woolen stuff became so heavy that we were hardly able to lug it along the next morning.

The morning we left Covington Ky. Corporal George Ney [Nye] of town Freedom reported sick. The doctor thought the muddy water of the Licking river had produced his disease. He was left in hospital in Covington where he died shortly after. He was the heaviest, and next to Phil Rose the tallest man in the Comp. He oppened the long list of deaths of diseases which happened in the Comp. afterwards. He had a jounger brother in the Co. Bill Nye. a tall slim built boy who was taken sick three months later at Murfreesboro Tenn. and died there. . . . [6]

There were about 20,000 fresh soldiers gathered around Louisville to welcome Bragg. On the second afternoon the advance of Genl. Buel[l']s army arrived, who in forced marches had come all the way from Chattanooga Tenn. to head of[f] old Bragg. Buel[l']s troops, in consequence of continued forced marches, were in a sorry plight and needed some rest badly. As I stood looking at the passing troops, all covered and gray with dust, their clothing torn, some almost barefooted, I noticed one Captain limping along painfully, using his sword as a staff. Looking at him closely I was surprised to recognize in him a dear friend from Appleton, August Steffens by name.[7] He probably did not recognize me in soldiers garb, but when I called his name he stared a moment at me and then blurted out,

"Jehosaphat, Otto, you here!" and in a moment I was surrounded by a dozen more former friends, which altogether made me almost break down with handshaking. Since they were not allowed to stay behind, and I had no leave to go along with them, I promised to hunt them up as soon as I could get leave to do so. . . .

While I [y]et was talking and shaking hands with the friends of the 24th Ill. orders came for us to pack up and be ready to move. While busy with that performance I noticed that Sergeant Williams took some kind of wirecloth out of his knapsack and tried to roll it up in a package. He acted somewhat sly about it, as if he did not wish anybody to see it. When he found that I observed his operation he winked and whispered to me not to tell anything about it. It was a mail waistcoat, made of fine steel wire and quite heavy. Only the front parts which cover the breast were made of wire. I suppose the manufactures of the article took it for granted that in warfare the bullets only came square from the front. Sergeant Williams found the article to[o] heavy to lug along in the knapsack and he intended to wrap it up and put it in the Quartermasters wagon, supposing he could get it any time he needed it. Poor chap; he made the bill without the host. About two weeks after in the battle at Perryville Ky. the Quartermasters wagon with the steel waist aboard was miles in the rear and Sergeant Williams was shot in the breast. And even if he had worn the thing it would not have saved him, because he was shot from behind while the Regt. was making a move. He did not die but remained a poor, suffering Invalid ever after.

This time we were marched to the East side of the city. The following day was Saturday and we were set to work digging trenches and building breastworks. At 4 P.M. my squad had finished its allotted share of work and for the rest of the day we were free of duty. I went out to find my friends of the 24th Ill. I had not far to go. The brigade of which the 24th. formed a part was encamped about a quarter of a mile south of us. I found the boys easy enough and time passed quick in exchanging news on both sides. Before I left for our camp, I made arrangements with Steffens how we should pass the Sunday. We concluded to take in the sights of the City. . . . Steffens who had been in Louisville a full month the year previous could act as guide. The only drawback in the plan was: would Captain Jewett give me a pass for the day? I felt quite sure if I went alone to the Capt. he would refuse me. I informed Steffens of my situation and requested him to come to our Camp next morning and go with me to the Capt. Jewett, as a matter of courtesy, could not well refuse Captain Steffens plea and I got a pass. I watched Jewett closely while he wrote the pass and noticed by the twitching of the muscles in his face that it went against his grain, and he did made me pay for the favor. The next day I had to go on picket duty although it was not my turn to do so. That prooves conclusively what mean tricks he would adopt to gratify his petty malice. . . .

Returning from picket the following morning I found everybody busy packing things together for a move. This time we marched about two miles to the south of the City to what was called "Camp Buckner" because the land belonged to the rebel general [Simon Bolivar] Buckner. For three days we had to dig ditches and construct breastworks. We had to work day and night by reliefs; two hours work two hours rest. Frank Stowe met here with a sad accident. He worked with a spade or shovel and Curtis Mitchell who used a pickaxe by accident struck Stowes right hand just behind the knucles of the two midle fingers, driving the pickaxe clear through. The surgeons wanted to take the two fingers out as the bones and coards in the hand were all smashed but Stowe would not let them. The result was the fingers became stiff and bended inward in the palm of the hand. Being disabled for further service he was discharged.[8]

Several more days were spent with Comp. and Regiments drill, with testing the abilities of our austrian rifles in a target shooting match; as also a scout ten miles out in the Country along the Louisville and Nashville R.R. Gen'l. Buel[l']s troops had been sufficiently rested; new clothing and shoes were issued; the army wagons were replenished and filled with hard tack and bacon; batteries supplied with cannisters, round Shot and shell. The army had been reorganized, that is, the new Regts. were distributed among the older troops. Our Regt. for instance was assigned to the 28th Brigade commanded by Col. John C. Starkweather of the 1st Wis. Rgt. The brigade consisted of three old Regt. wich had already seen a years service, viz: the First Wis. Regt., the 79th Penn and the 24th Ill. Our Regt. 21st Wis. was the new Rgt. in the brigade.

A short description of the different Regt. of the brigade will be interesting as far as the future history of the brigade is concerned. The First Wis. had been organized under the call of the President for 75,000 three months men in April 1861. In July the same year their term of service expired, but most of them reinlisted for three years and with the addition of new recruits the 1st Wis. Regt. was formed, commanded by Col. John C. Starkweather, as brave and reliable a soldier as ever entered the field. The Regt. consisted of members of different kind of nations and so we may call it a mixed concern. . . . The 79th Penn. was a composition of the so called Pensilvania dutch, born here of german Immigrants; german born men who having immigrated to America had become Citizens here; and a sprinkling of Americans and Irish and Scotch. Its Colonel a certain Hambright was a trained military men, a West Pointer; tall, heavy built and of erect carriage like a bean pole. He was a brave, well meaning man whose only fault was that he stook to[o] pertinaciously to the West Point regulations which could not be applied to the Volunteer soldier.[9] The 24th Ill. . . . was an exlusively german Regt. composed of Chicago Turners.[10]. . . Finally our Regt. the 21st Wis. was the only new Regt. in the brigade and consequently styled by the other Regts. as the "greenhorns, or suckers"; but it did not take very long they dropped thus [this]complimentary title. The Division was commanded by Genl. Lovel H. Rousseau, a Kentukian by birth, a lawyer by profession, and a splendid soldier. The Army Corps (14th) at that time was commanded by Genl. D. M. McCook, a splendid fighting soldier. . . . Our Army was commanded by Major Genl. Don Carlos Buel[l],[11] also a Kentukian and a graduate of West Point. He was said to be a good, able General but during this campain he did not come up to that mark as will be seen further on. My wish to be assigned to the middle or western army was fulfilled. Our Army was then Known as the Army of the Ohio.

On the first of October, the army was to start on the hunt after Bragg. He was directing his march towards Cumberland Gap East Tennessee. If he succeeded in bringing his army through the gap before we could reach him he was safe. Kirby Smith meanwhile had formed a junction with Braggs army, thus bringing the strenght of Braggs army to nearly 50,000 fighting men. But it was not Br[a]ggs intention to fight us, but to bring his plunder in security. And just here is the point where Genl. D. C. Buel[l] failed in not following close enough on the heels of Bragg; and prevent him from bringing his army through Cumberland gap.[12]

On the 30th of September, the day before we started, the regt. surprised Major Schumacher by presenting him a splendid black horse and equipment which they purchased in Louisville for $500.00. The Regt. was drawn up in line when the present was tendered. The always so jolly Major was so overcome with emotion that he was almost unable to speak. Towards evening all the doubtful fellows had to report to the surgeons and such as were found to be wanting in physical strenght were sent to the hospital in Louisville, or New Albany Indiana. James Orr . . . tried hard to convince the surgeons that he was unable to go through the Campain, but the surgeons could not see it and sent him back to the Comp. Finally, as a last trump he asserted his front teeth were loose and he could not bite off a cartridge, nor could he successfully cope with the hardtack. The surgen knocked about

PREPARING FOR ACTUAL WARFARE

his teeth awhile and finally said he himself would be glad to possess such a fine set of grinders. So Orr had to stick to it but he told some of the boys he would make them feel sorry for it; and he kept his word, but of that by and by. Corporal Amos Lawrence also tried hard to back out but he also had to go along.

Considerabl dissastifection existed among the men on account of the rations we had received up to this time. Indeed it seemed strange that we, being so near railroad and water Communication, had never received anything but crakers, bacon, Coffe, salt and sugar. It certainly was a sudden change and very trying for the men, most of whom had been used from childhood to a rich, varying diet. Besides the nauseating Effect, it produced diarrhia, blody and white flux, disentery, piles, scurvy and other diseases. Add to this the filthy stagnant water we had to use most of the time, no better plan could have been adopted to disable and break down otherwise robust and healthy men.

CHAPTER THREE

~

Progress and Incidents of
Our First Campaign

~ Oct. 1st 1862, at 4 A.M. bugles and drums brought us to our feet and
remined us that to day we were to start on the actual war path. How long
that path would be, when, where, and how it would end; who would be the
lucky ones who would retrace their steps and see their homes and embrace
their dear ones again, who could tell? Alas! Thousands and thousands of
those who shouldered their rifle and stowed away the 60 rounds of cartridges on that bright October morning never saw their home again. . . .
Bullet and cannister, shot and shell took considerable, but more succumbed
to diseases in various form, a consequence of untold hardships, exposure,
poor rations and water and defective treatment when sick, did far more.
The rebel prison pens, those wholesale starving establishments, guerillas
and bushwhakers, all were united as it were, to kill off the hated yankee,
dutch mudsills and Lincoln hirelings.

At 5. A.M. the troops took line of march. Our Corps on the Bardstown
Pike in a south eastern direction from Louisville. At first the boys felt
cheerfull and would sing and crack jokes; even Phil Rose could not suppress his desire to once meet a live rebel; but when it came towards 9. A.M.
unmistakable signs of flagging were apparent. The day became exeedingly
hot. The dust on the pike was hand deep and became almost unbearable. It
had to be swallowed with every breath; it clogged up the nostrils, it settled
finger thick on hat, knapsack, and uniform. The uniform became saturated
with sweat and made the dust stick so much the better. The stretching of
the column grew to an alarming extent. Repeatedly the order close up!

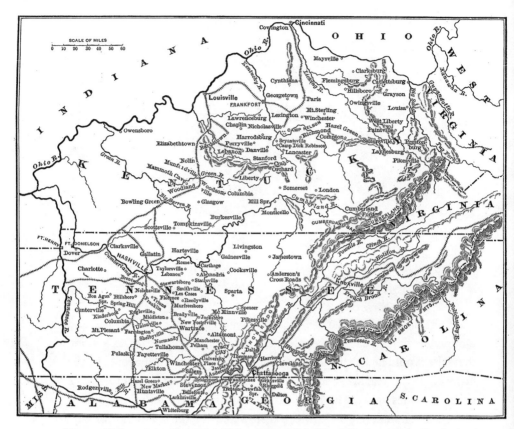

"General Map of the Campaign," from Henry M. Cist, *The Army of the Cumberland* (New York: Scribner's, 1882). (Courtesy State Historical Society of Wisconsin)

boys, close up! was heard but without much effect. This stretching out of a Column while marching is one of the greatest evils of new, unexperienced soldiers. A division of soldiers of Infantry in line of march, if the Regts. are complete, cover a road for two miles in lenght, exclusive train. Now by a little carelessness of each file of men to alow the space between them and the preceding file to increase 18 inches the Division will stretch out 4 miles in lenght, or double that of its proper lenght. What exertion that takes for the troops in the rear to catch up, anyone may find out by letting a person march 2 miles and then try to overtake him. He will find it a tough job I warrant, even if he has not to tote 40–50 pounds luggage along as we had to. . . . If there were two or three divisions on the same road the stretching would increase accordingly.

The men soon began to throw away their Overcoats, to lighten their burden, some even disposed of their blankets in the same manner; a verry imprudent act for which the[y] felt verry sorry afterward. The water in the Canteens was soon gone and no water to be found near the pike. If a well was met with occasionally it was dry in a short time, as an unusually dry season had brought the water very low. Whenever fruit was found the men would eat it greedily, wether ripe or not, and complain of pains in the stomach and bowels afterward. At about noon a halt was made partly for reason to take dinner and partly to give troops in the rear chance to close up. Dinner was a mighty shabby affair. The most could make no coffee as there was no water near. Of course dry hardtack and a slice of raw bacon may be under certain circumstances a very desirable Object but under the present condition it was the poorest substitute possible for a refreshing meal; but we had to become reconciled and used to such every day fare, and the sooner that was accomplished, the better.

After about an hours rest we went on again. We passed through Bardstown, a long straggling village. Woman and children stood alongside the street. It was easy to see and to hear which party they favored. The rebel inclined would scowl and sneer and their young ones hoot at us, while the union Ladies, some crying, some laughing, offered us water and fruits. One old lady assured me that she had three sons in the Union army and that the rebel Bragg had been there a week ago and his men had taken everything they could carry or drive away; while a rebel women hoped Bragg would take us all prisoner, or kill every one of us and send us to hell where we belonged.

Slowly and painfully the afternoon wore away. Tiered and foot sore the boys stragled along. The Officers had ceased long ago to order the men to close up, because it had no effect. It seemed the men were entirely worn out and unmindfull what might become of them. Good many fell out and squatted down in fence corners. Long Phil, who was so jubilant when we started in the morning and hoped to meet a live rebel, I noticed had also quitted the ranks. Capt. Jewett, although he had nothing to carry but his sword and canteen walked like on eggs. I undertook to draw him in conversation and asked him if he did not think the march to[o] long for new troops not used to it, but he did not think it worth while to reply so I gave up the trial. . . .

The Stars already twinkled from the clear sky and still we, or what was left of us, strugled wearily along, a scattering, despairing mass of humanity. Not untill ten at night did the head of our brigade file to the left in a large field, where the Regts. were drawn up in line, arms sta[c]ked and informed that we would camp here to night; to be ready to march next morning at five, and were strictly forbidden to use any fencerails for firewood.

We were further informed that half a mile south of the road was a creek where water could be had. I had noticed that the front of the Regt. seemed so short and counted the files of our Comp. Twenty seven had disappeared who were either camping somewhere on their own hook, or strugling on the road to come up with us. After the order to break ranks almost every one laid down in the first convenient place, Capt. Jewett among the first. Of course no one of them knew anything of army life and followed their first impulse, which was decidedly wrong. I advised them to make a cup of coffee but very few did so. I went to the german boys and told them what the result would be. Chas. Lymer and Van Stratum had fallen out. They were all willing to make coffee. So we all started for the Creek, each taking half a dozen Canteens along. After filling the Canteens we washed our feet, then gathered some dry driftwood which lay along the bank of the creek.

Arrived in camp we soon had a blazing little fire and coffee made and I can assure anybody that we relished the hot black beverage. All that had taken but half an hour. I made an other cup for Capt. Jewett. He seemed to be in a swoon, it took me so long to shake life into him. He stared at me for a while and then said: "You?" But that was all. He took the cup and I left him to bring an other cup to Lieut. Turner. I advised Turner to induce the Capt. to detail a man from the Comp. whose business it was to prepare the coffee for the Officers which after a while they did. While we were taking our coffee some of the man rose and stared at us. "There is the fire boys, set to work." I advised them, which they did as long as the wood held out but no one was willing to go after wood. I further warned them that if they did not provide for wood now they would not be able to make coffee the next morning, but to no purpose; not a single man went. We hauled us some more wood and water and then wrapt ourselves in the blanket and went to sleep. But up to 2. A.M. the following day the stragglers were coming in and laid down to have a few hours rest. We had marched that day 27 miles. That is not much, good many will say; but let any try to travel that much and tote fifty pounds along I want to see how he will feel at the end of the journey.

The following day was a true copy of the first one with this exeption that we had to travel 30 miles. When we halted at noon for dinner it happened that alongside our Regt. not far from the road was a sort of pond in the field. It was the drinking place for a lot of cattle, mules and swine. It contained a muddy, filthy warm mixture, with a slimy cover on the surface but, by way of compliment I suppose, was called water. As the boys had no other choice they went for it. Scarcely had the boys cleared the scum of[f] and were filling the canteens, when our Adjutant, Lieut Fitch, coolly rode

his horse in the water to drink. The horse was restles and unruly and consequently made the water very rily. "Get out of here" the boys shouted; "You
can water your stag when we are through." As usual in such cases a number
of profane epithets and requests were hurled at the Adjutant, but he did
not stir. The men, not willing to be treated in such a hoggish manner, applied a lot of little stones and lumps of hard Clay in the direction of the
Adjutant and his horse, which made him wheel round in a hurry, swearing
as he did so, he would report them to the Colonel. He did so. But Colonel
Sweet had more sense. Instead of reprimanding the men he ordered the
Adjutant under arrest and made him walk in the rear of the Regt. for the
rest of the day. Colonel Sweet made a big score that day in the opinion of
the men.

It was late in the evening when we halted for camp. The men were even
more demoralized than the night before. But when we were informed that
we should have rest the next day the feeling of misery gave vent to hearty
cheers and renewed courage. A small creek wound its way through the
camping ground. There was not much water in it, but it was clear and pure.
The wood also was not far of[f] and before long the "dutch squad" were
enjoying their Coffee, bacon and hardtack. The other men were crowding
around our fires again and finally we moved back and left it all to them. As
the fire was not extensive enough for so many men they soon began to
quarrel about room and in the melee many cups and small kettles were
upset. Only Richard Baker and his son and the Walker brothers[1] had provided wood and fire for themselves. But that could not go on in that way.
Our men saw the old Regts. building numbers of fires but they did not
seem to mind their example, or perhaps they thought somebody else would
do it for them. Capt. Jewett either was to[o] proud, or to[o] indifferent to
look after the welfare of his Comp. and whatever he did say was said in
such a bluff, repulsive manner that the boys seldom cared to heed it unless
compelled to.

I had a long conversation with Lieut. Turner and advised him, since the
Captain did not do it, to take the matter in hand himself and see that the
boys take better care of themselves. Our Orderly Sergeant, Chas. Fay was
the same as the Capt., aristocratic and indifferent. Lieut. Turner, for different reasons and excuses, put the job on to me. He argued that Captain Jewett as the head of the Comp. might think him to[o] forward, or putting on
airs, etc. Further, he said, that as he was acquainted with nearly every on[e]
of them, and as he did not know more about soldiering as they did, they
might resent his suggestions. On the other hand they all knew that I had

been a soldier in an European army they would listen to me sooner than to him. I tried to argue that point with him, because at that time, (and good many times to day for that matter) a german, or dutchmen, as they called us, was of no account exept to stopp a rebel bullet. Further I was only the third sergeant; what authority could I produce to justify, or claim obedience to my suggestions? And could not the Capt. at any time step up and tell me to mind my business? But I concluded to try the experiment in a different way. Accordingly, before we laid down I enticed the dutch squad to help me to get wood enough to build fires for the whole Comp. next morning. They readily consented. We also built the fires next morning and while they were sipping their coffee I had a half hours talk with them. They all listened with great attention, although I noticed on many a face an expression of doubt or contempt. When I had concluded I met Capt. Jewett, or rather, he met me. He must have heard my remarks, because he told me in plain and clear English that if I in any manner would further interfere with the business of the boys, or the Comp. he would have me reduced to the ranks. "Very well, Captain," I replied: "do not be bashfull; go right along. But you cannot forbid me to give advice to the men if their welfare is thereby advanced." He did not say a word, but the look and expression he measured me with I will never forget.

After the [encounter] with the Capt. I went down the creek expecting to find somewhere a good place for a thorough washing below the camps of the troops. About a miles walk brought me to a bend of the creek where the same formed a sort of pond. I went back immediately to the Regt. and informed them of my find. The greater part of the Regt. went along and I am sure none of them ever regretted the exercise.

During the forenoon a couple of runaway negro slaves came in camp asking for protection and work. The negroes all had the Idea that if they were with us they were free. Some of our Officers felt inclined to keep them as cooks and men of all work, but the Emancipation proclamation had not [y]et been issued and Officers and soldiers were strictly forbidden to encourage runaways, or ha[r]bour the same. Shortly after the niggers had come in, two citizens on horseback, armed each with a long whip and, as I noticed later, with a navy revolver in the sadle pocket, rode into our camp. They inquired for the Colonel and wanted him to deliver over to them t[w]o negros who were their property, they had run away during the night and were now hidden somewhere in our camp. How they knew they were in our Regt. I do not know, unless there was some niggerhater in our Regt. who had given the information. Colonel Sweet wanted to know how they knew "the property" was in our Regt. They refused to give any direct answers but insisted that the niggers were hidden in our regt. Colonel Sweets dander got up. He spoke very decisive now. "Gentlemen! by whose authority do you come here to ransack the camp of my regiment? What do I know but you are common thiefs or tramps trying to find some United States money among my mens bagage. If you have no authority to produce I advise you to get out of here as fast as you can." The fellows sat still and did not answer.

Now I must remark that it was not now merely a matter of our regiment. Our brigade was encamped in column, that is our Regt. and the 79th Penn. were in the first or front line, the 24th Ill. about ten rods in the rear of our Regt. and the 1st Wis. in the same line behind the 79th Penn. Communication was easily kept up at such short distance. The trouble was soon known in the entire brigade. When the nigger catchers began their parlay with the Colonel the music band of the 24th Ill. was just playing "Hail Columbia." but they soon stopped. A big circle of boys of our and other Regts. had gathered around the slave hunters; their behavior and language did not signify anything pleasant for the citizens. The Colonel, fearing the soldiers might go to an ex[c]ess, gave the slave hunters leave to search in the Regt. There was not much to search though. The boys had built some shade huts of cornstalks; some blankets lay round loose and some army wagons and ambulances in the rear of the Col. headquarters. The fellows looked carefully enough and went over the ground twice but failed to find their property. They began to utter abusive language, spoke about damned blackguards, Abolitionists, thiefs and beggars. That was to[o] much for the boys. The twenty fourth boys who were nearest to us mingled freely with us. Cries of: "Get out you niggerdrivers! take them down! let's hang them!" were heard among the Crowd; and as by command the air filled with corncobs and other missiles, hitting horses and riders. The fellows seeing the unhealthy condition drewe their navies. Instantly a number of revolvers were pointed at their heads and they ordered to drop their navies. They did so. At that instant Van Stratum tickled one of their horses with a jackknife behind, which made the horse give a sudden start, nearly throwing of[f] its rider. Both dashed towards the pike, but not home. They went directly towards Genl. Rousseau's headquarters to look for help.

General Rousseau, himself a [Kentuckian], was a strong Union men.[2] Although no slave owner himself, he did not favor the sudden liberation of the slaves, nor the Idea to give employment to slaves in the army. The slave catchers therefore felt sure of the recovery of their property if they appealed to him. As the Genl. commanded the Division he had authority in the matter. Consequently a quarter of an hour later an order came from Div. Headquarters for our brigade to fall in and take arms. Hardly had we done so when Rousseau with his staff and the nigger catchers rode into camp. Our Regt. was ordered to stake arms and march 20. paces backward. The 79th Penn. was moved next between us and our rifles and ordered to load, facing towards us. The 24th Ill. was placed in our rear; the 1st Wis. on our right along the road and Capt. Stones Kentuky batterie on our left flank. So we were properly enclosed for execution if necessary. The Genl. then took position in front of us and in a loud voice asked the Regt. where the two slaves who had been seen in our Regt. could be found. No answer. He repeated the question. No result. "Now 21st Wis." he roared, "will you obey my orders or not?"

All was quiet but a distint voice from the left replied in a clear voice: "Yes General, if consistent with our duty and Concience, but no slave catching." He gallopped to the left and wanted to know who the men was who made such impertinent reply. He could not find him; Nobody seemed to know. He dashed back to the front. It was plainly to been seen he was mad. Finally the boys who had thrown the corncobs were ordered to step forward. None came. He repeated the request. Br[a]ton Newel [Newell] and Foster Pearson[3] from our Comp. and 3 of another Comp. stepped forward. The Genl. then ordered two of his Orderlies to bring them to his headquarters under arrest. He then put all line Officers of the Regt. under arrest. The noncommissioned Officers and privates were confined to the camp and a strong guard detailed to enforce orders. The General then went back to his qua[r]ters, the nigger cat[c]hers going along with them. The funniest in the whole proceeding was that during the whole proceeding the two slaves were within the camp grounds.

The topic about which conversation in camp turned now was: What would Rousseau do with our Regt. and specially with the men who had pleaded guilty of the throwing of corncobs. Lieut. Turner and I went over to the 24th Ill. to hear what they thought about the matter as they had a hand in the affair. They took the matter very easy thinking the General would drop the whole thing like a hot iron. . . . They all said that if the General should prosecute our boys their whole Regt. would step up and plead guilty of having thrown corncobs; and so thought the 79th Penn. and the 1st Wis. Nay, it would have set the whole Division against him, which would have forced him to resign, or to be transferred to some other part of the army. And he seemed to understand the matter perfectly, because that same night the plantation buildings of the two slavehunters went up in smoke and we never knew who had been the cause of it, nor did the General undertake to investigate. This Intermezzo had given him to understand that the northern soldiers had not enlisted to catch slaves like a bloo[d]-hound, for the rebel niggerdrivers.

In consequences of our arrest we had no chance to get wood for supper fires and breakfast; on account of the trouble, we even had had no dinner. But the 24th boys hauled wood enough for our Regt. We made an early supper. After that the 24th boys had a surprise in store for us. That Regt. had a fine music band, the only one in the brigade. This band took position between their and our Regt. and played martial and other pieces. In the intervals the Turners performed acrobatic feats and the song clubs sang american and german Songs. It was not long before the 79th Penn and 1st Wis. came to see the "Elephant" as they said. The 79th had a minstrel troop in their Regt. These fellows would blacken their faces and hands, wearing oldfacioned, longpointed paper collars, a battered old cylinder on the artificially curled wool, a long swallowtailed coat of old patched up overcoats and uniforms. Their make up looked real and armd with fidle, banjo and bones and being good singers they performed as fine a niggershow as I ever have seen travelling afterward. Soon the brigade was together and finally most of the Division. Genls. Mitchel, Terrill and Colonel Starkweather wanted to know all about the exitement and soon became infected with the general spirit and heartily endorsed and joined the merryment. Some of the 24th boys had been on a private scout in the country and had struck Oil (distillery) and bought, (or confiscated, I dont remember which) an 8 gallon Keg of Bourbon. Of course that stimulated the merry feeling, but when sometime afterward an other keg made its appearance the Officers became alarmed anticipating disorder, or a row. The jubilee continued until 9. P.M. when "Taps" reminded us to squat down on the usual soldiers homestead. . . .

Next morning at 5. we filed out of camp for the days trip. Officers and men released from arrest, even the 5 boys who had been taken to headquarters, and nothing was said about jesterdays affair. But when we turned on to the pike, there was Genl. Rousseau with his staff, watching with a rather sour face the ranks as they passed by, hoping perhaps the darkies mig[h]t pop up. But there came none and finally he turned the horses head and dashed to the front, that is to the head of the Colum. But still the darkies were with us and the Genral might easy have found them if he wanted to. But I believe he did not want to and was glad to be out of the trap as we never heard any more of the affair. The darkies did not march but rode in an

PROGRESS AND INCIDENTS OF OUR FIRST CAMPAIGN

ambulance, covered with straw, knapsacks of the sick boys etc. They remained in the Regt. as Officers servants and packmules in general.[4] The day again became viciously hot but passed with out any incident exept the usually stretching & straggling and a lively tussel beneath a big apple tree which refused to supply everybody with a peck of poor apples. The march was moderate, 22 miles, but certainly enough considering the heat and dust. . . . We went into camp about 6. P.M. There were not so many stragglers as the previous days and those all were in by 9 o clock. After supper we drew for 5. days rations.

Oct. 5th. That was a good stretch. 30 miles, measured by the fox, the tail not counted in, as Walker Fish remarked. A great number of straglers was the consequence. For me it was the hardest day I had experienced [y]et. I had made a mistake when we received shoes in camp at Oshkosh. I could not find a pair which suited me exactly and as I had a good pair of new boots I did not take shoes. The boots were well enough for every day wear at home, but for a 30 mile tramp on a hard gravel pike and in a steady hot sun, they were to[o] small and to[o] hot. The feet would swell and burn like a red hot block of Iron. But that was not all. When we left Louisville I felt some pain in the left armpit, but as it was not severe I did not pay much attention to it. The second day it worried me considerable, as the shoulderstrap from the knapsack pressed somewhat against it. In camp on Sunday I examined the matter and found I was hatching a handsome bile [boil] there. I could not stand the pressure of the shoulderstrap again[s]t it. I went to the surgeon who made room for my knapsack in an ambulance. During the afternoon I even had to take off the coat, as the tailer making the same, had given no allowance for a big bile. I rolled the coat in a bundle, tied a string around and hung the bundle on my rifle. But, as the saying has it: "A good thing seldom comes alone." It certainly did not in this case. Like most of the men, I had unusually often private business the other side of the fence. Well, on one of these occasions I put the bundle aside, leaned the rifle against the fence. Being in a hurry to catch up with the regiment, I grabbed the rifle as soon as relieved, cleared the fence and went for the regiment, leaving the coat behind the fence doing guard duty. I never thought of it until after going several miles, Sergea[n]t Williams inquired if my coat was on the wagon. There! I would not go back for the coat; walking was to[o] hard work just at that time; so I concluded to go minus coat hoping the Quartermaster might have some on hand [y]et.

Past 10. P.M. we humped into camp. More than ¼ of the Regt. were behind; even Capt. Jewett was not there. Lieut. Turner was nearly played

out and I not less. Fred Borcherdt our 2d Lieut. who had served a year in
the Potomac Army said: they never had made such trips there. But we
managed to get wood and water and had coffee in short time. But not half
the men took the trouble to make coffee. It was a poor rest that night.
Untill the small hours in the morning the straglers came in inquiring for
their brigades and Regt. running here and there against a sleeping form,
setting the same cursing and swearing until the air seemed full of brimstone. Besides the bowels would claim immediate attention several times.
When we got up at reveillee I felt as though I had slept on a stone and the
way the boys acted I knew they were not better of[f], perhaps worse. At
roll call not all an[s]wered to their names. They had camped somewhere
along the road, hoping to catch up the next day. At sick call a long string
winded its way towards the surgeons wagon. . . . The most complaint was
on account of diarrhea or sore feet, or both. In aggravated cases they would
be sent to the Ambulances to have a ride that day; others would have the
priviledge to put their rifles, accoutrements and other things on an army
wagon and thus relieved follow in the rear of the Regt. Chas. Lymer and
Van Stratum were sent to an ambulance. Both were so badly chafed as to be
almost raw over the entyre body. They had a somewhat tender skin and
sweat, dust and the friction produced by knapsack and accoutrements had
produced the result.

Oct. 6th[.] Our Regiment had considerable easier marching today, because our Regt. was at the head of the column whereas we had been in the
rear the day before. That makes a great difference because of the stretching
process, as I have explained before. We marched twenty five miles and
camped not far from Taylorsville. For the first time our Regt. had to furnish
a detail for picket duty. Our Orderly Sergt. ordered me with the detail of
our Comp. It was not my turn as Sergt. John Dey ranked me he should
have been the first on the detail. I inquired of the Orderly why he did not
take Sergeant Dey. I explained to him my situation, but he simply replied I
had to go as Sergeant Dey did not feel well. I left and went to Sergeant
Theodore Clark and asked him if he would go on picket for me to night I
would take his turn next. He knew my situation and readily consented and
I informed the orderly of our agreement; he in turn reported the same to
Capt. Jewett, which was not necessary at all as such exchanges among comrades are not forbidden at all. But the Capt. sent for me and reporting he
asked: "I heard you refuse to go on picket; why not?" I explained and during
the time he noticed I was in shirtsleeves. He wanted to know why I did not
come in Uniform. I explained again. That made him mad and he used very

hard language. As soon as I had a chance I remarked; since it was myself who had to pay for the coat I could not see why he should fly up so about it; besides I had not lost, or thrown away the coat by intent or malice. That knocked the bottom out of the barrel. He sent for Sergeant Clark and ordered him not to go on picket for me and pointing to me shouted: and you lazy dutchman go immediately and report for picket or go in arrest. "Capt." I replied, "I am a sergeant; and if you should have forgotten that I will take occasion to remind you of the fact." "A cheat you are," he returned and I went off, but not to report for picket, but to the surgeon. I stated the case and asked him for an excuse from duty. He took a carefull survey of the pet in my armpit. That fellow had by this time grown fat, about the size of a hens egg cut in two. The surgeon said it had not come to point [y]et and he did not like to lance it, nor did I want him to. He wanted me to report to him next morning and he would find a place in the ambulance for me. Then he took a slip of paper and scribled a few words on it and handed it to me saying: "That will do." The paper read: "Excused from duty untill further orders. R. Carlin Regts. Surgeon 21st Wis."

So far all was right but I was not satisfied [y]et. I went to Regts. head-quarters and reported to Col. Sweet. I explained the whole affair and that I could wear neither coat nor knapsack. "You go to your quarters, I will tend to this," was all he said. I had not reached the Camp [y]et when the Ser-geant Major run past me direct to Capt. Jewett. I saw him go with the Sergt. Major to the Colonel. Meanwhile the various picket details assembled at brigade headquarters. Everything was correct but the detail from our Regt. was not there. It happened that Major Schumacher was in charge of the brigade picket line that night. When Capt. Jewett was at Regt. head-quarters the Major came galopping to the Regt. and wanted to know what caused the delay. I had already informed our Orderly of my excuse and he then ordered Sergt. Clark for the duty. While Clark was getting ready and the men in order I told the Major how the delay had happened. "Er ist ein dummer Teufel" meaning Capt. Jewett, remarked the Major in german, "but he will get smart before long or quit." The detail being ready they marched off just when Capt. Jewett returned from the Colonel. Lieut. Turner informed me the same evening that the Capt. was mad enough to take poison and never forgive me the point I had made. . . .

Oct. 7th. I did not make use of the ambulance which the Doctor had promised me. I thought there might be boys more in need of it than I. We strugled along as usual; the same burning hot sun, the same dust, the same nasty slimy water or non at all. What puzzled me somewhat was that during the afternoon we stopped almost every mile, or half mile. Besides Genls. Mitchell, and Terrills Brigade had to turn to the left and march contiguous with our brigade. Guard details were kept in the rear to hurry up the straglers and keep the troops closed up. That were sure signs that we came in close proximity of Braggs Army. How long it would take untill Bragg would turn round and show his teeth depended merely when we would come near enough to bother his rear. Bragg had to fight to save his plunder he had gathered. He could not make so long marches as we, being to[o] much bothered with that stuff. My diarrhea had stopped but it left me so miserable and weak that it seemed to me sometimes I had to double up. I could not bear to have the left arm hang down or swing it as [one] usually [does] in walking, but had to put the hand on the hip and keep the ellbow in line with the body. After dinner the country became more broken and hills and mountains lo[o]med up against the sky in the distance. About 7 P.M. the brigade turned of[f] the pike to the right and up a high ridge on which we camped for the night. We were not allowed to build fires on the ridge but might desent the western slope make coffee and return to the crest again. The water was nearly a mile off in a deep ravine. As it was only a small spring it was midnight before the brigade got through with their coffee.

I did not have any appetite that evening but August Peirrelle [Pierrelee][5] had managed to confiscate a chicken and a four Quart tin pail, and he brought me a cup full brooth which was a god send to me. Capt. Steffens came over and informed me he had learned from Col. Mihalotzy that very probably we would have a brush with Bragg to morrow provided he did not back out again; but nothing was to be said about it to save unnecessary anxiety in the new Regts. After we had turned in Phil Rose again was seized with one of his blowing fits. He wanted to know why we were dragged over all creation and never have a chance to get at a live rebel. He thought the general were only playing "seven up" to kill the time and draw big pay. I asked him if he was sure to be there when the dance came off. This raised the laugh on him and somewhat angrily he replied that if the Officers were not such cowards we could have whipped Bragg out of his boots long ago; where upon Curtis Mitchel[l] asked if the marches had not been long enough to satisfy his patriotism and Ephr[ai]m Walker made the modest proposition to declare Phil Commander in Chief, but a strong protest against this move was raised on the ground that we would not be able to keep up with Phils long legs if he schould find it convenient to concentrate himself to the rear. Finding that he could not successfully compete with the sarcastic rallies of the boys, Phil found it wiser to sleep and so did the rest.

~

CHAPTER FOUR

The Battle of Perryville,
or Chaplin Hills

~ Oct. 8th. At break of day reveille called us to the days duty which for many of them was to be the last one. But happily all of those were as [y]et ignorant of the rapidly approaching fate. It was our turn to day to guard the Div. [wagon] train. As the greater part of the train is always in the rear of a Div. Corps, or Army, in order to keep the troops more close together, the whole Div. had to march out before we moved. Accordingly it was 7. A.M. before we came in motion. Col. Sweet was unwell that morning so the command of the Regt. depended on Major Schumacher as Lieut. Col. Hobart was absent on leave. . . . The day became exceedingly hot again; more than any day previous. The Major enjoined us most urgently to keep well closed up and he did not want to see any straggling that day. About 9. A.M. a rumbling noise was heard at short intervals, like distant thunder far of[f] towards the East among the hills. Some of the boys thought of a regular, good sized thunder storm and jokingly remarked that would settle the dust and give us pure water. But not the sign of a cloud could be detected on the horizont. Well did I know the meaning of all but I kept my peace. Soon enough the men would realize the real cause. About 10. A.M. as the distance diminished the men could not help but to gues[s] the cause correctly. They took it cooler [than] I had expected for the most part of them. Some even would crack jokes about it. "Free admission to the circus, boys"! jelled Walk Fish. "McCook is tickling Braggs hinder" drawled Eph Walker. . . . The men then tried to keep up their spirits with light talk, but their expressions belied their jokings an[d] ere long every one was left with his own reflexions.

Not a drop of water had been found along the road thus far. Knowing by experience the value of water on a battlefield, especially after a battle when the wounded and dieing, delirious with fever, ar laying in the s[c]orching sun. I went to Capt. Jewett and advised him to sent a Corporal and 6 or [more] men with as many canteens as the[y] could carry in search of water. Surely in some of the deep gulches water must be found. "Go to your place and tend to your business," was his short reply. I went to Lieut. Turner and informed him I was going after water the Capt. might punish me for it or not. And besides the Capt. had no control over me to day as my ex[c]use from duty by the Surgeon had not expired yet. Looking over the country both sides of the road, I detected southward about half a mile from the road, a small house just where a narrow ravine cleft the ste[e]p hills. If people could live there there must be water. So I informed Turner that if the Capt. should inquire for me to tell him I would be up with the Comp. in time. I took Turners Canteen and eleven others and went across the field.

Reaching the house I did not see anything alive on the premises and feared the hut might be abandoned, but when I took a peep through the open door and my eyes got used to the darkness within, I discovered five human beings; a midle aged male and female sitting on a wooden block, both smoking a corncob pipe, with just enough raggs dangling about them to cover the greater part of their hide. Three dirty, almost nacked urchins of about the same size sat digging holes in the clay floor. No one of them semed at all surprised on seeing me. I inquired for a drink of water, when the male got up, went to a dark corner, took a gourd from a nail and a big jug from the floor, poured it full and brought it to me. It was good water only to[o] warm but that was not his fault. I then inquired if there was any water round here. He shook his head sadly and replied: "I reckon not stranger; been as it is so dry right smart along, the well is gin out this jer long time, but I calkerlate you mout get some in that thar gully," pointing towards the split in the hills. "How far is it about?" I asked. "Right smart half mile twixt the ould saw mill timbers." he replied. I thanked him and gave each of the urchins a craker out of my haversack. They all at once tried to thank me by going to dance a gigger while I backed out of the door to start on my mission. . . . I went doublequick towards the gap. It was a cool, shady, under the circumstances delightfull spot. Tall trees crowning the hills from foot to top. I should have preferred to camp here all day to take a good, solid rest, but I must hurry on to cat[c]h up with the Comp. I hastened along with all speed in my power. It went for what seemed to me more than a mile, but no old sawmil, no timbers would heave in sight. I began to calculate how long

THE BATTLE OF PERRYVILLE, OR CHAPLIN HILLS

a genuine Kentuky right smart half mile might be, when the ravine made a turn to the left and sure enough, some rods ahead was the old, tumbled down sawmill. I could not see the spring at first, but after carefull inspection I discovered signs of a blind path leading among the old timbers. I had to run over and creep under the timbers to reach the spring. It was then but a small affair, perhaps also on account of the dry season, but the water was clear and cool. With my tincup I filled the canteens but it took me certainly half an hour as I had to be carefull not to rile the water.

Going back was not an easy matter. the thirteen canteens weighed, filled, 45. pounds and such weight does not at all agree with fast walking. Coming on the hight of the field again, I calculated on a short cut in order to gain some [on] the Regt. I did not know the correct run of the pike but all at once I discovered in the distance what seemed to be a village. It struck me that the pike must touch the village, so I took the direction in that way. Just then the booming of the cannon increased suddenly and much nearer than before. On I went, allmost on a double quick. I reached the village. It was called Maxville. The pike went through there. I met quite a number of stragglers but non from our Comp. They informed me that the Regt. was far ahead [y]et; that they had been ordered to double quick march and they had done so until they could do it no longer. I left them behind one after another. The noise of the cannon became louder and more distinct; finally I could distinguish the rattling of the musketry. Now I was stopped by several stragglers who wanted water. I told them it was for the men at the front; that they might hunt water for themselves, since they did not do anything else. But they insisted and when I saw they intended to use force, I forthwith put the bajonet on the rifle and cockd it and leveled it at them. That increased the distance between us in a moment and I went on. The fools might have known my rifle was not [y]et loaded, but I did so now while walking.

Next I met Ephr[ai]m and Jim Walker, both of our Company and good boys to[o]. They sat a side the road with shoes and stocking off. Ephs. feet were right enough but he was generally played out; Jims feet were nearly raw. I washed them which relieved the pain somewhat. From them I learned that Phil Rose and several others from our Comp. had made across the field for the woods. "Just what I expected," I said and went on. James P. Orr was one of them. The roar of the battle increased. I could see the smoke curling cloudlike in the air and then hovering like a dark gray sheet over the bloody drama enacted there below. I overtook Charles Lymer wadling painfully along, afraid he should come to[o] late to have his share in the fuss.[1] It was now past twelve o.clock. A half mile further I saw the train drawn up in the field on one side of the pike, the mules all in harness. The Regt. had moved on towards the scene of action. But just then a lull came in the fearfull contest. They needed a breathing spell it seemed. Once in a while a shell would explode high in the air and some scattering rifle shots in the skirmish line was all what was heard now. Another half a mile and I found the Regt. and brigade, the arms staked, the boys squatted on the ground chewing hard tack and raw bacon. I handed the canteens to the Orderly who gave each man a solid drink and it just rea[c]hed for the Comp. and was received with profuse thanks.

A quarter of a mile northward, between the pike and the hills was a little hamlet called "Perryville" from which the battle bears its name. The hills are called the "Chaplin hills" which name is also given to the battle in some reports. The hamlet consisted of perhaps 30 or 40 little buildings which were already filled with wounded. There was a spring there but it was closely guarded to prevent any men from getting water unless it be for the wounded. We were about half a mile from the battlefield and the wounded such as were unable to walk were brought in on stretchers continually. I looked for Capt. Jewett and found him and Old R. Baker somewhat to the rear sitting and leaning against a log. I offered a cup of water to the Capt. which he drank greedily but never said a word. Baker took a cup and having disposed of it remarked: "Otto, I wish I had he[e]ded your advice at Appleton; if that has to go on in the way it has done since we left Louisville, I hope the first bullet which comes in my direction will kill me." The Capt. smiled grimly but did not reply. . . . Baker then relieved his mind by cursing the rebel leaders who brought about this Rebellion. But not alone the southern rebels, the northern democrats of fugitive slave renown, who had fostered and encouraged southern Ideas and principles got their full share and he hoped all of them would meet their deserved fate. Capt. Jewett, who always had been a hardshell democrat got up and went away. I suppose he felt that to a certain degree he was responsible for the existing state of things.

Probably an hour or more had passed as it was nearly 2 P.M. when all at once on the right the batteries began the fearfull concert again. Shells exploded above and behind us and the boys began to look anxiously around. Presently Col. Starkweathers well known bugle sounded its shrill notes. Colonel Sweet, who aparently had put aside his indispo[si]tion seemed full of life. "Take arms! load"! was the order. Many a cartridge, destined to kill or disable some human being, was rammed home with trembling muscles and strained nerves. Drummer and fifers run ahead to lay of[f] fences for the regiments to pass through. We followed double quick first to the right, then to the left about fourty rods. The rebels wasted a great amount of shels and solid shot but it seemed their gunners fired to[o] high and took to[o] long a range to hurt us. I did not notice a single man being hurt during the advance. We were brought in line in the folowing order: . . . The 24th Ill. on the right to connect with the line that had been fighting during the forenoon. The 79th on the left of them, Our Regt. on the left of the 79th, and the 1st Wis. on the left of us, its left wing well thrown forward. The 24th were on a ridge in a open field with woods about 25 rods in front; the 79th down the slope of the ridge and woods at the same distance. Our Regt. and the 1st Wis. were on more level ground. The woods stretched along the entire front and further on. But our Regt. had a serious disadvantage. While the other 3 Regts. had a clear open front and could see when the rebels sallied out of the woods we stood close to the edge of a cornfield and considerable ahead with the front of the other Reglts.[2] The corn was at least 10–12 foot high consequently we were not aware of their coming untill they were nearly upon us.

As soon as we were in line the order "lay down" was given. Our scirmishers in the woods soon became heavily engaged. Capt. Stones 4th Kentuky battery[3] took position behind our Regt. on rising ground some 40 rods in our rear threw lustily shells in the woods among the rebs. The rebel gunners soon got a better range and their shels began to explode so close to our line as to make it decidedly uncomfortable. Major Schumacher, at the left of the Regt. called to [the] boys to keep cool and not to fire to[o] high when the order to fire was given. Our scirmisher[s] came running in now and said the rebels were advancing. Bullets came zipping and whizzing through and over the corn in lively manner, the first time the men became acquainted with that peculiar hissing "zipp" a bullet only can make. Suddenly I felt a thud and then a sharp pain in my left armpit. I straigthened up immediately and felt with the right hand for the reason. On with drawing my hand all was clear. I had to laugh right out. The hand was covered with bloody pus from that long cherished bile. "My goodness! Are you wounded?" exclaimed Sergeant Williams who was nearest to me, when he saw my bloody hand. "That pet is busted." I replied but I wish to know how it happened. Looking donward I saw a piece of stone, about the size of an egg, but not round and, as one side indicated, fresh broken from some other piece of rock. I looked back a little and found the solution. A shell from our batterie for some reason had exploded before it had passed our lines. A fraction of the shell had struck the rock on the ground a little behind me, broke of[f] a piece and the force drove it right under my arm. As it was I felt thankfull for the operation, besides it might have been worse.

I laid down again. The other Regt. right and left began a lively fire now; the noise became allmost deafening. Half a dozen batteries were roaring, shells exploding everywhere; thousands of rifles kept up an incessant rattle. Still we did receive no order, or if we did we could not hear it. I got up to get a look around. The 79th and 24th were all enveloped in smoke; the first Wis. I could not see on account of the corn. I looked to the front. All at once I saw a rebel flagg, that is, the upper part of it above the cornstalks and not far away neither. I sat down on my right knee and said as loud as I could: "Boys be ready! they ar coming"! They got on their knees; some looked forward, some back at me. Instinctly I jelled: "Why do'nt we fired?" I looked to the right, no Colonel was not there; I looked to the left, no Major was not there. I levelled my rifle at some butternut coleured jacked which I saw among the stalks. Instantly the Comp. folowed suit. The rebs stagered a little and in their turn saluted. . . . I saw some of our men fall forward and backward. Now was the moment to fix bajonet and charge. But no order of any kind. Then the right of the Regt. gave way and ran back. The scare speedily run along the line and soon the whole Regt. was running back. As if our Regt. had been picked out for a stool pidgeon that day it happened that just before the left turned on the retreat we received a heavy flank fire from the left, and that from our own comrades of the 1st Wis. but that we did not know at the time.

So we were on the run. Almost every time when a column or Regt. turns to run or retreat from close quarters, the loss on the retreat is more heavy as it would have been had they faced the enemy to the death. So it was with us. In running backward we had to go somewhat up hill, on the hight of which stood Stones battery. About midway between us and the battery was a high rail fence which we had to climb. They were firing lively after us while we were trying to increase the distance between us. Right behind thus fence had been a good place to rally the Regt. but there was no Officer who undertook to try it. While running back up hill and climbing over the fence the men fell like leaves from a tree in the fall. While trying to mount the fence the strings of both my haversack and canteen were cut in two by a bullet and both fell on the wrong side of the fence. I jumped back to pick them up and just then Sergt. Williams tried to get over the fence. He did not succeed. A bullet hit him from behind in the back passing through the right lung. He fell forward from the fence. . . .

THE BATTLE OF PERRYVILLE, OR CHAPLIN HILLS

When we came to the battery we found it silent and deserted. Most of the artillerie men being dead, or wounded.[4] The Capt. and some of the unhurt gunners had deserted the battery. The Capt. was afterward tried by a court martial and cashiered.[5] When we came up to the batterie Loewenfeld of Comp. "F." looked in the caissons, or ammunition chests and found them well supplied with cannister and shells.[6] He had served in the artillerie during the revolution in Germany 1848–49. He asked if any of us could help him serve the guns. I for one could. We found lots of others who were willing to assist under advice. It took but a short time and four pi[e]ces were loaded with double rations of cannisters. (two pieces were disabled.) The rebels were just tearing down the fence intending to capture the battery. They got the compliment from the battery right among them. Just then the 79th and 1st Wis. poured a terrible flankfire from both flanks into their ranks. They staggered for a moment then turned back on the retreat ju[s]t when we had the second charge ready, which they received as a farewell. When they got out of reach of cannister we loaded shells and hurled the same after them as an acknowledgment of their friendly visit. Col. Starkweather came along and on seeing Infantry handling the battery, inquired: "Who runs this concern"?—"Colonel" I replied. "We are running this business on shares; but here Loewenfeld serves as a Captain without a commission."—"Well, give them hell!" he replied and dashed to the left.[7] Two days later, Loewenfeld was appointed Sergeant for bravery. It did not do the brave fellow much good. Eleven months afterward in the battle of Chickamauga Ga. he was one of the silent squad and rests since that time in a grave marked: "Unknown."

Some 8 or 10 rods behind the battery the Regt. formed again. It was considerable less in number than an hour before. Good many had not stopped retreating [y]et; in fact, did not stop until they got clear back to Louisville. Our Comp. had its share of such heroes. Wm. H. Wood, the would be first Lieut. James Orr, H. A. Bennett, Amos Lawrence, the former enrolling clerk and Lieuts. candidate; Phil Rose also, the renowned rebel killer had not been there and never came to the Comp. afterwards. Dorset Smith and Remick Knowles[8] also belonged to those brave defenders of the country. There were others which will appear in proper time.

Before the Regt. could be formed the Companies had to be formed and roll call held. Roll call is said easily enough, but if there is nor orderly to call the roll, nor any [roster] to call the roll from, what then? I will, and must leave the other Comp[s]. alone as I have no business with them, and merely relate about our Comp. Capt. Jewett was "non est," that is "Not present." Lieut. Turner called the Comp. to form into line. The men who were there did so. But there was no Orderly Sergeant to call the roll. Finally some one said the Orderly Sergeant had been wounded. Turner then called for the second Sergeant John Dey; he was not there. So the third Sergeant was called, that was I. Turner ordered me to call the roll and bring the Comp. in order. Yes Sirree; but how will you manage to call the roll if you have no [roster] or list. I hinted the fact to Turner on the sly. "Well, form the men in line as good as you can" he said. Accordingly I shouted for Comp "D" men to fall in, and by degrees they did so. I found there were 66. men in line out of 90 with which we had started from Louisville. But where was our Colonel? where was the Major? We learned soon enough. The Colonels left arm was smashed, besides a dangerous wound in the back of the neck, and Major Schumacher was killed. That explained why we did receive no orders while in line, awaiting the rebels. Soon, Cpt. Goodrich of the first Wis. came and took command of our Regt. by order of Coll. Starkweather, [commanding the] brigade.

As soon as the Regt. was in order again we advanced. The Johnnies had withdrawn in the woods. So when we reached our former place in line we were halted. But before we reached that spot again, what a sight!—There, friend and foe, union and rebel soldier were laying side by side. The flank fire of the 79th and 1st Wis. as well as the cannisters from our improvised battery had made sad havoc in their lines. But there was no time now to look for, and take care of the wounded; on we went. Our scirmishers soon got into a lively scrimmage with the rebels but this time there was no backing out. Our men now were on even terms with the rebels and wished to get on square terms with them. . . . Meanwhile, towards the center and right the fight had been taken up again and raged furiously now. Bragg, perhaps thought that while assaulting our left, Genl McCook[9] had weakened his right and center but such was not the case. Three times Bragg hurled his men against McCooks lines, but only to be repulsed every time. . . .

Our brigade was moved back now ¼ of a mile and regimental details made to look after the wounded and bring them to the hospital. That sounds very big but one must not expect to[o] much of a hospital behind a battlefield. In this case the hospitals consisted of a few small houses in Perryville, two small log barns in the rear of the battlefield and one big hospital tent. The barn nearest to the line was used as an amputation room; that is wher arms and legs were sawed off. The boys called it the "butchershop, or barnjard." others gave it the very proper name of "Uncle Sams Sawmill." The other barn was used or intended for the more slightly wounded. Probing for bullets and dressing of wounds was mainly performed here. As soon as they were tended to they were put out doors on the ground, covered with a blanket and left to themselfes to indulge in wholesome meditations over the beauties of patriotism and liberty; but such who were able to endure transportation in an ambulance were directly sent back to hospital in Louisville.

While ruminating over the battlefield it was found that water was the first article needed. There was no water anywhere near there exept the small spring at Perryville and there we could get none. I went to Capt. Jewett, who by this time had returned to the Comp. again and begged him to send at least a half a dozend men to hunt up water; But true to his ridiculous obstinacy he bade me to let him alone, and so I did. I made up my mind to take a squad of men and hunt for water, Captain or no Captain. I spoke to Lieut. Turner of my intention, so that he at least should know where I was. He agreed with me and said: "go on." I asked Sergeant Clark who gladly assented to be of the party; Charles Herb[10] also offered to go along and we three, armed each with thirteen Canteens and our rifle went in search of the invaluabl beverage. . . .

It was past midnight when we arrived near the battlefield. The wounded had been all brought in and the balance had nearly all laid down. But as soon as we came in they got up lively enough and began to make coffee which example I followed and then laid down to gather a little rest which I needed very much. Shortly after, and before I fell asleep, I heard Sergeant John Dey come in and inquire for Capt. Jewett. As I laid but a little ways from the Capt. I heard every word spoken. Sergt. Dey informed Capt. Jewett that while on the battlefield looking for wounded men, he had been taken prisoner by the rebels; they had taken his sword and gone back with him to a rebel Officer who had paroled him and given him two hours leave of absence after which time he was to report again within their lines. . . . The Capt. did not say much but grumbling something about a lucky dog getting out of a scrape. I thought to give good advice to Dey, as at that moment I believed his story to be true, and told him he need not go back to the rebels as they did not want to bother with him and for that reason had paroled him. He should go right back with his parole paper to Ohio where the paroled prisoner camp was located, deliver his paper there and when Exchanged return to us. Capt. Jewett, who had heard the conversation, broke out with: "Sergeant Dey! you go where you are ordered to." That settled the matter. Dey went. But not long after he returned, saying he could find no rebels. "Bully for you" some of the boys remarked, "so you can stay with the Comp." But Sergeant Dey felt different. The proceedings in the afternoon had prooved that staying with the Comp. was an unhealthy busines sometimes and just then a number of ambulances being ready to transport wounded men to Louisville, he went aboard of one of them and slipped off. I wish I had know[n] the true story just then.

It soon was daylight again and while we were busy preparing coffee, Chas. Lymer whispered to me he had something to communicate to me alone. Accordingly we took coffee and haversack and sat aside to breakfast. Lymer nodded to Chals. Buck to come along, which he did. Lymer then began: "You suppose that Sergeant Dey has been taken prisoner involuntarily?" Not knowing what to answer on such a question I stared at Lymer wondering what he meant. "No such thing," he went on. "Here Buck and I were wittnes to the operation and we can tell you all about it. Besides Corp. Sylvester Greeley and John Buboltz[11] were there and saw all of it." So he related how he, Buck, Greeley, Buboltz and Dey had been together looking for wounded men. When they came to the spot where our Regt. had been in line they became curious to know if the rebs had left many dead there. They advanced cautiously saw lots of rebel dead and finally saw a party of Johnnies looking for wounded. They halted at once and warned Dey not to go any further, as they belonged to the other side and he might be taken prisoner. Dey thought they would not do him anything and he wanted to have a talk with them . . . so he went straight up to them. Lymer and Buck wanted to know what Dey had to say to them and cautiously krept forward within hearing distance. The Johnnies heard and saw Dey coming and one of them spoke out loud: "Look out Yank! you better make yourself scarce or we'l take you in." But Dey went straight up to them and said: "How do you do boys?" and then followed a low conversation which Lymer and Buck could not understand. Shortly after Dey took off his sword and handed it to one of the rebs who then went back with Dey. None of the rebs had a rifle or other weapon. That was the whole of it. I asked both, Lymer and Buck, if they would testify so before a courtmartial which they said they would and were anxious to do so. To say that I was surprised is not sufficient; I was astonished, dumbfounded, so to speak. Here was a clear case of desertion under aggravating circumstances; and that by a man forty years of age and one of the first men among the farming population in the country. Besides a man who at every spare moment would draw out his little pocket Bible and read to the boys and teaching them to trust in God who certainly would fight on the right side. . . . Perhaps Sergeant Dey lost his share of patriotism there in the cornfield, or on the retreat and concluded to let the other boys do the fighting. The mode he adopted to get out of the scrape was well planned to scatter sand in

THE BATTLE OF PERRYVILLE, OR CHAPLIN HILLS

the eyes of the other men of the Comp. had it not been for the four witnesses. Greeley and Buboltz both corroborated the statements of Lymer and Buck. Dey was the only prisoner taken from our brigade that day. . . .

Oct. 9th. After breakfast was disposed of we had to go to work to bury our dead. It was a difficult matter as the soil was so rocky we could dig not deeper than 18 inches. The corpses were wrapped in a blanket, laid in the ditch and covered with mother Earth. Major Schumacher, the beloved on[e] in the Regt., was ridled with bullets. One had passed clear through the head and six others had passed through chest and legs. His body was sent to Milwaukee, where his familie lived, for burial. Poor Richard Baker! How soon his wish was fulfilled. "If that has to go on in the way it has done since we left Louisville, I hope the first bullet which comes in my direction will kill me." The bullet had passed nearly through his heart. He had crept up to a stump against which he leaned in a sitting posture. Our Comp. ("D") had been lucky as far as the killed are concerned; Richard Baker was the only on[e] killed but we had 17 wounded most of them seriously, who afterward had to be discharged from service. The Regt. lost a total of 46 killed and 163 wounded making a total of 209 in the Regt.[12] It was our sacrifice for the initiation in the misteries of humane warfare. . . .

Having performed the last rites to our dead comrades . . . we returned to the camping ground of the Regt. and found that a little surprise was awaiting some of us. During our absence some fellows had taken an Inventory of our stock on hand, and as the opportunity was favorable, had confiscated such articles as they needed most. I did not miss anything exept my blanket. . . .

We were informed that we would stay here the rest of the day and during night, so I set to work cleaning my rifle and darn[ing] my socks. While thus busy I noticed that a transport of wounded was getting ready at the barn hospitals, bound for Louisville. I went to the hospital and took leave of them, as good many of them belong to our Comp. Sanford Rexford, an old friend of mine, who was shot through the left upper arm, had his coat hanging over his right shoulder.[13] I asked him to sell me his coat as he had no use for it and could draw an other one in hospital. He at once was willing to do so and I was glad to be once more the owner of that valuable article. After dinner I hunted up a shady spot and indulged in a sound nap as other boys did who had no further duty. When I awoke it was nearly sundown. A part of the Regt. was busy again stowing away dead comrades near the barn hospitals. It was the remains of the unhappy fellows who had died in consequence of their wounds.

~

CHAPTER FIVE

In Which We Chase Bragg Again, Which Amounts to Nothing

~ Oct. 10th. At seven A.M. we started after Bragg again. But this time we did not take the pike. We marched on the common land or bush roads as the case would happen; but they are very tiresome for a large body of troops to travel. The road led us over the main part of the battlefield where Braggs men had fought all day. It was an extremely sickening sight. The rebels had buried none of their dead. Everywhere the dead bodies lay scattered and as they had lain under the burning sun a day and a half, were fearfully swollen, face and hands black and emitting an unbearable, sickening odor. Some lay on their back, some on their faces, others in cramped positions, or leaning against trees; some were minus head, leg or arm; others had the skul smashed, or were otherwise fearfully mangled by shot or shell. A solid shot had hit an Orderly, while on horseback, in the flank; passing through the horse and cutting of[f] both legs of the rider. Horse and rider were laying as they had dropped. In one place, alongside of the road they had build a pen of fencerails, 2 rails wide and three long, four rails high; it was filled with dead bodies packed close together to the top rail. Why that had been done, nobody could guess. How relieved we felt when we reached pure air again. . . .

Twenty two miles was our allotted tramp for the day. About sundown we halted in a fine grove of tall black walnut and maple. The trees hung full with nuts and the ground was covered with them. The boys could hardly await the order to stake arms to begin the attack. . . .

We camped here on historical ground. The spring where we got the water was called "Mill Springs." Here it was w[h]ere nine months before [on] Jan. 19 and 20th, 1862. Genls. Geo. H. Thomas and Willich whipped the rebel Genl. Zollikoffer [Zollicoffer] and Col. Fry killed him.[1]

Oct. 13th. The Regt. was train guard again for the day. Untill the troops and train had strung out on the road we busied ourselves with cracking walnuts. It was nearly 8 o.clock before the train was on the road and in motion. About ten A.M. we once again came onto a turnpike. It was the Danville and Crab Orchard pike. During the afternoon we passed through Danville, a large, stragling built village and mostly inhabited by rank rebels. . . . The day was very hot and the dust, after all the troops, batteries and teams had passed over the pike, ankle deep. Twenty five miles was the stretch and as we were in the rear of the Corps, it was nearly midnight before the train had parked and we were allowed to camp sore and wery.

Oct. 14th. Shaked and rolled blankets at 5. A.M. and half an hour later we were on the pike again. All of us felt more or less stiff and sore; it seemed though as if our limbs would never get used to the business; but even the toughest mule can be driven to death. But for all that we had to make our thirty miles that day. Ridiculous as it may appear, it seemed that Genl. Buel[l] was trying to spring the trap after the fox was gone. . . .

Oct. 15th. This morning we were allowed to dooze [doze] untill 6. O.clock. At roll call the very welcome information was given that we were to stay here to day. The men indulged in a very lusty cheer and most of them squatted down again. I held a consultation with the squad which resulted in our having a change of shirts and a great washing in generl. Some ladies might find it difficult to go through this process without boiler, washtub, hot water, soap, and other handy articles, but we did all the same. Sure there we had one advantage. There were no friendly neighbors to call and critizise our job, and since that was left to ourselves, we followed the example of the Creator when he had finished his six day job: we looked at everything we had done and, "[Lo], it was very good." . . . We drew for five days rations, cleaned our rifles and the days works was done.

Oct. 16th. At the morning roll call Sergeant Clark had to order a detail for provision guard. The detail consisted of one sergt. on[e] Corporal and 12 privates. As I was the only Sergeant in the Comp. besides Clark himself there was no choice. About a quarter of a mile east from our camp a pike branched of[f] Southwest in the direction of Stanford and Lebanon. Just at the fork of these pikes an immense pile of craker boxes, bags with oats or corn, boxes filled with bacon, barrels and other stuff was piled up, which

we were sen[t] to guard. It had been assertained that Bragg was near the
Cumberland Gap and there was no use for us to chase him any further. The
guard duty was an easy matter, but as nowhere a shady spot could be found
it became altogether to[o] hot to be pleasant. I therefore sent four men to
the woods to cut poles and brush as much as they could carry, and soon we
had a confortable, shady hut constructed. To pass the time for those not on
duty, we trimmed our hair one another and besides I indulged in a clean
shave, the last I had for a long while. During the night the guard boys had
a surprise in Store for me. Geo. Rawson and Henry Knowl[e]s.[2] called me
aside and whispered the information in my ear that many of the barrels
there contained hams and shoulders. They were anxious to examine the
stuff, "yust to see, you know, if they are cured right." I thought the experiment dangerous since the barrels had to be opened and closed again carefully which could not be done well without some noise, and as the Quartermaster and Commissary were liable to come round at any time, I did not
feel like to authorize the job. I told them so plainly and they went off, seemingly satisfied.

Not long after I heard Knowl[e]s say: "All right Doc," and said Dock
Gilbert[3] and Walker Fish stepped forward with a ham each hidden under
their coatflaps. The rascals had finished the job without my consent, as
they knew well enough that I could not give my consent. They judged right
enough that I would not go back on them. I examined the barrels and
found the job so nicely done that no danger of detection was likely. The
hams were speedily cut up and distributed in the haversacks of the guard.
During the distributing of the hams, Walk Fish had made an other investigation on his own hook and presently came back with the news, he had
discovered among the different barrels some which were loaded with genuine commissary. (Bourbon Whiskey; usually in charge of the Doctors.) He
had already drilled a hole through one of the staves with a penknife but
had as [y]et no sucking apparatus. But that was to[o] serious a matter to be
taken slightly. There must not be tipsy men on guard. I at once forbid them
to tuch the stuff and let me handle the matter. I made a spout by taking a
thin stick or twig, splitting the same in two, cutting a grove in each half,
and after binding the two parts together again, fitted the same in the drilled
hole. Then rolling the barrel sideways and holding the cup under the
improvi[s]ed spout, regulating the flow with a finger, I drew for each on[e]
a good swallow. Next I filled two Canteens and my own, rolled the barrel in
position and plugged the hole carefully. The canteens I took care of and
issued the stuff as I thought proper. The boys understood the necessity of

my proceedings and were fully satisfied. During all this time I placed a special sentinel on the road from camp to guard against any surprise. The night passed plesantly and without any trouble.

Oct. 17th. At nine A.M. we were relieved by a detail from the 24th Ill. The Sergeant and several of the men belonged to Captain Steffens Comp. all whom I well knew. Before I left for camp I informed the Sergeant in what manner they might draw extra rations. I learned the next day they improved on our method by smugling a dozen canteens full in camp. . . . The following night Steffens, Turner and I paid a visit to the provision guard and drew some more extra rations. I must say here that I became somewhat uneasy about the matter, because if we were to stay here a week or so it would have been mighty rough on the co[n]tents of the barrel. I stated my fears to Turner and Steffens. After some consultation we agreed to a plan which certainly would prevent discovery. We simply filled the empty space in the barrel with water. I often have wished to know how the Commissary Sergeant, or the Doctors found the Bourbon afterward. In the afternoon the Quartermaster issued shoes to such who needed them. The soles of my boots were worn out so I took a pair. T[h]ey were good ones but by the time we were through Kentuky they were played out. . . .

Oct. 20th. Another long stretch until dark. My feet were very sore on account of the new shoes. Laid down as soon as the last bite was swallowed. I had just fallen asleep when Capt. Steffens darkey, "Sambo," pulled my blanket saying: "Sah! Sah! Mass Stebben done want yu rite ob." I hated to get up but as I had an idea what I was wanted for I went along with Sambo. I was disappointed but still became satisfied. Some of his men had confiscated a lot of firy "Apple Jack," a tremendnous fi[e]ry stuf, strong enough to upset a mule at 40 rods distance. Mixed liberally with water and sugar it makes a splendid beverage, always provided there is no better at hand. As he had plenty of the stuff I bathed my feet with it several times and it did cure them for good. . . .

Oct. 21st. On we went as usual. Up and down, up and down all day long. About noon we halted in a smal valley but were not allowed to make coffee as we would not stop long enough. While I sat munching hardtack and raw bacon, Van Stratum came to me saying he felt very queer. I saw plain enough something was the matter with him and advised him to go to the Doctor to be put in an Ambulance, or have at least his straps carried along. But while we were speaking a sudden paller overspread his face and he sank down at my side in a dead swoon. Chas. Herb ran for the Doctor while I loosened knapsack belt and coat. The Docktor poured some liquid between his teeth and held a little flask under his nose and when he revived he was put in an Ambulance and sent to Lebanon in Hospital. A half a year had passed before I saw him again. . . .

Oct. 22d. When we arose this morning we found quite a hoar frost and some blankets even were frozen to the ground with the edges. It is a remarkable fact that in the Southern States even after very hot days the nights will be very Chilly. We passed through Glasgow, a smal City which looked considerable worsted at that time. A short time ago the rebel freebooter John Morgan had a row here with some of our troops and got worsted. As Morgan had [a] position in and about the City, the latter had suffered considerable during the fight; good many houses being burnt, others ridled with shot and shell.[4] As it was a prominent rebel community we had not much sympathy with the people. It was past ten P.M. when we went in camp and the straglers and footsore came in one by one untill past midnight. Capt. Steffens again was on hand with two Canteens of Applejack which I gladly donated to the footsore comrades. . . .

Oct. 24th. Was one of th[o]se days the boys said ought to be marked red in the Almanach. At morning roll call the Capt. said that all such who could not march 20. miles should step out. The boys laughed and said if they would let us off with that much they were satisfied and none stepped out. The first couple miles we followed a sort of blind bushroad until it led us right into the dry river bed. . . . That we followed upward untill four in the afternoon when we emerged out of it on the pike. It was said that by following the river bed we could save three miles tramping. Who ever got up the story he did not know a bit about the marching trade. If we saved the three miles we certainly paid dear enough for them. It was a foolish move. The river bed, although dry enough, was covered with gravel corse and fine interspersed plentifully with boulders of rock. River gravel, like quicksand, has the faculty of slipping away under ones feet, because of it[s] rounded peble form produced by the constant action of the water. Whoever has undertaken to walk any lenght of time in loose gravel can apreciate the dificulty and its Effects. Besides we had to stick to the river bed as it was impossible to march on the banks on account of the nature of the ground and dense brush and briar. At noon a short halt was made and there was not a man not tired enough to welcome an undisturbed rest of twenty four hours. We were not allowed to make Coffee. Some of the men tried to make fun of the matter but with poor success, it did not take. On again we went, how many miles I do not know untill about 4. P.M. we climbed a high bank and suddenly stood on a pike. A train of an other Division was just passing and we squatted down until it had passed. . . .

As soon as the train was by we followed. It seemed something of a no[v]elty to walk once more on a solid level road without fearing to knock a two or three pounder out of the way with tender toes. But there is nothing perfect in this world, even if the creator has made everything good, and the pike made no exeption to the old rule. Thousands of troops and horses and mules, and batteries and wagons had passed this same road and the dust was half a foot deep. By the constant stirring of it the air became so filled with it as to make the sun appear like a big round Slice of a watermelon. To a short[-]breathed person the dust was most inconvenient and more dangerous than sore feet. We had not gone far when the lines began to lenghten. Not a word was spoken. Everyone dragged wearily along busy with his own thoughts and troubles. Even Walk Fish was serene and quiet. Men would get mad if some one else came in his way. It is in such trying times that the true character of a person reveals itself. I was thinking about this and how in the prussian Army under similar circumstances the drummers and fifers had to play once in a while, "to grease the joints" as we used to say, and how effective it always was. I wondered why they could not do that here and on a sudden impulse shouted: "Drummer and fifers to the front"! But none came. They had betaken themselfes to the wagons. But all at once the 24th Ill. Music band struck up a march. A deefening jell arose from the ranks; Like as by magic the men straightened up, took [step] and to all appearances stepped as easy as on parade ground. The 24th marched behind our Regt. Col. Mihalotzi had heard the call for the drummers and seeing that none came had ordered his band to play. When the music ceased their drummers took it up and in that manner we went along in good style.

. . . at 10. P.M. we went in camp where a bridge spans the "Rolling fork" a river of considerable size. They called the place "New Market" but no City or village could be discovered. Only 25 men of the Comp. were present to stake arms. Even the "dutch squad" was "demoralized." Grunert, Herb, Lymer, [Pierrelee] and Molitor[5] were not there. I was one of the first down at the river for water and was lucky in finding a lot of dry driftwood along the bank. I hastily piled a heap together and when the other men came I had gathered sufficient for supper and breakfast. After supper I took a bath in the river and squatted.

Oct. 24th. When the bugles call broke our slumber and reminded us that an other day was at hand to distribute [its] joys and sorows I turned to one

Lt. Col. Harrison C. Hobart. (Courtesy Carlisle Military History Institute)

side and found, or rather imagined that someone was holding my blanket to prevent my turning to one side. Upon examination I found that the blanket was frozen to the ground and covered all over with hoar frost. Since we had left Crab Orchard the nights had cooled down considerable no matter how hot the days had been. It was an unpardonable neglect on the part of the Government not to provide us with oilcloth or rubber blankets to spread on the ground to prevent the moisture arising from the soil every night to poison the mens limbs and bodies. Even if we did gather fencerail and brush to sleep on[,] the vapor woud get through blanket and clothing. It has been the death of thousands and many more came home crippled with rheumatism, lung diseases, chronic diarrhea, heart disease and other incurable maladies. And [y]et to day the copperheads and stay at homes call the old soldiers frauds, humbuggers, paupers and other vile epithets. The old Regts. had oil blankets but we received them when it was to[o] late.—

IN WHICH WE CHASE BRAGG AGAIN

Oct. 25th. Long before the bugler sounded Reveillee I was up and tramping. The night was to[o] cold to feel comfortable under on[e] blanket. We were to stay here an other day. Lieut. Col. Hobart came up during the day to take command of the Regt. Since the battle at Perryville the Regt. had been commanded by Capt. Goodrich of the first Wis.[6] Hobart had not been with us [y]et. It was whispered among the Officers that Hobart had aspired for the Colonelcy from the start, but that Sweet got ahead of him and procured the commission, Both were lawyers from Calumet Co. Wis. and wel acquainted but Hobart was the older of the two; both had served one year as Capt. in some Wis. Regt. in the army of the Potomak. It seems that Hobart considered it an insult to his dignity to serve under an Officer who was jounger member of the bar than himself. Besides Hobart had been a Candidate for Gouverneur on the democratic ticket five years ago and was beaten by the republican Candidate Randal [Randall].[7] Sweet was a strong Republican and that probably had some influence with Gouv. Randal to give him the Colonels commission. Be that as it may; since Col. Sweet was disabled from any further service and Major Shumacher killed, Hobart was the sole commander of the Regt. But as far as soldierly discipline and efficacy is concerned the Regt. would have won a far better reputation with Col. Sweet as its commander as it did with Col. Hobart. The one was every inch a solder, the other an easy going, do as you please,—school teacher. But in other respects, Col. Hobart was a fine man. He did everything in his power to make it easy for his men and the welfare of them was always uppermost in his mind and actions. . . .

Oct. 26th. It had stormed and snowed until near 4. A.M. when the skye cleared and the storm ceased. The snow covered the ground near 10 inches deep. At near 8. A.M. one of those sudden changes for which our climate is remarkable, set in. It got warmer and warmer and by noon the snow was transfixed in a s[w]ampy mire. . . .

Oct. 27th. Early in the morning orders came to be ready to move. . . . We left camp at 7. A.M. The roads were muddy [y]et from the late snow, by noon every trace of it was gone. It became very hot, only the cold nights and the recent snow reminding us of the coming winter. We trotted along lively as the three days rest had taken the dry river experience away. But a good many were among us who needed more than [three] days rest to set them right again; and a good many whom nothing would, or could save from a so called patriotic grave. . . .

Oct. 28th to Nov. 3d. Those 6 days we had to travel without a single day's rest. And such a miserable road in the mountains and every day from 25 to 30

Surgeon Samuel J. Carolin and 2d Asst. Surgeon Sidney S. Fuller. From a lithograph, "Col. B. J. Sweet's 21st Wis. Vol Regt. Located at Oshkosh, Wis. 1862." (Courtesy Oshkosh Public Museum)

miles. There was no use to attempt to keep the lines together; they would stragle like sheep and come in camp at midnight or later. I noticed that Capt. Jewett used the ambulance more frequently as usual. Settlements between the Mountains were scarce and chances for extra rations very slim. . . .

Nov. 4th. Shortly after daylight we were ready again. There was no bridge at that point and so we had to ford the river. It was not very broad at that time but waist deep, and the water ice cold. It had been a very cool night and the cold water set us fairly dancing. Good many of the men took severe cold and Am[a]zi[e] Pollack [Pollock], Wm. Knowles, David Peebles and young Harry Simpson[8] never got over it. We marched about 6 miles and went in Camp in a large plain two miles east of Bowling Green. They called the place the "Yankee Cemetary" because a number of Union soldiers were burried here, who had been killed a year ago in an Engagement wich resulted in the occupation of Bowling Green by our troops. But why it was named "The Yankee Cemetary" is not very clear, as the rebel dead were burried along side the Yankees. It was about 9 A.M. and right glad we were to find a chance to rest and dry up again. But wood and water was two miles of[f] and had to be hauled in with wagons so it was nearly noon before we could build fire.

Nov. 5th. Untill further orders we will remain in camp here, was the news at morning roll call. That was welcome news but neutralized somewhat by the additional information that Doctor Carline [Carolin], our regimental surgeon[,] had been found dead on his couch in the morning. That was sad news indeed. Dr. Carline was a Dane by birth and much esteemed by the men of the Regt. for his amiable Qualities and untiring zeal for the welfare of the men. The immediate cause of his death was said to have been heart disease. So the sanitary welfare of the Regt. was for the time being left in the hands of assistant Surgeon Fuller,[9] a conceited, overbearing brute. Sometime we will learn more of him. After coffee we went to the woods and cut poles and brush which were hauled into camp, and brush huts soon decorated the same. The afternoon I spent with [a] private detective service. Dear reader! do you know what that means? The pest[-]like, terrible little graybacks were rapidly conquering the entire army; from the private up to the General, even proud Capt. Jewett was not exemted. Before we left Bowling Green I detected him once with his back against a tree trying to scratch that part of his body. I asked him if he was trying to squeeze the lousy dutchmen. He laughed aloud and said: "Well Sergeant, I never expected it would come to that." That was the first time he had spoken to me in a civil manner since we left home. It was indeed a sorry plight. Wearing the same garments day and night, no chance for washing thoroughly, dust and sweat poisoning the garments; it was no wonder the [vermin] got the upper hand. O, how I wished to see the perfumed, bejeweled big boys whose patriotism never went further than the pulpit, the speakers platform or the sidewalk, in the same plight. . . .

Nov. 6th. . . . An order from the War Department was read to us during the day which relieved our commander General Don Carlos Buel[l] from the comand of the Army of the Ohio and appointed Major General W. G. Rosecrans his successor.[10] Henceforth our army was to be known as the army of the Cumberland, composed of . . . the 14th, 20th, and 21st Army Corps. The 14th to wich we were assigned under Major Generl. Geo. H. Thomas; the 20th under Maj. Genl. McCook, and the 21st under Maj. Genl. T. Crittenden. Each Corps had three Divisions, each Division three or four brigades, each brigade from four to 6. Regts. A battery of 6 guns was usually assigned to e[a]ch brigade.

Nov. 7th. The vacancy of Regimental Surgeon was filled by the appointment of Dr. J. T. Reeves [Reeve][11] formerly of Depere Wis. He was a worthy successor of Dr. Carline and soon won the esteem of all the men of the Regt. A special field order by Genl. Rosecrans informed us of his having taken command of the Army of the Cumberland and that he would inspect the army on the 9th of November. Preparations for inspection were begun at once.

Surgeon James Theodore Reeve. (Courtesy State Historical Society of Wisconsin)

Nov. 9th. At half past seven we marched out for parade and inspection. It was to come of[f] in a field of several miles extension just east of Bowling Green. The different Corps were drawn up in line by brigade columns. At each Division the General made a short speach at the close of which he promised us a good commissary to begin with, as he said. Genl. Rosecrans was a splendid looking man. His sharp defined roman nose indicated energie and perseverance. When he bid us good by, defening cheers filled the air. The commissary was issued the afternoon as also an order to march the next morning at 7. A.M.

IN WHICH WE CHASE BRAGG AGAIN

The reason why our Army was so glad in having General Rosecrans for commander was to be found in his past [career]. He was the first on[e] who upheld the Stars and Stripes in Western Virginia and teached the rebels there to have respect for the same. It was him who after the miserable campain of Genl. Halleck against Genl. Beuregard [Beauregard] at Corinth Miss. defeated with a small army the united armies of the Generals Price and Van Dorn at Corinth and Iuka Miss. "Old Rosie," as the boys used to call him, had won the heart of the army of the Cumberland. . . .

Nov. 10th. As ordered we marched at seven. Bowling Green is quite a respectable looking city but just now it was in deep mourning. The union shot and shell the year previous had made sad havoc here. Many houses were in ruins. The able bodied men being most all in the army, either rebel or union, the population consisted mostly of old men, women, children and darkies. We marched about twenty miles and as we had passed the mountains the trip was not so very exhaustive. Drew ration[s] by the light of the campfire.

Nov. 11th. It was not daylight [y]et when we left camp. That indicated a long march and so it prooved to be. Capt. Jewett was unable to march and had to resort to the ambulance. The road was good but very dusty. At noon we passed the state line between Kentuky and Tennessee. So we had entered exclusive Confederate terriorry, for a good many of us destined for a burrying ground, for others a starving prison, and for others as a tramping, camping and fighting arena, which we would not quit untill secession was smashed as flat as a Kentucky pie. No time was given for dinner and about that time we heard lively fighting way off to our right. We were ordered to close up and wondered what that could mean. Bragg could not be there unless his army had taken wings. We were not aware of any other rebel army in that vicinity to dispute our advance. We were soon enlightened when an O[r]donnance of Genl. Thomas informed Genl. Rousseau that we need not disturb our line of march as he was fully able to take care of the rebs. It was that rebel freebooter John Morgan who with several thousand Cavallery had undertaken to dispute "Pop Thomas['s]" advance. He had selected the wrong man however, for, after a twenty minutes sharp conversation with Thomas he was glad to get [away], leaving several hundred of his dashers with Thomas to take care of.[12] We marched untill five P.M. when we arrived at Mitchel-ville, a little village, Station and depot on the Louisville and Nashville R.R. A dense brush wood was selected for our camp grounds and we had to set to work right of[f] to clear the grounds. That done it was as dark a[s] we ever could wish it to be, and shortly it began to rain lively.

Nov. 12th. That had been a miserable night. It had rained steadily until morning and in spite of the fires we had kept we were soaked to the skin. At roll call we learned that our brigade was to stay here for a while as depot guard. A supply depot was to be established here and we had to build temporary sheds and unload the cars and pile up the stuff in the sheds. The rest of the army moved on to Nashville leaving on[e] brigade at Galatin 10 miles south of us. The boys used to call this our lucky day, because we received tents; the so called "Bell Tents." For the purpose of shelter against rain and snow they were well enough but in the way of comfort they were nowhere. From eight to twelve men were assigned to one tent. In the middle of the tent 4 or 5 men could stand errect but the balance had to squat on their haunches. But it was better than nothing and we were right glad to have that much.

During the afternoon Lieut. Turner came to me with the news that Sergeant Clark had resigned his place as Orderly Sergeant and positively refused to do duty as such any further. He further said that Captain Jewett intended to make one certain Private Miles Fenno Orderly of the Comp.[13] Now Miles had enlisted from Lawrence University but he was one of those patriots who thought it degrading to carry knapsack and rifle in the ranks or take part in a days march. From Louisville on he had managed with the consent of Captain Jewett to steal rides in Ambulance or wagon; the battle at Perryville he with many others had viewed from a safe distance. But still he was all right with Capt. Jewett. The boys called him the Captains pet, or the Captains Chambermaid. But that did not disturb him the least; he was so conceited and arrogant as to shun to speak with a common soldier. How he succeeded to install himself to such an extent in the grace of Capt. Jewett I am unable to say. But then nobody could form a correct judgment about Capt. Jewett exept that he was a spitefull fellow. I belive that his desire to recommend Fenno for orderly Sergeant was to spite the Comp. as he well knew that none in the Comp. liked neither him nor Miles Fenno.

Lieut. Turner wanted me to see Capt. Jewett about the matter and press my claim.—"No" I replied, "I shall and will do no such thing. Capt. Jewett has broken his promise once and ever since the Comp. was complete has treated me like a cur of a dog. But I will teach Capt. Jewett that he can not create Orderly Sergeants at his will. He can recomme[n]d a men for the position, but it is the Colonel who issues the Commission. Further he can not set aside Corporals and Sergeants provided they are able to do the duty. Instead of going to Capt. Jewett I will go directly to Col. Hobart and state the case to him." "Wait" Turner replied "until I come back." After while

Turner came back and said the Capt. wanted to see me. I went and saw Miles Fenno come out of the Captains tent. I found the Capt. laying on some blankets looking ghastly pale. I waited for him to speak and after while he began, "So you want to be the Orderly Sergeant?" "No Captain." I replied. "I am not seeking the position, but since Sergeant Theodore Clark resigned I claim the place as belonging by right to me; by the right of regular promotion. Besides your promise for services rendered, you not alone broke your promise, but treated me ever since as if I had been an Idiot. You know I can fill the Office as good as any in the Comp. and now you intend to fill that place with a good for nothing vagabond. Do as you please." I waited a minute for answer and as none came turned to leave; he then roused himself and said: "You may have it" and then turned on his side as if he hated the sight of me. I went to Lieut. Turner and informed him of the result. I requested him to go to the Adjutant, get an Orderly Sergeants Commission, have it filled out properly then go to Col. Hobart and have it signed; all of which was done in a quarter of an hour.

Sergeant Clark had no papers to turn over to me. In fact there were no Comp. records at all. Capt. Jewett said he did not know where they were. Lieut. Turner, [who] since the Capt. was sick, had to take command of the Comp.[,] ordered me to take the best course I could as he did not know how to proceed. I at once went to Regts. Headquarters stated the case and was allowed to take a copy of the Co. [roster] on file there.

At roll call evenings I found that 66. men answered to their names. So we had lost for some reason or other 31 men in the Comp. since we left Oshkosh.

Nov. 13th. At roll call I ordered the different details for camp guard, picket, wood squad and provision squad. At sick call 16 men reported sick. Four of them were sent to the Hospital tents; the others were mostly ex[c]used from duty. Braton Newell, R. Pearse, Henry Simp[s]on and Walton Baker were the ones sent to hospital.[14] Capt. Jewett was allso found to be very sick and was placed in a small frame house near the depot, the inhabitants having run away on our approach. Mead H. Seaman was detailed as nurse with the Captain. Today was also the day to draw rations. I had found in the regulations to what rations a soldier was entitled and what should be done with that part the soldier did not receive. The regulation provide[d] that the Orderly Sergeant shall fill out a requsition in duplicate stating how many men are present for which he must draw the rations. Such requisitions must be countersigned by the Comp. commander. The requisitions are handed to the Quartermaster who states on the face of them what articles he can issue and for how many days. The duplicate is handed back to the Orderly Sergt. who has to keep them on file, he also has to keep an account of them in a Journal furnished by the Government for this purpose. Every Quarter these Journals are verified and approved at Brigade headquarters and the amount [authorized but not issued] paid at certain times by the Paymaster at Corps headquarters. Such savings belong to the enlisted men who can dispose of them as they choose. That never had been done [y]et in our Regt. I went to Col. Hobart and called his attention to it. He at once was willing to issue the necessary orders for the blanks and Journals. Since the time we had left Wisconsin we [had] never received more than half rations and not always that. That was 15 cts per day due each man, making for two months or up to date $9.00 per head, for a year at that rate $54.00. an item surely worth[while] to look after. I had a little trouble with the other Orderlies before they caught the run of the business and Hamilton the Quartermaster was real mad because it made him some worrk and deprived him to some extent to cheat the boys and goverment. For the first time full rations were issued to day. Besides the usual hard tack, bacon, coffee and sugar there were beans, rice, vinegar and molasses. Three campkettles were given to each Comp. which came very handy. A campkettle is made of heavy sheetiron and holds a little more than two pails. The beans and rice and coffee were cooked in bulk now and distributed afterward. Henry Van De Bogart [Vandebogart] acted as cook.[15] The beans he baked in a hole in the ground filled with live coal and they were just splendid. . . .

To keep my papers, books etc. in proper shape and out of the hands of curious boys I constructed a little bookcase out of crakerboxes which I could lock up. On the march I put the case on the Comp. wagon. The evil results of the exessive marching and other hardships cropped out now more and more every day. Every morning the sick list increased and as there was no room in the hospital for half of them the man had to stay in the tents. Breton Newell was sinking very fast; the Dr. thought it to be typhoid fever. Richard Pearse was a clear case of exhaustion the Doctor said. Capt. Jewett allso sank rapidly.

When all the details were ordered there were usually from 20 to 30 men of the comp. left able for duty. To give them some exercise and prevent their laying in the tent all day I concluded to drill them in the manual of arms and Comp. drill one hour before and on[e] hour in the afternoon. I did that in the Comp. street. Colonel Hobart would pass through these streets unawares to see how the business in general was conducted. One day, while I was drilling the men the Colonel had been a silent observer from behind a tent. That afternoon he sent for me and on Entering his tent said: "Take that chair Sergt." pointing to an empty crakerbox. "I wish to have a talk with you. What would you say if I helped you to a good Office?" As I had not the least Idea about his drive I replied that my present Office gave me sufficient exercise. "I suppose so" he replied "but still think I ought to promote you; but mind, there is no money in it, no money, only the honor and—the trouble. To come to the point: I noticed this morning your drilling of your Comp. and the way you instructed the men convinced me you are an old hand in the business. Now you know how much in need the Regt. is in drilling and instructions. In this respect Officers and men stand on the same footing. Now what I intend to do is, to make you instructer of the Regt. that is Instructor of the Officers and Sergeants: they in their turn can later on drill and instruct the men. The Officers have to take muskets the same as the Sergeants; they must know all the details in order to teach the men. That can not be learned out of a book; that needs practice. What do you say"?—

If I had given my opinion as I felt it, I would have simply said: "No." But that could not well be done. I had no objection to drill the Sergeants and Corporals, but the Captains and the Lieutenants, some of which had im- bibed such an amount of pride and conceit, all on account of the little shoulderstraps, that they never would speak with a Sergeant, exept in a way of an order. I thought to explain that to the Colonel and get clear of the job. First I tried to excuse myself with having no time. But he promtly met that by saying I should drop the company drill and instead of that should drill the Officers one hour mornings and afternoon. Seeing that would not work I stated my fears about the willingness of the Officers to be com- manded by a Sergeant. He looked somewhat surprised at me and finally said: "Tutt, Tutt! I have thought about that and admit you are quite right, but you see, I will make them mind you; and dont you forget it. You choose your hours convenient to you and I will tend to the balance." I saw there was no escape and chose froom 2 to 4. in the afternoon; that left me the morning free for our Comp. . . .

Nov. 19th. During these days Breton Newell had steadily declined. I had called on him every day and he always seemed full of courage, but to day it was different. As soon as he saw me he stretched out one of his emeciated arms and said: "So good of you Otto to come. You see I must go. Will you write to my father and mother and tell them all? Take my knapsack and sent the contents home. Give them my love"—Here he had to stop for exhaustion; a heavy caughing set in which ended with hemorrhages of the lungs and that ended his youthfull carreer. He was the only son, or child and a good boy. His remains were bedded in a plain Coffin and burried at the edge of the woods with military honors, the only of the Companies dead to whom we could afford the same, because of lack of time and chance. The ceremony made a deep impression on all comrades. He opened the casualty list and before long many others were to follow.

Nov. 20th. Went over to Capt. Jewett but found him delirious. He did recognize no one. He died during the afternoon; ending a mistakin carier which his constitution could not uphold and for which he had no abilities. The short service had only been a burden to him.[16]

From there I went to see Richard Pearse and found him in bad circumstances. The Doctor told me there were no hopes for him. Lieut. Turner telegraphed to Appleton the demise of Capt. Jewett and reply came that somebody would come for the body of the Capt.

Nov. 22d. Richard Pearse passed away quietly, so quiet indeed that I who happened to stand near him had not noticed his departure; only when I bent down to moisten his lips I noticed the glassy stare of his eyes which told all. Although only thirty years old his hair had turned almost to silver white. He also was one of the best comrades in the Company. He was burried alongside of Breton Newell.

Nov. 23d. A dull rainy day. Late in the afternoon Tom Hood, a joung member of the Appleton bar arrived to take home with him the remains of Capt. Jewett. Hood brought me some presents of my wife and several letters from wife and friends. The presents consisted of: One phial of Perry Davis painkiller. 2d. One square tin two quart bottle labeled: "PainKiller limited" which I, in my innocent ignorance, mistook for brandy; 3d. last, but not least, one pair of stylish heavy fur gloves reaching clear up to the elbow, but which I could not use, because of their clumsines, they were in the way everywhere. The label was marked $5.00. When we moved again I put them on Quartermasters wagon but when the rebel cavallerie Genl. Wheeler saw fit to capture our train, the gloves went along. Who knows what dirty rebel made proud with them afterward. Next morning Hood went home with the remains of Capt. Jewett.

Among the men who reported sick every morning and were regularly excused from service, were two dirty looking young men, named: Joe Woodland[17] and Doc Gilbert. Gilberts proper name was Eleanor Gilbert, where he had picked up the "Doc" is more than I know. I had watched these young men for a while and found they were either cooking and eating, or lying curled up in their tent. They did not speak to anybody, so nobody spoke to them. They were mere sceletons and so filthy and dirty that nobody dared

IN WHICH WE CHASE BRAGG AGAIN

to come near them. I undertook to cheer up those two boys. It semed to me they had no special disease. I would speak to them sometimes jokingly, sometimes earnestly. They would listen patiently, now and then a deep, sad smile would flitter across the sunken cheeks but they seldom spoke a word. Finally Woodland whined: "I want to go home."—"I want to see mother." Gilbert chimed in. There I had the solution. The boys were homesick. No Doctor can help there. No medicine has ever been invented to cure that disease. I spoke to Dr. Reeves about the boys and he said he would sent Woodland to the Hospital in Bowling Green but Gilbert, he thought was not so far gone [y]et and advised me to keep pegging at him. Woodland was sent to Bowling Green from where he was discharged and sent home. There he recoverd quickly and afterward enlisted in a Cavallery Regt. and made a good soldier. I kept pegging away at Gilbert and one day he surprised me with the question: If I had any thing [for him to do]. "Certainly Gilbert, and fine work to[o]," I replied. "Come along with me." He came. I went to the Quartermaster and selected a pair new drawers, shirt, pants, blouse and socks for him[,] put them up in a package, then I went to Johnston and got a bar of soap, then calling on Charles Lymer and requested him to go with Gilbert down to the Creek, see that he had a good bath and make him put on the new clothing and throw the old ones in the woods, and come home with him on a run to warm him up. They followed my advice to the letter. At their return I treated him with a dose of "Painkiller," and then sent him to the campfire. The next day he went with the woodsquad to work. He became one of the best soldiers and we will meet him again some time. Years after the war I met him once in New London and shaking hands he said: "Captain! You have saved my life in Tennessee; but for you, I can shake hands now." An other case was that of William Knowles; but there was nothing to do with him. His case was the more remarkable as he had two older brothers with him. But they made it the more bad because they always kept talking of home with him. He was discharged and sent home; but he was past help. He died a week after he reached home.

Nov. 24th. John Molitor and Walton Baker were sent to hospital at Bowling Green. John Molitor was discharged there and sent home. He recovered there and enlisted again in the first Wis. Cavallery. In May 1864, I met him at Snake Creek Gap in Georgia. That was the last time I saw him. When Genl. McCook in Aug. 1864. made that raid south of Atlanta Ga. Molitor was killed in a charge. Walton Baker who had been so disheartened since his father was killed at Perryville died in the hospital shortly after his arrival there. So father and son sleep in Kentucky soil. . . .

To create a little diversion in our regular routine of duty and perhaps to replenish the empty haversacks of his guerillas from our supply, John Morgan concluded to pay us a visit. Nov. 28th just at noon when our Cook was issuing the baked beans, the pickets suddenly began to pop of[f] their muskets. A lively time followd. Beans and bacon had to take the back seat. In less than five minutes the Regt. went to the place of the disturbance. The reserve picket post was station behind a railroad dam and was firing as fast as the muskets could be loaded. The First Wis. 79th Pa. and 24th Ill. had not so far to march than we had and were already blazing away when we came into line. But the rebs seemed to be [d]etermined to inspect our provision supply and dashed forward. I will not enter in details here but the end of the fracas was; They left a great number of killed and wounded on the field, for us to take care of. We burried 45. of their dead, and it took ten cars to bring their wounded back north. Arriving in camp again we found the beans sufficiently coold to be eaten without ceremony. . . .

Dec. 6th[.] Received orders to move next day. Rations issued for five days. Our caretridges were also replenished to 60. rounds per man. The sick were also sent back to Bowling Green. There was quite a number from the Comp. W. Geary [Gerry], afterward discharged for disability; Anson Tollman, discharged for disability. Nelson Draper who returned after a while but never amounted to anything, Ephriam Walker also returned and did the best he could, Allen W. Ballard was on[e] of the soft kids, discharged, Daniel B. Cushman, a good man but broken down, discharged, Levant van De Bogart, a stout able fellow whose disease is not in the surgeons register, e.a. Laziness; transferred finally to the Invalid Corps; Geo. Herrick discharged for disability; Henry Simpson who died shortly after in hospital; were those of our Company.[18] During November it had rained considerable and most always had been of a chilly temperature. The last night we were here it froze slightly and about 6. inches of snow fell.

Dec. 7th. At 6. A.M. we struck tents and started. We passed through Gallatin, where an other brigade who had been on duty there, joined us. At about 10. A.M. the snow began to melt and the marching became miserable. It was said we had only to march 20 miles, but if tha[t] was so, I never found them so long. A little after dark we arrived at Tyree Springs where we went in camp in a muddy field. For some reason our train was far behind and we could put up no tents. It was a cold night and wood verry scarce. My feet got so cold I was obliged to tramp around half the time to keep them warm. There was one consolation however, if it can be called so; I had lots of company in the misery.

IN WHICH WE CHASE BRAGG AGAIN

Dec. 8th. Shortly after daylight we were in motion again. Tyree Springs where we had camped received its name from a big spring near a splendid plantation mansion. No village or City is to be seen. The marching was better than the previous day as the roads had dried up. We passed through Smyrna, a good looking little City on the Louisville and Nashville R.R. In a big square in the centre of the City was an [arrangement] for the sale of negroes, the whipping post close by. There were no niggers to be sold just then. The dispute the rebels had provoked with Uncle Sam had decreased the value of the black property immensely. The northern barbarians had put their sacrilegious hand on the divine southern rights. But there was an immense stock of young, growing black property staring at, and running along with us, indicating that a considerable trade had been going on in this line. The city seemed to be evacuated. If any of the houses was inhabited the white people took well care to keep out of sight, least they might be infected with some dreadful disease the northern mudsills are heir to; i.e. personal liberty. When we passed the market square, close by the whipping post, some of the boys started: "John Browns Body" in which all joined. That was certainly very disrespectfull and provoking but in perfect harmony with the spirit of the times. . . .

About an hour before dark we arrived at Edgefield where we went in camp. As our train had been able to keep well close[d] up we were able to put up tents which prooved to be a good thing as it rained hard during the night. Edgefield is a little City on the north bank of Cumberland River about a mile and a half north of Nashville.

Dec. 9th. Before break of day we had to start. We naturally made up our mind for a long trip that day. . . . We marched across the Cumberland and through Nashville about 5 miles south of which we went into camp. The camp was called Andy Johnson, in honor of the then military Gouvernuer of Tenn. and later President of the United States. . . .

The army remained here untill Dec. 26th. The time in the Intervall was improoved by drilling and speciall scirmish drill. Lieuts. Weisbrod, La Count,[19] Adjutant Fitch and myself being the instructors. Since our arrival in Camp the weather was like spring, warm and pleasant without a drop of rain. . . .

Dec. 24th[.] Mr. Spaulding arrived from Appleton with several big boxes and Compliments for the Comp. from the Appleton Ladies, and a "Merry Christmass." The boxes contained eatables of good many different Kinds and it puzled me considerable how to distribute the stuff among the men. There was stuff enough to give each man a square meal but there was not enough of each article to give every one a test [taste] of it. . . .

Capt. Rudolph J. Weisbrod, Company E, 21st Wisconsin Infantry, from quarter-plate ambrotype. (Courtesy Oshkosh Public Museum)

The Commissary also thought to surprise us with a good Christmass dinner. Christmass Eve he issued for the first time vegetables. It was queer looking stuff, pressed into cakes a foot square and 2 inches thick, and consisted of all possible garden greens: Cabbage, beet, rutabaga, and turnip leaves, beanpods, Onion vines and sliced Onions, parsley, sage and cellery, sliced turnup, carrots and cohlraby, culliflower and last but not least—red pepper.

IN WHICH WE CHASE BRAGG AGAIN

Capt. Joseph La Count. From a litho-
graph, "Col. B. J. Sweet's 21st Wis. Vol
Regt. Located at Oshkosh, Wis. 1862."
(Courtesy Oshkosh Public Museum)

These ingredients had been slightly boiled before they were pressed in the form. When to be used they were soaked in water over night which dissolved the cakes. It needed a tremendous boiling to get it done, Some bacon or greese was added and it was ready to be served; but nobody ever could tell exatly how it tested because there were so many tastes to it that it was difficult to give any one the preference; exept, and all agreed in that: it was hot, hot like blazes. Walk Fish called it the "hot Trinity." When you begin to eat it is hot, when you are half through it is hotter, and when you have done with it is just hottest. Wherever the stuff was manufatured; red pepper must have been of no account or they would not have been so liberal with it. But for all that it was a healthy stuff if they would only have issued it oftener. We drew it several times that winter and never after.

During the 24th warning was given to prepare for moving. Some more men had become sick and had to be sent to hospital in Nashville; thus were: Dor A. Gurnee who was discharged from hospital as unfit for service; Governeur M. Davis also discharged; Edwin Bowen discharged; Walk Fish, discharged; Seymour Dickinson who died in Hospital; Robert Logan, died in hospital; his brother Tom Logan discharged; Wm. Priest discharged; Andrew Sherwood discharged; Wm. Smith discharged but died shortly after at home; John Tupper, died in hospital; Thomas S[i]mpson died in hospital and David Peebles who also died in hospital.[20] But some of those left sick at Louisville, Lebanon and Bowling Green had returned as also some of those slightly wounded at Perryville.

Capt. Steffens had been shot through the calf of the left leg at Perryville but he would not go to the Hospital. He would ride in an ambulance or wagon but the leg would not be treated in that way. When we left New Market he took a sick furlough and went home. There his wound healed quickly and on the 24th he was with us again. My shoes were worn out. For the winter I wanted boots but had no money to buy them with. A pair of high Cavallery boots cost $13.00 and Steffens advanced the money. It were splendid boots only I had bad luck with them.

IN WHICH WE CHASE BRAGG AGAIN

CHAPTER SIX

~

The Battle of Stone River,
or Murfreesboro

~ Dec. 26th. Dark and cloudy the day opened. Not a very flattering omen for the opening of a campain. . . . Our Div. formed in a field not far from Camp, but long before we strung out on the pike the clouds burst and the rain poured down in torrents.

The twentieth Corps (McCooks) marched somewhat to the right and ahead of us. During the afternoon they develloped the enemies outpost and some scirmishing and shelling took place but the rebels, being only small detached commands, soon withdrew. But the rain held out all the day, there is no fighting against that. In the afternoon we waded in the mud ancle deep. No rubber blankets had been issued [y]et so the soaking process went on undisturbed. Dinner was taken cold and consisted as on all such occasions of crakers, bacon and water. We went in camp on a wooded ridge a little before dark. It ceased to rain now. The train was behind so we busied ourselfes by building big fires in order to dry up somewhat. But that was a ticklish job; the wood all green and wet and no fence rails near. (Burning fencerails was no crime now since we were in actually enemies terrytorry.) But perseverance conquered and after an hour the logs were blazing. Finally the train howled up and we put up tents. Before we turned in a good sized Commissary was issued which helped us to warm up.

Dec. 27. It had not rained during the night, but we were hardly on the road when it started again. We marched on the Franklin Pike but about 9. A.M. we were ordered to strike for the Nolansville or Triune pike four miles to the left. There was no road leading to that pike so we had to go just across the country and through the swamps as it would happen. It rained steadily and the soil had already soaked to such an extent that the wheels of wagons and batteries sunk down to the hub. The boys had to stretch out and help the teams along. A dozen were with each wagon and whenever one got stuck they had to help it out. If some of our promoters of subtle, tender language had been present on that occasion they would have been surprised at the amount of slang and brimstone poesy which can be manufactured in a short time.

The Nolandsville pike was reached at noon. Horses and mules were so exhausted that they needed absolute rest for a while, but the men marched on until 4 P.M. when we reached Nolansville where we camped. Hardly had we staked arms when our Regt. got orders to fall in again. We were to go out on a Scout or reconoitering party. We marched forward on the pike about two miles when we came to a steep, high ridge, the road leading through a narrow Cleft or gap. Here we climbed up the hills on both sides of the gap and formed somewhat in line of battle. A considerable fight had taken place here as trees and limbs were much scarred and torn. We remained in line half an hour or so looking down in the valley the other side, for what exactly I could not find out, and then went down again and towards camp. During the afternoon the rain had been light, but when we returned it came down with redoubled fury and by the time we reached camp the water stood three inches high on the road.

The train was not in [y]et. That was the more inconvenient as our haversacks were allmost empty; we having drawn for only three days rations at camp Andy Johnson. My only hope was now the success of [Pierrelee] and Herb who had my leave for a private scout when the Regt. went out on the pike. I [had] gladly assented and sent Miles Hoskins, a lively young fellow along with them.[1] We all were working lively to get in a good supply of wood and rails for the night which promised to become pitch dark. It had ceased rajning but it was turning cold, which was felt the more severe, because we were wet to the skin. But it did not take long before we were steaming in the neighborhood of several blazing big fires. Ere long, Charles Herb pulled my sleeve, and going aside with him he informed me that two sheep, two geese and a pailfull of honey had been confiscated. I directed him to bring the sheep to the fire but hide the geese and honey for future use. As our wagon had not arrived [y]et I went to the 24th whose team had come up and succeded in borrowing three campkettles there through the help of Capt. Steffens. . . . I apointed John Buboltz, Herb, Lymer, and Hoskins as temporary cooks. Next I asked the men to shell out all the

THE BATTLE OF STONE RIVER, OR MURFREESBORO

crakers they had which they did without a murmur. Every men of the Comp. and Capt. Steffens included, got mutton and soup enough to satisfaction. . . . It was near midnight when we were ready too squat down, fencerails and pieces of old boards serving as bedsprings.

Dec. 28th. At 8. this morning our train finally arrived and we drew for five days rations. Old "Sol" once more unveiled his friendly "Phiz," the first time since Christmass. As nothing was said about moving I advised the boys to draw the charges out of their rifles and clean the same. Most of the charges were soaked through and worthless. Nolansville was a miserable poor village of perhaps 3 dozen one[-]storied frame Shanties, all unpainted and most of them in a tumble down condition; no gardens or fruit trees, or shrubbery around the buildings; a regular City for the "poor white thrash." But there were several extensive plantations in the vicinity.

About 2 in the afternoon we were to move. The two geese and honey I had carefully stowed away on our wagon, as also the fur gloves. . . . I left John Buboltz to take care of the same who under the plea of not feeling well was permitted to do so. Again we had to strike across the Country to the Murfreesboro and Nashville pike, but this time it was ten miles across. We went across fields, pastures and through woods untill about dark when we entered an immense cedar swamp. A red cedar swamp is unlike his northern cousin. There is no danger of sinking in the water or mire, or bottomles mud; contrary, the soil is nearly solid rock, but it is a very tiresome marching nevertheles, Boulders seem to have been thrown round in a reckles manner. The protruding roots of the mighty red cedar trunks are running in every direction. There was no regular road through the swamp, and as the night happened to be pretty dark, especially in the woods, we had a sweet time of it. Besides considerable brush was scattered between the trees. The front man would bent the brush aside, let it carelessly fly back and it usually would whack the next man in some tender spot where it was least wanted. We always could tell, without seeing, when such happened by the solid expressions which were sure to follow. I never shall forget little Chas. Buck who, after a smart whack across his dial, spouted out in correct german: "Himmel Donner wetter!" which made the woods resound with laughter and mirt[h]. "Got a bite Charly"? one askes. "Pass it along," another advised. "He! Charley! that was witchhazel, it draws water," an other remarked who probably spoke by experience. For a long time afterwards Charley went by the soubriquet of "the little Donnerwetter." Marching through brushy woods was styled: "Bushwhaking." Some of the men met with serious accidents. Nelson B. Draper a 43 year old fellow of heavy limbs and a clumsy walker, had a fall which disabled him for several weeks.[2] Midnight we landed on cleared ground and shortley after at the Nashville and Murfreesboro pike where we camped. The camp was named: "Wilsons Creek." others Call it Steward Creek because that crossed the pike a quarter of a mile to the South.

Dec. 29th. . . . As soon as we had staked arms we laid down as it would soon be daylight. But I was not suffered to rest long. The brigade commissary was issuing beef and the orderlies had to be there. The manipulation took so long that it was nearly daylight when I returned to camp. Fortunately we did not march that day so after breakfast I indulged in a sound dooze. As it had not rained for the last thirty hours it seemed to be time for an other sprinkling and accordingly at 10. A.M. it began in regular southern fashion and kept it up until 3. P.M. As the train had not arrived we had no tents and patiently we submitted to the soaking.

At 6. P.M. Genl. Starkweather was ordered to procede with his brigade along the Jefferson pike towards the bridge across the little Stone river. The Jefferson pike branches off from the Murfreesbor[o] pike near Wilsons Creek to the left in a south easterly direction. Accordingly we started at sunset. The road, in past ages probably was intended for a pike or perhaps had been one, we found it a succession of mudholes filled with water. My big cannon boots did exellent service. It was a ten mile tramp and we arrived at the bridge at midnight and as plenty of rails were to be found built fires and had a cup of coffee and after pickets had been posted, squatted down.

Dec. 30th. We had no Idea where our train was. It had not arrived at Wilsons Creek when we left there the evening previous. We should soon find out however. We were busy preparing dinner, when Adjutant Fitch came running from the rear shouting with all his might "fall in! fall in![3] The contents of cups and pans flew in the fire and in two minutes we were flying along the road which was inclosed on both sides with high rail fences. About forty rods back, Chas. Warner[4] who drove Regts. headquarters team came dashing on, whipping the mules u[n]mercifully; some ten rods further we saw the next wagon, the mules on the ground being shot, 4 rebs busy chopping away at the spokes of the wheels but seeing us coming jumped in the sadle and gallopped away. Three of the fellows were brought down by our bullets, the other got away. In a fence corner lay poor Ben Turney from Hortonville, the driver shot through the bowels.[5] "Oh, boys, don't leave me!" he begged but we had to go on. The wagons on the road as far as we could see were ablaze, or already burned to cinders. About a quater of a mile further on a narrow belt of woods extended to the pike on both sides.

THE BATTLE OF STONE RIVER, OR MURFREESBORO

Capt. Simeon B. Nelson. From a lithograph, "Col. B. J. Sweet's 21st Wis. Vol Regt. Located at Oshkosh, Wis. 1862." (Courtesy Oshkosh Public Museum)

It was full of rebel cavallery, some on horseback, some on foot. It seemed they were not ready [y]et to leave. We went into the field deployed in line and went for them. They began a spirited fire with carabine and revolvers. We reached a fence running across the field and within fire range of the rebs and at once began to retaliate with a will. Then came a section of our battery and opened fire on them. They concluded to leave the field in a hurry. They left 82 dead and wounded behind.[6] How many wounded they had was never known as they had taken most of them along.

It was a bad pi[e]ce of business for us. Eighty wagons and twelve ambulances with tents and provisions and other material was in ashes. Four hundred mules had been captured. No special guard had been detailed with the train; but there were nearly two hundred men with the train all well armed, some footsore, some suffering with slight ailments but all able to resist a short attack of Cavallery. The responsibility and fault rest altogether with Capt. Nelson[7] of Neenah, of Comp. "I." He felt indisposed when we left Nolansville and therefore was given the command of the train. He allowed all the men to lay on the wagons an fall asleep, as he did himself, so several of the men present informed me afterward; and consequently when the Cavallerie came they were surprised and hardly a shot was fired. All were made prisoners including John Buboltz, the geese and honey guard. He and Remick Knowles were mounted together on a barebacked mule and mostly in a trot had to ride 35 miles before stopping. They were sent to Libby prison in Richmond and exchanged in April 1863. . . .

After we had driven of[f] the rebels the other Regts. came up to assist us but found nothing to do but to look at the ruins. Genl. Starkweather in an Special Order Complimented our Regt. for its promt action. Four of our Regt. were slightly wounded by spent balls. Robert Hutchinson[8] of our Comp. on the wrist and Charles Bu[c]k, the "Donnerwetter," mortally in immagination. Whil[e] we were busy at the fence popping at the rebs, Charly all at a suden uttered a loud cry: saying he was shot, holding his hand in his left side just over the hip. T[h]ree or four rods behind us stood a little empty log shanty. I went with him behind the Shanty, took of[f] his knapsack and waistbelt, he all the while repeating that he would die. I could not discover a bullet hole in the blouse but after I had removed all the clothing I found a blue spot above the left hip. The ball had been nearly spent and had not force enough to penetrate through; had it done so it very probably would have been the last of little "Donnerwetter." It is a remarkable fact however that a merely stunning, or blunt ball creates a vastly more intense pain as a bullet which makes a wound. I can vouch for the thruth of that as I have experienced myself. . . .

Dec. 31st. The last day of the second year of the rebellion was to inaugurate the blody battle of Stone river or Murfreesboro. Without making coffee we started at day break for the old bridge. Arrived there we were informed that if any had a desire for coffee to go about it in quick motions. While busy we heard the faint boom of cannon far to the right which quickly came nearer until it was direct in our front and perhaps two miles ahead. Just as we began to cross the old rickety bridge, a lot of scared straglers from Genl. T. Crittendens corps came running back which were promtly stopped by Genl. Starkweather who told them to go back or be shot on the spot.[9] As usually these fellows had the most horribly stories to tell; how Crittendens Corps was half killed and taken prisoner and the other half scattered in all directions in the woods. And all that at the beginning of the battle. Presently a section of a battery came dashing on, followed by two line Officers, a Capt. and a Lieut. They also were halted. Starkweather took the Officers names, Regt. and Comp. held them a short peppered speech and then ordered them to take command of the straglers and Artillery and report with them to Genl. Crittenden or Re[y]nolds and if they should fail to do so he would see that they were dealt with according to the articles of war, which was death. . . .

Scarcely had the straglers left when a courier from Crittenden dashed up to Genl. Starkweather handing him an order to immediately join our division. In order to do so we had to retrace our way to Wilsons Creek 10. miles, and from there ten miles forward again on the Murfreesboro Pike. It was impossible to march across the country, as impassabl swamps blokaded the way. The move began immediately. We passed by the charred remains of our train and arrived at Wilsons Creek a little past noon. We had traveled fast and the men needed some rest. A half an hour was given and a cup of coffee was prepared. Harrold Galpin, who also had been taken prisoner, joined us here; he was one of our drummer boys and but 14 years old.[10] He was to[o] smart for the rebels and had slipped the halter. Col. Hobart proposed three cheers for the drummer boy which were given with a will.

On we went again. Towards 3. P.M. we were nearing the scene of action. On the right the contest seemed to be fearfull, while in the centre and on the left it seemed to be moderate. Before we enter the fray we will take a short recess and see how the ball oppened and how it went on during the day.

Genl. McCook commanding the 20th Corps held the right wing, being almost its entyre length in a cedar swamp, Genl. George H. Thomas with the 14th Corps formed to the left of McCook, being the center of the army. This corps was nearly all in open ground. On the left of Thomas was Genl. Crittenden with the 21st Corps partly in open ground, partly in the woods. Between our army and Stone river was Genl. Braggs army well entrenched and both of his wing[s] resting on the river, the bridge across the river behind his centre. Our troops had made no breastworks at all; it was not customary with the western armies at that time. Of course it has cost us many lifes before we came to it. But after a while we had to come to it, because the Johnnies most all the time fought from behind breastworks of some kind. We had but a few Regt. of Cavallery and they were poorly equipped, whereas the rebel Genl. Wheeler had 6000 men well equipped.

Before daybreak on the morning of Dec. 31st. the rebels made a furious attack on the Division of our right wing[,] McCooks corps. Were our men prepared? Were they ready? Not a bit of it. They were making coffee; Artillery as well as Infantry. The pickets were soon overwhelmed and the result was an indescribable panic; Our men had barely time to grab their rifles, [a] good many did not even that. The faint hearted run away, others were shot down or taken prisoners. The best class fell back a distance and then tried to form again to stem the tide. . . . Meanwhile, while pandemonium was reigning here, a furious onslaught was made on the next Division (Sheridans.) but here the thing was different. The Johnnies received a wellcome wich made them see stars; but as Sheridans right was uncovered by the repulse of the Division on his right, he was obliged to withdraw his right in order to escape the enemies fire from flank and rear. The soldiers of the first Div. had somewhat formed again but were to[o] weak to resist the rebels. Genl. Rosecrans, as soon as he learned of the State of affairs sent troops from other points of the line where ever they could be spared, but Bragg did the same. Braggs object was to drive our right wing back across the Murfreesboro and Nashville pike, take possession of all our trains and cut us of[f] from Nashville our nearest base of supplies. The battle here was [waged] fearfully all day, but our troops were pressed back slowly all day so that finally our right wing stood allmost at right angles with the regular line and only half a mile from Nashville pike. So matters stood when I broke off for a retrospect.

When we arrived on the same hight, or as it were, in the rear of the right wing which was parralel with the pike and about a half a mile off, our brigade filed to the right of the pike and formed into line and halted. The rebels kept up an ugly artillery fire and shells exploded in the air like popcorn, but here I must say that the Johnnies were either poor judges of distance, or they did not want to hurt us. None of their shells hurt any of us. But for all that it had a certain effect, "makes on[e] shake in his boots" as the boys used to express it. We saw troops coming from the centre, evidently for the purpose to reinforce the strugling right wing. The coming troops formed on our left. We were cautioned to keep well closed up and reserve our fire for a good hitting distance. There was hardly any musket firing at that time; it seemed the rebels were preparing for a final charge. We were ordered forward to our thin front line, passed through that line and laid down. Four batteries in the intervals of Regiments or brigades went along with us. The pieces were loaded with cannister. "Fix bajonet." was the next news; that meant a charge on our part. As the Johnnies also laid low we could see nothing exept their batteries.

The sun had disappeared and the shadows of night were fast approaching, covering field and woods with a mystic hallo. All at a sudden the rebel lines rose up and with a fearfull jell charged forward. The distance then I judged at about thirty rods. Our batteries spat their deadly cannisters at them and, the roar of cannons [y]et vibrating in the air, Genl. Starkweathers roaring voice broke forth: "Attention! Ready! Aim! fire! Charge bajonet! March! March!" The volly rattled and with a deafening "Hurrah!" the line charged forward. I expected a furious hand to hand fight with bajonet and butt of rifle; but suddenly the rebs turned and run. Some held up the muskets and surrendered, others threw them or threw themselves on the ground. We followed as close as our legs would carry us but they outrun us. Arrived at the edge of the cedar swamp we were halted as it was nearly dark. Just

THE BATTLE OF STONE RIVER, OR MURFREESBORO

when we were ordered to charge, a column of rebel cavallery came dashing towards us from the right. Nobody of us had seen them but Colonel Mihalotzi, who was on the extreme right, had. Quickly wheeled his Regt. to the right they received a reception which utterly disgusted them and made them turn and get out of danger. A [Confederate] battery had been captured; how many prisoners I can not say.

Our brigade returned again to join our division. When we reached the spot where the rebels had received our volley and the volley of the batteries, an indescribable sad scene met our eyes, or to have it correct, our ears, for the night did not allow us to see distincly. The dead and wounded were many, some groaning, some praying, some swearing and cussing the [damned] Yankees. In our Regt. were but four wounded as the rebels foolishly had fired while we were laying down. Arrived at our division we were placed in reserve in a cedar swamp. The strugle had ceased along the whole line. We were not allowed to make fires. The night was cold and grew colder as it advanced. There was no thought of laying down; we had to keep moving in order to keep warm. Our clothing soon froze stiff on our limbs. That was a long night. Tired and sore from the forced days march we would stamp our feet on the ground and tramp round and then lean against a tree and dooze.—

1863 Jan. 1st. "Happy New Year!?" Not much;—in fact, nobody thought of it. Everybody thought of his own misery. Happy indeed.—A host of rebels in front inviting us in their usual hospitable way to a superb dinner a la Chevalier, the bill of fare consisting of shot and shell, of grape and Cannister, of bullets and bajonets, all finely garnished with an enticing view of Libby prison and "la belle Isle" in the background; musical entertainment thrown in free. Added to that empty haversacks, a couple ears of corn and a handfull of coffebeans for the enjoiment of a craving stomach and the happines seemed complete.

There was not much fighting to day exept some scirmishing and here and there an artillery duel. In the centre and on the left the rebels had met with severe punishment. The temporary advantage they had gained on our right did not justify their heavy losses. Positions were changed during the day; ammunition replenished and one days ration drawn. About noon our hospital Stewar[d] was badly wounded.[11] (Hospital steward is the druggist in the Regt.or brigade.) A percussion shell struck against a tree and exploded. It was one of those looky accidents which so often happen in active warfare. Several [dozen] of us were, some sitting on logs or rocks, or standing in close vicinity of said tree. The shell struck the tree about ten feet

from the ground and, while exploding[,] might have disabled a dozen men.
At noon it began to rain again and kept at it steady until next morning.

I was ordered to go on vidett duty for the night. Videtts are sent in advance of the picket lines; their duty is to crawl up as near as possible to the Enemy to assertain if any moving is going on in the Enemies lines, and in general note everything which can be heard or seen. They are not relieved during the night, but must stay, or rather lay there, all the time and return to Camp Shortly before daylight and report the result of their observations. It was not my duty to go, as an Orderly Sergt. is exempted from such duty, but as Sergeant Clark, the only Sergeant in the Comp. was quite sick I voluntarily took his place, as he had done the same for me while in Kentucky. I took three trustworthy men along and went up to our picket line. When dark we went cautiously forward, having no Idea how far off, or how near we were to the rebel picket line. We were in a cedar swamp but there was very little or no brush. Cautiously we advanced, halting and listening every few steps. We could not see over five feet ahead of us; and to make things worse, we could not tell in what direction we went. No moon or star was there to guide us. The rain poured down steadily. We concluded to stop and listen awhile. We laid down with the ear on the ground. There was no danger to fall asleep. The situation was to[o] interesting, to[o] ex[c]iting, to[o] dangerous to fall asleep. The entire body, the whole body seemed to be converted in one big ear. . . . Finally we heard the braying of a mule which was followed by others; we heard the rattling of wheels on the roads and rocks; every quarter of an hour railroad trains came in, or left Murfreesboro, although they did not whistle.—

But what was that? Something seemed to investigate my lower garments and came snuppering along my body as if to assertain where it would end. I was on knees in a twinkling, you may be sure, and discovered what?— "Little Brick." the hospital dog whom I had often patted and treated to a piece of cracker or pork rind. He was a little mite of a fellow and the pet of the Regt. He had followed our track on the sly and his behavior indicated that he was mighty glad of his success; but I was not. Having not the sense, or instinct to comprehend our dangerous situation, he with his joifull demonstrations might bring us in serious trouble. I therefore took hold of his snout and with several well applied puffs and cuffs convinced him that to be quiet was the rule of the time being. He nestled close to me for a while but soon became restless and sniffed the air. Finally he began slowly to whine and showing signs of uneasiness. I quieted him again, but soon afterward he repeated the same operation, seeming anxious to be off towards the right. I took my handkerchiff, rolled it up and tied it closely about his neck in order to secure a better hold of him. He semed to understand that no barking was allowed but kept on slowly whining and sniffing. I next crowled to the right my comrades following. They had not noticed anything unusual. But it was not long before "little Brick" got uneasy again and wound of[f] a long, suppressed growl. Taking hold of his snout I put my ear to the ground and listened again. It seemed to me I heard something creeping, or dragging along the ground. At that moment Geo. Rawson pulled at my heel and whispered: "Something is coming." It seemed to be not more than a rod away from us. I had trouble in keeping "Brick" quiet whom I held squeezed under my left arm. Next we heard whispering and then a hardly perceptible rustling or sliding noise. "Brick" again made a violent attempt for liberty but was resolutely suppressed. I was convinced now that a party of rebel friends were on the same Errand as ourselfes. For a moment I thought to give "Brick" a chance to investigate but abandoned the Idea as unpracticable. It would create a great noise, set both picket lines firing at each other, and alarming all troops unnecessarily, besides endanger our own lives.

Henry [Vandebogart] and Geo. Rawson had crawled close up to me, but Eph. Walker the other man of our party was not with them, nor did they know where he was. Another move was heard and I concluded to stop it. "Not an inch further Johnnies, or we fire." I said in a supprssed voice and the click of our rifles must have convinced them of the possibility of the assertion. Now we could not distinguish any thing in particular to fire at, exept here and there a big cedar tree the branches of which extended in a horizontal line to within 6 or 7. foot of the ground. For a short time everything was quiet only "Brick" kept up his strugling protest. Then a low voice said: "Are you uns Yanks"?—"We are."—"Don't fire. We will leave our arms here and come in."—"How many are you?"—"Three of us."—"Come in one at the time." And so they did. But a fourth fellow came and inquired: "Wont you fellows take me to[o]?" That was an unexpected surprise, but we knew the drawling voice of Long Eph. Walker, to[o] well to ask who stood there, the three rifles the Johnnies had left behind, in his arms. He, like a sleuth hound, had scented and located the rebs and when he found we would tend to them in front, had sneaked around their flank in their rear, determined if they should choose to fight, to tickle them from behind. "He is a good one" the rebel Sergeant remarked, "he would have made us a heap of trouble."—"How far are you ahead of your pickets?" I asked. "About thirty or forty rods I reckon" the Sergt. replied. We retreated about the same distance towards our picket line and sat down under the branches of a big cedar and then the Johnnies related their experience, or as much of it as they deemed proper. Little "Brick" seemed to understand that peace was declared and contentedly squatted down at my side.

The Sergeant was born in Mississippi, and raised in the same township where Jeff. Davis owned a plantation and a lot of niggers. He, the Sergeant, belonged to the poor white trash, to[o] poor, or unwilling to buy niggers. He had learnd the mason trade but was unable to read or write as there was no schoolhouse in the county. When the rebel leaders declaired Mississippy out of the Union he was working in Macon Ga. The common white people were not asked about their opinion as they had no right to vote. Only thoose who owned a certain number of Slaves, or paid a certain amount of taxes were allowed to step up to the polls and cast their vote. But when soldiers were needed, when armies had to be raised to fight the northern mudsills, they called on the poor white thrash to fight the battles for the nigger barons. "I was no secessionist," the Sergt. said. "Although I was unable to read or write, I saw, or rather felt that the slave owners wanted to control our country; but what could I do? and thousands others who only could choose between enlistment or death?" At first the rebell Government employed him on building factories, wharehouses etc. but when they found out that the yankees were going to fight the thing out, they stuck him in the 10th Ga. Regt. At Perryville was his first battle. His brother and a cousin were killed there. Then he had made up his mind to get out of it the first safe chance he could find and was right glad the thing was done. "I tell you yanks" he concluded, "if Braggs men over yonder had their pick what to do, mor'n half on em would be in your lines befere sun riz to morrow morn." The other two fellows had not much to say. They were both Georgians and, although not specially friendly to the Yankees, were glad to be out of the fuss, as they expressed it. They thought it was the rich mens war and they [the rich] might fight it out.

The Sergeant wanted to know if they would be compelled to enlist in our army. I answered him: "No." But everything depended on how they wishcd to be reported. If as prisoners, they would in course of time be ex[c]hanged and they would have to serve in the rebel army once again; but if they reported as deserters, they could go north and work there and earn money and never being asked to join the Union army. The Sergeant pondered for a little while and then said: "You see, my ole dad and ma have done gone for good, but thar is two sisters I mought be able to do a good turn to sometimes." They concluded to enter our lines as deserters as that

THE BATTLE OF STONE RIVER, OR MURFREESBORO

would leave them free to do afterwards as they mind to. "In that case" I said "you will have to take the oath of allegiance that you never will take up arms again against the United States."—"Bully for us" the Sergeant replied, "we just now have surrendered our arms and never want to touch them again. What do you say, pards?" addressing his companions. Both of them nodded a silent assent.

I informed them that President Lincoln had issued the Emancipation Proclamation and that from the first of January 1863. every slave in the Confederacy was a free men. They were greatly surprised at that. They never had heard of it, although the proclamation had been published in Sept. previous. It seemed to tickle the Sergeant hugely. "Wont the negger bosses be a swearin and cussing" he exclaimed. "But say," he continued, "that Lincum of yours must be an allfired plucky cuss, being as it is that the English are cuming hyar to fight the yanks." That was important news to us and we naturally were anxious to hear more about it. The Sergeant said it was a common belief in the rebel army, and so proclaimed by their Officers that before April a powerfull English Army would be landed in Canada and from there overrun the northern states, and if the yanks would not submit annex the whole north to Canada. Besides the almighty Napoleon III would come from Mexico and take New Mexico, and California, and Nevada, and Arizona, and Texas, and Utah, and Colorado and form a coalition with the rebel states and make a big slave empire there. That was no special news to me. That plan had been adapted and worked on by England and France since, and even before the rebellion broke out. It might have been undertaken and carried out, had not in May following (1863.) a powerfull fleet of russian men of War appeared suddenly in New York harbor and remained there for a long time. That was a mighty cooler on Johns Bulls and Napoleons enterprising spirit and they wisely concluded to wait a little while and see what would turn up next. The famous "Locke" of the "Toledo Blade" made "Petroleum V. Nashby" exclaim: "Napoleon smels Waterloo and England mourns the loss of Canada."—[12]

That nasty, drizzling rain did not cease all night. The cedar boughs offered no protection, [to the] contrary they increased the evil. They gathered the fine rain, formed large drops of it, and the least wind moving through the branches would pile them unto us. . . . As soon as it was light enough for our pickets to recognize us we went back to camp. I reported with the rebs to brigade headquarters. Genl. Starkweather examined them and in turn forwarded them to Genl. Rosecrans, wher without doubt, they were pumped to the utmost regarding strenght, position etc. of the rebel armies.

Jan. 2d. I set to work immediately for a cup of coffee. With that also my last craker was consumed. While I was chewing the craker, Maurice Grunert cried for hunger. He was an insatiable eater and never could make his rations meet. He would chew all day long, if it was not tobacco it was crakers. Whenever I could make it possible I gave him extra crakers, or gave him of my part but now I had nothing to give him exept a couple of ears of corn and which he quickly thrust in the fire for parching. Having been without an hours sleep for two nights and three days my eyelids felt pretty stiff and stretching out I was doozing in less than no time.

A little past 8. A.M. someone was shaking and calling me for quite a while. I felt and heard all but it seemed impossible to wake up. When finally my senses became able to comprehend something I found that rations were to be issued. That was good news. Taking three men along we went [to] the Commissary, but—fudge!—a cup of flour was issued for each man present for duty and that was called a days ration. Having distributed the flour, order came to fall in. The first time since we left camp at Nashville the sun shone bright and clear; but below everything was mud and water. Our Corps (The 14th commanded by Pop Thomas, as the boys had christened him) held the centre of the line which (the Corps line.) extended nearly two miles from right to left. The right wing of the Corps was in a dense Cedar swamp, but our Division and the Division to our left were in open ground, as also was Crittendens Corps to the left of our Corps. Our brigade was placed in reserve and at the same time had to support two batteries. Capt. Loomis battery was just in front of our Regt. Supporting a battery is usually considered a light duty, but it is nevertheless a darned hot place as long as the artillery duels last. Of course we laid down in the mud and hugged the dirt as fondly as possible. The Nashville and Murfreesboro pike run throough our lines at right angles; the left of our Regt. resting on th[e] pike and the right of the 24th Ill. extending from the pike to the left. The front line, some 30 rods ahead of us, had dug a rifle pit, or ditch about two foot deep through the entire lenght of the field and thrown the dirt in front as a sort of cover; but the ditch was full of water which made it decidedly unpleasant for the men to stay in there.

As soon as the lines were formed 40 rounds of extra cartridges were issued. It had been more appropriate to issue forty rounds of crakers. As I remarked before, the field was nothing but a continous bed of mud; the first days battle had converted it in that shape. But under such circumstances one is not very particular and therefore we found the mud as convenient as a featherbed. But Gus. [Pierrelee] just then found he had a serious attack

THE BATTLE OF STONE RIVER, OR MURFREESBORO

of fever. Lieut. Turner told him to report to the Doctors behind in the woods which he did and did not return. But Henry [Vandebogart] wanted to know if I had an Idea what kind of fever was troubling [Pierrelee]. I replied I never had been inside of a medical colledge and could not tell. But Henry laughed and said: "Cannon fever." That made the boys laugh but it did not last long, because just then our rebel friend sent their compliments in the shape of six shels, which exploded nearer to us a[s] we wished them to. At the same time the skirmishers got up a lively fire[,] most of the bullets coming over to us. That stopped joking and laughing, and as our batteries were working lively to return the rebel compliments, our though[t]s were turned in an other direction.

Toward our right one battery after an other took up the Challenge and soon things became very interesting from the centre to the extreme right, but on the left everything kept quiet and cool. We wondered if the battle again was to be fought on the right and centre as on the first day.

Shortly after the batteries had oppened fire, one of the man of Loomis battery, whose duty was to close the [cannon's] vent during the time the charge was brought home, was shot through the right arm by a rifle ball just at the moment when the man at the muzzle was ramming home the shell. The hand of the man closing the vent was removed by the force of the bullet hitting his arm and the gun immediately discharged itself, tearing away both hands of the poor fellow who was loading. Raising both bleeding stumps high, he turned round and coming toward us said: "Oh boys! please, let me pass through." I never saw the poor fellow again.

The duel of batteries and scirmishers kept going on steadily; the men speculating which party was to assume the offensive. Genl. Starkweather on his black charger came galopping from the left in our rear when just as he was crossing the pike, a pi[e]ce of shell struck the horses left foreleg, just below the shoulder, smashing the leg. Horse and rider went down in the mud, but the Genl. succeeded in clearing the stirrups in time, jumped up, looked a moment at the horse, which in vain tried to get up again, then drew a revolver and emptied its contents in the horses head. We saw he felt sorry as we all did. It was a fine, jet black stallion, presented by the brigade to the Genl. at Louisville. But as an old proverb has it: "the loss of one is the gain of another." prooved true in this case. The Genl. was hardly out of sight when young Charles Lymer went up to the horse and satisfying himself of its being dead, immediately set to work whittling out an immense pi[e]ce out of the haunches. The boys of the 24th Ill. to the left of the pike, seeing what Lymer was up to, quickly fell in and in less than half an hour nothing was left of the fine stallion but skin and bones.[13] During the process the boys were several time scared and scattered by bursting shels from the rebel lines but none was hurt. Chas. Lymer offered to distribute his share to such as who were willing to try the horse. One usually does not indulge in delicate notions when the stomach insist to be the boss, and consequently most of the boys took a junk and hid it in the haversack.

Apparently there was no change in the affairs [y]et; batteries and skirmishers did all the fighting but that compelled us to hug the mud all the same. We were getting very cold, and very stiff and longed for a change. The battery men had suffered severe loss and our brigade, especially the 79th Pa. Regt. which was on higher ground, had suffered much from bullets and shells. Still, at the left all was quiet. But all this time we had noticed a continuous stream of Infantry and artillery moving a quater of a mile in our rear t[h]rough the woods towards our left, where Genl Crittendens (21st Corps) was in position. This indicated that either Rosecrans intended to attack with strong force the rebel right, or he expected that Bragg would try to double up our left.

It was now 1. P.M. It se[e]med the Johnnies thought it dinner time, at least they moderated their fire and soon ceased altogether. Our troops followed the sensible suggestion and soon quiet raigned along the lines. We were allowed to go back to the Edge of the woods and make dinner, but were Cautioned to build only small fires so as not to draw the rebel fire and to upset the operation. Making dinner is not very difficult if a well filled larder is near by, but ours contained only water, a cup of flour and a chunk of horseflesh. Some had [y]et an ear or two of corn left. But we tried to make the best of it. Soon the water in the tin cup was boiling, flour was stirred in to make a soup or puding, according to taste. The horse was treated in different ways; some would put it on a stick and broil in the flame or over the coals; others tried to fry it on flat stones put in the fire; others again boiled it in the cups. I had picked up a shovel of which the handle had been broken of[f]. I cleaned the thing as near as possible, sliced the flesh and fried it on the shovel; but it was a bad job. I had no bacon or anything to gries the shovel with. As soon as the flesh touched the hot shovel it would stick to it like glued, it seemd to freeze fast. Do what I mind to I could not save the horse steak from burning. So the morsels were Coal out side and raw flesh inside. Some folks like it that way. I don't. We were out of salt allso and as horse flesh is particularly sweet that did not improve it. But hunger is an Exellent Cook and the flesh went down for all that and did not do any harm either.

THE BATTLE OF STONE RIVER, OR MURFREESBORO

Grunert, Herb, Lymer, Buck and myself were cooking at the same fire. We all had made pudding first, but Grunert, who thought the flesh the better of the two took that first. So when we were tending to the flesh, Grunert was brewing his soup. I happened to look towards the front when I noticed an object twisting round high in the air in a dow[n]ward course direct to where we were. I shouted to the boys and not a moment to[o] soon. About a yard in front of the fire the blasted thing burried itself in the mud throwing about a bushel of dirt forward over the fire and upsetling Gruners cup of soup. The missile had bored itself deep in the ground but we dug it up and found it to be a piece of a railroad rail about 15 inches long. I suppose the Johnnies had done that as a joke, but if so, it was a bad one. Grunert looked very sad, and very mad. I wish the Johnnies Could have heard his blessings he bestowed on them; and he was not much to blame neither; Grub was to[o] scarce to be wasted in such reckless manner. We others however came to the rescue and donated enough each to fill his cup.

It semed the rebels had sent this messenger into our lines as a notice of their intention to resume active business again. Not five minutes after[,] all their batteries along their line opened fire. Our batteries of cour[s]e followed suit. In a moment we were in our places again, hugging the mud. The Johnnies seemed to work their batteries with magic. The ghastly and sharp scre[e]ch, the short, tearing crash of the exploding shells, the booming report of our batteries, all together made the air fairly tremble and shake. A thick, heavy cloud of smoke covered field and woods and made the air so thick that it allmost produced a shocking sensation. I expected every moment a charge from the Enemy, or that our troops would be ordered to charge; but nothing of the kind happened. But something else happened. . . .

It was between two and three P.M. when suddenly a rattle of musketry in the scirmishline to the left was heard. Immediately after a cannonade began which no pen can describe. It lasted about twenty minutes and ceased abruply. Then the volleys of musketry followed in unbroken succession for perhaps ten minutes. Then cheer after cheer rent the air. It was started at the left of the union line and taken up from Regt. to Regt. from brigade to brigade untill it reached the extreme right. We did not know what for; we could not see anything exept the heavy smoke. But it were Union cheers and that was enough for us.

All at once the roaring voice of Genl. Starkweather was heard; "Raise up! by the right flank! double quick! March! March!" and away we went to the right. Troops in Reserve allways must expect such sudden movements; they are there to support weak points, or to repel a sudden charge. It was about a quarter of a mile to the cedar swamp on our right, Running in that soft field was a difficult undertaking, but it made us very warm, and very short of breath; The Johnnies made it still warmer with a liberal supply of shells and many in the brigade got a mark then and there. About half a mile through the swamp and we were at the desired spot. We were placed behind an unocupied low breastwork. We had just time to recover our breath when the scirmishers came running back saying: "The rebs are coming." Yes, they came, sure enough; but they allso went back again; but not all of them. They dropped by the hundreds and were taken care of afterwards by our Surgeons. An other big cheer went along the line but this time from the right to the left. Genl. Starkweather marched us back behind our Division as Reserve. The conflict of Crittendens Corps with the rebels during the afternoon happened in this way:

Genl. Bragg having come to the conclusion that our left wing probably could be easier overcome than the right, ordered Genl. Breckinridge to undertake the job. His Corps and one Div. each of Genls. Hills and Hardees Corps were to crush General Crittenden turn our left and in that way get possession of the Nashville pike. In order to be succesfull the crushing process had to be completed with the first charge. He therefore formed his troops in brigade Colums, that is in four ranks instead of two. Besides those he held one line in reserve for reinforcement if necessary. He evidently expected a stubborn resistance or he would not have formed his troops so en masse. After an preliminary short artillery duel his lines advanced in grand style. The ground they had to pass over was open with but few depressions, a fact which was a great advantage to our troops as Infantry and Artillery could sweep the whole ground. When they came within good hitting distance and our batteries (48. guns) and Infantry opened on them, they could not stand it very long. Every volley tore great opening in their close mass. Advancing they would close the gaps again but the same havoc was repeated over and over again and finally the[y] began to waver and show plain signs of loss of spirit. Observing this Genl. Crittenden at once ordered a countercharge which was undertaken by our troops with high spirits. Some of the rebels undertook to stem the tide, but that was impossible. They were thrown in complete disorder and soon sought their safety in reckless flight. Their reserve, which was coming up for help, was carried back with the running mass. Our men, elated with their success, followed closely Keeping up a steady fire. The rebels never stopped but went on to the river and jumped in. Those who could swim got over those who could not were partly helped across by their comrades, partly drowned. Others

THE BATTLE OF STONE RIVER, OR MURFREESBORO

who would not risk the river were taken prisoner. Then it was that grand cheering went up of which I spoke before as running from left to right.—

Night was setting in rapidly now. The sky, so bright in the morning, looked now dark and threatening; the temperature decidedly snowish. The Quartermaster called for the Orderlies to come for rations which we speedily obeyed, the men making fires the while. We received for two days hard tack, bacon, coffee and sugar together with the cooling notice that [this] must hold out for three days. Most of the men thought they could dispose of them in one day and not hurting themselves. While we were preparing the Coffee the clouds began to discharge in a lively manner a mixture of rain, snow and Ice. To make it more entertaining a lively northwestern set in, increasing almost to a gale, a comforting view for the night.

While sipping my coffee Bill, or Wm. Sweetzer[,] came and said he was plaid out; he could stand it no longer. I was convinced he spoke the truth and brought him to the Doctors. He was brought to the hospital tent for the night and next day was sent to hospital in Nashville where he died shortly after. . . . He was an exellent soldier and one of my best friends.[14]

After supper the brigade again had to fall in. This time we marched forward to relieve a brigade which had been in the rifle pits all day. It was so dark the rear rank could not see the front rank and we had considerable trouble in finding our places. When we finally were in order, the partly starved and benumbed comrades which we reli[e]ved were hardly able to express their gratitude for being relieved from a place which they had considered the portal to the grave.

Well, here we were. The so called rifle pit, or more correctly spoken, ditch was full of water; the level field all anckle deep mud. Snow, Ice and water coming down so fast as if the Clouds had intended to get through in a hurry and have done with it. There was nothing to do in order to keep warm but to tramp the mud back and forth, right and left, running against one another and indulge in profane language. If the politicians whose reckles ambition and cowardly behavior brought about the war; if the bondholders, contractors and other speculater[s] who waxed to millinaires while we were undergoing hardships which can not be aproximatily described had been here these four days, they perhaps would not now talk so loud about frauds, coffecoolers swindlers and government paupers. But now the "Devise" is: "The Moor has done his duty, the Moor may go."—[15]

To break the monotony and misery of our night watch a very ex[c]iting intermezzo took place about 2. A.M. Perhaps a half or three quarter of a mile to the left of us sudden and rapid musket fire broke out between the opposing scirmish lines. It has never been assertained which side started the racket but it was fearfull in its results. The firing was in front of a brigade of Ohio troops and did not extend to our brigade. The rebels immediately reinforced their pickets as we could hear by the increased rapidity of their firing. Genl. Willich,[16] who commanded the brigade on our side, a rather impulsive man and good fighter reinforced his line also, and shortly after folowed with the brigade in line, fearing the rebels might try to break t[h]rough our lines. The rebels, of course, thought, or expected the same on our part, and so it happened that in the deep darkness thus two bodies met and then a sad and most lamentable slaughter began. On account of the intense darkness the men could not distinguish friend from foe; blue and gray looked alike and as they became mixed up the slaughter became indiscriminate. Finally, both parties seeing the folly of the thing, endeavored to retreat to their lines which finally was acomplished.

When the related incident began we immediately fell into line. Genl. Starkweather allso sent reinforcements to our pikets but with the strict orders not to fire unless they were attacked directly. He then followed with the brigade within close supporting distance and halted. Our pickets kept cool, nothing happened in our front and we finally withdrew. The whole thing was inaugurated by some scared fellows who immagined the least noise they heard was indicative of a rebel attack.

Shortly after the clouds had exhausted their stock of nasty stuff, the sky became clear and bright and twinkled with millions of stars. And as a kind of compensation for the Egy[p]tian darkness we had passed through, the last quarter of the moon came up slyly in the East as if to look at the scene of disaster and ascertain what damage had been done. But we did not profit much by the clear Atmosphere. In less than half an hour our clothing was frozen stiff on our bodies, and it took renewed exertion to keep the blood in Circulation. Genl. Willich at once set his men at work to collect the wounded. They had to take the rebel wounded allso as no rebels came to claim them, or take care of them. That was a trick the rebels have often played on us; it saved them a great deal of trouble and medicine. The loss in Willichs brigade was near two hundred killed and wounded. The rebel losses were never ascertained. There was quite a number of rebel prisoners, or deserters who had gone back with our men on their own account. . . .

Jan. 3d. Very soon after daylight some of our batteries oppened on the rebels but did not receive any response. Our scirmishers were ordered to advance Cautiously and feel for the rebel line. They did and found the Johnnies had skedadled under cover of the night. (Scedadled was an expression in the army signifying: to sneak away, to give one the slip.) Ge[n]l. Rosecrans immediately sent Genl. Neglie [Negley][17] with his Division and a few Regt. of Cavallery in pursuit. They came just in time to save the bridge across Stone river which the rebels were trying to burn behind them. Our troops captured a battery and a train containing tents and ammunition. Our Cavallery was to[o] inferior in number to effect anything against the rebel Cavallery. Bragg had taken advantage of the dark night to slip away unobserved and it was well for him to do so. On the other hand we were glad to get a little respite. It was no use to follow up Bragg as the roads, after his army had passed, were so bad that no vehickle of any kind could get through the mire. The loss in those three days entertainments was near 13,249 on our side and 15,000 on the rebel side. . . . [18]

When it became known that Bragg had lit out the soldiers indulged in an other fit of cheers and a dance in half frozen mud. We were at liberty now to tend to breakfast and a squad from each company went for the cedar swamp to fetch dry wood for fuel. A great number of empty ammunition boxes lay scattered over the field which made exellent kindling wood. How pleasant it felt to once more face a cheerfull fire and feel its renovating influence. And when we had partaken of a cup of hot coffee, a piece of fried bacon and a couple hardtack we felt like new men. Thus it is that misery makes one apreciative and thankfull for small favors.

Towards 9. A.M. troops began to mass on and near the pike preparatory to cross the river towards Mufreesboro. But General Starkweather informed us that we would be among the last to leave and would not start before late in the day, or perhaps not at all to day. Old Sol was by this time diffussing a genial warmth so I advised the boys of the Comp. to overhaul their rifles which needed cleaning very much, setting the example myself by taking [mine] all appart and giving each part a thourough cleaning and oiling. Since we left camp at Nashville we never had found time to look them over exept an occasional wiping with the sleeve of the blouse; as they had been wet allmost all the time they were in a fearfull condition. The boys were soon busy with cleaning up.

Having done with the rifle I concluded to change my socks. As I remarked elsewhere I bought a pair of long Cavallery boots in Camp Andy Johnson. They had not been off from my legs since Dec. 26th. What was my surprise when, in trying to draw them off, both shafts broke right in two above the heel. Examining the leather I found it was burned to a crisp. I must have backed up to[o] close to the fire and the lether being wet got s[c]orched without my noticing it. Here indeed I was in a sore plight. There was no telling when the Quartermaster would be able to issue new ones since Wheeler had burned our train on the Jefferson pike. I was bound to have either boots or shoes and that speedily before we were to march. I finally adopted a course for which some of the boys blamed me, but dire need admits of no choice. As I have already stated our rifle pits run across a large old cotton field, certainly half a mile in lenght; to the right the line extended way off into a cedar swamp. The rebel line and works were perhaps 80. rods in front of us. During the first day of the battle Dec. 31st the rebels had repeatedly charged on our line but were repulsed every time. Of course they had a heavy loss of dead and wounded. The latter they removed the next day under flagg of truce but the dead they left on the field and in the woods. I thought it just possible to find there what I needed and which was of no Earthly use to any of them.

I went to Lieut. Turner commanding Comp. and informed him of my situation and the plan I had formed to get out of it. Like a good politician he kept on neutral grounds and did not say "jes or no." So I concluded to act on my own responsibility. I did not want anybody to know, or see what I was about and therefore went along the line to the right until I reached the Cedar swamp. Here I soon managed to get out of sight of the men, turned to the front and soon found an abundance of silent Johnnies to whom boots or shoes were of no further use. The battle must have raged fearfully here. In every possible position grim death had surprised the rebel Comrades. But in the woods they lay not half as thick as in the open field. The trees had afforded some shelter. It was a terrible sight. It requires considerable nerve to overcome a painfull, depressive, sickenish feeling. Involuntarily I asked myself: Will that be my fate?

For a long time I was sadly disapointed. I had imagined I would find plenty of the article I was in need of. But must of the unhappy sleepers had but miserable apologies for footwear; good many even had rags wrapped around their feet instead of shoes. Their late raid through Kentucky and East Tennessee had playd havoc with their footgear. I did not wish to be seen by any of our men and kept on in the woods until I came in a depression where I could examine the field unobserved by our men. Just when I turned out of the woods a pitiable sight made me stop and shudder. A handsome young man sat leaning against a tree. A solid shot, or a piece of shell had struck him across the body; the bowels were laying in his lap. In his right hand he held a letter, the envellop laid on the ground. Had he read the letter [y]et before he died? I took the letter and read it. It was dated: "Schelbyville Tenn. Dec. 26th, 1862." and began with: "My dear Bob." It

THE BATTLE OF STONE RIVER, OR MURFREESBORO

reminded him of his promise to come on New years Eve to a Sylvester dance at Shelbyville. It promised a splendid time as no dirty Unionist and Abholitionist would be admitted. Signed by: "Maud." What a cruel fate. That very same evening when his beloved was anxiously awaiting him he sat there mute and stiff, her letter in his hand, having been sent to Eternity only a few hours before the dance opened. (Shelbyville is only about 18 miles south of Murfreesboro on the Nashville and Chattanooga railroad. So if leave had been granted him he could be there in an hours ride. . . .)

I found at last what I wanted. An Officer, seemingly of high rank, judging by the profuse gold lace trimming on sleeves and collar of his coat lay peacefully streched on his back. It seemed death had overtaken him all at a sudden as his features wore a placid contended expression. I did not discover any wounds, or marks of blood at first. He wore a pair [of] fine, new high boots which I saw at a glance were about my size. With a mental apologie I confiscated the same, put them on and found them an exact fit. Later on I found an Etiquette, or label pasted inside on the lining of the shafts reading thus: "Barkley & Co. Manufacturers Birmingham G. B." which showed they were made in England and smugled into the Confederacy. That was some relief to me, as in this manner England had unwittingly done something for the Support of the Union. To give some compensation for the theft I had committed I managed to put the lower part of my boots on the feet of the dead Officer. Besides he wore a tightly rolled rubber blanket over his right shoulder extending over his chest down to the left side. I allso considered that a god send and took it off. While doing this I discovered that a rifle ball had passed through the close rolled rubber blanked into his heart. That had been his credentials for Eternity. Now some of the readers of thus sketch probably will say that I have been one of the so called "Hyenas of the battlefield." a robber of the dead. To all such I will say: "Put yourself, or think yourself in the same circumstances I was, and think what you wold have done." Would you have walked barefooted in the half frozen mud? perhaps for days or weeks? It is an easy thing to moralize in a snug home, surrounded by all luxuries and comforts money can buy, but when you are brought face to face with dire necessessity, things usually show an other aspect. That is all I have to offer for an Excuse. I might have gone through his pockets, but I never thought of it; I was glad to have footwear and the rubber blanket.—

I took my way back as I had come, through the woods. I did not feel well by any means. It seemed to me that every corpse I passed stared at me with an expression saying: "You are a sacrilegious robber." Involuntarily I woul[d] look right and left and turn round to assertain if perhaps some one had noticed my pilfering. I have often since wondered how robbers and thiefs can endure and suppress the upbraiding of concience; how thay can successfully hide an expression of guilt and shame. Moreover nobody seemed to pay any attention to me when I returned. The rubber blanket I had hid in my knapsack, and as I had pulled the pants down over the boots nobody thought of looking at them. But for Maurice Grunert, nobody would have been any wiser for it. Grunert, who had seen my burnt boots, inquired where I got those new boots. His shoes were also worn out and he was anxious to have a better pair. I informed him where I had drawn them and remarked there were plenty more of them. He cast a wistful, longing look across the field and finally said: "I will go." and go he did, but returned shortley afterward empty handed saying to me: "By God, Otto, I cannot do it; I am afraid. I can't stand see them mute fellows staring at me so." I could not blame him. I remembered to[o] well my own experience. But before an other year had passed, Grunert had different views of the matter.

CHAPTER SEVEN

~

About Our "Coozie" Winter Quarters, Light Duty, and Our Bully Picnic in General

~ Jan. 4th. [Murfreesboro] So here we landed about 10. A.M. the rain pouring down in a steady, determined way. The first thing to do after each Regt. had its share of territory allotted was to lay out the Comp. grounds and streets in order to put up tents. The latter part was a difficult job as it will be remembered that our rebel friend, Genl. Wheeler, had Captured or burned our brigade train on the Jefferson pike Dec. 31st. previous. So no tents could be put up and the firmament was our only shelter. Something over a mile west from our camp was a dense Cedar swamp. Thither we betook ourselfes and cut as much Cedar boughs as we could carry and toted them to camp. They were to serve as a foundation to keep us from sinking into the mud. When we returned we found that the inclination of the ground was not sufficient to carry of[f] the water as fast as it came down. The camp ground was fast assuming the aspect of a lake; ditching was necessary to keep us from drowning. All pickaxes, spades and shovels the Quartermaster could furnish were put in motion and ditches made lenghtways and crossways as the inclination of the ground required. Those ditches could not at once be made in proper shape as time was to[o] short, but were afterward Completed and bridges laid across at each end of Comp. streets. As there were not tools enough to keep all men busy the balance went after more cedar boughs. Next we had to provide for firewood, which for the night and next morning we found a mile off at the south end of the field where an eight rail high red cedar fence furnished exellent material. This red cedar will not burn in a green state, but dry it burns like tinder. It

100

has one serious drawback though. While burning it seemes that gases are developing in the wood which will explode with a loud detonation, scattering the coals in every direction, upsetting cups and spiders, or if blankets and knapsacks were within hitting distance, burning holes in the same. . . .

The night passed as comfortable as a steady cold rain, and no shelter can make it. I was the l[uc]kiest dog in the crowd because of my rubber. The next morning the Commisary informed us that he was able to issue for an other two days hard tack and coffee but no bacon. Very wellcome and thanks for small favors. After breakfast, call was made for pikets which took nearly half the Comp. The part of the picket line which our brigade was to fill was in a south western direction, four miles from camp and to the right of the Salem pike. The line was along a stream, or large creek, the most part of the line being in the woods; But a few plantations were inside and near the line. During the afternoon each Comp. received two Bell tents. Those tents were captured from the rebels after their retreat from the battlefield. That was a kind of an offset for the tents Wheeler had captured from us and burned. They certainly were very wellcome, but all the men could not be crowded in two tents. If the men would crowd together and sleep in spoon fashion, twelve men would fill on[e] tent. But there were 45. men for duty [y]et. To avoid personal unpleasintnes in assigning the men to the tents I went to Lieut. Turner and requested him to make the assignments but he ordered me to go ahead with the business and whatever I did he would approove of, as in fact he always did. Now the Easiest and most impartial way would have been to let the men draw lots for the right of tent, but I knew there were about a dozend who would break down soon, especially if the rain should keep on. Thus class I separated first and assigned them to one tent; the others had to draw lots [for] the other tent. At first it created some dissatisfaction but after a little talking they saw the justice of the matter and submitted. Besides there were usually 15 or 20 men on duty every night, either on picket, camp or provost guard, so that but a few had to stay out and they would ex[c]hange among themselves by sleeping in the tent by turns.

Regular details were made now every morning to provide for firewood. A mile and a half south was a strip of heavy timbered wood perhaps a quarter section [one-quarter square mile] in extent, covered with splendid oak, beach, maple, whitewood etc. The trees were cut down, made into certain lenghts and the Quartermasters teams would haul them into camp. We were not at liberty to take merely the best timber, but had to take everything exept the brush. To avoid quarreling among Regts. and Comps. each of them had a certain parcel assigned for their special use. By the midle of March not a single tree, or even sappling was to be seen on that spot.

The winter, or rather the rainy season, was very severe and of long duration this year. Up to the end of February a day seldom passed without rain, or a mixture of rain and snow. That was very unhealthy, especially as we had to sleep on damp ground. It did not make much difference if we piled up the cedar boughs a foot high we had nothing to prevent the moisture from working upward and poison the mens bodies. Combined with the poor rations we received, the effect soon became apparent. The second week Ephriam Walker and Wm. or Bill Nye opened the list. Walkers limbs swoll up dropsy like. He did not complain of any pain, but drowsiness and stifness in the limbs. He absolutely refused to be sent to the hospital. I prepared a mild dicoction of sasafras and wild, or black cherry bark mixed with some of the red cedar berry and coaxed him to a swallow every hour. He did pull through but never got over the effects of it and died of the same disease at his home shortly after the war. Bill Nye was sent to a hospital in Murfreesbore where he died shortly after his arrival; his brother George having died already in Covington Kentucky.

The next in turn were Abbott, Alfred. and Foster Pearson. The latter . . . was sent to hospital where he died the same week. Alfred Abbott was also sent to hospital, but he recovered to meat a worse fate than death in the hospital.[1]

Henry Spaulding was the next.[2] He always had been a bright young fellow, always willing to do his duty to the best of his ability. He also was sent to hospital, but being entirely b[r]oken down was finally transferred to the Invalid Corps at Indianapolis, Indiana where I lost track of him. . . .

And now came Sergeant Theodore Clark and George Mansur.[3] Clark was a man in the fullest sense of the word and one of my best friends. He had been fighting lung trouble for some time but this mud hole settled him. He was one of thus kind of man who would never say: "I quitt." George Mansur always had been a robust, healthy fellow. When I went to the Doctors with them Sergeant Clark was unable to walk without assistance. Dr. Fuller who had snubbed me so beautifully on the morning of the 8th of Oct. previous again gave vent to his brutish instinct.[4] He abused Sergt. Clark in most vile language and refused to give him medicine or sent him to hospital. Good many sick soldiers stood round awaiting their turn for examination. They in turn served the Doctor with very plain arguments and for some minutes I expected to see the Doctor receive a sound drumming then and there, which would have served him but right. I helped Sergeant

Clark to a seat on a box and went to Colonel Hobarts tent which was near by. To the Colonel I explained the matter in brief. The Colonel came along and administered a good lecture to Dr. Fuller, but having no direct control over the Doctor he could do no more at present; but he did do something immediately after. He went to Dr. Wagner, then brigade Surgeon, informing him that if the matter was not set right he would prefer Charges against Dr. Fuller and bring it up to the Surgeon General at Washington D.C. Well, Fuller was dismissed, but some way or an other he succeeded in getting an appointment as assistant Surgeon in the 24th Ill. But the Turner boys knew how to deal with him. Being in Camp next to our Regt. they heard and knew all about him and sent him warning to quit. But he did not mind that and undertook to snub the men there as he had done with us. The consequence was a liberal ducking in a ditch and some rough handling in general which brought him to terms. He resigned and that ended his military Doctors Carrer.

Sergeant Clark[5] and George Mansur were helped into an Ambulance and sent to hospital in Murfreesboro; Clark dying there the next day and Geo. Mansur a few days later.

Next in order were: Anson Tollman and Daniel B. Cushman.[6] Both sent to hospital and being totally disabled for field duty were transferred to the Invalid Corps.

Am[a]zi[e] Poll[o]ck, George Herrick and James Woolcott[7] shared the same fate. I must say here that August [Pierrelee], the cannon fever suspect, returned to the Company the day after the battle. The fever seemed to have disappeared. . . .

Murfreesboro is the County seat of Williamson County in midle Tennessee. According to its size it might have contained 2500 inhabitants; present there were scarcely 500. and that were mostly negros and poor white people unable to move away. A good many returned though after finding the yankees would not skin them alive. Those people became very agressive and impudent after a while. Of course they found here and there a hen coop or old stable missing, which probably had been confiscated for kindling wood. Chickens and other kinds of the feathered tribe also found it very unhealthy in the neighborhood of the yankees. The most carefull hidden sweet potatoes, hams, shoulders, or other eatables had mysteriously disappeared. The Courthouse, City hall and other suitable vacated buildings were seized and converted in hospitals, or the Quartermaster and Commissary would use them to store their goods in. Soon after the return of these scared rebels they poured in their claims for damage upon Genl. Rosecrans for articles

ABOUT OUR "COOZIE" WINTER QUARTERS

said to be stolen, damaged or destroyed. Of course they all claimed to be good union people, which seemed the more queer since they had run away when the union Soldiers advanced. They also wanted rations and victuals from Rosecrans. But old Rosey stopped them short. The actually poor which were found in the City at our entering it received rations, the others were informed if they could not support themselfes, to pack up their things and they would be escorted outside our lines where General Bragg and their great father Jeff. Davis would certainly do everything to fatten them up. And so it was done. No citizen was permitted after that to leave or enter our lines without a proper pass from Genl. Rosecrans countersigned by his Adjutant General. . . .

Genl. Bragg after his retreat from Murfreesboro had made Duck river the base of his line. This line included Tullahoma, a small city like Murfreesbor[o]. He built strong defensive works at Tullahoma and other points covering the Salem, Shelbyville, Manchester and McMinnville Pikes. Especially at Hoovers Gap on the Manchester, and at Shelbyville, on the Shelbyville pike were these works formidable. The extent of the whole line being about 14 miles from west to east and from 22 to 25 miles south of Murfreesboro. Our line necessarily covered the same distance. Our right (McCooks 20st Corps) reaching west to Franklin to the river. To the left of the 20st Corps came our (Pop Thomas 14th) Corps in the Centre extending to the left and east across the Manchester pike, from where Crittendens Corps (21) extended the line towards the McMinnville pike. Such an extended line required strong picketing and the call for picket came usually every third or fourth day.

The 10th of Januar[y] 1863. is another of those sweet days which deserves a red mark. The Quartermaster being unable to have feed enough forwarded from Nashville for horses and mules, had to fall back on fouraging in the Country. Accordingly on the 9th we were informed that on the next day a trip in the Country was to be made to gather Corn and fodder for the Quadrupeds of the Brigade, each Regt. to furnish 50 men, 200 men in all. The expedition was to start soon after daylight. The trip promised to be an extensive one, as Braggs troops had stripped the Country mighty clean both side of the river to a distance from 8 to 10. miles. Companies "D" and "E" of our Regt. were the looky ones to share in the trip.

At the appointed time we were in motion. Forty army wagons, some with four, some with six mules made up the train. It started towards the river in the rear of our lines. Something was wrong with the bridge and we could not cross. So we had to drive down along the bank a couple miles towards a ford. We jumped onto the wagons and after a lively shaking up on the uneven rocky river bottom landed safely on the north side, then up again the steep bank towards the road. We st[u]ck to the wagons, thinking it a big thing to have a ride out; but that pleasure was of short duration. Soon the teams took a blind road to the left which led directly into a cedar swamp. We soon were glad to scramble out of the wagons. The evil one himself could not ride in an army wagon box, en route in a cedar swamp for any lenght of time and keep his bones and wits together, provided allways, he had any. So we meekley plodded alongside of the rattling, bumping vehicles. That swamp must be of considerable extent as it was One P.M. when we landed out of it, right plump onto a big plantation, at least a square mile in extent. The buildings made the impression of a village; But the big, three storied mansion (basement included) of brick, and the unavoidable cotton gin and press with its heavy wooden press screw, capped with a steeple like roof, proclaimed it at once a typical southern Chevaliers Institute. Some forty, one storied building[s], about 16 x 30 in size, some frame, some of hewn logs and all whitewashed stood in two rows about 20 rods from the main building. A garden plot of half an acre surrounded each building. An immense frame barn stood somewhat apart from Gin and press and towards the barn the teams wended their way.

The Major of the 79th Penn. who was in command at once placed a guard at every entrance of the house and none of the Soldiers were permitted to enter the same, nor were they allowed to enter the nigger quarters. The barn sized 40 x 100 feet divided in two part with a passage in the Centre. One part of it was filled high up between the rafters with husked corn. I never before nor after have I seen such an amount of corn in one pile. Just think of it a room 40 x 45. 18 feet high. That space contains 32.400 cubic feet. Allowing two Cubic feet per bushel would be 16,000 bushels husked or 8000 bushels shelled corn. Our 40. wagons would not make a very great impression on that. One wagon would take 50. bushel, 2,000 bushel in all. Consequently it would have required 8. trips for our 40 wagons to haul away the pile. The other part of the barn was partly filled with fodder, that is; the dried leaves of corn tied in bundles which served as hay. The cattle are running out doors the year round and but little fodder is needed during the winter. But there was an emensity of hogs and dont you forget it. The hogs had to live and fatten on corn; the 4 or 500 niggroes in turn lived on the hog, cornmeal and Molasses, besides such vittels a[s] they raised on their gardenpatch. That patch was to a great extent abandoned to watermelons which, next to the Opossum, is the greatest luxury for the darkey. But not all

ABOUT OUR "COOZIE" WINTER QUARTERS

slaves had gardens. Only such planters who were inclined to treat their slaves somewhat like a human being would allow that luxury.

No time was given for dinner. Loading immediately began. A couple boards knocked out at the sides and end of the building enabled us to load 8 wagons at once; two in the passage in the barn and two on each side and end. When the wagon boxes were full, fodder was piled on top and bound down with a rope.

We did not see any of the inmates of the mansion. They perhaps felt to[o] proud, or what is about as likely, were to[o] much scared. But the darkies swarmed around like bees around the hive. They were of all sizes from the old croony down to the waddling picaninny. Good many of them were barefooted. From one of them I learned that "Ole massa was some big pumpkin in the rebel army," that young Massa was sick abed, he having come in the way of some yankee bullet in the battle at Stone river. And he "lowed that ole Missus heart was mos broke." He informed me also that there was a young missus who had a hard time of it, "b'cause young missus she took awfull to Massa Linkum," meaning that she was of Union senti-ment. The old fellow kept on chatting and rattling like a gander, so much so that I found it difficult to keep up with him, I felt sorry I could not understand all he said. Finally I approached a subject which was upper-most in my mind. I hinted that I would be willing to part with some real good coffee in ex[c]hange for some different eatable stuff. Hearing my offer his mouth and eyes suddenly oppened like barn doors in a storm. (Slaves never received coffee exept sometimes on thanksgiving day, Christmass and Easter.) "De Lor bress je, jes massa," he exclaimed, "ab what do Massa want?" In return I asked him what he had to give. "Coan meal and bacon, sah and lasses, an appels, an taters all you can tote Sah." I told him to do up about a peck of cornmeal and a couple dozen apples and come with them behind the woodshed which stood close to and in the rear of the house. I should have liked to take some potatoes but was unable to transport them. I took four haversacks and four Canteens from the boys of my Comp. hid them in my rubber blanket and went behind the woodshed; the darkey soon came with a bundle of cornmeal done up in a dirty peace of butternut jean and a peck of apples. I inquired if there was anything drinkable in the house stronger than water. He scratched his wool vigerously. "Da is sah" he said after a while and next made a dive in the basement. I suppose the kitchen was in the basement and the kitchen personal [personnel] in south-ern families always were negroes. He certainly had gone to find the lay of the ground, to scout.

Presently he came hurriedly back nodding his head. I handed him two canteens and back he went and did not stay long neither. "From young missus," he said "Massa allus drinks dat." But next he warned me not to say anything to the other soldiers as Missus could not satisfy them all. Of course the warning was he[e]ded; That was in my own interest. Now I handed the other two Canteens for "lassus." I was astonished at the darkies confidence bringing me everything without having his coffee. While he was after molasses I went to the Major inquiring if he would permit the boys trading with the negroes ex[c]hanging coffee for vegetables and tobacco. He had no objection and would give a quarter of an hour for that purpose after the loading was done. Next I went to Lieut. Turner, explained and we agreed over a [plan] to secure a good share for the boys of our Comp. He was to inform our boys quietly of the plan while I went back to my old nigger friend to complete arrangements with him. He was waiting for me in the woodshed and handed me the molasses while I handed him all the coffee I had, nearly a pound, but I told him I wanted the bag back. He danced a jig for a short time and when he got tired I spoke to him of our plan. He readily understood the drive and we went together to his house which was the second in the row. While I tried to entertain his spouse with but poor success he went round to the neighbors giving the word and soon they came in piling things around. Half an hour afterward the loading was completed and when the word was given the boys of our Comp. were at the head and I stood ready to conduct them to the exchange building. They all loaded pretty well, some one thing, some another and all were satisfied. We got even several bushel potatoes along which we put on a wagon.

The day had been sulky and cold, but the work had kept the men warm enough. It was half past three when we started on the home stretch. From the darkey I had learned that we were only 3 miles south of Nolansville, the very place where, the reader will remember Gus [Pierrelee] and Chs. Herb had confiscated a sheep, two geese and a pail of honey. We could not return the same road we had come as in the Cedar swamp we would have lost nearly everything. We had to take the regular road leding through the swamp towards the Murfreesboro pike. That was 6. miles and from the junction to Stone river it was 16. miles and from there to camp near 3. miles. Also a twenty five mile trip; very encouraging indeed. As soon as we were fairly started we began to munch our diner, as usual Crakers and a slice of raw bacon and as a special luxury some aples. When we rea[c]hed the pike it began to rain right smart, which, as the night advanced turned into sleet; it continued in that way until midnight when it cleared off and became very

ABOUT OUR "COOZIE" WINTER QUARTERS

cold. No halts were made. Steadily the mules plodded along scattering the mud profusely right and left, covering us, who just as steadily plodded along, with a coat of plaster from bottom to top and which soon froze on ouer clothing. Finally, after a seeming Eternity, we reached the river. We could not see it but heard it. We were over three miles higher up the river from where we had crossed the morning before. A halt was made for the purpose of finding a fording place nearer than that. I asked of Turner the time. He lighted a match and found it two A.M. To say I was tired would do no justice to the fact; I was simply broken down, played out, as the boys styled it. Turner said he was, all were. Some said they would not walk an other mile for twenty dollar. They had to do it though for nothing, or at the rate of thirteen per month in depreciated greenback. I sat down on a rotten pile of railroad ties, gradually laid down and fell asleep, or I fell asleep and sank down, I do not know which.—

Suddenly I awoke. It seemed someone or something had startled me. I was on my legs in an instant. But what was that? Where were the wagons? the men? Or was I asleep [y]et. No I was alone. Could they leave without calling me, or give me a good kick? Then I heard way up the river a craking of whips, jelling and shouting. They were fording the river. For the first time I sampled the Canteen the darkey had filled for me and then started in a run in the direction of the noise. How far it seemed to be; but luckily it always went down hill. Almost out of wind I came just in time to scramble on to the last wagon before it was in the river. I was so exhausted and ex[c]ited as hardly to be able to hold on to the rope in order not to drop in the river.

The oppsite bank was high and steep and of clay soil. They had to double teams in order to reach the level ground. That took time and was the means to bring me across because, without that I would have been left on the wrong side of the river. As soon as we reached the plateau we were ordered to "Skit." If I had been able to, I would have paid five dollars to remain on that wagon up to camp, but the teamsters dictionary did not contain the word "pity" and down I came with the rest of the men. I suppose the mules were tired also. Well I started but: Oh, my! It seemed all the joints were stiff and squeeling. I stopped and taking another sniff, said to myself: "Henry, you must stand it; root hog or die." And so I set the stiff limbs in motion again. But right here I must say that a reasonable dose of liqueur, applied, or taken at the right time beats all powders, pills or quinine in the United States. I dont care about all sophysteries and arguments of prohibition cranks and ministers. Experience is better than all theory. "Search and try everything and keep that which is best." During my walk towards camp I

gradually overtook and passed most all of the command. They were straggling pitiously. It was no wonder; we had marched 41. miles since 6 o.clock
the previous morning, without rest and only one scanty meal. That constitutes the good picknick times we had during the war, as the Copperheads
tell us to day.

I overtook Lieut. Turner nearly at the head of the stragling procession.
He had been on the first wagon to cross and that brought him in advance.
He was moving slowly along and I asked him if he was earning the twenty
dollar now which he had so liberally offered at the other side the river. "Yes"
he replied grimly, "and more than that. I am going to resign. Is it not enough
that we risk our lives and limbs by facing the rebel bullets and shells? Must
we sacrifice our lives in such a miserable way? Uncle Sam, or his minions
will never say: thank you, if we rot here in the Clay. The damned"—"Stop
a moment," I interrupted him, with an air of assumed dignity, and seizing
his arm made him stop. "I have an Elixir which will make you ashamed of
resignation and besides, if you do resign, old 'Rosy' wont let you, he will
put a stop to it." And having uncorked the Canteen I handed it to him. He
sniffed at the noozle first and then went in for it. Just then some soldiers
passed by and looked at him. He noticed that, brought down the Canteen
and: "Why" he exclaimed, "That tast's just like river water"!—"Capt." I
replied, "I could not find any other." That satisfied the soldiers and they
went on, and so did we. . . . After a while he began again in a sort of official
tone . . ."Sergeant, there is some important matter about which I must
speak to you. If you can find time to morrow, come in my tent, will you?"
. . . Another little swallow and we parted. . . .

Fortune was on our side for the next day, for there was no special duty to
be performed exept camp guard and so the men had time to nurse the tired
limbs and be ready for picket the following day. Heavy rain again during
afternoon and night. . . . After dinner (This time it was corn meal mush and
"lassas.") I went over to Lieut. Turner to hear what important matter he had
on his mind to unload. I put the Canteen under my blouse in order to
encourage and aid his mind and concience to fully unload itself. I found
him alone, stretched on a low bunk. "Oh, just in time Sergeant; please pass
that Canteen," was his greeting when he brought himself in a sitting posture. "Please take a chair," pointing to an empty craker box set on end. . . .
"Some evenings past," Turner began. "Col. Hobart called the Comp. commanders in his tent and informed us that it was necessary to complete the
promotions of commissioned and non Commissioned Officers in the Regt."
(This [these] promotions were in place of those Officers, Sergeants and

Corporals we had lost at Perryville in battle and others who had died of disease or were discharged for the same. There was quite a number of them.) "Before he forwarded the recomandations for Commissioned Officers to the Gouvernor of Wisconsin he wished that the Company Commanders would recommand such of the Sergeants and Corporals as by ability, Character and service were most entitled to promotion. Now you know that in the regular order of promotion I will become Captain of the Comp. Second Lieutenant Fred B[o]rch[e]rd[t] will step in my place as first Lieutenant, and you in [Borcherdt's] place a[s] second Lieut. I wish to change that program slightly. Lieut. [Borcherdt] is certainly a good fellow and able also, but he is to[o] slow, to[o] sleepy, no energy, a go-as you please fellow. I want you to take Commission over him as first Lieut. You have been worth half a dozen [Borcherdts] to the Comp. Now is that all right? Do you accept? I am sure Colonel Hobart will not object." . . .

That was a surprise indeed. Sure I had expected the promotion to second Lieut. in the regular order but to jump Lieut. [Borcherdt] had never occurred to me. It certainly would be of great advantage to me, but it seemed to me altogether a detestable trick and made up my mind to refuse at once and so I did. I thanked Lieut. Turner but begged him to let the matter rest. "Well," he replied, "If that is your decision I must submit, but remember what I promised to you in Cincinnaty that I would stick to you and anyway, I believe you will have to command ere long." We consulted for a while about the appointments of Sergeants and Corporals in the Comp. and then I left. . . .

The issue of rations had become regular now but only as far as hard tack, bacon, coffee, sugar and salt was concerned. We never received anything else. That was a great drawback on the health of the men. One of the worst features was the scarcity of tobacco, both, smoking and chewing. The Drs. incouraged the use of tobacco as they considered it a preventive against malaria and other fevers. There were several suttlers who had tobacco for sale but there was hardly an Officer or soldier who could muster money enough to buy a package or a plug. We had been five months in the field now but had not received a cent of Money [y]et since we left Oshkosh. Thousands of families at home were actually suffering for the want of it. When the soldiers enlisted it was always loudly proclaimed that the families should and would be taken care of, because from $13.00 dollars a month in depreciated greenbacks no family could exist, but when the soldiers were in the field the families usually were left alone with the care. Neither would the storekeepers trust the soldiers wifes much because, as they said, if the soldier should bite the dust where do we get our money? Such was the patriotism of the "stay at homes." who made money and got rich. Every day the soldiers received letters from their wifes complaining of utter want and poverty. And to day the northern rebels and copperheads loudly proclaim that the soldiers had received all they had earned. During January I received a letter from my wife saying the little money I could leave her was gone and she was not able to buy wood for fuel to keep out the cold. She had applied to the City authorities for temporary relief but was cooly informed that I might sent her money. . . .

Finally during February we were electrified by the order to prepare muster and payrolls immediately, as the Paymaster had arrived and was ready to begin paying off as soon as the rolls were completed. As we had received one months pay in advance at muster in at Oshkosh there was four months pay due us. At thirteen dollars per month that would bring for privates and corporals $52.00, the sergeants $15.00. per month $60.00. and the Orderly sergeant at $20.00 per month $80.00. Now it must be understood that we received this pay in greenbacks so called worth at home about fifty cents on the dollar in store pay, not in cash. Accordingly we did not receive half what was promised us. But enough of that. The veteran is the underdog in the fight, and is nothing more but a fraud, a swindler, or a government pauper, who has no claims whatever for saving the Union.

To avoid the danger of loosing the mony by sending it per mail home, an other course was adopted. Rev. Clinton, our Chaplain, a thrustworthy man, was given leave of absence and he was to take the money, the men wished to send home and delivered the same to the proper addresses.[8] Each. Comp. Commander had to make out a list in duplicate of all the men who wished to sent money home together with the amount to be sent. The original of such list was given to the Chaplain for his guidance, the duplicate was kept by the company Commander for reference. We always followed this rule and never lost a cent of money in such transit. Another sure way to get the money home was the Allotment system. While in camp at Oshkosh Wis. the men were asked if any one of them would sent any sum of their monthly pay to father or mother, brother or sister or wife, or any other person whom they would trust with the keeping of the money, they should give the proper directions and addresses. The amount of such allotment was not paid to the soldier but directly by the government to the Allottee. In this manner the danger of the trains being robbed, captured or burned by the rebel Cavallery or guerillas and the money taken was to a great extent avoided.

ABOUT OUR "COOZIE" WINTER QUARTERS

About this time there was considerable exitement among the Captains of the Regt. As related before, Colonel Sweet was so severely wounded in the battle at Perryville Ky. as to totally disable him from further field service. He resigned his commission as Colonel of our Regt. and was appointed Commander of Camp Douglass, Chicago Ill. where several thousand rebel prisoners were quartered.[9] He did valuable service there. . . . Lieut. Col. Hobart of cour[s]e took his place. As Major Schumacher had been killed at Perryville, Col. Hobart wished to have a man in his place he could rely on. In the regular course of advancement the ranking, or oldest Capt. by appointment in the Regt. would have been entitled to that position. But Col. Hobart knew them to[o] well to trust them with such an important Office. The only Officer in the Regt. best fitted for the place was Adjutant M. Fitch. He had served a year in the Potomac army and was a soldier by instinct, so to speak. But then, he was merely a second Lieutenant and the new fledged Capts. merely considered him a "non est subordinate." But Colonel Hobart kept his own Counsel. The senior, or ranking Capt. in the Regt. was a certain White of Fond dul Lac (Comp. "A.") who had kept a general store there. He was an easy going, good natured man but not fit to command a Corporals guard and he said so himself. The Captains of Comps. "B." and "C." were braggards but no soldierly qualities about them; the Capt. of Comp. "D." had died; of Co. "E" had been killed at Perryville; of "F." was a very neutral man who thought the war was an outrage on good american Citizens; the Capt. of Co. "G." had been severely wounded and had resigned; the Capt. of Co. "H." had been killed at Perryville; the Capt. of Co. "I." had been taken prisoner at the Jefferson pike when Wheeler burned our brigade train and was at present in board in Hotel "Libby" at Richmond; now Comp. "K." the last on[e] in the Regt. had the best Captain in the Regt. Chas. H. Walker of Manitowoc, the second ranking Capt. But he would not take the place because, as he said, he was not able to fill it satisfactoroly. We will meet him again. So, Colonel Hobart decided to recommend the second Lieut. and Adjutant Fitch for the Majorship.[10]

At this all the Capts. exept C. H. Walker got their dander up. They considered that action an insult on their dignity;—to have a mere second Lieut. promoted over them to Major. Capt. Godfrey of Oshkosh, (Comp. "C") an overbearing blunderbuss, even went so far as to call Colonel Hobart a rascally intriguant, a demagogue etc. Hobart at once requested him to resign, or he would have him tried by a court martial and cashired. Capt. Godfrey

Capt. Alphonso S. Godfrey and Capt. Charles H. Walker. From a lithograph, "Col. B. J. Sweet's 21st Wis. Vol Regt. Located at Oshkosh, Wis. 1862." (Courtesy Oshkosh Public Museum)

probably had not expected that. For once he had put his fingers to[o] deep in the soup and got them scalded. He took the best course left him and resigned.[11] But the other Captains also resigned excpt Capt. Walker Co. "K." Col. Hobart endorsed the resignations "For the good of the service," and Genl. Rosecrans promply approoved the same.

We received orders for an other fouraging trip. Our Quartermaster happened to issue Shoes and Clothing and as I did not wish to wear out my boots to[o] fast I drew a pair of new shoes to wear on the trip. This time the fouraging was to be in a southern direction between the lines of the opposing armies. As it was possible we might meet some rebel force, scouting parties . . . had to go in strong force; The whole brigade went out, the battery going along as also two Escadrons of Cavallery. We went out on the Salem pike and found the same in a condition impossible to describe. One Corps of Braggs army had retreated on this road and cut it up in a horrible way. A tenacious Clay soil made the matter more bad. The stuf would stick to and fill the wheels untill they had the appearance of immense rolling, flat disks; in the same manner it treated our legs. Every depression, or hole was filled with water, which after a little working over converted the hole into a vast, sticky dough. We were compelled [to] resort to the fields where ever there were any or go bushwaking which was far better than treading the Clay. Towards noon a halt was made for dinner.

We had hardly made 6 miles during so many hours. Colonel Hambright of the 79th Penn. who Commanded the Expedition must have become convinced that we could not load and return the same day. In the afternoon we made perhaps 4 miles more and went in Camp for the night. . . .

Early next morning we were moving again. We went perhaps two miles when a road was found turning to the right at right angles with the pike. It was no crossroad and therefore indicating that it led to some plantation. The head of the Column turned into this road the wagons and battery following. Our Regt. bringing up the rear, was ordered to proceed on the pike untill we reached a point where a road forked of[f] towards the left. Here we were to halt, watch both roads, and in case of attack hold the point until our train was back on the pike when we would be informed to return. Two parrot guns went along with us. We went accordingly and some miles further on found the fork. We were within five miles of the rebel picket line and as the immediate front of a picket lines is always patrouilled by scouts and Cavallery we had to expect to be discovered and attacked. We at once set to work and constructed a heavy breastwork across the pike at the point of the fork so as to control both roads. the parrot guns were placed behind the works. Light breastworks were built to the right and left in the woods. The fork of the roads was in the form of a Y so we could easily watch both roads from breastworks.

It was nearly two P.M. when we had made preparations to our satisfaction and now devoted a quarter of an hour to masticate some har[d]tack and raw bacon. While thus engaged we thought to hear faintly lively discharge of Musketry westward in the direction our train had gone. But the reports were so faint that we considered it an immagination of ex[c]ited brains, specially as we did not hear any Artillery. Colonel Hobart ordered Lieut. Weisbrod and myself to go forward on the roads to our advanced pickets and assertain if they per[h]aps had heard or observed anything. Weisbrod went forward on the branch road while I took the pike. The pickets were full ¼ of a mile in advance. They had made the same observation, but insisted that a fight had taken place. While we were speaking we noticed Cavallery approaching in a lively trot. We lost no time in running back through the woods to inform our men. We arived behind the breastworks without the Cavallery having seen us. The boys were in place in a moment and at almost the same time Weisbrod came in with his pickets. They came 6 abreast as the width of the road would not allow of more. We could form no estimate of their number as they rode on[e] after another and the wood prevented any side vi[e]w. It was well for them however that they could not deploy or they would have lost immensely. Whether they thought we were merely a small guard there I do not know but it was altogether a foolish move on their part. Their front section discharged their [carbines] and rev[o]lvers at us the bullets either striking the breastworks or going over us. Then with sabers raised high and jelling wildly, they came on in a dashing gallop. Poor fellows. It certainly looked very dangerous but: "fire" Hobart commanded and men and horses in the front section went down, causing the following sections to be thrown in disorder. An other volley was administerd and for a moment it seemed that all would pile up in a heap. Col. Hobart took pity on them and ordered: "Cease firing." ("It seemed to me like murder," the Colonel afterward said.) In half a minute they traveled back in quick style. But they did not intend to give up so easy. When out of range they dismounted and tried to fight us scirmishing in the woods. They were wellcome for that. They kept up a scattering fire for a quarter of an hour and then left.

We could not do anything for their wounded as we had neither Dr. nor ambulance with us. They had 10 killed and some 40 wounded. We had four slightly wounded during scirmishing. It was near night now and we wondered if the train had not returned to the pike [y]et. Colonel Hobart was ordered to remain there until ordered to come back. But he concluded to fall back on his own account to the point where the train had left the pike. Arriving their a small troop of our Cavallery came up informing us that the train was already several miles ahead towards camp. Severall miles further, almost on the same spot we had camped the night before we found troops and train in camp busy making coffee. The wagons were all loaded but when they were starting for home they were surprised by a spirited attack of rebel Cavallery They sent them on the back tramp easy enough, but as the attack was in open field we had twenty four wounded, one so severly in the upper right arm as to make amputation near the shoulder necessary. The rebel loss was never assertained. No Artillery was employed as Col. Hambright feared to draw more rebel reinforcements.

As it was possible the rebs might make an other trial the next day we were moving early. But we could make but little headway as the loaded wagons again and again would stick in some bottomless hole and had to be helped out by the men. So we went slowly along untill noon when a halt was made to feed the mules and make Coffee. When we were in motion again our Cavallery reported the approach of rebel Cavallery. Our teams kept on but the troops were quickly formed in line. We happened to be in open Country, high fences on both side the road. The fences were converted into low breastworks in short order while our Cavallery tryed to detain the rebels; but had to fall back as the rebel force was far to[o] strong for them. The rebels had not forgotten the lesson of the previous day but dismounted and deployed as scirmishers. They took well care not to come to[o] near us. Their Carbines were of not much account. But after a while the head of an infantry Column hove in sight and deployed. That put a serious aspect to the matter. It was a brigade, stronger in number than ouers, but they had no artillery with them. Their cavallery fell back and mounted again. The commander of the rebel infantry thought to do us up in grand style. As soon as his men were properly deployed he ordered a charge. Yes; they came, brave enough like good boys; but when our infantry, hidden behind a little row of fencerails, and the battery opened on them, it brought them in utter confusion and they went back out of range to form again. They undertook a second charge with the same result.

Meanwhile the rebel Cavallery had concocted a s[c]heme to get around our left wing and in our rear. If successfull in this move they were in a condition to make it warm for us. But Colonel Mihalotzi, who was on the left of our line detected their move quickly formed his regiment backward at right angles with front line, forwarded a strong scirmishline and sent them forward. At the same time Colonel Hambright had been informed of the affairs and sent a section of the battery to the left. The Johnnies soon abandoned this move and went back. As the rebell Infantry seemed to be tired of the job, Colonel Hambright ordered our lines to fall back in line and keep a strong scirmishline in the rear to repel, or give notice of any further attack. The rebel Cavallery thought they could improove on this arrangement and made several dashes on us, dis[c]harging their carabines and gallop back again. They did not do us much harm, but it was exedingly vexing and very tiring business. We had none killed, but a dozend wounded in the affair. The Johnnies loss unknown.

CHAPTER EIGHT

~

Expedition into East Tennessee

~ During the later part in Februar[y] heaven seemed to have exhausted its supply of shower baths. The rainy days and nights became gradually less and fine spring weather took their place. This meant an increased activity for the soldiers allso. Strong, extensive fortifications were build in the outscirts of the City and armed with the best guns and manned with artillery and Infantry. They served also as storehouses for army supplies. Extensive gardens were cultivated for the benefit of the Hospitals and convalescent camps. The garden work was mostly done by Invalids and convalescents. Company and Regiments drill as also scirmish dril became a dayly practice. The Austrian rifle was ex[c]hanged for the Enfield rifle which had a longer range. Genl. Rosecrans meanwhile exerted himself to reorganize his army and bring it to the most effective point for the coming Campain. He was sadley in need of more Cavallery. There were but a few small Regts. with us and they but poorly equipped and altogether unable to perform Effectively the service required of them. In fact, the government and rulers at Washington had but a poor opinion of the importance of active Cavallery service, hence the sad neglect in the organization. Genl. Rosecrans saw and felt, in the face of the overwhelming force of rebel cavallerie the necessity of counteracting that force. He organized four Regt. of mounted Infantry. They were taken from the Infty Regts. by Volunteering. They had first the Enfield rifle, but later on the breach loading Sharps rifles. They were able to fight either mounted or on foot. They also had light batteries of mountain howitzers, or Jack Ass batteries, as the boys called them. He kept bothering the

117

Second Lt. James H. Jenkins. From a lithograph, "Col. B. J. Sweet's 21st Wis. Vol Regt. Located at Oshkosh, Wis. 1862." (Courtesy Oshkosh Public Museum)

government until he got a division of Cavallery which he put under Command of Genl. McCook. Our Regiments had dwindled down to half their original numbers and Rosecrans wanted to have them filled up with recruits, but the fellows in Washington pretended to know everything better than the Generals in the field. Even General Halleck the commander in chief of all the armies in the field, with hea[d]quarters in Washington opposed the request of Rosecrans. They kept on raising new Regts. and in that way had chance to decorate their friends and influencial pets with shoulderstraps and secure fat Offices for them. Those fellows usually were to[o] hightoned, or had not patriotism sufficient to serve their Country in the ranks for $13.00 per month.

Lieut. H. Fitch having been promoted Major, Lieut. Howard Jenkins was made Adjutant.[1] He was a little dapper fellow, native of Boston and wanted everybody to understand it. Every thing was different in Bosting, everithing better in Bosting and "you ought to see Bosting." That procured for him the sobriquet: "Little Bosting Jim." But for all that, he was generally well liked. He was of pleasing accommodating temperament; had no Idea of rank and pride and allways ready for joke or fun. He had also a fine voice and was an exellent singer. This made him very popular and he seemed to be proud of the title; "Little Bosting."

The Sergeants and Corporals places were also filled up. After my promotion there was no sergeant in the Comp. exept John Dey who had suffered himself to be taken prisoner at Perryville and was absent. To fill my place as orderly, Private Egbert J. Scott was choosen.[2] He had enlisted from the College and was a fine and able fellow. From the eight Corporals but three remained: Sylvester Greel[e]y, Curtis Mitchell and Joe Holden, and they were promoted to Sergeants. Geo. Rawson, McKender Rawson August [Pierrelee] and Jim Walker and Lyman C. Wait[e][3] were appointed Corporals.

The first week in March we finally were assigned to a more pleasant camping ground. We moved to the East side of the City in a fine grove of heavy timber. The ground was high and dry and all fallen timber, brush and other obstacles removed, burned and the ground made as smooth and even as a parlor floor. North of the Camp and adjoining it was a large former Cotton field which extended to the Murfreesboro and McMinville pike. North of the pike was an immense Peach Orchard extending north nearly down to Stone river, the whole covering about a section of land.

At the same time we received new tents. It was a new invention and considered a great improoovement. I never could see the improoovements exept that we were obliged to carry them ourselfes while our former tents were carried on a wagon. The offi[ci]al name was: "Shelter tent" but the boys soon discovered a more appropiate name and simply called it "dog tent." In fact it resembled a dog Kennel more than any other thing. Each man received a sheet of light canvass, the size of a bed sheet. One sheet contained a row of buttons at one edge, while the other sheet contained corresponding button holes; consequently the men had to pair off by twos in order to complete a tent. Each man had to carry his half on the march and in this wise a great number of wagons could be spared who formerly had to transport the h[e]avy tents. They were quickley and easily put up which was one great advantage but for actual shelter during a campain they did not amount to much. Two poles, or sticks five foot long with a crotch at one End, a ridge pole to lay across in the crotches, all about the size of a bean pole was all. The crotch poles were stuck in the ground, crotch upward, the ridge pole laid across in the crotches, the two tent halves buttoned together and thrown over the ridgepole, both lower corners stretched out and fastened to the ground by means of pins passing through a loop at the lower four corners. In putting up the tent the wind had to be taken in consideration so that it struck the side, or roof of the tents as the end were open. On the March or Campaign in fair weather the boys never put them up but used them as a covering instead. If the prospect was fair, or we were sure we would stay a while in the same place things were arraigned different. If bords could be found so much the better, if not, straight grained

Oak or Chestnut trees were selected, cut into lenghts of 6 foot, split into strips or shakes from four to six inches wide and an inch thick. One end was driven into the ground a foot, one alongside the other, in that way forming the lower part, or uprights for four half tent sheets as the roof; four men being the inmates of such building. The inside room was usually 7 x 12. the gable ends were closed with blankets or anything found handy. At one end in the tent two bunks, one above the other, each for twoo men served for bedstead. That left room enough for a small table and a few small chairs. The officers were provided with the big wall tent which was necessary on account of their being oblidged to write considerabl, keep books and accounts, etc. . . .

Franklin, so to speak, was the Outpost on our e[x]treme right. A certain Colonel Wallace was in Command of the post. One day in April two Colonels in Union uniform reported to Colonel Wallace saying, they were Inspection Oficers sent by General Rosecrans to inspect the troops, Artillery, horses, camp equippage, ammunition etc. They allso presented an order from Genl. Rosecrans to the effect. They said they had to go from there to Nashville and were in a great hurry. They would begin at once. A Colonel S. who belonged to the troops of the post expressed his suspicion to Colonel Wallace of their being rebel spies, but Wallace ridiculed the Idea and said they were all right. The Inspectors looked at everything in a hurry and nearly condemned Everything, even if the things were in serviceable order. (Every three, or four months, as it may be necessary, the Div. Inspector examines every article and if found unfit for service condems the same. New articles are issued then and the old ones destroyed or turned over to an Officer designated for that purpose.) This seemed more suspicious still to Colonel S. and he again applied to Colonel Wallace to arrest the fellows but Wallace would not listen. When the Inspectors were through they mounted their horses and left on the pike for Nashville. When they had gone a little ways and Colonel Wallace out of sight, Colonel S. took the Adjutant of his Regt. and four men and on fleet horses went in pursuit. They must have ridden furiously as it took the pursuing party 10 miles to overtake them. They had turned off the pike and stopped with a planter who was known as a rank rebel. This strenghtened the Colonels suspicion and he secured the fellows while at supper and took them back to Franklin. He then sent to Genl. Rosecrans for instructions. Genl. Rosy replied he had sent no Inspectors. They should try the fellows by drumhead court martial and if found guilty, hang them. Overwhelming proof of their being spies were found and two days after they were hoisted.[4]

The later part in March Genl. Rosy was informed that the rebel free-booter John Morgan was in the neighborhood of Liberty, and Alexandria[,] smashing things in general and specially harrassing union people. Both places were on the Liberty pike 20 miles in our left rear. An Indiana Regt. was sent out to take care of them. The Colonel of the Regt. sent word by courier that Morgan was greatly to[o] much for him to be scared. He asked for reinforcements describing the spot where he had hastily intrenched himself. Colonel Hobart received orders to immediately march to the support of the Indiana Regt. [We] had just turned in when the order came. At ten P.M. we started, the courier being our guide. We marched very fast as it was of the greatest importance to arrive there before daylight. We had to wade the Stone river twice because the river winds in such confounded zig zag way that we had to cut off one of its immense Elbows in order to save the long tramp around. The water was not warm a bit, but the sharp marching kept us warm. We had no knapsacks or blanket to carry and could make good time.

We arrived in due time. Just at daybreak we observed through the woods the camp fires of the rebs. The courier informed us that the Indiana Regt. had fortified on a Knoll in the woods, being entirely surrounded. Morgan did not dare to charge on the Indiana boys as they from behind their shelter would kill off his men at long range before his carbines would have any efect. Morgans men were all Cavallerie but had dismounted. They were a brigade, outnumbered also the Indiana boys four to one. Morgan calculated on starvation, but forgot to calculate on reinforcements. So sure did he feel himself that he even neglected to post pickets. That was bad for him. Hobart formed a strong scirmish line and cautioned the men to advance carefully without the least noise, he following at a short distance with the rest. Of course we could cover but a part of Morgans line, but we were sure the Indiana boys would be lively as soon as they knew our presence. Major Fitch comanded our skirmishers and was to give the signal to fire.

We started. It went up hill but very little. When we came nearer we saw Morgans men busy about the fires some preparing breakfast, others sitting in groups eating. Unobserved we had advanced in the woods to about five rods distance. I looked back to see how far Colonel Hobart was behind with the rest of the regiment; but had followed close not more than ten rods behind us. Suddenly the crack of Major Fitchs Revolver gave the signal and a hundred rifles peppered the rebels breakfast. "Charge bajonet! March! March"! Hobart ordered his men and with a "hurrah"! the men dashed forward. What followed cannot be described. Hobarts troop fired and then we went for them with the bajonet. Some of the Johnnies had got hold of their carbines and discharged them at us; others started on the wildest run, and others went in for unconditional surrender. The Indiana boys had been on the lookout. No sooner had they heard our first volley when they jumped over the breastworks on the opposite side from us [and] charged down the hill. But the rebs did not wait for the meeting and could only be reached by the bullets of the Indian[a] boys. They soon reached their horses and were of[f] in a jiffy. It seemed the Indiana men could not stop cheering. Our men made prisoners by the scores. The rebs were so scared that they did not think of much resistance. There was no use to chase those who escaped as their horses soon brought them in safe distance. We found hams, shoulder, bacon and cornmeal enough to last us a week. They were stolen from the Country people of course. We had only three men wounded but some over two hundred prisoners who were set to work to bury the rebel dead of whom there were 35. and 75. wounded. Nobody had seen Genl. Morgan and the prisoners cursed him in bitter terms. That was the second time we met and whipped that renowned Guerrilla. At sundown we reached camp again amidts cheers from our Comrades, who were not a little surprised at the long string of prisoners as our escort. . . .

John Morgan, after we had spoiled his breakfast, had thought it wise to increase the distance between him and our army. He had united with Dick McCann, an other rebel freebooter and had turned towards McMinnville East Tennessee plundering and murdering Union people. Refugees came to Murfreesboro imploring aid and protection from Genl. Rosecrans. At the latest report they were in the vicinity of McMinnville about 40 miles east of us. Rosy concluded to drive them out there and an e[x]pedition was formed under the command of Genl. Re[y]nolds composed of the following troop: Two regiments of mounted Infantry and two Regts. of Cavalry with two batteries of Mountain howitzers under command of Colonel Minty.[5] General Wagners and Genl. Starkweathers brigades of Infantery. We were to take for five days rations in our haversacks and for two weeks on the wagons. It promised to become an interesting Expedition. We started on the 10th of April, the mounted Infantry and Cavalry ahead. We made but a short march that day, about 15 miles and camped near a village called Readville. As it looked somewhat unsafe in the west we thought it prudent to put up our shelter tents for the night. . . .

The following day the march was a long one. It was the more tiresome because of the steady upward tendency of the road. East Tennessee, aside from its vast mountains, commands a high level above the ocean. It was intended to come as near McMinville as possible. We camped a mile and a half west of the City. Early next morning the mounted Infantry and Cavalry drew out of camp on different roads. We received orders to march at a moments notice. An hour and a half passed quietly but then the mountain howitzers were getting up a lively racket. We formed in marching order but did not march. A while after 6. Ambulances filled with wounded and about 100 prisoners made their appearance. The wounded were dressed by the surgeons and then together with the prisoners sent under guard to Murfreesboro. From the wounded we learned that they almost surprised the rebels. A spirited fight issued and the Johnnies, being superior in number stood their ground well, although their loss from our rifles was telling. When the howitzers got in good position and opened Colonel Minty ordered a sabre charge. They could not stand that. Morgan retreated but Dick McCann stood his ground a little longer until he was knocked off from his horse by a Corporal of our mounted Infantry and taken prisoner together with the prisoners allready mentioned. The rebs then broke up in a big rout, our men following them up closely.[6]

McMinnville was of some importance to the rebel government on account of its factories who made the stuff for the cheap uniform of the rebel soldiers, its grist and rolling mills. While the mounted Infantry chased the rebels, the cavalry tended to the factories and railroad. The factories and mills and ready stoff were all burned, the railroad totally destroyed for a number of miles, all bridges burned, in fact, everything, exept private property had to go. It was a serious loss to the rebs but it was to become more serious [y]et.

The following morning we went on again but turned of[f] from the road in a north easterly direction toward the Snow Mountains. Morgan had taken his retreat in that direction probably with the intention to hide in the numerous Crevices, caves and gulches which abound in these Mountains, or to prepare ambushes for our troops. He probably would have succeeded in his scheme had it not been for the brave Mountaineers who, being all sound union men and know Every path and cave, guided our troops and frustrated all Morgans cunning.

We cleared near twenty five miles that day and at sundown when we went in camp the hights of the Snow mountain were visible in the distance. The people in this part of the country were very poor, having been robbed of everything by the rebels. Many of the homesteads lay in ashes. Many of the men had fled and joined the union troops in Kentuky, some were in hiding in the mountains. But the curse of the country were the prowling, thiefing, murderous outlaws; usually called guerillas or bush-whakers, who had no authority from either government, who were nothing but comon murderers and robbers; to[o] cowardly to fight in either army. They usually kept hidden when soldiers were near, but when they were gone they would commit the most atrocious deeds immaginable. The rebel authorities never did anything to suppress them. Some even had commissions from the rebel government as independent scouts and when captured would claim the right to be treated as prisoners of war. . . .

After a miles march the following morning the mountains receided to both sides, extending the width of the valley from one to three miles. Here the brigade divided. The 24th Ill. and 79th. Pa. following a more northern Course. The valley was well settled but many of the houses were in ruins. Woman and children would run to meet us, bid us good speed and—cry bitterly. They were so poor. Some had their husbands or sons shot or hanged because they would not go in the rebel army; others had run away in time and joined the Union army in Kentucky; Other[s] were hiding in the mountains [y]et. Everything not securely hidden was taken away or destroyed by the rebels or guerrillas. It made us feel mad, and soft too, to hear them recite in their queer mountain jargon the barbarous treatment they had to endure.—But relief was near at hand, thanks to brave Genl. Burnside who in July following captured Cumberland Gap and Knoxville. By this move he came in control of the greater part of East Tennessee exept the Counties adjoining West Virginia.[7]

While we were making dinner two men came out of the mountains and direct toward us. They were clad in homespun which hung in rags about their lean bodies. Each carried a rifle, powderhorn and shotpouch. They said they lived in an other valley several miles off and had been on their way to Knoxville to procure if possible some cornmeal or other eatables when they all at once run onto the rebels. They hid in the mountains during the night. What was their surprise when Early next morning the rebels were attacked by Yankees and whipped in les than no time. They had spoken with the Comanding Officer and when he had learned where they lived, told them to travel back as fast as they could on the shortest road and in the shortest time. They would find yankees in that vicinity. They should see the commanding Officer and tell him of what they had heard and in what direction they had run, "an hyah we uns is" they closed.

We invited them to partake of coffee, bacon and hardtack with us which they gladly did declairing it to be the first square meal they had taken for a long time. They were not the least bashfull and very amusing it was to see

how they could grind the hardtack. Genl. Starkweather had been informed
and he came and took a seat beside them. After they had told their story
the Genl. inquired about the direction and outlet of the roads in the mountains. The spokesman took the ramrod from his rifle and scratched a lot of
lines on the ground, exp[l]aining as he proceeded. "An durn it Kurnel" he
said at last, "You mout pick up sume of them dar gray Critters, ef you dun
keer bout sume what ub a race."—"Confound the race" the General replied
and jumped up, "I hope you will go along and show us the way."—"And dat
we will," both replied, "just a bit of biz for dease," patting the long rifle
barrels. "Boys, get ready" shouted the Genl. and went for his horse. In five
minutes we were on the tramp.

We kept up a lively gait all the afternoon on a road skirting the Mountains to our right. Near five the guides turned to the right where a narow
gap afforded a passage through the mountain. The gap extended far in the
mountains and led out of the same south eastward. The guides expected
that the rebels, or at least a part of them, had taken this road to escape the
yanke Cavallery. We followed this road, which was quite narrow for about
four miles when it became so dark that we could proceed no further. The
guides felt very satisfied and said we were far enough for the night. A picket
of twenty men was sent forward, one of the guides himself went along to
stay with them. The guns were advanced somewhat where there was more
room in the gap, turned round and loaded with grape and Cannister; the
canoniers bunked under the guns, while the rest of the men lay to both
sides at the foot of the Mountains. These preparation made, we proceeded
to munch some hardtak, which with raw bacon and an occasional swallow
of water had to satisfy the inner man.

The night passed quietly along as was expected. An occasional screch of
a fouraging owl would be heard now and then, that was all. But at day
break suddenly the report of a rifle and then a dozen more, roused repeated
Echoes among the mountains and brought us endways in a hurry. We heard
the Clatter of galloping horses, but it was not light enough [y]et to see
distinctly. We went forward toward the pickets. The guides said it had been
the advance of the rebel Cavallery. "Ef thar aint no yank at t'other end we
shan't see em again," one of the guides remarked. Half an hour later when
it was light enough to see clear, a troop of grays came riding towards us,
making signs with some kind of a rag held high with a sabre, for us not to
fire. We stood at a ready. When near enough the leader said in a loud voice:
"We come to surrender." The Genl. ordered them to dismount and deposit
their arms on the ground. They were put under guard and questioned by

the Genl. but he did not get much out of them. He asked them if there were any more of them on this road. They said No, the others had taken an other road. The guides thought that was a lie. They wanted us to get out of the gap that the others might escape. But we did not leave the gap as [y]et. The prisoners. 20. in number and the horses were sent back under guard to the entrance in the valley where they should await our return.

The Genl. concluded to examine the gap further. We had not avanced a mile when a number of riderless horses came dashing toward us. They all were sadled and bridled and stopped readily when they came up to us. There were some thirty of them. We did not know what to make of it exept that a fight had taken place somewhere and the horses made riderless, but the guides did not think so and held an earnest consultation together in a whisper of which we did not catch a word. Ere long more horses came but this time there were a lot of riders among them as leaders. We were not a little surprised to discover the riders to be from Companies of our mounted Infantry. The matter was somewhat explained but not to satisfaction. They said they had been in pursuit of the rebels since day before jesterday, but the rebs, being better acquainted with the roads, had got the slip of them once and before they found the right trak again they were over an hours ride ahead. About an hour ago they had met these horses running backward. "The rascals have taken to the mountains where we cannot touch them." Starkweather said. "Yaas" one of the guides replied, "de is in the mountuns Kurnel." (they allways called the General "Kurnel") "but I calkerlate we mout lay hands on de durned critters, Kurnel, You just git dem thar hosses out ob de way an we uns can go foh 'em." That was an easy job and soon done. The major who commanded our mounted men said he could hardley take care of the horses as he had orders to reach the Liberty pike in the shortest time possible, as it was thought Morgan himself might try to escape by that road. Starkweather told the Major to march right along he would take care of the horses. The Major, after consulting the Guides about the shortest road to reach that point rode on with his command. There were just a hundred horses. They were tied together by fours, A Captain and 30 men detailed to bring them back to where the prisoners and guard were and await our return. We then dumped Carbines, revolvers, bowie knifes an sabres in a wagon and went forward, the guides leading.

I do not know if the guides had informed Genl. Starkweather of their suspicion and plans, certain it is none of us knew anything about it. After advancing about a mile they took a Company and went with them to the right up the steep mountain side; we soon lost sight of them among the brush and bowlders. Returning they took another Comp. went half a mile forward, again turned to the right and up the mountain. Returning again they held a lengthy conversation with the Genl. and Col. Hobart and Goodrich after which the greatest part of the troop were deployed in a strong scirmish line right and left facing the mountain to the right. They were not to advance up the mountain side but to remain on the spot and capture or shoot any rebel who should undertake to escape. The remaining part, to which I belonged, went up the mountain under the direction of the guides. First we followed the road for perhaps a quarter of a mile and were warned to be as quiet about it as possible. Starkweather and the other mounted Officers had dismounted and were near the head of climbing line.

It was a ticklish job to clamber upward without noise. There was no sign of a path, or trail, nothing but rocks bowlders, brush and here and there a tree pryed its roots in the clefts and fissures of the rok. When up somewhat about 30 rods the guides halted and motioned us to do the same. They then crept behind a dense chestnut brush and one shouted: "You ones is to kum outer dar, an right smart to, an surrendah evry durned un of you." No reply, but a carbine was discharged, the ball whizzing over us. Instantly both men discharged their rifles through the brush in the opening of the cave and came back. The bullet had hit one of them slightley in the left upper arm. A hankerchif was tied around the arm to prevent to[o] much bleeding. Starkweather wanted him to go down to the surgeon, but says he: "No Kurnel, I'll be durn'd ef I do, I'll see them blasted varmints out of dat dere hole fust." They then told us all about the Cave in the Mountain and the Entrance behind the clump of Chestnut brosh. The rebs had sacrificed the horses to hide in the Cave and save themselves, expecting for certain not to be discovered; and they surely would not have been, had it not been for the guides.

Starkweather told us to kneel or lay down and watch for a sudden dash by the rebs out of the Cave. He next went up sideways to the entrance and said in a strong, loud voice: "Se here Johnnies in the cave there! I give you five minutes time by the watch to come out unarmed and surrender." "Go to hell! we will never surrender, we can stand it as long as you"—"Well," the Genl. replied, "if that is the last you have to say, all right. Do as you please; but in that case I must inform you that the bread you will eat is all cooked." And creeping down he ordered a soldier to hurry down to the battery and tell the Capt. there to send up half a dozen fuse shells. Three canoniers came with the shells, the Capt. of the batterie with them. The Genl. told them to throw them into the opening. The guides jumped forward asking permission to throw the shells as they knew in what direction they ought to be thrown. That was granted. The fuses were cut on quarter minutes time but before they were lighted, Genl. Starkweather called again: "Boys do you surrender?"—"No"! came back. "Go ahead then" the Genl. said, "I feel sorry for the Johnnies."

The guides grabbed the shells and several matches. Again a carbine was discharged from out of the rocks but nobody hurt. The guides came running down somewhat paler than usual. Unconciously I found myself counting to know when the quarter minute was gone. It did not take long. A full, deep rumbling noise and a gust of air was forced out of the cave which bent the brush clear down in front of the cave. Then a thick volume of smoke followed and curled slowly upward. Then it seemed we heard groans and curses. Not a word was spoken, no one felt like speaking. I watched the guides and noticed even them shake.—In no battle have I ever felt so mean or miserable as I did in these five minutes. As the smoke decreased the groans seemed to grow louder. Starkweather hollered again: "Do you surrender? be quik about it." Some on[e] replied: "Sir, I wish to say a few words to you."—"What is it?" The man came around the brush in full view and raising his right arm up high exclaimed: "In the name of allmighty God I protest against such barbaric treatment, It is against all usage of warfare."—"Stop Sir" Starkweather thundered; "You dare to talk about barbarism and usage of war? You who with all your crew ought to be hanged to the highest trees that ever grew under the sun? Have you ever cared for the usages of war? Ask those citizens here. But I cannot stop to argue with you. Return to your men; in five minutes I must have you[r] decision." The Officer, for such he was, bowed and went back.

"Stern necessity is not much of a virtue," is an old proverb. But in this case the rebels made a virtue out of necessity. The cave poured forth its motly crew. They came out one after another in a long string. They had left their Carbines and sabers in the cave as ordered, but good many had their ugly bowie knifes [y]et, but they were quickley taken away. A goodly number of tough looking customers were to be seen among them. Compaired with our men they looked every inch a bandit. Their atrocious deeds among the union citizens were plainly written on their features. It was no wonder. Morgan liked to recruit his command from desperadoes, outlaws, escaped convicts, etc. No respectble men wished to join his command. When the Officer reached the Genl. and handed him his sword he remarked: "Sir you had the best of the bargain this time, but I hope to live to revenge this outrage."—"Sir!" Starkweather replied, "I hope you will be smart enough to stop your unjust remarks, or you will furnish a handsome ornament to that tree over yonder." He stopped; but a forbidding scowl remained on his features. The prisoners were marched down to the road and formed in two ranks. There were 90 of them. The first Wis. was ordered to take them to the valley where the others were. In a loud voice the Genl. charged the men to shoot down any one who should try to escape.

All the troops out were now recalled exept a strong piket up the road. Then we went to investigate the cave. The brush in front of the entrance was cleared away. The guides had prepared some torches but we found enough tallow candles in the Cave to dispend with the torches. The entrance was about 3 foot wide and 7 foot high. It soon widened in a spacious chamber of oval form perhaps 40 x 60 in the largest part. It had an irregular vaulted ceiling from twelve to thirty foot high. Partly in the entrance which was perhaps 10 foot long lay a corpse. He was shot through the breast by the guides. The powder smoke had not all escaped [y]et; the entrance was to[o] low for speedy Egress. But in the cave when it was lighted, we met a dismal sight. Five more mangled corpses and four wounded lay scattered around. The wounded were taken out and the surgeon busied himself with them, but three of them were bejond his help. They had closed their accounts before we left there; the fourth was only slightly wounded. The shells had done their terrible work.

But the greater surprise was the Commissary department of the Cave. Around against the rocks was piled up a great number of bags of cornmeal and corn, bacon, hams shoulders, potatoes, even a lot of home made cotton jean, tobacco, smoking and chewing, several large and small barrels of whiskey and other trinkets. Arrangements were made at once to convay as much of the stuff to the Wagons as we could load. A line was formed from the cave to the road and the Stuff passed from hand to hand. We had two empty wagons and two half loaded ration wagons. First the meat department was tackled. It was a delight to see the hams and shoulders fly from hand to hand. Meanwhile Starkweather had a small cask of Whiskey tapped and soon everybody had his smack. Our wagons were packed as close as possible and still the Cornmeal was not half loaded and the corn not even touched [y]et. Perhaps a hundred or more bushels of sweet potatoes were allso left. The General asked the guides if they had means to bring that to their homes. They thought they would find means for that purpose. They allso said they had been aware of the stuf being there but could not get at it as the rebels had kept a strong guard there. The Genl. kindly allowed the boys an other smile and then we started on the backward trip.

It was two P.M. when we arrived at the place of rendezvous. Two wagons were immediately unloaded and with a strong detail of men sent back to load corn for the captured horses. Four of the horses were given to the guides to transport stuff home with. The Genl. specially warned them to divide the things among the most needy class. Among the soldiers articles were distributed in the following manner. One ham to every 6 men. One bushel potatoes to every 10 men. There was considerable more chewing than smoking tobacco. The chewers each got 3 large navy plugs, while the smokers each got a pound smoking tobacco. Every 6. men got a Canteen of Whiskey or a half pint per head. All other stuff was given in care of the guides for distribution among the poor in the valley. The prisoners received for five days cornmeal and bacon. We camped here for the night and had a high time in general in which everyone, exept the prisoners took active part. . . .

The following day about noon the 24th Ill. and 79th Pa. joined us again with a number of vagabonds in tow. The two Regts. of Wagners brigade who were not in [y]et arrived shortley before su[n]set. They allso had a crowd of the same stamp. About a dozen fugitive families, mostley women and children and old men, were with them. As they had nothing to live on at home they were going to Murfreesboro to be supported by the Government. Three fellows among Genl. Wagners crowd created considerable attention. Their hands were tied behind their backs and all three tied together by the arms. The boys told us the following story regarding them. Day before jesterday a girl of eighteen had appeared in their camp[.] She inqu[i]red for the Comander. Brought to Genl. [Wagner] She told the following: Her name was Annie Weaver, lived about three miles from camp. That on the 9th of March previous a certain W. A. Selkirk with two other men entered her fathers house and ordered him to immediatly come along with them and join the rebel army. Her father replied that he was past 60 years old and not able to do field service and besides that he was exempted by law. Whereupon they knocked him down and beat his brains out. Her mother and younger brother were also killed and mutilated; she escaped by jumping through the window and hiding in the woods. The murderers then took everything of value, set fire to the house and outbuildings and destroyed everything. She however had kept track of the murderers and they were now hidden within a mile and a half from Camp. She begged the Genl. to capture the murderers. The Genl. at once ordered a Capt. and thirty men to go along with the girl. But before she went she asked for a loaded revolver which was given her. But the Genl. requested them to cap-ture them alive if possible so that they might be hung. They found the culprits in the act of changing camp, that is, their hiding place. A half an hour later and they would have been in security. The fellows had made a desperate fight and were not secured untill their ammunition had given out. They might have killed them, but as stated, they wanted them alive.

Just before dark Lieut. Bill Wall who had left us in the morning [with] 10 men and a Citizen as guide came in with five jayhawkers; as ugly, brutal looking Custumers as it ever has been my look to see. Every one was se-curely bound and were not released during the night. Thre[e] citizens, all-ready old men, accompanied them as witnesses. I never have learned exactly for what crimes they were taken.

An other little surprise was in store for the fourth Indiana battery boys. That battery was attached to our brigade. The morning when we were west of McMinnville and the mounted Infty made their attack on Morgan, the battery Orderlies found one of their men missing. As they had been in no fight he must have gone of[f] voluntarily. As he did not return during the day he was considered a deserter. They considered him a bounty jumper. He had served in an Infantry Regt. before and had told conflicting stories of his former service. Some of the battery men standing near the fence looking at the prisoners thought the[y] saw a fellow among them strikingly resemble the deserter David Blazer. "I say Will! isn't there Blazers double"? asked one battery boy of an other. Blazer must have heard the remark be-cause he tried to hide among the other prisoners. But the boys went over the fence and soon were up to him. He wore a dirty rebel gray Cavallery suit which made the boys at first doubtfull in their suspicion but when brought to the fence they all recognized him. "Poor David," Starkweather said to him. "Your bread is nearly cooked." He had him securely bound and put under seperate guard.

The command beeing together now we started next morning on the homeward trip. With prisoners, horses and Citizens the column was over two miles in lenght. There were nearly 300 horses and mules, (Some mules had been given to citizens to cultivate their fields) some fifty bushwhakers, and nearly a hundred refugees but, a strange fact, no niggers. The lojal East Tennessee people did not fancy human cattle. They were bound to earn their living themselves. The ambulances were well filled too. [The] mounted Infty. in their several fights with Morgan had ten killed and fifty wounded. Our brigade had no casualties and Wagners had one wounded, he being hit by a shot from the murderer Selkirk. We marched about 20. miles that day to the banks of Snake Creek a tributary of Stone river. Annie Weaver was at Genl. Wagners headquarter. She was bound, as she said, to tie the hemp collar about the neck of her families murderers. At noon the following day April 25th we reached camp again. Major Genl. Rousseau with his staff and a music band met us some distance from Camp and proffered the escort of honor as an acknowledgement of our successfull expedition. The trip had taken 15 days. . . .

The murderer Wm. A. Selkirk and his two companions, whose names I do not remember were tried before court martial and found guilty of murder.[8] They were sentenced to be hung. Genl. Rosecrans promptly approoved the sentence. The gallows was erected only about 15 rods from our camp in the field. On the fifth of June the leader Selkirks time was up. At 2. P.M. the Provost Marshall and guard, the criminal between them marched through an immense crowd of soldiers who had gathered to witness the imposing circus. The Culprit, a brutish looking fellow, did not seem to be much affected. He mounted the ladder with firm steps and with a forbidding scowl looked over the immense mass of heads. Miss Weaver mounted the platform after the Provost Marchal. The marchal asked the prisoner if he wished to say anything. but he merely made a sign of refusal. The death sentence was then read and Miss Weaver stepped forward, adjusted the black cap, then put the noose carefully around the neck and stepped back.[9] The marchal cut the cord and the culprit dropped four foot. I dont know whether his neck was broken or not but his limbs twisted quite a while. His two partners in crime were hung together a few days later. One of them was a sort of Mulatto, quite a fine looking fellow. The mulatto went up the latter with firm step, but the other had to be helped; he could hardly stand on the platform alone. The Mulatto spoke for about five minutes. He admitted that his death was just, that he never had done any wrong until the rebels had promised him large sums of money and falling in the Society of Selkirk and others. The other fellow did not say a word. Both dropped the same moment. The mulatto apparently died easy, he did not move after the trap had fallen, but the other strugled long. There were not so many spectators as the first time. Seen once is usually enough for most men. I for my part have no desire to see the performance again.

The five fellows Lieut. Wall had caught were also hung but not on those gallows. This wholesale hanging made it more safe for the union people in East Tennessee, at lea[s]t in that part.

The deserter, David Blazer, was tried by court martial and found guilty of desertion to the Enemy.[10] He was sentenced to be shot June 20th between ten and twelve A.M. The brigade was formed in an open square. . . .

The ranks were opened to admit the passage between them of the wagon containing the Provost marchal, the condemned and execution guard. The culprit sat on his Coffin. The wagon passed between the opened ranks of the square and emerging out of the square passed to the midle and about fifty yards to the front of the open side where the grave was allready dug. Here all alighted. The coffin was placed aside the grave, the delinquent sat down on it facing the execution troop who had formed six steps from and in front of the Coffin. The delinquents eyes were bandaged. The execution troop consists of 12 men. 6 rifles are loaded with ball cartridge and 6 with blank cartridges. The Provost marchal does the loading and distributes the rifles among the soldiers before they start from prison. No command is given. The Marchal lifts his sword, and the soldiers take aim, he drops the sword, that means "fire" and the thing is done. It was an impressive Ceremony and has no doubt saved many from a like fate.—The captured bushwhakers were sent to the military prison at Nashville where they were kept at hard labor during the war. The other prisoners were sent north as regular prisoners of war.

~

CHAPTER NINE

The Tullahoma Campaign

~ Shortly after we were encamped at Murfreesboro a citizen came in camp pedling army songs, dime novels, envellops, paper, postage stamps, pens and ink etc. He had a pass or permit from Genl. Rosecrans. He was a splendid singer, a fluent talker and story teller and soon became a favorite with the men. He went from camp to camp wherever he pleased, in the Forts and hospitals and was welcome everywhere. Shortly after our return from the East Tenn. Expedition I came on picket on the Manchester pike. He came to us where the Reserve was stationed and offered his stuff for sale. He did not sell much and I remarked to him that the picketline was a poor place to do business. He admitted that he had come out for exercise more than for business. The next time I came on picked [picket] at a different place and again he came there with his stuff. I noticed that before he went away he had a long chat with a soldier who was some distance away from the rest. Finally he handed the soldier some paper and Envellopes and left. I took that soldier alone and inquired what their conversation had been. He told me readily. The pedler had inquired where and how far it was to the next reserve, how strong it was etc. "How much did you pay for the stuff he handed you" I asked. "Nothing he gave that to me." That increased my suspicion about the fellow being a spy. When relieved I went to Genl Rousseaus Quarters and expleained the matter as also my reasons for my suspicions. "You are the second who calls my attention to that fellow" the Genl. replied, "I will attend to the matter at once. Thank you." A few days later the fellow was arrested in Genl. Sheridans Division. Correct drawings of our fortifications, the lay of our camps and picket lines and outposts, with number of troops, the number and size of the batteries in the forts and in the army etc. were found on his person; and to settle all, a pass from Gel. Bragg to go in and out of the rebel picket line at any time. The following day he was hoisted in Sheridans Division. . . . [1]

On the 9th of May we were paid for three Months, that is for Feb. March and April 1863. At the same time all such who had been promoted to commissioned Officer since we left the recruiting camp were mustered into the United States service as such by a regular mustering Officer of the United States. I was the first Officer in the Regiment so promoted. In this manipulation either the Government, or the Paymaster swindled me out of $375.00. . . .

We were paid in bran new Greenbacks fresh from the press. Th[e]y looked very fine and imposing but were not worth much after all. The Officers had to buy their own rations and clothing. We were compelled to have two suits; one for dayly service and one "Undress Uniform" for dress parades, guard mounting Inspections and Reviews. For the latter I had to pay $95.00 wereas in gold I might have had it for $40.00. The difference went into the pockets of the bondholders, contractors, speculators etc. A sword I got per chance very cheap. A Capt. in the fourth Missoury was promoted to Major and thought the occasion important enough to indulge in the luxury of a new and stilish weapon. I procured the old one for $4.00. I[t] was not much to boast of but good enough for a beginning. . . .

Early one morning before reveille we were disturbed in our slumber by a soldier coming in the tent and sit down on a crakerbox. "Capt," he began "I have got the blues, what shall I do"? We looked at him somewhat surprised and saw he had a flushed and scared countenance. We knew the men not to be one who wanted a holyday, or to play off. It was Henry [Vandebogart], a good hearted, jolly fellow who on many a tiresome march had with his harmless, amusing tricks and funy stories cheered the men and was a favorite with all of them. He was now with a guard detail at brigade headquarters. "When did you come off from post?" Turner asked. "Just now." he replicd. (4 A.M.) "the last two hours seemed endless to me. O, I am so tired and so, so afraid." and the poor fellow allmost cried. "Don't be discouraged Henry" Turner said. "courage and a stiff upper lip is half the victory. I will give you an order and you go immediately to Sage, the brigade Suttler. He will give you something which probably will set everything right. If by 6. O.clock you dont feel better dont fail to report to the Doctor. Meanwhile I felt Vans pulse which was greatly ex[c]ited; his eyes also had an unnaturally firy glance. He left. "Turner" I said "Van is laboring with a high fever, his pulse went at a double quick." "I saw it in his eyes" he replied, "but I hope Sage will break it." Now Sage was a druggist by profession and had saved many a man from the hospital, or perhaps the grave. But this was to[o] much for his skill, or perhaps had not the medicine he needed.

[Vandebogart] was sent to the hospital at 7. A.M. At four P.M. I went to see him. He held out his hand to me and—"Well, Lieut, I am going to leave you," he began with a cheerfull voice and a smile on his face. "Will you please write a few lines to my father when I am gone"? Such are very trying situations. Of cours, I promised that, but at the same time tried to direct his thoughts into an other channel but, "What is the use"? he interrupted me. "It is as well now as any other time." He then directed me what to write and to take the two photographs out of his knapsack and enclosed them in the letter. He allso handed me a ten dollar bill for which he had no more use he said and his old father was sadly in need of them. One of the photos represented his father and mother (the mother being dead.) the other himself which he had taken in Murfreesboro. I promised to be back at evening and went to camp. I informed Turner of Vans situation. He went over but soon returned. He had inquired of the Dr. about Vans case and had been informed that it was a case of malignant typhoid fever with little chance of recovery. After tattoo I again went to see him and found him highly delirious. He did not recognize me and remained so all night. Even in that state he could not quit craking jokes, or trying to sing funny songs. After daylight reason returned and as soon as he recognized me said, "O. Lieut. how good of you to come. I am much better now. I will be with the Comp. soon." I made him a glass limonade which he drained to the bottom. I was glad to find him so full of courage although there was something undescribable in his face and look. He went on talking for half an hour when something seemed to attract his attention. I noticed that his eyes assumed a leaden hue. Just then reveillee sounded. "Ha, ha"! he said, "that means rollcall but I can't be there this time. The commanding Genl. beats the call for me." After a minute he began as if in a hurry: "Otto, tell the boys to remember me kindly, and my brother"—Here he stopped short and never spoke again. He had responded to the last roll call. . . .

One night we were suddenly alarmed by several shots being fired in quick sucession near the guard tent of our Regt. A fellow dressed in butternut garb, had been caught by our pickets while trying to crawl inside our line between the pickets. He said he wanted to go in town after a Doctor. But if that was his intention he might have kept the open road and not crawl round in the woods. The Officer sent him under guard to camp where he was placed in the guard house to be sent to headquarters next morning. The fellows concience must not have been at ease for shortley after he had been put in the tent he stealthily crawled out below the canvas intending to escape to the woods. But Miles Hoskins, the sentinel espied him and ordered a ha[lt]. The fellow jumped up and in quick succession fired two revolver shots at Hoskins, one ball passing through the muscle of the right arm. But that did not stop Hoskins from giving him a dose out of his Enfield and bringing him down too. He died an hour afterward, but before he quit he told us that he was one of Braggs spies and had been in our camp before.

Inspection of arms and accoutrements, of Camp and garrison Equipments, as allso Brigade and Corps reviews were now the order of the day. If any article was found damaged, or unserviceable it was condemned and replaced with new ones. This was a sure sign of the approaching campain against Bragg.

While our Division Review was in progress a funny diversion happened which, as good look would have it, afforded us great merriment and satisfaction. The place where the revue was held was a large field about two miles outside of our picket line on the west and east of the Manchester pike. Heavy woods enclosed the field on all sides. We started Early in order to get through before the greatest heat began. By eleven A.M. everything was done. Two brigades had allready drawn of[f] on the pike for the homeward march. The three batteries were to follow next and our brigade was to bring up the rear. Two batteries were in the woods allready when suddenly two niggers mounted on bare mules came dashing on and shouted: "De rebs am comming! de rebs am coming"! Genl. Baird who commanded the Division now had gone back at the head of the other brigades so Starkweather was in command. "Where are they"? he inquired. "Bouf haf mile off in dem woods dah Massa." "What, Infantry or Cavallery?"—"Bof massa, and right smart of em too, an cannon too, allow six on em."

The Genl sent at once his aid de camp to inform Baird of the game the rebs intended to play and then took measurs to receive and entertain our visitors in proper style. Two regiments were to take position in the edge of the woods two to the wright of the pike the other two to the left. The battery allso had to hide in the woods. No shot was to b[e] fired until the bugle sounded. We all laid down. That all was done in short order. Not a men was to be seen on the pike. We had not to wait long. A squad of 12 Cavallery men appeared at the opposite side of the field. They advanced cautiously but seeing nothing Entered the woods within our line. They were quickly taken and disarmed without firing a shot. They were so taken by surprise that they never thought of firing in order to warn their comrades untill it was to[o] late.

Shortly after the rebel Infantry appeared. But they were more cautious. As soon as they cleared the woods they filed to right and left of the pike and formed in line. It was a brigade about the size of ours. Next a battery appeared and unlimbered in the field. Another brigade of Infantery appeared and took position behind the first. The head of a column of Cavallery could be seen on the pike but we could not judge of its strenght. They threw out scirmishers about ten rods in advance and the line followed at about the same distance, the second line in close support of the first. As soon as the lines advanced their battery opened fire and threw shells in the woods behind us. The scirmishers were not more than five rods away when Starkweathers little bugle talked. Hardley had its first notes died away when infantry and Artillery fired simoultaneously. The cannon had been stuffed with cannister. That was terrible for the Johnnies. The skirmishers were all down and their first line had suffered terrible. They staggered and suddenly turned back. But their second line had not lost courage [y]et. They now came forward in a run, yelling like mad men and most of the first line turning back with them. But we had loded again and just now an other brigade of our division came running up and formed close behind us in line.

Again the contents of rifles and cannon went on their death errand and with more deadly effect than the first time. It was downright slaughter. Hardly had the deafening roar died away when the bugle sounded the charge and with a thundering "hurrah" we went for them. But they did not wait. It became a race for life across that field. They did not remember it seems that their rifles were all loaded while ours were empty; by simply turning round and fire they would have done great damage to us. But they were only thinking and striving to reach the woods, their only hope of safety. A good many of them got out of wind before they got there, threw away their rifles and surrendered. Their Battery tried to get off but left two guns and caissons in our hands. They did not form again in the woods as we expected, nor even sent out a skirmish line to protect their rear, but kept up their race for home. Our battery sent a dozen Shells after them as a parting salute. Genl. Baird came up now with the other brigade and batteries, but their was no use for them now. Genl. Baird sent one of the prisoners after them with the notice that they could sent a detail to bury their dead under flagg of truce. . . .

The scene on the field was absolutily sickening. Some thre[e] hundred wounded were picked up and taken along. I never have learned the number of dead but it must at least have been a hundred. 120. prisoners were taken. So that little picknick cost the Johnnies over 500. men. Our brigade had neither killed nor wounded, but the brigade which came first to our support had one killed and nine wounded by the shells the rebs had thrown into the woods. . . . This little engagement is one of the many not mentioned in history. . . . [2]

On the 22d of June orders were received that all men not able for field service should be sent to convalescent camp or hospital. Our Comp. had three of that stamp. Levant [Vandebogart],[3] Anton H. Van Stratum and Nelson B. Draper[.] The latter was an inco[n]siderate Glutton who in a single meal had put himself outside of a canteenful molasses and a spiderfull of crakers fried in bacon grease. That got up such a racket in his bowels that the Surgeons despaired of his life.

Our Div. Commander Genl. Rousseau was relieved from comma[n]d at his own request and Genl. Absolon [Absalom] Baird filled his place. He was an entire stranger to us and seemingly a quiet, unobtrusive man, but he proved to be an exellent soldier. . . .

June 26th 1863. Genl. Braxton Bragg had his main line established along on the north side of Duck river. Tullahoma was strongly fortified and the whole line well protected by breastworks. Shelbiville, severall mils in advance of his main line, was held by several brigades of Infantery and a brigade of cavallery and allso a battery. The whole rebel line extended perhaps 8 miles from east to west. His army, it was said[,] numbered 60,000 men. Ours contained about the same number.[4] So the deceision of a battle did not depend on the number of men. But Bragg had one advantage which was worth a full army corps of soldiers, his men were all protected by good breastworks. But Rosie did not intend to have his men killed off before the works but resorted to strategie to compel Bragg to quit his works and accept battle on equal terms or skedadle. Our right wing, all of the old 20th Corps. Genl. McCook commdg. and a Division of Cavallery was to advance on the Salem and Shelbiville pikes, take Shelbiville and take care of the rebel left in general. The centre, comprising the 14th Corps. Major General Geo. H. Thomas commdg. was to advance on the Manchester pike to the left of McCooks Corps which would bring the right of the 14th Corps nearly opposite Tullahoma and the right of Braggs army. The left wing, 21st Corps Major Genl. Crittenden commdg. was to march east towards McMinnville then turn south and work around Braggs right wing

THE TULLAHOMA CAMPAIGN

and into his rear and cut of[f] Braggs line of communication with Chattanooga and destroy the Chattanooga Railroad. The latter place is a 100 miles
southeast of Tullahoma and was Braggs main supply depot. Genl. Crittenden, who had the longest road was to start on the 24th McCook the
25th and the 14th Corps, which had the most direct road, on the 26th. We
felt very sorry indeed to part with our habitations, which we had come to
consider our second home; but such is soldiers lot. The weather had been
splendid for the last month and struck us as very singular that just to day at
about 10. A.M. it began to rain in good style, but as we were provided with
rubber Ponchos now we did not care much. About noon we heard far to
our right the booming of cannon and knew that Genl. McCook had found
obstacles in his way.

As mentioned before, Shelbiville was an advanced post of Braggs main
line. It was well fortified, but it seems Bragg had neglected to man it with a
force strong enough to withstand a determined asault, or he did not care
much for the place. The garrison consisted of about 2500. infantery, a small
troop of Cavallery and 2 battery of six guns each. Behind their works, they
were able to resist treble their number. Genl. McCook sent one brigade of
Infantry, the name of the Col. I do not remember, and two brigades of
Cavallery one commanded by Col. Mitchell, the other by Col. Minty both
exellent Officers. The cavallery of course had to fight afoot. Mintys brigade
was used to that end as it consisted mainly of mounted Infantry. The
works were carried in the first charge, 600 prisoner, a battery, a lot of small
arms and a considerable quantity of Commissary stores were captured.[5]

This was the noise which we heard 5 miles away. Of course we did not
know at the time what it meant, or what the result would be. We received
orders to stake arms along side the pike and make Coffee but be ready to
move at a moments notice. It was about 2. P.M. now. The rain had ceased
and old sol wore his kindest and hottest smiles. We lost no time in making
Coffee, but an hour passed and no order to advance came. Our brigade
Suttler Mr. Sage had followed us. In a short time his big tent was up and
everybody knew what that meant. He had five or six barrels of beer on hand
which he was anxious to dispose of before they would sour on his hands. He
send word that he would sell the stuff at reduced prices to get rid of it. As an
enlisted man was not allowed to buy any distilled or fermented liquors
without an Order from the respective Comp. Commanders the latter gave
such an order to all who called for one. Very soon there was a big crowd
arond Sages tent, every on[e] holding in one hand a slip of paper, in the
other a tin Cup or Canteen awaiting their turn to be served.

Now it happened that our brigade commander Genl. Starkweather was not with us that day and Col. Hambright of the 79th Pa. commanded the brigade. He was a West Point graduate, or regular Officer and a good soldier, but like most of his class, had a very slight opinion of Volunteer Officers and men. He claimed to be a strict temperance man and wanted the men to be the same allthough the Officers of his Regt. knew that none appreciated a hearty stimulant better than himself. Perhaps he was afraid the man might get drunk on a pint of beer and a tussle with the rebs to be expected at any moment, enough, he forbid Mr. Sage to sell any more beer to the soldiers even if they had permission to buy from the Comp. commanders. As the crowd about the sutlers tent did not disperse readily, Hambright ordered the brigade guard to charge bajonet on the crowd. That of course dispersed the crowd but it made the suttler mad. He tried to argue with the Colonel that he had a right under the regulations and his commission and license from the government. But Hambright would not listen to any argument and simply told him to "shut up." He did "shut up" but he acted nevertheless. He set his clerks to work to pack up everything he had. He had three barrels of beer and two of cider left. These he gave to the line Officers of the brigade to do with them as they pleased. Next he stradled a mule and went forward on the pike. Nobody had an Idea of his intention. While the Officers were in consultation what to do with the beer, as they had no right to sell or give away the stuff, Col. Hambright who had watched the proceedings, came up and ordered the Officers to set the beer adrift and destroy the barrels. This was roundly refused. Then he threatened to put us all under arrest. This was accepted and we all tendered our swords, knowing he could do nothing with a brigade without Officers. He did not accept our swords but ordered the guard to destroy the barrels.

Matters took a serious turn now but all at a sudden a troop of horsemen came dashing up the pike. Ahead of them on his mule was Sage; following were Genls. Rosecrans and staff, Pop Thomas and staf and a lot of Orderlies. Col. Hambright turned to meet them and make his report. But Rosie cut him short by asking: "Colonel Hambright! Has Mr. Sage violated any of the rules laid down in the regulations for the guidance of Suttlers and Officers alike"? "No, General, but he refused to obey my orders."—"Is that so Mr. Sage"? Rosey inquired. "No General," Sage replied, "I stopped selling beer when the Colonel ordered it, but I undertook to convince him that I had a right to sell beer according to government commission and license; The remaining beer I have made a present of to the Officers of the brigade."—"Colonel Hambright, no doubt you thought to do right, but you

THE TULLAHOMA CAMPAIGN

were wrong. Do you really suppose that these men after a 20. miles walk will get drunk and unman[a]geable by taking a mug of beer or cider? Sir! that looks much like an insult to your men for which you ought apologize. And now," turning to the Officers, "Comrades, will you sell us a mug of your beer? I must admit I feel as dry as a tinderbox."—"No, General" Capt. Whittacre replied, "We have not had time yet to apply for a Suttlers comission and license, but we surrender all our rights on that beer to Mr. Sage; he may do as he pleases." Sage understood the hint and in a moment, with the assistance of his clerks, he was handing out the glasses to them. When Rosey turned back again he asked the men who had crowded round: "Boys! how is it, Is your powder dry? You will need it soon."—"Yes! you just try us" they jelled. "Then tend to your beer as fast as you can; you wont be here long" and with that they dashed down the pike again. I[t] took several minutes before the hurrahing and noise ceased and in an quarter of an hour beer and cider belonged to the things that have been. Mr. Sage came and bade us good bye and good speed. We felt verry sorry to loose him, because he was a perfect gentlemen and honest in all his dealings. We never saw him again.

Genl. Rosecrans warning had not been idle talk. Near five P.M. we went on again. After marching about three miles our advance met the rebel pickets and a few shots were exchanged. Strong skirmish lines were thrown out, but they were instructed not to advance, nor indulge in any firing if not attacked, as no engagement was wished for the night. Two brigades of the Div. then went up onto a steep high ridge which extended at right angles with, and to the left of the pike. The other brigade went to the right of the pike on more level ground. On the ridge we formed in line of battle. From our elevated position we were enabled to take a good survey of the ground, right left and front. We were in front of the so called Hoovers Gap. A mile and a half in front of us a considerable high ridge extended to the right and left of the [pike] for many miles. There was but one Porte or gap through which the pike passed. The rebs had build breastworks at the foot all along the ridge and their batteries were posted on the top. The ridge was not in the regular position of their line. Like Shelbiville it served as an outpost, but it was amply manned, and able to repulse strong attacks from the front. But we were bound to have ridge and Gap in order to get our artillery and train through.

We were not allowed to built fires as they might draw the rebel fire. Those who wished to make Coffee had to go down hill to the rear. A little before dark the rebs let us know that they knew where we were, because a half dozen shells and shot made their way through the trees above us, but they had taken the range to[o] long and the missiles exploded far in our rear. That night we slept on our arms, that is, we laid down in ranks without unbuckling anything, with the rifles alongside of us. I dont know what posessed the rebs that night but three times they sent us a shower of shells which busted so near that it became very unhealthy. I suppose they challenged our batteries to find out where they were situated; but our batteries did not reply.

It seemed Pop Thomas believed in the saying: "The early bird catches the worm" because he began so early. At least an hour before daylight we were moving down the hill to the right of the pike nearly a mile. I do not know what troops were to the left of the pike. We were then formed in line and advanced half a mile through meadows and were halted untill it began to dawn. It seemed strange that we had met no rebel pickets and scirmishers. As soon as we were in line two more brigades formed on our right. This was all done without a loud command, on the sly I may say. We were ordered to fix bajonet and squat down. A faint streak of light in the east told of the coming new day. Would there any be missing at night?

It was very quiet in the lines; a gravelike stillness. It seemed one did not dare to breathe. One could hear his heart beat if not his neighbors. Orders passed quietly along the lines that no shot was to be fired until we came to the Enemys works, not a word or sound must be heard. Thus passed a long quarter of an hour. It did not get much lighter. A fog or mist arose from the moist soil which completely hid everything from view. All at once the rebel batteries far to our left opened and it extended fast enough to the right. But this time our batteries were wide awake too. Five of them opened at once and the reports of the cannon and the explosion of shels made an infernal music. It was at the same time the signal for us to advance. The order was quietly given and away we went. About twenty rods further we suddenly came to the banks of a considerable creek, but without hesitation the men plunged in holding high the cartridge boxes in order to keep the powder dry. . . .

So forward we went. From the meadow we came in a wheatfield; the wheat stood in shocks. The artillery duel was still going on, but as the batteries were firing at each other and as the rebel batteries stood so high and they could not see us on account of the fogg the shells all passed high over and behind us. We reached the end of the field but still could not detect works or ridge. Presently we came to a depression in the ground and saw dimly what seemed to be merely a dark line. We heard the rebel Officers speak and give orders. We heard one say plainly: "if only that damned fog would lift." Now, loud and clear Starkweathers bugle sounded the charge. "Hurrah" and on we went. A volley from the works but luky for us we were not out of the depression [y]et and most of the bullets went over us. I saw some drop but only a few as I could not see far along the line. Another "hurrah" and we were at the breastworks. The rifles were discharged over the logs in the face of the Johnnies and the next moment we stood inside the works. Some of the rebs tried to use their bajonet, but the most of them turned and run up hill; others threw down their rifles and raised their arms in token of surrender. We speedily followed up hill in pursuit but it was hard work, the ridge was so steep. We found many rebs sitting down willing to surender.

The Artillery fire had ceased. When we reached the top of the hill we found no fog there. The sun, just risen, dispersed allso the fog below on the plain. The battery which had been just opposite us had fared hard. Four pieces were disabled. Twelve of the batterymen had been killed or wounded. Looking to the left towards the gap I saw signs which assured us that our comrades there had been equally successfull. Far away towards the front I saw a long string of our Cavallery gallopping along gathering in prisoners and other trophies. Finally the Call to assemble was heard and the some-what scattered men went to their respective Regts. and Comps. While the men were forming I saw Dorset Smith coming slowly up the hill. I thought he was perhaps hurt but found that he had laid down in front of the works and kept low until the game was ended. Our casualties were but small. The brigade had 15 killed, the number of wounded I do not remember. Our Regt. had seven wounded, none killed.[6]

An hour was spent for breakfast and then we went forward again. Nothing was to be seen of the rebels. We marched four miles and halted at a place called "Beach Grove" where we camped over night. It is a lovely country here and the more the pity that cruel war, partly out of necessity, partly wontonly crushed everything under foot. That night the boys conversed anxiously about the coming day as it was expected that tomorrow we should have to meet Bragg behind his works. A good many letters were written, expecting to be the last. Some very apprehensive fellows instructed other Comrades, or Officers what should be done with this, or that, after their dead. Jim Walker even took a little pocket Testament, (in which he never read.) a pocketbook with a few shillings, a ring and photograph, made a package of it and handing it to me requested me to forward the same to his wife in town Grand Chute. I laughed at him, asking if he thought I was bullet proof. He scratched his head a while and finally said. "Well, I should like some one would take care of it and tend to that little matter for I am sure the next fight will be my last." To put him at ease I took the package and assured him it should be attended to even if I should drop myself. At the writing of this Jim is living on a farm in Kansas drawing $14.00 pension per month. Although he was in many battles and smaller engagements he never received a scratch.

At the first glimpse of daylight next morning we formed in line of battle and "by the right of Companies" went forward, skirmishers at the front, expecting every moment the advisory: "Pop, Pop, whiz!" of the skirmishers and facing the solid front of the Enemy. Judge therefore of our surprise, when suddenly the Order: "Countermarch by file left." came from Starkweathers bashfull lips. We marched back to "Beach Grove," staked arms and were advised to make ourselfes comfortable. Soonn the boys were sitting or laying in groups, discussing the reason and meaning of the abortive movement. Right here I will remark that the boys considered it as their inherent right to discuss and pass judgement upon all orders and movements of their superior Officers. Naturally there was a great deal of "Buncombe" in such Councils of war, but at the same time I must admit that sometimes one fellow or an other would hit the nail right square on the head. So here. Corporal Geo. Rawson of my Comp. who had been a silent listener during all the arguments pro and con, suddenly jumped up and holding a greenback high aloft delivered himself in this wise: "Se here boys! that's the last greenback I have left from last payday; the balance I sent to father. Now, I have observed there are about as many opinions among you, as heads. Now to end this controverse I make you an offer. Here is a new five dollar Greenback. I will bet against any one, or any club of you, that our brigade, or our army will not fire a shot at Bragg or his army this side, or north of the Tennessee river, but the Cavallery allways excluded. Capt. Turner to be stakeholder."—"Hold on," Turner interrupted. "I can not be stakeholder as I will take up your bet myself, but I propose Lieut. Otto to be stakeholder." Rawson and Turner handed the greenbacks to me. The result will be seen later.

Shortly before 11. A.M. we were told to make dinner and at twelve we started again, but not in line of battle. We went straight to the Manchester pike and then forward. Whil marching during the afternoon we learned that our worthy friend Braxton Bragg was in full retreat toward Chattanooga. . . .

The following day brought us to Manchester after a 15 miles tramp. The name of the town is promising but in fact it is but a miserable looking, tumble down village. . . . Just south of the village we went in camp.

THE TULLAHOMA CAMPAIGN

The following day it was near noon before we started again, marched near ten miles and camped in a big grass field. . . . Just after dark, and dark it became like darkness itself, the thick misty vail broke, discharging in true southern style a torrent of water, nor did it slack up much until near morning. We were in a bad plight, as just before the affair at Hoovers gap we had put our dog tents on the Quartermasters wagons, to be not incumbered with them. But even if we had them with us they would have done us no good. The field was a flat, dead level with no drainage and before half an hour was gone we stood ankle deep in the water. There was no higher ground round where we could move to and so we had literally to stand it out; no thought of laying or sitting down. That was a long night and with delight we hailed the order a[t] daybreak next morning to fall in. Of course none had been able to make breakfast but for all that we were glad to get out of there.

Today our Div. was to be in advance again. We marched perhaps 6 or 7. miles and suddenly stood on the banks of Elk river with no bridge, or ferry, or ford to cross it. Orders given to make breakfast.

This was the 2d of July 1863. I never can forget that date. It came as near as I ever was to cut short my carrier [career] on this globe. Our Div. was to cross here, how? we could not imagine at present. The river, owing to the heavy rain last night was fearfully swollen with a current so wild and turbulent that even the most expert swimmers would not venture to cross it. Some where a heavy, stout rope was secured, perhaps taken along for such occasions. The river was at least 200. yards wide across; the banks from 10. to 30. foot. A coup[l]e men on horseback swam the horses across with one end of the rope bound the same securely around a tree. The same was done on this side. But owing to the ropes own weight it could not be drawn taut, or even nearly straight. Although it was fastened to the trees so high that it took a good jump to reach it, in the middle of the river it was a play of the current, bobbing down and up stream like a thread of a sewing needle. But it constituted the only means of crossing and business began immediately.

I sat down on an old log to watch proceedings on the new hanging and floating machine. Rifle, cartridgebox belt and haversak had to be strapped securely across the shoulders behind the neck to keep dry. The men would go in squads from ten to fifteen, jump upward to get hold of the rope and tally off towards the right hand by hand. Hanging on the sagging rope their feet soon tuched bottom. But the depth of the water soon increased to shoulderhight and as the current increased towards the middle of the river the shorter ones would first loose their hold on the bottom and suddenly their bodies would bub up horizontally, like a stick of wood to be tossed up and down and hither and thiter by the current. Tallying off with their hands they worked slowly across. None succeeded to keep their feet on the bottom. I noticed that by keeping so close together the current acted on them with greater force as it would do on a single man. That put the perverse Idea into my head to try the experiment alone. Acting on the first impulse I jumped for the rope when the preceeding squad had passed the midle of the river. I went on splendidly at first; the current near the bank being more slow and regular. I kept the feet on the slippery rock until I had passed about the third part of the river. The water reached now up to my armpits. By this time the preceeding squad had reached their destination. No sooner had they jumped ashore, releasing thereby the rope when my trouble began and I at once realized the foolishnes of my notion.

The slakend rope all at a sudden jerked me first down, then up stream with irresistible force now above and then below the foaming waves. I had kept my footing on the bottom but now I laid horizontally a pray[er] to the tubulent waves. But still I crawled along slowly untill I came in the midle of the river, then the cup of my misery was filled to the brim. And what was it that caused the perilous situation? Nothing more or less than my innocent haversack. That innocent looking pouch contained for 3 days rations tobacco, pocketbook, paper and envellopes and other numerous smal necessaries and together with sword and belt was strapped across my shoulders to keep it dry if possible. The fellow who tied the thing must have been careless for, all at once when the rope made a lurch down stream, it the haversack suddenly bumped over my head the current forcing it immediately under my body. The strap remained behind my neck and the force of the current pressing on the bulky bag actually tied me to the rope. I was unable to move onward an other foot. I slipped my left arm over the rope so as to have the same under my left arm and with my right hand tried to get the haversack forward and over my head on my back again, but it was no go; I had not power enough in one arm to force the thing forward over my head against the current. I worked for dear life, in fact I was sweating in the water. I bethought me of my knife intending to cut the strap but that allso was in the haversack. I looked towards the shore thinking that an other squad would come over but they seemed to be waiting for me to get across.

I was calculating how long I would be able to stand that sort of business and trying to get the strap from behind my neck and let the whole concern take a trip to New Orleans when I heard shouting from the south bank. Looking in that direction I saw a man walking along the rope, his back

THE TULLAHOMA CAMPAIGN

Capt. James M. Randall. From a lithograph, "Col. B. J. Sweet's 21st Wis. Vol Regt. Located at Oshkosh, Wis. 1862." (Courtesy Oshkosh Public Museum)

against the current, I recognized him finally as Capt. Randall of Comp "G." of our Regt.[7] He was a Wisconsin river man and nearly as well at home in the water as a fish. He stepped opposite me breaking the current thereby, brought the haversack on my back, assisted me to plant my feet at the bottom and so we marched face to face towards the bank. I felt so relieved after once more feeling terra firma under my feet that I was hardley able to thank Capt. Randal for his timely aid. But he would not hear it and laughed at me and called me a sandturtle, all of which I meekly assented to. But in course of time I had my revenge and got even with him. . . .

About 1. P.M. the Div. was all across, the clothing and other things had speedily dried in the burning sun; Coffee had been made and we were ready to tramp. But before we started ammunition was distributed to such men whose cartridges had become wet. It had been ascertained that a strong force of rebel Cavallerie was prowling round in the neighborhood and it would not do to enter in conversation with them with the powder wet. They did not come near us though that afternoon and after a march of perhaps 8 or 9 miles the brigade went in camp on a big plantation. . . .

[July 3.] They made us tramp "right smart" that day, 25 miles if anything and "old Sol" did his best to keep perspiration in order. A little before sundown, tired allmost to exhaustion we finally came to a halt. Shortly after the Quartermaster drove up with our dogtents. But the men were to[o] tired to put them up, and in fact there was no use for it. The sky was as clear as a globe of Crystal, so we wrapped our tired limbs in the blanket and Poncho and slept the sleep of the just.

July 4th 63. Our great national holiday. Would we be suffered to celebrate the same? For certain it was not celebrated by the rebs. They were striving with all their might to substitute an other holiday for the Celebration of the suppression of liberty and human rights. Shortly after coffee we were ordered to clean our arms and after that we were at liberty to celebrate in grand style but we were not to go outside the picket line and use no firearms.

At 9. A.M. the band of the 24th Ill. began to play all the national tunes they could think of and something besides. At 10. A.M. a batterie fired the national salute. Our camp being alongside a highway, a big crowd of niggers and "poor white thrash" crowded around to find out what all the noise was about. They knew about as much of the fourth of July as they did about the man in the moon. They soon skedaddled helter skelter, and this is how it came about:

Genl. Forest [Forrest] in command of a Div. of rebel Cavallery was hovering on our flanks and rear watching his chances for a successfull dash. He probably had heard the noise in our camp and guessing the meaning of it probably thought us all out of order; perhaps drunk, concluded to put a damper on our hilarity and make us sober. Consequently about 11. A.M. our attention was called to a number of picket shots following each other in quick succession, the pickets running for dear life towards Camp. Now, across the road and in front of our camp was a large stublefield extending towards the front about a quarter of a mile and several miles to right and left; bejond the field all was open woods; that is there were trees but not much underwood or brush. Of course, no sooner had we heard the reports and saw the pickets coming back in such a hurry, than we jumped for rifle stakes and made for the fence across the road. A long line of Cavallery dashed out of the woods and reaching the open field came forward in a gallop. I suppose they did not see us as we were crushing behind the fence, the rifles thrust through between the rails; but they certainly could see our batteries getting ready. The line was certainly half a mile long. As soon as our pickets were in the bugles signal was heard and the next moment the fence was converted in a flame from the dead dealing rifles and immediately after the batteries unloaded their cannister into their ranks. The scene at once changed from the heroic to the tradgic. Heavens! what a confused mass that line presented But only for a moment; then they went back just when a second line appeared at the edge of the woods to support the first, but seeing how matters stood, thought it the wiser part to let us celebrate the fourth after our own fashion. Some of the Johnnies had lost control of their horses and came right up to the fence where they were made prisoner.

To enliven the retreat of the Johnnies our batteries threw a dozen shells after them in the woods which probably had the desired effect.

Although this friendly call of Genl. Fo[r]rest had not been in our program of celebration the boys felt much elated of its result. But there was some work connected with it. The rebel dead had to be burried and the wounded and prisoners taken care of. Forty five bodies were burried; the wounded were more but I have not the correct number on hand. After the details for this work were made the boys were going to take up celebration again when suddenly at the right of the Div. a most Enthusiastic cheering and hurrahing began. We were at a loss to account for it and looked anxiously about thinking the Johnnies were trying to spring an other trap on us. Regt. after Regt. was infected with the Craze untill Adjutant Jenkins came and read a comunication from Genl. Rosy to the effect that Genl. Lee had been whipped at Gettisburg Pa. That was reason enough for a hearty cheer and the Regt. did full justice to the occasion. . . . [8]

July 8th[.] No order to march but instead of that an order to lay out the Regts. camp ground in regular shape and order. Besides pickets, a regular camp guard was mounted and a guard house put up. That indicated we were going to stay here for a while. The men worked like beavers that day. All who could be spared went to the woods and chopped small saplings and brush which the Quartermaster hauled to camp with his teams and by evening every tent was so closely shaded that not a drop of Sunlight could enter it. The reason why a halt was made was very obvious. Bragg, on his retreat had, as far as possible, destroyed railroad and bridges and as our Construction Corps was not [y]et complete, they could not be repaired as fast as we advanced; consequently rations, ammunition and a number of other things an army in the field needs, could not be forwarded. In fact, the first ten days we were here, rations were so small that we had to fall back on berries and corn to fill our stomach. Ahead of us was a tunnel which to a great extent had been blown up and which allso had to be repaired. Taken in all we had a tolerable good time here. Occasionally an hour drill early in the morning before the oppressive heat came on, now and then a picket or camp guard and sunday dressparade constituted about all the duty. Yes, once we had to go to Winchester, Alabama to meet a ration train and act as train guard back to camp. That was a hard trip; 30 miles forth and back and nearly allways in the glaring sun.

That virtually ended the Tullahoma Campaign, the lightest we ever had proportionally but its results nevertheles were grand. The loss in our Corps (14th) amounted only to 206. . . .

General Rosecrans wished to keep up the numerical strenght of his army and issued an ordre that all Compagnie Commanders should sent a list of all absentees, stating for what reason they were absent, where they were and how long they had been absent, to his headquarter. After a few days the reports were returned with the instruction to drop all such on the Comp. rolls as deserters whose names were marked with a red cross. There were six of that class from our Comp: Sergt. John Dey, Corp. Amos Lawrence, A. H. Bennett, Joel Prince, Chas. Warner and Wm. H. Wood. Of Dey, Warner and Wood we will hear soon and get acquainted with them, the others I have never seen again. . . . [9]

A few days after our arrival here news was received of the capture of Vicksburg and Genl. Pembertons Army by Gennls. Grant and Sherman on July 4th. That, so to speak, cut the confederacy in two. The western part of the Confederacy, Arkansas, Texas and Louisiana, which had heretofore furnished the greater part of supplies necessary for the rebel armys[,] were henceforth worthless for them. The garrison of Vickburg which was surrendered to Grant numbered 34.000 men. which were paroled. A great number of field and siege guns as well as small arms, ammunition, Commissary and Quartermaster stores were allso captured. . . . [10]

Some Appleton boys belonging to the 1st Wis. Cavallery paid us a flying visit. They never had been near enough as [y]et for that purpose. Among them was a certain A.B. Evarts.[11] I must say I was much surprised to see Evarts in the garb of Uncle Sams boys. He was a smart lively fellow; had been Sherif several times and was well liked generally. He allways had been a rabiat [rabid] democrat with all the proclivities which make up a Copperhead, or northern rebel. When I enlisted he swore solemnly, rather than to fight for old Abe and the north and the damnd nigger he would go south and fight with the rebs. He still cussed the government and the black Republicans. I asked him why he had enlisted at all and hinted that it was time [y]et to join the rebels. I believe he would have deserted and joined the rebs if he had not feared the consequences. Fear for the draft had driven him in the army but I saw plainly he felt sorry for it. He served to the close of the war though, but the hardships of the service had scattered his con stitution and he died a few years after discharge. . . .

On the first of August Genl. Rosecrans inspected our corps and gave us a hint at the same time that tramping would be the order of the day again. That made me shudder, not because of the tramping but, because of the heat. Even now, standing for only a couple hours in an open field we allmost suffocated. There is a vast difference between the heat in northern and southern states. Even if the Thermometer in the north points to 90 or 100 in the shade there is almost allways some wind, some circulation of air which enables one to breathe freely, but not so in the south. There the air is during day time mostley a dead calm, thick and oppressive, nothing moves, or stirs, no leaf trembles. The very air quivers as if heated by a monster blast furnace. One feels a choking sensation while the perspiration runs in streams down the body. . . .

The following day appeared the usual order to clear the comps of sick and such unable to stand the campain. The first who reported himself as being unable to stand the trial was my friend Dorset Smith. I could detect nothing wrong about him bodily but Dr. Reeve thought with a sly hint at sarcasm that it perhaps was better for the service to sent him to hospital and I fully agreed with him. That ended his military carrier for he managed to slip into the Invalid Corps where there was no danger to run against some stray bullet. Nex[t] came big Rimick Knowles. He belonged to the same class as Dorset and was sent back allso. Next came Sanford Rexford. He was an exellent soldier. He was severely wounded at Perryville and had returned to[o] soon from hospital, the wound having broken open anew. Then was his brother Jacob Rexford.[12] We had him employed as Officers cook but even that he thought he could not stand. Besides he was not worth much as a soldier on account of shortsightedness. Since our arrival at Cowan Station I had been in command of the Compagnie as Captain Turner was acting Major and Fred B[o]rcherdt detailed in some capacity at brigade headquarters.

~

CHAPTER TEN

The Chickamauga Campaign

~ Finally on August 4th early we broke camp and tramped. At first it was cool and pleasant but as the day advanced became decidedly hot. After marching 6. or 7. miles we came among the spurs of the Cumberland mountains which, climbing up and down, made the busines much more difficult and trying. After a twenty stretch we camped in a narrow valley between high ridges. A good sized creek with plenty of water was near and most of us took a refreshing bath. The following day was to be a trying one. Nearly the whole day the road followed the southeastern slope of a mountain ridge. There was hardly ever a specter of shade and the sun burned against that ridge with double fury. Towards noon the men dragged along as in a dream, as if dizzie, or drunk. Finally a halt was made, partly to enable the long stretched column to close up, partly to make dinner. That was a difficult matter as the men had drank the last drop of water and the nearest water a mile off. Here Capt. Turner and Adjutant Jenkins came to the rescue. They gave their horses to some of the men and by means of a little contrivance each horse fetched 30. or 40. Canteens the trip. During the time the men contrived to make some shade by stretching tent sheets and blankets over the bajonets. We heard soon that in the regular brigade three men died of overheating, or sunstroke. That was mostly due to the unreasonable strictness and brutality of their Officers.

It is astonishing how much invigorating power is hidden in a cup of strong Coffee. No one can appreciate that unless he has been on the verge of Exaustion. We wer allowed a two hours rest. The march was then slowly taken up. The men were cautioned to keep well closed up in order to avoid any undue exertion in closing up. But in spite of all this some men were overcome by the heat, among them Sergt. Lyman C. Wait[e] of my Comp. He suddenly began to stagger, threw the arms wildly about him as if to lay hold of something and dropped. Fortunately there was water enough in the canteens to give him a good soaking. He revived and was taken along by an ambulance. But he suffered for months with headache and dizziness.

About 7. p.m. we passed through a handsome, aristocratic looking village. It was a cluster of stately, f[a]ncy buildings and everything around the houses kept scrupulously clean and neat. It seemed to be deserted. The shutters were closed, nobody, not even a nigger or pickaninny, no dog or cat, or any other animal was to be seen. An other thing struck me forcilly [forcibly]; no store or grocery was to be discovered. I took it to be some kind of a sommer resort for the rich Nabobs in the vicinity who did not wont to see the hated yanks, or be seen by them. I think the name was Anderson station. A mile further we went into camp. . . .

Before daylight we were busy brewing Coffee. Nobody grumbled because all knew it was the best time for marching. We went in a lively gait untill 9. a.m. when we came to "Craw Creek." We were marched of[f] the road, a little ways up the slope of a long and lofty Mountain staked arms and were ordered to pitch tents in regular Comp. order. Details for pickets and camp guard were allso made which indicated an other stop. I heard afterwards we had to wait for pontoons to cross the Tennessee river.

The first two weeks we were here we received hardly half rations. All kind of berries and especially field corn had to fill the place. But the corn was to[o] ripe and would not get soft by boiling it a week; it took a good set of teeth to grind it but it had to be done. Some of the boys were anxious to know what kind of a country there was at the other side, or east of the mountain. They asked for a pass, or leave to go over, but as it was outside the picket line that could not be granted. So half a dozen watched their chance and went on a tour of discovery on the sly. That was by no means an easy undertaking as the mountain was not only very high and steep, but it was a continuous climbing over rocks and boulders, now right, now left, with here and there a meager brush to take hold of. I climbed up once and had enough of it. But the view from the summit was worth the trouble. So when the boys reached the top and saw the valley on the East side dotted here and there with dwellings, surrounded with what seemed to be fruittrees, they concluded to go down to see the people. When they returned they had a lot of the finest peaches I ever had seen; some were nearly three inches in diameter and a flavor, Oh, my! All the men wanted to go but th[at] was not to be thought of. Moreover the returned boys said that was not necessary as they had told the people to bring all the peaches they could spare in camp where the men would buy them. And sure enough, the following afternoon two Butternuts came around the mountain with a horsecart drawn by a mule the cart heap full with peaches. They had packed the fruit carefully between leaves, straw etc. to avoid their being smashed. They sold the big ones two for a cent, the smaller ones five for a cent. And they were glad to get greenbacks. After that they came regulairly with two carts full every afternoon. That helped our rations along somewhat. . . .

One day I was highly surprised to see Wm. H. Wood step into my tent, putting down a satchel and stretching out his hand. It will be remembered he was one of the deserters of the Comp. who quitted business at Perriville. He had run away before we came into battle, made his way back to Louis-ville under the pretex of being sick, and from there made his way back home to Appleton. He cooly took his former position with Chs. H. Fay as foreman in the taylor shop. I soon found out where he was and wrote to him, as allso to Charles Fay informing them it would be better for Wood to return or he would come in trouble, but none an[s]wered. From Cowan Station I informed him that he had been dropped as a deserter and might expect to be arrested any day. That seemed to have moved his Concience and here he was, all smiles and politeness, and so glad to see me again and find me well and hoped the boys were all right etc. Meanwhile he had oppened the satchel and fished out a Quart bottle of brandy and putting it on my little table said: "I thought to bring some Fox river juice along for you and good look to you." The rascal. My wife had bought the brandy and requested him to take it along for me. He probably thought to use it as a bribe to secure my good will and service in mitigating his case. He inquired if I had arms and equipment for him. I told him that he did not need any equipments at present; that his case must be tried before a Court martial; that he should report now to the Orderly sergeant under arrest and not leave the Comp. grounds without permission. That was a damper on his hilarity. And when I offered him a drink and avised him to behave so as to gain the respect of Officers and comrades his buoyant spirits deserted him and he asked somewhat doubtingly. "Will they do anything to me you think? You see I returned voluntarily." "Have you not deserved anything"? I replied, "Why did you run away when your Comrades were fighting? Have you come to draw a years pay and go home again? Go ask the boys they will tell you their opinion straight and plain." He went. Next morning the customary charges and specification were forwarded to Corps Headquarters.

As Wood had returned voluntarily the court possibly would treat him leniently, but his restles, mischivous spirit led him into more trouble. Already on the second day he broke arrest, that is, he left camp unobserved, went over the mountain into the valley bejond and behaved in a very bad manner. Among other things he insulted a young lady in a ruffian like manner. He came quietly back to camp and had nothing to say. I intended to send him to Div. headquarters where soldiers under Court martial Charges are kept under guard, the next day. but before I came to it a tall Citizen in butternut garb and a comely girl appeared and wanted to see the Commanding Officer. They were shown to Genl. Starkweather. They stated their grivances and were asked to what Comp. and Regt. the Soldier belonged. Of course they did not know. If they would recognize the soldier? Both said they would. So the 24th Ill. had to fall in first. None was recognized in that Regt. Next came our Regt. drawn up in Comp. fronts. Wood stood in the rear rank as he did not belong to the taller class, his hat drawn a little deeper as usual over his eyes, looking persistently at his feet. The girl went ahead of the man. She did not look long at the soldiers but went right along in usual gait. When she came opposite the file where Wood stood she pointed over the shoulder of the front rank men saying: "Thar he is." That settled the matter. Wood was immediately conveyed to Div. headquarters wher he was kept under close confinement. A special court martial was conveened and Corp. Wm H. Wood sentenced to: I. To be reduced to the ranks. II. To forfeit one years pay and emoluments as allso the bounty. III. To make good the time of service lost and. IV. To be kept at hard labor with ball and chain attached to one leg for the period of two months. Immediately after sentence was passed Wood was conveyed to the delinquent work squad, the chain riveted to [t]he left ankle. It was a severe lesson but it did not break his wicked spirit as will be seen later. . . .

The long looked for Pontoons arrived at last. They were of the old fashioned pattern, made of wood about 25. feet long each. Every boat required a long stretched wagon to transport it. Other wagons carried the joi[s]ts, planks, ropes, etc. It was a train of several miles long. . . .

One afternoon the Officers of the Regt. were assembled at the Colonels tent for a general chat when the conversation drifted into politics. Of course, political views were different and allthough good many who had enlisted as democrats had by this time embraced the republican faith, some would obstinately uphold the argument that the south was right and the north wrong and the republican party was responsible for the war. Conspicuous among those was one young second Lieut. C. Morgan of Co. "F." Allthough a good comrade and soldier in general, he could, or would not admit the argument that the republican party was right in suppressing the rebellion and upholding the Union. Neither would he admit that slavery was wrong and at the bottom of the rebellion. Morgan was a good schooler and fluent speaker, but without practical experience. In the heat of the debate he mounted a craker box and soon was lost in a eloquent argument in favor of the oppressed poor Southern people. Captain C. H. Walker, who was an ardent Republican and opposed to slavery, quietly slipped out of the tent but soon returned with his cook, a bright young mulatto, as white and fair as any Caucasian can be, only the slightly curled hair indicated some remote nigger blood. Placing the mulatto in front of Morgan the Captain suddenly interrupted him thus: "Lieutenant, here is my Nigger! Look well at him. A year ago he was a Slave, a Cattle, simply a piece of property worth so many dollars and cents. twice he has been sold at auction; he has no Idea where his father and mother, his brothers and sisters are. They are sold. That is all he knows. Would you buy that nigger, that man as you buy a mule, a dog or a hog? to use and dispose of him as you dispose of your hogs? Supposing that nigger was a girl. Would you buy her, perhaps with the intention to satisfy your lust and breed new stock for the slave market and sell your own offspring in order to fill your pocket?"—Lieut. Morgan looked at the Mulatto, then at the Capt. He seemed confused, dazed, then jumped off the box and made for the tent opening. But the Capt. stopped him saying: "Lieutenant, a good lesson for you would be to spend a few months among our prisoners in the southern prison pens and study the principles of humanity from your rebel friends." This forcible and unimpeachable argument of Capt. Walker brought the sociable to a sudden close. Outside, Capt. Randall, allso a good democrat grabbed my arm saying: "Otto, I know you left the democratic ranks a while ago. You were right. Captain Walkers mulatto argument knocks all democratic points into a cocked hat. I am one of yours now."

I have often thought of this meeting and argument of Capt. Walker and his allusion to a rebel prison as a means of instruction to Lieut. Morgan because ere a month had passed Morgan was a prisoner in the hands of the rebels with many other Officers and soldiers of the Regt.[1] And to give them ample time to ponder over the blessings of freedom and personal liberty, they were kept there untill we, while on the march from Savannah Ga.

through the Carolinas northward in Feb. 1865. were the indirect means to their liberation. I learned afterwards that Lieut. Morgan lost his southern sympathies somewhere in the southern prisons, whether by accident or design I do not know.

Sept. 2d found us pressing forward again. After a stretch of 18. miles we reached Stevenson, Alabama on the Chattanooga and Nashville R.R. The place has a big name but in reality is a conglomerate of several dozen miserable looking shanties erected in a barren sandy plain. Nevertheless the place was selected as suitable for a suply depot and numerous big warehouses were built for the storage of provisions, ammunition and other necessary articles for the army, as allso blockhouses and forts for the soldiers to guard the same.

From Stevenson to Bridgeport is but a short march which we easily managed on the third. The pioneers immediately began layning the pontoons across the Tennessee. An other delay followed here. There were not enough pontoons to span the river; consequently so called Eprons, [aprons] or piers had to be built on both bank in lew of pontoons. . . .

The route to be taken by different Corps was as follows: Genl. Crittenden with the 21st Corps was to march on the north side of the river, cross the Wauseca mountains, then up the Sequatchee Valley and threaten C[h]attanooga from the front. That was a difficult and long route; 70 miles. McCook with the 20th Corps was to cross the Cumberland Mountains to the right, aim for Rome Ga. and destroy all factories, machine shops, railroads and bridges there and then join us again south of Look out mountain, while our, 14th Corps was to cross the mountains so as to land in the southwestern part of the valley between Lookout mountain and Missionary ridge and threaten Brags left flank and rear. It was a difficult and dangerous undertaking but it was well executed.

On the morning of the 6th crossing of the Tennessee with our Corps began. It was somewhat slow work as they did not dare to test the capacity of the pontoon bridge to the utmost. The night we camped several miles south of the river. During the night Ephriam Walker was seized with colics and cramps in the bowels which doubled him up fearfully, but luckily I had a little phial of painkiller left and a spoonfull of that set him right.

The following morning a miles walk brought us to the foot of the first mountain range usually called "Pidgeon ridge," and preparation for the Crossing immediately began. The title "Ridge" is decidedly a misnomer, as we found when we had measured its hight step by step. I had been bothered with diarrhea for several days and felt somewhat weak in the knees.

The men staked arms untill the batteries and teams had drawn up. Near the foot of the ridge a clear crystal like stream of water emerged out of the rock about 5 foot above the level of the ground. For a distance of half a mile it formed a little creek but, singular enough, lost itself in the ground without leaving a trace behind. While Turner, Fred and I were taking breakfast George Rawson stepped up and reminded the Capt. of the pending bet which had hung fire since the affair at Hoovers Gap. "All right Geor[g]e" Turner replied, "You have earned every cent of it. But will [you] take an other bet on a fight now"?—"Not much" Rawson replied, "I am satisfied with the five dollar. He who undertakes to grab to[o] much will loose that what he has got."

As soon as the batteries and wagons were drawing up the Regts. were counted of[f] in squads of ten, each such squad had to go along with a battery or team to furnish help if required. I went to Capt. and told him I wished to go ahead in order to go more at ease as I felt very mean. I would wait [on] the ridge for the arrival of the Regt. He readily consented and so I started with the first batterie and troupe which opened the assent. I must remark here that the day before one brigade had already ascended to act as pickets and guard against any surprise.

The road up the ridge, if it can be called a road, for the most went in a snake line making it four times as long as it actually was. At first the direction was southwest for perhaps a qua[r]ter of a mile, then with a short curve would double on itself and go in an opposite direction and so on up to the top. In those curves it was the men had to grab the spokes for all they were worth. Each gun had six heavy horses but in the curves the leaders could not pull to any advantage and the wheel horses hardly able to hold their own. With the wagons it was worse [y]et because being drawn by mules who are more afraid, unruly and baulky than horses it became often dangerous to round a short, steep curve; and the danger increased the higher we came. At first the road was, if not smooth, at least passable, but soon it turned in a sucession of bowlders and holes; levers and pries had to be used to lift the wheels up the rocks. The last third of the road grew worse and worse; the ascent became more abrupt, the curves steeper, therefore more difficult and dangerous; chasms and precipices would jawn on one side or the other; in many places the road was so narrow that the men could not walk alongside of the wheels. As with a blanket of snow were the horses covered with foam, the soldiers gaping for breath and bathed in sweat. Slower and slower we advanced and finally, being nearly exhausted I went ahead to gain the summit for some rest.

It was three P.M. when I stepped onto the crest and was surprised to find it to be a large plateau extending far to right left and front. I sat down to rest a while but being afraid to get to[o] stiff I soon arose and looked around. Not far of[f] I espied what seemed to be a clearing and went to examine it. It was a large field but neither house nor any other building could I discover. Neither was there any crop visible. While wondering how people, if any lived here, got their stuff to and from marke[t], my attention was directed to, what seemed to be a fresh[ly] broken piece of land. I investigated and found dry potato vines laying here and there. Since we had left Murfreesboro I never had seen a field with potatoes, or "Murphys" as they are called here. Wonder if they had found them all. With my sword I began to stir the ground and soon had the satisfaction to bring to light some of the size of a hickory nut or a small egg, but none bigger. That in fact, was a "small potatoe" business but the prospect to have potatoes for supper kept me stirring. If I only could find enough.

I put aside my straps and blouse and set to work as dilligently as ever a digger for gold has done; but it was slow progress. Getting somewhat disgusted I looked round and discovered at the edge of the field near the woods an untouched row of potatovines. That nearly took the breath out of me. Were they forgotten? or were the people scared away? No matter. They were mine now and I speedily set to rooting. They were small indeed. In Wisconsin not many people would have spent the time to dig them, but then we were not in Wisconsin just then. While digging I was calculating like an impatient kid how long it would be before they were cooked; and what eyes the boys would make. Now I heard the first of the batteries come up on the platteau. Would the boys detect me and perhaps come and rob me of my mine? But they could not see me from the road and were certainly to[o] tired for much investigation. If only the artillery did not park in the field. But no, they went on. Our Regt. I knew would not arrive before an hour [y]et. Time went by and my potatoes were dug without an accident. I gathered them in my poncho and found I had a good half bushel. I thought myself rich with that bundle of marbles. I shouldered my treasure and under cover went as near the road as I dared and hid them there, then setting down near the road awaited the arrival of the Regt.

Team after team went by but none of our Regt. hove in sight. The sun had passed behind the horizont and was relieved from duty by a bright full moon when I heard well known voices among the boys who were endeavoring to push a wagon around the last curve in the road. Jumping for my bundle I joined the Comp. and cheared the tired fellows with the prospect of a good supper. That made them allmost forget their aching limbs and after a miles tramp we went into camp. I immediately sent two men for the campkettles, others for wood and water. The ballance helped peeling the murphys. Every man had to donate a piece of bacon and in the course of an hour every one had two tin cups of potato soup fit for a king to eat, allways provided he is hungry and has nothing better to fall back on.

Decending the ridge the following day was even worse and more dangerous as the ascent had been; but as we had begun with the rising sun we arrived in the valley at sundown. The valley was from one to thre[e] miles wide and well cultivated. Here we camped for the night. A mile from our camp another ridge loomed up high which we had to overcome. It was a repetition of the first one. This Ridge was called "Racoon, or sandy ridge" allthough there was precious little sand in its construction. An other day of hard toil brought us on to the back of this Racoon where we camped but this time we missed the potatoe s[o]up. An other day brought us down again in Lookout valley where we had one days rest. The valley is situated between Racoon ridge and Lookout mountain from two to five miles wide and some twenty miles long. . . .

The following day we had to cross Lookout mountain. That historic pile rises at the very bank of the Tennessee river and abruptly rises to the hight of 3200. foot. following a southwestern course for about 15 miles, gradually sloping down to the level of the Country. We crossed his shaggie sides and back about 8 miles from the highest point. When we reached the top we halted for dinner. It was the 12th of September, the aniversary of our departure from Oshkosh, from home a year ago. I called the boys attention to the fact which called forth some sad reflections and conversation. Then we counted a thousand stalwart men, just dismissed from the Doctors scrutinizing examination and who all thought to be able to stand the rough usages and hardships of war. That illusion had speedily been destroyed; it was a thing of the past. Not one in the Regt. now but who realized that to morrow may be his last day. Of the thousand who dined at Oshkosh a year ago not 500 dined that day on Lookout Mountain. Over two hundred had allready been assigned to their final resting places in Dixie, a great number were discharged on account of disability and diseases, or were scattered in diverse hospitals. Of the latter class, I must admit, was a goodly number who thought the hospital the safest place against bullets and hardships unavoidable in warfare. At sunset we landed in the valley between Lookout Mountain and the spurs of Missionary Ridge and is a continuance of the Chattanooga valley. We had entered now the State of

Georgia which made us considerable trouble before we had mastered it. Before we begin we will see what had become of the 20th Corps.

Genl. Crittenden with the 21st Corps had arrived at his place of designation, that is, opposite Chattanooga on the North side of the river on the Eleventh. He had thrown a couple shells across the river into the rebel works, as to let them know he was there. Then he made faints here and there a[s] if trying to cross the river but did not cross. By this time Genl. McCook with the 20th Corps had successfully crossed the mountains and was well on his way towards Rome. Bragg had expected our whole army to come in front of Chattanooga and considered Crittendens Corps as the advance. He therefore cooly prepared for an attack, which behind his strong works was no easy thing. But when next day he was informed by his scouts of McCooks move and that Rosecrans was in the lower Chattanooga Valley, and an other day would bring them allmost directly in his rear, he lost no time to clear out. In forced marches he fell back on the Lafayette road in order to escape the clutches of Rosecrans and await the reinforcements which were on the road to join him.[2]

The hasty retreat of Genl. Bragg from Chattanooga changed the aspect of the situation materially. Crittenden had moved into Chattanooga immediately after Braggs retreat, left Genl. Wagners brigade there as garrison and with the Corps followed Bragg. Rosecrans wished now to have [t]he army together for two reasons. First if Bragg should attack him before McCook was back, Bragg would be to[o] much for him; but if McCook was back in time he could attack Bragg before his reinforcements arrived and perhaps give him a good thrashing. He therefore ordered McCook to come back in haste and join him at Crawfish Springs.

Meanwhile Rosecrans had to maneuvre to connect with Crittenden. In order to do so we had to pass through Taylors Gap which cleaves the spurs of Missionary Ridge. (Some call it Dug Gap, others Stephens gap I dont know which is right) and which we had to pass in order to be on the same side of the ridge with Crittenden. But Bragg had expected such [a] move and had sent a Division to hold the gap. But lukily Genl. [Negley's] Division of our Corps and our brigade of Bairds Division got "thar fust." The other troops of our Corps having passed some five or six miles to the left through another gap. When about a mile and a half out of the Gap we were ordered to make dinner in a hurry. Two Regts. of our brigade the 1st Wis. and 79th Pa. were sent out as scirmishers. They had hardly reached their destination and we had started dinner when they became heavily engaged. Genl. Starkweather at once ordered the other two Regiments 21st

Wis. and 24th Ill. to reinforce the scirmishers. We held the rebs in check for half an hour when they advanced in solid double line of battle. Stark-weathers bugle ordered us to retreat but keep up the firing. We were not more than 3 or four yards apart in our line and did good execution. We did not retreat towards the gap but in a more easterly direction.

It seemed queer to me that we did not see anything of Negl[ey']s Division; they must be somewhere sure. We had dodged from tree to tree for about a mile when suddenly the woods ended and we stood before a 4 foot high stone fence stritching right and left as far as we could see. A large field being on the other side. Behind this fence we found Negl[ey']s Div. deployed busy at work to break loopholes in the fence. As soon as we arrived they held out their hands to help us over quick. We turned round immediately to await the rebs. (Some 10 or fifteen rods before we came to the fence I saw Capt. Randal[1] who helped me across Elk river, stagger and stop. I went up to him and he said that he had been shot in a leg. There was not much time to loose so I stepped in front of him and told him to hang on to my shoulders. He was lifted over the fence in safety. "I suppose we square accounts now," he remarked. "I am glad to be even" I replied and that settled the matter.) When they came in sure hitting distance they received our first salute. That staggered the first line but not the second. They pressed forward in a charge only to receive an other at about 5 rods distance.

That settled the matter. Those who did not drop discharged their rifles at the stone wall but did not hurt us and immediadely took the back track. While they were running back, our artillery threw a lot of shells in the woods to Enliven their gait. After a little while a strong scirmish line was sent after them, partly to assertain if they would return, partly to find our wounded who had dropped during our retreat. We did not meet any John-nies. It seemed they had disappeared somewhere; but we found 10 of our wounded, several of whom died during the night. None of my company was hurt. We found allso the body of Genl. Starkweathers aid de Camp, but the rebels had taken everything away from him Except drawers and shirt.[3] When we returned, the balance of the Div. had picked up the rebel wounded and were burrying their dead. Their loss was very severe for so small an affair. I have forgotten the exact number.

The troops were now marched acros the field in the woods where we camped that knight. It had been a very hot day and combined with some hot work the men felt tired; besides as the rebs had given us no time for dinner we felt somewhat uneasy about the region of the stomach. But there was one advantage, we could combine dinner and supper and delight in a good rest if the rebs did leave us alone. Proper precaution against surprise was taken and at sundown most of the men were at rest. The night was a cool one and towards morning the men hoodled closer together in order to combine the animal heat in the warming pr[o]cess.

That day we tramped for a while in all directions in the woods and finally struck a blind wagon road leading in an eastern direction which we followed. Shortley after noon we were halted and informed we were to remain here for the day and night. Soldiers in the field soon learn to procure ease and rest because they are bound to as they are allways liable to be called upon to perform some extra feats of endurance. So the men hunted shady spots and squatted down, some writing letters, others making notes in their diaries and others again were discussing the possibilities and probabilities of the pending row with Bragg. Our drummers and fifers and buglers had organized themselfes in a committee on the conduct of the war. They claimed this priviledge on the ground that they had access to and were familiar with the cook's and h[o]stlers of the Generals and Colonels and therefore learned and knew more about the secrets of the campain then any line Officer or Soldier. The soldiers, appreciating the humorous in the matter, were attentive listeners and encouraged them in the Enterprise. So here little drummer Payne [Paine] and fifer Owens [Owen], the latter the ugliest but bes[t-he]arted fellow and for thus two reasons a sort of pet in the Regt. had started the rumor that Rosecrans had Bragg in a bag and all what was left to do now was to tie up the bag and pound him to mincemeat.[4] They claimed to have it direct from the Colonels hostler and he in turn had it warm from Genl. Starkweathers headquarter Cook. So the authority was unimpea[c]hable and the boys listened with awe and pleasure to the good tidings. I asked Geo. Rawson, the looky better [lucky bettor] of Hoovers gap, if he was not going to bet on some point. He replied with the question on what point I would bet. I said that if there was any bag ready made among the hills that we perhaps were nearest to the open end of it and the tying and pounding might be done by Bragg. Capt. Turner leaned to the same view and Corporal Rawson could not see plainly the drummers bag, no bet was effected that day. How narrowly we escaped being tied in a bag by Mr. Bragg will soon appear. As far as the pounding was concerned it was mutual in general, but Bragg decidedly got the most of it. . . .

The following day we took a more southern course and about six in the afternoon debauched out of the mountains into a more level country. We staked arms and in a little while the other Divisions arrived from other directions so the whole Corps was together now. We received two rations of beef, the second time in three months and the last for a half year to come. The boys set immediately to work broiling or frying the stuff. . . .

We had now recovered feeling with Genl. Crittendens Corps, that is, Genl. Crittendens right was near the point where our Corps was broiling beef. Crittenden, knowing that McCook was not back [y]et and Thomas with the 14th Corps was alone facing Bragg, had hastened to join Thomas and prevent his being driven by overwhelming numbers in the mountains. McCook was expected that very day by Rosecrans. Now Genl. Crittende[n]s March to join Thomas was certainly a timely move but there was great dange[r] connected with it. There was but one road leading back to Chattanooga passing through Rossville gap in Missionary ridge. The left of Crittendens Corps did not meet that road by several miles. It was of the greatest importance that we should have and hold that road in order to have Communication open with Chattanooga and have a road to fall back on in case of necessity. Now it happened that, while the boys were chewing and discussing the tough beef Rosecrans was informed by a scout that Mosje [Monsieur?] Bragg was sending a Corps to seize the Chatanooga road. Bragg knew that McCook had not [y]et returned; he knew allso of the Gap between Crittenden and the road. He therefore wisely undertook to steel a march on us and cut us of[f] from Chattanooga. If he then could avoid a battle untill his reinforcements arrived he had all chances to drive us in the mountains and take possession again of Chattanooga. He at the same time strongly calculated that Genl. McCook could not join us in proper time.

No sooner had Rosy received information of Braggs clever move than the drummers beat the long roll in the whole Corps. "To move in five minutes," was the order. The stir and hustle which at once took hold of the Corp would have been interesting to an observer not familiar with it. It seemed like an anthill upset by the foot of a malicious boy. For a few minutes all seemed dire Confusion, a complete mob; but as if by a magic wand the Chaos was converted in a mass of straight lines like the rows in a Cornfield and immediately the first, or the leading brigade moved on followed successively by the others. Our Div. took the lead; our Brigade the third in line of march. Genl. Johnsons Div came next, Genl. Reynolds last. We were not informed of the whereto, but we were to march fast and a good ways was whispered in the ranks, by whose authority the rumor was started nobody knew. But at the end of it we found that we had passed in the rear of Crittendens Corps to take hold of and keep the Chattanooga Road at all hazzards. It was to be a race between Braggs troops and us. If Bragg had known of our move he certainly would have beaten us, as he had much the better and shorter road. But believing Thomas Corps still on the right of Crittenden, the rebel troops possibly had marched easy and taken some rest during the night.

When the drummers beat the long roll I was just going to eat my portion of beef. I hastily wrapped the beef in a piece of paper and shoved it in the haversack, the coffee I poured in the Canteen. Dock Gilbert, our mess cook dumped the raw beef left in the messchest, locke[d] the chest and handed me the key. Coffeepot and coffee he allways carried with him, the Coffeepot on top of the knapsack, the coffee in the haversack. It was well for him to be ignorant of the fate awaiting him. When fairly started on the road I bethought myself of the interrupted dinner, and supper too for that matter, and finished the same at leisure.

Shortley before we entered the woods again Genl. Rosy and Staff rode past us. Capt. Weisbrod and I marching a little outside the road were speaking in german about the reason of the fast move. Major Schlucter, a former prussian Officer who belonged to Roseys staff heard some of our remarks and slackening the speed of his horse, leaned towards us a little, said, allso in german: "I will tell you gentleman what it is: It is a silent wager between Bragg and Rose who gets there first; You must prepare for a solid tramp to night." "Get where?" Weisbrod inquired. "Chattanooga Road" he replied and dashed on. That was the first and last hint we received about the reason and destination of the night march.

A little after ten at night we arrived at Crawfish springs. We were warned to take our fill of water and allso fill the Canteens. As it was a big spring forming a good run of water that did not take long. About two miles further a halt of 20 minutes was made to allow the troops to close up. It was a clear bright night; but never in my life have I experienced, or suffered so much on account of dust. In the road it was ankle deep and stirred up by the feet of horses and men formed a thick cloud which totally eclipsed stars and everything. But on we went in quick step; no one speaking or inquiring. It allways has been a wonder to me how the men stood it. Of my Comp. none fell out and I did not hear any of the other Comp. complain. All seemed to understand and appreciate the necessity of the move; that our lifes depended on the success of the same. There is certainly something unfathomable in certain phases of life. Here was hardly a line Officer or man who knew the importance of this movement, but all seemed to agree silently that it must be made. No murmer, no complaints were heard. One and all plodded on silently, patiently through the dust. Once more a halt of 20. minutes was made and on it went again. . . .

At daybreak we seemed to have reached our destination. We were ordered to stake arms and make coffee in a hurry with the smallest fire possible, and extinguish the fires as soon as we were ready. After that we were placed in brigade column, that is, two regiments in the front line and two Regts. in the second line, the rear line about three rods behind the front line, the battery being placed in the interval in the Centre of the brigade. The formation being completed we staked arms and laid down behind the stakes to indulge if possible in a snap sleep. . . .

At two O clock that morning the advance of McCooks Corps had reached the right of Crittendens lines. These boy[s] had allso experienced rough times. During two nights and one day they had marched allmost incessantly with occasionally an hours rest and had traveled nearly 65. miles. It was to be expected that these men were exhausted and needed rest, but that word was not in the program just then.

CHAPTER ELEVEN

~

The Battle of Chickamauga, Georgia

~ Sept. 19th 1863. About 9. A.M. suddenly the report of a heavy volley of small arms was heard perhaps a mile to our left and front. We were called to arms, scirmishers advanced and forward we started in the woods. There was not much brusch in the woods but on account of logs laying in every direction, the batterie had much trouble. The firing on the left had increased and the artillerie was taking a lively share in it. On our immediate left all was quiet, nor could we see any troops there. Far off to the right business also seemed to be lively. That indicated that McCooks Corps was felt for. We had advanced perhaps half a mile when we changed direction by a half right wheel. As the scirmishers in our front were not informed of the Change, they of course kept right along in the former direction and in this way our front was soon uncovered and unprotected.

Advancing perhaps half a mile further, all at once and without the least warning a heavy volley was fired into our ranks at a distance of about 30 yards. The Johnnies were low and therefore could not easy be seen. Oh, shades of Jupiter! what havoc that made. The 79th Pa. and first Wis. who were in the front line suffered more than the 24th Ill. and our Regiment who were the second line. The battery horses fell like flies, more than half; the batterie men sitting on horses and limbers were to a great part either killed or wounded. In vain did the Officer who commanded the battery and the remaining men try to unlimber and bring the guns in position. We, as soon as the volley was fired knelt down and returned the fire; loaded again and fixed bajonet. Lieut. Chas. Searls [Searles], Genl. Starkweathers Aid de Camp was killed.[1] I saw him raise his cap to the Genl. saying "Good bye, Genl" and drop from the horse. Colonel Mihalotzi was shot through the right wrist. He put the rains for a moment between his teeth, with the left hand then put the sword in the scabbard, had a handkerchief tied around the wrist and remained there.

Meanwhile the Officer commanding the rebel force had lost the best chance to make the business profitable for him. I had expected the rebs would make a charge as soon as the volley was delivered; at least they ought to have done so. During the first surprise and at such short distance they certainly could have made some prisoners and perhaps had captured the battery. Our men were laying low, such as who had no shelter behind the trees and kept firing with a will. The wounded who were able to walk had retreated to a safe distance. And now we heard a sharp command behind us. "Double quick! Right oblike, march, March!" It was the 11th Kentucky which was ordered after us as reserve.[2] It was a full Regt. allmost as strong as our brigade. The plucky little Colonel came in double quick on our right flank and Starkweather giving the order "Charge bajonett" we went with a "hurrah" for our rebel friends. They fired a few stragling shots and then turned for the rear. Quite a number were taken prisoners. A section of the battery (two guns) was allso captured.[3]

The most ridiculous things will happen among the most trying circumstances. Just after we had rec[e]ived the salute from the Johnnies and everybody was in the highest grade of ex[c]itement, the boys dropped on the right Knee and fired at will as per order. I stood edgeways behind a chestnut tree a little bigger than a common stovepipe close behind the ranks. I could see the Johnnies plainly among the brush and behind the trees and expected a charge every moment. I cautioned the Comp. to look out and keep an eye on the rebs. Maurice Grunert who kneeled close in front of me looked back and up to me, probably to better hear what I said. Just at that moment a big, white battery horse came dashing back directly to where Grunert sat. It came so sudden that I had no time to warn Grunert. He, looking back at me, did not see the horse which, with tremendous force with his forelegs struck Grunerts Knapsack sending him spinning, heels over head, backward like a little rubber ball. He picked himself up though immediately, stared wildly about him and suddenly ran back as fast as his legs would carry him, leaving rifle and cap behind him.

None of the other boys had seen this little incident and I did not say anything about it because there was no time and besides, I thought Grunert would return as soon as he got over the scare. But I was disappointed. He did not return that day, nor the next; but the third day about noon just before we formed line of battle on Missionary Ridge near Rossville Gap. he turned up. The orderly Sergeant was issuing hard tack and coffee to the men clustering around him. I sat a little ways off in the shade of a bush, when some one tapped on my shoulders from behind. Looking round I beheld among the brush the ghostly features of Maurice Grunert. His face allways belonged to the lean, emaciated order but now it looked frightfull. I went round the brush and found he was minus Everything Exept pants and shirt. In his frency to get away he probably had thrown knapsack, haversack, canteen and accoutrements, even the blouse away. "Have you any water"? was the first he said. Handing him my canteen and several hardtack he drained the first to the last drop and then went for the hardtack. "Will I be shot"? was his next question. Knowing that, according the articles of war, running away in the face of the Enemy is punishable with death, had prompted this question. "No" I replied, "Just keep mum, Dont say a word about it to anybody and come along with me." A little ways back I knew were a number of wagons filled with rifles, acoutrements etc. picked up on the battlefield. Theither I conducted him, picked out everything he needed exept blouse and Cap which I procured from the Quartermaster, and then told him to go among the boys as if nothing had happened and call on the Orderly for rations.

It worked all right. Afterwards when I asked him why he was absent so long and why he had lost everything he replied that the only recollection he had of the matter was that he had been struck by a cannon ball and sent whirling through space. The only recollection after that was that he found himself in the mountains, tired to death and minus everything. In the distance he heard the roar of the battle and hid himself under a dense bush. He remained that night on the mountain hungry and thirsty and shivering for cold. The next day he saw from his high position when the battle opened again and the furious contest; he saw how Sheridans Div. was cut off from our right wing, and driven into the Mountain directly to where he was. Fearing he would be arrested when found, he started again, allways keeping on the hight of the ridges, until night when exhausted by running, hunger and thirst, he laid down. He had eaten some brush Chestnuts to squench the hunger and thirst but found the[y] did not agree with his empty stomach. He thought of suicide but had neither gun, knife or rope to accomplish that feat. He could not sleep, because of the thirst and cold. He chewed green leaves to moisten his tongue and throat. Finally after midnight he heard a rumbling noise as if batteries or heavy wagons were passing over a rocky road. Careless now what might become of him if he only could procure a drink of water, he started in the direction of the noise. He could make but slow headway, being weak and finding numerous boulders an[d] Crags which he had to circumvent. At daybreak he arrived at the narrow road leading towards the gap but the troops were gone. He did not dare to take the open road but stumbled alongside it through the brush untill he heard familiar voices of some of our Comp. and found means to draw my attention to him. None of the Comp. ever knew what had happened to him.

But while relating this "little act between" I have almost lost track of the proceedings in the woods. It is a pity such moments of intense ex[c]itement can not be written and explained sufficiently in so short a time as they happen; Nor can the different feelings and emotions which they stirr up in different persons according to disposition and character of the Individual be described. And none can understand such emotions who has not experienced them. Nor can any one predict how he would behave on the battlefield, or by a surprise of that kind, as he never had an opportunity to give his nerves a deciding test. Saloon rows, street fights, or any other brawl current in civil life are no tests at all.

When the Johnnies were out of range, lines were formed again and the wounded conveyed back. An other brigade came up to relieve us. We were marched back a quarter of a mile and a little ways towards the left and placed in reserve of General Willichs brigade. Willich had not been engaged [y]et so we staked arms and sat down behind the stakes. On the extreme left the fighting had been severe and obstinate. The rebels sent there by Bragg the previous night to take possession of the Chattanooga Road were surprised bejond measure to find the road in possession of our 14th Corps and intent to keep it. Said a rebel Capt. who had been taken prisoner there, afterward to me in Chattanooga: "Why, we sooner had expe[c]ted to see the moon drop from the skye then to find you there. When we started that afternoon for that road you uns were reported to be eight miles southwest of Crawfish springs." "So we were" I replied, "but by daylight we were at the road all the same."—"That we found out or I would not be here, but see here, I am born and raised in this part of the Country and know every crook and corner. Do you know that, as the road twists and turns between the hills you have marched a good 35 miles that night?" "I don't doubt it," I replied, "at least we judged it to be about that much by the way our joints squealed, but if it had bee[n] ten miles more we were bound to get there. But what made you tarry so long? I understand you had a good road."—"Road? A good smooth road, the Lafayette Pike, Sur"! And then

THE BATTLE OF CHICKAMAUGA, GEORGIA

he added somewhat sulkily: "But nigh on midnight the men began, at first low and grumbling like but, by and by loud enough to swear and cuss about being driven like a crowd of niggers. Genl. Hill who thought we had time enough, 'lowed them three hours sleep. Yes sur, we uns got a good rest an you uns got the road; that's all the difference there is in it. . . ."

When we staked arms in the rear of General Willichs brigade, Willich had not been engaged [y]et. The most severe fighting had been on the left in the vicinity of the Chattanooga road. But the most determined onslaughts of the rebs ha[d] been coolly met by our men. But now it seemed they intended to try an other part of the line. While on the left the battle now cooled down to a lively scirmish fire and an occasional shot from the batterie, they began to feel whether we were there or not, or perhaps asleep. They began to throw shells profusely all over the woods. They wanted our batteries to take up the Challenge in order to judge of our whereabout and position, but our batteries kept still. That was kept up for an hour greatly to our anoyance. Good many shells would explode to[o] near and kill or wound a man here and there. Solid round shots would crash and tear through the tree tops scattering the limbs broadcast. It allways could be heard a few moments in advance when those fellows were making their way through the limbs by the peculiar crashing noise produced by the breaking of the limbs. It was amusing sometimes to watch the antics of the boys trying to dodge the falling splinters and limbs.

As all good things must come to an end so did this. The rebels, perhaps tired of wasting ammunition or supposing we were sufficiently scared, cooled down. But shortly after our skirmisher began a lively racket. That of course meant busines and we stood to arms. Soon the skirmishers came running in reporting the rebs were coming in solid lines. If the rebs had been anxious to find out our wherabouts they found out soon. There were three batteries with us. As soon as the rebel lines came in sight they opened a murderous fire with case shot and cannister on them. T[h]e boys of Willichs brigade were still laying down. The rebs were by no means dismayed at the terrible fire from our batteries, but quickly closed up the gaps and steadily advanced. A second line of rebs could be seen now advancing in support of the first. Now Willich bugle called to fire which was done at the moment. Starkweather ordered us forward at a double quick. Arrived at the front line we fired at a distance of perhaps 15 or 20 [rods]. Then the order came charge bajonett; but Willichs men who had loaded again fired an other volley and then the charge was made. The front line of the rebels fired now and many of our boy had to go down but it was not half a volley as their ranks had become very thin. They did not wait for our charge though but turned and ran towards their second line. But that line had not fire[d] a shot [y]et, neither had it lost much.

Here a Regt. of Willichs Brigade saved us many lives. This Regiment was armed with the Henry breachloader sixteenshooter rifle, that is 16 cartridges could be placed in a groove in the stock and after each discharge a contrivance in the lock loaded the rifle again.[4] The men had bought the rifles themselfes, the Government having promised to pay for the same at discharge. This Regiment now opened such a destructive fire on the rebs, that made even the second line confuse and hastily discharging their rifles at us in a reckles way turned and run. To our great surprise we received the order to lay down, but quickly found out what for. The batteries which had followed us oppened and threated the running rebs with all the cannister and shell they wanted. When the battery ceased firing the Henry Regt. was deployed as scirmishers and we had a chance for a little breathing and take care of our wounded and dead.

About the time we were preparing for the charge the two brigades on our immediate right were allso called upon to mind their busines. They were in full work now and Starkweather sent an orderly over to inquire if any help was wished for. They did need no help at present, was the reply and in a little while after their front was as clear as ours. So the rebs tried from left to right for a soft spot but without success. On the far right of McCooks corps the fight must have been very severe judging by the continued reports of Artillerie.

Genl. Starkweather now wanted Genl. Willich to retire in Reserve and he would take the front line but Willich refused. As if to give his refusal more weight he called on his brigade if they wished to go in reserve. An unanimous "No" was the response. Willichs men knew to[o] well the Genl. wished to stay and they loved him to[o] much to disappoint him. Starkweather who was junior to Willich, had nothing to say and moving us back a little ways we staked arms.

Genl. Willich was a proud man and had reason to be. Not that he was in the least conceited, or overbearing. Contrary he was a most pleasant and sociable fellow and everybody felt at ease in his company. But he was proud of his brigade and his successfull performances with it. And the brigade was proud of him and loved him. During its four years service that brigade has never been whipped allthough sorely pressed some times. It consisted of four Ohio Regts. one exclusively germans, the others mixed. Willich had been an Officer in the prussian army I think and had speedily advanced to Brigade Genl. here. But there he stopped. It was understood among the boys of the Division that his nonpromotion was due to jealousy of his superior Officers. The brigade was known as the bugle brigade, because Willich carried a little silver bugle with him with which he directed most all movements of the brigade during action. This was a great advantage as in the roar of battle even the most powerfull voice cannot allwas be heard, or if heard, not plainly understood; but that little bugle could allways be distinguished amid[st] the noise and din.

It was now perhaps 4. P.M. In our front it was as quiet as in a graveyard; Even the scirmishers did give no sign of life. And in fact we were in a grave-yard of imense size. Details were busy to bury our dead, other[s] carried our and the rebel wounded to the rear; but the rebel dead we could not burry.

As it was only a short distance to where we had the brush with the rebs in the morning I concluded to go there and take a look at the place. I informed Col. Hobart of my intention and he bade me to be quick about it as it was uncertain when we might move. So I started immediately but had not gone far when I heard our Chaplain calling me. He and a couple drumer boys were busy about three rebel wounded whom the[y] were trying to lift on to stretchers. One of them would not let the yanks tuch him. They were tryin to lift him on a stretcher but he would scream and cur[s]e like mad. He was shot in the loin, a painfull and dangerous wound. I said to the Chaplain loud enough for the fellow to hear, to let the fellow alone if he did not wanted help; it was just as well for him to die here as anywhere else. Then one of his wounded comrades said: "Look a heah Ben, 'pears to me you is making this blasted fuss foh nothin and a mighty fool of jerself. Dem frins may take me away this very minute and thanks in the bargain." That seemed to strike him as common sense and he consented. I leaned my sword, which I had unhooked and carried in my hand, against a tree and helped to lift him on a stretcher. Then I hurried on never thinking of the sword.

I found the spot and found ten hills [i.e., mounds] which denoted where our Comrades were burried. But there were more than one laid in the same grave as the hills were considerable broader as the grave for one man would require. There were allso the cadavers of eleven horses, one of them sitting on its hounches like a dog the forelegs straight and stiff. leaning with the shoulders against a tree. It had been shot in one eye. Just now I discovered I had no sword. I hurried back but found the sword gone. I supposed the Chaplain or the drummers might perhaps have seen it and taken it along but such was not the case. I never saw it again. The following evening when retreating from the battlefield our Sergeant Major picked up a steel scabbard sword which he borrowed me until I could buy a new one. . . .

It was getting dark now and our days work seemed to be nearly done. . . . When daylight had vanished, which in the south is nearly Identical with sunset, the scirmisher[s] became restless again. Was it carelessness of the scirmishers? Or were the rebels intent on a night circus since we had treated them so unhospitable during the day? Anyway, since the scirmishers had began the amusement the rebel batteries took it up and sent a shower of shells. But this time they did not have it all their own way. Our cannoniers returned them heaped measure and that seemed to produce more peaceable notion with the rebel friends, for after a half hours duel they quit and so did ours and the scirmishers also thought to keep better quiet.

During the duel a certain Schroeder of Capt. Steffens Comp. came to inform me that Capt. Steffens had just been killed by a piece of shell hitting him square on the chest probably injuring heart and lungs. I went along with him to take a last look at him who allways had been one of my best and truest friends. But I came to[o] late. When we arrived at his Comp. place some of his men had allready carried the body back to the Doctors tent to be sent from there to Chattanooga as his Comp. wished to sent his body to his parents in Appleton. Three days later while we were marching from Rossville Gap to Chattanooga across the plain whom should I see standing alongside the road but Capt. Steffens stretching both hands towards me. Tears stood in his eyes and it seemed he was unable to speak; so was I at first. But desiring to put a jovial face on the matter finally said: "So uncle Peter had no room for you above there I see."—"No, not [y]et," he replied. "I knocked loud enough at the door though." And he opened the vest, parted the shirt and what a sight! The whole left breast and part of the right was a mixture of different shades of coleur, green, blue, yellow and black. The piece of shell probably had spent i[t]s most force, but [y]et strong enough to force all the wind out of him. "You must have a breastbone like an Elephant to stand such knocks," I remarked. "Well" he said "Doctor Wagner told me he worked a full hour before he could set the machine running again." . . .

It was II. P.M. Most of the men had fallen in a dooze behind the gunstacks. Again the scirmishers got up a racket and thereby compelling the drowsy men to jump up and look for the rifles. But this time the batteries did not join in the con[c]ert. But all at once we received a scattering fire direct from the left flank and not far away neither. Genl. Starkweather and his ordlies immediately rode out that way and soon returned and we learned that the firing was a mistake by our own troops believing us to be rebels.

An Orderly from Genl. Willich informed Starkweather that the rebs had left the front. Our wat[c]hfull scirmishers having noticed the rebel scirmishers withdraw had given them a farewell salute. Having delivered the news the orderly proceeded to Genl. Thomas. And shortly after began a series of movements and countermarches right and left and back and forth, which looked to me as if we were searching for something which we could not find, and lasted over an hour.

Genl. Rosecrans had learned that Braggs reinforcements had arrived. They consisted of Genl. Longstreets Corps from the army of Virginia, the reputed best fighting corps in Genl. Lees Army, a Corps which never had been beaten. Further Gen. Popes Corps from Mississippi. In the latter Corps were over 10.000 paroled prisoners which Grant had captured at Vicksburg and who had not [y]et been exchanged; but the rebel authorities had forced them into service again. The rebels had no right to do this, but the rebel leaders never cared for any right. The two Corps numbered over thirty thousand fighting men. Besides there came some smaller organisations which were gathered from all over the southern seaport garrisons which amounted to about 7 to 8000 men. This enabled Bragg to put a force of between 70 to 80,000 men against our 50.000. So at best we had to fight two against three. But it was well we did not know it that night and not untill the next afternoon. Rosy was therefore compelled to keep strickly in the defensive.[5]

It seemed what we were looking for was finally found. We staked arms but were forbidden to make any fires which could be seen from the distance. The night became very chilly. How good a cup of hot coffee would be. But to make coffee water is a very important factor and that we had none. Chicamauga river was nearly two miles away; we did not know even where to find it exept by going behind the lines towards the left. I asked Sergeant Greeley to take 8 men, take all the canteens in the Comp. and try to find water. He went and after an hour returned with water. Meanwhile the men had got up contrivances to built small hidden fires. The rifles reversed, sticking the bajonets in the ground, buttupward and tying the outspread ponchoes along the rifles made an effective shade. The shine of the fires could not be seen in the bright moonlight especially as we took care to keep the fires low. So we had our coffee but we had to be carefull with the hardtack which were nearly all [gone] and it was uncertain when an other supply could be had. Then we laid down to catch a little sleep as it was past two A.M. . . .

Sunday Sept. 20th 1863. . . . Reluctantly I undertake to give a little scetch of this historical day, of the hardest fought and most obstinately fought contest during the Rebellion; where the weaker part fought with the courage of despair never once entertaining the thought of submitting and the other part, exultant with the assurance a great superiority in numbers always imparts, fought recklessly, desperately in the hope of anihilating us, wiping us from the face of the earth. The best descriptions can not convey a correct impression of the reality. The best executed battle scenes on canvas are merely inanimate, lifeless forms representing a certain moment in a contest usually fails to give a correct Idea of a battle because, there is no life in it, the figures are immovable, dead; there is no change in the situation, you can not see the Expressions of passions, of hope or despair, of joy or doubt, of reckles bravery or hesitating fear, of hate and revenge. You can not hear the infernal roar and noise of all the batteries and small arms, the shreeks and moans of the wounded, the groans of the dieing the cries for help, for water.—The liveliest immagination can not realize the situation in real battle.

We were aroused at break of day shivering, cold and stiff, although we had slept but two hours. Everything was covered with a film of hoar frost. Again we were shifted towards the left and finally directed to the spot the brigade was to occupy. We did not come in the wood this time but on the left of the brigade the woods began again. Our Div. the first 14th Corps Genl. A. Baird commding, held the Extreme left on and across the Chattanooga road; our brigade being the fourth in line from the left. To the right of us Brennans Div. then Re[y]nolds, and next Negl[ey']s. These four Divisions constituted the 14th Corps. Next came Crittendens Corps 21st and McCooks 20th on the Extreme right. Our line, that is for our brigade and the brigade to our right, (I could not see further) was at the south end of an abandoned field somewhat overgrown with short chestnut brush, sassafras, persimmon etc. The field in our rear rose gradually so as to form a ridge. In our front a level strip of pasture 20. to 25. rods across skirted the woods at the opposite side. From the edge of the woods an other ridge arose along our front. As there was no undergrowth in the woods we could see through between the big trees and notice everything going on, on the ridge. This was the view in our immediate front. But as our line in acordance with the formation of the surrounding country was formed slightly in the form of a horse shoe, the centre curve outward and the wings drawn backward,[6] It was impossible for us to observe anything further as what happened in front of our two brigades. The extreme right of our line rested on the spurs of Missionary ridge, 5 miles away, so as to make a flanking there impossible.

THE BATTLE OF CHICKAMAUGA, GEORGIA

How it had happened I do not know, but a rumor had got afloat among the boys that large reinforcements had arrived for Braggs army. Nobody could tell it sure but the strictly defensive preparations strongly suported the rumor. We were advised to arrange some sort of shelter against an attack. Heretofore we allways had fought from the level ground face to face before, and this order indicated severe busines and aroused suspicion. Then a rumor ran along the lines, (by grapevine mail, of course) that Longstreet with his invincible Corps had arrived from the east to show the western greenhorns how to conduct and behave in a fight.[7] Now I must say right here that thus rumor, instead of discouraging, or scaring our men, just put them on their mettle. To be scared by eastern tramps? Never. But this rumor convinced the men that some kind of protection would be a good thing. But with what to make breastworks? Half a dozen good sized chestnut trees stood in a stragling way in our front. Those were soon down and rolled into line; several more were rolled out of the woods in front and those logs arrainged in single lines formed our breastworks. Behind them, flat on the ground, the men squatted down, when necessary, and fired over the log. The battle line was formed in two lines, each line having twoo ranks, the second line about 20 yards in the rear so as to enable them to fire over the front line. The batteries stood several rods in the rear so that the elevation of the ground enabled them to fire over the 1st line. Our brigade had two batteries; the fourth Indiana (Capt Loomis) and a regular battery the number of which I have forgotten.[8] Ammunition was issued so that each men had 120. rounds or more. So provided the men sat down and awaited events.

It was half past eight A.M. and we had no Idea [y]et of the designs and whereabouts of the rebs. The frost had melted long ago and old sol began to look down in a way which promised he would keep us warm and comfortable. August Pierrelee asked me for leave to see his Uncle Capt. Steffens who, he had heard was wounded. As [Pierrelee] was quiet sick I let him go. McKend[ry] Rawson who also had been very unwell for a week I detailed to supply the Comp. with water. (We were then about a mile from Chickamauga river.) Spencer Orlup, ("Old Carefull," the boys had nicknamed him, because he allways was so extremely cautious whenever there was prospect of danger, allthough not a coward.) hearing this said: "Oh, I wish I could do that." Whereupon Rawson said: "You go Orlup in my place." Orlup took a number of canteens and started on his first trip. But we never got a drop of water through him that day; nor did we get a sight of him until the afternoon the following day on Missionary ridge and even

then the canteens were all empty. He got an ugly wellcome from the boys.
He undertook to justify himself by asserting that he had got lost, but they
called him simply a mean sneak. He was amply repaid in his own Coin
afterward to the great satisfaction and amusement of the Company. Old
Charles Buchholtz [Buchholz], the grandfather of the Comp. (He was 45.
years old and the senior in the Comp. and commonly called the creeper,
because of his short legs.[9] He allways had trouble to keep up when a resolute march was made.) came to me again with a bundel of premonitions he
had gathered during the night, as he had done before at Hoovers gap. He
had the little package ready which he wished me to sent to his wife. He was
sure he would be killed as dead as a rat this time. To avoid unnecessary
arguments I took the package and slipped it into my haversack. Jim Walker allso had some misgivings about being bullet proof but reminding him
of his first failure in premonistic prophsies he withdrew.

We were suddenly interrupted in these little arrangements by a spirited
rifle firing at the left of the line. It did not last long; nor did any big guns
take part in it. The cause and result in short is this: Genl. Bragg was ancious
to assertain our exact position and strenght in the vicinity of that one road,
and if there were any chances to get possession of it. He sent a brigade to
recognoitre with the ins[t]ruction not to enter into any serious engagement. Well they did "recognoitre" and were speedily sent home. This, for
the time being, satisfied Brags curiosity about the affairs on our left.

When I said the affair on the left did not last long I did not intend to
insinuate that with its ending we had secured safety, for, hardley had the
echoes died away when the sudden explosion of numerous shells before,
above and behind us and the following reports of the dis[c]harging cannons notified us that the circus had begun; free admission to all and no
humbug about it. So the boys squatted down behind the logs awaiting developments. The batteries did not return the challenge. "We will see them
first" Captain Loomis said, "and then show our goods." A pi[e]ce of shell
broke the ramrod a canonier held in his hands; he looked at the stump a
moment, then threw it away and grabbed an other one. Now several batteries appeared on the hights opposite us. Immediately our batteries oppened
on them with such effect that none of them fired a shot but withdrew. But
now our scirmishers discharged their rifles and came running back with all
speed. Over the ridge came rolling down the rebel lines, banners and flags
proudly waving. Now our cannoniers began to warm up and show their
mettle; it was surprising how fast they could load, aim and fire. But now the
rebs came in exellent range for the Infantry and the rattle of thousands and

thousands of rifles comingled with the deefening roar of the batteries. From left to right as far as we could hear the very hell seemed to be in uproar. No single report of rifle or cannon could be distinguished.

Soon the smoke enveloped everything in a inpenetrable gloom through which even old sol himself could not penetrate to see what we were doing. We could see no more rebels. Were they coming? or were they there yet? We should soon know. A shower of bullets from them added their hissing noise with the general uproar. They could only be heard when passing very close ones head because the general roar of Cannon and rifles was deafening. They could not hurt us much though. If they fired low the bullets would hit the logs, if the[y] fired high the[y] would go in the ground behind us. That was really an amusing sight in the deadly busines. Each bullet striking the ground raised a little cloud of dust and by the immense number the rebs threw at us it appeared as if heavy raindrops had fallen in hot ashes. Judging by the report of their rifles they were perhaps twenty rods away. They kept it up for about fifteen minutes when they stopped. We could not tell whether they were gone or not. Scirmishers were sent forward who crawled on hands and knees. They did not return, a sign that the Johnnies had gone.

Soon the dense smoke lifted and we saw clear again. No rebs were to be seen exept those laying on the ground. Many of their wounded who were able to walk came up to us and begged to be taken in; some even would crawl in. That was readily granted and they were treated like our wounded. But the rebels had taken advantage of the time the smoke was so thick and had mounted several batteries on the ridge and now all at once began to treat us to volleys of shells. That set our batteries to work again and they cleared the ridge a second time. Then came a short lull and gave the boys chance to stand up a little while as it was nearly burning hot on the ground. Charles Buck was the only wounded in the Co.[10] The bullet had grazed his right chin and cut off the lapel of the ear; a close call indeed. It bleed profusely and looked more dangerous as it actually was. I told Chas. Lymer to go back with him to the Doctors. They went, but after going a few rods Buck began to run and Lymer, not being much of a runner, turned back saying: "If you are able to run like that you may run alone, It is to[o] hot for me to run for nothing." The poor battery men had suffered severely. They had no shelter at all. Six of them were wounded, two of whom had to be carried back, the others refused to go. The Capt. was wounded twice slightly but: "plugged up the breaches" as he said and remained all day. A tree about a foot in diameter was left standing about two rods in the front of the

battery it being not heavy enough for a ground log. As it was in the way the
cannoniers shot it away and falling the top reached the 24th Ill. killing
Captain Mauf [Mauff] and severly bruising two men.[11] Captain Mauf[f]
was the oldest, or ranking Capt. in that Regt. . . .

We soon found the rebs had not forgotten us. Every big tree at the slope
of the hill, or ridge hid one or two sharpshooters who were deliberately
trying to pick of[f] our Cannoneers. But that was not for long. A shower
of shells thrown among the trees soon drove the poor fellows up and across
the ridge; in doing so our scirmishers at the base of the ridge acelerated
their speed.

Perhaps twenty minutes had passed in this wise. Then our scirmishers
came running back again. Two lines of rebels could be seen crowding over
the hights. It was the same thing over again with this difference that we
could see more clear as the smoke more readily ascended upwards as before, and they did not lay down this time at the foot of the ridge as before.
They were determined to see us face to face. So they kept straight on across
the narrow plain. Meanwhile some batteries had again taken position on
the brow of the hill pouring shells over us and trying to disable our batteries. An indescribable pandemonium ruled supreme for about five minutes;
a long time under such circumstances. In spite of their severe losses the
rebel lines advanced to within ten rods of us. Those poor, brave, but deluded men, probably were told that we would run if they only came near
us, had to suffer for the hightoned deceit of their leaders. At the distance
mentioned such a tremendous fire was poured into them which seemed to
me would bring them all down. Involuntarily I shut my Eyes and when I
looked again they were running back, batteries and Infantery firing after
them with the utmost speed.

During the attack Genl. Starkweather was severely wounded in one
ancle.[12] He did not leave the field though but had the wound dressed as
good as possible and remained with us to the end. McKend[ry] Rawson
was allso shot through an ankle and helped back as he could not step on the
foot. John Shokey [Shockley] was shot through the left hand.[13] Rawson's
rifle and accoutrements I appropriated for my own use. The Canoniers
allso had two severely wounded and Infantry men took their place.

In the centre and on the right the strugle allso was fearfull. Anxiously
we listened to the directions of the battle roar. All at once it seemed as if
our men had to give way there. More and more the tumult of the fearfull
combat seemed to come in our rear. Anxiously we looked backward but the
hight behind us impeded the view. Capt. Bill Wall, now Starkweathers aid

Capt. William Wall. From a lithograph, "Col. B. J. Sweet's 21st Wis. Vol Regt. Located at Oshkosh, Wis. 1862." (Courtesy Oshkosh Public Museum)

de Camp went up to assertain what could be seen.[14] He came back soon and reported he could see nothing but according to the direction it seemed sure that the wing was beeing driven. The centre was all right but how long would it be before it would be flanked and compelled to retreat? Oh how anxiously we listened; but steadily the tumult kept towards our rear. Then we heard far away, faintley, but [y]et distincly a tremenduous long drawn "Hurrah"! and knew thereby that some of our troops were making a desperate charge. But sudenly the rebs told us to tend to our business. A volley of shells told us that much. This time they seemed more determined than ever. Arriving on level ground they fired a volley at us which we duly receipted, battery and all. Quickley filling up the gaps in their lines they charged with a terrible yell in[t]o the very jaws of death. But they could not advance very fast because of the many dead and wounded laying scattered on the field. At about two rods distance a sheet of flame burst from our line and batteries allmost in their very faces. "Charge bajonet" clear and loud rang Genls. Starkweathers and Brennans voice. But there was nobody to charge at. The poor fellows were running back with all possible speed; followed by a number of shells from our batteries. Several dozend had thrown away their arms and came in as prisoners; a great number of wounded allso came in. It was a sickening sight to look over the field in our front. There were dead and wounded enough laying there to make a respectable line. And then to hear their groans and cries for help, for water.—

We will now look back and ascertain what had happened to our right wing half an hour before. For two long hours the rebel had tried in vain to find a weak, or unguarded spot in our position without success. But about noon during a tremenduous unslought on our right center that fatal order came to Genl. Wood to withdrraw his brigade from the line and hasten to the left to support Genl. Bairds (our) Division. Wood of course immediately withdrew his brigade and that fatal step decided our fate. There were no troops available to fill the gap made by the withdrawal of Woods brigade. (This fatal order business has remained a mistery to the present day and probably forever will. Both Rosecrans and Thomas deny to have given such order, which must be believed as both well knew that such a move must proove disastrous to the army. On the other hand Genl. Wood has proven that he received such order, but in the hurry of the moment did take no notice who the Orderly was who delivered the ordre. Genl. Wood was a brave, efficient and reliable Officer. I believe that as the Order was a verbal one, the Orderly who delivered the ordre misunderstood the same and perhaps was killed afterwards and could not explain matters.)[15]

The rebels soon discovered the gap in our line and poured through column after columns. Genl. Sheridan on the right was furiously attacked in flank and rear and in spite of the severest resistance pressed among the mountains. Genl. Negl[ey']s Division on the left of the Gap allso was attacked in flank. It seemed that Negl[ey] lost his head, or rather presence of mind which he always had shown on former occasions. Instead of withdrawing right wing so as to form a right angle with the main line he withdrew his whole Div. and marched them back to C[h]attanooga. Rosecrans, seeing the terrible state of affairs and seeing no means to stop them considered the day as lost and now only thought of saving as much of the army as possible and save Chattanooga. He turned the command over to Pop Thomas directing him to fall fighting back to Rossville gap and Missionary ridge. He himself went to Chattanooga to make arrangements for its defense, at the same time ordering back all rolling stock as, provisions and ammunition trains, hospital and headquarter trains, ambulances etc. to make the road clear for the troops. Pop Thomas did not like the Idea of giving up, as his Corps had not given an inch [y]et; nor had he any means to stop the encroaching rebs.

One of Thomas staff Officers espied a moving Column in the distance and called Thomas attention to it. Watching the column through his field glass he suddenly exclaimed: "That's Gordon, that's Gordon! Hurry over and tell him to hasten forward and to form his Div. for a charge while marching." It was indeed Genl. Gordon Granger with a reserve Division just coming up from Chattanooga.[16] Genl. Gordon Granger was by nature an impulsive man and dashing soldier which sometimes led him to reckless daring, but in this case it was just the thing needed. He did need no encouragement to hasten. His men seemed to have caught his spirit. In a sharp run they struck Longstreets men, the invincibles from Virginia, fired their rifles in their faces and then set to clubbing and stabbing without mercy and rest until they, by force, gave way and run. And then cheer followed cheer untill the air seemed to vibrate. That was what we had heard when the rebs called on us the fourth time. As our lines could not now be extended with infantry up to the mountains a number of Cavallery dismounted and did duty a[s] Infantry for a while with good Effect.

It was one P.M. now. It seemed the rebels needed some rest; or were hatching new plans to bring us to terms. It became singularly still and quiet along the whole line. If Pop Thomas had been anxious to sneak away, now had been the time; but he was not built that way. We all felt that something more was to be done [y]et, that was mer[e]ly the calm before the storm. The boys had not much water left but what they had they poured into the rifles and by violently shacking tried to remove the dried powder smoch [smoke] gathered from the continuous firing and which made the loading very difficult. I sent a couple trusty men for water with a lot of canteens, men who I was sure would return. Then we went among the dead and wounded and robbed their cartridgeboxes and try if their bullets would fit our rifles. That was a dire necessity as our ammunition was getting scarce and our supply train had gone to Chattanooga.

The unnatural stillness became oppr[e]ssive. It seemed something terrible, undefinable was to happen. And still good many of the boys fell asleep especially the jounger ones. Genl. Starkweather limping along with a stick behind the lines together with Col. Hobart spoke to and encouraged the men with good assurances, which they themselves probably did not feel. So time dragged on until between 3 and 4. P.M. when volley after volley of shells announced the coming storm. We instinctively felt the decisive moment was near at hand and grabbed the rifle more firmly. Our batteries did not reply; they allso had to husband their ammunition. When they reached the edge of the woods they received the first salute of rifle and batteries. They returned the fire immediately but did not stop. With their screeching cry: "Hec-e, Hec, hurrah for Longstreet!" they dashed forward over dead and wounded. Another volley at short distance tore through their lines, but they still came on. "Double rations" shouted Captain Loomis and a moment more and an other volley of double charged cannister tore through the ranks. Mercy! how they tumbled and dropped. I thought nothing could

persuade them to move further. But I was mistaken; they were bound to
show they were Longstreets men. They came to the logs. But the first line
stood ready; the second line close up. The cannoniers who could not fire
now came with their long hand spikes (ramrods) and a reckless stabbing
and clubbing took place which defies all description and immagination. It
did not last long though. Even Longstreets men were only mortals and
streamed back without cheering for Longstreet.

On the left the rebs seemed determined to have their own way. In fact it
seemed as if our troops had to give way there. Starkweather, now on horseback, ordered the rear line of our brigade, being the 79th Pa. and our 21st
Wis. Regt. to follow him at double quick. The rear line of the brigade to
our right had also to follow, forming together a brigate. The distance was
fully ¾ if not a mile. It was a hard trip to perform in a trot in such a heat,
but it was done. The last brigade in line on the left had been compelled to
withdraw their left as they were flanked by the rebels; our Cavallery having
been unable to resist the onslaught of the rebel Infantry. Arriving we found
the last brigade swung around backward fighting furiously for every inch of
ground with the rebs. In a run we had to form into line and immediately
charge bajonet. As our rifles were loaded the first discharge at close quarters
made a bad impression on them and as we still pressed forward they turned
and run. The Colonel commanding the Cavallery, meanwhile had ordered
his men to mount and now came dashing along and hallored to leave the
rebs to them. It was a brigade of Cavallery and we could not see the end of
it. They made bad work among the retreating Johnnies and gobled prisoners by the hundreds. A battery which could not get out of the way fast
enough was also captured. The original line being restored we were ordered
back with the same speed as we had come to our place in line arriving just in
time to help repelling a charge the rebs had again undertaken.

"Great heavens! what is to become of us"? Capt. Loomis of our battery
exclaimed, when a gunner reported that only ten rounds of shell and cannister were left for each gun. And our men were nearly out of cartridges
also. They again began to examine the cartridgeboxes of the dead and
wounded and divided the result equal among themselves and then laid down
to await developments.

At the extreme right meanwhile the battle had gone on furiously. Bragg,
seeing he could nowhere break our lines, resolved to overpower our wings
and roll up our lines by the flanks. His great superiority in number of troops
enabled him to do so. Again as at noon the right was giving way. The cavallery which after Sheridans disaster had closed the gap was not able to

THE BATTLE OF CHICKAMAUGA, GEORGIA

repulse the heavy charges of the Infantry, because of the inferiority of their arms. I have often wondered [why] they held out as long as they did. The withdrawal of the cavallery gave the rebels a chan[c]e to mass troops on our right and bring them around to operate in our rear. Genl. Thomas seeing he could do nothing to prevent their sheeme [scheme] concluded to withdraw the troops and leave the battlefield to the rebs. He therefore gave orders to the Div. Commanders to fall back successively from the right to left but keep up the fighting. But of all this, we on the left were ignorant of at the time. Bragg, perceiving our right was withdrawing, thought that by a vigerous assault on the left he might throw us in disorder and make a lot of prisoners. Once more they made a furious dash and got nearly all of our ammunition left, rifle bullets, shells, cannister and all free of cost. That seemed to fill the bill and they went back again. I had spent the last cartridge of Rawsons supply which I had anexed in the morning. The rifle being of no further use to me I struck the same across the log which made it unfit for further service and threw it after the rebs.

Capt. Loomis, having spent his last cartridge now limbered up and went to the rear. He and his men almost cried when they left us. Half of their men were disabled, three killed, but still the rest was full of fight.

All the Divisions on our right had gradually retreated now. We also received orders to face about and retreat slowly. Scarcely had we faced about when on the left again the rebs made a furious onsllaught on front and flank. This time it were Genl. Turchins and Reynolds brigades who, being a little in our rear on the retreat made an impetous charge on the flanking rebels, charged through their lines, and facing about made nearly more prisoners as they themselves numbered.

Our Division was the last of the army to leave the lines; the only Division which had not budged a step the whole day. Slowly we fell back up the incline, the rear rank now in front. The rebels, noticing our retreat, bothered us considerable with a scattering fire from the rear. Arriving on the hight of the level field among the short brush, bullets came thick and fast from the former right, now our left, striking us in flank. Our Regt. now on the left of the brigade was nearest the rebels. Looking in that direction I saw over the brush, the rebel flags advancing not twenty rods away. A rebel batterie was turning round preparatory to open fire on us. I shouted to Captain Weisbrod whose Comp. was next to mine [on] the left: "There they come! We must get out [of] here! Company 'D.' right oblike! double quick, March!" Weisbrod ordered his Comp. the same. But Colonel Hobart who usually walked with the head down looking at the ground said: "Boys follow me"! But mine and Weisbrods Comp. were already making good time; others followed and for good half a mile we made the fastest time we ever had made in the army, or ever made afterward. All thus who followed Col. Hobart, the Adjutant 14. line Officers and 75. Non commissioned Oficers and privates were taken prisoners by the Johnnies and were sent to the rebel prison pens where two thirds of them starved to death.[17] That satisfaction I have I saved the greater part of the regt. from a worse fate than death. . . .

As soon as we got somewhat out of range we slackened our speed to catch some breath. Here we found thousands of soldiers who had been scattered during their retreat from the right and centre and were trying now to find their comands and organize again. Suddenly Genl. Steadman came dashing along, bareheaded but a flag in his right [hand]. Close behind him Genl. Gordon Granger and nex Pop Thomas. All shouted about the same. "Form in line men! We must chase these dogs from our track. Form on the flag men"! And without a murmur it was done. To the right and left of Steadman the line was quickly formed without regard to Comp. or Regiment. The line contained more than a good sized Division. They marched us a little forward and told us to kneel down and fix bajonet. The sun had gone down behind the mountains and it was getting dark fast. We had not been there more than five minutes when we heard the orders the rebel Oficers gave their men. We heard the rattle of a battery coming forward on a run, and then we saw dimly a line of men advancing. Granger had gone to the right, Baird to the left, Steadman in the center as colorbearer a foot. Thomas behind the center gave the command "Charge"! and "Hurrah"! we went. Not three rods we were from the rebs. Those who had a bullet in the rifle gave it to them. The surprise was so complete that they not even fired their guns at us but immediately turned and run. Good many prisoners fell in our hands, four cannon and two caissons; the cannon were quickly turned round and fired after the grayhounds. That were the last shots fired on the famous battlefield of Chickamauga. They left us entirely alone for that night. A short mile further we reached the road and the men directed to look for their respective Commands, an hours stop would be made for that purpose.

This charge, in the night allmost, was a good lesson for the rebs. It explained to them the old proverb: "A wounded game is still able to bite or kick." General Thomas for his heroic defense against overwhelming numbers received the honorable title: "The Rock of Chickamauga." and his Corps the 14th was given the Acorn as a corps badge, a symbol of endurance and heroism.—

THE BATTLE OF CHICKAMAUGA, GEORGIA

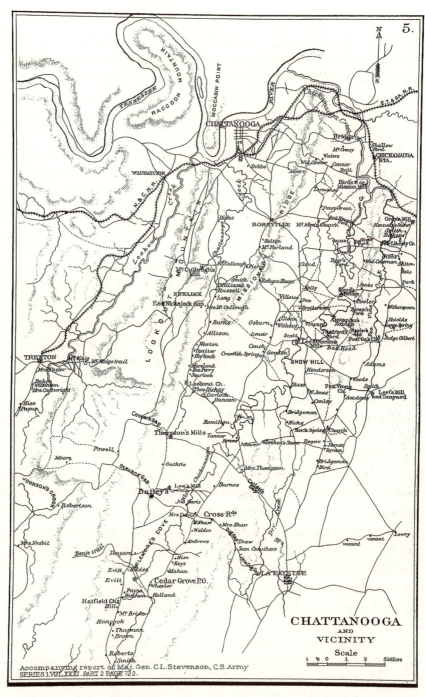

"Chattanooga and Vicinity." From George B. Davis, *Atlas to Accompany the Official Records of the Union and Confederate Armies* (Washington, D.C.: Government Printing Office, 1891–95), plate 50, no. 5. (Courtesy Wisconsin Historical Society)

CHAPTER TWELVE

~

Chattanooga:
Battles of Lookout Mountain
and Missionary Ridge

~ Our brigade was pretty well together [y]et, that is, what was left of it; consequently we had no hunting or organizing to do. John Buboltz told me he was going for water and asked for my Canteen. We were at the foot of the Mountains and Wood plenty so we built fires as the air was getting chilley. It had been a day of unusual exitement and exertion. Now when the overtaxed nerves and muscles had a chance to relax, when we felt somewhat at ease, we became aware how tired, how hungry, how thirsty, in short, how dead broke we were. After ten minutes three fourth of the men were fast asleep. I did not like to sleep, because, as we had to march soon I would only feel the worse for it. To keep awake I kept walking up and down. A cluster of rebel prisoners came and stopped at our fire. I did not see a special guard to watch them as usually was done and watched them closely in order to observe if they had a mind to sneak off which they easily might have done as we were so near the woods and mountains, but they seemed to be glad to be allowed to warm themselves. . . .

The Order to march soon came. . . . The road wound through the narrow defiles of the craggie hills. After a stretch of perhaps three miles we entered an extensive cornfield enclosed all round by mountains. The corn stalks were still standing tall and upright. Between the rows our lines were drawn up. We staked arms and were informed we might make coffee. The dry stalks furnished exellent material for that purpose and we began at once. John Buboltz and I had three crakers between us two and while munching them I thought I heard the bass voice of General Starkweather a little to the right of me. I had not seen him since the beginning of our retreat and as his wound would not allow of much walking, or riding either, I thought he probably had found an ambulance to come along in. I went over in that direction and surely there he sat nursing his ancle, two sticks laying aside of him by the help of which he had traveled along. I asked him if a cup of coffee was welcome—"Wellcome?" he replied. "Why! after such a day allmost any thing is wellcome." And he managed to do away with two of them. I asked him why he had not sent for an Ambulance. He replied that Bill Wall had gone for one. His leg and foot was very much inflamed and swollen. This midnight repast was the first one since the night before.

After an other three mile stretch we arrived at Rossville gap a little after daylight monday morning. This gap leads through the main part of Missionary ridge into the extensive plain which surrounds Chattanooga on the southeast of the Tennessee. We halted in the gap and the men immediately laid down behind the arms to catch a little sleep if allowed to. At 10. A.M. crakers, coffee, bacon and sugar as also ammunition, was issued. After dinner we were marched, or rather climbed, up on the ridge to right and left of the gap and again formed in line of battle. The batteries and cassons had to be houled up by hand as the ridge was to[o] steep for horse or mule to ascent. About two hour before sunset the rebels began to feel for us with their batteries throwing a number of shells and some cannisters. They wanted to know whether we were there or not. Of the cannisters but few reached us as the distance was to[o] great. As our batteries did not reply they came nearer and then here and there a stray ball would loose its way among our ranks.

And so it happened that I was to be a victim of their pranks. Before we climbed up on the ridge I was ordered by Major Walker (commdg. Regt. since Col. Hobart was taken prisoner) to take command of Comp. "A" together with my own Comp. Lieut. Edwards in Command of that Comp. had not been seen since the beginning of our retreat and was supposed to have been taken prisoner. But we were mistaken; The day we came into Chattanooga he turned up. . . . I put that Comp. on the left of my Comp. and as we were ordered to lay down I lay in the midle between the two Comps. A stray Cannister bullet, an inch and a quarter in diameter struck the ground in front of me, ploughed through the ground nearly the lenght of my body, rubbing severely against the inside of the right knee, then tearing of[f] the sole of one shoe, not wounding but hurting the foot considerable by the force. The bullet stopped just in front of a men of Comp. "A." who laid behind me. I had at the moment no time to look after damages as I was busy scratching the dirt out of Eyes and neck, the missile in striking the ground had covered me very liberally with the same. The fellow in my rear hollered: "Be the powers Leftenant! And I'll be blasted if yer shoe is'nt knocked in'ter smethereens. And here is the critter as did the same; a good keepsake." "Let me have it" I said, "I will take care of it." It was only after much persuasion that I got hold of it. I still keep it as a relic and in thankfull acknowledment of its friendly intention. By investigation I found that on the knee I bore a three inch long blue mark of honor which felt a[s] if burnt by steam or hot ashes. The foot showed no signs of being hurt but soon began to swell and causing much pain. The knee also began to swell and become stiff.

As our batteries did not deem it worth while to reply to the rebels challenge, and Bragg probably did not think it profitable to create a rumpus during the night, we were informed towards 11. P.M. that we were to fall back towards Chattanooga. We were cautioned not to make any noise, were not even alowed to speak above a whisper. The batterie wheels were muffled with blankets and carefully brought down. As our Division was again assigned the honorable post of covering the retreat we were the last ones to leave and consequently did not start untill daylight the next morning. It was about four miles from the gap to the works at Chattanooga. I had made a couple of sticks to serve as substitute for my homesick leg but soon found I could not keep up. I halted and awaited the arrival of a batterie when a pitying cannonier helped me onto the limbers of a gun. So I rode proudly in the coveted fortifications of Chattanooga.

No sooner had we arrived there and staked arms than the men were armed with spades shovels and pickaxes to strenghten the old, and add new breastworks and forts to those already there. While the boys are thus employed let us see what losses we had sustained. My Comp. was very lucky in so far there were none killed. The following were wounded:

1. John [Shockley], shot through left hand.
2. Charles. Buck, wounded in head.
3. Michael Hammond, shot in back while retreating.
4. Charles Herb, shot through the mouth knocking out teeth in upper jaw, also shot through leg below knee and taken prisoner.
5. Sanford Rexford, stabbed through arm with bajonet.
6. Sergt. Sylvester Greeley, bajonet wound in t[h]igh.
7. Miles Hoskins, bullet wound in left leg.
*8. McKend[ry] Rawson, shot through ankle.[1]

CHATTANOOGA

*Thus were out of a total of 40. men also one out of five. The following are those who thought it better to follow Col. Hobart than me and were taken prisoner:

1. Orderly Sergeant Egbert J. Scott.
2. Sergt. Curtis Mitchel[1].
3. Corporal Mead H. Seaman.
4. Private Henry Knowles.
5.   "   Samuel Turney.
6.   "   Eleanor Gilbert. (took the coffeepot of my mess with him)
7.   "   Charles Herb.
8.   "   Alfred Abbott.
9.   "   Almiran Kling.[2]

Of those the following starved in the prison pens of the south

1. Ordly. Sergt. E. J Scott, on Belle Iland Virginia.
2. Corp. M. H. Seaman. in Andersonville, Ga.
3. Priv. Henry Knowles.   "   "   "
4.   "   Saml. Turney.   "   "   "
5.   "   Alfred Abbot.   "   "   "[3]

Accordingly the number of men lost in the Comp. out of 40. was 16. Certainly a big figure, two out of five but there were Comps. and Regts. whose loss was even more. The loss in the Regt. is as follows: Killed: 29. wounded: 107. taken prisoner: 1. Col. 15. line Officers, 75. enlisted men. missing: 3. total 230. That number was lost out of about 400. men leaving about 170 men for duty in the Regt. A regt. can not stand many such knocks even if its numbers are complete to 1000. men. . . . [4]

Towards evening the Regt. was ordered to fall in. It was a pitifull sight to see that little group assemble. So many familiar faces were missing; there was hardly a mess which was not broken up. But old Charles Buchholz, who was such an expert in getting up premonitions was still alive and kicking. In spite of his short clumsy legs he had managed to outrun the rebs when we retreated from the battlefield. After it had been assertained how many were missing a little example of military discipline was enacted. Sergeant Murphy of Comp. "C." was the Color bearer the first day of the battle.[5] When we run so suddenly on the rebels and received that volley, he dropped the flag and run back but came back again during afternoon. Major Walker, who

now commanded the Regt. called him before the front, faced him about so
as to face the Regt. and then told him that, as he heretofore always had been
a good soldier, he would not bring him before a court martial which, according the articles of war, would certainly sentence him to be shot to death, and
that the least he could do was to reduce him to the ranks. Two Corporals
then were ordered to tear of[f] the Sergeants cheverons from his sleeves of
his blouse and he ordered to step back in the ranks. Murphy cried bitterly,
but he had to be thankful to Major Walker, for, if he had been brought
before a court martial his life would have been forfeited. We all pitied him
because, he always had been a brave, fine fellow, never had shown any signs
of fear or cowardice and it was plain he was overcome with a sudden fear
which he was unable to control.

One of the man of the Comp. who was reported as deserter reported to
me for duty. It was Chas. H. Warner. He had been taken prisoner by Wheelers Cavallery the first day of the battle at Stone River Dec. 31st 1862. He
was paroled by the rebs and sent to parole Camp at Dennison Ohio. There
he applied for leave of absence which was granted with the ins[t]ruction to
report every forthnight by letter, giving his Post office address so that in
case of his ex[c]hange they could notify him of it and he had to return to
the Comp. He went home and reported regularly as directed. He was
ex[c]hanged in April 1863. but they failed to notify him of the fact so he
remained at home. In July 1863. he was dropped from the Comp. rolls as a
deserter by order of Genl. Rosecrans. So in due time he was arrested by the
Provost marshal with a lot of others and sent under guard to Stevenson
Alabama where they were put in a big bull pen for the night. But Warner
did not want to return to the Comp. under guard, as he did not consider
himself a deserter. So he scaled a ten foot bord fence, and eluding the sentinels made the fifty miles to Chattanooga afoot alone. He wanted his case
investigated before he was ordered before a court martial. So we went to
Brigade headquarters from where we were sent to Div. headquarters and
from there to Genl. Thomas headquarters. He everywhere told a straight
story and as I was in honor bound to give him a good testimony as to his
behavior previous to his capture, Genl. Thomas annulled the charges against
him and without any fine or punishment was restored to duty again. He
had been absent 9 months.

It was quite a different thing with our friend Sergt. John Dey. The Provost Marchal had got hold of him also and three days after Charles Warner
he was brought in under guard. . . . The following morning I went with him
to Regiments headquarters but neither Capt. Turner nor Major Walker

could give or promise him any relief or hope. A week after a court martial sentenced him to the loss of pay and emoluments for the time of his absence and three month of loss of pay extra, to be reduced to the ranks and to make good his time lost.

The day after sentence was passed Sergeant John Dey was led before the front of the Regt. He had brought with him a new Uniform and regulation Cap. The chevrons or sergeants stripes on the sleeves of his blouse were of extra fine quality. He looked splendid in the new outfit. But when he stood in front of the Regt. facing the men, and the sergeant Major had read charges and sentence, and Major Walker had explained to him in plain but telling language how he had skirked his duty when the other boys were fighting and die[i]ng and bearing the hardships of warfare, and the corporals tore the chevrons off from the sleeves of his blouse and threw them into the dust, he broke down and wept like a child.—[6]

All is well that ends well. John Dey became a new man and good soldier. He did his duty promptly and well. But it seemed he had become a misanthroph. He kept alone. He never would join in the sports and frolics of the other men. Whenever he could spare a moment he would take his pocket bible and seek consolation in perusing the same. Whether he thought himself wronged I do not know; he never said a word about it. To encourge him I made him Corporal on Cristmass Eve and intended to give him a Sergeants Commission the next sommer but it should not be. During the siege of Atlanta the following year he was shot through the t[h]igh and that ended his military career. . . .

A few days after our arival Bragg had completed the enclosure, or rather ¾ enclosure. He did not dare to attack us as he knew to[o] well he never would have got us out of the works by direct asault and only would butcher off his men needlessly. He concluded to obtain by starvation what fighting would not give him. His line stretched in a big ¾ circle from the Tennessee on the east along the crest of Missionary ridge and Lookout Mountain to the river on the north, a line of perhaps eight miles in lenght. The lofty position his army occupied enabled them to see and watch everything we did below in the open plain. Although not completely surrounded, Bragg had control of our line of supply. The railroad as well as the wagon road to Bridgeport and Stevenson Alabama, where our supplies were stored run along the left bank of the river and close to Lookout Mountain and adjoining hills and valleys, consequently no cars, or wagons, or boats could pass without being captured or destroyed by the rebels. True, we had an other road left open to Bridgeport but that led in a round about way over the Wausaka mountains and was 75. miles to Bridgeport, whereas the river route was only 45. to 50 miles and mostly on level ground. But there was no choice; the mountain route had to be taken. We had hardly for two weeks supplies when we reached Chattanooga and the first thing done was to put the army on half rations. The feed suply for horses and mules was nearly exhausted and the teams which were sent after supplies could take no feed along on the road. They were to find feed along the road. But the barren mountains did not furnish any eatables, either for man or beast and the small valleys between had been stripped of everything a month before. Consequently the poor beasts who were nearly half starved when they started fell by the thousands on the road. Not a fifth of them who started on the trip ever returned. Charles Warner who was one of the lucky ones who returned with his team said there was hardly a rod of ground alongside the road which was not covered with the carcass of a dead mule, which filled the air with a deadly stench. The reports give the losses of mules on this road alone near ten thousand.

I must relate here an occurrence which illustrates the brutal and barbarous inclination of some of the rebel Officers and men. When we retreated from the battlefield we had to leave thousands of wounded men which we could not take along for want of transportation. It is customary in warfare among civilyzed nations to treat the wounded, whether friend or foe, alike. A helpless enemy is no longer an enemy, but simply a man who needs assistance. We always acted on that principle in Europe, we were so instructed here and always acted on that principle. But what did Bragg do? Here it is: The day succeeding our arrival in Chattanooga Rosecrans sent an Officer under flag of truce to Genl. Bragg requesting permission to bury our dead and bring in the wounded, but Bragg flatly refused. Only the third day he gave permission to look after the wounded but would not allow us to bury the dead.

It is sickening to think what these poor men must have suffered during these four days and nights on that lonely battlefield without shelter or shade in the burning sun, without water, without food, without any assistance whatever. The men who were sent out to bring in the wounded were unable to describe the horrible scenes they had met there. The dead were all stripped, even most of the wounded were robbed of their blankets, blouses, hats or caps. More than half of the wounded had sucumbed to wound feavers and blood poisening. Most all of theese man might have been saved but for that inhuman monster Bragg. Those still living were nearly all unable to speak; their parched and swollen tongues as to nearly filling the cavity of the mouth, many delirious and dying; others seemingly dead only the slow heaving of the breast indicating a glimmer of life. The dead bodies swollen to an unnatura[l] size, emitting allready an unbearable odor; thousands of flies and beetles swarming and crawling about them; Vulturs and carion crows circling in the air uttering ever and anon their dismal "Chaw, caw; craff, craf," waiting for a chance to sit down to their loathsome repast; and over all, for miles and miles in extent, that horrible, sickening stench which cannot be described. This barbarous act forever brands Bragg as a hellborn fiend in human disquise. . . . [7]

Our sojourn at Chattanooga prooved to be the trying ordeal of our heroic little army. It was in fact our babylonic Captivity with the fasting thrown in as amusement. A few days after we had been put on half rations the allowance was further reduced to a third, and finally to a quarter which alowed one craker for a meal. And the duty was very exhausting. Besides the heavy picket duties the work on forts, casemattes, breastworks etc. went on by day and night. Three extensive forts were built: Rosecrans, Wood and Negl[ey]. A bridge was built across the river as also half a dozen scows for ferry purposes. All had to work which called for increase rather than decrease of rations. Consequently a good many got sick and got thin, and emeciated and looked like walking specters.

It can not be immagined to what desperate means man will resort to satisfy the craving hunger. They would go to the places where the rebs had butchered weeks and months before and dig up the rotten heads and legs the rebs had thrown away, scrape of[f] the thousands of maggots they were covered with, wash them in the river, boil and eat the nasty, stinky stuf and call it: "stewed beef," they swallowed the stinky brine with great gusto and seeming relish and call it: "Professor Liebig's improoved meat extract and beef tea." They would hunt the horse and mule stands, turn over every bit of accumulated dropping and dirt for some stray corncob which perhaps might hide a few Kerrnels of corn the mules had missed to find, which kernels were also washed, parched and eaten. They dug in the mud for clams and crabs and mudturtles and whenever one of the latter was caught the lucky captor thought himself richer than Croesus. And it was not untill the 12th of November that hope of more hardtack, no matter how wormy, was dawning. Seven week[s] had we endured this hell and had well nigh come to the conclusion that it would end in starvation. . . . [8]

The first of my Comp. who succumbed were Ephriam Walker and August [Pierrelee]. Both tried hard to hold out untill finally they were hardly able to rise up from the blanket. Walker was bloated and swollen as if in

the last stage of dropsy, whereas [Pierrelee] looked like a mere skeleton.
Then they were lifted into a wagon and sent to Bridgeport by the mountain road. From there they could take the train and go home provided they
could stand it. They both had a sick leave but I never believed they would
reach home alive. I tried to persuade the Doctor to sent them to some
hospital but he replied curtly: "What is the use? both of them will die
anyway." Before they were put into the wagon I told both of them that, as
soon as they had recovered a little at home, to report to the military hospital at Madison and get a discharge and stay at home afterward. But they
did not. The following Febr. they both returned seemingly all right. Next
summer [Pierrelee] was shot in the leg, sent to hospital in Murfreesboro
and discharged. Eph Walker kept with us to the close of the war, but completely broken down. He died shortly afterward at home surrounded by his
wife and children.

It is revolting to know and to consider that the greater part of this misery was the result of the ambition, the jealousy and unrelenting hate of one
man. That man was Maj. General Hall[e]ck, then the Commander in Chief
of all the Armies of the United States, subject only to the President and in
some cases to the Secretaire of War. . . . We will see how he managed that.

After the battle of Stone river Rosecrans undertook to reorganize his
little army and bring it in such shape that the coming Chattanooga campain should be a sure success. But whatever he undertook to improove was
sure to find opposition in Washington. He wanted to organize an effective
Cavallerie Corps, or at least a Division to check the well organized rebel Cavallerie which did us more damage than all Braggs Infantry could do; but
no. He was informed he had to get along with the few Regiments he had.
He asked for recruits to fill up the thinned ranks of the Regiments, but to
no purpose. Genl. Halleck eased his mind by saying that Genl. Burnside
with a strong Army was on the way to Knoxville to capture that place and
from there was to march for his support. But Burnside had only 7. to 8000
men and thus he needed all to keep and defend Knoxville. When Rosecrans
called Hallecks attention to that fact and again asked for reinforcements he
was coolly informed that no troops could be spared anywhere. Such an
infernal lie. Why could the troops be spared three weeks afterward when
we had sacrificed a third of our army? Then four Corps were sent and not
missed anywhere. That were more troops than our army numbered the first
day of the battle. If they had sent us one Corps in time we had played ball
with the rebels and would not have lost so many men. . . . After the battle
of Gettysburg the Army of the Potomac lay idle at the Rappah[a]nnok,

waiting to see what Lee would get up next. Could not an Army Corps have been spared there? The rebels could spare Longstreets Corps to fight us at Chicamuaga. The Army of the Tennessee, 13th 15th 16th and 17 Army Corps after the surrender of Vicksburg July 4th 1863. lay nearly idle in the vicinity of Vicksburg and Memphys. Could not a Corps have been spared there? But after the child was drowned, Halleck was in a hurry to cover the Well. He found all at once that the 11th and 12th Corps of the Army of the Potomac, and the 15th and 17th Corps of the Army of the Tennessee could be spared without detriment to the service. And they stood with us to the end of the war. Could they not have been sent three weeks earlier when Rosecrans needed them so badly? But Hallecks plan was well calculated and we will now see how he managed to escape the responsibility.

As soon as the result of the battle and the retreat of Rosecrans to Chattanooga became known in the North, all the Copperhead papers began a tremenduous howl about the loss of a great battle, the cutting to pieces of a splendid Army, of the loss of Chattanooga, and that the whole campain had been useless; (The reader must remember that we never before had occupied Chattanooga, that we started from Murfreesboro to get that place, and did get it and kept it, to[o].) and that Bragg now would swoop down through Tennessee and Kentucky and take Louisville and Cincinnaty and sweap over Ohio and Indiana and God only knows where he would stop. And all on account of an inefficient upstart of a commander; General Rosecrans. They said the war was a failure and should be stopped immediately. If some well informed men undertook to explain the reason of our retreat to Chattanooga the[y] were set down as falsifiers and liars. Genl. Rosecrans report and assurance that Chattanooga was safe, was called a fabrication of falsehoods. They knew better than he. He ought to have handled his troops in a different way; he did not know how to treat his Generals, etc. They finally trumped up a charge which ex[ce]eded in fiendishness anything heard [y]et. They charged Rosecrans with being a confirmed, exessive Opium eater and that he had been so overcome by its effects on the second day of the battle as to be compelled to leave the battlefield like a drunken sod. . . . They loudley called on Lincoln, Stanton and Halleck to dismiss him from Service.

That was what Halleck wanted, what he had been looking for. Now was the time to speed the bolt. And he did not wait long. Under the excuse the people demanded it, Rosecrans was relieved from the command of the army of the Cumberland Oct. 20th 1863. (Genl. Geo. H. Thomas to succeed.)[9] and ordered to take charge of the Dept. of the Missoury where he did exellent service in spite of all the Opium in the Universe. Halleck also had a severe grudge against Grant and Sherman, but as both, on account of their successfull campain against Vicksburg were very popular just then he did not dare to touch them just now. Grant escaped his clutches but how he tried to give Sherman a parting kick I will relate in proper time. It is thus Halleck succeeded not only in disgracing Rosecrans, but also in nearly destroying the Army of the Cumberland and sacrificing the results of a half years hard Campaign.

Just inside our picket line and near Rossville Gap stood a large and fine brick mansion. As it stood in the way of our batteries in raking the gap it was concluded to level it to the ground. It happened I was with the Comp. on picket there when that was to be done. We were informed when the racket was to begin, in order to keep at a safe distance. As it was before the time given we concluded to asscertain what the house might contain. The people being good secesh, probably had left the house in a hurry and left some articles which might be welcome to a hungry soldier. We busted a door and the first thing we met was a big lean black tomcat bounding past us towards the opening, evidently glad to regain liberty. We were glad to find the people had left everything behind. Costly furniture, fine bedding and wearing apparel; but that was nothing to us. But that larder and cellar were well provided with an abundance of choice articles which gladden the inner man and set our pulses beating. This fact was more pleasing to us at the moment than any amount of Uncle Sams greenbacks could have been. Lots of cured hams and shoulders and bacon, a barrel of rice, a dozend bags of cornmeal, several barrels of dried aples, hominy and flour, about twenty bushels of sweet potatoes, 50 cans of condensed milk, a barrel of corned beef and a good lot of dried beef and numerous small articles, as allso a cask of peach brandy were stored in the celler or basement. We lost no time in removing these articles to a safe distance and then investigated for other articles. We found silver table services which were distributed. There were allso costly pictures and a well selected library, but we had no use for them; besides time was nearly up and we had to hustle to get out of the way unless we might get hoisted or scattered by the artillery. Twenty minutes later the fine structure was a heap of ruins. In consequence of thus god send, there were a few happy days for the boys of the regt. and we regretted very much there were no more buildings in the way of the Artillery.

My former cook "Doc Gilbert" had unwittingly played me a shabby trick. When we retreated from the battlefield of Chicamauga he was among them that stuk to the Colonel and consequently was gobled up by the rebs.

As he allways had the coffeepot with him that shared the same fate. . . . Since Doc Gilbert had granted himself "Absence without leave" I promoted John Buboltz to the dignified and responsible office as chief cook for our mess, Fred B[o]rcherdt, myself and John and I must do him the Justice to state that he was not alone the best cook in the Regt. but allso the washwoman and the best fourager. He filled this responsible and most difficult situation to our entire satisfaction until the close of the war.

When we arrived in Chattanooga our Comp. wagon drove up soon and I took of[f] my little desk and Mess chest. On opening the latter I found that the beef which Gilbert had hastily put in it without salt when we had so suddenly to start on that famous night march before the battle, I found millions of maggots crawling over everything and a perfume arose which drove the boys allmost out of camp. . . .

On the 25th of Sept. Fred B[o]rcherdt, now the Adjutant of the Regt. handed me an Order from Maj. Walker commanding the Regt. that I was to take charge of Comp. "C." in addition to my Comp. Now it seemed to me Major Walker was stretching his authority a little to[o] far. Such duties are allways given to older, or ranking Officers. I was the oldest 2d Lieut. in the Regt. but there were 4. Capt. present in the Regt. [y]et who certainly ought to have been appointed to that honor, or rather trouble, for that was all it meant. Besides Comp. C had a second Lieut. Julius P. Bissell [Bissel] who was in command of that Comp and had been all summer.[10] But he was not fit to take care of a Corporals guard much less a Comp. His men made a fool of him and did not mind his orders, neither did he know to enforce them. Besides he was not able to keep the Comps. books and accounts in order, nor to make out the payrolls and monthly returns to the Quartermasters and Ordnance Department at Washington. And by all that he was a conceited coxcomb who thought himself a "big Injun." It was true that Comp. "C." contained more "Toughs" than any Comp. in the Regt. They had to a great extent been recruited out of the lumber camps in the region of the Shioc, Embarras and Wolf rivers and considered themselves entitled to more liberties than other mortals. Their first Capt. Godfrey, himself a lumberman, had done nothing to correct or supress this notion and consequently the men thought they were right. But for all that, as far as fighting is concerned, they were not behind any in the Regt. But I did not fency to bother with them if I could possible escape it. So I went to Major Walker and had a talk with him. But he overruled all I said and even throwing in a little flattery saying he knew no Comp. Officer in the Regt. who got along with the men as smooth as I. That seemed a clumsy bait to me and I told him so. But he only laughed and said I should go and take the Comp. "And have I to keep the books and accounts etc?" I inquired. "Certainly" he said. "Lieut. Bissel will shortly start for home." Now I understood. They were going to order Lieut. Bissel to resign for the good of the service and sent him home. So I took an Inventar [inventory] of the Government property in the Comp. ex[c]hanged Invoices and receipts with the Lieut. who shortly after was dismissed and went home. . . . When 6 months later I was ordered to turn over Comp. "C." to Lieut. Jaeger the men petitioned the Colonel to let them remain with my Comp. but it could not be granted.[11]

The rebs on Missionary ridge annoyed us considerable by throwing shot and shells. The distance was four miles and most of the missiles fell short of the mark, but now and then some came so uncomfortable near as to create a decidedly unsafe feeling. The Nashville, Chattanooga and Atlanta R.R. run along our camp and nearly parrallel with the ridge. The Embankment for nearly ½ mile was from 8 to 12 foot high. Whenever the rebs thought it nescessary to stir us up, we would run for this embankment where we were at least safe against solid shot. While there once someone suggested we might built a sort of bombproof for beast and man against the grade. The Idea was a good one and carried out in a few days. But again a few days later our brigade was moved a mile towards Lookout Mountain. That brought us out of the reach of the guns on Mission ridge but instead of that we came in range of the batteries on Lookout mountain, that is, we jumped from the frying pan into the fire.

In this dilemma Captain Truesdell who commanded a Wisconsin battery came to the rescue.[12] The river at the foot of the mountain makes a sudden bend northward, doubling on itself, forming a long narrow peninsula, describing the form of a mocassin from whence the name Mocassin point. On this point on an elevation or hill, about 150 feet high, the Capt. erected a battery. Everybody thought he would be unable to elevate the guns sufficiently to bring the balls or shells up to the nose of the mountain where the rebel batteries were placed. But his calculation prooved correct. The rebel flagg which waved so proudly from this pe[a]k, came down at the third shot. The rebs tried to get him away [from] there and returned with a terrible cannonade, but they could not depress their guns enough to hit him. After two days trial they gave up the game.

To increase the suffering we endured for want of food came now the scarcity of tobacco. Many may smile who read this and condemn the use of the obnoxious weed as a nasty habit. I will not dispute their opinion, they have a right to that; but I deny that they can be a competent judge in the matter. In the first place good many Doctors advised the use of tobacco as a pr[e]ventive against feevers, or that fearfull disease disentery or flux. Second; I have watched and observed the men who did not tuch tobacco and could never discover they were able to endure more hardships than those who did use it, contrary some were far inferior in that respect. And last but not least; I have many a time soothed the craving pangs of the empty stomach with a pipe of tobacco. Some Doctors insist that tobacco irretates and exites the nerves. That may be true but it never made me a hundreth part so nervous as did the indigestible blue pills of the enemy.

Chewing tobacco was not so scarce as smoking. But as I allways had an aversion for chewing I gained not much by that fact. After considerable speculation to overcome the difficulty I hit upon a novel plan. The chewers were constantly throwing away quids who had passed through the mill. It struck me these disregarded quids might do some service [y]et. On the sly I gathered a few of them, bathed them good in water, dried and tried them and found them superior to fresh cut leaf tobacco. The bitter, oily nicotin having been sqeezed out of it, it had a far sweeter flavor and taste. "Eureka," I said to myself, now I will be soon out of trouble. My smoking comrades soon wanted to know where the dickens I got all that good smoking tobacco as I seldom refused them to fill their pipe. For a while I kept the secret, feeling somewhat delicate about its origin and manufacturing process. But the steady inquiries as well as the bother of preparing so much decided me and I busted the secreet. The manufacture of "Exelsior" as the boys soon called it, devellopped to a fine art. Every smoker would enter in a sort of contract with a chewer or two who would bind themselves to save the finished quids for him. Quid hunting was allso sharply practised. Many a chewer did not suspect, while rolling the plug over his tongue, how keenly he was watched by some smoker waiting patientley for the dropping of the valuable quid.—Now I suspect good many will sniff their noses and call this a vile, nasty and vulgar proceeding, but to all such I most humbly sugest to consider that it was not a whit more vulgar than the eating of rotten, stinky meat and sowbelly, the chewing of hardtack alive with fat, blackheaded maggotts. It was simply making "virtue out of mud." . . .

Since November 1862. the Comp. ration Savings funds had never been distributed or anything expended of it. The commanding Officers of the Comps. had to keep book over such savings and verify the accounts with the Commissary, after which the Colonel approved them as correct. The Comp. Commander could use such money in such a manner as the members of the Comps. might direct. The total amount for Comp. "D" footed up to $310.00. Comp. Cs account was only partley kept up and that in such a bad shape that no payment could be realized on it. Early in November I came on guard at 14th Corps Headquarters guarding Quartermasters and Commissary Stores. Lieut. Wm. Starkweather cousin to Genl. Starkweather asked me if I had any Comp. funds due. I said I had. "Jou better hurry up then" he said, "to morrow is the last day that any such funds will be paid." And he handed me the New York Tribune pointing to an article in the Congressional proceedings which repealed, or annulled the law in regard to the payment of comutation for rations not issued and received, fixing a date when the repeal of said law was to take force. Sure enough, next day was the last and I would not be relieved untill 10. A.M. next day.

On the way to camp next day I met Lieut Fargo commdg Comp. "H."[13] and informed him of the news and in Camp I found only Capts. Weisbrod and Smith of Comps. "E." and "I." whom I allso gave information. Then taking the saving account book I ran to the Commissary to have it verified up to date, then to the Colonl to have it approved. A certain Colonel Paul who belonged to Genl. Thomas staff was the man who paid out such funds. I arrived there at 2. P.M. got the money, went home and distributed the money among the boys. Comp. A men hearing that other Comps. had received their saving funds inquired of their Capt. Edwards if he had not drawn any funds. He replied that he had come to[o] late and was refused payment. The Orderly of the Comp. was not satisfied with the excuse and went to Col. Paul to investigate. He was shown the records which proved that Capt. Edward had drawn the Comps. funds regular every month since he was in command of the Comp. That proved him to be an embezzler and on complaint would have been held to make good the loss to the Comp. being cashired and dishonorable dismissed from the service. The men of the Comp. were for putting him through but he begged so doggishly and promised to refund the money the next two paydays, that they let him alone. . . .

Capt. Steffens had recovered from the murderous assault of the rebel shell at Chickamauga. But it seemed he was no more the same man. Somehow, the Idea had taken hold of him that he certainly would be killed if he remained in the service. A bullet had found its way through one of his legs at Perryville Ky. but that did not disturb his humor. But that piece [of] shell seemed to have squeezed all the courage out of him. I tried my best to argue the Idea out of him, especially because his prospects for promotion were very bright, allmost sure now. Since Capt. Mauf[f] was killed at Chicamauga he was the ranking Capt. in the Regiment. As there was neither Lieut. Col.

nor Major in the Regt. he was sure to have one of the two. But all my talking did not shake his resolution. He sent in his Resignation. As I had expected it was returned "Not approved." No resignations were accepted at this time exept on most urgent grounds, the best of which was: "for the good of the service." like Lieut. J. P. [Bissel]. I could not help but congratulate him on the good sense of Genl. Thomas to order him to stay and accept a promotion. He shook his head and replied. "No, no, I know a way to get out and nobody can stop me." He remained silent and I would not press him any further and went away. I wondered though w[hat] reasons he would put up to make Thomas accept his resignation. A young man with no family, nothing to bother him. The same day he went to town and accidentally met Col. Mihalotzi of his Regt. He passed proudly by the Col. without giving the customary and obligatory Salute. The Col. good naturedly turned round and said: "Hello, Capt! are you dreaming? or have you forgotten your duty as Officer and Soldier to salute a Comrade"? Steffens proudly replied: "I do not salute a horsethief." and went his way.

The insulting reply was no insult as far as Colonel Mihalotzi was concerned. Steffens had told me several times how the Colonel, after the capture of Bowling Green Ky. in Feb. 1862, had send half a dozen valuable, full blooded horses to Chicago and had them sold there for his benefit. Steffens and other Officers in the Regt. knew that and if they had reported the Colonel he would have been cashired. The Col. did not intend to have Steffens punished but went to him expecting Steffens to apologize. But instead of that he insulted the Col. worse than before. So the Col. sent the Adjutant to demand the Capts. Sword and put him under arrest. Ignorant of all this I went to the Capts. tent the next day to have a chat with him. I found him unusually bright and talkative and inquired what had happened. "Why, Dont you know?" he replied. "I am going home soon. I have made an aplication now which will be approoved." I did not understand him looking inquiringly at him. "Dont understand that, He? Well, I dont wonder. Dont you miss anything here?" I looked round and finally saw his swordbelt lying on a little table but saw no sword. "Where is your sword, I inquired"—"The Colonel wanted it." he replied. I began to dawn under my scull and asked: "What for? what have you done"? He explained the whole affair and added triumphantly: "Don't you think that will work? It is not a fine trick? I have told the thruth which nobody dared to and they will send me home."—"Jes" I replied, "cashiered and dishonorable dismissed the service."—"Oh, nonsense," he replied, "they don't know anything about it at home." ... I could not agree with his views and plainly told him so, but that did not disturb him a bit. I went home and did not see him again during his service. Genl. Thomas had let him down very easy. He said in his decision: "That in consideration of his previous good conduct and exellent service, Capt. Steffens was merely dismissed the service."—That was the least punishment Genl. Thomas could give. Perhaps he suspected Steffens motive for his unsoldierly conduct and pittied him.

The unexplainable, if not to say mad conduct of Capt. Steffens is still a mistery to me. Steffens was, so to speak, a born soldier. He had been a soldier since he was 16. years in the belgian army and was Sergeant Major. When his parents, brothers and sisters emigrated to this Country he quitted the service and came with them. A few years later the Rebellion broke out and he intended to go at once but was prevented by his family. A few months after he, while digging a well saw a dozen young men pass by who hailed him and jokingly asked him to come along to Chicago and enlist in the Hecker Regt. He replied he had no money. They offered to pay the fare. He threw aside shovel and pickaxe and in shirtsleeves went to Chicago and enlisted. He was very ambitious and loved military pomp and glory. He often told me that, when the war was over he would take service in the regular army and remain a soldier for life. I encouraged the Idea since, as he had no trade no experience or inclination for agricultural pursuit, he probably would remain a drug [drudge] his life long. He allways was brave, never had shown signs of fear of death. And still that piece of shell had effectually upset, anihilated all former ambition and calculations. After the war I told him that if he had remained in the service he might have been the Colonel of the Regt. he replied: "I know that; that was one reason why I could not stay with you. I was afraid I might turn a coward."[14]

Finally our captivity and resulting hunger cure was to be ended. The twelft of November was the day which is marked in our Almanck, not with a red mark, but with gold star and laurel wreath. At break of day we were surprised by the report of cannon and the faint rattle of small arms some miles down the river north west of Lookout Mountain. We learned soon however that it was Genl. Hooker who had found the way from the Potomac to the upper Tennessee and who was now hammering at the rebel detachements who blockaded the river and the roads near it. It can easily be immagined how ex[c]ited our nearly starved little army was; how anxiously we watched the progress and interruptions of the fight. Slowly it became more and more distinct and, as to inform Genl. Hooker that we were alive and kicking [y]et, Capt. Truesdall on Moccasin point treated the rebs on Lookout with a lively dose of shot and shell.

CHATTANOOGA

At noon all was quiet again, but who can describe our feelings when about two P.M. three river steamers, each with a transport in tow came tooting around Moccasin Point. Instantly the river banks were lined with hungry men, some cheering, others praying, some crying, others dancing, according to inclination or impulse. The rebel batteries on Missionary ridge, who, with the help of fieldglasses could observe everything opened a tremendous fire but they could not hurt us. In our transport of joy we were even willing to accept it as a celebration of our deliverance from starvation. We knew, and perhaps they felt, that their days on missionary Ridge and Lookout would be of short duration. And therefore we stored no grudge against them. Before two hours were gone we drew for five days rations which, as Genl. Thomas order said, had to last at least three days. Pop Thomas meant well and wanted the boys to have their fill, but he had done better to gradually increase the rations, because a good many did not know when the shrunken stomach had enough for digestion and had to pay for their indiscreet indulgence with complaints of the stomach, colics and other bowel complaints. Good many had to be sent to the hospital and not a few died of the consequences. I noticed Maurice Grunert getting up quietly several times during the night consulting the contents of his haversack. His five days rations did not last him three days and I had to come to the rescue as so often before. But he did not get sick. That man had a stomach like an Ostrichs gibbet. Sole leather and tacks would not incommodate him.

Nov. 24th 1863. Genl. Joe Hooker cleared in a few days the hills and valleys on the north west side of Lookout from the rebs and his scirmishers were pushed ahead to the foot of the mountain. Genl. Grant had been appointed Commander of the department of the Mississippi, which comprised the Ohio, Tennessee and Cumberland armies and Departments. He came up himself now to take command of the whole operation. But he waited for the arrival of the troops from the Mississippi under Sherman. On the 22d of November Sherman arrived in Chattanooga and the advance of the 15th and 17th Corps at the same time within two miles of Chattanooga at Browns ferry. Grant made now the following dispositions of the troops in order to compell Bragg to move to safer quarters. Hooker with the 11th and 12th Corps and Osterhaus Division of the 15th Corps was to drive the rebels from Lookout next day then from there cross the spurs of Missionary ridge well to the right and try to envellop the rebel left. Genl. Sherman at the same time with the 15th and 17th Corps and Jeff C. Davis Division of our Corps (in lieu of Osterhaus division which was to assist Hooker) was to march well up the right bank of the river, keeping concealed by the Wauseka mountains, and during the night throw his Corps across the river and try to envellop the Braggs right. Thomas with the old boys of the Cumberland as usual in the centre and facing missionary ridge; McCooks 20th Corps on the right at Rossville gap, the 14th Corps, now commanded by Genl. Palmer in the Centre, Crittendens 21st Corps on the left.

But I am running ahead of the passing events, because before we move to the assault of the ridge, Lookout must first be cleared of the rebels. So, on the morning of Nov. 24th Hooker sent a strong scirmish line, beginning two miles on the northwestern side, thence around the Point along the south eastern side about a mile, troops following in supporting distance. On the northwest side the accent was specially difficult on account of the uneven broken surface. In fact it looks here as if an immense mass of boulders of all shapes and sizes had been thrown together at random out of the middle of which, high up rose a towering wall of solid rock which [seemed] to be ready to tumble down at any moment; the whole up to the wall grown with bryars, wild laurel and small trees. At the point and south eastern side up to the midle hight it was not quite so rough. When the line was in position the ascent began without any resistance on the part of the rebs untill about 30 rods had been passed when they woke up and were soon in good working trim. They could not be coaxed to go back as rocks and trees afforded them abundant shelter from behind which they sent bullet after bullet. As charging was out of the question, because of the many obstacles in the way and the steep incline, our scirmishers were strongly reinforced so as to nearly form a compact line. Slowly, very slowly the rebels fell back defending each rock, every tree with great obstinacy. Men would fight from the opposite sides of the same rock and by strategie try and get the best of each other.

About midway between the foot of the mountain and pallisades or nose, stood a solitary frame building called the "Craven house," which looked from below as if some big bird of the forest had glued his nest against the rocks. It was two O clock when our troops had pushed the Johnnies up to this point. I do not know if the rebs had received reinforcements but here again they absolutely refused to budge an inch. Our brigade had been formed in line at beginning of the scirmish, then staked arms and stood, or sat down and observed the contest with great interest. Now and then a squad of prisoners would come down under guard and passed to Chattanooga. Wounded allso were constantly brought in. At the Point the mountain is 3200 foot high above the Tennessee; deducting the palisade or Nose 150 foot leaves the slope 3050 foot perpendicular hight. Half of that our troops had overcome, but the ascent now became more abrupt, more rocks and caveties.

CHATTANOOGA

Our brigade was now called on and we began to climb up. But we were halted in good supporting distance and told to take shelter for the bullets. Capt. Truesdels battery had not dared to fire up to this time, because they were afraid they might hurt our troops as well as the rebs. But now they opened throwing the shells over our lines and well behind the rebs in order to harras, or disperse the rebel reserve troops if they had any. This lasted for half an hour during which the scirmishfire had nearly ceased; then it stopped. Our line was ordered to try again and they did; some crawling upward while others lay hidden watching every move of the Johnnies in order to get a chance for a fair hit. Shortly before dark several brigades came up to relieve the fighting line, but they declined to be relieved; so the brigades crawled among the others and helped to increase the noise. Colonel Hambright who commanded our brigade, (Genl. Starkweathers leg having become so bad that the surgeon feared it would have to be amputated) waited anxiously for the order to join this front line but, instead of that he received Ordre to bring the brigade down towards the road, which leads from below along the south eastern slope upward and lands on the top about two miles from the point. Here we were to watch that Bragg could not throw any more troops up the mountain during the night. It was dark when we arrived at our destination and set to work at once to prepare Coffee.

The night set in with a clear bright skye and a promise to be very cool allso. The friendly business between Johnnie and yank on the mountain sides was going as lively as ever. We below could no longer distinguish the special features of the mountain, we only saw the huge, unshapely towering dark mass against the starlight skye. But we saw slowly creeping higher and higher along the side and around the point a continuous stream of darting flames like so many fire bugs or shooting stars darting up and down and right and left against the dark background. But between 9 and ten P.M. the skye became covered with clouds which, like a giant vail, envelloped the upper part of the mountain, hiding from our view the only visible sign of the bitter contest. We only could hear now and then the faint rattle of rifles. Some what after two A.M. we thought to hear faintley the usual yankee cheers and "hurrahs" but were not sure of it. The first rays of the sun saw the stars and stripes proudly waving from the point of the mountain and no armed rebel has set foot on it again after that. Over 1000 prisoners, two batteries 200 barrels of cornmeal and a considerable of English ship crakers were the secondary fruit of the victory. This engagement is set down in history as "the battle over the clouds" and justly so, as it certainly closed, or terminated over the clouds. But in other respects is this battle remarkable.

MEMOIRS OF A DUTCH MUDSILL

No battle has been fought in such a manner during the four years strife. Allthough there were about 20,000 men engaged in it, it was done on the scirmish plan from beginning to end. It was hide and seek, but a desperate killing business nevertheless.

Nov. 25th. Lookout Mountain was ours, but the greater task was [y]et in store for us. Missionary ridge with two heavy, well constructed lines of breastworks, one nearly at the foot of the ridge, the other on the crest with a hundred cannon and defended by 60,000 veterans was still proud and defiant.[15] Genl. Sherman had succeeded in crossing the river during the night and at nine A.M. was allready fighting among the hills on Braggs right and rear. Genl. Hooker early in the morning had started with his two Corps and marched through the gaps between the spurs of Missionary ridge in order to get around Braggs left and cut off his retreat from Ringold, or rather through Ringold Gap. Towards noon the army of the Cumberland to escape the fire from the enemies batteries on the ridge, pressed close up to the foot of the ridge under cover of the woods along and in front of the ridge. McCooks 20th Corps on the right at Rossville Gap; on the left of him and forming the center the 14th Corps and to the left of that Crittende[n]s 21st Corps. Gens. Grant[,] Thomas and staff were on Orchard Knob, a lone, conical high hil, rising out of the plane near the left centre of our line.

It was two P.M. and still we were laying quiet, no orders to move. Grant was waiting for Sherman and Hooker to work well around. Finally, at 3. P.M. we received Orders to charge the first line of works at the base of the hill. It was the reverse from Chicamauga; there the Johnnies did all the charging and we did the repulsing business. We were calculating if the Johnnies would defend their works as stubbornly as we did our single logs at Chicamauga. We were ordered to fix bajonet at once and not fire a shot untill we were close up to their works. In case the works were taken at the first assault we were not to follow the rebs but to stay in the works. Now we heard the report of a single gun from Orchard Knob. That was the signal to advance and orders were given accordingly. We advanced in common route step. The rebs kept their fire well. They intended to be sure and have us near enough in order to hit their man. We were not more than thirty yards away when bugles called for the charge. The usual "hurrah" deafened by the volley from behind the rebel works and a quarter of a minute later we were at their works. Some of our boys fired over their works but most of our men clambered right up and fired in the faces of the rebels. And then the stabbing and clubbing began, but for only a very short time, they did not want to measure their skill with us but turned and clambered up the ridge. Some shots were fired after them and then we sat down behind their works.

It seemed the rebs had not learned anything from us at Chickamauga. We allways opened fire at eighty, or at least sixty yards and fired usually twice before they began to charge. But we allways took care to have a pill for them when they came to[o] close to be comfortable. Their volley had done less damage as was to be expected. I had but three slightly wounded in the Comp. Capt. Weisbrod only four. But there was some chance luck in the matter. Weisbrod and my Comp. were in a slight depression of the ground the moment the rebs fired and that saved us from many a scratch. Other Companies had not escaped so easy. . . .

When the retreating Johnnies had reached their breastworks on the ridge the rebs oppened with some of their batteries and threw a perfect storm of shels over us. Allthough they could not depress their guns sufficient to hit our lines directly the scattering pieces of exploded shells hurt some here and there. The men all preferred to storm the ridge immediately than to lay here and be killed off just for the sake of show. Perhaps Grant knew that Hooker or Sherman had not reached their destination [y]et. We had lain under that fire half an hour when all at a suden and without any order or command from the Genl. the long line of men started up hill. We could not advance very fast on account of the steep incline. In most places the brush was used as a means to draw up the body. When we had made three quarters of the distance a halt of about five minutes was made to gather breath. The rebs had changed for cannisters now and all their guns were working with a will. When we started again the rebel Infantry allso began to fire. It was a deafening tumult and roar. The whole crest of the hill miles to right and left was a dense colum of smoke. The very ridge trembled and the air vibrated. That were trying minutes for the Clambering men. But they went steady upward. The nearer we came the less dangerous the cannister were, and their Infantry did not take time to aim at a man. That was a good thing for us else good many more would have bit the dust. The dense smoke was allso a god send to us, becase the rebs could not see us untill we were up to the works. And the rear line quickly lifted the front line up the works and they fired their rifles right into the faces of the rebels, the rear line followed immediately and repeating the same. Then with bajonet ahead a short hand to hand tussle began during which many comic taunts and sneers were thrown in gratis. "Here is your Chickamauga! Here is your hardtack! When are you going to Nashville? He hip! for Longstreet! Dont stop this side of Atlanta! Give old Braggard our compliments" etc.

Exept many who thought it a good chance to stay with us they soon took to their heels and run for dear life. Half their batteries were captured and quickly turned on the flying mass.

We intended to follow the rebs but were ordered to remain. The ridge at the other side decends very gradually and is well cultivated. Genl. Bragg had never dreamt that we would undertake to storm the ridge, much less that we would [b]e able to carry it. His headquarters were in a house of a well to do widow whose house could be plainly seen from Chattanooga.[16] When we took the first, or lower line of the rebel works the widow had asked Genl Bragg if it would be safe to stay there any longer. "Be at ease Madame," Bragg had replied, "There are not Yankees enough in Amerika to take thuse works." This unconditional confidence in the bravery of his men and the supposed feebleness and want of confidence of the Yanks in themselves probably was the reason that we captured his entire headquarter outfit and he himself barely escaped capture. The yankees were inside the works and the Johnnies allready running when he escaped through the back door, stradled a horse and dashed back.[17] It was looky for him that none of the men had loaded, or had a breachloading rifle or the Confederacy would have been relieved of that inhumane Monster.

The immense amount of plunder captured must have been a serious loss to the rebels. 44. cannon with limbers and caissons; hundreds of wagons loaded with provisions, ammunition, feed for horses and mules, Clothing and shoes etc. thousands of small arms and many mules and horses, for all of which we were duly thankfull in proportion as the long continued cheers and "hurrahs" testified. The boys indulged freeley in dancing and singing and no wonder. It was a big step, allmost incomprehensible; from starvation and despair to a decisive crushing victory. It was all so sudden, so unexspected, so grand, that at first it semed allmost a delusion, a dream. The army of the Cumberland had effectually quieted and wiped out the slandering remarks and abusive languadge of northern Copperheads and their papers. The stubborn bravery they had displayed at Chickamauga against an overwhelming majority was still there and unsullied.

I remarked that our men moved onto the rebel works on the ridge with out waiting for orders. That semed to be a fact because Genl. Grant was very indignant when he saw the lines had nearly reached the crest and inquired of Genl. Thomas who had ordered the lines to advance. Thomas replied he did not know, he had not. Inquieries were made by Corps and Division Commanders but not one had given the order. It is said that Grant distrusted the Cumberland Army and doubted their ability to carry the rebel works.[18] If he had mistrusted them he certainly was cured now of the doubt because in an order which was read to us the following day he complimented us highly for the bravery in scaling the enemyes works and routing the enemy.

Genl. Bragg had but one road on which to gather and retreat his scattered forces; the road leading through Ringold gap. The gap is about 13 miles south of Mission Ridge. Genl. Hooker, as stated before had been sent around Braggs left to seize the Gap and cut of[f] Braggs retreat but on account of bridges burnt he did not reach there in time to prevent their escape. Hooker nevertheless had a spirited fight with them at dusk time for half an hour during which several batteries and a considerable number of prisoners were taken.

The loss in our Regt. was light. 3 killed and 47. wounded. My Comp. 5. wounded of which but one went to the hospital. The total loss in the whole army during Nov. 24–25th is as follows:

Union killed:	757.	Confederate killed:	361.
Union wounded	4529.	Confederate wounded.	2181.
Union Missing	330	Confederate prisoners	6142.
total	5616	total:	8684.

I must remark here that the rebel losses have never been learned. The number given here as killed are those we burried; allso the wounded we found and took care of. It is safe to say that their losses aggr[e]gate a 1,000 more including those they lost in the fight with Hooker at Ringold gap. . . . [19]

The 14th Army Corps. was again put in Camp in the vicinity of Chattanooga. The 11th and 12th Corps, beeing both small in number, were consolidated and henceforth known as the 20th Corps. The old 20th and 21st Corps were allso consolidated and formed now the fourth Corps. The camping ground of these two Corps was south of Mission Ridge to the right and left of the Atlanta railroad. Bragg had withdrawn to Tunnel Hill 8 miles south of Ringold Gap, where he reorganized his scattered forces. But he met the same fate as Rosecrans only he had deserved it. Perryville, Stone river, Tullahoma and Missionary ridge had gone against him and the loss of Chattanooga was a loss to the Confederacy which never could be regained nor repaired. Allthough a favorite of Jeff Davis the rebell Congress forced Jeff Davis to dismiss him and appointed Genl. Joe E. Johnston as his successor. The obstinate Jeff had to give in but to spite the rebel Congress he called Bragg to Richmond and appointed him Commander in Chief of all the rebel forces exept Genl. Lees army in Virginia. . . . [20]

The politicians at Washington had concocted and partley succeeded in hatching out a plan which, if carried through, would have seriously crippled the army. It was nothing less than an order from the Secretaire of War (How the sagacious and obstinate Mr. Stanton could fall into such a trap and issue such an order remains a mistery) that all Regts. and Comp. below the minimum number should be consolidated to the maximum number, and if there were any more commissioned or non Commissioned Officers as such consolidated Comps. or Regts. required, the former should be mustered out and the lat[t]er reduced to the ranks. To explain: the minimum number of a Comp. was 50. that of an Regt. [w]as 500. There were very few Regts. in our army who numbered that much. Our Regt. had not 250. men for duty. Now such Regts. were to be thrown together so as to contain a thousand men the Comps. 100. If every Regt. had two third, or even one half of the proper number of Officers on hand, a great number had to be mustered out, and a great number noncommissioned Officers would have been reduced to the ranks. The ordre further said that in order to keep up the strenght of the army, new Regts. should be raised and forwarded. There is where the trick of the wirepullers came in. They had a lot of good for nothing dudes at home they wanted Offices for with good salaries. They were to[o] high born, to[o] tender, made of to[o] costley material to be spoiled in the ranks. In this way they would get rid of many a numbscul or blockhead. Up to this time when a line Officer was needed he was promoted from the best seargeant, and the Sergeant from the best Corporal, and the Corporal from the best private. In that way a good class of Officers was secured who had grown up with the service and knew what to do. Again: Put recruits between old soldiers they soon will become good soldiers, whereas a new Regt. with new Officers will need a years experience or more to become reliable soldiers. All thus the wirepullers knew, but they did not care for the country.

As soon as the Ordre was received both Thomas and Sherman baulked and kicked. Especially Sherman got his dander up. In his well known spicy, sarcastic way he wrote an open letter to the powers at Washington in which he, as the common phrase has it, gave them a piece of his mind. "Why," he said. "reducing a noncommissioned Oficer to the ranks is only done for some crime, or gross misbehavior, but you with one stroke of the pen reduce them for galantry and bravery displayed on many a blody field. You cooly dismiss experienced, tried and brave Officers without reason, without fault of theirs and without trial simply to gratify and please a hungry horde of Officeseekers." And at the end he gives them to understand that if they were determined to promulgate the Order they might sent the green Officers to the front to fight the battles and let the old soldiers go home and rest on their laurels. In conclusion he says: "Fill up our thinned ranks with recruits and they will soon become good soldiers among the Veterans but leave us our Officers and let us select them from the heroes in the ranks and we will have an Army worthy of its name."[21]

It was never attempted to carry out the Ordre in our army. In the Potomac it was to some extent but not thoroughly. Both Lincoln and Stanton valued the services and military capacities to[o] high to interfere to[o] much with their wishes and arrangements. . . .

But an other move which originated in Congress found universal applause and satisfaction. With the beginning of the coming year hundreds of Regts. would be discharged by reason of expiration of service. That would take the best men out of the army and throw us back on new men drafted to a great extent. Congress therefore passed a law to the effect that all veterans who had served 2 years or more and reenlisted again for three year[s] unless sooner dis[c]harged, should have leave of absence for 30 days and $400.00 bounty. Most of the veterans reenlisted and that saved our army.

To fill up to some extent the depleted ranks of the Regts. recruiting Officers were sent north to enlist new recruits. From our Comp. Capt. Turner and Sergeant Lyman C. Waite[22] got six weeks leave of absence for that purpose. They left Dec. 1st and the latter part of January Sergeant Waite returned with 19 recruits for our Comp. among which were some Oneida Indians from the Reservation in Brown and Outagamie Counties. The Regt. received 220 in all. This brought a respectable front to the Regt. and if during the winter the sick and wounded returned from the hospitals we would have a good beginning the coming Campain.

It seemed Capt. Turner found it more pleasant in Wisconsin as at the front for he did not return. He managed to get a detail as member of the Court martial at Madison Wis. That certainly was a more pleasant and dangerless duty as facing the Johnnies and as he drew Capts. pay right along, in all respects a soft snap. He enjoyed that for nine months. . . .

Dec. 2d. our Brigade received orders to make a scout on Lookout Mountain. We left camp in the valley about 3. P.M. and arrived on the high platteau just before dark, where we camped for the night. Early next morning we took the road south west. . . .

When we arrived on the Camping ground of the previous night we were informed that our and the 78th Pensilvania Regt. had to remain on the Mountain untill further orders. The other Regts. went down to Chattanooga. It was my luck again to come on picket that nig[h]t. As no pickets had been established [y]et, Col. Blakel[e]y of the 78th went along and we posted the pickets across the plateau from one side to the other about a mile in extent.[23]

The first job we had to do, after we had set the camp in order, was to build a passable road for teams up and down the mountain. The old road began at the foot opposite the point and wound alongside the mountain over and between crags and boulders upward untill it reached the plateau 1¾ miles from the point. In many places the narrow road led along deep gulches and there was danger, if the mules were unruly, that mules, men and wagon would tumble down the rocky sides never to rise again. It was an ugly job as all the rocks had to be blasted but after two weeks hard work the road was passable and nearly dangerless. But a tipsy fellow would have done better to leave it alone.

Next we were set to work to built two strong forts and bomb proofs. The timbers were all of heavy oak and we were forbidden to use any Oak for firewood exept the branches and chips. This was very annoying as besides Oak, Chestnut was the only heavy timber growing on the mountain and for firewood that is even worse than swamp ash. But after the forts were finished we were allowed to use oak.

We lived now so to speak in an other Climate. At such an elevation the air was allways pure and keen and nearly allways, especially at night time, a lively wind blowing. Here is a fine place for a summer resort but I would not recommend it for the winter on account of the steady Cold winds. It had indeed been used as a summer resort on a small scale. A quarter of a mile from where the road enters the plateau and toward the point was a little village named "Summerville," which contained a fine, big hotel with all modern improvements. The hotel was now used as a signal station, the flags being worked on the top of the flat roof. There was allso a couple dozen fine dwelling houses, but now deserted. A few were used for hospitals. Colonel Fitch and Colonel Blakely each took one, as allso the Quartermasters and Commissaries. The balance were used for storerooms. . . .

The cornmeal and ship crakers captured on the mountain were distributed among the two Regts. I received a half barrel meal and as much crakers for the share of our mess. It was amusing to see the experiments the boys went through in making puddings, hoecakes, doughnuts, buiscuits all of cornmeal. But none could beat John Buboltz in coocking corn bread. He had confiscated somewhere, what is designated in the south a "dutch Oven." That sounds big enough but in reality is a small affair; merely an Iron pot 10 to 12 inches diameter and 5 or 6 inches deep, with bail and heavy cast iron cover. The pot is well greased inside, the dough for the bread put in the pot and placed on a bed of live coals, the cover put on and allso covered with coals and a fine round loaf of bread would be turned out in time. The difficulty was not in the cooking so much as in preparing the dough and that was Johns secreet. Warm cornbread with fried bacon made an exellent breakfast or supper. But the cornmeal was better adapted for that purpose a[s] our northern meal. It was as white as flour and finely ground. That dutch oven had a hard time of it. It never got cold as long as the cornmeal lasted. Allways somebody was wanting it and John, to escape the bothering, told them he had no right to dispose of it as it belonged to me. But that did not save the oven. I could not well refuse the men the use of it, and so made araingements that from 4 to 7. A.M. allso from 10. to 12. A.M. the oven belonged to John; the remaining hours it was for use of the Comps. . . .

The camping ground our Regt. occupied was not satisfactory; it was to[o] uneven and contracted. After we had been there two weeks Capt. Weisbrod and I were ordered to select a better site, lay out the camp ground and streets, the line officers places and parade ground. We found an exellent place ¼ of a mile from the old ground. Here the boys fixed themselves comfortable and as the wind continued to grow colder and more severe, special care was taken to keep the wind out. In my wall tent I built a sort of fire hearth or oven in this wise: First, I dug a ditch 4 foot long 1 foot wide and 6 inch deep, reaching one foot outside the tent. I had procured some plates of heavy sheetiron from a burnt rolling mill down in the valley. Two of these I put edgeways on each side in the ditch, then filled the ditch up 3 inches to make them stand on edge, an other plate was put across the top and stones put on the edges to keep the joints closed and prevent the escape of smoke. Outside I built a chimney of rock and mud reaching a little higher as the tent. It worked admirable and in quiet weather kept the tent warm enough, but if the wind had his dander up it was of not much account. I could roast myself in front and shiver behind. I made me a bunk to sleep on, filled it up about 8 inches with dry leaves, on them a rubber blanket, an inch thick of wrapping and newspaper, on that a woolen blanket double. For cover I had two woolen blankets, a rubber blanket and overcoat. I expected that would be sufficient to keep me warm, but it did not. When old Boreas was whistling round he kept me shivering all night. John

Buboltz was better of[f] in that respect. He put his tent close up to mine on the south end and as the wind usually came from the north or northwest it did not strike his tent so much. So when it became untenable in my house I sought refuge in the kitchen department. . . .

All the veterans, who were at the front that time remember that cold winter from 63 to 64 and especially New Year. The Officers of the Regts. had made arrangements for a new years dance. It was Capt. Bradish turn to go on picket from our Regt. New Years Eve. Knowing I did not care for the dance he asked of me as a favor to take his turn and he would take my turn whenever I wanted. I promised but felt sorry for it. Such a cold night I have seldom experienced. The wind blew a perfect gale and no matter how big a fire we made it did not do us much good. I had the picket relieved every hour instead of every two and [even] then the men were nearly frozen stiff. It semed I was doomed never to enjoy a decent New Years day during the war. The first New years night we spent in a cedar swamp after the first days battle at Stone river. That allso was a cold night. We were all wet to the skin and not allowed to make a spark of fire. This was the second and the third I allso spent on picket at Savannah on the south Atlantic coast. But here was reasonable fair weather.

The Christmass days however treated me more fair. The first we spent south of Nashville where Mr. Spaulding surprised us with several big boxes Christmass presents from the ladies of Appleton. The second was here on Lookout and allthough it was not the most pleasant weather, John had contrived to make up for that in an other way. He had been visiting the sweetzers [Swiss] who lived on the western slope of the Mountain. I had procured a pass for him which enabled him to go outside the picketline. He had made several scouting expeditions but on returning allways complained that the people were all to[o] poor. But on Christmass morning we had sweet potatoes and ham and eggs for breakfast, and at noon a couple chickens proudly adorned the rough table; neither was that all. He had even tried his skill on apple pie and I must do him the justice to state that I have eaten poorer stuff in boarding houses or hotels for that matter.

When the inner man was satisfied John produced a gallon jug and smiling requested us to help ourselfes. It was not commissary [-issue liquor] what sparkled in the tin cups, but pure wine. It was not Champagner but certainly superior to the vinegar sugar and water mixture which we pay so enormous prices for in the liquor stores and hotels. My third Christmass was at Savannah, but of that I will report when we get there. While we were sipping the wine, which had been raised and made on Lookout, John was carefully putting away for supper the chips which had been left from the chickens. I remarked that they raised a big kind of chicken in the South. John laughed at my remark and said: "Did you eat them for chicken?" We stared at him while he shook with laughter. "Well, what is it?" Fred asked, "No carion crows, or vultures I hope"—"No, no" John replied, "I could buy thuse cheaper as the chickens and as they weigh more I thought to give them a trial." "But sure, they are no Ducks or geese?" I inquired. "No" said John. "They are Guinea hens and the eggs were of the same familie."— Fred stretched himself and said: "Well John bring us some more in time. I will swear off the chicken as long as I can have the genuine Guinea to fill up with."

I will mention he[re] how I drifted in the Commission Merchant business. Buboltz had bought the stuff and paid for it with greenbacks. The man he bought the wine from had hinted that if he could get money for it, he knew where some more was to be got. So I spoke to Lieut. Col. Fitch and Major Walker and both were glad to take some if the price was not exorbitant. I went out to the fellow. He lived four miles from camp. He called himself Weiss (White) but he was black as night. He was a sprightly little fellow and got round mighty fast, even if one leg was two inches shorter than the other. That defect had saved him from the rebel army. Three of his neighbors, allso were sweetzers. They had successfully hid themselves among the crags and caves of the mountain. They were all Union men and since we had possession of the mountain there was no danger for them. Weiss had his wine hidden in the caves as well as other household articles. Everything kept in the house the rebels had taken away.

I found it an easy matter to close a bargain with him. He asked only $1.50 per gallon if paid in greenbacks, but $40.00 if paid in Confederate scrip. The reason he offered the wine so cheap I suppose was mainly the fear that we might come and confiscate his stuff and pay him nothing. The question now was how to get the stuff in camp without the pickets and men seeing it. Here Weis came to the rescue. He knew every rock and corner on the Mountain. He went back with me to near our picket line. I pointed out to him the direction of the line from one side of the mountain to the other. He inquired where the last picket on the south eastern edge stood. I told him on a high bluff overlooking the deep valley between Lookout and Missionary ridge. He thought there was a chance. He went up there, then back a little and then disappeared among some wild laurel bushes downward. He called on me to follow and I went. A narrow ledge went downward gradually perhaps a hundred feet in perpendicular line, then it went nearly level for about 20 rods and then upward again, entering the plateau among a wilderness of laurel brush and, what was best, inside our picket line and unseen by the Picket.

The problem was solved. I went back with him the same way. The next day he was to bring the first installment, 6 gallon and hide them in the laurel bushes where we would find them. Then he was to bring every Saturday afternoon 6 gallon unless ordered otherwise. Then we parted. I took the ledge path back again. It was not alltogether without danger as the ledge at some places was very narrow and not very level neither. It was much like walking on a narrow scaffold alongside a mamoth building high up in the air but without any thing to take hold of for support. When I stepped on to the plateau again I made marks which I could not mistake in order to know where I had to enter the thicket and went to camp. I informed John of the agreement and he was anxious to see the poacher road at once. I went with him and he tramped it over several times in order to get used to it, as he said.

As soon as it was dark enough the following evening we set out for the goods. The wine was to be delivered in gallon jugs. We had provided us each with a piece of rope the ends of which were tied to the jugs and the rope slung behind the neck. One jug we had to carry in the hand. A poncho thrown over the head concealed the jugs. We took two candles along to light on the ledge if the wind would permit. Going out the candles burnt all right as we could shade them with the hand. Examining the designed storeroom the jugs were there, but two carefully wrapped and tied bundles wer there besides. One, we felt were Sweet potatoes but the other we could not make out first when John untied it and discovered a fine dressed guinea fowl. All very wellcome indeed but we could not take it all along. We had to make a second trip.

On the return trip both candles went out before we were half way. We lighted them again only to be blown out again. So keeping the left hand against the rocky wall we went slowly foot for foot forward arrived safely, but wery warm on account of fear of danger on terra firma. Here we made a short rest and John made motion that, as such feat deserved a treat, every one might help himself, which motion was heartily seconded on my part. Each of the jugs had to stand its treat, we hoping that our Customers had no access to quart or pint measures to detect the steal. I charged $2.00 per gallon for the wine as a commission of 50 cents per gallon was certainly not to[o] much for the negotiation and the danger implied to get the stuff into camp. I divided the net proceeds with John who certainly earned his share.

CHATTANOOGA

I smugled in and disposed of 66 gallons, Colonel Blakely being my best customer. Even our good old prohibition Chaplain, who was severely down on Commissary stuff, declared it a harmless, but invigorating, not intoxicating stimulant. To proove that his opinion was sincere he invested in thre gallons of it. But I had to pledge my word of honor as an Officer and Gentlemen that the men should know nothing of it. Mr. Weiss felt so thankfull that from time to time he presented us with 6 guinea fowls and several bushels of sweet potatoes.

One of the swiss neighbors of Weis had several comely girls of which on[e] was captured by the sergeant of the signal station. He allso married on the mountain and then sent the young wife to his parents in Indiana; but thereby hangs a tragic tale which may find room here. Shortly after New Year a photographist came up the mountain and put up his tents near the nose of the mountain. He was a cripled soldier named Roper having lost a leg a year previous in the battle at Stone river. He did a good paying business as nearly all the soldiers on the mountain and down in Chattanooga had their likeness taken together with a view of the palisades of the mountain. Shortley before the Sergeant married he intended to sent her photograph to his folks and inquire how they liked the looks of the bride. Accordingly he betook himself with the bride to the Artist. The latter placed the couple in proper position. The instrument stood near the precipice. The artist, having no artifical leg walked on crutches. While adjusting the Camera one of the crutches slipped on the hard rock and he fell over the edge of the precipice, down several hundred feet on to the rocks at the foot of the palisades. No help could reach him in less than an hour and a half, and no help was necessary as he certainly was dead before he came to a halt. He was picked up a mass of unrecognizabl broken bones and lacerated muscles. And very near had the young bride shared the same fate. She had her eyes on the artist when he fell over. The sudden danger and fear overpowered her and with a cry she fell fainting towards the abyss, but luckily the Sergeant got hold of her dress and saved her from a terrible fate.[24]

Captain Otto and an unidentified soldier on Umbrella Rock, Lookout Mountain. The photographer's studio can be seen to the right. (Courtesy George Otto)

21st Wisconsin Volunteers on Lookout Mountain. Top row (left to right): John Buboltz, Spencer Orlup, John Henry Otto, Lyman C. Waite, Andrew Jackson, William H. Wood, Joseph D. Holden, Charles Lymer, and Sylvester Greeley. Middle row (left to right): Charles Buck, Miles Hoskins, George J. Rawson, Nelson B. Draper, Miles Fenno, Lewis H. Sykes, James P. Walker, and John Dey. Front row (left to right): Harold Galpin, Jacob W. Rexford, August Pierrelee, Maurice F. Grunert, Ephriam Walker, and Charles Buckholz. (Courtesy State Historical Society of Wisconsin)

Field, staff, and line officers of the 21st Wisconsin on Lookout Mountain. Standing, left to right: Lt. James E. Stuart, Company B; Lt. Alfred H. Harding, Company G; Lt. John Henry Otto, Company D; Captain R. J. Weisbrod, Company B; Lt. Fred W. Borcherdt, Company D; Seated, left to right: Lt. B. J. Van Valkenberg, Quartermaster; Lt. Albert B. Bradish, Company I. Inset: Sam H. Fernandez, Quartermaster Sergeant. (Courtesy Oshkosh Public Museum)

~

CHAPTER THIRTEEN

Preparation for
the Atlanta Campaign

~ Early in February Col. Hobart returned from rebel prison. It will be remembered that he was taken prisoner at Chickamauga. He was sent to Libby prison where all Officers were confined in one room on the first floor. Among them was a Colonel Straight [Streight][1] of an Indiana Cavallerie Regt. who had been captured during a raid in Mississippi 1863. He was a daring fellow and matured a plan to give the rebs the slip. He took four trusted Officers in his confidence and disclosed to them his skeme. They went heartily into it and agreed not to speak of the plan to any other prisoner until all was finished. This was necessary for the reason to avoid probable detection. The plan was to dig themselves out. The prison was bounded on the north side and east end by streets, while on the south side was James river and west the approach to the bridge. Opposite and close to the street at the east end was an old shed without doors containing all sorts of old refuse matter such as old wagons, barrels, boxes etc. Below their room was a cellar partly filled with empty barrels and other stuff. A stairway, covered with a trapdoor led down into the cellar from the inside of their room. Here they began their mining operation. They could work only during night time when the other prisoners slept. They dug across under the street at the east end and came out among the old rubbish in the shed. It took them the best of two Months to finish the job but they came out where they had intended to.

When they were ready to escape they informed their fellow prisoners of the Chance but cautioned them if they wished to strike for liberty not to go more than two together, to avoid the Sentinel in front of the prison and not to enter the city. 150. got out that night of which about fifty reached the Union lines on the Rappahannok, the others being recaptured. Col. Hobart said he never would have reached the Union lines if it had not been for the negros. It took him three weeks to cover a distance of seventy miles. He dared to march only during the night times, laying low during the day. Being in winter, the rivers and creeks were much swollen. He could not take the bridges as they were guarded by rebel soldiers. He had to cross the Pamunky, Chickahominy, North Ann, Rapidan and Rappahannok and numrous streams and creeks. He remained a month at home to recover somewhat from the exhausting trip. He said he felt well but his usually ruddy, blooming cheeks were changed to a pale hue and never recovered their former healthy aspect.

In the latter part of February Genl Banks at New Orleans made preparations for his Red river campain; Genl. Sherman allso was to make his famous Meridian raid into Mississippi. To prevent Genl. Joe E. Johnston to sent any troops to oppose Sherman or Banks, Genl. Thomas concluded to stir Johnston up a little in order to prevent him from sending away any troops. The 14th Corps was selected to make demonstrations in front of different parts of Johnstons army or position. Our two Regts. were not called on to take part in the expedition. Johnston had, since he took command of Braggs army, choosen a different position for the same. From the line near tunnel hill he had m[o]ved southward to Dalton behind Buzzard roost, or Rocky face ridge. His lines and fortification stretched from Buzzard roost past Dalton to Resacca on the Ostanaula river, a distance of eleven miles. Genl. Palmer, now commdg the 14th Corps, made faints here and there but was instructed not to bring on a general engagement. But at Buzzard roost gap where the land and railroad pass through the ridge, a spirited engagement took place which lasted from 1. P.M. untill after dark. When at night Col. Mihalotzi of the 24th Ill. was placing his picket he was mortally wounded, the bullet entering the left side above the hipp. He walked back half a mile unassisted, when he was put in an Ambulance and brought to Chattanooga.

That was on Washingtons birthday. The next day I went down to Chattanooga to see how Michael Hammond, who was desperately wounded at Chickamauga[,] was getting along. Peter E. Dane of our Comp. who was hospital steward informed me first of Col. Mihalotzis dangerous state.[2] He was quartered in a house and I went to see him. Several Doctors were there who refused my request to see the Colonel as he was to[o] sick to converse with anybody. But Dr. Wagner who came just then out of the patients room and who knew me, said he would anounce me to the Col. but I must not stay over ten minutes. (Dr. Wagner had been the surgeon of the 24th Ill. but was promoted to brigade surgeon. While we stayed at Murfreesboro, he, the Colonel, Capt. Steffens and I had played many a party of Domino together.) When I entered, the Col., laying on a low couch, extended both hands and in a laughing, resolute voice said: "He' Lieut. you see? I have lost the game. Some one of the darned rebels fired just once to[o] much."—"I hope Col." I replied, "you will have your revange this summer."—"No, No," he replied. "They have done their work to[o] well. It is no use to deceive myself; I know better. The Doctors too are trying to conceal my real position and perhaps they act right, but why should I try to deceive myself? I am not afraid to die. If I was I would not be here. Every soldier must expect it. It may be your lot the next fight you come in. I have telegraphed to Chicago to my wife to come. If I only can speak to her for ten minutes, I am ready. But I must not be sent back to Chicago. I will be burried here among the comrades who have gone before. . . . He! is the time up Doctor"? he remarked suddenly when Dr. Wagner stepped into the room. "How jealous you fellows are when a minutes time is in question. Give me your hand, Lieut. for the last time. If the ministers are right we will meet again; if not, then goodbye and good luk to you." So I left that true soldier, deeply moved by his artless, good cheer and unconcerned easy philosophy about the future.

Outside I waited until Dr. Wagner came out again. He told me there was absolutely no help for the Col. The ball could not be found and had probably hurt liver and kidneys. He was glad to find the Col. so cheerfull and resigned, another proof he said, that a freethinker can look death in the face as calmly and unconcerned as the most orthodox minister. The evening after the Cols. wife arrived and had an hours time to co[n]verse with him, when he died. He was burried as he had wished, with military honeurs among his brave comrades.

When it was acertained that we were to stay on the mountain during the winter months I wrote to my wife to sent me some provisions viz: Cervelat [sausage], onions, smoked halibut, sourkrout and tobacco, the latter to be done up in a tin box to prevent its spoiling the other articles. When I sat writing the letter, Charles Russell[3] came in and informed me that he had applied for a leave of absence as his mother was very ill. (Chs. Russell belonged to our Comp. but was detailed on hospital duty. He was allso from Appleton.) He wished to inquire if I, in case the leave should be granted, wished for anything he could bring along. That fitted my case exactly. I told him no better service could be done me just now, but I was afraid it would put him at to[o] much trouble. But he insisted he could tend to all my wants. So I began to enumerate. First: The box with provisions, second: I needed a watch very bad. Third: I needed a sword and belt as allso a leather haversack. fourth: I needed a good leather valise to keep books and papers in, as we had been informed that no transportation would be furnished for our desks during the coming campaign, but a valise would be transported.

By this time I looked slyly at him expecting his "phiz" would assume a somewhat elongated shape, but he merely asked: "Is that all?" That beat me but I replied: "No, I want a lot of stationary and post stamps, a bottle of turpentine and Alkohol, and some prussian blue, and vermillion and some chrom jellow but thuse Articles I will leave for my wife to enclose in the box." Well, he said he would tend to the matter and left. I did not send of[f] the letter untill I should know of Charles. success. Two days later Russell came with a pass for leave of absence for 20 days outside the department line, that is from Nashville. We sat down and talked a while about what style of sword, watch and valise I wanted and then he left to make his own preparations. The following morning he left for the north. The same train which carried Russell carried my letter home. In it I informed my wife about the agreement I had made with Chs. Russell. Then I figured at what time Charly would return.

In due time Chas. Russell made his appearance. He had fullfilled the orders to the letter, but said that he never would undertake such a job again. The sword, watch and valise was nothing as he could carry that with him, but the box was what made the trouble. At Indianapolis it was thrown of[f] and put in the baggage room, and he had to lay over a day and treat the baggage master to get it aboard the next day. At Louisville and Nashville the same ceremony was repeated. On that account he came three days behind time but nothing was said about it. Next day was Sunday and John began early to boil down [a] mess of krout. It wass just splendid and went well with halibut. That tattle tale, Fred B[o]rch[e]rdt could not rest untill he had given the news to Col. Fitch and Major Walker what an exellent feast he had partaken of. The Consequence was they sent me notice inviting themselves as my guest at the next souerkrout dinner.

That made John mad, and me to[o] for that matter. I told Fred in plain words he might hire his own cook and eat at headquarters where he belonged. That Lieut. Col. Fitch and Major Walker both had families and plenty money and were well able to provide for their own wants. Moreover if they had anything special they did not dream of inviting poor, simple second Lieut. Otto to be their guest. The next thing we would hear would be the talk about the "dutch souerkrout." Fred felt very sorry but the thing was done and could not be recalled. So I instructed John to do his best on coming Thursday so that at least the sugarcoated tongues of the illustrious yankees might not run the danger of being blistered. It happened that John had the last guinea fowl on hand and some sweet potatoes were allso left. When John got over his dark mood he promised to do his best. And so he did. I instructed John if Questions were asked where chickens and sweet potatoes were raised not to forget that they came from home.

Well; the guests came and worked with a will. They felt not the least bashfull but put themselves around the good things in such a style as to satisfy a fence rail splitter. At the close Lieut. Col. Fitch remarked that he had never expected sourkrout to be such a respectable dish as thus had prooved to be. "Oh, then you are behind the times," Walker exclaimed. "Why, in Manitowok I used to have stated places where I got my fill of Sourkrout regularly. But here John beats them all in preparing it; I would take every day my dinner of it." I concluded to rub Col. Fitch down a little. I had heard him at Louisville when he was [y]et our Adjutant call a german who could not speak English fluently "dutch souerkrout." I therefore said: "Gentlemen! I am under much obligation to you. It is a great consolation to find and to know that gentlemen of your standing do not approove of the aprobium which usually is laid in the sneering remark: 'Dutch sourkrout.' by the Americans." I saw that Fitch felt the thrust when he replied. "Oh, well, circumstances alter cases. We all have our prejudices, which sooner or later must be overcome."—"Now" Walker replied, "it seems to me that the people who use such language with the intention to hurt ones feeling show a very limited extent of common sense." Lieut. Col. Fitch did not like the drift of the conversation and expressing thanks suddenly arose and went to his quarters. Maj. Walker spent a half hour in friendly conversation. A few days after a ration of sourkrout was issued to the men by the Commissary. Each man received a quart. Here was proof how intensely the yankees dispised the nasty stuff. No sooner did they get hold of it than they devoured it raw using the fingers as a spoon or fork. [The] german boys put theirs together and boiled it thoroughly with a liberal supply of bacon and when they sat eating it the yankees stood by with longing looks, which clearly indicated their willingnes to swallow an other dose. It was the second and last time that sour krout was issued.

One morning at roll call Wm. H. Wood did not answer to his name. His tentmates said that he had left the tent the previous night right after taps and had not returned. Wood, it will be remembered, was the deserter who was sentenced at Camp Dawson Ala. for desertion and too close attention to free love matters and who, after the expiration of his term of penalty had been returned to Comp. Some thought he had deserted again but I thought different. Desertion to home would be a difficult undertaking from here and he was to[o] much of a coward to desert to the Enemy. My suspicion was correct. A little after roll call a Corporal with two men brought him in Camp from the picket line, reporting that at 2. A.M. a sentinel had arrested him while trying to creep inside the picket line. As the pickets that night were of the 78th Pa. Regt. they did not know him. They had not seen him going out. I asked Wood what he had been up to and he replied he only intended to hunt up some fourage. He had a considerable bruise on one side of his head which indicated he had been in a severe tussel; his blouse allso was torn in many places. He begged hard of me to let him go, but that was out of the question since he had been a legally absentee with out leave. I told him so and added that he probably needed an other dose of ball and chain. He was confined in the guard house.

Towards noon one of the sweetzer [Swiss] farmers and a girl were brought in by the pickets. The farmer wanted to see the commander of the Regt. As I suspected what he come for I requested him to come along to the Colonel. Here in very funny English he unloaded himself of the following story: About midnight he had been suddenly waked up by a scream of his daughter. He run into her room and saw a fellow trying to escape through the window. He seized the fellow and dragged him back and next they had a lively tussel in which the fellow got worsted. The fellow, as he allways called him, had finally begged him to let him go. As he had felt by the buttons that he was a soldier he had let him slip. The girl told the following: She thought she heard a slight noise at the window, but as it was very dark she could not see anything. She finally sat up and asked "who is there"? when a man rose up aside the bed and said: "Be still and I want [won't] hurt you, but if you scream I will kill you." She then screamed with all her might and the man seized her by the throat and tryed to strangle her. When the door was burst open the fellow made for the window.

The Colonel inquired if they would recognize the man. They said they could not as it was to[o] dark to see his features plainly, but the father thought the fellows head would show the stamp he had put on it. If that could not be found he would go home and say nothing. He allso held a piece of the blouse which had been torn out in the engagement. We went to the guard house. Besides the bruises on the head Wood bore, they recognized him by his voice. That piece of blouse the man had kept allso fitted exactly in Woods blouse. All this and his absence from camp that night proved him guilty. Wood was sentenced by a court martial to 3 months hard labor with ball and chain attached to one leg. That lasted until the Atlanta Campain. He was sent down to Chattanooga to the convict gang where there was plenty work for him. . . .

By April 17 men had returned from sick leave, hospitals and convalescent camps. With the 19 recruits received Comp. "D." once more presented a respectable front. We numbered now 55 men for duty. How many of them would get through the coming campain the future only could tell.

April 1st. Lieut. Jaeger of Comp. "I." who had been absent during the winter was ordered to take charge of Comp. "C." to relieve me of double duty.[4] The boys of Comp. "C." did not like the change and got up a petition, which every men in the Comp signed, to let them remain with Comp. "D." but Col. Hobart thought it better to have the Comps. separated. Lieut. Jaeger however was not long with the Comp. Their first Sergeant Hubbard was promoted second Lieut. and took charge of the Comp. . . .

During the winter a great number of immense Government workshops and machine shops were built as well as large magazines for the storing and safe keeping of the tremendous amount of Provision, ammunition, Clothing, fourage, and other things necessary to provide for and sustain a large army. Chattanooga henceforth was to be our supply depot when moving southward. Thousands of darkies from the southern States and mechanics from the north found employment here; The mechanics earned from 4. to 6. doller per day.

Some smart yankees in Massachusets undertook a smart move to escape the draft. In the enlistment law passed by Congress was a clause which permitted the States to enlist men for the Union Army in the southern states. Now these puritan Yankees reasoned that, as the Negroes were man as well as the white people, Ergo, they might enlist negroes, fill up the Regts. with them and keep the white people at home. Several agents from the New England States presented themselves to Genl. Sherman with a letter from President Lincoln in which Sherman was requested to allow thuse Agents to go on with their work and support them as much he could. But Sherman could not see it. He wrote to the President that, if Niggers had to be enlisted as soldiers, he would respectfully propose that they be organized in separate Regts. commanded by white Officers who had served in the field. That our soldiers were not ready [y]et to be mixed up and sleep with the niggers. But if it was ordered so, he would not risk his reputation by commanding such a checkered army. In other words, he told them that if they put the nigger in the ranks with the white men, he would go home, rather, than to command that spotted Crew. But the niggers could be made usefull in many other ways. We used thousands of teamsters which were all taken from the ranks. The niggers could drive the teams and the white men returned to the ranks. Niggers might load and unload cars and boats and do all the work in and around the Magazines and Storehouses; they could build fortifications and blochouses, work at bridges and other places necessary.[5]

That letter had the desired result. No niggers were put among white troops. Negro Regts. were organized and first put in places where not much fighting was to be expected. The New England papers were loudly blaming and abusing Sherman for his untimely interfeering with their s[c]heme, but he cooley answered them in an open letter that they better not proclaim their cowardice so broadcast. Everybody knew that they had their full share in provoking and bringing on this murderous war, and now, when they had what they wanted, they tryed to shirk their duty and escape the consequences of their abolition tyrades. He challenged them to come to the front and fight and prove that they meant what they preached. That helped. They let Sherman alone from that time. They found he was as bad to handle as a porcupine, full of needles all round and wherever they touched him he would leave a sting behind. But that was not all. The Massachusets men calculated to Officer the new nigger Regts. with green Officers from home. Again Sherman stepped in the breach and insisted that the Officers be taken from the best soldiers in the field. And so it was done.

On the 15th of April the usual orders preliminary to a Campaign were read. The Officers were informed that no desks or messchest would be taken along; neither the parade, or Undress Uniform. All such things were to be stored in Chattanooga under tents and to be guarded by Invalids. Only one valise was allowed to each Officer. This was done to limit the wagon trains to the smallest number. It was a great saving on mules, wagons, fourage and men. Besides large trains are a nuisance to an army. They must be guarded by a sufficient force to repel any attack by the enemy and besides they are allways in the way. All sick men were to be sent to hospital. Of this men I had but one, Maurice Grunert. He had a violent attack of Diarrhea which in time changed into flux, which threatened to become chronic. He was sent to hospital in Nashville. . . .

PREPARATION FOR THE ATLANTA CAMPAIGN

With the beginning of the Atlanta Campaign our Army was completely reorganized. The army of the Cumberland having formerly acted independent became now a part of the army of Georgia as it was officially called.[6] Our Regt. allso was assigned to an other brigade, being the first brigade, first Division, Army of the Cumberland. The latter army being nearly two thirds of the entyre army. . . . It was supposed that Johnston had about 55.000 men to oppose this army with; only a little more than half our number.[7] But it must be born in mind that Genl. Johnston acted on the defensive. Further, the broken, mountanous country up to Atlanta was exellently fitted for defensive warfare; then, all his defensive lines were ready made beforehand. If he was driven, or flanked out of one line he only had to fall back and quietly settle [behind] the next works. Thousands of negroes under the direction of skilfull engineers were steady at work to provide for the most effective defensive means in Johnstons army. As we were allways the attacking party, we necessary must loose a far greater number of men and by this means Genl. Johnston calculated to reduce our army so much in numbers that finally he could engage us in open battle with fair show of success. And again it was easy for Genl. Johnston to draw reinforcements if there were any troops to spare somewhere else which was not so easy with us. Further; we had but one line to furnish us with supplies, where Johnston had three; we were allready over 600 miles from our main basis of supplies and were increasing the distance with every step we made. Would it not be possible for Johnstons Cavallery to get in our rear and efectually destroy our communication and put us on a starving footing or force us to run back as fast as possible? There was no fourage and feed enough in thus mountainous country to keep a brigade alive much less a 100,000 men with a large number of horses and mules attached. So it will be seen that Genl. Johnstons prospects were not so very bad and our Chances of final success by no means so sure. . . .

On the first of May we left Lookout, passed through Rossville gap to Graysville on the Chicamauga river. Distance about 7. miles. With much regret we left the dear old mountain who had become allmost a second home to us, and who was just beginning to devellop his real advantages during summer time. On the way we passed several Brigades of eastern troops who had staked arms near the road in order to let us pass by. These boys, who had read a great deal about Indians, but never had seen any live ones, were much surprised and amused when my Comp. passed by and they discovered the duskey fellows. Now it happened I had a man in the Comp. named Jim Walker who was of genuine English ancestry but who nevertheless could pass for a full blooded Injun. He wore a heavy mess of coalblack hair, had a towny, coppercolored skin and big, bulging eyes. Besides he was not a special friend of water, soap and comb which made the matter so much worse. When the boys discovered the Indians they began to yell: "Look! look at the Injuns look at this one! and this one with the calfs eyes"! pointing to Jim Walker. That made Jim so mad that he fixed bajonet and threatened to stab the first man who dared call him an Injun. That of course made matters worse and poor Jim had to stand the consequences of mistaken Identity as well as he could. The afternoon as soon as we went in camp he went to the drummer Paine and had his hair cut short, and next he went to the Chickamauga river and rubbed his hide down to half its thickness and sure enough, he looked all the better for it.

The following day we marched near to Ringold where our Corps was to assemble. Here we remained to the 6th when the whole army was to move forward. Here our Regt. was assigned to the first brigade, first Division. We were no longer to associate with the 1st Wis. 24th Ill. and 79th Pa. Genl. Starkweather had been oblidged to resign, being no more able for duty. Our brigade was now Composed of eight Regts instead of four, viz: 21st Wis. 10th Wis. 15th Ky. 33d Ohio, 104th Ill. 42d Indiana and 88th Ind. and 94th Ohio. The brigade was comanded by Brigd. Genl. Carlin, a West Point graduate.[8]

The day before we left this camp R[e]mick Knowles came to me and in a whining voice said he was not able to go with us on the campain, he was sure he could not stand it, and he began to enumerate a long list of complaints, enough to disable the thoughest mule. Now I knew there was nothing the matter with the fellow. He was a regular deadbeat. He allways had managed to be sent to some hospital whenever the future was pregnant with dangerous duty. He had returned from hospital shortley before we left Lookout and was one of the healthiest and jolliest fellows in camp; and even now he wore a rosy, full moon face. He had a special knack in describing his ailments and shortcomings and his simpering, whining voice together with the pitiable working and twisting of his facial muscles would deceive anybody who did not know the fellow and make him believe the fellow was sure a candidate for the grave. Having studied his character and observed his rumping and playing qualities and especially his ability in digesting any amount of eatables without the least objection of his stomach, or any unpleasant consequences, I made up my mind to make him stick to it at least for a while. I tried to appeal to his manhood and honor, to make him feel how ridiculous and dispiseable his behavior must be to his comrades;

what he would say to his familie and friends after the war was over and they should happen to inquire about his doings. I pointed to Little Chas Lymer, a mere schoolboy who had not missed an hours duty yet. He had no answer to that and finally slunk away. To make sure however I went to the Doctor and had a talk with him and he promised to look out for him.

But an other real good boy became dangerously ill. John Buboltz complained of tormenting pains in the bowels. He was not the man to play off and had allready a history. At Perryville Ky. he was quite seriously wounded over one Eye but he refused to go to the hospital but went right along. On Jefferson pike he was taken prisoner by Wheelers Cavallery and sent to Libby prison. Being exchanged after three months he might have gone home on leave for a month but he immediately reported for duty. During the night the disease increased to such an extent that I had to call on a Doctor who administered opiates to deaden the pain. The following morning he had to be carried to the ambulance which brought him back to Chattanooga. The Dr. told me we probably might not see him again as he feared inflammation of the bowels had set in. Remick was there allso trying to convince the Dr. of some terrible disease he was the victim of. The Dr. good naturedly advised him to take good exercise for a few weeks that would improve his case enormously. At the same time he handed him a box with pills of which he had to swallow, one mornings and nights.

At 6. A.M. May 6th we wended our way southward. We passed through Ringold and the Gap south of it and went in Camp about 5. P.M. We had to sleep alongside our arms as it was known that the rebels held Tunnel Hill [y]et which was only two miles ahead of us. The following morning our Regt. was deployed as skirmishers. We were in dense woods with heavy undergrowth. As we were thrown out to clear the flanks we had no reserve behind us. The guide was left, that is, from the left we had to keep distance and direction[.] As our Comp. was on the right of the Regt. we were on the extreme right of the line. Before we started I cautioned the men to allways keep the file on the left in sight or we might get lost. I could not overlook the line of the Comp. in the dense woods, the line being perhaps 25 rods long. After having advanced about a mile or so I noticed that the line pressed unusually to the right. I worked to the left to assertain the cause. I found it. It hapened that a creek ran diagonally with our line of march in a direction from our left and rear to our right and front. The men on the left met the creek first and the men had to cross whenever the[y] arrived at it. None of us had any knoledge of the existence of the creek. The last file in the Comp. were two recruits to whom the business was new.

When I arrived there I found them working alongside the creek which, by the direction it run, I saw at once must be crossed. "Where is the Regt." I inquired. "On the other side the creek." Schneider replied.[9] "When did they cross the creek."—"Oh, a while ago."—"Why did you not cross it"? "We were lo[o]king for a bridge."—"You are a set of Idiots." I exclaimed. "Have you an Idea where the Regt. now is"? No they had not.

I hastily called the Comp. together and explained the situation. We crossed the creek which was not more than a rod wide and not deep and by going in a left oblike direction I hoped to catch up with the Regt. But it is a very difficult thing to march in any given direction in Close woods. We marched and marched with no other result than becoming very tired. I halted for a little rest. We could not see or hear anything. All at once half a dozen reports of Cannon were heard but at quite a distance. "Forward march!" I ordered. "We have to find thus [these] cannon be the[y] union or rebs." Now it seemed we heard the rattling of small arms but it was very indistinct. We took the direction toward the sound heard and strugled forward with all our might untill we were nearly played out, with no result. We struck a steep high hill. We must climb that hill; perhaps we can see something from there.

It was 2. P.M. now. The firing had ceased long ago. The skye was cloudy, no sun to be seen. We climbed the hill but could not see anything on account of the woods. I called for a volunteer to climb a high tree. Jack Rheiner voluntered and soon was in the topmost branches of a towering white-wood.[10] "Do you see any clearings?" I inquired. "Only one."—"Nothing in there?"—"Cannot see anything." "Can you see a high ridge somewhere, higher than any other"?—"Yes, there it is." "Can you see a break or gap in it?"—"Yes, right there," pointing towards it. "Can you see a hill a little this side of the gap"? "Yes."—"How far is it?"—"Guess about two miles."— "That is Tunell hill and the high ridge with the gap is Buzzard roost. We have to stear in that direction to find our Regt. Point out the gap again." He did so and I noted exactly the dirrection he pointed out. "Hold on" Rh[e]iner shouted. "I see smoke rising out of the woods in that direction."—"All right. Stay there a little while and observe. We will make now Coffe and yours to[o]." After a while Jack hollered again: "I see some black lines moving in the clearing; they are very small though."—"All right, watch them what they are doing." The coffee water was nearly boiling when Jack called again. "The black lines are gone now; It seems they are all running wild now."—"So much the better; the[y] will camp there and you will soon see smoke rising." A little while after Jack reported: "They are building

PREPARATION FOR THE ATLANTA CAMPAIGN

fires now, the whole clearing is full." "How far is the clearing away?" "About a mile."—"In what direction?"—"Just the same as the gap."—"Come down now Jack and take your dinner."

After a little rest we started again. I did not dare to risk the good luck direction again. I started Jack ahead in the given direction, then an other men to follow in Jacks steps at a distance so as not to loose sight of Jack. I following as the third in line, was then enabled to see whether Jack was swerving from the given course right or left. and give him directions accordingly. It was slow work, but it landed us at the clearing and to our great joy found our brigade encamped there. The Colonel had given us up for lost and laughed heartily when I explained why, and how long we had been chasing round in the woods. The brigade had not made more than four miles in a straight line and we had made at least three times that distance. . . .

The following morning we advanced towards Buzzard roost, or properly Rocky face ridge. Some call this a spur of the Alleghanies, but where its connections with the Alleghanies come from I never could find out. It is a high ridge perhaps 20 miles long from east to west. To the west of the Gap the crest is crowned with a high wall of solid rocks rising perpendicular, which nowhere could be scaled, the top being well lined with Johnnies. Mill Creek, the Chattanooga and Atlanta R.R. and a wagon road pass t[h]rough a cleft in the ridge called "Buzzard roost gap." This gap as well as the ridge was strongly fortified and if Genl. Johnston expected Sherman to force the passag[e] he was mistaken. True, Pop Thomas was making demonstrations as if he intended to force the passage but that was only make believe. The 4th Corps, Genl. O. O. Howard, was massed to the left of the R.R. and Gap. Our Division went up the side of the ridge on the right of the road. A shower of shells was thrown by the rebs from the ridge but we soon got close enough so as to be rather under the protection, than in danger of their batteries. At first the rebel musketry anoyed us somewhat killing a Colonel of a Iowa Regt. but the higher we came the less they could hurt us. The rebs seemed to know that and ceased firing; but we were not allowed to come near the long rocky Cappice crowning the ridge. T[h]ey rolled heavy rock over the precipice, which would roll down the ridge in all directions, compelling us to be on the steady lookout for them.

We remained here overnight and experienced a regular Cloudburst; the clouds discharging the water with such a force, and such a quantity that we were hardly able to keep on our feet. It had been ugly hot the previous day, so much so, that several men were sunstroke while ascending the ridge. The following noon we descended again and went into Camp behind an Elevation in front of the ridge. Meanwhile some batteries of the fourth Corps amused themselves with throwing shells into the gap and onto the ridge.

Our climbing the ridge as well as the presence of the 4th Corps at the gap was merely intended as a blind by Genl. Sherman. A little south and behind Buzzard roost is Dalton, a respectable village containing at that time perhaps 1500 inhabitants. About twelve miles further south is Resaca on the Ostanaula river where the Atlanta R.R. crosses the river. Between thuse places was a station called Tilton. This distance from the roost by Dalton, Tilton to Resacka was strongly fortified. This prooved that the rebels expected Sherman to force the passage through the gap and attack them from the east and front of their works. But Shermans plans were different. Twelve miles west from Buzzard roost gap was snake creek gap, allso in the same ridge. While we were crawling up the ridge, Sherman sent Genl. McPherson with the 15th and 17th Corps through Snake Creek gap with instructions to press forward, if possible to Resaca and try to get hold of the railroad and bridges there.[II] It must not been forgotten that this was in the rear of the enemy. Genl. Hooker with the 20th Corps was to follow him, but face to the left when the gap was cleared so as to come in the rear of Dalton. Our, or the 14th[,] Corps was to follow and fill up the intervall between Hooker and McPherson. Genl. Howard with the fourth Corps and Scofield with the 23d Corps were to remain at Buzzard roost gap but to press through as soon as the rebels should abandon the gap and ridge.

Genl. McPherson arrived at Snake Creek gap just when a rebel brigade of Cavallery had arrived to fortify and defend the same. The Cavallery was easily brushed aside and McPherson went through with out any notable resistance. After the 20th Corps had followed McPherson our Corps followed on the 12th of May. By this time the passage through the gap, nearly two miles in lenght, was utterly cut up (there never had been a road) so much so that hardly a man, much less the horses, mules, batteries and teams could get through. However by dint of hard work we succeeded to pass the gap in one day. At dusk we had cleared the horrible passage and went in Camp immediately.

The thirteenth we spent in scrambling and crawling through the woods, over and among the hills to find and connect with the left of McPhersons and the right of Hookers line. Not an acre of clearing, nor a shanty or building did we see that day. Nothing but hills ravines and—woods. Finally, at sundown our Regt. was drawn up in line on a steep hill and down again. We could not stake arms, the stakes would not stand on the steep incline. Bajonets were fixed and thrust into the ground, but[t] end of rifle upward. We were ordered to go down in the ravine and make Coffee and make but small fires, make no noise and having done with the Coffee to exstinguish the fires and lay down behind our arms. We rested that night under amusing difficulties. The big hill was so steep all around that no matter in what direction we laid down, lenghtways, or crossways, when asleep, some one would make a sudden move dowward and would not stop, either, unless some friendly bush or small tree interfered with his reckless downward course.

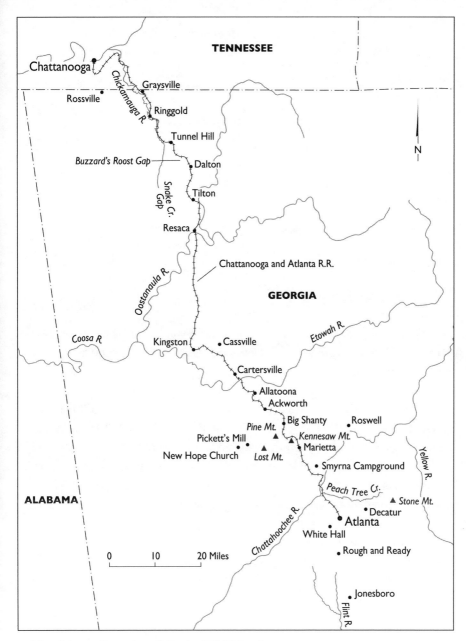

The Atlanta Campaign. (Map by Bill Nelson)

~

CHAPTER FOURTEEN

The Battle of Resaca:
Tedious Skirmishing and
Final Advance

~ General Johnston must have been sadly surprised when he learned that nearly our entire army had passed Snake Creek gap and were now endeavoring to cut of[f] his retreat. It was a great mistake on his part not to take care of that gap even if it was 12 miles from his lines.[1] However as soon as he found out he evecuated Buzzard roost gap and Dalton and concentrated his army in the works from Tilton to Resaca. General Howard moved the 4th Corps now through the gap to Dalton and Schofield with the 23d Corps and formed on the left of Hooker.[2] Thus our whole army was south of the ridge and well connected. I can now only give the proceedings of our Regt. as the nature of the ground did not allow much observation.

About 8. A.M. we went forward in a right oblike perhaps a mile and formed in line of battle. Again our Regt. came on a ridge which stretched half a mile from right to left. Line being formed we were ordered to lay down. Nothing was heard as [other than] now and then a word of command; Neither could we see anything as we lay a little dow[n]ward behind the ridge. Again the farseers or [prescient] made their last will, among those old Charlie Buchholz, Remick Knowles and a recruit Frank Extine.[3] Presently two batteries came up and took position in front of the line and loaded. Next, far to the right, the booming of cannon indicated that McPherson had opened conversation.[4] It came nearer and nearer and now Scofield Howard and Hooker to our left and front allso became restless. Col. Hobart went along behind the line telling the men to keep together and well closed up. "Raise up! forward march!" A few steps brought us over the brow of the hill and as the decline was somewhat steep we could see over the brush and between the trees what was ahead of us.

At the foot of the hill was a large grass field, slightly rasing at the opposite end. There, in the edge of the woods were the rebel works. The leng[th] of the field towards the works was at least a quarter of a mile. If we had to charge these works, not half of us would get there. They could pick off all of us before we could get there. Moreover we had started and were carefully working down the steep incline. No sooner were we down low enough to be out of the level range of the batteries when they opened on the rebel works. Oh, what a tumult it was. It seemed the brush was swaying and trembling under the pressure of the forcible agitated air. I can not blame the Indians who never had seen nor heard a Cannon; who had no Idea of its force and destructive Power, beeing allmost paralized with fear. Peter Green,[5] the oldest, who acted as a kind of father or chief among them, turned round and cried: "Ugh! big gun, big gun"! and then some in Indian vernacular which I could not digest, but all the Indians came round him looking as scared as burnt chickens. I expected when I perceived the terror in their faces they all would run away and it was only when I assured them that down at the foot of the hill we would be safe, they started again to catch up with the Regt.

When we came at the foot of the hill we found something which we had not noticed in coming down. First there was a creek about 2 rods wide, Camp Creek, as it was called. It had a gravel bottom and only 4 to 7 inches deep water. That was no hindrance but the grassfield opposite rose perpendicular 3 foot higher. The edge of this bank or shore was overgrown with wild laurel, briars and other thorny vines so thick and close interwoven that not even a cat could slip through. Now in order to make the situation clear to the reader I must beg excuse for a little digression. On the right of our brigade that day was the 33d Ohio, next came our Regt. then the 104. Ill. etc. The hedge mentioned extended only in front of the 33 Ohio and 4. Comp. on the right of our Regt. E. D. I and C. from there and toward the left, the entrance to the field was not obstructed; the left of the brigade being again in the woods. As the Creek and field were not exactly parallel with our advancing line the left of the Regts. entered the open field before we came to the hedge. When we reached the hedge some one ordered a halt, (I believe it was the Col. of the 33d Ohio) but the men on the left of us being in the open field were allready in bitter combat. The grass in the field was over knee high and about 20 rods from the entrance in the field lay a line of rebel soldiers hidden in the grass who opened a tremendous fire as soon as our men entered the field. Our men quicke lay down and returned the fire.

Just about when that happened we came across that close hedge. To advance any further was impossible. A few steps from the right of our Comp. was a small gap or opening in the hedge through which a footpath led into the field. Lewis Sykes[6] and Andrew Jackson coming just in front of this spot immediately clambered up into the field, only to drop back instantly, Lewis Sykes being shot clear through the head made two steps backwards an fell on his back into the creek; Andrew Jackson being shot through the upper left t[h]igh limped back and squatted behind a tree. I forbid at once any further attempt to enter the field at that place but advised the men to make small openings in the hedge and watch for any head that should appear ab[o]ve the grass. They were not slow in following that advice. Every pocket and penknife was put in operation to clear a small spot for rifle and eye, and very soon the game stopped to be all on[e]sided. Charly Lymers rifle was formed in the shape of an Elbow by a bullet; but he apropiated Sykes rifle and went on with the business.

Allmost immediately after Sykes and Jackson fell, Remick Knowles and Nelson Draper asked leave to escort Jackson back to the Doctors. I did not fancy the Idea of Knowles going, because I felt about sure he would not return but stay back under some excuse. But as none of the other men volunteered, and he begged so earnestly I let him go but assured him that, if he did not return to Comp. I would report him a deserter. I noticed he did not like that clause, but his cowardice got the upper hand and he went. It was by no means a desirable stopping place behind the hedge allthough we were out of sight of the Johnnies. They knew we were there and the bullets whizzed incessantly through the hedge and compelled us to keep low behind the projecting bank. The men had widened the little loopholes gradually to such an extent as to allow them to crawl through. Genl. Carlin, seeing that a charge through the open field would be to[o] murderous, had more artillery massed on the ridge behind us, who treated the rebel works with round shot and threw shells behind the works. We could plainly see how the logs in their works were scattered in all directions.

The bulletts soon became remarkably less and now we began to climb up the bank and crawl forward in the grass. That part of our Regt. which had entered the field from the start were about some fifteen rods ahead of us but we soon had crowled up in line with them. It was a bad business at best. Allthough the musketfiring from the rebel works had mostly ceased on account of our batteries keeping up a incessant fire, the Johnnies hidden in the grass were not willing [y]et to give up the contest. However we were on equal terms now and paid them honestly in their own coin. We kept on kreeping forward, firing all the while, whenever a hat, or disturbance in the grass denoted the presence of a Johnny. And here I must remark that the Indians seemed to be in their element. They did not stay back now but contrary were allways ahead. They seemed to delight in the hide and seek business and used all kinds of tricks to induce the Johnnies to show their heads. But the fact soon revealed itself that not withstanding we kept creeping forward we did not come nearer the rebs. The fact was, they were as anxious to get out there as we were to get in.

Finally we reached the line they had occupied first and found some dead and wounded. The latter begged piteously for water which was given to them as far as possibly. It was no wonder they felt dry. It seemed old Sol had espicially selected that field for his target, and hidden in the grass his arrows were piercing with double power. Order was passed now quietly from men to men to be ready for a charge when the command was given. We had passed the middle of the field and it seemed their breastworks had been damaged to such an extent as to make it easy for us to get over them. The rebels did not fire a shot from their works and it seemed to me as if they were deserted. The order to charge did not come but an other brigade to relieve us and they charged immediately, we falling in behind them as second line. The rebel skirmishers were all taken prisoner. With a "Hurrah" we went for, and over the works and found—nothing but a goodly number of dead Johnnies. Our brigade was ordered back to the creek, w[h]ere we immediatily set to work to bury the dead.

One would hardly call this a battle and still our Regt. lost heavy. We had 35 killed and 90 wounded.[7] It will be seen that the number of killed is unusual large compared with the wounded. Usually there are 5 or 6. wounded to one killed, but here it was more than one killed to three wounded; a loss which selldom has happened during the war. The Comps. who came behind the hedge at the creek did not suffer so much, but the other Comps. who came from the ridge directly in the open field suffered so much more. My Comps. loss was Lewis Sykes killed, George Rawson, Colorbearer killed. Andrew Jackson, Aug. [Pierrelee], and Henry Jenkins wounded.[8]

The last rites over our fallen Comrades being over we were allowed to consider the state of the inner man. It was sunset now and would soon be

THE BATTLE OF RESACA

night. We were reminded officially to "sleep on our Arms." . . . I was soon fast asleep but was suddenly aroused by a lively discharge of musketry and artillery. It seemed to me we had not slept an hour, but consulting my watch I found it to be 2. A.M. "Fall In! Fall in!" and immediately we were double-quicked towards the rebel works where our advanced line was making the racket. The enemies batteries seemed to be about two miles away in, or behind the wood and their shells came in such a liberal way as to convince us they had enough of them to spare. Fortunately they did not find the correct distance and range and the shells went whooping over us, exploding in the vicinity of the creek where we had slept. So it prooved fortunate for us to have moved forward, else we might have met with serious loss.

Coming up to our batteries we laid down rifle in arm. We were sent forward to support the batteries. Our Infantrie, who were a quarter of a mile ahead in the woods gradually ceased firing and so did the batteries. Some wounded came back who informed us that the fuss was started by a rebel scouting party who had tried to steal through our skirmish line. They were taken prisoner but not before they had discharged their rifles and in this wise set the mutual serenade agoing. We slept here the remaining part of the night untill 5. A.M. when we were marched not forward but back to the Creek again where we made breakfast. There was considerable Speculation about this backward movement but we had to submit to the higher powers that were.

May 15th. Precisely at 8. A.M. business was started again way off to the left, which was spedily followed on the right. Ere a quarter of an hour had passed there was lively work more or less along the whole line. We were ordered to fall in and marched between and around the hills untill we came to a miserable wagon road where our brigade train was drawn up. The men were ordered to put their knapsacks on the respective Regts. Wagons. Here I found Remick Knowles and Draper among the teamsters. I inquired if the Drs. had been so far away that it took all day to get Jackson there. But they had an ex[c]use ready. They had got lost between the hills and finding the train here in the afternoon they had thought better stay with it. I had no opportunity to reprimand them much, as the boys did that in an able and cutting way. Knowles even had spunk enough to request to be allowed to stay with the wagons to guard the knapsacks, which of course was refused.

We were hurried towards the right now in right lively fashion. It was about three miles and the nearer we came the more furious the contest seemed to wax. Finally we marched by the left flank and drew up behind two batteries who had taken position on a slight prominence and were pegging away at a big formidable work just in front of Resaca and the R.R. bridge. We stopped behind the batteries as support. I went up to the Crest to have a look at the front. The rebel works seemed to be immense Earthworks on which our round shot did make but little impression. The balls would bore themselves into the dirt, got stuck and stay there without doing much damage.

About a mile to our right flank was a round, conical hill of considerabl size called: "Bald Hill." The rebels had twoo batteries stationed on the hill which found the range on our position and soon made it dicidely unpleasant for us. Genl. McPherson wanted that special hill very bad, not alone to stop their firing on our line and flank, but to occupy it himself, as the hill commended both Resaca and the bridges across the Ostanaula river. He selected Genl. Peter Osterhaus to take his Division and see if he coud coax the Johnnies to leave "Bald Hill" to him. Osterhaus . . . was a former prussian Officer . . . a good Stratigian [strategist] and cool and brave under all circumstances. He was a favorite in the Army of the Tennessee and the men of his Division adored him. He brought two batteries in position to engage the batteries on the hill; the Infantry he brought under cover of the woods nearly to the foot of the hill. About midway between the foot and the top of the hill was a ring of breastworks around the hill held by the rebel Infantry. As soon as his batteries began to play the batteries on the hill lost their interest in us as they had their hands full now tending to Osterhaus.[9]

We watched the hill, which was in plain sight, with deep interest. Allthough we did not know at that moment that Osterhaus was preparing to storm the hill we suspected that from the sudden ceasing of firing onto us, and their rapid firing on some other object, that some danger was threatening the Johnnies on the hill. For about ten minutes the rebel batteries worked convulsively, so to speak, enveloping the top of the hill in a dense cloud of smoke; then gradually their fire slakened and ceased nearly alltogether. Why? were their guns disabled? Or the Cannoniers killed and wounded? We found out soon. A blue ring, like a big ribbon suddenly envelloped the hill about the third part from its base where the Johnnies had their breastworks. And now an other and still another and now a faint rattle of musketry was heard. "They have got them! Every one of them"! the Captain of a battery shouted, who had been watching the proceeding through his fieldglass. "No one has escaped" he added. "See? they are hoisting the stars and stripes now." Yes, we saw the flagg and allso a crowd of dark, small objects crowding around and up the hill, but to[o] small and uncertain to distinguish friend from foe. But before night we knew that our men had taken 1200. prisoners and 12 Cannon.

During this time the fighting in the centre and on the left had gone on steadily. Judging by the sound, our troops were steadily pressing around the rebel right and rear. If McPherson should succeed in throwing the 15th and 17th Corps across the river to our right and gain the roads towards Kingston, Genl. Johnston could not get out and had either to fight as long as he could or surrender. It was a bad country to fight in especially in the offensive. Large body of troops could not be employed to any advantage and that saved Johnston.

From about 1. P.M. to 3. our batteries ceased firing as allso did the rebel batteries. The battery men buried their dead and brought back the wounded. But at three O clock they set to work again. I wondered if those works in front of us were to be charged and if we were to take part in it. The works were perhaps ¾ of a mile in front of us and allso on elevated ground. A broad girt of abattis protected the works as allso a line of palisades and a broad and deep ditch. (Note. Abattis are constructed by falling trees in such a manner that the tops or branches point outward. The small branches are then trimmed of[f] and left on the ground. Other branches of the size of an inch and upward are then sharp pointed. If there are trees enough such an Abattis can be made impregnable. Pallisades are logs usually 10 foot long, sometimes round, sometimes hewn on two [sides], set endways 2 or 3, foot in the ground and a few inches apart for loopholes. Sometimes they are strenghtened by strong girths on both sides. They are usually put outside the ditch or Moat.)

Two lines of our men were laying in the depression between the elevations constantly looking out for some curious or careless Johnny who should expose his scalp more than desirable. I have no Idea how many men were behind and in these works, but if they had to be taken by assault it would lay low many a yanke soldier. The Captain of one of the batteries was so kind to lent me his fieldglass and I studied the thing carefully. It was built in the form of a five pointed star with somewhat obtuse points; all made of dirt, the embrassures for their batteries made of sandbags. The ditch seemed to be a rod wide, how deep I could not see. The Palisades were more than half knocked down by our batteries but the abattis were close and formidable. A good bombproof was inside for storing ammunition and other articles. A strong breastwork Extended right and left. There were 18 guns in it but some seemed to have been disabled by our guns. If the abattis had not been there it might have been successfully assaulted, but as it was it would be at best a foolhardy undertaking.

But it seemed Genl. Thomas had no Idea to charge the Fort. The afternoon wore away without any order to that effect. A[t] six P.M. the Capt. ordered the gunners to sent the Johnnies six rounds of shells and then retire the Cannon out of range. The Cannoniers obeyed with a will and it must have made the Johnnies hunt their holes if they had any. Shortly after we were ordered down to make Coffee. After supper we were taken up to the battery again and told to lay down with the rifle alongside of us. I could not sleep for a long while. The roar of the Cannon all day had made my head so confused that it seemed to me they were booming still.

May 16th. At daylight we were surprised by our fifers, buglers and drummers sounding the reveillee in regular camp fashion, a thing which is never done in the presence of an enemy. The reason we soon learned. The Johnnies had scedadled. Johnston, seeing that before an other day was gone he would be bagged, had taken the wiser course and left the field, a lot of provision and ammunition to us. McPherson had indeed succeeded during the night to cross the river but he did not reach the Kingston road in time to prevent Johnstons escape. After a short time our train came up and as soon as the boys had their knapsacks we started after the rebs. . . .

On the 18th Johnston held a very favorable and commanding position on a succession of hills in front of Cassville. Our army closed up that day and on the morning of the 19th Sherman intended to attack him, but on account of some misunderstanding among the rebel Corps commanders Johnston thought it best to fall back crossing the Etowah river at Cartersville, burning railroad and wagon bridges and retreating to Allatoona Pass which he could hold against any force. Sherman allowed us a few days rest here at Kingston in order that rations might be brought forward. As the railroad bridge at Resaca had been burned we did not know how long it would take to rebuilt the same. It did not take long though; because on the evening of the second day we heard the lusty tooting of the Engine.

Genl. Jeff C. Davis with his Division joined us here again. He had been sent off from Resaca on an expedition to Rome Ga. This is situated near the confluence of the Ostanaula and the Etowah rivers, forming the Coosa river 30 miles southwest of Resaca and 12 miles from Kingston. Rome is connected with the Chattanooga railway with a side branch. It was so far of importance to the rebels as there were a number of mills, factories and foundaries wich furnished war material for the rebel armies. Jeff C. Davis succeeded in capturing its forts with 10 guns of heavy Callibre and everything else.[10]

While here we had heavy picket duty to perform. Every day half the men allmost would be detailed for that duty; so the men actually had but ones days rest out of two. One day several men came to me and made complaint that Miles Fenno had not done any picket or guard duty, nor any other fatigue duty since we had left Lookout mountain. The Orderly Sergeant, who has to tend to such details, was Lyman C. Wait[e] was a special friend of Miles H. Fenno. The latter was a smart, well educated boy, but not worth the salt as a soldier. A big Officers Bee was bumming in his hat which made him believe he was to[o] good, and above doing duty as a common soldier. He had not done much duty in the Comp. as he allways succeeded in getting some kind of light detail work with the Quartermaster, or Commissary, or trainmaster etc. but after the battle of Chickamauga he was returned for duty. He hated me honestly because he had not succeded in stealing the Orderly Sergeancy from me at Mitchelville Tenn. He allso had an Idea that a man not born in America, was [not] fit for anything but to stop the rebel bullets and do all the nasty work; in short he was a conceited Kno[w]nothing.[11] The Orderly Sergeant has no right to excuse any men from duty. As soon as the Complaint was made I sent for the Orderly and questioned him about the matter but he at first denied the change and said the Dr. had excused Fenno. I went to the Dr. and inquired. Th[e] Dr. said Fenno had not been there. I went back and called for the plaintiffs and Confronted them with the Orderly. He had nothing more to say. I intended first to have the orderly reduced to the ranks and I told him so but his instant begging and promises to do better, but most of all, he was really an exellent soldier and that prompted me to let him off with a reprimand.

When John Bubol[t]z was taken sick so suddenly at Ringgold I had to look round for an other cook. I selected a certain Jack Rexford who, on account of his being very nearsighted, was but a poor soldier. But I soon found him to be a failure. He had not the least Idea of preparing the most common meal, next he was to[o] lazy, and last but not least, he was alltogether to[o] dirty to suit my taste. I therefore dismissed him and took young Chas. [Lymer] who just now felt somewhat sick. He did fairly well and I kept him untill he got tired of it.

Genl. Sherman did not intend to attack Johns[t]on from the front at Allatoona pass. It would cost to[o] many men with but poor show of success. He decided to make a flank movement far to the right and endeavor to gain, or reach Johnstons rear and at the same time keep him occupied so as to prevent him from attacking the communikation in our rear. If that could be done successfully, Johnston would be oblidged to quit the pass. As we had to quit the railroad during this move, the wagons were loaded with 20 days rations besides 5 days rations we carried in our haversacks. I can not enter upon minute details during this great flanking process, but so much I will say that the Country is one of the most god forsaken I ever had the fortune to pass through. No fields, nor meadows, no houses or barns, no people or beasts, nothing but mountains and hills, and gulches and ravines, with no roads, or at best very poor ones. It is evident that the army could move but very slow in such a country, mostly on account of the wagons and batteries and the great amount of labor it implied for men and beast.

On the morning of the 22d we began the move. The Corps all took separate roads in order to get ahead faster, the 15th and 17th Corps on the extreme right, Hookers 20th Corps on their left, the 14th Corps (Palmers) on Hookers left and Schofields 23d Corps on the extreme left making a faint on Allatoona Pass. We had to travl six miles before we reached [the] Etowah river and before we got there Jake Rexford fell with sunstroke. It happened that an Ambulance and Dr. followed the Regt. so he was speedily taken care of, but it took him a fortnight before he was able for duty again. But, Oh! was it hot that day. We took the leaves from the black Jack oak, which grow sometimes to the size of half a sheet of foolscap paper and put them in our hats or caps and in an quarter of an hour they would be black and scorched.

When we reached the river we found we had to wade it. The 3d Division was allready crossing it. The river here was about 200 yards wide, the water reaching up to the hip with a strong current. One m[a]n alone could hardley go through, the current would take him off his legs. But three or four men joining hands could manage it well enough. Some took off their shoes and stockings, others did not. I pulled them of[f] because I thought it would be hard marching after with wet socks. But I felt sorry for my supposed smartness. The river bottom was all rocks, big and small, high and low, covered with a slimy, slippery substance on which the feet could take no halt and the slipping hurt the feet. We could not land directly on the opposite side on account of high, rocky banks but landed on a small Island near the bank. The channel between the Island and the mainland was about 40 foot wide with a roaring current. A big tree had been felled from the shore towards the Iland which served as a bridge. As the opposite bank was much higher as the Island the tree laid in a pretty sharp incline which made the

THE BATTLE OF RESACA

passage rather difficult. It was a ticklish job to ascend the bridge. If on[e] looked down at the roaring current, which swept past like a millrace he was sure to become dizzy. The boys fixed bajonet and used the rifle as a balance pole which was of great help. A Mr Bartlett a recruit of Comp. "F" between 50 and 60. years old became alarmed and dizzy when about half way up.[12] He quickly dropped on his knees, but dropped his rifle allso, and grabbed the tree with his arms and crawled up in that manner. Not so lucky was a man from the 104. Ill. He allso tried to seize the tree but missed hold, dropped down and was swept away. They never saw him again.

We marched about ten miles further on miserable roads, up and down the hills and were sufficiently tired for a good stout rest. But something else was in store for us. We were ordered to make coffee on short notice and must be through with it in half an hour. We expected to be called on for an other stretch but such was not the case. Pretty soon a wagon drove up and unloaded a lot of axes, picks, spades and shovels and we were informed that each Regt. had to make a breastwork in its front. This was alltogether a new departure which was strictly adhered to henceforth. It made no difference whether an enemy was in front or not, breastworks had to be built. If no timber was near, broad ditches were dug and the dirt thrown up towards the enemys side. The country from here to Atlanta was nearly dug up and filled with riflepits, breastworks, battery embrazures, etc. for an average wid[t]h of from 10. to 15. miles. We lacked on[e] instrument which would have saved us a great deal of trouble and labor and that was the Canthook, such as is used in the lumber camps. Our Quartermaster promised to order some but they never came. The heavier the trees were, the more solid the works. The trees were seldom cut into logs, because a long log offers more resistance to a cannon ball than a short one. In all cases a ditch run along the inside of the breastworks and the dirt thrown over to the front.

The following day we ran against an enemy on which we had not calculated. He was not the least scared by our rifles and batteries and besides he made us "Git" quick. Our Regt. happend to be in advance. Near the narrow road lay a half rotten smal brush pile. I do not know whether some of the boys had disturbed the pile, but this I know that a colony of jellow Jackets, or wasps had their domicil in there and they claimed the exclusive right of way. They got it to[o] without much dispute. It did not take a minute and the whole Regt. was whisking through the underbrush trying to loose them little devils. The troops in our rear, in order to escape them, made a considerable flank mo[v]ement.

It was an awfull hot day again. We marched perhaps 10 miles, built works, made coffee and laid down. All that was done at sunset. We were in antici- pation of a solid nights rest. Meanwhile the sky became decorated with queer looking clouds, such as usually come before a heavy thunderstorm. Soon it was as dark as pitch. We were sure we would have a plenty of rain and felt sorry not to have put up tents. But it was to[o] late now; in the inky darkness one could not see the difference between a tent pole and a tree. Well, we adjusted our Ponchos as good as possible, determined to have some rest [even] if it rained pitchforks. I dont know how long we had slept, but the Sergeant Major from somewhere hollered: "Fall in 21st." I need hardly say that that was a difficult job. I and the Orderly laid just behind the first stake of rifles and therefore knew where the right of the Comp. was. By calling names from file to file the Comps. were formed. "Right face, March." Slowly at first lightning began to illuminate the woods and a rum- bling noise advertised the coming storm. And it came fast, very fast indeed. Presently their was no intermission between the glaring, almost blinding lightning strokes. Crash upon Crash made the very Earth trembling.

I looked at the watch. 11. P.M. A peculiar whispering, murmuring noise was now moving in the tree tops such as allway preceedes a tempest. It came sudden and with a force which seemed to bent the tree tops half way down to the ground. Such a force would have unrooted any tree in the north, but it seems the roots take better hold of the ground here as [than] they do in the north. And with the wind came the rain. Not a rain either; a waterfall is the proper name, which rattled against our Ponchos as if driven out of the hoose of a fire engine. Presently we came in an open clear place which, as far as I could notice might be about 20. or thirty acres hemmed in all round by hills, but whether field or pasture or merely wild ground I could not decide, for just now it looked more like a lake than anything else. The water stood 3 to 4 inches everywhere, only here and there a little black Iland would denote an Elevated spot. The brigade was halted here untill the storm abated, the rain keeping on moderately for a quarter of an hour more when the skye became bright and starlit once more.

After a little while we started again. We were cautioned as we had to wade a creek at the foot of the hills. The creek was much swollen, the water pouring in from the hills on all sides. The men were told to take of[f] their cartridgebox belts and hold the box high. The boys knew a better way. They bound box and haversack on the riflebarrel and carried them high on their shoulders. At day time the thing would have been simple as then the

THE BATTLE OF RESACA

original creek bed could have been located which was now impossible. For rods we waded knee deep in the water to be suddenly dumped up to the neck into the original creek bed. It was not dangerous as the creek was narrow and the opposite side high. Good many got badly scared though but the most made fun of it and helped each other to a ducking which under the circumstances was just as good as crying. We tramped about four miles farther and finally staked arms on a lofty ridge and immediately squatted down for an other nap.

Why thus [this] night tramp was made is only known to the leading powers that were. In campaign life it is much as in Religion. As we are thought [taught] that everything which transpires, however vexing and unwellcome it might be, is to our ultimate best, so in field life. Every order, every move, must be accepted by the subordinate as absolutely necessary and for the good of the whole, and if anybody should dare to enter a protest, well, he would get hurt. I never forget how the Sunday after the battle at the Chickamauga, our old Chaplain Rev. Clinton tryed his best to convince us how necessary and how good it was for us, and how thankfull we ought to be to god Allmighty for the sound thrashing we got and consequently had now the consoling privilege to starve to death. There were not half a dozen men in the Regt. who believed it, and he himself did not, because I heard him later, when his mule got caught with one leg between some cypress roots and broke the lege, and he had to travel on foot, cuss and swear like a good trooper. Why? Because he knew that Providence just then kept no mules on hand for him, and he had to hunt for one himself, or have some one else do it for him. But I will drop that and try to sleep.

We were left undisturbed untill 7. A.M, when half an hour was allowed for coffee. It was a long tripp that day but we did make not much headway for all that. I[t] semed we were much like a flock of sheep, wandering at random. Now right, then left and once in a while a little forward. The storm the previous night had been of some good. It had cooled the temperature wonderfully. At 6 P.M. the fortifying process began and at nine we were ready for the Coffee. But the following morning at 4. we were ready to start.

For a number of miles the road went along on the top of a long ridge and was in good passable condition, but then it decended to the lower regions and the winding and twisting began again. It was allso much warmer as the previous day. Finally the road took an upward course to an immense plateau. Some small fields were seen and here and there a little log hut. . . . We halted here to make dinner. . . . At half past 3. we were suddenly stirred

up by cannon shots towards our right and front. More reports followed and
we were soon in quick step. We could not hear any firing of small arms as it
was to[o] far away. We had gone about a mile when a Courier came from
the front bearing orders for Genl Johnson our Division Commander. We
turned of[f] from the road and took a right oblike direction. Our advance
Div. Genl. Geary[']s had met a rebel Brigade of Cavallery who had undertaken to stop their Advance but were quickly pushed aside.[13]

We had worked forward in the new direction perhaps two miles when
on our right front the Circus started in earnest. There seemed to be something else than Cavallery. In less than 10 minutes there were at least half a
dozen batteries at work. That was on the road Genl. Hooker was moving;
the place called "New Hope Church." Hooker had unmasked Stewar[t's]
Division of Hoods Corps who were behind good works. Hooker had but
one Division in hand, and with that alone he could not undertake to attack
and carry the works. When his other Divisions finally came up he made
preparation to attack the works, but a dark stormy night setting in, he had
to wait for the coming day. We were moved out there to protect Hookers
left flank and when on the same hight with him formed line of battle,
posted pickets and slept on our arms. It was again a stormy night but not so
bad as we had experienced a few nights ago.

May. 26. We were not allowed to make coffee this morning. Raw bacon,
hardtack and liberal allowance of water is sometimes a good meal, especially
if no better victuals lay round loose. We marched forward in line of battle
front, scirmishers in advance. That is miserable work. One wing of the Regt.
would be in a gulch, while the other was high up on some hill or ridge.
About 9. A.M. we formed brigade colum and holted. About 10. Hooker took
up the game which had been interrupted the previous night. It was a very
obstinate affair and it took Hooker untill 3. P.M. before he could convince
Stewart that he must get out of there. At 2. P.M. the fuss began on the hills
in our front and was soon in full working order. Johnsons and Jeff C. Davis
Divisions had it with two Div[s]. of Hoods Corps. We were advanced to
supporting distance and sat down. The 2d and 3d brigade of our Division
formed on the left of our brigade. The fight became furious. The wounded
were coming, or caried down the hights in great numbers. About an hour
before dark we were brought forward to relieve the front lines. The rebel
had breastworks while we were laying on the ground unprotected. Our
Artillerie tried hard to demolish their works, while we tried our best to keep
the rebel Infantry low. It was more of an artillery fight than anything else

THE BATTLE OF RESACA

and most all our casualties were the result of e[x]ploding shells. When night set in the firing ceased. During the night they fell back to an line of works a mile south of Pumpkin vine Creek. Thus engagement is called by some "New Hope Church"; by some "Picket Mills," from a few rotten timbers which in bygone times had belonged to a Mill on the Creek.[14]

Again the night grew dark like an underground dungeon. We went down the hills and were led round several hours this way and that, as if we had been in search of something which was not there. Finally, it seemed, nobody knew where south or north, east or west was to be located. Pickets crept forward several rods and the balance laid down. . . .

When daylight next morning enabled us to take a view of the situation we found we had taken position with our back toward the rebels. We were only about 15 [rods] from the Creek and the rebel pickets on a ridge at the other side. The first thing was to countermarch and to bring the different comands in their proper places. That done it was learned that our train was in danger of being attacked by rebel cavalry. We had to double quick nearly a mile to learn that our Cavallery had treated the rebel Cavallery to a regular "Hail Columbia." We took a little more time going back and next made coffee. We had not tasted coffee since the night before last and was therefore double wellcome.

When that was done Genl. Carlin, commanding our brigade[,] had come to the conclusion that we ought to have that ridge the other side of the creek which was now occupied by the rebel scirmishers. Well, we went through the Creek, (which, by the way is something of a stream and just now contained an abundance of a yellow, muddy fluid.) and up the ridge and tried to convince the Johnnies that we ought to have that ridge. They seemed not to understand the case; they seemed to think; "Come and get it if you dare." They argued their case with a very stubborn but able manner. But finally under our repeated an[d] stronger arguments they looked at the case from a different standpoint and gave us quit claim Deed of the ridge. . . . To secure our right of possession we imediately set to work and built good breastworks and several batteries were soon in position.

General Carlin came looking round again and informed us that after dinner he had an other job for us. In front of us and only separated by an abrupt and deep ravine was an other long ridge, similar and parallel with the one we were on now. On the other side of that ridge, it was supposed, the rebel works were situated somewhere. That was what Carlin wanted to know. The rebel scirmishers were on the ridge now and their sharpshooters were ex[c]hanging compliments with ours right along. Genl. Carlin was of a greedy disposition; he wanted that ridge allso. He acted on the principle: "The more on[e] has, the more on[e] needs." On the strenght of that he ordered that two Comps. from each Regt. be taken who were to deploy as scirmishers and buy that ridge at any price.

Col. Hobart chosse for the part of our regt. Comps. "D." and "E." mine and Capt. Weisbrods. The comp. of the other Regts, 16 in all came to the place of Rendezvous. Capt. Weisbrod had the Command of the right half, and a Capt. of the 42d Ind. of the left half. We deployed and at a prearainged signal started down the one ridge and up the other. The preliminary arraignments and debates as to our right of possession did not take half as long. When the[y] found we were willing to argue the matter with the bajonet they faced about and went down the other side. But I imediately discovered two unpleasant facts. My Comp. held the extreme right of our brigade line. Now, no sooner had we reached the hight of the ridge than we received a flank fire from the right. Next, Some raskals were firing at us from the rear. From the right of my Comp. the line was to be extended by scirmishers from the first Wisconsin. But they were not there, and the Johnnies still in possession of that part of the ridge. I withdrew half a dozen files of my Comp. to a right angle with the line, which enabled them to take care of the rebels in flank. Next I told the Orderly to take care of the Comp. untill I had things straightened in the rear. Then I went down to see about the backsliders in the rear.

When nearly down in the ravine, I was suddenly startled by a shot only a few yard away. There, behind a chestnut bush sat R[e]mick Knowles loading his rifle again. I told him that he could not hurt a rebel from here, but that he easy might kill some of his comrades and wanted him to go up and join his comrades. But he smiled and said he woud shoot over the ridge and rather wait untill the boy[s] came back. He was just about putting a cap on the rifle when I put my revolver within 6 inches of his head and told him to start. That straightened him instantly and he began moving slowly upward. I followed him closely until I was sure he would not squat again. A little further back I found behind a big log Sergeant Joe Holden, and two recruits John Sutschutz and John Darby [Derby].[15] I inquired what business they had here. The recruits replied the Sergt. had asked them to stay with him; the Sergeant said he had not heard the order to go forward. I gave them the choice between going forward immediately, or a court martial. They went.

Then I went to see about the first Wis. scirmishers. Th[e]ly were still on the line from which we had started. I inquired of the first man I met why they had not advanced. They said their Lieut. would not let them. I found the Lieut. The first look told me all. A young, haughty looking fellow who told me he would not move a step unles ordered by the Col. of his Regt. I undertook to explain to him that this advancing the scirmish line was not a matter of one Regt. but a detail of number of Regts. and that he was ordered with two Comps. of his Regt. to take part in it. Then he began to use high language and wound up by directing me to the devil. I turned to report to Genl. Carlin. Happily I met him and Col. Hobart overlooking the grounds. "Whats is up?" Hobart asked. I explained our situation on the ridge, the conversation with the 1st Wis. Lieut. and wound up with informing Col. Hobart that our men were nearly out of ammunition. "I will tend to that" he replied and I went back to the Comp. Shortly after the 1st Wis. boys came up, but the young Lieut. was not with them. He was cashired by a court martial and dishonorable dismissed [from] the Service.

This ridge was one of the hottest scirmish places I ever was in. . . . We remained here 8. days and the first four days either mornings before daylight or evenings, just after dark the rebels would make a dashing charge, sometimes dislodging our line and sometimes being sent home with blody noses. It was a hard service at best. We relieved mornings at daylight and evenings at dark so that 12 hours passed on steady duty. During the day the men had to lay low and watch all the while. The least carelesness would provoke the rebs to spill a pill. Of course it was tit for tat, as our boys and especially the Indians were as wide awake as the rebs. But they had one great advantage. Our blue uniforms and brass buttons and blue Cap or hat could readily be seen at a distance, whereas their dirty gray stoff could not be detected when not in motion. The old trick of rasing a hat, or cap and pick them off while shooting at it, was practised so often here that it became an old chestnut and did not draw a pennys worth.

The 3d night was my turn to stay out all night. It was bright moonlight, allthough the folliage of the trees cast a shadow it was bright enough to see one moving if not to[o] far distant. The Johnnies seemed to be very spitefull to night and kept on popping, close over the brow of the ridge. Near midnight I went along the line behind the men of my Comp. I kept beneath the crest of the ridge so as to be safe for bullets. Allmost to the left of the Comp. were Chas Buck and James P. Orr. . . . He had played crazy for a while thinking he woud get a dis[c]harge and was altogether an ugly customer.[16] . . . When I came behind them a reb happened to send a bullet over there. The bullet whizzed over us, but at the same moment Orr got onto his knees, turned round and fired at me. That would have certainly settled my carier had not Charles Buck, at the moment Orr pulled the trigger, with a quick move of his arm pushed the rifle upward exclaiming: "Orr, what are you doing?!" The bullett whizzed close over my head. "God dam you" Orr cried "I dont want you to shoot at me."—"I did not shoot at you Orr. Buck and others can testify to that. The bullet you heard came from the rebel lines. Now hand me your rifle." He refused to do that and began to load again. I sprang at him, got him by the nape of the neck and held him down while Buck had to use all his force to wrench the rifle from him. I ordered Charles Hilfert[17] to guard Orr until we were relieved, and at the same time instructed him to fix bajonet and pin Orr to the ground, or shoot him if he should move. I knew Hilfert had [would have] done it if necessary because Orr had bitten him in one hand while on Lookout Mountain, which nearly had cost him that limb.

The night wore slowly away. Towards morning I again went along the line and warned all to be on the sharp lookout for the Johnnies. Sergeant Sylvester Greeley and Henry [Jenkins] I instructed to crawl carefull forward and observe if anything unusual was going on in the rebel line and report every suspicious sign. I took Orrs rifle and cartridges to use them myself if need be. The Johnnies had not fired a shot during the last hour. I told the men to fix bajonet now in order to be ready in case of emergency. . . . Presently Sergt. Greeley returned and said he believed we soon would have a lively surprise party. . . .

The suspense and anxiety allways present before an expected attack or charge did not last long. I soon heard their movements in the brush. When they came among the open timber they tried to advance from tree to tree, but their Officers found that to[o] slow and ordered them forward. I said to the boys loud enough that the rebs could hear it: "Boys! Our friends are coming for their crakers. Give them full rations."! Then I fired the first shot and winged on[e] and immediately the boys followed suit. "Charge bajonet"! And that was promtly done. The Jonnies were so surprised at the counter-charge that hardley half of them discharged their rifles, but turned and ran down hill. Others even forgot to turn back but remained with us. When we returned Col. Hobart and Lt. Col. Fitch came running up with the relief party. "We heard you had a surprise party and hurried to have a hand in it, but I see we came to[o] late" Hobart said. "Come behind the works now and have your coffee."—"But what have we here?" seeing Hilfert standing guard by Orr. I explained the story. Orr was sent to Division Headquarters under guard. Lieut. Stewart [Stuart] of Comp "B." relieved me in the scirmish line.[18]

THE BATTLE OF RESACA

While I was speaking with the Col., Lieut. Col. Fitch had been looking over the ridge, now turned round and said: "There is somebody coming with a white rag on his sword."—"Flag of truce probably." Hobart said. Presently he came up and inquired if we would allow them to carry of[f] their wounded and bury the dead. "Certainly" Hobart replied. "how long time do you want?"—"An hour."—"well you have it, see that your men mind the truce and the time. By the way. You had bad luck this morning."—"Yes" the officer replied, "And what is worse than that: We deserved it. What is the use of such petty warfare? It only serves to kill off and disable so many men and that is all the good it effects." Seing a half dozen prisoners whom he well knew, standing there, he asked them if they were not sorry to be prisoners. "I ain't" one said resolutely, but the others looked at their toes and said nothing. In front of our Comp. the rebs had to bury three and carry off 16 wounded. I[n] my Comp. Julius Weinert[19] had a slight hip wound Jake Rh[e]iner had his canteen smashed.

While going back to our works I remarked to Col. Hobart that if we were to stay here much longer it would pay to make some little works for shelter on the ridge and make the rebels tired of their foolish charging. "Rifle pitt you mean"? he said. "No, that log shanty there is the thing for it." I replied. "Well," he said. "take as many men as you want and set to work."

In front of our works, but down in the ravine stood a log building 16 x 24. and 16 foot high. When we came there the building was packed full of leaf tobacco bundles. That was a very wellcome article, because since we left Resaca we had to rely for smoking tobacco on the self manufactured "Exelsior" invented and patented at Chattanooga as allready related. The only door was securely fastened but that was no hindrance. Evidently the building had been put up there for the purpose of saving the tobacco from the thievish yankees. It was new; there was no road leading towards it and no farm or plantation near it, in fact, it stood in a wilderness. I took two men from each Comp. 20 in all and within an hour the building lay scattered on the ground. None of the logs was over 10 inches through. I had them al chopped in 8 foot lenghts and carried up the ridge. When the transportation began, all the men of the Regt. who were not on duty had to lay hands on. When evening came the logs were all up but I could not put them in shape during the night. Shortly before dark Lieut. Stewart sent in notice that he believed the rebs were going to charge again and asked for help. Lieut. Col. Fitch called for Volunteers who soon were on hand.

In Comp. "I." was a certain Robinson who allways volunteered as scirmisher but this time he kept back.[20] The men of his Comp. called on him but he shook his head and said: "Not this time boys. If I go with you you will have to bring me back." Of course they all laughed at him and, to stop their laughing, he grabbed his gun and said: "I am going. It is just as well now as any other time." We were hardly over the works when the racke[t] began. We ran down as fast as legs could carry us. Down in the ravine Lieut. [Stuart] met us, bare headed, running back at full speed like a scared deer all alone, while his men were up on the midle of the ridge, stubbornly fighting the rebs. Next came a French Canadian of Comp. "E." with the lower jaw shot away.[21] We worked up the ridge untill we came in line with the fighting men. Ordre went from file to file to have guns loaded and fix bajonet. Then: "Charge bajonet." The rebs fired before we were fairly on our legs, because not a shot was fired while we were clambering upward. They all were running down when we came on the crest of the ridge. We went back again and the relief party was sent out to relieve the night detail. Robinson of Comp. "I" was shot through the heart during the charge. A lucky death. This is the only instance which ever came under my observation where presentiment held proof. . . .

The following morning I set to work on our defenses. It was simple enough, but very Effective. The line for the little defensive works I established about 5 to 6 rods down the ridge on our side. The prepared logs I put up in the shape of a flat ^ the point towards the enemy; four logs, or about 3½ foot high. Between the two upper logs a space was left to fire through. They were about 6 rods apart from each other. We put up 15 of them; all the timber would allow. Eight or t[e]n men found shelter in each and they could fire to the front right and left as occasion might require. When the Johnnies came the next time they did not know what happened to them, but that was the last time they came.

The move of Genl. Sherman had compelled Genl. Johnston to abandon Allatoona Pass in order to protect his rear. Sherman now moved troops to the left and seized the Pass and Ackworth Station. Johnston seeing he could not prevent Sherman now from pressing forward along the railroad, fell back to the Kennesaw Mountain line to cover Marrietta. Before we followed him Col. Hobart received a letter from James P. Orr in which the fellow begged for gods sake not to bring him before a court martial. He spoke of his wife and children and promised everything good for the future. Hobart asked me what I thought of it as the matter rested with me to decide. I hated to comply with the request because I knew the m[a]n to[o] well. If he had been a unmarried man I certainly would not have consented to his request, but as the matter stood I told the Col. to have him released. . . .

THE BATTLE OF RESACA

During the night of the 6th it rained allmost incessantly. The rebel scirmishers had opposed our advance most stubernly, so much so that w[e] litterally had to fight for every foot of ground. On the morning of the 7th it was Capt. Edwards turn to tend to the scirmish line. He reported sick. Next after him came Capt. Bradish turn. He allso reported sick. Next came my turn and I received ordre for the duty. As this was the third time the two Capts. played that trick on me, and as they allways managed to be sick on the same day, I became suspicious of a well arraigned plot between the two to escape their duty and make me their stoolpidgeon. I went to the Doctors to ascertain if they had reported sick. I allso noted the dates of their supposed infirmities in my diary and should my suspicions proove to be correct, to give them a good lesson in proper time. I went as ordered and found a very hot place. I could not help thinking that the knowledge of this had something to do with the indisposition of the two brave Capts.[22]

It happened that our scirmish line was in a low marshy flat, sparsily covered with here and there a willow or alder brush. The rebels were on high ground and protected by good riflepits. Besides they had a stronger line than we had. It was expected that we should drive the rebels away so that our troops could take up line of march. I soon discovered that we could not scare the Johnnies a cents worth and sent a Sergt. to Genl. Carlin asking for more troops, when just at that moment Capt. Buckskin came with two parrot guns. The men drew the guns by hand as no horse could travel in the marsh. "Wait a moment!" Capt. Buckskin hollered to me; "We will give these fellows some real hardtack." And so he did. A couple dozen rounds induced the rebels to lay low and when we made a Charge they thought best to quit. This Capt. Buckskin was a brave fellow. I believe fear was unknown to him. His right name was Dilger. He had been an Artillery Officer in the Bavarian army in Germany, but had taken leave of absence for the purpose to fight in our war. The boys, allways eager to improove on names, had christened him: "Buckskin, or Leather breeches." because he allways wore buckskin pants and boots the shafts of which reached above the knees. He originally belonged to the Eleventh Corps and had at the battle of Chancellorsville saved that Corps from serious disaster.[23] He came with Hooker to our army. He was a dare devil fellow, the best Artillerie Officer in the Corps, and known in the whole army. His men would go through the fire for him. He spoke but imperfectly English and when pressing business was on hand, or in the heat of action he would rattle off commands and curses in regular south german style, but the soldiers knew [how] to interpret that and everything went smooth and slick.

CHAPTER FIFTEEN

~

Advance on Atlanta

~ Kenesaw mountain is 3 or 4 miles north of Marietta. The Chattanooga and Atlanta R.R. winds around its eastern slope between Kennesaw and brushy hill. The Mountain stretches westward for about a mile and a half. A mile southwest is Pine mountain, not quite so imposing as Kennesaw and an other mile northeast is Lost mountain; so called from its isolated position, rising like a giant molehill out of the level country. Those three mountains form a flat triangle and constituted Johnstons Line of defense. His right rested on brushy hill, east of Kennesaw and the railroad, thence extending westward and along the mountain toward Pine mountain and thence to Lost mountain. They were very formidable works and the mountains, especially Kennesaw, bristled with batteries. From the lofty hights they were enabled to overlook and observe all our movements and discern their intentions. Just north of and at the foot of the mountain was a little railroad station called "Big Shanty," well known by the capture of a rebel Lokomotive by Union Soldiers dressed in butternut garb, during the spring of 1862.[1]

On the 9th we arrived within four miles of their works and were opposed by strong scirmish lines who allways were protected in riffle pits. Especially the batteries on the hights were exedingly annoying. Once, our brigade had just been relieved from half a days skirmish, when the Commissary began issuing rations. He had [t]he craker and bacon boxes unloaded in an open spot, and the men detailed to bring the rations to camp gathered around to await their turn. It was over two miles from the rebel batteries; but the[y] must have espied us, because a big shell found its way to the spot and burried itself in the ground close to the crowd and then exploded, covering men and rations with an abundance of dirt and prompting several mule teams near by to hunt for a safe place. If the fuse had been cut a mite shorter the men might not have escaped with a mere scare.

An other time, we allso had been relieved from the scirmish line, we had laid down to catch a little sleep. It was about 9. A.M. The 42d Indiana were in an open pi[e]ce of ground and as the weather was very hot some of the men had put up shelter tents just for shade. Of course the rebels saw these from their Elevated Position. A Captain and Orderly Sergeant laid alongside in one of these tents. A solid round shot struck the ground a little ways from the tent, bounced up again and passing crossways through the tent passed over the Capt. who laid straight on his back, but the Orderly, who allso laid on the back with the knees high up, lost both leggs above the knees. The Doctors sawed off the stumps but the poor fellow had lost to[o] much blood and died shortly after. The men of his Comp. did not mourn much over the loss because, they said, he was the only Copperhead in the Comp.

Another fellow of the same Regt. received a severe punishment for his foolhardishness. A round ball was rolling along the ground having spent its flying force. The soldier, seeing the ball coming along, jumped in the direction of the ball, and putting the right heel firmly on the ground lifted the toe end to stop the ball. Good many called on him to get out of the way but he did not mind them. Before he knew he lay sprawling on his back, minus the right foot. A severe lesson indeed.

We did not give the Johnnies much rest, either by day or by night. About the fourteenth we had pushed so close up to their works that no more scirmishers could be sent out. We allso had constructed good works and the firing was done from one breastwork to the other. At some places the works were so close together as to be allmost within stones throw. It can easily be understood that this became a very delicate and tiring business. The coffee we had to make in the ditch behind the works because anything seen moving would draw a lot of bullets; in short we had to keep low. Sergeant Julius Hesse of Neenah Wis. while making Coffee thoughtlessly jumped out of the ditch to grab a few sticks of wood which lay only a few yards off.[2] A bullet struck him across the back and although breaking no bones, tore the skin from shoulder to shoulder, inflicting an exceedingly painfull wound. It never healed and when I saw him 15 years later it was still and steady discharging.

Both parties finally got tired of the vexing business and the men came to some kind of agreement. Mornings, at noon and evenings, one party or the other would hang a rag on a stick, plant the stick on the breastwork and holler: "Hello Johnny! Hallow Yank! Time for breakfast." and the so called party allso would hoist a rag and the truce was made and concientiously kept. ¾ of an hour was usually the time allowed, when one, or the other party woul[d] shout: "Hello! Yank, or Johnny! time is up! Look out," and the dodging was the rule again. After dark every Regt. would sent out a couple of videttes outside the works to guard against surprise. The Johnnies of course did the same. These videttes soon established commercial intercourse. They would barter coffee for tobacco; the Johnnies having no Coffee and we were short in tobacco. They allso would get hold once in a while of a rebel newspaper which allways ex[c]ited our curiosity. They were printed mostly on browen wrapping or wall paper. I remember receiving once the Charleston Mercury and Courier, the worst secesh paper in the South. It contained a lenghty, furious article about the Atlanta Campain and Closing glorified in the Certainty how Genl. Johnston would crush us and wipe out Shermans "Hessians" when he had deluded them far enough away from home. That paper created much amusement among the boys.

On the 15th the rebel Genl. Polk was killed on Pine Mountain by one of Hookers batteries.[3] Genl. Sherman had been standing near the battery, observing pine mountain through a fieldglass. He noticed a group of Officers on the Mountain and requested the Officer of the battery to fire a shot at them, "to make them lively, you know." The Officer after ascertaining the position of the rebels adjusted carefully the cannon, and that shot settled Genel. Polk. Before the war Polk was a Bishop of the southern Methodist Church in Mississippi. He was one of the most rampant rebels in the Confederacy and that had enduced him to exhange bible and Gospel for the sword and blood. I wonder what old Peter said when that many colored chamaleon reported for admission to the realms of the meek and tenderhearted. A minister of the Gospel of Love and peace and good will, and a defender of tyranny, slavery and war.—

On the morning of the 16th Pine mountain was found to be abandond and on the 17th Lost mountain was allso deserted. Johnston had withdrawn his left wing to a line of small hils allso strongly entrenched and connected with Kennesaw.

As allready stated Johnston had effectually destroyed all bridges across the Etowah river. It was by no means an easy job to rebuilt those bridges. The river was at least 600 foot wide and the banks on both side of the river from 50. to 70. foot high. We left the Etowah on the 23d of May and when we came near Big shanty on the 8th of June the carrs allready brought stores for the army, the bridges having been replaced in eleven days by our Construction Corps which allways followed us. . . .

Genl. Sherman now concluded to drive the rebels out of their works by charging them. June 27th was the day appointed. On the 26th in the afternoon our brigade was suddenly ordered to accompany a brigade of Cavellerie on some kind of an expedition. We had a hard time of it but we escaped the charge on the rebel works. What for we had been out I never learned. We returned next day just when the Charge was going on. It was mainly made on the centre with the intention to break through there. Some 30,000 men took part in it. It was a pitifull sight to se[e] the men drop like apples from a tree during a Hurrycane; and poorly managed besides, the suporting troops to[o] far behind the advance. They might as well have charged Popocatepetl as those works. Those who were not shot down as soon as they reached the Abattis tried to pick of[f] the rebs when the[y] fired over the works. The supporting line returnd but had lost considerable. All day the wounded and maimed had to lay in the burning sun without help. After dark we were allowed under flag of truce to take them inside the lines and bury the dead which took us all night. Our loss amounted to over three thousand killed and wounded, while the rebs being behind good cover had about fifteen hundred.[4] It was next to murder and Sherman made the lame excuse that he had to do it in order to keep the soldiers used to fighting. If Genl. Sherman ever made a cruel blunder it was on that occasion.

Genl. Sherman now fell back on his flanking movements again. The Effect of it was that Johnston during the night from the second to 3d of July evacuated his strong works and fell back to an other strong line on the north bank of the Chattahoochee river, about 7 miles north of Atlanta. On the morning we followed in his tracks. We passed through Marietta, an aristocratic looking little City. On the big market square a lot of women felt delighted to hoot at us, making faces and giving us all sorts of titles and names which are not down in Websters "Unabridged." In one corner of the Market square, four or five bords were fastened together and set upright. An ugly looking chap in yankee Uniform running for dear life, a rebel General after him whose swordpoint tickled the yank at the seat of his trowsers, was painted in glaring colors on the boards. Underneath was painted in large letters: "The brute Sherman on the homeward track." Of course we found the thing very apropriate, cheered and laughed, asking the woman occasionally if this looked much like a retreat.

Marietta was a venomous secesh nest, so much so, that Sherman some weeks later sent an order to Genl. Kilpatrick, Commander of Cavallerie, to destroy the nest which order Kilpatrick litterally obeyed. It was a pity, but it had to be done. They harbored Guerillas, bushwhakers and cutthroats and had poisoned and abused a number of our sick and wounded soldiers. A while before the same thing had happened to Cassville a little City not far from Kingston at the Etowah river. It was the Custom of the guerillas and bushwhakers to follow at a safe distance in our rear and destroy bridges, culverts, telegraphes and railroads and hang and murder Union Soldiers whe[n]ever they had a chance. Of course they must have places where they could hide and find subsistence. After considerable watching and figuring it was found out that Cassville was such a place. Sherman sent them warning to stop that matter or some one else would, but they did not stop. So it was completely demolished, so thouroughly that hardly a rat could find a living there. It was just such aristocratic nest as Marietta.

Such measures, cruel as they seemed to be, had a wholesome Effect on guerillas and Citizens. A half dozend bushwhakers were once caught murdering a Union familie. They all were strung up on telegraph poles and left hanging, a warning for others. They had an other ugly way in hurting us. They would hide in the brush alongside the railway and fire at Engeneer and firemen, or on the soldiers on top the cars if any were there. Sherman found a remedy for that allso. A number of rebel Citizens were caught, dressed in our Uniform and then tied to the Cab near the Engeneer and firemen, as allso on top of the carrs. It was no very pleasant riding for the fellows, even if the fare was free but then it had a wholesome Effect on the bushwhakers. "What will the brute do next"? asked the Charleston Courier and Mercury when he heard of it. ("Brute." was the name Sherman went by among the rebels and northern Copperheads) and Sherman replied: "To try the experiment on yourself if you will only stay long enough untill we can get round." But the Courier man did not wait. When we got Charleston the following winter, the bird had flown.

On the morning of the fourth we met the rebel rearguard and scirmishers at Smyrna Camp grounds. As the fourth of July had to be celebrated we unfurled the stars and stripes and pressed them very hard. The Johnnies were in for an all round celebration and for a while we had all the celebration we wanted, but after repeated coaxings and flatteries they took to their heels. We followed them up untill we came nearly in reach of their batteries in their works at the Chattahootchee.

On 4th of July the year previous we had a little celebration, good news regarding Gettisburg and Vicksburg and a little fight with rebel Cavallery. This year we had neither exept the fight. Shortley after we had staked arms the Sergeant Major came with the mail. As a kind of curiosity I regarded a letter, or rather petition, from one Levant [Vandebogart]. This Levant was a perfect counterpart of Remick Knowles. They would have made a perfect team and any one would have been puzzled to decide who was the laziest of the two. Over a year ago when we started from Murfreesboro he was left in Convallescent Camp there and I had not heard anything of him since. Now in a long tirade he told a pitifull story how the brutal Commander of the Post had set them to work in the gardens and fortifications for 4 and even 6 hours a day. How they even were forced to take a rifle and go behind the ramparts when the rebel Cavallerie was round. He thought that outrageous; he had not enlisted to be abused and driven round to work, by an upstart. He might as well be in the field and make us happy once more with his presence, if I would be so kind to secure a place for him as a commissioned Officer. If nothing better could be obtained he would even accept a second Lieutenancy. I sent the letter to the commander at Murfreesboro with the request to return Levant [Vandebogart] at once to the Comp. for duty. He returned the letter saying that [Vandebogart] had just been transferred to the Invalid Corps. . . . [5]

To charge the rebel works at Chattahoochee would have been as big a folly as it was at Kennsaw. Sherman therefore sent McPherson and Schofield up the river to effect a crossing somewhere, march past Johnstons right wing and take a good position in the direction of the Augusta and Atlanta R.R. while we at the same time were working up to the rebel works. During this process I was one day with a party of scirmishers when orders came to charge the rebel scirmish line and take their riflepits. Some reinforcement were sent us and the order carried out to the letter. But the Johnnies being mad of loosing their ditches kept up a sharp firing which compelled us to be very carefull. Shortley after Chas. Lymer brought me my noon Coffee. I sat down behind a big tree, put my hat aside of me, and attacked the frugal meal. Capt. Cook of the 42d Ind. wished me good appetite whereupon I invited him to partake of the repast. He sat down on my left side. Some of our batteries behind us were busy throwing shells over us in the rebel lines. One shell with a bad fuse exploded before it had passed our lines. One of the fragments struck the ground in front of the Captain, covering us with dirt, another struck my old hat and spilling the crown in good shape. An other narrow escape.

That night, Genl. Johnston finding he had again been serieously flanked, fell back across the river in the outer defensive works of Atlanta. As usual he burnt the bridges behind him. Sherman now concluded to give the army a few days rest and so we had only picket duty to do. . . .

In Comp. "C" was a fellow Chris Sergent [Sargent]. He was a machinist and, when not on duty, allways tinkering at something.[6] He carried files, screwdriver, cold chisels, small bitts etc. in his knapsack. He was now on Reserve with us. As usual he hunted round for something and finally came back with two unexploded percussion shells under his arms. He sat down, took a screwdriver and cooly began to unscrew the cap to see why the shell had not exploded. But before he could make a turn I had snatched the tool out of his hand and held him a lecture about his careless doings. He merely grinned at me saying: there was no danger. I told him if he was willing to sacrifice his life for the Country in that manner to do it alone and not endanger the lifes of other man. He took the shells and went about 20 rods aside and began his investigations. He soon came running back with an open shell and sure enough, instead of with powder the missile was loaded with sawdust. He went back again and tried the other. But the dust of that one was of a different style. It busted, but singular, it did not hurt him any further as to burn hands, face and clothing somewhat; bad enough though it was. His ambition was gratified. He did not look for more shells.

While on Lookout he was allso the indirect cause of a painfull accident. He made an Engine which he christened: "The Confederacy," and connected it with a miniature sawmill. The thing worked admirable and amused the boys much. The boiler he had made of a Campkettle holding two pails of water. In the same Comp. was a young drummer named Norman van Nostrand [Norman W. Northam], a reckless-I-don't-care fellow. One day while the men were all out on some duty what should [Northam] do but get up steam and start the sawmill. Careless as he was he did not look for the amount of water in the boiler. Finally he found the boiler getting red hot, let on the water when the thing busted scalding him fearfully. At first it was thought he would loose his eyesight but that misfortune was averted. . . . [7]

The short rest which we were enjoying now was badly needed. We had been incessantly working day and night allmost for 70. days. Shoes and boots were worn out, Pants and blouses torn to shreeds by brush and briar. But that was not the worst of it. The continued sameness of the diat [diet], bacon, craker and coffee had produced what they called the Army disease; properly "Scorbait" scurvy (Blood rotting.) to an alarming extent. The men would be at first attacked with a tired, drowsy feeling, becoming weak in all limbs, loss of Appetite and a careless and indifferent feeling in general. In this stage it could be easyly cured if a vegetable diat coud be procured. The next stage was the swelling of face and limbs and the skin would assume a pale, ashy hue. They would walk as in a dream, not caring for anything. The gums would become loose and bleed profusely. The tongue would swell up enormously, allmost filling the cavity of the mouth. In that stage death soon relieved them. No Doctor could help them in the field. And it was so easy to cure them. A fortnights vegetable diat would set them right.

An other very troublesome complaint, though not dangerous, made its appearance while we were in the Allatoona mountains. It made itself known by an uncontrollable itching all over the body especially when laying down. It would attack leggs and arms first, but soon would extend over the whole body. Whenever the itching took hold the skin would turn red like scarlet. At first it was thought to be the result of our miserable laundry busines, that is to say, of the total absence of any laundry. We never could undress, nor even take off our shoes either day or night. During the four months campain I had my shirt washed twice, if it can be called washing by rubbing in cold water and without soap. Some Doctors having observed the disease carefully, finally solved the problem. It turned out to be a parasite of the smallest order; in fact a single on[e] of the small insects could not be seen with an unarmed eye, except on a white sheet of paper and even then it took a good eye to detect the beast. It grew on the leaves of a certain brushy plant, where it covered the lower surface of the leaves by the millions, giving it a scarlet appearance. As we were most of the time dashing about in the woods we stripped the little beasts of[f] with our clothing; They got through that easy enough without even making a hole and settled down in the skin to grow fat and increase. The Doctors soon furnished an Ointment which the little fellows did not like and they left. Another great nuisance were the wood tics. Some fellows coud raise and fatten them up to the size of a small marble, but the same ointment was poison for them. . . .

Capt. Turner returned from his nine months leave of absence hale and hearty. . . .

By the 15th of July the men were provided with the nescessary articles and the 17th was set by Genl. Sherman as the day for general advance. The very same day Jeff. Davis made an other great mistake as he had made many before. He relieved Genl. Johnston from command and put Genl. J. B. Hood in his place. Hood was a dashing fighter but a poor Strategician. As will be seen later he sacrificed the best part of his men merely for the sake of the fighting without any reason for a possible success.

On the 17th of July we once again took to the warpath. We had to march 5. miles up to Powers ferry where a pontoon bridge was laid. Here we saw for the first time the newly invented pontoon. The hull, or sceleton is of light frame work, which can be taken to pieces and put together again in a few minutes. The covering is of waterproof heavy canvass, which is drawn over the boat frame like a nightcap over the head. One wagon can carry 4. to 5. pontoons where formerly one made a load. At the bridge for some reason or other we had to wait several hours before we could cross. During this time a heavy thunderstorm arose. It seems that the gunstakes and batteries which all were closely massed attracted the lightning. Several dozend rifles were bended and splintered and some barrels partly molten. Five men of an Iowa Regt. were killed. We crossed the river in the afternoon, marched about 4 miles in the direction of Atlanta and halted.

In the neighborhood of Powers ferry where we crossed lay the village of Rosswell. Several large Cottonmills were at work there day and night making Cloth for the rebel army. Some 400 girls were working there. Sherman ordered General Garrard who commanded a brigade of Cavallery to destroy the Cotton mills, which was promtly done.[8] Some of the northern ministers and especially the Copperheads condemned this in unmeasured terms as a wanton, brutal and barbaric act, but Genl. Sherman as usual answered them in a manner which, if it did not satisfy, at least quieted them.

About five miles northeast of Atlanta is Peach tree Creek, a stream of considerable size and tributary to the Chattahoochee. Its banks are high and precipitous. It winds its way among a mass of densely wooded hills. On theese hills the rebel army, now Commanded by Genl. Hood lay strongly intrenched. . . . On the morning of the 20th the 20th Corps crossed the stream. A bridge of logs had been constructed but, because of the high aproaches it took the Artillerie some time before they got over. Shortley after noon our Corps began to cross. The 20th Corps had made their way through the woods and took up position partly on the Edge of a large field. They immediately built little breastworks of fencerails and small timber. Our Division of the 14th was the only one of the Corps which had crossed and could extend the line on the right of the 20th Corps. But their was no open field in front of our Division; neither had we time to mack any works.

It happened that our brigade was the last in the Division to cross Peach tree Creek and only half of it (4 Regts.) had formed in line when Hood sallied forth in colums without any preliminary Artilillerie firing. They first s[t]ruck the 20th Corps which they only could reach through the open field. Genl. Thomas had massed a number of batteries there who did a terrible work. The battle was going on furiously, while our Regt., the 33d Ohio, 42d Indiana and 86th Ill. were tearing through the brush in order to extend the line to the right. The 104th Ill. was the last Regt. wich had come into line on the right previous to the assault. The rebs overreaching our line, swung round to take the 104th in flank and rear, when luckily we came near and immediately charged the wheeling rebels. One volley we gave them allmost in their teeth and then for about five minutes it was Chickamauga again; a mixture of clubbing and stabbing, of damning, cursing and swearing, for about 5. minutes more or less, (On such occassions one forgetts to consult the watch,) when the Johnnies concluded to go home. Most of the 44th Georgia Regt we took prisoner. One smart looking, perhaps 16 years old boy, wept bitterly and asked me: "Will we be killed sir"?—"No my boy. We do not kill prisoners if they behave. You will be taken care of."—"You see" he said. "father has been killed and I am his only boy."—"Where was your father killed?" I inquired. "Right here" he replied pointing to the front and sobbing again. Such is war. Hood seemed to be satisfied for the time as he did not return.

The battle, considering the time it lasted, had been a very severe on[e]; Especially in the open field in front of the 20th Corps had the rebs suffered fearfully. Their total loss was a little over 5.000. while our total loss was 1710. They had four Genls. killed: Featherstone, Long, Pettis and Stevens.[9] The 104th Ill. had suffered more than any other Regts. on account of the flanking of the rebels. Poor fellows. The following day they went home to be mustered out as their time was out. At the beginning of the fight their Adjutant, a fine young man, had cheerfully said "Boys, this is our last fight, let us give the rebs a good farewell." He had spoken the truth for himself for, he was forever relieved from all fighting and trouble, shot through the head. . . .

Hood did not care much for his wounded and killed; he never asked time to take them away or bury them. By the time we had our and the rebel wounded away it was dark and rain had set in which lasted nearly all night. The following morning the burrying began which took all day, there were so many of them. Towards evening I came on picket in front of the rebel works. The night passed quietly as the Johnnies seemed to have no desire to stir up any fuss.

General Hood had certainly shown poor generalship in this dash. He knew that by noon only the 20th Corps had crossed but were not in position as [y]et. If he had made the attack at 11. A.M. in stead of 2. P.M. he would have found that Corps alone and no other troops near to support it.

A rich harvest slipped out of his fingers here. Dash is a good quality in war but it cannot allways overcome blunders. Johns[t]on would not have been guilty of the same.

On the morning of the 22d we advanced carefully towards the rebels works. We were much surprised to meet with neither scirmishers or pickets. But smoke was arising here and there behind the works. Carefully we picked our way through the abattis, carefully we peeped over the works to find the Johnnies gone; the smoking embers testifying their recent presence. A cheerfull "hurrah" told the troops behind what was up and soon their long lines came winding along. Hood had fallen back to the last works immediately around Atlanta. The boys called them: "Hoods last ditch." We took up line of march and followed him. A short tramp of three miles brought us as far as prudence and Hoods boys would let us and lines were formed again.

This was July 22d. Genls. McPherson and Schofield had meanwhile worked up towards the Augusta R.R. on the east of Atlanta and destroyed the same from Stone mountain to Decatur and towards Atlanta for a distance to 15 mil[e]s. They then wheeled to the right and closed in on Atlanta from the East. Genl Schofield (23d Corps) on the extreme left; To the right of him Genl. Dodge (15th Corps.) To the right of him a Division of the 16th Corps; then Genl. Blair with the 17th Corps; Howard 4th Corps came next; Hookers 20th Corps following and the 14th Corps on the extreme right, thus forming a half circle around the rebel works, extending from the Augusta R.R. east over the Chattanooga and Atlanta R.R. well to the west. . . . [10]

Our brigade lay across the Chattanooga and Atlanta Railroad and the land road which led to the City from the north. Close to the road stood an old monster Oak tree with large, spreading top and branches. The restless Buckskin planted his Parrott batterie near this tree. Next he accended the tree and from its hight had a good view of Atlanta. He requested permission to train his battery on the City and fire into it but was refused. But the permission was to come soon. We had just disposed of the dinner crakers when far to left a tremendous Cannonade and a steady rattling of musketry was heard. Hoods plan was to throw his whole force again[s]t our left wing, swing it round and roll up our line from that flank. Sherman who probably understood Hoods plan, ordered all the batteries to open fire on the rebel works and Buckskin was permitted to throw a dozen Shells in the City. He mounted his lofty seat again. He ordered one cannon to be loaded, stated the lenght of the fuse and direction of aim. Putting the field glass to the eyes to observe the execution he ordered "fire." Again the gun was loaded under his direction and fired. He repeated that a third time. Then he shouted: "We have it now boys; give them the ballance." He felt sorry he could not fire any more but he was not allowed to, because it is customary allways to first request a City to surrender, before bombardment is resorted to. This trial was merely allowed to convince the rebels, Citizens as well as soldiers, that we could make it warm for them.

The battle of Atlanta was a very serious affair. Hood with his usual impetuosity hurled line after line against the Tennessee Army [Army of the Tennessee] on our left, driving them back sometimes, only to be driven in turn. The old boys of the Tennessee Army were not of the stuff to cry: "Quit." About 2. P.M. the brave Genl. McPherson, who commanded that wing, was killed, but Genl. John Logan, the next in rank, took command and ably did he sustain his reputation as a brave and able soldier and leader. Until near 5. P.M. the storm raged with the highest fury and then, seeing that victory was not to perch on his banners, Hood withdrew behind his fortifications. Our loss in this battle summed up to a total of 3641. The Confederate loss as given in Hoods report was killed: 1482. wounded 4.000. Missing or prisoners: 2017. total: 9000. Besides Genl. McPherson we lost Genl. Greathouse killed.[11]

Genl. Sherman assigned Genl. O. O. Howard successor to Genl. McPherson. Genl. Hooker who was older in rank than Howard felt insulted at this, resigned and went home. Genl. Slocum took command now of the 20th Corps. Genl. Palmer who had commanded the 14th Corps allso resigned and Genl. J. C. Davis took his place.[12]

On the 24th suspicious signs indicated that Hood might try to flank us on the right. As Sherman intended to move gradually to the right in order to get hold of the West Point R.R. he ordered the 15. 16 and 17th Corps to the right flank. Our Division of the 14th Corps allso went to the right. On the evening of the 27th our brigade received order to move immediately. The night was cloudy and dark and that was the reason that we got lost in the wooded country. We tramped all night on a distance of 5. miles arriving at our destination on the left of the fifteenth Corps at 7. A.M. The troops there had their breastworks allready built and we began the same as soon as guns were staked. At 10. we had them done and proceeded to make coffee.

In the battle at Peach tree Creek the Officers of Comps. "F" and "H" were all wounded.[13] Col. Hobart now put Capt. Turner back in Command of Comp. "D" and I had to take "F." and "H."

Shortly after noon the Johnnies came over a low ridge in our front. There was but little brush in the woods which enabled us to see quite far

ahead. They advanced in splendid shape. It seemed a pity to scatter those
solid ranks with cannister and bullet, but: kill, or be killed is the severe
"Motto" of warfare. With a deafening jell they started in the charge only to
go back, broken and scattered. Five times they repeated thus sucidal charges
and everytime with the same result. It seemed the men were mad or incited
by liquor. Proof of this assertion may be found in the following: Just before
the last infantry charge, a full batterie came dashing up to our works and
unlimbered within 15. rods from our works. Our men were, so to speak,
dumbfounded. They did not believe their eyes seing a battery running to
certain dead and destruction. Not a shot was fired by our men, untill the
batterie man had unlimbered the guns, when in less than a minute, men
and horses of that batterie were down. The batterie, of course, was appropriated by Uncle Sams boys.

In the last charge of the Infantry a good many came up to our works,
and attempted to get over only to be killed or h[au]led over and be taken
prisoner. Hood was satisfied now. At four P.M. he left for Atlanta and sul-
lenly sat down behind his works to await further developements. The dead
and wounded he again left on our hands. Shortly after we of the 14th
Corps went back to our Corps where we arrived at 10. P.M. glad to get
some rest as we had not slept a wink the previous night. This affair is named
the battle of "Ezra Church" from a little log meeting house where the
darkies used to congregate and sing their "Hallelujahs." Thanks to our good
works our loss was but slight. The loss total was not quite 600. Comps. "F"
and "H." had one killed and five wounded; the Regt. 7 killed and 34.
wounded. The loss of the rebels I have never seen stated but it certainly
cannot be less than 3000. taking it at the lowest figure.[14] Thus Hood had
sacrificed during the 11 days he had been in command: 16,796 men while
our total loss during the same period of time amounted to 5950. No wonder he lost some of his dashing courage, settling down behind his works,
awaiting in turn our attacks. . . .

In the meantime Sherman had ordered and received heavy siege guns
from Chattanooga and he was now ready for practical siege work and
bombardement. The bridges across the Chattahoochee had been rebuilt in
a good substantial way. A brigade was stationed there as bridge guard. On
the 29th an Officer with a flag of truce was sent to Hood demanding the
surrender of the City. Hood said: "No." That was to be expected from Hood,
for he was by no means so bad off as to be forced to surrender. We could not
force his works without loosing more than half of our men. After receiving
the refusal Sherman sent the same Officer right back to Hood, giving him

48. hours time to remove women and children, and such of the Citizens who wished to leave, out of the City, to avoid unnecessary misery and bloodshed. Hood protested in a letter of decided strong language against such cruel and barbarous measure, and did not send the people away.[15] But before long most of the people went on their own accord. Sherman was not the least moved by Hoods peppered protest but precisely at 9. P.M. July 31st the screeching messengers of destruction went into the doomed City. Half an hour later a voluminous red glare rose at the horizon a sign that fire in the City was added to the horrors of bombardement. As soon as the fires lighted the horizont, Sherman stoped the firing, but ordered one solid shot to be thrown in the City every five minute[s] untill 12. P.M.

Hard work was in store for us now for a long while. In order to shorten the lenght of the besieging line we had to work up to the rebel works as close as possible. The Johnnies were brave fellows and contested our advance inch for inch. The guns in the rebel work were steady throwing shot and shell. Three lines of works we built successively untill we were allmost close up to their works. In order to make the siege a success it was necessary to enclose the Entire City and to cut of[f] all supplies. Starvation means surrender. Atlanta is entered by 4 R.R. from the four quarters of the Globe. The Augusta from the East; but that was efectually destroyed and morever in our possession; the Chattanooga and Atlanta from the north, allso ours; the West Point or Mississippi from the West for which we were reaching now and the Macon and Mobile road south. As the rebel works were in a great Circle around the City the line naturally was a long one. It was 16 miles from the Augusta road round to the Macon road. The bombardement was repeated occasionally, but only at night time. The rebel works and their defenders allso got their full share. Severall hours every day it seemed the very hell was holding carnival amids the roar of guns and the screaming and explosion of shells. At such times we had to keep low, because the Johnnies were not slow in returning compliments. . . .

On the 6th of Aug. we were shifted about two miles to the right. Here the scirmish line was not so near the rebel works and consequently we had to advance them. The next day a little after dinner we were ordered to take the rebel riflepits. In front of our work was an open field sloping downward to a small run or brook. The brook on both sides was lined with brush. At the Edge of the brush the rebels had their pits. On the right of the Regt. the woods began which extended down to the creek. By charging through the open field we were greatly exposed to the rebel fire. But Col. Fitch, who commanded now the Regt. ordered the men in the field and with a right oblique make for the woods. If he had faced the Regt. to the right the man could march clear into the woods. The five Comps. on the right jumped over the works. I had the right of the left wing and immediately ordered "Right face!" and in a sharp run went along the works in the woods. The Comps to the left of me knew what it meant and gladly followed me. In the woods we met the other coming out of the field. We then went down untill we were only a few rods from the rifle pits. then turning by the left flank we rolled them up so to speak and took most all of them prisoner. Those Comps. who had been in the field had many losses. I had watched Co. "D" and they were not 2 rods in front of the works when Capt. Turner fell; allmost the same time John Dey and James Orr fell. Miles Hoskins came a little farther when he fell shot through the bowels. He was the only son and child of a widow and a model of a soldier. Since Capt. Turner had fallen I took hold of Comp. "D" again.[16]

Shortley before night we were relieved and went behind the works again. Whom should I meet here but James Orr sitting at the fire frying bacon. I asked him where he was hit as I had seen him fall. He grinned at me and replied: "Well, you see, I saw Hank fall (meaning the Capt.) and John Dey I thought as they were hiding I would do the same." I assured him if he played the trick a second time he would not play anymore.

As nobody could give me any information as to what extent Turner and Dey were wounded I went to the Doctors to inquire. Both had allready been sent to the train for Chattanooga. I learned though that Capt. Turner had apparently been shot through the neck from left to right, but in fact the bullet had turned on the muskels and made its way between skin and muscles around the throat, coming out below the ear on the right side. It nearly had cost him his life though. When in Hospital at Nashville, gangrine set in and the Doctors, seeing they had not the stuff to cure him sent him quickly home where he pulled through. John Dey was shot through the left thigh and finally discharged for disability. Miles Hoskins was dead.

On the 9th we were again shifted to the right about a mile, but here our predecessors had worked up Close Enough, so we had only to occupy their works and continue business. Chars. Lymer found that he was tired of brewing coffee and frying bacon; There was no variety in the business he said and he preferred to handle the rifle again. It happened that Henry Hilfert was unable for active duty on account of a big bile [boil-]like promonition which covered nearly the whole surface of his left hand. He was willing to tend coffee and bacon to kill the time. So Lymer got his discharge from that responsible Office.

ADVANCE ON ATLANTA

It was an unavoidable duty for every Comp. Commander to write at the end of every month 3 copies of Muster and payrolls of the Comp. as allso the camp and garrison equippage and Clothing Account with the Genl. Quartermaster Department at Washington, the Ordonance return etc. At the end of June and July we had been so busy with tending to the rebs that we even did not get time to open the valises much less to wr[i]te. So as soon as possible I set to work. Of boards from bacon and craker boxes I made an exellent table, not counting it[s] shaking qualities. During the afternoon, I was nearly ready with one muster roll, the Johnnies got into a fit of throwing bullets over the works. I had put up a shelter tent to write under shade. A bullet bored through the canvass, upset my patent inkstand and spilt its last drop on the finished payroll. It was a spent bullet; it did not even roll from the table. If it had struck me one the back instead of on the inkstand, I might have straightened up a little, but I would have kept my temper under controll; as it was I fear I did not. . . .

While making coffee that evening a boy of the 33d Ohio was hit by a bullet on the left side of the neck cutting the jugular vain. Instantly the blood spurted fingers thick. We tried to shut off the vain but with poor success. Doctors were on hand quick enough but he died under their hands.

Shortly before night I received a letter from home. I suspected that it would contain bad news, because I had received a letter but a few days ago. It told me in short words that on the fourth of August the house had burnt down with everything it contained. That I should come home and make araingements for a new house as they could find none to rent and lived now in an old horsebarn. I immediately made application for leave of absence for one Month and forwarded the same to Genl. Thomas the following morning. Thomas returned the same with the following indorsement: "Not approved. A new application to be forwarded to these HQ. as soon as a contemplated move has been successfully made." What was meant by "the contemplated move" of course I had no means to know, but sure it must have something to do with the taking of Atlanta. All there was for me to do was to await in patience coming events.

Again we were shifted to the right on the 15th. Here the works were not so near the Enemies lines as the former, and therefore we had to have a skirmishline out steady. We were not called upon to advance the line and consequently the duty was very hard and tiresome. One day, a certain Henry Fink of Comp. "A" undertook to b[r]ing the boys of his Comp. some Coffee for dinner.[17] That was a thing seldom done because of the danger. But Fink wanted to surprise the Comrades. So, kettle in hand he went over the works.

He was warned of the danger by many voices but he said the rebs could not hit an Elephant. He had gone several rods when he returned to the works saying: "Boys, lent me a hand, I am done for." We helped him over and inquired what ailed him. He pointed to his stomach and sank down. He was brought to the Doctors who found the bullet had passed through the stomach and stopped at the spine. Dr. Reeves told him that he had not long to live. "I know it" he replied and beckoned me to come to him. I had been well acquainted with him and all his family in Appleton. He allways came to me when he wanted to sent a letter to his father as he could write but very poorly. He told me what to w[r]ite to his father, then handed me his pocketbook which contained $30.00 in greenbacks to sent in the letter and then bade us good by. He lingered untill evening and suffered greatly. He was beloved by all his Comrades for he was one of the most cheerfull and kindhearted boys I ever met.

Genl. Sherman had now stretched the army to its utmost capacity, but still there were over four miles uncovered. He clearly saw that with the army he had he could not encircle the City. So he came to a bold conclusion. To raise the siege, march rapidly south, destroy thoroughly the Mississippi and the Macon railroads and attack Atlanta from the south. The 24th of August the move was to begin. Genl. Slocum with the 20th Corps was sent to guard the bridges across the Chattahooche as allso to prevent Hood from escaping north. The wagons were loaded with 15 days rations and for five days we had in the haversacks. All sick were sent back to Chattanooga. Meanwhile the business in the rifle pits, skirmishline and behind the works went on as usual so that the rebs could not smell a rat. At 10. P.M. all krept out of the works and quietly fell back to a road about 3 Miles in the rear where the train had drawn up. The skirmishers were to remain untill an hour before daylight. They were to fire a shot once in a while to assure the rebels of their presence. To make the deceit more complete two Cannon were left in position who were to open fire briskly at daybreak and after firing a dozend rounds the Cannon were to be left and Cannoniers and skirmishers were to follow us rapidly. So complete was the deceipt that Hood when he learned the following afternoon that our works were empty, really believed we had taken the back track to Chattanooga. He sent a troop of Cavallerie towards the Chattahoohee who found Slocum there. That made the Illusion complete. We had escaped north, Slocum was our rear guard. That night their was great rejoicing in Israel. The Hessians running away. Atlanta free once more. Hallelujah! Poor deluded souls. How bitter must have been their disappointment.

ADVANCE ON ATLANTA

The night seemed to have been specially made for our enterprise. It was dark [y]et light enough to find and keep the narrow road. When day came we halted and made Coffee. We were allowed to sleep till noon and then went on again. At night we arrived near the West Point or Mississippi R.R. and remained there. We were between 15 and 20. miles west of Atlanta. Next morning after Coffee we set to work to destroy the R.R. That was done in good style for over 20 miles. The ties were burnt, the rails made red hot and twisted, bridges and cattleguards burned, culverts destroyed; Cuts filled up with earth and rock and shells put in prepared as torpedoes which would explode when undertaken to clean the cuts.

We had to make a grand left wheel now in order to strike the Atlanta and Macon road south. As the 15th and 16th and 17th Corps were on our right they had the largest circle to describe. Genl. Howard on the extreme right was to strike the railroad south of Jonesboro 20. miles South of Atlanta. All were to destroy the road whenever they came at it. Hood, who had finally learned that we had not run home, had immediately sent Hardees and Stephen D. Lees Corps to Jonesboro to intercept our progress, while he kept Stewarts Corps in Atlanta. On the 31st while Howard was trying to get possession of the bridge across Flint river south of Jonesboro he was furiously attacked by Hardees Corps which resulted in Hardees repulse.[18]

On the 1st of September our brigade had to serve as train guard. During that afternoon matters came to a crisis. The rebels were slightly intrenched at the edge in the woods west of Jonesboro. The 2d Div. of the 14th Corps charged the rebels behind their works, carried them and took Genl. Gowans brigade prisoners, as allso a number of guns and flags. Thereupon Genl. Hardee fell back and when night set in operations were suspended; but the 4th and 23d Corps were moving all night to get around the rebel forces and cut off their retreat; But old Hardee was to[o] sly. He got out of the trap before it could be sprung on him.

We came in camp south of Jonesboro in a large field. As it was getting dark we made Coffee and went to rest. At about midnight we heard thunder-like, rumbling reports which continued untill daybreak. The reports were in a northern direction. Various speculations as to the Cause were advanced. Some thought that Genl. Slocum had advanced from his position at the Chattahoochee and attacked Atlanta; others thought that Hood had attacked Slocum. But, singular, none hit the nail in the right spot. The following day we were to know. Hood having found Atlanta untenable had left the same and destroyed everything which could be of any value to us. When the news spread among the army it seemed the men had gone stark mad. The cheering, singing and dancing would not cease. There was ample reason for this mad jubilee. What would have been our lot if our mission had failed? And what would have been the Effect in the North and on the coming presidential Election? I shudder to think of it. We had marched, and labored, and fought incessantly for four months; we had advanced 150. miles in the Enemys Country without any support within reach. We had lost a small army in killed, wounded and disease; we had worked hard and suffered much to attain this result and now when it was there, when we held it in our grasp, it seemed allmost to[o] much to realize it. . . .

The following morning the pursuit of Hardee southward was taken up, but having Effected a Crossing over Flint river during the night was out of reach. The pursuit was left to the Cavallerie and we returned to Jonesboro. Not far from our Camp I had noticed a great many persimmon loaded allmost to breaking with lucious looking fruit. I was well acquainted with their horrid, astringent qualities, but thought that perhaps they might be made palatable by adding plenty of sugar. So I procured a lot and instructed Hilfert to boyle them down to a sort of sass [sauce] and spare no sugar. While that was going on night set in. The persimmon enterprise turned out a failure. A barrel of sugar would not convert a quart of persimmons into anything enjoiable.

While grumbling over the miscarried speculation; agravated by the malicious remarks of Fred B[o]rch[e]rdt and Hilfert, the Sergeant Major stepped up and in his usual smiling and obliging way said: "Lieut. Otto, I have the honor to invite you to a free picket party for to night; place of assembly: brigade headquarters; time: half past nine." Fred B[o]rch[e]rdt laughed outright and said: "That comes just handy Otto. You take some persimmon sass along; it will keep you and the boys awake and lively." I pretended not to hear his advice but turned to the Sergeant Major and asked: "Excuse me Sergeant, but is there not a mistake?" "Not at all Lieut." he replied. "I called on Capts. Adams and Bradish whose turn comes before you[r]s, but both gentlemen are sick." I reflected a minute and then said: "Sergeant, you know all about [this] sick busines; I can not go on picket. I am sick myself." The Sergeant Major was a real good hearted fellow. He said: "But Lieut. there are only three left beside you and they have been on picket lately." "I know it" I said. "I want to have that sick business stopped in the way it is conducted, or I will quitt."—"But Lieut, I shall have to report this to the Colonel."—"Exactly. That is what I want you to do." The Sergeant Major left. "Now you have done it. They will cashire you and kick you out of the service." Fred B[o]rch[e]rdt said. "Well let them" I replied. "Do you suppose Fred, I am so stook on the service as to be willing to be a stoolpidgeon for any conceited playing off Coward? If they do kick me out it saves me the trouble to apply for a leave of absence."

So the dice was cast. I had made myself liable to be cashiered and dishonorable dismissed the service of the United States. I was in the same box now as Capt. Steffens had been in Chattanooga. True I had insulted no superior Officer. But I had s[h]ir[k]ed duty without reason, which was about as bad. It must not be t[h]ought that I had acted merely on the spur of the moment. By no means. I had contemplated such a move for a long time. If I had not done it, it would go on in that way as long as we were in Service. Capt. Edwards and Bradish both hated me for different reasons. Edwards dated back to Oct. 26 1862 when he put me under arrest while sergeant of the guard which ended in a signal failure on his part; and again at Chattanooga when I refused him a loan to cover his [theft] of the Comps. fund. Bradishs reasons were even more Contemptible. He hated me because I was a foreigner; because I was able to manage my affairs myself, which he could not. I had drilled him and other Sergeants and Officers which was not to his liking; In short, he knew I would not take any water from him and that was the thorn in his flesh. I did not care a fig for their likes or dislikes as I did not need their help, but It became clear to me during the Campain that they had formed a sort of combine to annoy and bother me. Ever since we had left Lookout [Mountain] and during the Campain, when their turn came for skirmish or picket and the weather was disagreable, or it seemed to be specially dangerous, or we had performed an exhausting march they would simply skirk their duty by claiming they were sick, but they never went to the Doctor giving an account of their ailments. As in the [roster] my name followed after theirs I had to soup [*sic*] what they did not like. That is the reason why I concluded to bust the combine and committed such a gross blunder as regards military dicipline. Whatever the result might be I was glad to set the ball in motion. I slept sound and well for all that.

The following morning I prepared myself fully for the trial. Of course I did not know whether Col Fitch would give me a hearing, or would simply put me under arrest and report me to Genl. Thomas for trial. Fred B[o]rcherdt, the Adjutant informed me that he found the Col. very cross that morning. Finally the Sergeant Major came informing me to report to the Colonels headquarters at once. I went. I saw Captains Edwards and Bradish take their course that way allso. By and bye all the Officers of the Regt. came. The Col. was not in the tent but soon came. He loocked daggers, took a seat on a campstool and began: "Lieut. Otto! Did you receive an Ordre to go on picket last evening"?—"I was detailed for that duty Sir."—"Did you go?"—"No Sir." "Don't you know you have to obey Orders?—"I do Sir." "Why did you not go then"?—"For two reasons Sir: First; This was not a direct order but a detail for duty; details are allways made in the Order as the names appear on the rooster and no discrimination should be made without proper reason. And second: I charge Captains Edwards and Bradish with conspiring to skirk [shirk] their duty and put the same on the shoulders of their Comerades." Here the Colonels eyes grew big and in a very severe tone said: "Lieut. You are making grave charges, but Explain yourself." I took my diary out of my pocket and read off the days and dates of the month when they missed their turn under the plea of sickness. "Call in the Sergeant Major," the Colonel said. The Sergeant came. "Sergeant, have you got your detail rooster since the Regt. left Look out"? "I have Sir."—"Compare notes with Lieut. Otto and see if you agree." We did so and agreed exactly. Seven times they had played off and this was the Eight. "Colonel" I said "I make charges for conspiracy for the following reasons. First: They allways were sick on the same day and the same time. Should their Constitutions be so exa[c]tly formed alike that they must get sick the very same hour and minute? Then their disease has allways disappeared when the picket or skirmish duty was performed. They never have been to a Dr. stating the nature of their disease. Second:"—"That will do now." the Colonel interrupted me, and then made us a short and sharp speech and at the close said: "I will consider what is to be done in the matter. You may go now; Capts Edwards and Bradish remain." What he had to say them I never learned. When we were fairly outside Lieuts. Fargo, Hubard [Hubbard], Vredenburg[19] and other shook hands and promised they would set them up the first chance they could find to do so.

During the afternoon I went to the Adjutants tent and found the Colonel there. "Hello Lieut." he began. "I have forwarded charges against you." —"Allright Col." I replied. "So I can go home and build a house for my family. Shall I bring in my sword"?—"No you may keep that. I only wanted to see if I could not scare you. I will let the matter rest; but I should have done so if your case had not been so strong and your retreat so well covered. And besides it would have been a disgrace for the Regt. But you may rest assured there will be no more playing off. But why did not you report the matter to me before?"—"I hate to make complaints of that kind Colonel; It looks to[o] shabby, to[o] little. And then If I had done so the matter would probably have ended between you and me and the two Capts. Now, they have been exposed before all the Officers of the Regt. and that is all the punishment I desire them to receive. I knew you would not report the matter because your sense of justice is to[o] keen for that." He took the Compliment smilingly but did not reply. Strange to say, the Capts. did not seem to bear any grudge against me; they appeared more friendly and sociable than before.

On the 6th of Sept. the Arme began the March to Atlanta. Funy, we came from the north to capture it and got into it from the south. It fell to the lot of our brigade to cover the rear of our Corps. A brigade of rebell Infantry and a lot of their Cavallery had been waiting for this. They wanted to give us some parting salutes along on the road. We deployed as skirmishers and as soon as our troops marched we followed, allways skirmishing. We had three pieces of Artillery with us and if the Johnnies became to[o] arrogant the Cannoniers would quickly treat them to a lot of hardware, which would cool them of[f] somewhat. They kept that up for 5 miles when they got tired and let us alone. One this Occasion I lost one of my Indians, Cornelius Endone, of which no one knows what became of him.[20] Probably he remained to[o] long behind a tree or log and was killed, or wounded and taken prisoner. We marched 10. miles and camped at a station named "Rough and Ready."

September 7th. It was now only 8 miles to Atlanta. We wondered how things would look there in general. We came soon to the underground, or Cave City. When Hood refused to sent the families out of the City the Citizens thought perhaps he was right. But when shot and shell came screaming into the City and tearing through the buildings converting parlors and chambers in ruins and setting wooden structures on fire, when the scattering shells would strike down indiscriminately young and old, woman and men, Soldier or Citizen, then they were glad to leave on their own account. They went south of the City out of reach of our missiles. They dug holes in the ground and covered them with timbers and dirt. In the deep cutts along the railroad tracks they would dig caves supporting them with timbers. They called those structure very properly "gopher holes." For a distance of two miles this novel City extended. Our Division was assigned a place for camping ground on the Macon R.R. called "Whitehall," just south of the City. The army was mostly distributed in the rebel works. But as Sherman intended to keep the place as a military post he had works made Close to the City which could be defended by a small number of men. The old works were partly used for the Construction of the new ones. . . .

The day after our arrival I went into the City. I can not undertake to give a correct pen picture of the ruin and desolation I met here. War is cruelty and barbarism on a large scale. And still it is argued and upheld stubbornly that the mercifull, Allwise, Allmighty God ordains and conducts wars to obtain his ends. Is there not a considerable sprinkling of pure, genuine blasphemy hidden in such arguments? . . . A great part of the destruction had been caused by Hood at the evacuation of the City. On the east along the Augusta R.R. a great number of Mills, Foundaries, Machine shop, warehouses and other buldings were blown up and burned what ever would burn. Seven long trains had been gathered on Sidetracks an burned and nothing remained but the tracks and other Iron work. Seven Engines were all converted in[to] old Iron; hundreds of Cannon of all sizes and Calliber were laying round spiked, muzzled and otherwise injured. Tons of shells and small ammunition had been exploded and rifleballs could be shoveled together by the bushel. Carloads of riflebarrels, from which the stocks had burnt away, lay round in big piles. Enough material had been destroyed to equip a moderate army. The destruction our guns had caused was mostly in the business part of the City but here it was bejond description. Not many Private houses had suffered. . . .

Genl. Sherman intended to make Atlanta a military Post which could be held by a comparative small garrison and Enable him to use the larger part of the army elsewhere; it allso was to serve as a suply depot. The subsistence of such garrison and the storing of supplies was of the greatest importance. As soon as we moved into Atlanta a great many of the Citizens, especially the poorer Class returned; but they had nothing to live on. The few stores left had not much to sell, nor had the people any money to buy with. Work was not to be found and not a cent could be earned. We could not feed them as the single road was taxed to the utmost to supply the army with the most necessary articles. They should not starve. Midle and southern Georgia and Alabama had an abundance of provisions and there Sherman concluded to send them. Acordingly on the 5th he issued an order that all Citizens who could not support themselfes had to leave the City. . . . [21]

The 1st Wisconsin Regt, having served three years was sent home to be mustered out. Such of their men who had not served three years were transferred to our Regt. The list of the men who were assigned to my Comp. bore 39 names but only 29 were present, the others were absent in hospital for some reason or other. John Buboltz allso returned from hospital and I at once installed him in his former Office as cook again.

The "contemplated move" to which Genl. Thomas had referred on my application was now Completed. Directly after our arrival at Atlanta I forwarded a new Application together with the old one. After a weeks delay a Pass for a furlough of 20. days outside the Department line (from Nashville) was in my hands.[22] Sergt. Joseph D. Holden had allso applied and was granted the same lenght of time. We calculated to make the trip together. Neither of us had a cent of money. We did need none for transportation as the fare was free but we needed some sustenance, as we could not take rations along. I tried to negotiate a loan somewhere but it seemed everybody was dead broke. So we fell back on the tramp principle: "The world owes us a living." On the 18th of September we went to Atlanta but could get no transportation. No passenger coaches were on the trak south of Nashville at that time exept hospital coaches which were Exclusively for sick and wounded. Every one had to take his chances on top of a fr[e]ight car. We were disappointed day for day untill on the evening of the 22nd we fought our way up on the roof and left northward bound.

~

CHAPTER SIXTEEN

The Army Found Again.
Savannah.
A Valuable Christmas Present

On the night of September 22 Otto and Sergeant Holden left Atlanta for Chattanooga, traveling on top of freight cars. Because of the scarcity of transportation, it
took them five days to reach Nashville, where Otto was able to draw half-pay
after waiting another four days. He used the time to visit invalids of the regiment in hospital there. The travelers arrived in Chicago on October 6, and on
October 7 at 2 A.M. they arrived in Oshkosh, only to find that no trains were
running that day, it being Sunday. They walked the remaining twenty miles to
Appleton, arriving there at 2 P.M. on October 7.

They found Appleton in "a crazy feverheat" over the draft and the upcoming
presidential elections. Those willing to enlist were already in the army; of those
remaining to be drafted, Otto says, some were hiding out in the woods, and some
had gone to Canada, while those who could afford it paid between five hundred
and a thousand dollars for substitutes. With most of the staunch Republicans
away in the army, the Democrats were agitating fiercely for the election of Gen.
George B. McClellan, "that renowned military imbecile," as Otto calls him. Otto
got into an altercation with the speaker at a Democratic political rally who denied that Atlanta had been captured and had to take to his heels to escape the
wrath of a crowd of copperheads.

Otto found building materials very expensive and skilled help impossible to
find, as all the skilled workers were either working for the government or in the
army. He finally had to hire two Irish brothers, "carpenters in name only," for
five dollars a day, to build a house for his family. By the time the arrangements
for the building were completed, it was time to start back to the regiment. Otto

left Appleton October 16 with a satchel containing spare socks, corned beef and crackers, four bottles of blackberry wine, and a pair of boots. Otto and Holden were held up in Nashville by General Thomas's troops, preparing to follow Hood north. They arrived back in Chattanooga October 24 and were reunited with the army at Kingston on November 6.

∾ On the 5th of November we were, about a thousand of us put on bord a long string of flats and steered carefully towards Kingston; it was allmost night when we started and we did not arrive at Kingston untill 9. A.M. next morning. We came just in time to vote for Lincoln for President. Besides the paymaster was there with greenbacks which pleased the boys very much. Since March they had not been paid. The Sergeant Major found work for me at once. The following day I had to go with a comand of 75 men on a fouraging Expedition. Quartermaster Van Valkenburg[1] had espied some place where a fine lot of corn and fodder coud be had just for the trouble of loding it. But as it was 10. miles off he needed a guard to protect the teams from bushwhackers and guerillas. We started so as not to be belated. It was not far from Cassville the former noted bushwhaker haunt. We passed through the streets of the ruined City. It had been burned and sacked by order of Genl. Sherman a couple months previous because of its bush-whacking propensities. The city presented now a meloncholy sight. The high, roofles[s], black brick walls with their gaping doors and windows looked desolate and forbidding. No living soul was to be seen exept in the outscirts of the city among some negro shanties, which had been spared, some darkey urchins were rolling in the sand or roming around. An old darkey came out to us and warned us to look out as only yesterday "Kurnell Tuttle" had been seen with his gang and "he am powerfull keerless bout handlin yanks" the darky said. I sent out flankers to both sides as soon as we came to the woods. Van Valkenburg, his Sergeant and two soldiers who were on horseback kept a qua[r]ter of a mile ahead to guard against ambush.

We arrived at the designated place without disturbance. Pickets were posted and loading began at once. We had only 25 wagons to load which would not take long. A promising looking house was not far off. Van proposed an investigation and I readily assented but taking the precaution to inform a Sergeant of our project and instructing him to keep a sharp look on the house and if any signs were made to come with half a dozen men and rifles. We entered the house and found two resolute looking females whose looks did not promise a friendly wellcome. But Van, being an exellent talker, did not despair and began at once to parley. He felt so happy to

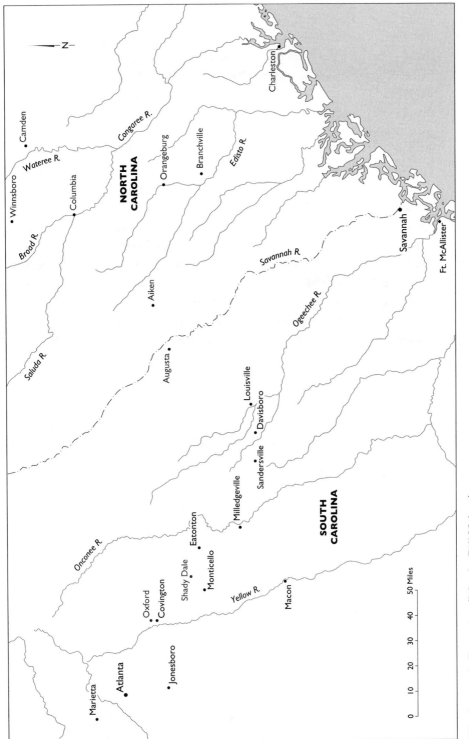

The Savannah Campaign (Map by Bill Nelson)

make the aquaintance of such amiable ladies etc. and wound up with inquiring if they had anything to dispose of in the line of chickens, geese, hams, sweet potatoes etc. for all of which he was willing to pay either greenbacks or graybacks whatever they might choose, but;—"Dry up! you red haired son of a devil." the younger sweet thirty began. "I will see you bust first before you get anything here." Thinking Van to be able to entertain the ladies alone, I set about on a private Inspection. In a room the other side of the hallway I discovered a trap door in the floor, which I raised and went down. A goodly pile of sweet potatoes was the first I saw. A further search disclosed a lot of bacon, hams and shoulders. I took a ham and threw it up on the floor at the same time calling for Van to leave off courting the woman and come and help me. I went for an other ham but before I could reach it, bang! went the trap door and I sat in a pitch dark trap hole. I heard a tramping and scufling overhead and the door was thrown open again. I lost no time in getting to day light. Just then Van bent down to pick up the ham when the younger woman sprang forward and hacked him with [a] carving knife across the right hand making a long cut. Van dropped the ham like hot Iron and with the wounded hand gave the woman a thrust which sent her headlong against the wall and down to the floor. I ran out doors and swung my hat as a sign for the Sergeant, then hunted round, found a towel and dressed Vans hand. The woman all the while wagging their tongues as if propelled by steampower.

The Sergeant came with six men. When the women saw the soldiers coming they run outdoors, but I had them spedily brought back and put a guard over them and told him to let them talk as much as they wanted but if they tried to get out to use the but of his gun. One soldier I sent back for blankets to carry the stuf in and at the same time to bring two more men along. The other went down celler to bring up what they found serviceable. The woman, seeing that resistance was useless quieted down. We took 6 hams, all there was of them, and 4 shoulders but left them the bacon and plenty of sweet potatoes. When we left, Van stepped up to the women and said: "That will be a lesson to you. If you had been decent we woud have taken two hams and a few bushels [of] sweetpotatoes enoug to make us dinner and would have paid you good money for it. Now you will have nothing and you may be thankfull we do not take all."

When we returned the wagons were loaded, and we started immediately on the return trip. After going about half way with large fields on both sides of the road and a small creek crossing the same. We concluded to make dinner here as we could not easily be surprised. Plenty of Fencerails within reach, the ham was soon frying and sweet potatoes baking in the ashes. It was 2. P.M. when we started again. On the right the wood soon reached to the road again and flankers were detailed. Van led again. Presently on[e] of the flankers came running and reported there were butternut bushwhackers in the woods but he could not tell how strong they were. I sent a Sergeant with thirty men to deploy in the woods as scirmishers and keep the train covered, and make report as soon as possible, with the rest of the troops I marched behind the train. Now I could not believe that bushwhacker would attack a force of our strenght. They usually are la[y]ing in ambush, fire off their guns and run. They are the meanest enemies one can have. They are great cowards but cruel and unmerciful if successfull. I thought that perhaps rebel Cavallery had dismounted and if that was the case they might make serious trouble if there was enough of them.

The firing soon became brisk. I took the men I had with me and went in the woods. But the firing ceased now and when I came up the bushmen had fled. Some of the boys were out to fetch in one of the fellows whom they had winged. He was badly wounded in one knee. He was not much given to talk and refused to answer any question. Van thought it proper to hang him at once and have done with him. But he finally agreed with me, since the fellow could not run and needed no guard and no damage was done, to leave the hanging business to General Sherman. Guerillas and bushwhackers are not considered soldiers but merely murderers and robbers and are usually strung up when caught. The fellow had a good rifle and lots of ammunition. He had expected to be hung but when he found he was not to be hanged he thawed up somewhat and told us they had been thirty in number, but they had not learned soon enough of our trip to prepare an ambush. They would not have fired at us in the woods, as they were not enough to beat us but that the soldiers began the fire. But the boys gave him the lie and he backed down. Without further trouble we arrived in camp at 5. P.M. As we passed close by Shermans headquarters we left the prisoner there. Sherman sent him to Chattanooga to work in the Chaingang when able. . . .

Preparations were going on for the intended march to the sea. Genl. Corse destroyed the machineshops and factories at Rome. The wagons were loaded with twenty days rations; but these rations were not to be issued only in the direst case of necessity. We were to fourage and live on the Country. No baggage wagons were allowed for the Officers, but every Officer might keep a mule, provided he could catch and confiscate and feed one. Genl. Ste[e]dman was to destroy the R.R. from Atlanta back to Dalton.

THE ARMY FOUND AGAIN

All sick men were sent back. The 10th Wis. Regt. whose term of service ha[d] expired was sent home and their recruits transferred to our Regt.[2] My share for the Comp. was ten.

On the 12th Nov. we left Kingston, crossed the Etowah on the bridge near Cartersville, went through Allatoona pass and camped on the old battle-grounds at Big Shanty, having marched 25. miles. The following day we passed through Marietta again which was now a heap of ruins. The women did not hoot at us and cutting faces as they did 5. months ago when we passed through the first time; in fact, we did not see many but darkies. We camped at Smyrna church where we had been fighting on the 4th of July. The third day we passed through Atlanta and camped on the east side near the Augusta R.R.

On the 14th the 15th and 17. Corps who were to take the right wing marched out towards Macon. On the 15th the 20th Corps, which was to take the left wing started towards Stone mountain. Chief of Engineers, Capt. Poe had been ordered by Sherman to destroy Atlanta but let churches and dwelling houses unmolested. Consequently on the night from the 15th to the 16th there was a grand Illumination in doomed Atlanta. As no soldiers were to remain there Sherman did not want it to become a danger in our rear. It was now dangerless. No Cars could reach it within 60. miles of it and if even the citizens did return, there were no Stores left to buy anything.

At this time Genl. Sherman was by no means sure at what place or port on the South Atlantic or gulf he might bring up. That might depend on the force of troops the Enemy could throw in our way. He had to avoid fighting as much as possible since we had no communications anywhere where the wounded could be sent; nor would we have been able to provide for a living during a Campain. Small forces we could brush aside, but heavy forces we had to avoid. The rebel cavallery under Wheeler was 8000 strong; ours under Kilpatrick about the same. Our Infantry numbered 60.000 men.[3] How much Infantry the rebels could gather to oppose us was not known. But we had to march far appart on different roads in o[r]der to fourage enough for man and beast to live. Shermans aim was Savannah, but his course was so exentric, so crooked and fence shaped that the rebels never could tell where he wanted to go. Some days it would seem as if he was aiming for Charleston, S.C. and next it would seem Savannah or Florida was his object. He kept the Enemy always in hot water. Of course such zig zag Course increased the distance to travel over. In a straight course we could make Savannah in three week whereas it took now a month. We cut a path through Ga. of an average width of 45. miles.

On the morning of the 16th our Corps took leave of the ruins of Atlanta. Col. Hobart, having been promoted Brevet Brigade Genl. commanded now the brigade. Genl. Carlin the division. I must say here that I confine myself exclusively to the movements of our Div. and Corps, which came more under my observation. This day we had an easy march, only 15. miles. Fouragers were sent out but returned empty handed. We were to[o] near Atlanta [y]et.

"Shermans bummers" has become a significant byword in the history of the rebellion. To better understand this fouraging, or bummer business I will shortly explain how [it was] conducted. A good many people believe that the whole army was let loose bumming round like a lot of vagabonds, robbing and murdering and God knows what else. That was not the case. Why, we would have been gobled up, and taken prisoner, or killed within a short time by the rebel troops. On the contrary. Our Divisions, brigades, Regt. and Companies were kept compact and as well in hand as before, allways ready for a tussle with the Johnnies. This is the way it was managed: Every evening details were made for the following day, viz: Six or eight men had to provide for the Compagny; from twenty to 30. men had to provide for brigade and regimental headquarters. Those details were allways under command of a commissioned Officer or Sergt. They were forbidden to destroy, or to take anything they did not need; allso they must not take all forage they found in a house or outhouse, or on the premises, but leave enough for the family to live on. Families in the South then usually consisted of woman and children and a lot of negroes; the men and boys up to 15. years were either in the rebel army or followed the noble trade of bushwhaking. The fouragers were informed where the Corps would encamp the following evening in order that they might find them. They would start early usually before the troops. This was necessary, because as they had to spread over the Country, sometimes for miles off from the road. they had to travel many miles more than the troops on the road.

Foraging was at best an exhausting and dangerous service. As they were sometimes ahead, or on the flanks of the army, they very often had to fight with rebel Cavallery or bushwhackers. The former, if not in to[o] great force, were most time driven of[f], or if captured by them the men were mostly treated as prisoners of war, but with bushwhackers it was different. They did not fight on a fair scale. They killed the soldiers from secure hiding places and if a soldier was so unlucky to fall in their hands alive they would in many cases, Indian like, first torment, mutilate and then hang him. It is not to be wonderd at that under such circumstances the boys would resort to reprisals which were by no means models of humanity. But this state of affairs was not so bad in Georgia as afterward in South Carolina. The people of that state had lost all regard for the usages of war as well as for humanity; they seemed to have settled down to the very depths of incarnate brutality.

But we did not entirely rely on the good luck of the regular fouragers. We would, while on the march, take such things along which came within reach and handy to transport. And when we got clear of the suburbs of Atlanta everything became plenty. It was just the right season of the year. Every thing was ripe and had been gathered; beasts of all kind were grown and fat. Midle Georgia, unlike northern Ga. is a fertile, rich farming Country and quite well settled by planters. It was full of large, well stocked plantations, such as we had seldom met with in Kentucky. No armies, either rebel or yankee had ever been here; and as the people never even had dreamed that yankee soldiers would penetrate that remote country they had taken no pains to get anything out of the way, to hide or conceil anything. And as we came all on a sudden they were completely taken by surprise. They were nearly paralized.

The first evening we had to fall back on the regular army grub. I was detailed for fouraging the next day. The Corps would camp next evening at, or near Rankins Ferry at the yellow river. The night was ugly as it rained steady. At 6. a.m. we started taking a south west course from the road. Up to noon we had not found anything [y]et, and as we were a good ways off the road we shaped our course so as to reach the ferry before dark. During the afternoon we run on to a plantation and here for the first time our star shone bright and radiant. The first thing the boys took hold of was a splendid 200 pound grunter. While they were busy with him I looked in one of the barns and found a splendid gray mule and a coop with a lot of turkies. I went and called John Buboltz who was busy dressing the hog. I asked him to leave that to the other boys and come along. He made a big jump when he saw the mule and lost no time to put him in harness. To make a long story short, when we left there the mule was loaded—well, like a mule, and every men carried as much as he could besides.

During all the time we had seen no white person but lot of negroes crowded round watching the proceedings and staring at us. They were not at all afraid but seemed to take great delight in the work. They told the men where they could find the sweet potatoes, molasses, honey and cornmeal. Besides the hog we had two sheep, a dozen turkeys and a dozen Chicken. Of the other stuff I can give no account, but as we were 36 in number it was considerable. A darkey showed us the shortest road to Rankins Ferry. But we had not gone a mile before the same darkey overtook us. "Massa" he began "I'se gwine 'long with you uns." Now Genl. Sherman had forbidden to take, or allow any nigger to follow us, exept such as who were able to work on curdoroys, breastworks, etc. as others would be a bother to the army. But as this was a stout, burley specimen I allowed him to go along. And well did he do his part the time he remained with us. He was of great service in fouraging as he allways knew where to look for stuff. He stook to our Company and no one could coax him away. He became a favorite with the men and all felt sorry when we had to part with him at Savannah.

We arrived at the yellow river nearly the same time with the Division at 5. P.M. The boys cheered lustily when we passed into camp but they allso had gathered considerable along the road. The Orderly Sergeants were busy distributing the confiscated articles. But John was not satisfied. With mutton and fresh ham and turkey and sweet potatoes and cornmeal laying around him he grumbled. On my inquiring what was lacking he groaned; "Oh my Dutch oven"! The dutch oven we had to leave at Chattanooga at the beginning of the Atlanta Campain. But he had a spider to fry in, and we had camp kettles to boil sweet potatoes; the only trouble was with the Cornmeal bread. Fresh ham and sweet potatoes is an exellent match and I never heard any having got tired of it. That night Genl. Hobart called the Officers in his tent and informed us that considerable rebel Cavallery was swarming round and wanted us to instruct the boys to be watchfull and cautious when they were out fouraging.

Nov. 18th. We crossed yellow river on two pontoon bridges laid during the night. The fouragers had gone ahead a little more in number on account of the rebel cavallery. John did not go along but Dan went along. (That was the darkie's handle.) John said he had stuf enough for several days to come and Dan would probably bring more. We passed through Covington a large, stragling village of unpainted frame houses and Streets 6 or 7. rods wide. Never did I see in a place of that size so many women and Children, white and black, than here. They mostley all were of the poorer class and had never seen a live yankee. They probably had heard much of them lately and all wanted to see them as close as possible. They were not at all afraid and passed close up to the ranks. They seemed somewhat disapointed as the yanks looked pretty much like other folks and "had no horns at all." Some of the boys told them that, in order not to scare them we had taken them off and put them in the wagons. We camped that night at the [Ulcofauhachee] river. Shortly after we had staked arms the fouragers came in well provided but they had met some rebel Cavallery and a man of Comp. "G" was well clipped on one arm but no bone broken. They had ousted the Cavallery in good style though. Dan had loaded himself well down with household furniture. Besides a turkey he fetched a frying pan, a dutch oven, a light soupkettle and several tin plates, which he completed next day by a tin pail to keep the lard and gries [grease] in. John was now in his Element and he would be up till midnight, cooking, frying and baking; Dan allways helping, looking for good wood, fence rails, water, tending the mule etc.

Nov. 19th. Crossed the river with the ugly name on pontoons Passed through Oxford during the day. Oxford is the opposite from Covington. It was the abode of the aristocracy, the nigger-drivers. Not a white person was to be seen in the streets. Doors and blinds were shut and the City seemed to be the "City of the dead." Some one started "Hail Columbia, hail." Next one intonated: "We will Hang Jeff Davis on a sour appletree." but to no purpose. If any were living in the stately mansions they felt it to be below their dignity to pollute themselfes with a look at the "hessians." The march to day was somewhat longer, about 25 miles. We camped at a place called "shady Dale" but no village or houses were to be seen. Our Camp was in the edge of a wood, large Cotton fields in front. In one part of the field, specially fenced off a number of hogs were busy rooting. There was sport for the boys and ere long their hogships given a passport for Eternity. . . .

The soldiers were forbidden to destroy or burn anything exept fence rails for cooking purposes and campfires. But a brigade of mounted Infantry was specially entrusted with this business. Their duty was by no means an easy one. Besides the destroying business they had much scouting to do and would get entangled in numerous fights with rebel cavalry. They were properly named the "destroying brigade" but the men had a special knack of improving on official titles or expressions and called them: Barnburners, Levelers, Firebugs, torch brigade, destroying Angels and other appropriate Epithets. But they were by no means allowed to destroy indiscriminately. The first thing to be taken care of was cotton. The rebels had declared: "Cotton is King." Consequently war was declared to the knife to the King. Cotton had just been picked and baled. A great amount was stored Everywhere. It could not be shipped to England as all the sea ports were blokaded. It was held by the rebels for John Bull as payment for hundreds of millions of Confederate bonds England had so freely invested in. Every pound of cotton was equal to 50 cents in gold, every bale was worth from $300 to $350.00. Over 100,000. bales were burned making an average loss to John

Bull of 35.000.000 dollars. We were, so to speak, whipping the bag but hitting the mule; but it served John Bull just right If he had kept his finger out of our pie we would not have burnt them and the rebellion would have died out. He is still hugging the Confederate bonds watching to catch Brother Jonathan asleep and to make him saddle the old mare, but all chances are that Jonathan wont dooze much.

The next articles which came under the care of the firebugs were Confederate government factories and machine shops and such private Enterprises wich furnished articles to sustain the war. Furnaces, rolling mills, cotton mills, factorries of any kind, gun and wagon shops, Depots etc. and last but not least, the property of the most prominent rebels who had been active in promoting secession and their leaders, and the leaders who fought so strenuously to uphold the rebellion. Special attention was paid to those who, having received their education at government expenses, had turned traiter and joined the rebel army. Among those who lost large fortunes were: Jeff Davis, Floyd, Toombs, Benjamin and a lot of others whose names I do not remember. But no dwelling of the "poor white trash," or the negroes were ever destroyed. We always could easily tell when and where a cotton sacrifice was taking place. The cotton bales were allways closely piled up likes bricks in a huge wall. If set on fire they would emit a dense black smoke like rosin. Huge, dark clouds would curl and roll skyward but never a flame would be noticed. Such smoke could be easily recognized ten or 15 miles away, as no other Clouds wear such black aspect.

Nov. 20th Brought us to Eatonton factories. When we started John handed me a bundle saying: "here is your dinner, Dan and I are going on a hunt, but let me have your revolver, you wont need it to day." I handed it to him. He then filled my canteen with Coffee and we parted. It was a rough day on us because at about 10. A.M. we came to a railroad which had to be destroyed and that was done in this manner: The leading brigade would draw out along the track in line and halt. The following brigades would pass by and begin where the first ended and so on. If we were in a hurry the track would simply be turned over. Otherwise the rails were torn from the ties, the ties put together in piles and the rails laid across it, the ties set on fire which made the rail red hot. Then with huge tongs, which were made for that purpose, the rails were grabbed at both ends and twisted like a rope. If trees were near enough the men would sometimes twist them around the trees and leave them there. That was called hooping. More than a dozen such hoops, or collars were sometimes found on a single tree. The ties burned readily as they were mostly of pitch pine, which never rots and burns like tinder. Bridges or trestleworks were burnt and culverts broken up. By 5. P.M. ten miles were destroyed and the men thoroughly tired. Happily we had but a mile to the camping place. . . .

Nov. 21st. It had been a very cold night for this latitude. When we crept from under the blanket we found everything coated with frost and smal pools of water had even a thin shell of Ice. An old saying is that hoar frost must be washed off by rain. In this Case it prooved true because about 9. A.M. all the fountains of heaven seemed to spring a leak at once and it rained merciless most of the day. The roads were transformed in[to] mud beds and as the soil here consisted of a sticky white Clay we had to carry klumps along on the feet the size of a peck measure. It could not be shaken off and had to be carried along patiently untill it fell of its own weight. Wagon, Ambulance and battery wheels were merely enormous lumps of rolling Clay gathering and growing with every turn until the enormous weight would cause it to drop only to begin anew. . . . Many a shoe stook in the clay to day which had to be pulled out by hand.

At about 5 P.M. we came to Murder Creek which was so swollen that we were unable to ford it. As the wagons could move but slowly the Pontoons were far behind and it was nearly 7. P.M. before we could cross; but as soon as we had crossed we camped in a high field. I noticed here and there persimmon brush and while John was preparing the evening repast I went on a scout and found a good ways off a big persimmon tree in a fence corner. Its branches were loaded with the shriveled fruit, the frost of the previous night having seasoned the same. Good many had dropped and trying some of them I found them delicious. No humbug about them now, if they did look shriveled. They have a taste similar to figs we buy in the groceries. I lost no time in gathring my haversack full. John and Fred found them just to[o] good. John wanted us to hurry with supper so we could get some more before it was to[o] dark. The tree could not be seen from camp and I suppose that was the reason that nobody had been there, and an other reason was, the men were to[o] tired to indulge in extra tramping. Dan went up the tree and shook them off, John and I gathering. We got over a bushel of them.

Nov. 22d. The roads were very bad [y]et. It was learned to day that three men were missing of the 33d Ohio. They had been out fouraging but no one knew what had become of them. It was hoped they might merely be lost and might turn up sometime, but hope was idle. They never were seen again. We camped for the night at Cedar Creek. At supper John surprised us with a specimen of his culinary art which consisted in a big persimmon pie which met our hearty approoval. John had long been known as the best Officers Cook in the Regiment and he knew it and was rightley proud of it. This pride, I suppose, tempted him to try his skill at mince pie. On his repeated fouraging tours in which Dan allways took part, he had managed to gather all such spices necessary to warrant success. And he did make a success of it as far as I was concerned, but Fred, who had a particular Faculty for detecting flaws in any kind of pottage, found that not all was right with the "Pie." John was perplexed. He enumerated carefully all the ingredients contained therein. Suddenly his face brightened. "I know what it is"! he burst forth. "Brandy" And Brandy it was, sure enough, for when next day with the assistance of Dan he had confiscated a jug persimmon brandy Fred pronounced the "Pie" perfect to a dot. John felt so elated with his success that he manufactured a special pie and sent it by Dan together with his compliments to Genl. Hobart who, in return, highly complimented him for his skill and even hinted that a medal for distinguished service had often been given for deeds of less merit. . . .

A remarkable feature in the difference of living in the southern states was the absence of so called "garden sass" or vegetable. Arou[n]d the manor buildings of the plantations there were splendid parks and gardens with all sorts of tropical flowers, plants and shrubbery; but hardly a specimen could be found of such articles as beans, peas, carrots, lettuce, cellery, parsnips culliflowers or anything with which the gardens in the north abound. Even onions could seldom be found but garlic grew wild in the fields. Even the poorer class of the white people were to[o] lazy to raise such things. At the best they would have a little patch of corn, sweet potatoes, pumpkins and gourds. These poor people were always to be found on the poorest land, or hid away somewhere along the hills and mountains.

Another fact which seemed str[a]nge to me was the way the Aristocracy lived here. One should naturally think that in such a warm Climate a fatty, greasy diat [diet] would be unwholesome, but that seemed not to be the Case. All year round bacon, saltpork, ham and shoulders was the staple article together with fixtures prepared from cornmeal. Wheat flower had to be imported from the north and was used sparingly. If they wanted fresh meat or a beafsteak they sadled the horses and went hunting a beast. Their stock was all and allways running at large. They were branded with the owners mark or name and they had to hunt until one of the right mark was found. Many did not know even how many cattle they had. The pasture ground was seldom enclosed, nor was any hay made as the Cattle were outdoors and found their living all the year round. They did not care much for milk and butter, but some would keep a milch cow in a pasture near home. But that is all different by this time. After the war northern Capital and the thrifty northern Emigrants have revolutionized the mode of Southern agriculture and living.

Nov. 23d. Having crossed the Creek we pursued our way leisurely. Exept in low places the roads had dried sufficient to make marching agreeable. The [weather] was fine and pleasant. Nothing worth of note happened during the day and at four P.M. we drew up and camped near the outskirts of Milledgeville the capital of Georgia.

The good people of Milledgeville were in a State of wild consternation and despair. They had known nothing of our advance or coming. Gouverneur Brown had just called an extra session of the Legislature to meet and consider what means were best to be adopted for further defense of the State.[4] That august body was in session in the halls of the Capitol of the State. While these wise men were discussing the gravity of the situation, some one came running into the halls shouting: "Save yourselfs! the Yanks are coming in the City!" Some of them stepped to a window and sure enough; there, up the broad Avenue, the stars and stripes proudly floating to the breeze, a solid, endless looking Column of bluecoats pressed steadily onward. The wise Statesmen for once lost their heads. Without adjourning they rushed out of the halls pell mell down the stairs and out doors, and did not stop, nor look back until they had cleared the City at the other end. The brigade soon after filed into the park which surrounded the Capitol, staked arms and camped here for the night. . . .

Nov. 24th. We did not start before 8. A.M. because a Division of the 20th Corps came in our way. From here our Corps took the left wing and the 20th Corps our place, the centre. We passed the town and the people, seeing that no harm was done them filled the streets and stared at us. South of the City we crossed Oconee river on a good bridge, the first found undestroyed since we left Chattanooga. John and Dan went on private business again. We undid an other stretch of railroad and at 6. P.M. camped at Black Springs. When the fouragers came in they brought as extra 3 Johnny cavallery men and one bushwhacker, p[r]isoners. As the latter had shot at and wounded one of our men from ambush, Sherman ordered the provost Marchall to have the fellow swung up. The foragers had all more or less to fight that day which was due to the absence of Kilpatricks Cavallery who was operating with the right wing. John Sutschutz and Sergeant Leland Amadon [Amandon] of my Comp. were both slightly wounded. . . .

MEMOIRS OF A DUTCH MUDSILL

Nov. 26th. After a few miles marching we heard the foragers were again in dispute with some rebels. Not long after our advance met with an obstacle. They found the Johnnies behind slight breastworks and seemed unwilling to get out of the way. Scirmishers were forwarded but they were treated very resolute with musketry. A few brigades were quickly formed in line of battle for a charge; A battery allso was quickly at the front and began business at once. When the cannon balls scattered the fence rails about the Johnnies ears and the shells began to pop among them they beat a hasty retreat without waiting for a charge. Abou[t] a mile further on was Sandersville, a place with some pretensions of a city. Our brigade staked arms on the market square while the other troops went on.

That square was a big one; containing at least two acres. There was nothing remarkable about it but a long, one storied frame building with a large porch running all around it, stood in the midle of it. That was the slave mart where niggers were bought and sold. Near by stood the whipping post where refactory niggers received instructions in human rights and personal liberty; the only kind of schools the southern Chevaliers ever established for the education of the darkies. Around the square were splendid brick and stone mansions but in all other parts of the City one only met with unpainted frame houses and hovels. . . . I learned we had to wait for our wagon train which we had to guard for the rest of the day. . . . [By the time the train arrived,] the slave market in the centre of the square was burning lustily. The whipping post was cut down and thrown in the flames. . . .

We marched about 8. miles that afternoon, but as the train is usually in the rear of the army it was dark when we came to camp. It happened that our Regt. came in a park of a lordly looking stone structure. Hardly had we passed through the wide entrance gates when a pack of firce bloodhounds, perhaps ten or twelve of them, came dashing out of their kennels and with blood curdling howls came for us. But they had mistaken their men. At least thre or four bullets went for every hound and before they had passed half the distance up to us, every one of them was harmless. Bloodhounds, whereever met with, were treated in the same manner, and it did make no difference, whether grown or puppies, they were dispatched, "Put onto the scent" as the boys said. Thousands of the beasts were disposed of and the niggerdrivers ought to have been thankfull for it, since the niggers were free they had no more use for them. . . .

Nov. 27th. Again we were trainguard to day. Before we came in motion we learned that the firebugs had done their work in Sandersville, but we did not learn to what extent. A great hindrance, if not to say nuisance, became worse from day to day. It were the nigger who followed us, and the crowd, like a rolling snowball, would increase from day to day. There were not many able bodied man among them; mostly women, children and old people. They would not leave us if told to do so. They followed the train. Where they lived from I dont know, but they managed to live somehow. There were thousands of them and I wondered many times what would be done with them. Being tired nearly to exhaustion we went in camp near Davisboro long after dark.

Nov. 28th. Train guard again and rain nearly all day. About noon a strong troop of Whe[e]lers rebel cavallery wanted to know what we carried along in all thus wagons. We were not slow in giving them the desired information and issued a goodly portion of blue hardtack to them which satisfied their curiosity to such an extent that they left about a hundred killed and wounded and a goodly number of prisoners in our hands. Crossed the Ogeechee river on pontoons during the afternoon. Camped near Louisville which was a place of perhaps a thousand inhabitants. Five men reported missing from fouragers of the 2d Brigade. Never heard from again.

Nov. 29th. We were relived from trainguard to day and mighty glad we were. We had marched 10 miles and were just through with dinner when a Courier on a foam covered horse came dashing up inqu[i]ring for Genl. Carlin. A minute after the brigade was hurried forward on the road about a mile, then a turn to the left kept hurrying along mostly allways in a double quick. We could not learn anything about the reason for this sudden move. Finally after an houres run we were drawn up in the edge of the woods opposite a big field. As we afterwards learned, a part of Kilpatricks cavallery had been nearly surounded by Wheelers Entire force. We had not long to wait when a great string of rebel cavallery came charging past us; there left wing only a few rods away from us. Poor fellows did not know what was hidden in the woods. Now a single shot warned us to fire, and fire it was. From right oblique left oblique and flank our bullet pirced their ranks. The confusion was terrible. They wheeled the horses round to retreat but the mass of fallen horses and men made that naturally difficult; and our men kept on pouring led into them. Finally the rest succeeded in getting out of reach. As the rebels did not return we marched back. Kilpatrick in his report gives the number of prisoners taken as 500. and the dead and wounded as 300.

Nov. 30th. Turned out to be a nasty fellow. Shortly after we had started a fine drizling rain set in which gradually develloped to a regular soaker and continued till 10. A.M. Then we struck a railroad and the usual demolishing process began. This road was built in a very substantial way such as I had never seen before. Instead of laying and nailing the rails direct onto the ties, solid, square stringers 8 x 8 were first laid across the ties dropping an inch and a half in the same. On the stringers the rails were fastened. It was an expensive way of building but certainly a good one. It had many advantages over the common built roads. It kept the road bed more even, prevented the spreading, or breaking of rails, and as the cars were raised 6 inches higher over the track, a man may lay with safety between the rails and not being hurt by a passing train. But it made us mor work to destroy the road, but I suppose it had not been built for that purpose. We kept up the work untill 3. P.M. when we came to an other wagon road followed the same. We camped at a place with a big name and very little show, a kind of pocket edition City which were so frequently met in the south. "Sebastopol" was the pretensious bait which had so far failed to draw Capital and develop a healthy enterprise. The combined Turkish, English and French armies who, during 6 months, wasted their energies to reduce and take the famous russian Sebastopol in 1855. would hardly have noticed this one. . . .

Dec. 1st. It was my turn to go with the fourage party to day. I induced John and Dan to come along and advised them to gather as much as possible. The reason was thus: Up to this time we had been on the high tableland to a certain extend well cultivated and stocked, but to day we were beginning to decend the slope towards the south Atlantic Coast. Gradually the Cotton and Corn plantations disappear and Rice and Sugar cane plantatation take their place. On the higher ground sweet potatoes cotton and corn is raised. With the country the vegetation changes in generel. The sturdy, tall whitewood, beach, soft maple and Chestnut give room for the life oak, red cedar, Cypress, magnolia and Palmetto. The swamps are covered with a tropical vegetation, so dense that not even a cat would find room for passage. The higher, sandy tracks are covered with the tall, stately pitch pine, which is such an exellent firewood and the smoke of which turn the whitest man into a nigger in less than no time and, what is the best of it, no amount of water will take of[f] the soot. As soap was an unknown quality with us the reader can immagine what a dusky, smoked looking set we were after a weeks tramp in the pitch pine Country. Indeed, when we arrived in Savannah there was not much difference in coleur between us and the motley Crowd of Africans which followed us. And not alone did face and hands undergo the transformation, but the confounded stoff would penetrate the clothing and stain the body as nice and perfect as if mother

THE ARMY FOUND AGAIN

nature had done the job herself. Neither was that all. A sharp, pugnant odor, which one allways reminded of a tarbarrel, was everywhere. The boys now, in conformity with the circumstances[,] adopted the title "Billey Shermans smoked yankees." . . .

Our success in gathering fourage was not very promising. Not that there had been any lack of plantations, but it seemed that wherever we came Kilpatricks, or Wheelers Cavallery had been there and taken the cream away. It was allready past noon and but very little had been realized. Dan informed us that he learned from a nigger of an allmighty big plantation where we might find plenty stuff but it was several miles off. We could and did not expect the people to bring us the stuff in the road ready to be picked up. So we started at once and after several miles tramp we found the nigger had spoken the truth. It seemed a city on a small scale lay before us. From the side we entered the field, the Mansion, and outbuildings and negro quarters were fully half a mile distant and situated on a rising Plateau nearly in the midle of the immense field. First we met a peanut patch comprising perhaps twenty acres the rows being turned by the plow, the roots with the peanuts scattered for seasoning. That looked very nice but that was all we could get out of it, for a raw peanut is a mean thing to eat and as we had no Contrivances to roast them we let them alone.

The mansion, or palace, as I ought to call it, was surrounded by a park, enclosed by a cast Iron fence. I sent most of the men towards the outbuildings to see what could be found there, while I with ten others passed through the main gate towards the mansion. The building was of gray stone, three stories high, the lower, or basement, being half under ground. A broad, double stone stairway, with marble bannisters, garded by two marble lyons led to the first floor. The massive casings of the portal and windows were of marble and eleborately carved. Over the portal, on a large oval marble slab was engraved the coat of arms of some brittish lord and the legend: "Erected A.D. MDCCCL." Coming near the steps we stopped to study the facade of the house when suddenly one of the folding doors opened and three ladies stepped on the plattform. One was a stately, proud looking figure of midle age as it seemed, holding in her right hand carelessly a light but fine looking breech loading rifle; the second was young and of delicate frame, probably daughter or sister. The third was a [quadroon], semingly the chambermaid, a picture of face and form. Had not the exessive whiteness of her complexion and the long raven black, curly hair disclosed her ancestry, anybody would have taken her for a caucasian. In the background, but inside the hall appeared the unavoidable clumsey, fat "Dinah" the kitchen dragoon, a big turban around her head and an enormous set of Ivory white teeth glistend dangerously between a pair of gaping, bloodred lips.

For a minute they gave us time to study the picture and I was mentally calculating whether that ladies rifle was loaded or not, when the creature suddenly struck an imposing figure and pointing with the raised left arm towards the gate exclaimed fircely: "Clear out of here, you bastardly robbers!" There was so much of the comic in the situation that made the boys laugh merrily and: "Thats right mother, give it to them," advised one. "You better fix bajonet old girl," an other. "But isn't she a daisy"? queried a third. That was to[o] much for our heroine and up went the little rifle but, before she could pul the trigger the watching quadroon was at her side and with a quick move threw the muzzle upward and the ball went high into the air. There was no more fun in the busines now and in double quick time we flew up the steps from both sides, but before we could reach the platform she managed to crack off an other pill which, thanks to the lively quadroon, was harmless as the first. I took hold of the rifle near the muzzle and holding it upward requested her to let me have the rifle, but it took two of the boys to induce her to give it up.

They went back into the house, we following. The young lady and quadroon followed the hallway but the older lady turned to the right in what seemed to be a reception room, I following close upon her heels to prevent her closing the door in my face. She sat down in an armchair and covered her face with her hands. I ins[t]ructed the men to find the entrance to the basement as that certainly was the place to look for rations; but warned them to leave the other rooms alone. Jacob Rhiner I kept with me as a sort of witness of what the lady might say, or do. I took the remaining cartridges out of the cylinder, put the rifle in a corner and took a seat. I did not intend to disturb the old lady and was glad she kept quiet. I began to muster the fixtures in the room, all of which were of the most luxurious style. A life size portrait in Oilpainting of a very handsome, but proud and commanding looking gentlemen hung over the mantelpiece. It probably represented the lord of the manor.

After a few minutes however the lady straightned up and haughtily said: "What are you sitting there for like blocks of stone? What do you want anyway? If you want to rob and plunder why do you not go to work and relive me of your odious presence"?—"Softly. Madam" I replied. "softly. There is time enough and we need not hurry. Let us take one thing at a time. I did not wish to disturb your reflections, nor hurt your feelings with untimely remarks. We do not intent to rob you nor plunder, as you please to

THE ARMY FOUND AGAIN

express it. We only came to take so much of your bountifull viands as we need for supper and breakfast and will spedily relieve your gracefull highness of our odious presence. I know that tastes differ and every person has a right to follow his inclinations, as far as decency and law admits. I am well aware madam that you prefer the society of the dusky, odorous african and do not feel any disgrace on that account"—"Stop"! she said ex[c]itedly. "Can you blame me? Our servants I can order what to do and how to behave, and can make him to obey orders, but you are nothing but a set of lawless, voracious, cruel barbarians who will stop short for nothing and respect neither person, property or propriety. Oh, mercy! that it should come to this." And she again covered her face and seemed to be overcome with emotion. . . .

At this moment the howls of some bloodhounds, then three or fo[u]r shots and yells of the hounds were heard. The lady, who had not stirred during my short sermon, jumped up exclaiming: "What does that mean?"— "Do not be frightened Madam," I replied. "the boys are only executing your police, your nigger catchers. You see that is a custom with the men to dispose of all the bloodhounds that come in their way. They have that foolish notion that it is barbarous and brutal to hunt a human being with voracious wild beasts. I suppose it is a ridiculous, sentimental notion but they stick to it all the same and can not be con[v]inced otherwise." The lady stood a little while as if listening intently, then raising her eyes to the portray over the mantelpiece and clasping her hands she broke forth: "Oh, my Hector, Hector! why do you not step down and slay those brutes who pollute your sacred premises." Jack Rh[e]iner laughed aloud and I came very near being guilty of the same rudeness when the lady suddenly pointed her long index finger at Jack and, a strange gleaming light in her eyes exclaimed: "Jes, you may laugh, you monkey! you brute! That man, represented on that canvas, was one of Gods noblest Creatures, worth a thousand of you. If he were here you would not stay there and mock my grief and live. Curses upon you"! "Where is he now Madame?" I inquired. "Where is he now?" she repeated. "Where none of you can hurt or insult him. You have killed him, murdered him. Do you hear? Do you understand? You mu[r]dered him. May all the devils tear you to pieces; May you burn forever in the deepest pit of hell." Jack involuntarily stepped back as if afraid and I feared the lady might work herself into histerics or fits. But she sank down in the chair again and covered her face. "Madame" I said "I symphatize with your grief, but let me tell you there are a great many in the same boat with you. There are thousands of widows, of fathers and mothers, and sisters and brothers in the northern states who bewail the losses of husbands, fathers, sons and brothers. They all feel their loss as keen as you do. But the misery was forced upon them, whereas you, and the likes of you are responsible for it. The sooner you come to realize this the better it will be for you."

The boys were gathering in front of the stairs outside indicating that they were through with their mission and were waiting for me. When stepping in the Hall I noticed the young lady, Quadrone and Dinah coming from the other end of the hall as if to see us depart. I found the boys had done well. John and Dan had their mules well loaded and the others had a number of bags and boxes and baskets, enough to load them down. The party who had been investigating the outbuildings allso came along outside the fence having found two mules which were well loaded. The ladies exept the older one, who did not come out, stood now on the platform. "O, see"! the young lady exclaimed. "there go our last mules, what shall we do now"? "Is these all you have" I asked. "Yes sir. The Confederates took all horses and mules we had a while ago."—"If you will send on[e], or two darkies along I will return the mules to you."—"Will you? thank you sir." Speaking a few words to the [quadroon] the latter went into the house. The young lady then said: "Sir, I am so much oblidged to you for your kindness. The other things we can spare very well but without the mules we would be as poor as Job. And we could not buy others as our money is not—not very good. I suppose you know all about it." She stopped, but I saw she had something more to say. Finally she said in a half whisper: "I hope Sir Mother has been no more rude to you? You must excuse her she is so full of grief." I assured her that I did not blame her mother and expressed the hope that time would heal the wounds. Two darkies came round the corner and the young lady said to them: "Dave and Caesar. You take up some of this bundles and carry them for the gentlemen and you will return with the mules, will you?"—"Shuah Missus, dat we will." And we started off, the ladies calling severel "Good by's" after us. . . .

Before we left the field we passed by the family graveyard. I stopped to read the inscriptions. The tallest monument, a massive granite pedestal with marble shaft bore the legend: "Colonel Hector Burton, 12th. Ga. Regt. killed in battle at Stone river Tenn. Dec. 31st 1862.[5] Age 45. years 9. months. He died a patriot and a hero, giving his life for his country and liberty. Peace and honor to his memory." What queer notions people have of Liberty. I could not help to remark. That man fought and died for the liberty to perpetuate Slavery. . . .

THE ARMY FOUND AGAIN

It was dark when we came to the Regt. and fires were burning brightley. The mules were quickley unloaded and I hastened the Niggers away with them, because I feared that if the Quartermaster should get an Eye on them, he should seize and confiscate them. . . .

Dec. 3d. Was in so far noteworthy as the men were enriched by a some what ridiculous Experience. We passed several fields of sugarcane, the first we had ever seen. The darkies would cut of[f] a stalk, peel of[f] the rind and chew the marrow. The men soon followed their Exemple and as the stuff is of pleasant taste indulged freely therein. In a raw state the juice acts as a physic and the men being ignorant of that fact, and besides beeing not used to it became the more readily its victim. After a few hours it was amusing to observe how anxiously the men would dodge aside in the woods or swamps which was the cause of much joking and merriment. During the afternoon we crossed Buckhead Creek on pontoons. The Creek might have properly been called a river for its size and depth. The darkeys had wellnigh become an unbearable nuisance as there was a whole army of them. Genl. Sherman concluded to check their Crowding us and gave orders to stop the niggers at the bridge and after the troops and teams had passed to take up the pontoons and leave the darkies at the other side. It seemed to be a cruel measure but under the circumstances can not be censured. But the darkies were not to be outwitted so easy. They were left on the wrong side of the river sure enough, but when we broke camp next morning they were there again all the same. By what means they had crossed I do not know.[6] We camped that night at Lumpkins Station.

Dec. 4th. Shortley after leaving Camp we struck the Savannah and Augussta R.R. and of course were ordered to attack the same. After fixing the road after our own fashion for a distance of five miles we took a road east. Soon we entered a forest of exclusively pitch pine trees. This pine is different from the northern pine. It grows very tall and straight with but few branches at the crown. But it is in the foliage the difference strikingly appears. The nedles grow in tufts or small bundles and are about a foot long and as the[y] drop every year, will cover the ground foot high or more. The tree is so saturated with pitch that a mere match is able to set a tree on fire. The troop ahead of us had set the droppings on fire which made such a thick, heavy smoke in which no man could breath and live. There was nothing left for us but to go around the burning woods which added five miles to our days tramp. Just before dark we Crossed Bryar Creek and went into Camp.

Dec. 5th. Was a hard working day for man and beasts. The ro[a]ds were well enough for us to walk on, but i[t] seemed there was merely a thin crust or shell over an underlying strata of quicksand or mire. After a dozen wagons or batteries had passed the same spot the wheels would cut the crust and disappear untill the axles rested on the ground. Nor was there much chance for the teams to spread as the roads were to[o] narrow. What an amount of work that meant for the men cannot be described. Good water was allso becoming scarce. Springs were out of the question; the water in the swamps and mar[s]hes was but a black, thick fluid. Consequently we were thrown back on the creeks and that more or less mixed with the swampy fluid. The fouragers had allso met with poor success and only brought in a lot of rice; but that was better than nothing. We camped that night at Buck creek Postoffice.

Dec. 6th. Again I was detailed on a fouraging Expedition. It was with but very little hope of success we started. The country seemed to[o] poor to raise anything except cypress and pitch pine. I did not know in what direction to turn in order to realize anything. I knew the Savannah river could not be far towards the East as we were informed that the Division was to camp in the vicinity of Hudsons ferry. I concluded to go in that direction; hoping that near the river we might find some more habitations. We traveled some five or six miles through a godforsaken Country where a crow would hardly make its living. Beaver dam Creek slowly felt its way toward the river. It was one of thuse runs often met with in low Countries which are neither creek nor river, the water nearly stagnant, so that one is at a loss to tell for a certainty, in what direction it flows, or where its banks begin or end. This was certainly half a mile wide and as there was no bridge we had to cross as best we could, that is to say, we had to wade it, for the knols and moss hills which peeped here and there above the water were often to[o] far apart for a jump. We were well soaked when we reached higher ground. Instead of decending down to the river we slowly went up hill and soon found a small plantation; but it was of not much account. The people had left and the few darkies told us there was nothing to be gotten but some sweet potatoes and unt[h]r[e]shed rice. Well, it was better than nothing at all so we took a couple bushels of potatoes and knocked of[f] a bag of rice and went on. I had learned from the darkies that it was only one mile to the river and 7. miles down to the ferry. We met several more small concerns but nothing was captured. Finally the boys succeeded in capturing a 100. pound pig which was duly dispatched and quartered. This was

THE ARMY FOUND AGAIN

the last fresh pork we captured on the Savannah trip. We found more rice stakes but as we had plenty of it we did not bother with it.

But somehow it was decided in the council of the gods that we should not return empty handed. After a continued long tramp it seemed to me the 7. miles to the ferry must be nearly done away with if the darkies had told the truth. We came to an old road, now partley overgrown with brush, which led in the direction of the river. I requested the men to rest here while I would go and have a look at the river. It was only one eight[h] of a mile to the river but it could not be seen on account of the woods. When I got down the first thing I noticed were two boats run partially unter the brush and tied to the same. One was quite a big affair and had four oars in it. Looking up the river I saw a scow or transport coming down the river with the stream or current; they allso had a sail hoisted. It seemed to be a big concern but it was to[o] far off to judge of its dimensions.

I made up my mind to get that craft if possible and went to the boys telling them what was in sight and my intention to capture it, provided they would take a hand in it. Of course they would. They all felt happy over the sport in view. I left two men in charge of the baggage and knapsacks and with the rest, 28. men went to the river. The craft had neared considerable. We kept conceiled untill the craft came in striking distance. Thee boats were unfastened and made ready for service. When the scow was near enough I ordered four men to fire over the scow the first time. There were only t[w]o men to be seen, one at the rudder and one on the foreport. As the scow floated in midstream the distance was not over hundred yards. I ordered all in sight now and hailed the Craftsmen. They stared at us a moment and immediately a half dozen men came on deck. I ordered them to heed [head] this way. But they did not mind and tried to heed the vessell for the opposite bank. I ordered the four to fire. That did not have no effect. Some of the sailors run below deck again. The craft swung slowly round; the sail was lowered. I counted off 6 men to fire to kill. The helmsmen and an other fell. But a fellow with a broad plank came up from below; and the other had taken the rudder and he with the plank held the latter in such position that it covered them both.

"Quick in the boats now," I said and twelve sprang in the big and six in the small one, I going in the bigger. The ten men left I told to remain and if necessary I would send the big boat for them. The men plied the oars with a will and the boats shot swiftley over the water. As the sailors did not dare use their poles for fear of being shot and the scow, coming out of the current had no propelling power, was allmost helpless. We soon overtook them and went immediately on board being only 18 inches above water. The boats being fastened to the stern we looked round. The helmsman lay [y]et where he had fallen, dead; another was wounded in the hip. I asked the fellow who was at the rudder now if he would steer the scow to the other side now. Yes he would. "But be careful sir," he said, "there are eight men in the hold [y]et and all of them have navys [navy pistols]." "Oh, have they. Why did they not use them when we boarded"?—"I dont know" he replied. With the help of poles we swung the scow around, hoisted the sail and slowly the unwieldy box swam for the other shore. I had closed the hatchway to prevent the fellows below from mischief. "What have you loaded"? I inquired. "Different things," he said. "Some stuff for the hospitals in Savannah, Some grub and clothing for the soldiers, some tobacco and I dont know what all." When we neared the shore we were surprised to see so many soldiers and Officers coming down to see the Elephant, shouting and cheering like posessed. That happened this way: This place was the very Ferry where our Division was to camp. They had been there when we arrived, only half a mile away. Our firing had been heard by some of them and two Orderlies on horseback had been sent to investigate. They found the two men guarding the baggage and heard the story. They saw when we were chasing the scow in the boats and went quickly back to camp with the news. So everybody wanted to see the pri[z]e.

When we landed allmost half the brigade was gathered among the trees at the river. Genl. Hobart, Col. Fitch and Maj. Walker were allso on the spot. John and Dan as a matter of course. Genl. Hobart claimed the scow as a pri[z]e for the brigade; Col. Fitch claimed it as a pri[z]e for the Regt. because all of the crew belonged to his Regt. the booty should be treated as fourage[.] The two got up quite an argument when I thought it time to add my mite to it. So I told them frankly they were disposing of a piece of property of which they could give no tittle. That according to the laws of nations and war, every vessel captured from the enemy in time of war belonged as a pri[z]e to the Captors, untill the pri[z]e mony had been decided and paid. Maj. Walker at once took my party and he was an able partner. After a little good natured scirmishing in arguments it was decided that it should be left with the captors to say what should be done with the vessel and its contents. I called the party together to hear their opinion. They left it all to me. So I put it this way: First: the prisoners on bord the scow were to be turned over to the proper authorities. The scow was to be unloaded and if found that there was more than the Regiment needed the surplus to go to the brigade, but before distributing should begin the captors should

THE ARMY FOUND AGAIN

be allowed to pick out for themselves whatever they pleased. The scow and such goods and articles which were of no use to the soldiers should be burnd. Everyone was satisfied with the decision. . . .

The scow was quite a big one. It was twenty foot wide by 60 foot long. The hold was seven foot deep. Soon the Quartermaster and Commissary came with teams and unloading and loading was done at a lively rate. I sat down and observed the men who worked as lively as so many bees. After a while Dan came with the notice that supper was ready. That was very wellcome, because it was the first meal since 4. A.M. John felt well to night seeing his larder so well supplied. The unloading and distributing took untill midnight and had to be done by the light of the campfire. It was no easy job either. There were so many different Articles. Sweet potatoes. corn meal, shelled rice, hams, shoulders and bacon, dried aples and peaches; eggs, hundred barrels of sourkrout made not from the regular Cabbage but from the so called Bore Cohl or Brussels sprouts; smoking and chewing tobacco; Peach, and Persimmon brandy. But one thing I was looking for in vain was butter. Not an ounce in the whole concern. Well, we had lived without that article for two and a half years and could do without it now. The Peach and Persimmon Juice was not distributed at once for fear of making the men to[o] happy I suppose. . . .

Dec. 8th. Our Division brought up the rear today. Being the last in line we did not come in motion untill 8. A.M. We labored forward untill about 10. A.M. when the Column stopped. Morgans Division, which led the advance had entered Ebeniezer swamp & had been obliged to halt. Thus swamp is very extensive. Ebenezer creek runs through about the midle of it and the creek was spanned by a long bridge. From both ends of the bridge a curduroy road extended through the swamp. But the rebels had raised "Hail Columbia" here in general. The curduroy was torn up the whole lenght; the bridge burned and not satisfied with that they slashed the Cypresses from both sides across the road and making a complete tangle of it. Colonel Buel[l] with the Engineer worked all night but had only been able to clear and build the curderoy up to the Creek and was constructing the bridge out of unhewn timbers. Finally at five in the after noon the passage was clear and the troops moved on again. But we had not been allowed to be idle during that time. The 20th Corps being some 8. or 10 miles to our right and unable to come to our assistance on account of the impassable swamps, the Johnnies, who had been hovering in our rear for several days thought to profit by the occasion and suddenly attacked our rear. It was a poor position to make a decent fight on account of the swamps, but the rebels insisted on having a row. It was a mean business to fight in the swamp and the rebels perhaps thought we did not know how to behave in there. But if such was their opinion they were mistaken. After a few hours of sharp scirmishing they quitted and withdrew. We krept out of the tangled mas of cypress knees and vines towards the road. It was found that our loss was 10 killed and 120 wounded. It was 10. P.M. when we went in camp at Ebenezer Church close alongside the cemetary.

Dec. 9th. . . . At about noon we came to the Augusta and Savannah R.R. We were ordered to make dinner and then set to work destroying the track. We were kept busy with that amusement until 4. P.M. when we went ahead again. After a couple miles walk the advance reported breakers ahead. We were just entering a somewhat extensive swamp. At the opposite side of the swamp the rebels had build a strong field work and seemed disposed to dispute our advance. Our Artillerie opened on them but as it was getting late an attack was delayed untill next morning.

Dec. 10th. On investigation it was found that the rebs had thought best to abandon their works and retreat towards the Savannah. But they had left some strong evidence of their friendley feeling behind. Having passed their works several torpedoes exploded under the feet of the men, wounding several of them severely. The torpedoes were burried in the ground even with the surface. The cap would project just a little above the ground, but being loosely covered with sand or dirt could not easyly be detected. But the person who stepped on such a thing was sure to be immediately hoisted and perhaps mutilated or killed, besides others who might be hit by the scattering fragments. Of course halt was made and carefull investigation of the road begun but Genl. J. C. Davis had a better plan. We had quite a number of rebel prisoners who had been escorted along under guard. These, Officers and soldiers[,] had to march ahead of us. During the first ha[lf] mile three more exploded killing two Johnnies and wounding several more or less. No more were found then.[7] But Genl. Hardee was informed under flag of truce and notified of the measures we had taken to discover the torpedoes. At the same time he was warned to desist from that practice. Hardee replied that the torpedoes were planted without his knowledge and should not happen again. At the same time he would see that the perpetrators were properly punished. We camped that night at ten mile house.

Dec. 11th. We had now arrived within dangerous proximity of the fortifications of Savannah. It was now a shifting right or left to gain the proper position in the encircling line. The 20th Corps began at the Savannah river north east; on its right the 14th Corps e[x]tended the line towards the Ogeechee river; the 15th and 17th Corps on the right of the 14th due south towards Kings bridge and Fort McAllister. Savannah could hardly be taken by assault on account of its peculiar situation. On the north east it was protected by the Savannah river, on the west and South, and distant about 4 miles from the City, by impassable swamps through which only small causeways led to the plateau on which the City is built. On the rim of thus plateau, facing outward the Fortifications were built. The few roads leading into the City were well protected by good works. Our brigade lay alongside a Canal conecting the Ogeechee with the Savannah river and furnishing rice fields with the necessary water. The canal was in our immediate rear.

The most important question for the moment was ration and fourage for men and bea[s]ts. There was nothing to be found in the vicinity of Savannah as the Johnnies had taken care to clear everything. But Argyle Island in the Savannah river was one big riceplantation and it was found out that a considerable quantity of fourage could be found there. But the rebels had troops and artillerie there to defend the Island; besides we had no boats or any other Contrivance to reach the Island. It would have been an easy job for our artillerie boys to drive the rebels away from the Island, but that would have implied the entire destruction of the property, because our shot and shell woud have destroyed much and the balance would have been destroyed by the Johnnies before they left the Island. And the stuff there was just what we wanted. But the 20th Corps was equal to the Emergency. They constructed a number of rafts above the Island unseen by the Johnnies and in the dead of night floated silently down the river and landed at the northern point of the Island. They completely surprised the Johnnies and all were taken prisoners allmost without firing a shot. An imense lot of unshelled rice, severall hogshead of molasses, sugar, cornmeal and bacon was found there.

At first the rice was issued to us in the husk but the 20th Corps fellows had soon the husking, or shelling mill in operation and we got the rice all ready for the kettle. To shell, or husk the rice the men adopted different methods. Some would hew a sort of trough in a log, pour in a lot of rice and stamp it lustily with clubs held vertical or endways. The cleaning or separating the chaf was effected by winnowing in the air. In this operation we usually had to raise the wind, which was done either with the hat, or big fan made from old tent cloth, bags or any kind of rags we could get hold of, stretched on a frame. The stamping and winnowing was repeated until the kernels were free of shells. An other way was to take bags, fill them about a quarter full of rice, tie the bag and place it on a bord or large flat rock and thrash it lustily. This process was more slow but no rice was wasted, which could not be avoided in the stamping process. The rice so prepared was considerable bigger and fatter than thus we usual buy in the groceries. It is moreover a nourishing and healthy food, but we had not the ingredients to prepare it in a proper tastefull way. Boiled with salt and water we took it with gries, or without, but one becomes soon tired of and disgusted with it if eaten three times a day. How the Chinese and Japanese get along with it is more than I can account for. . . .

Before we left A[t]lanta Genl. Sherman had requested the Government to keep lookouts on the Atlantic in front of Charleston, Savannah or Fernandina and be ready with a fleet of supplies for the army. Especially had he cautioned to keep watch in Ossabaw Sound opposite the mouth of the Ogeechee, as Savannah was the point he would turn up if the Rebels would let him. But no ships could pass Fort McAllister at the mouth of the Ogeechee. A union fleet had formerly tried to reduce the fort but had failed. The rebels had a garrison and heavy Artillerie there. The fort had to be taken before any vessel could come up the sound and enter the river. Genl. Osterhaus was assigned the job to take the Fort. Kings bridge across the Ogeechee had been burned but was substantially rebuilt within three days by Col. Buel[l] and the 58th Indiana Regt. under the supervision of Capt. Reese of the Ingenier Corps. Genl. Osterhaus with the 15th Corps crossed to the south side and made preparations to attack the Fort which was three miles down the river.

During the afternoon of the 13th the scirmishers of Genl. Hazens Division of the 15th Corps had worked up to the abattis of the fort followed by a good suport. We heard the heavy guns of the fort but could see nothing. Half an hour afterwards signals told us that the Fort was ours. Hazens Div. without further firing had rushed through the torpedoes and Abattis which obstructed the approach to the fort, and gaining the parapet after a short hand to hand strugle the garrison had surrendered. Hazens loss in killed and wounded was 90, the garrison had 50. in killed and wounded and 150 captured besides 22 pieces of artillerie and a large quantity of ammunition.[8] So the last barrier between us and the Ocean was removed. Admiral Dahlgreen [Dahlgren] with a flotilla of steamers, tugs and transports was waiting at the entrance of Ossabaw Sound out of reach of the rebel cannon, for signals that the fort was ours and the road clear. On the 20th we again drew the usual amount of hardtack, bacon and coffee.

Meanwhile we had no very serious work to do. The situation was such that no small arms could do much execution. In front of our brigade line was a narrow strip of heavy timber. At the further edge of the woods was an extended open mar[s]h, now deep under water. At the edge of the woods were our pickets. At the opposite side, ¼ of a mile distant where the higher land began, were the rebel works. A narrow causeway led through the march towards the rebel works and was defended by a rebel batterie.

Allthough we had no trouble with musketry fire, we were not alltogether out of danger. The Johnnies used their cannons liberaly, especially their big mortars created a holy terror. They were of twelve inch bore and threw a junk of 300. pound weight. When those fellows busted, scattering their Contents profusely around, it made the air tremble and set the limbs on the trees shaking. We allways had several men on watch for them as they could plainly be seen sailing in a long bow through the air. At the Alarm Cry: "Camp-kettle, ho"! every one jumped behind a tree, or dodging behind the bank of the canal. At night time we could watch them by the burning fuse des[c]ribing a firy streak in the air like a shooting star. It was lucky for us we were behind the woods out of sight of the rebels, for had they known we were so near then they would not have thrown the shells so far behind us. As it was but few pieces would reach occasionally our Camp. The first day the rebs began the game I spoke to John about building a small bombproof against the bank of the canal. No so[o]ner had I mentioned the Object than he and Dan set to work chopping down the smaller trees for the purpose. When the boys of the Comp. saw what they were about they set to work. The other Comps. caught the fever and by noon the next day the whole Regt. had a good shelter which, at least saved us the jumping during the night. But one fellow allmost got the best of us, bombproof and all.

It was near noon and the men busy preparing their rice. The rebs had rested for an hour, perhaps they were taking dinner allso. But: "Camp-kettle, Look out"! came the warning. Yes, look out. The huge monster was allready so near that we thought we heard the hissing of the fuse. Before we could cross the space of a rod to the log sheds the thing had buried its big nose in the canal bank. A tremendous explosion followed immediately and a deluge of dirt and mud followed covering everything within a radius of fifteen to twenty rods. It extinguished the fires, filled rice kettles, spiders and coffee cups, and—what was that? A stream of water came pouring into the campground. The canal was 4 foot higher than the campground, and the Explosion having torn a piece out of the Embankment, the water soon would drown us out. Luckily a dozen or so of short logs had been left from the log sheds and thuse were hastily thrown in the breach and with grass leaves, dirt and brush we managed to fill up the gap. . . .

MEMOIRS OF A DUTCH MUDSILL

General Sherman at first was speculating to get hold of Savannah with-out direct assault on the rebel works, which meant the sacrifice of thou-sands of lifes. The weak spot in the defense of the City was on the north, or river side from the South Carolina shore. There being only the river be-tween City and land and no fortifications. If he could throw a Corps over there he could starve Hardee and the City in submission. It was calculated that Hardee had 20,000. soldiers behind the works. Added to that 25. 30,000. citizens they could not subsist long when we were in possession of the river above and below the City. True we held the river nominally above the City but we could not lay a bridge there as the rebel gunboats would destroy them faster as we build them. But he found an other way. As soon as the fleet at the mouth of the Ogeechee had unloaded he put the 15th and 17th Corps on board the same and sent them along the coast east of Savannah round to Port Rojal South Carolina. From thence they had to fight their way southward to Savannah again. They soon took the works on the Cosawatchee and Tullifinny rivers and prepared to march towards Savan-nah. It was now for General Hardee to decide whether he would stand siege and final surrender, or slip out in time and try to escape to Charleston.

But it seems Sherman decided at last to take the City by assault. His desire to capture the City before Christmass in order to surprise President Lincoln with a valuable Christmass present may have been the motive for it. Be that as it may, on the 20th orders were received to prepare for an assault on the rebel fortifications. A number of heavy parrot siege guns had been received from Port Rojal and put in position. Hardee had been requested to surrender and had refused. I feel a cold shiver [y]et when I think of that order for the assault before daylight Dec. 21st. To wade in the cold water waist deep for half a mile in the night, to attack the rebel strongholds of whose strenght we did not know anything was not very encouraging. Every one had to provide himself with a 30. inch long pitch torch which was to be stuck behind under the waistbelt. A dozend matches were given to every man to light the torch with when the order was given. How the scheme was to work I never could solve, nor have I ever met one who could tell.

That afternoon Capt. Weisbrod and I with our Companies were or-dered on picket. All the afternoon the rebels kept up an unusual heavy artillery fire, as if they had known of our intention and were trying to scare the wits out of us before we were undertaking the assault. Neither did the night interfere much with the noisy racket. It was ten P.M. and still they were blowing away. "It seems" Weisbrod said, "the Johnnies are going to charge us instead of we them."—"Or" I replied, "it is a blind to cover their retreat."—"By Jingo. I believe you are right. Let us listen closely" he replied. A half an hour more and the firing ceased. But we could not hear the least disturbance. At twelve when the Outposts were relieved Weisbrod asked me: "What do you think about investigating the matter"?—"I am ready." I replied. Informing the Sergeants where we intended to go we went for the Causeway. One of the sergeants, Sylvester Greeley followed us and begged us to let him go along. We did so and went briskley ahead at first. When approaching the battery which was behind the works at the end of the causeway we slowed up and listening did not hear the least sound. The last 30. yards we crept on hands and knees until we were close up to the works. Still all was quiet as in a grave. We rose. There were the portholes, and there stood the cannon. Allso not gone [y]et. I put my Cap aside, put a foot on a projecting log, drew myself up and looked over the top log. Small heaps of dimly glimmering coals were here and there but no human being could be seen. If there were any there they surely would be near the works. I whispered to the Sergeant to give me a lift so as to get over without noise. The first thing I did was to feel for the vent of the cannons. They were spicked [spiked, i.e., plugged]. That was proof enough. Weisbrod and Greely came over now. They were allso satisfied that the birds had flown. Run away and left the guns. They probably were afraid we might hear the noise and at the same time the guns would detain their hasty flight. Being satisfied on that point we went back to the picket Reserve.

We concluded to report the news at once as it was nearly two A.M. and the attack would soon be made. When we arrived at Col. Fitchs tent he was just about getting up and when we informed him of the news he thought it to[o] good to be true. I asked if I might call in the picket. "Certainly, if you are sure the rebs are gone" he said. So I went to the picket and Weisbrod went to brigade headquarters to inform Genl. Hobart. But at the same time with him an Orderly from 20th Corps headquarters arrived with the same report. So it semed that the 20th Corps on the left had discovered the news as soon, or sooner as we. Hardee had crossed the river on a pontoon bridge into South Carolina and narrowly escaped the clutches of the 15 and 17th Corps. He fell back to Charleston. When I arrived in Camp with the picket the boys were wild with ex[c]itement for every one knew that a great trial had been averted. So elated did they feel over the timidity of the Johnnies that they even forgave them that unpleasant mud and water bath.

Dec. 21st. At daylight we crossed the causeway and entered the plateau. We were not however to enter the City to day. But the 20th Corps which had a much shorter route was there allready. Genl. Slocum had, as soon a[s] the rebel retreat was known to him, hurried forward his Corps hoping to catch some of Hardees rear troops but Hardee had managed his exit so deftly that when Slocum appeared the pontoons were allready taken up. We marched about four miles to the main road which leads from Kings bridge north to Savannah. Here, near a large plantation we went into camp. and were informed we would remain here for the day. . . .

Dec. 22d. Three miles walk brought us to the, at that time, largest and finest City in Georgia. The first object which called my attention was the so called Pulasky square in the southern part of the City, with a splendid Equestrian Statue of the Genl. of like name who was killed here during the revolutionary war. Savannah has very wide and very streight streets which all cross at right angles. It contains many fine squares and many fine structures. The houses, exept near the wharf at the river, where most all the business is transacted, are all built several rods back in the grounds; nor are they build near together. They all seem to be build in small parks. These are filled with evergreen trees, plants and flowers, so much so that in many cases the buildings are hidden from view. This gives the City a country like appearance or, as I might say: It is like walking in an artifical forest with avenues cut through at regular intervalls crossing at right angles. It was very quiet everywhere. Very few people were seen in the streets. But the people of Savannah were different from the people in other southern Citys. After they became used to our presence we never met with that defiant, proud, hatefull mien, or the insulting remarks which we had to endure everywhere before.

We passed through the City from the south to the north down the wharf street at the river and then turned to the left. . . . We went into Camp in a fine grove half a mile west of the City. . . .

While we were busy putting up tents we received the news that Genl. (Pop) Thomas had wiped Hoods army out of existence at Nashville. Dec. 15 and 16th. That created such cheering and ex[c]itement among the men it seemed for a while they had lost their senses. And it was no wonder. What an immense step was made towards crushing the rebellion. 500. miles north of us 6. months ago we left Chattanooga in the face of a formidable, well equipped army commanded by one of the ablest Generals in the Confederacy. Numerous rivers and streams, Mountains and mountain Passes obstructed our way and were scillfully and obstinately defended by the enemy. During four months we had marched, scirmished and fought day and night untill we called Atlanta ours. Stung to madness the enemy undertook to force us back by mere Strategy, take Nashville and perhaps carry the war in

THE ARMY FOUND AGAIN

the north. The movement was dictated by and through despair. But: "If Hood will go into Tennessee, I will give him his rations." Genl. Sherman had said when he gave up chasing Hood through Alabama.[9] That army would not bother us any more. And at the same time we had Cut of[f] such a big slice from the Confederacy as to leave it but little more than two empooverished, starving States, North and South Carolina and a fraction of Virginia. If the rebel leaders had not been posessed of such an infernal hate of all and Everything which came from, or reminded them of the free States, if they had been able to reason cooley and rationally; if they had been accessible to a spark of humanity and pity, they would have stopped now and saved thousands of lives and untold misery which their death strugle brought about. But no. They were bound to drain the cup of humiliation to the last drop. "Those whom the gods will destroy, they blind first."

Immediately after the capture of Savannah Sherman sent the following brief Note to President Lincoln:[10] "I beg to present you, as a Christmas gift, the City of Savannah, with 150. heavy guns and plenty of Amunition, and allso about 25,000 bales of cotton." But after subsequent Inspection and count of the guns it was found there were 168 guns. . . .

Savannah is actually 13. miles from the Ocean; but as below the City the shores on both sides receede, a large Bay is formed which has the appearance of being a part of the Ocean. This bay and river was obstructed with a network of torpedoes. A narrow channel for the passage of ships was left, but this was only known to certain pilots in the rebel service. To enable northern vessels to navigate the Bay and come to the city, these torpedoes had to be removed. As the citizens were anxious that commerce should be opened again the pilots were soon found, as allso the charts and diagrams of the torpedo network, and in a few days the bay and river was cleared for navigation.

In order to dispose of the army of negroes who had followed us Sherman issued the following ordre: "The abandoned Sea Ilands from Charleston South, the abandoned rice fields along the river for thirty miles back from the sea, and the country bordering the St. Johns river, Florida are reserved and set apart for the settlement of the Negroes now made free by the acts of war and the proclamation of the president of the United States.

Young and able bodied negroes must be enabled to enlist as soldiers in the service of the United States to contribute their share towards their own freedom, and securing their rights as Citizens of the United States."[11]

In that manner these negroes were at once changed from slavery into titled landowners. They received title on the land from the United States.

They allso were furnished the necessary subsistence, implement and seed untill the first crop was gathered. Those who Enlisted were organized in separate regiments, commanded and drilled by white Officers.[12]

Dec. 25th. Christmass Day. The third we observed while in Uncle Sams board. Some of the men were talking about the difference between our dinner and the dinners the people at home coud enjoy. Among the different tempting articles named, Oysters played a pr[o]minent part. Some Curious niggers from the City who were loafing about in Camp heard the desire of the men for Oysters. They at once offered to supply them with all the Oysters they wanted if they would send a couple dozend men along. Asked where they would get them. "Oh, the Bay is full of them." they replied. Accordingly two men from each Comp. went along with them. They allso got a wagon from the Quartermaster for the transport. In the afternoon they returned with a wagon load and everyone could have as much as he wanted. But it was a poor business after all as we had nor pepper or butter. At evening we were to have a gill of commissary each, (Whyskey) but that allso prooved to be a failure as we were informed that the barrel intended for our brigade had sprung a leak at brigade headquarters. Consequently we had to be satisfied with a small half gill. Most of the boys had their own Ideas about that "leak," and I had myself for that matter, as it was well known that prohibition principles found no favor at brigade headquarters.

Dec. 27th. The first Steamer landed at the wharf to day with our mail abord. We had no mail since Nov. 11th because we were cut off from all comunication with the north; neither did the people in the north know anything about us. During 5. weeks we had been the "Lost army." It afforded us great amusement to peruse the back numbers of these papers. The different theories they advanced what Genl. Sherman was about, where he would turn up, how the army would subsist and a number of other questions. The republican papers were full of hope that all would turn out right and Sherman would prove that the confederacy was but a shell, while the democratic papers to a great extent predicted the contrary. A well known Chicago Copperhead paper was so full of glee that it hardly could find words expressive of its feeling. It said that this would be the proper end of the "brute Sherman and his band of marauders; Lost and forgotten." It was confident and sure that the brave Hood would come north and wipe out the black Republicans and their monkey government at Washington. It called on all good and true democrats to organize and be ready that, whenever Hood came up they might join him in the good work of saving the country from utter ruin.—But the papers of the next mail? I have ever felt sorry for not being able to preserve Copies of them. The Republicans were jubilant and saw the end of the fearfull strugle near at hand. The Copperheads just like their brethren in the south, cursed and swore to give vent to their pent up rage. The Chicago Copperhead had two colums dressed in black, in which it said that the heroes of the glorious cause, the defenders of Liberty had suficient reason now to be anxious about the final result; that the old girl, with the [Phrygian] Cap, the godess of Liberty had veiled her face and was leaving this once glorious country, and more such nonsense which, when read to day would make one both blush and smile. Well, we could afford now to laugh at their silly ravings, but a year or two ago it was different.

Among my letters was one in a big official envellope. It contained my Commission as First Lieut. Col. Fitch sent for me and inquired if I would accept the Captaincy of Comp. "F." If so he would sent immediately for my Commission so that it might reach me before we left Savannah. I refused. I had made up my mind to stay with the Comp. to the End. They had made me such an offer a year ago on Lookout mountain. Then I was to take Comp. "H" but had refused on the same ground. The Colonel laughed and remarked that he missed one military Quality in me: "Ambition. Why," he said "there is not one Lieut. in the brigade who woud refuse such offer." "Well Colonel" I replied "that depends much on how the term 'Ambition' is interpreted or analized. My ambition is to stick to the boys with whom I enlisted to the last, unless I am transferred by a positive Ordre. We are grown up together, so to speak, and are more like a family than boss and servant. I know and understand the men and they me, and the result is harmony. With two exeptions, one of which is a half idiot and the other a chronic 'player off' there is no man in the Comp. who will not go a great lenght to do me a service. Is not that worth something? To me at least it is a great satisfaction and I am proud of it."—"You may well be." he replied. . . .

Jan. 1st 1865. I had to begin the new year again by going on picket. That was nothing new to me as I had done the same on the previous New Years. The picket was a mere matter of routine duty as there was no rebel soldier within 20 miles of us. Some of the soldiers soon discovered a patch of peanuts which had been turned out but not gathered. We spent most of the time in rosting and cracking them. A good portion went to camp.

Jan. 2d. When we arrived in Camp after being relieved[,] Orders came to strike tents. The 20th corps which up to this time had done provost duty in the City was sent across the river and we took their place. We were quartered in the large brick warehouse buildings along the river. This was the first time we had an other roof over us than a thin Canvas. But it was not much of an improvement after all. Most of the windows were either broken or entirely gone and that created an unwholesome draft, by no means pleasant nor healthy. But we were only two days in here when we were ordered to put up tents on the flat between the warehouses and the street. That was a ticklish job. The flat was paved with quadrangular stones and we could drive the tent pins only in between the joints. Our duty was various but not very hard. Guarding supplies, patroulling the streets day and nights, guarding the wharf and load and unload ships. . . .

Exept the cool nights we had steady, pleasant weather. The fall season had been unusually long. Winter, that is the rainy season begins here usually about the 20th of December and now we had Jan. 8th. But on the 10th the sky became a gray, ashen hue and seemed to settle down. Towards evening the vail broke and business began in good style. It poured down steadily until the following noon when a short respite set in; but the sky did not change its dull aspect and soon it began again. Allmost without interruption it kept it up untill the afternoon of the 16th when old sol tried to take a look at what had happened since his absence. A great change had come over the landscape indeed. The Country on the north, or South Carolina side of the river was much lower as on the south, or Georgia side. Farther than the Eye could reach these low lands were an immense lake, in fact now a part of the atlantic Ocean only that trees and the higher brush looked out of the water and indicated the coast lines. . . .

On the afternoon of the 15th steamers and transports came up the bay and landed Genl. Grover and his Division of the 9th Corps which were to relieve us in Savannah. . . . During the months sojourn here the army had been suplied with new wearing material. The wagons were filled with 30. days rations this time as it was expected that fourage would not be so plentifull in South and North Carolina as it had been in Georgia. But nevertheless these rations were only to be issued in case of the greatest necessity. The few sick among us were put on board the steamers and brought to the hospitals at New York. From my Comp. Ely Gray, Gale Cram and Orville Coddington[13] were of that class. The first two died in the hospital. I wanted to send Ephriam Walker allso but he would not go. He would rather die at the roadside than go to hospital. The darkies had all been taken care of. I allso had lost Sam; he had enlisted in a nigger Regiment and sent to Newburn [New Bern] North Carolina to be drilled. On the 19th we received orders to march.

THE ARMY FOUND AGAIN

~ That afternoon we received the last mail from the north. I received a letter from Capt. Turner who was stationed at Ringold in northern Georgia. It will be remembered that on the 7th of August 64. at Atlanta he was badly wounded in the neck. He pulled through however and intended to report to the Regt. but as we had left Atlanta he was assigned to duty with other troops. He informed me of his intention to resign in order to make room for me for the place I had so well deserved and held in trust so long.

~

CHAPTER SEVENTEEN

Facing Northward:
Averysboro. The Battle at Bentonville

~ During a pelting rain we slung knapsacks and filed off from the wharf square Jan. 20th 1865. On account of the high water on the Carolina side we were oblidged to march some 30. miles backward on the Georgia side of the river to sisters ferry to find a pro[per] place for a pontoon bridge. We could make only 10 miles today. It kept on raining and after leaving the City a few miles behind we came in the low country where water, mud and mire was the rule. We had to stop to wait for the train and went into camp. We remained here next day, the train having not been able to work through the mud. It was here I felt for the first time the beginning pangs and twitches of rheumatism in the legs which was to make my life miserable for the future. I did not mind it at first as I thought it would pass away in time, in fact, I had no Idea of its being Rheumatism as I never before had made its aquaintance, but it soon made me understand who was to be the boss.

The 21st. rain again more or less all day. The boys set to calculating how many miles we woud have to tramp before we reached Richmond or Wash-ington. Orderly sergeant Holdens immagination predicted that by the time we reached home our legs would be worn off clear up to the knees and we would be obliged to walk on the stumps. "Never mind Joe." Charly Lymer replied soothingly. "Old Abe will supply us with rubber legs which, by the way, is just the thing to dance those new fangled jigs with."—"You just wait youngster." Holden warned. "Johnston and Hardee and Wade Hampton may [y]et give you all the jig dancing you desire before we get there."

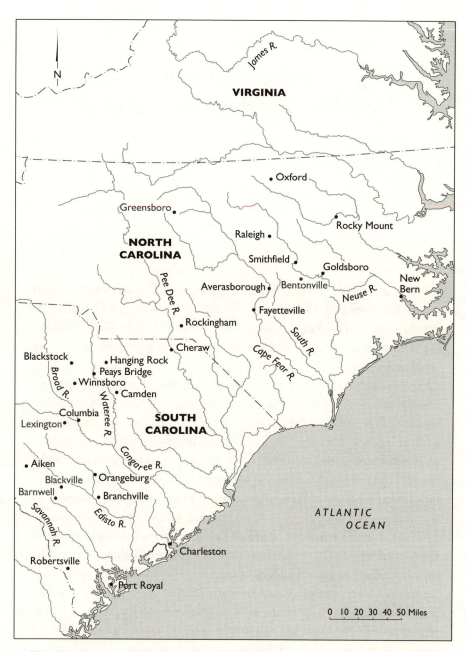

The Carolinas Campaign (Map by Bill Nelson)

Jan. 22d. After a few miles of mudslashing we reached higher ground which enabled us to make better headway. It did not rain the forenoon but the afternoon made good the neglect. Shortley before dark we reached Sisters ferry, the place selected to cross the river. It was not a very encouraging sight to look at. At our side the river bank was high and dry but on the other side we could see no bank, in fact, we could not see where the river ended, exept by the trees which indicated that at some time during the year there was dry land there. The pontoon laying was begun the following day. But it was not untill the twentyeight (28th) [that pontoons] were laid across up to the woods. To prevent the rebs from sending gunboats down from Augusta to hinder our laying the pontoons, the gunboat "Pontiac" had been sent up from Savannah to look out for such an ocurrence. When the Pontoons were laid our work fairly began. The road being 2 to 3. foot under water, and never having been a good one, had to be curduroyd. There was no help for it; we had to go in the water, chop the trees, cut them into proper lenghts and float or carry them to the road. The water was by no means warm and most of the time it rained lustily. For three miles such road had to be built, sometimes piling the logs three high to reach the surface of the water. It took us untill the 5th of February that we reached higher ground near Robertsville, a hamlet of a couple dozen Shanties, where we camped. During those 8. days we had not a square inch of dry clothing on the body, soaked from head to foot like a dishrag. It was enough to take courage and grit out of any man.

The norther[n] Copperheads had predicted that as the rebels knew now where Sherman was going they would mass an army in his front strong enough to crush him. It was their wish, their hope which prompted this theory, or rather, prophecy; in fact and practice it was far different. The same principle which had worked so admirable in Georgia held good in South and North Carolina. Sherman could choose between three roads each of which would eventually bring him to the desired Point, and each of these roads led to points which it was of great importance for the rebels to hold. He could march on the Atlantic Coast and threaten Charleston; he could take the middle road and threaten Columbia, the Capital City; or he could take the western road and threaten Augusta, Charlotte or Saulsbury. In fact, all of these roads were more or less used by Sherman to confuse the rebels and further his Ends. The rebels had to keep strong forces in all those places to defend them and so scatter their forces. It was no use to sent forces in our rear, because there were no railroads to destroy as we did that ourselfes; our base of supplies could not be captured or destroyed, because we had none. Our train they could not much endanger, because being reduced to the greatest minimum, it was allways between, or near the Army Corps. and easily defended.

Genl. Hardee was at Charleston with about 25.000 men; Wade Hampton was at Columbia with a Division of Cavallery and some Infantery the number of which I have not learned; at Augusta, it was said, were about 10.000. Besides an Army Corps was stationed near Branchville under Cheatham to watch the movements of Sherman and act accordingly. But so deftly and quickly were the movements of the 15th and 17th Corps. directed and executed that Cheatham had to run to escape capture. In one respect the rebels were ahead of us and that was their Cavallery force [, which] outnumbered ours two to one. During our march to Savannah Wheelers Cavallery Div. was the only one against Kilpatricks Div. but now the rebs had besides Wheelers Div. Wade Hamptons Div. and a brigade of Buttlers Div. Consequently Genl. Kilpatrick had a difficult job on hand, partly to keep our flanks clear, as allso to avoid engagements with a [force] greatly superior in numbers to his own. But he seemed to be just the man to understand and take hold of the situation and to his clever management and undaunted bravery Sherman is greatly indebted to the successfull termination of this remarkable campain. . . .

Sherman followed the same tactics here as in Georgia. The right wing 15 and 17th Corp formed the wright wing moved so as to threaten Charleston direct. When they started they had several hard encounters with the rebels at the Pocotaligo and Tullifinny rivers, but they drove the Johnnies soon out of sight. The 14th and 20th Corps, forming the left wing, with Kilpatric[k] on our left made a faint towards Augusta. At the proper time both wings directed their march towards the Center and pounded on to Columbia. But I will take up the proceedings of our Div. and brigade in detail.

The 14th Corps took the extreme left and marched on the Barnwell road. Owing to the miserable roads we cleared hardly 15. miles that day. Nothing of special interest happened exept the hard work to get the batteries along which is allways very interesting for the men. The following day was my turn for fouraging, that is for brigade and Regts. headquarters I was told. Seventy men were detailed to that end, more for the purpose of dealing successfully with rebel Cavallery and bushwhakers, should we meet any, than for fouraging. The latter was conside[rably] more difficult and dangerous as it had been in Georgia, allthough it was bad enough there. In the first place; South and North Carolina had been severely taxed to provide Lees army at Petersburg with provisions; next the people of South Carolina had been warned of our approach and had ample time to hide, or destroy everything moveable so as to get it out of our reach, and further, the people of that State were such radical, uncompromizing rebels that they would endure and suffer anything, even starvation, if it would hurt the cursed yankees and put them to trouble; and last, but by no means least, that the rebs had considerable more troops to oppose our advance as [than] they had in Georgia and especially Cavallery. They could make Kilpatrick all the trouble he could manage and having enough Cavallery besides to watch all the roads burn all stores and bridges, obstruct the roads and lay in wait and watch our fouragers, and pound on to them when they thought it safe to do so. Not a day passed without some of our fouragers had more or less severe fights with them or with the bushwhackers. Usually they were beaten, but such scrimmages are more or less dangerous and cause loss on both sides. It became a matter of importance for our men to study the Country, roads and crossroads, woods, clearings, hills and ravines and, when a plantation came in sight where they Expected to find fourage, to look out and guard against surprise. But in general our soldiers had little fear for the rebel Cavallery. "Go for them, it is but rebel Cavallery." was a common expression and when a fouraging party returned without having been molested by Cavallery or bushwhackers it was considered a failure.

There is another Item which I must mention here for a better understanding of the situation since, at that time it created severe command [comment] in the northern Copperhead papers and from the pulpit who converted the title of "Shermans bummers," which we had gained in Georgia, to Shermans robbers, bandits and barbarians. As will be remembered, in Georgia the destroying, or burning anything was done by special order and by troops designated for that purpose. The fouragers never medled with it by brutal treatment or treachery. The same order which governed in Georgia was supposed to be in force in South Carolina but it seemed the men had forgotten all about it. South Carolina allways had been and still was the leader in the rebellion; here secession was conceived and breed; it was the first State to pass the secession Ordinance and declared rebellion legal and right; here the first gun was fired; the South Carolina papers were the most blatant and arrogant in the Confederacy; in every issue they incited the rebel soldiers and citizens, woman and children to deeds of cruelty and barbarism; they conceived the fiendish plan to starve the union prisoners in the rebel pens and which was so successfully carried out. Even now when we were advancing in the State the Charleston "Mercury and Courier" which one could not read without a cold shiver running down along his spine. But these same Apostles of barbarism were Cowards enough to refute their own doctrines, to "die in the last ditch[,]" and ran for dear life when we came near enough to make it uncomfortable for them. Was it any wonder that the men hated South Carolina and put in practice the very rules and teachings laid down by them? This feeling was universal in the army and no sooner had the men Entered the state when the work of retaliation and destruction became general. What ever could be destroyed, whatever would burn or breake had to go, exept nigger dwellings. And Genl. Sherman? Did he feel the same as the boys did? Or was he con[s]cious that he could not stop it? Anyway, he did not say a word. If he had undertaken to stop it he would have been oblidged to put the whole army under arrest and that would have been a dangerous proceeding. But no sooner had we stepped on North Carolina soil when the ravages stopped. South Carolina had been severely punished. There was no special grudge against North Carolina and nothing was disturbed but under special order. . . .

Feb. 9th. We started early. It was raining lively and judging by the appearance of the sky, was likely to continue for some time. We were informed that the Div. would camp that night in the vicinity of the crossing of the Augusta and Orangeburg road calculated to be about 16 to 18. miles ahead. Knowing the dificulty to keep track of the different intersecting roads in a forei[gn] country and the numerous rebel Cavallery swarming round I went to brigade hedquarters and asked for a map or chart of the district to be guided by. (In South Carolina a County is called a District, in Louisiana a parish.) But I was jokingly informed that maps, charts or diagrams were only furnished to Staff Officers, and that it was expected of every line Officer to find their way by their acute senses of sight and smelling. That was poor consolation, but of course, I had to go. Leaving the tent one of the Orderlies held out a small pocket compass, asking if not that might be of any service to me. I would not have accepted the offer had it not been for the insinuating mean smile accompanying the offer. I took the little thing and went out. I need hardly say I never returned the thing, nor did he call for it.

About two miles out the road divided, the main taking its course somewhat to the west while the other turned a little eastward. In order to cover more territory I divided the force; thirty men and two Sergeants I sent on the main road left and west cautioned them to stop at the Crossing of the Augusta and Orangeburg road, with the other I took the right, or branch road. After some miles travel we found a big plantation and expected to do

a big business there but were muchly mistaken; it did not pan out at all, as
the miners would say. We found a lot of sorry looking old and little negroes
who were nearly scared to death. It took considerable coaxing to make them
speak and greater difficulty still to understand them. After a while we learned
that the rebel Cavallery had taken the most stuff and the balance Massa had
taken to Augusta. The poor beings had hardly anything to eat themselfes.
We suspected that some stuff might be hidden but the close search did not
reveal anything. We found the road ended here but the negroes pointed out
where a blind road led through the woods to an other plantation, way off as
they expressed it. When we reached the woods I looked round and saw the
main buildings in flames. Who had put the match to it I did not know and
did not want to.

In the woods the boys found two pigs in pretty good condition, perhaps
a hundred pounds each; a little further a yearling heifer was confiscated.
That was a pretty beginning and we felt quite elated, especially as at about
8. A.M. it ceased raining and old Sol smiled pleasantly on the landscape. . . .

A mile and a halfs walk brought us to the plantation. Nobody was to be
seen around the stately mansion. With a few men I went in. The first room
we found an aged woman was laying on a sofa. At sight of us she fell in
histerics, screamed and cried murder and help. I believe I was as much
scared at her behavior as the old woman was of us. A younger lady came
rushing in whom I at once assured that not the least insult was intended nor
any harm was to be done. While she was busy with the old lady a stout,
robust looking fellow rushed into the room several negroes behind him. He
pointed a big revolver at me, but Henry Craft [Krafft], seeing his intention,
with the butt of his rifle gave him such a lift under his arm that the bullet
went high into the Ceiling and the revolver dropped to the floor.[1] I took
hold of that and the fellow run out and went straight for the dog kennel
and opened the door. A large pack of hounds tumbled, one over the other,
out of the opening, and Encouraged by the voice and hand clapping of the
enraged fellow, with savage howl went for the boys scattered in the park.
But the fellow had made a mistake in playing this trump. That was just the
sort of sport the boys liked to indulge in, and ere a minute had passed every
hound laid low stretching his trembling limbs as a last farewell to slavery
and rebellion. A large crowd of half nacked, barefooted africans of both
sexes, old and young big and small had gathered round to witness the performance. Their behavior was ample proof of their Sympathy with the
wholesale execution. The older ones cheered and shouted, while the younger

and more limber ones indulged in turning sommersaults and other gimnastic exercises. Some of the boys had espied the whipping post in one Corner and were busy in piling all kinds of burnable stuff around it and then set it on fire.

All this had taken but a short time. I had kept an Eye on the rascal since he had set the hounds free. I took him to be the Overseer of the concern, because he looked and acted to[o] brutish for a full blood Chevalier. The summary and quick Execution of the hounds seemed to paralize him; he stood erect and stiff like a statue, never moving a limb or saying a word, looking over the scene as one in a trance. But when the whipping post began to light up the scene he seemed to come to life again. Shaking his fists in a threatening manner he turned and run towards the cotton gin. Not knowing what he might be up to this time I told Sergeant Greeley to take some of the men along and secure the fellow and if he should offer any resistance to tie his hands and make him travel at the point of the bajonet. That was water on Greeleys mill. He had served six years on board a whale ship and had nothing soft or sentimental about him. Then calling the men together I directed some of them to look up some kettels and spiders as we were going to camp here tonight. But after second thought I considered it more safe to camp some distance away from the buildings. Sergeant Greeley had been obliged to tie the fellows hands with a gun sling and showed me two revolvers which he had taken away from him.

About a quarter of a mile from the mansion and on the same road we come, a low strip of ground, or Slew some 30. rods wide crossed the road. This slew was densely covered with a growth of briars and vines and be-sides well filled with water. The road through it was allso well under water, but to enable foot passengers to cross, some heavy logs were placed along-side the road which served as a bridge. At the foot of this slew, on the rising ground I concluded to Camp for the night as it afforded protection against surprise from one side at least. I posted two pickets acros the slew on the rising ground in the field and one at the entrance to the building grounds. It was night now and allthough the moon was full, the drifting Clouds would allow but an uncertain, fitfull light. Fires were soon blazing and as we had an abundance of pro[v]isions, preparations for a good supper in full blast. And we were in need of that as we had not taken time to make dinner; but we had munched some dried aples and peaches. Besides we were very tired. We had travelled, as near as we could judge, 22. miles. Now that is not much, good many will say; but it is one thing to travel with free and unin-cumbered limbs and body, and quite an other thing to tote a lot of straps and goods along. There was not a man there who had not carried at least 60. pounds during the greater part of the day, No one can form a Idea of the strain this lays on the bones, muscles and nerves unless he goes through the performance himself.

Our brave friend from the plantation, whom I shall call the overseer, who singlehanded had undertaken to defy and scare us had been taken along and was well taken care of. With his hands still secured behind his back he was given a seat of honor on a rotten log near the fire. We undertook to draw him in conversation but he was as sulky and obstinate as a mule. Seing we could get nothing out of him he was let alone. Having taken supper (the sulky prisoner did not want any) the pickets were relieved to tend to the inner man. Detailing a guard to watch the prisoner we laid down to rest. . . .

It need hardly be said that we soon were in the relm of dreams. How long we had slept I am unable to say. Enough, we were suddenly aroused by several rifle reports. As we never took off our clothing or shoes at night, we of course were ready for a fray in a moment. The sentinel informed us that the reports came from the other side of the slew where our pickets were. Our Overseer allso seemed quite interested in the matter for he worked himself in a upright position and it seemed to me his "phiz" expressed the hope the rebs were there to make us get out [of] here. I ordered him down in short order and told the Sentinel to pin him to the ground if he should try to rise again. We then walked in Indian file over the logs acros the slew and up to the pickets. They said that on the opposite hight they had seen several figures advancing which they thought to be Cavallery[.] They had challenged them but receved no reply and that they retreated behind the hight, where upon the pickets fired in order to notify us.

We went towards the height and were Challenged in turn by someone laying low. I replied: "We are perhaps friends but who are you"? "A live Yank, if that will satisfy you" he replied somewhat snappishly. "Then come and shake." Three figures rose and came towards us. When Close enough we saw they were Union Cavallery men and the Countersign settled all doubt. They were Carefull though because they held their Sharps repeaters in hand ready for action. After mutual legitimation the leader, a Captain, asked me, somewhat surprised, why we were so far in front of the army. I explained we were a fouraging party had overshot the mark and were hunting for the fourteenth Corps. "Why" he replied. "The 14th Corps is back on the Orangeburg road. We are a scouting party to see if any rebels are lurking near that road."—"But where is the Orangeburg Road"?—"Somewhere

East" he replied. "and it can not be very far off." "Then we have crossed it yesterday" I said "and have to go back again." I invited him to come to our Camp to which he consented. He called for his troop to avance and soon 30. riders came up, one of them leading three horses. Arriving in camp the fire was stirred up and replenished and examining our watches found it allready past 3. A.M. As it was so near morning we concluded not to lay down again, and compared notes while the men busied themselfes with preparing breakfast. The Cavallery men secured their horses at the fence along the slew and fed them out of the nose bag.

In the course of our conversation the Capts. attention was suddenly directed to our prisoner. The latter, laying there covered with a blanket, would have been taken by any on[e] for a sleeping soldier. But all at once, the Overseer came to a sitting posture, staring somewhat wildly about, evidently surprised at the big crowd of Yankees around. Clad in his butternut garb he certainly was an object for Capt. Whitcombs curiosity. (That was the name the Capt. had introduced himself with.)[2] Looking a few moments sharply at him, he blurted out: "By the holy Moses, where did you get that fellow"?—I related the little rumpus of the previous evening, the Capt. all the while keeping his eyes fixed on the prisoner. I noticed the prisoner becoming uneasy and restless. He hung his head and finally turned his back to the fire.—"Why did you not shoot the raskall"? the Capt. asked ex[c]itedly. I admitted frankly that I did not like summary proceedings with non combattants or Citizens. "Oh, fudge"! he snapped. "You would rather see your Comrades hung, or shot from ambush, would you? You Infantry fellows are alltogether to[o] soft, to[o] tenderhearted with those devils. But I can not blame you much. You do not come over the Country as much as we do; you do not know to what barbaric deeds these people will resort to vent their devilish hate. You missed hundreds of Comrades who went fouraging in Georgia and never saw them again. You simply report them as missing but you have no Idea what became of them. I know, because I have found many of them; I have found some not merely shot or hung, but their body mutilated in the most shocking manner; their entrails, lungs and heart torn out and scattered around. You probably do not believe me, but ask here Sergeant Dixon how they treated his brother whose mutilated and scattered remains we found near the Ogechee river and burried there. Let me tell you what we saw and did only yesterday." But as breakfast was anounced ready we fell too to do justice to the same.

While eating the captain related the following incident: "Early yesterday morning we started on a scout towards and along the Aikin road, as it was learned that the rebel Genl. Wheeler was massing his Cavallery there in order to protect Augusta and to harass the 20th Corps which is marching on that road. About noon we suddenly run onto a party of three bushwhakers who were just about to hoist up a boy in blue. Their horses were thethered near by and when they perceived us they made haste to get away. Two of them we captured but the third succeeded to get away. The bullets we send after him missed the mark and your prisoner here is that man." "That's a damn lie" the prisoner exclaimed, the first word he had spoken since he was bound. "I have been at home all day yesterday."—"Be quiet, sir," The Captain replied. "We will not do you any wrong. But if your guilt is prooved you can not expect mercy." Several of the Cavallery men boldly asserted now that the prisoner was the same fellow who escaped the day before to which the prisoner did not reply.—"To finish my story" the Captain continued. "I asked the soldier why he was all alone. He replied, 'We were three of us; two were shot down from ambush a little ways back; they must lay there [y]et. I got away for a moment but could not run as fast as their horses. I turned fired and brought one down but there were three more and before I could reload they were upon me.' You can immagine," the Capt. added, "that our temperature rose high. We took the rope which was dangling from the Soldiers neck, and hoisted the assassins to the same limb they had selected for the soldier. We then went forward with the soldier to the place of the ambush but before we came there we found the body of the bushwhaker shot by the soldier. He was not quite dead [y]et and able to give vent to his hate against all yankees in red hot maledictions and curses. Assuring myself that the fellow could not recover, the bullet having passed through his bowels, I informed him what had happened to his fellow murderers and then left him to his fate. A little further we found the bodies of the murdered Comrades. They were ridled with bullets. We buried them as good as Circumstances would permit and pursued our route."

The recital of this tragedie had filled all listeners with consternation and desire for revenge. For a while nothing was said, but everyone scanned the prisoner. I knew then that, should the charges against him be correct, his life was forfeited. The Capt. meanwhile had taken a memorandum book and taking a folded paper out of it, unfolded the same and handed it to me. It was an Order from Genl. Sherman to find a certain Hawkins plantation somewhere between the Augusta and Orangeburg roads, to destroy everything there Exept the negro quarters and subsistence for them to live on. If the owner, Hawkins could be taken alive to bring him to hedquarters. "Thus [This] Hawkins." the Capt. said "has been and is one of the vilest and most cruel rebels in South Carolina. I wonder who lives here on thus plantation; do you know"?—No, I did not; never had inquired. "Say, prisoner"! the Capt. spoke. "What is the name of the owner of this plantation"?—The prisoner would not talk. "Never mind" the Capt. said. "Let him alone. He can not gain anything by sulking. We will find out without his help."

It was now broad daylight. It was the first day since we had left Savannah that the sun rose bright in a cloudless sky, giving promise of a fair day. The Capt. was anxious to finish the scout and ordered his men to the horses, I looked towards the Park and noticed a lot of negroes behind the fence enclosing the park, looking curiously at us. I went up towards them hoping to get some information out of them. But, great Scott what a sorry, miserable looking set they were. I never had seen such like them allthough I saw many like them later in South Carolina. I asked them several questions and though they answered them readily Enough I could not understand their jabberings. In fact, some of them were hardley able to speak at all. I gave up in despair and looking round saw the Captain coming with his troup. I told him now was his time to find out all he wanted to know, provided he was well versed in foreign languages. He halted his troop and went at it immediately, but with little better success than myself. Finally, and [an] old, scarred, lame fellow, whose upper half was bent forward nearly at right angles, came forward and from him we learned that Massas name was Hawkins and the man we held prisoner was "Bill" the nigger driver and whipper. That Massa and Bill left early the previous day both having riffles. They were on horse back. That Bill returned alone in the afternoon informing Mrs. Hawkins that Massa had been killed by a yankee soldier. That upon that Missus had been taken sick and had not left the sofa since. "That's enough." the Capt. said and turning to me continued. "Comrade, that fellow belongs to me. You must quit him. . . . I do not know what to do with him [y]et, but if I have time we will bring him to the very spot where they waylaid our men and hang him over the graves of the Union Soldiers. Squadron, forward, March!—Trott, march!"

We tarried [y]et for half an hour which the boys improoved to fry some meat to be used for dinner. Then we took the road back which we had come. But hardly had we passed the park an eight of a mile when we saw a single horsemen coming in a wild gallop towards us. Soon we saw it was one of the Captains men. Coming up to us he informed me that they had run onto a large body of rebel Cavallery to[o] much for them to handle and that the rebs were pressing them. The Captain wished me to take position somewhere and with our help we might whip the rebs. I choose the fence, because it was admirably adapted for a good defense. The fence was of Cast Iron fancy work, resting one a stone and brick foundation about 15. inches high. Laying behind this wall we were safe for the rebel bullets and could easily fire through the fancy work. At the top the fency stuf ended in pike like points which no rider would dare his horse to leap.

We were not more than behind the fence when we heard scattering shots and soon saw the Cavallery coming on at full gallop. But what was that? that was not our Cavallery; that were a great deal more in numbers and soon we could see they were very lively rebels. The Cavallery man who had remained with us was as much surprised as we. Instead of the Johnnies chasing our men, our men were Chasing the Johnnies. . . . I cautioned my men not to fire untill the ordre was given and fire to kill, allso to put some Cartridges handy in order to reload quick. When about fifty steps distant I ordered to fire. The result was all we could wish for. Saddles emptied, horses tumbled and fell. For a minute there was great confusion. It was plain they were entirely taken by surprise. But suddenly they turned out of the road half to the right and made for the slew. But before they had cleared many rods an other volley reached them with fearfull Effect. When they came to the slew and found they could not get through fast enough, they again turned to the right to gain the woods at the further End of the field half a mile away. But the Captain, guessing their intention, made a short cut across the field and with drawn sabers pounced onto them. The Johnnies still out-numbered the Captain greatly in numbers but they seemed to be so scared that not any of them offered any rescistance. Quite a number of them es-caped in the woods, the others surrendered. . . .

The men sent out to bring in the wounded and riderless horses had returned and reported 15. dead and 47. wounded. . . . The ambulances allso made their appearance accompanied by a troop of cavallery. The negroes were set to work to bury the dead. It was eight A.M. and time for us to be moving or we would not be able to catch up with the Corps to day. I hastily took leave of Captain Whitcomb. . . .

We traveld the road back towards the Orangeburg road. After a few miles travel the boys discoverd a number of sheep way off in the field. It seemed impossible to pass by without taxing them. Accordingly half a dozen were quickly dressed and divided among the men. Looking backward I saw in the distance heavy black clouds curling upward. Captain Whitcomb was executing Genl. Shermans Ordre.

It was near noon when we arrived at the road. The corps had passed but the train [was] lumbering along in the mire, guarded by a brigade of Infantry.

FACING NORTHWARD

We thought we could march faster as the mules went, but being oblidged to walk through fields and woods, as the road was to[o] narrow to allow marching alongside the teams and the splashing of the beasts threw the mud in all directions, we could not make headway very fast. Still we were struguling along manfully untill sundown. We all were Completely broke down on account of the extra weight we had to tote along. I did not know how far it was to camp [y]et. We came to the entrance of a low swampy wood the road through which was a common Curdroy, or log road. I called a halt and inquired of the men if it would not be better to stop here and rest and start early next morning. They all agreed at once. So we went a little ways aside of the road and staked arms. As it is but a short time from sunset to dark in these lattitudes I warned the men to prepare supper quickly so that the fire might be extinguished after dark.

Perhaps 25 or 30. rods back, but close to the road stood an on[e]story, unpainted frame house. While the man were busy at the fire I went to take a look inside. I found two shabby looking midleaged women both busy supplying their jaws with snuf tobacco by means of a little wooden stick. The house contained but one room but that was divided in two by means of a curtain which extended across the room and up to the ceiling. I looked behind the Curtain but saw nothing there but a poor looking bed, a square box, a couple stools and some womens clothing hanging on the wall; the front part contained four stools, an old square table, an oblong square box set on the high end against the wall and allso closed with a curtain, or rather a dirty pi[e]ce of butternut cloth, the box serving evidently for a cupboard. I inquired if they lived alone here to which both nodded but did not deem it worth while to speak. So I left them enjoying their tobacco thinking that it perhaps constituted their supper. When I oppened the door one of them suddenly found her tongue: "Say, do you ones tote any snuf terbaccer 'long"? I shook my head and went along.

When supper was taken the stars twinkled bright in the sky. I selected six men, who had done no duty the previous night[,] to stand each an hour on picket and by that time we had to be up and off again. We then squatted down for the needed rest. We had lain perhaps a quarter of an hour and most of the men were asleep when Henry Kra[f]ft touched me and whispered he had something to tell me. I went aside with him and his story was this: He had seen a dim light at the window at the back end of the house. Unobserved he went up there and as the rag which served as a curtain did not cover the window fully, he saw two women and a rebel Cavallery man in conversation. One of the woman held a pitch pine torch which served as a lamp. He could not hear what they said but by their gestures concluded they were speaking about us. After a little while the cavallery man left.

So for Henry Kraf[f]t. All though a young Chap, I knew him to be reliable, and well able to make cool observations. I must remark here that the last teams of our train had passed half an hour before. The train guard allso was without [out of] reach and we had to rely alltogether on our own resources. Allthough it seemed to me imprudent for rebel Cavallery to make a night attack on Infantry they had in so far the advantage as they were informed by the woman of our position and strenght. I concluded therefore to pass on and if they should persist in following us, well we could fight them at any place. I called up the men and explained to them the situation. I left it to them to decide whether we should remain here and fight it out, or march on and try to join the Corps, at the same time informing them of my Opinion to go forward. All accepted my views Exept three who resolutily refused to go a Step before next morning. . . . Of the three who refused to march, two were drafted and the other was a substitute who had sold himself for a cool $1000.00 to serve for some rich Copperhead or Coward. Upon my question why they would not go along the substitute replied that he would not move an other step untill it pleased him to do so. Not wishing to enter into any argument I thought best to let them have their own way for the present, took their rifles away and informed them they might stay here as long as they pleased and started with the rest of the man on the road.

The road through the woods was mostly curduroy, or log road. While marching I instructed the men how to act in case any rebel Cavallery should follow us. The matter was talked over untill everybody understood it perfectly. We had gone perhaps half a mile or more and were thinking we had been scared without reason when all at once we heard the Clatter of horsehoofs on the Curderoy behind us. Immediately we were in the woods on one side of the road and deploying as skirmishers, I going with the first file, Sergeant Greeley with the last. Allthough it was not very dark we could not see very clear if they were of our Cavallery or rebels. They rode two abreast. When the first file was nearly opposite me I called the usual: "Halt! who comes there?"—"Friends." was the reply and the speaker drew rains. "Dismount one, advance and give Countersignn." I demanded. Instead of that the fellow fired at me, the bullet lodging in a small tree behind which I stood. I had carried two of the rifles which I had taken from the bolting man, one of which I held at ready. The report of his Carbine was immediately followed by the discharge of my rifle and his horse fell in a heap. Half of my men followed suit and more horses went down. The balance immediately wheeled round and gallopped back. One of the riders was pinned down by the fallen horse, the others had managed to get free of the horses and had scampered off in the woods.

Four horses were liing in the road; whether there were any more men or horses wounded we could not tell. We relieved the fellow from under the horse and took him along. He was a born South Carolinean and felt very bad about being taken prisoner in his own State. Thus [This] Cavallery belonged to the same troupe we had scattered in the morning. Wondering why the rebels had so carelessly gone into the woods without an advanced guard, I asked the prisoner if that was their Custom in warfare. I explained to him that we might have killed and wounded a good many if we had so minded but he did not reply. The haughty, proud spirit of the South Carolina Chivallery was predominant [y]et. Being taken prisoner by Lincolns mudsills was certainly a heavy punishment for him. The boys teased him about the bad luck he had experienced to day with the yanks but he never said a word and they finally left him alone.

After a while we heard shouts behind us. That could not be enemies, because they would not make their presence known by shouts and noise far in the rear. "I bet" Sergeant Greeley said, "there comes our Ki[c]kers." To make sure I ordered the men aside in the wood and with Sergeant Greeley and two men I remained in the road. Sure Enough. The three miscreants were glad enough now to go along with us. To scare them a little I told Sergeant Greeley with three man to keep them under guard and after arriving in camp to bring them to Division headquarters to await a Court martial. But when we Came near Camp the fellows begged so much that I finally returned them their rifles and let them go. But after that they were allway willing to do their duty and one of them, five week later in the battle at Bentonville, North Carolina, was severely wounded of which he felt not a little proud.

After an other mile stretch we came out of the woods on higher ground. In the distance we saw a long string of light against the horizont which indicated the Camp of our Corps. . . .

Feb. 10th. About 6. A.M. we were on the tramp again. We passed through Barnwell a snug little City of perhaps 2000. inhabitants when all at home. Everything was still and quiet as in a grave; curtains drawn, doors and blinds well secured. But the omnipotent darkies would not be suppressed. They filled sidewalks and Alleys staring at us as at so many circus beasts, all the

while jabbering and jawing like parrots of which we understood but very
little. Many of the ragged fellows followed us again in spite of our trying to
drive them back. Towards evening we arrived within a few miles from
Blackville on the Augusta and Charleston railroad where we camped. . . .

Feb. 12th. The troops ahead of us had played us a nasty trick this morning. Either by design or carelessness the woods had been set on fire. That
made a smoke which i[t] was impossible to face and live. We were obliged
to face about and make a circuit of several miles in order to flank the fire.
But for all that we were well smoked and the sobriquet of "smoked yankee"
became a fact here well established.

During the day we passed through a place called Lexington. Whether it
was a village or a City, I cannot say but it certainly was big enough to take
care of a City charter. But in spite of its extensive territorry and numerous
buildings there was no sign of any Enterprise or prosperity. The buildings
most all of one story and unpainted had the appearance of old ruins,
weatherbeaten and forlorn. No building of either stone or brick was to be
seen. Attempts [to] built sidewalks had been made in times long past but as
they were now it would have been an decided improvement to tear them up
and burn the stuff. But very few darkies were seen here. It was plain this was
a City of the poor white thrash. No Slaveholder or Chevalier would dare to
live or associate with such common rabel. And still the fathers and sons of
this despised people fought, or were forced to fight for the extension and
perpituation of slavery. What surprised me most was that these people had
not left their habitations at our approach as mostly allways was done by
slaveowners and good rebels. I suppose the poor people, having not much
to loose, were not afraid to stay there. And further a great number of poorly
clad woman and children would wave selfmade small Union flags and cheer
and encourage us to bring the rebels down. It seemed as strange as an Oasis
in a Desert to find a City, or village with union sentiments in South Carolina. Such unusual demonstrations, which we had not met with since we
left Kentucky two years and a half ago were heartily responded to by the
boys and more than that; appreciating the sentiments and good will of the
people not a thing was touched or destroyed here.

While walking along the rickety sidewalk I saw a Cluster of women and
children waving little flags and talking al the while. One of them held a
sheet of brown paper in her hands, the only kind of paper then in use in the
Confederacy. When drawing near I heard the woman inquire whether we
knew any yankee Officers whose names were on this paper. I took the paper
and was greatly surprised to find some names of Officers who had been

taken prisoner at Chicamauga Sept. 20th. 1863. who belonged to our Regtt. Capt. Randall, Adjutant Jenkins and Lieutenants Watson and Morgan.[3] The woman told me that all the Officers whose names were on that paper she had given dinner to a year and a half ago when they were on their way to prison in Columbia. With some pride she showed me a few greenbacks which the kind Officers had given her for cornbread, sweet potatoes and bacon, all she had been able to give. "The poor Critters were so hungry" She remarked. She inquired if the 42nd Indiana Regt. was with us. One of the Officers among the prisoners had learned that she had been born and raised in Indiana and after some inquiry had told her that possibly her brother was in that Regt. as he knew a man by that name. I informed her that that Regt. was the second one behind us and that she must inquire of every Compagnie or she might miss him. Whether she was successfull I do not know as I had to hurry forward. That night we again camped in a pitch pine woods.

Feb. 13th. To day our brigade was to be trainguard. It was eight A.M. therefore when we came in motion. The roads were terribly cut up; the soil a reddish Clay with the usual sticking quality. We of course, when ever possible took to the fields and woods, but when we were oblidged to march along the teams it was not much of a picknick. . . . During the afternoon we passed more burning plantations. Towards evening the soil became more sandy and dry which enabled us to go ahead faster. At 10. P.M. we caught up with the Division. The train parked in a large field where we allso camped.

Feb. 14th. After several miles tramping we entered again a low, Swampy Country through which the South Edisto river slowly winds its way. It rained all the day and together with the former heavy rains the low country was allmost impassable. Long stretches of curduroy had to be laid which retarded our advance. In the afternoon we crossed the South Edisto, two miles north of which we went in Camp.

Feb. 15th[.] Earley this morning Crakers, Coffee and bacon for three days was issued because, the fouraging parties had not been able to realize enough to feed the tenth part of the army. The south Carolinians did the utmost to make good their threat to starve us before they would begin to attack us. The citizens and their Cavallery destroyed and hid everyting which could be of any value to us. The best thing in the matter was: if they could stand it, we certainly could. Near noon we crossed the North Edisto and marched until we reached the Congaree River, about 10 miles further and camped.

Feb. 16th. We were now in sight of Columbia, the Capital of South Carolina. We expected to take, and march through the City, but the 15th and seventeenth Corps, coming from the right, were a little ahead of us and were making preparations to advance on the City. It did not make them much trouble. A little skirmishing induced Wade Hampton and his troops to seek safety in a quick retreat northward. We crossed the Congaree on a pontoon bridge and were halted to await developments of the 15th and 17th. Corps and, if necessary, to take part in the circus. At noon we took up line of march in a northwesterly direction and later on Crossed the Saluda at Harts ferry on pontoons and went into camp. . . .

Expecting not to occupy the City Sherman had given written Orders to Genl. Howard regarding the conduct of the troops.[4] These instructions were: to destroy absolutely all arsenals and public property not needed for our own use; all railways, depots and machinery usefull in war to an enemy, but to spare all dwellings, Colleges, schools, asylums and harmless private property. In company with Genl. Howard Sherman was the first who rode into the City. The day was clear, but a perfect tempest of wind was raging. The brigade of Colonel Stone was allready in the City and properly posted. Citizens and Soldiers were on the streets and good Order prevailed. General Wade Hampton who commanded the Confederate rear guard of Cavallery had, in anticipation of the capture of Columbia, ordered that Cotton, public and private, should be moved into the Streets and fired, to prevent the yankee invaders from benefiting by its use. Bales were piled everywhere, the rope and bagging Cut, and tufts of cotton were blown about in the wind, lodged in the trees and against houses, so as to resemble a snowstorm. Some of these piles of cotton were burning, especially one in the very heart of the City, near the Courthouse, but the fire was practically subdued by the Efforts of the Union soldiers.

Before a single public building had been fired by orders, the smouldering fires, lighted by Hamptons men, were recindled by the wind and got bejond the Control of the brigade on duty in the City. The whole of Woods Division was brought in, but it was found impossible to check the progress of the fire, which, by midnight had become unmanageable, and raged about untill 4. P.M. when, the wind subsiding, it was got under Control. Sherman himself was up nearly all night, and with Genls. Howard, Logan, Hazen, Wood and others, labored hard to save houses and protect families thus suddenly deprived of shelter and of bedding and wearing apparel. . . . [5]

Feb. 18th. We were allowed a rest to day which was very wellcome. A general cleaning up was gone through with as far as circumstances would allow. Captain Randall and Lieutenants Morgan and Watson who had been taken prisoner at Chickamauga joined us here again. They had been kept in

~ prison at Columbia all the while. (A year and a half.) They had escaped several times, but through the help of hounds had been as often recaptured again before they could reach our lines in Georgia. After that they were watched so closely that escape became impossible. They were to a great extent ignorant of our operations in the field, as all thruthfull information was denied them. Lately, when the rebels began to concentrate an army in, and about Columbia they mistr[u]sted that something was wrong in the neighborhood, but still they did not know that we had taken Savannah and were advancing through South Carolina. Finally a Copy of the Charleston Courier and Mercury lost itself in prison, in which paper the people were entreated to oppose with all power and means the advance of the brute Sherman and his horde of barbarians. But nothing further they could learn.

Finally late on[e] afternoon a week ago, they were taken out of prison and conducted on board of freight trains to be shipped to Saulsbury [Salisbury] North Carolina. That made plain to them that Sherman must be in the vicinity. Again they thought of a scheme to escape and as soon as dark enough they set to work. They had to work very Carefully as there were t[w]o guards in each car. With pocket knifes they cut a hole in the half rotten floor of their Car, and when the Engine stopped to take in wood or water, crawled through and lost themselves in the darkness. They made their way backward, hoping to fall in with some of Shermans Cavallery. During the day they hid in the woods. The second night out they learned from a negro that the Yanks were coming; the third day they heard reports of Cannon in the direction of Columbia. The same day they saw from their hiding place the rebel soldiers retreating from Columbia northward. The following day they met a troop of our Cavallery with whom they stayed overnight and were then by them directed to our Division.

They looked very poor, very ragged, and very dirty. The treatment received had been all but human. Captain Randall especially, formally [formerly] a picture of manhood, was a pitiable looking sceleton. A look at him was Enough to fill ones heart with hate and disdain for all rebeldom. A little satisfaction I had out of Lieut. Morgan. Before he was taken prisoner he was a solid demokrat and claimed that the south had a right to own Slaves and go with them wherever they pleased, in fact, he maintained that the war on the part of the north was all wrong. I had many arguments with him on that point, but was unable to shake his views in the least. In all other respects he was a very amiable fellow and a good Comrade. I now asked him, since he had been in slavery for a year and a half how he liked it. "So much," he replied "that if I saw the niggers hang all their masters I would not lift a finger in their defense."—"That is strong." I replied. "But I hope you are not the only one who has come to his senses by Experience." . . .

Feb. 19th[.] Early in the morning we crossed Broad river on a pontoon bridge, passed through Allston and immediately began destroying the Spartansburg railroad for 14. miles northward and went in Camp tired and hungry. A very pleasant, and alltogether unexpected surprise awaited us here. While the men were building fires the fouragers returned. They had struck it big this time. In a mill they found a lot of corn meal, and an old negro had told them where they could resurrect a barrel of rice and a number of hams. John had been along and the gray mule was loaded down with the good things which were wellcomed with cheers by the men.

Feb. 20th. It was my fourage day again. We set out early on the Camden road. The prospect for business was poor. The most part of the Country was covered with dense woods; and the few plantations here and there were all stripped or burned and nothing left for us. About noon we overtook a party in the woods who were transporting a safe from some bank in Camden. When the driver saw us approaching they unhitched the horses and scedadled, their guard following suit, leaving the wagon with the safe standing in the road. We threw the safe off, broke the lock with a good Charge of powder and proceeded to look for spoils. No doubt some of the boys smelt piles of gold and were allready calculating to how much their share might amount to. Well the shares were big Enough, but it happened the stuff was of the wrong metal. Confederate scrip of all denominations by the thousands, of which every one was at liberty to help himself, but the precious metals were Conspicuous only by their absence. Disappointed and disgusted with Jeff Davis financial system we travelled on. During the afternoon we found in a barn a lot of so called niggertoes in the pod, of which we threshed a goodly lot and that was all we found that day. The niggertoe is a black bean much of the shape of a pea with a thick, hard skin. It is issued to the niggers as a part of their ration. It is hardly fit to be eaten on account of its acrid taste and leatherlike skin. When we arrived in Camp it began to rain and it kept at it all night.

Feb. 21st. Crossed Little River about noon. The roads were very bad because of the rain the previous night. We passed by Monticello where we learned that Kilpatricks men found 6. of our fouragers hung from the same beam in a cotton gin building. Gens. Kilpatrick and Sherman sent notice to Genls Wheeler and Wade Hampton that, if those outrages were not stopped, they would retaliate by hanging rebel prisoners. They replied that it was not their, but the bushwhakers and Citizens doings, and if any of the rebel prisoners were hung, they would hang so many yankee prisoners. But the soldiers took the matter in their own hands as will appear further on. We went in Camp near Winsboro.

The capture of Columbia made Charleston untenable for the rebels. Genl. Beauregard who had command there had been reinforced by Hardee when he left Savannah. After the surrender of Columbia they evacuated Charleston and our troops from Morris Island took immediate poss[ess]ion of it[.] So this hot bed of secession and rebellion lay prostrated at the feet of "Old Glorie." The Courier and Mercury, which for more than five years had incited the southern people to all immaginable outrages, was a fugitive and did not appear again for a long time to come. The rebel government became now thouroughly alarmed. Jeff Davis was forced again to put Genl. Joe E. Johnston, our former antagonist during the Atlanta campain, to command the forces which were to check our further advance. They were very diligent in uniting all available forces. . . .

Feb. 22d. Winsboro is on the Charlotte and South Carolina railway, 70. miles south of Charlotte N.C. In this direction we took line of march this morning, destroying the railway as we went along as far as Blackstock, or Blackstokes station, 65. miles south of Charlotte. General Johnston massed his troops therefore in the vicinity of Charlotte.

Feb. 23d. In order to keep up the delusion Kilpatrick advanced further on the roads towards Charlotte but we suddenly turned to the right, or northeast. I again was with the foragers and as before, we had poor luck. During the afternoon we discovered an old gristmill in a deep ravine. It was on[e] of the oldfashioned hopper concern with one set of stones. The power was furnished by a small Creek acting on an immense big undershot waterwheel. The concern was at rest and no people were to be seen. After investigating quite a lot of shelled Corn was discovered. We soon set the big wheel a moving and tried our skill to reduce the corn to meal. While thus busy an other party of fouragers from an other brigade joined us and inquired if we would take all the Corn there. No, we could not carry it all. So they waited untill we had our fill.

During the time some of their men went further up the ravine in quest of discoveries. They had not gone far when we heard half a dozen reports of rifles. Leaving a few men to tend the mill, we all went spedily in that direction. Having gone perhaps an eight of a mile a Sergeant came running back and reported, a lot of butternuts had opened fire on them. In fact, the firing was still going on. I doubted his statement as to the fellows being butternuts, or bushwhakers, as those fellows seldom had the courage to keep up a prolonged fight with soldiers. But the Sergeant insisted on his version, saying that he had plainly seen some of them but he did not know how many there were of them. Our plan of action was soon formed. We were forty men in all. With half of them the Sergeant was to go to the right in the woods and try to get in their rear, while I with the others was to reinforce the 8. men who were allready busy with them. It was understood that I was not to press the matter untill I heard from the Sergeant. I went forward in the narrow road untill I came in the rear of our boys who were engaged. Then I sent 12 men still further forward with the instruction to try to get in the bushwhakers flank. With the others I krept cautiously forward so as not to be seen before we reached our men. The firing was kept up slowly indicating that non of the parties were willing to waste ammunition for nothing. They must have noticed our Coming, because they ceased firing and were seen to slip back from tree to tree. We followed slowly, listening eagerly to hear from the Sergeant.

Suddenly severall scattering volleys were heard in the direction where I the sergeant supposed to be. We went forward immediately. The firing ceased abruptly and shortly afterwards the Sergeant and his men brought in four butternuts, and the detail which I had send on the flank, two more. I intended to bring the prisoners to Shermans headquarters, wher, I was sure they would be hung but the men all insisted to hang them on the spot. The rememberance of our men having being hung at Monticello a few days previous was to[o] fresh [y]et in the memory of all. And to add to this desire of revenge came the discovery that two of the prisoners were supplied with ropes to hang union soldiers with. These ropes were to seal their doom. During the exchange of bullets two of our men had been slightly wounded and one bushwhaker killed. When the bushwhakers understood what was to be their doom they began to threaten, saying that enough of them were round [y]et to take fearfull revenge. That made the matter worse and immediately preperations were made for execution. I did not feel like taking a hand in the affair and left with the soldiers of my command.

During our absence the men left at the mill had ground corn enough for us to carry and we prepared to leave at once. But before we left the grounds the Sergeant and his men returned and reported that the bushwhakers were at rest and never would lay in ambush for a yankee again. We took leave of them and started in quest of Rocky Mount the place of our destiny, which we reached just before night. Scarcely had the cornmeal been distributed among the comrades when Pluvious again blessed us with an all nights rain.

∽

Feb. 24th. It was still raining when Reveillee called for the usualy days business. A look at the skye did not promise any improvement. Having partaken of mush and coffee for breakfast we started again. After a three mile march we reached the Wateree, or Catawba river. This is a broad and turbulent stream. The day before the 20th Corps had crossed here and to day our Corps was to follow. But the heavy rain had swollen the river to such a degree that, just as we were beginning to cross, the wild current tore the pontoon bridge to pi[e]ces, part of it went down stream out of sight, and part swung round downward along the banks of the river. And worst of all, it began to rain again in good style and kept at it all day. So our Corps was left alone on the south side of the river; Kilpatrick with the Cavallery having crossed the same day with the 20th Corps, and the 15th 16th and 17th Corps having crossed about 10 miles below at Peay's Ferry. On the morning of the 25th the pontoneers worked strenuously to throw a bridge across but all attempts prooved futile against the mighty force of the roaring current. Finally about noon on the 26th a bridge had been built in a half circular form, the bow of the circle up stream so that the force of the Current acted on the bridge like the pressure of masonry on an arch.

The crossing began. But Genls. Wade Hampton and Buttler had found out our predicament and thought to profit by it. Scarcely had the crossing began when they appeared from the direction of Rocky Mount with a Division and a half of Cavallery determined to hurry up the Crossing and take some prisoners if we would let them. Our brigade was assigned the task of rear guard to keep the rebs in Check while the other troops Crossed. Exept some 25 or 30. rods back from the river the Country was more or less covered with brushwood and small trees. The cavallery had dismounted and, scattering among the brush, opened the dance with a brisk skirmish fire. Our brigade had deployed in a half circle, both wings being drawn back and resting on the river, the radius being about ¼. of a mile distant from the approach to the bridge. It was good for us the Johnnies had no artillery. Their scirmishers, allthough they were in close line and kept up a spirited fire, we held in check easy enough. About 5. P.M. the troops and teams had crossed and we had to come in line and cross allso; but there was no rear guard to cover our Crossing. We retreated slowly which necessarily contracted the half circle untill we stood in Close order. The Johnnies thought now was their time when we would begin the crossing. They came out of the brush and crept forward on all fours. We kept pegging away at them and many a one of them paid dearly for their rashnes.

A big old log barn stood at the edge of the clearing and thither the Johnnies went and soon filled it up. There we could not well reach them while they fired at us through the cracks between the logs. But Genl. Carlin commanding our division had posted two batteries on the high banks opposite the river and they suddenly began to throw shells among the Johnnies and one solid shot after the other through the barn, breaking, and knocking the logs in every direction. That settled the dispute at once. Our Johnny friends were in a hurry to get at a safe distance from us. We crossed the river in peace and left Wade Hampton and Buttler to speculate about more effective means to prevent our advance.

After the bridge had been taken up, a more formidable enemy than Hampton and Buttlers Cavallery interfeered with our advance. It was like jumping from the frying pan into the fire. We were to make forced marches to catch up with the 20th Corps which was 3. days ahead of us. We started but that was about all we did. The repeated heavy rains of late had soaked the soil thouroughly, which here consisted of loam and clay. The 20th Corps in its passage had allready broken up the ground completely, and the rain following filling up all rots and hoofprints had soaked the soil to the very bottom. Wheels went down in the dough like mass untill the hubs dragged the mud; horses and mules sank down into the sticky stuff, untill they were unable to recover their legs. Eaven the men were hardly able to walk. We had seen and passed good many tough places but this carried the price of all. After two hours of hard labor we had covered a mile and had to stop, mudbound. We worked all night to cut a new road through the woods, partly made of curdoroy for a distance of 8 miles, but it was of not much account. After a couple dozend wagons, or a battery had passed on bare ground, it was the same again. At night, after steady hard labor we had gained about 10. miles. On the 28th however, the soil having dried up some what, and being composed of different material we were enabled to cover 22. miles and camped at 10. P.M.

March 1st. Foraging again. It was not my turn exactly but the Officer who was to go felt rather lame so I took his turn. It was to be a hard day for "Hanging Rock" must be reached that day and that was 30. miles distant by the direct road, and we had the additional pleasure in making that distance by bumming right and left all over the Country, and then find nothing worth toting along. In the afternoon we were somewhat reconciled with our bad luck by finding a lot of niggertoes, a half barrel of molasses of the black strap order and a half starved cow. A little later on we secured an abandoned Cavallery horse which helped to carry the stuff to camp. Of course it was near midnight when we arrived at Hanging Rock and found the boys all asleep.

March 2d. We were now abreast again with the 20th Corps which had waited for us to come up. Again it began to rain and kept at it, and soon the roads were converted into a quagmire. We were approaching "Lynch Creek" one of those peculiar institutions which sometimes may be jumped or forded by a child, and again, allmost without warning, will swell and expand to formidable and dangerous streams. It took us two days to cross the 5 miles wide Expanse of water; working and wading in mud and water, day and night, and rain thereon in the bargain. On the afternoon of the 4th finally we emerged from the overflowed, godforsaken swamp, and once more marched on solid terra firma. At sunset we came in sight of, and camped on the banks of the Great Pedee [Pee Dee] at "Sneedsboro." . . .

March 5th. The great Pedee bears its name justly. Next [to] the Mississippi it is one of the broadest rivers in the southern states, at least so where we crossed it. It is wider than the Ohio at Louisville. It is the boundary line between North and South Carolina. The soil here is poor, white sand. The day was exeptionally fine. the Pontoons were soon laid and the crossing began. The 14th and 20th corps were to cross here, while the 15th 16th and 17th Corps crossed near Cheraw about 12 miles below. Where Sneedboro is I am unable to tell, unless half a dozen miserable looking hovels scattered on a section of land claimed that honor. At night we camped on North Carolina soil.

March 6th. The weather was exellent today. Hopes were freely expressed that the weather would finally settle down to a more agreable condition. We marched about 20 miles and camped in the neighborhood of a little village called Rockingham.

March 7th. Our cherished hopes for continuous fine spring weather turned to water again. We came now in the celebrated North Carolina pitch pine district where the gathering of pitch and the manufacture of turpentine and rosin is the only business and means of living for the people. It is mainly all a low, level country and a continuous pitch pine forest. . . .

[S]canty rations was beginning to tell on the enduring power of the soldiers. True, fouraging was kept up, but might as well have been abandoned, as it did not realize anything. There were no plantations in the pine woods, and the poor pitch gatherers who lived in small, dirty log hovels were nearer starvation than ourselves. The rectifying of turpentine and manufacture of rosin had wholly stopped during the war; the able bodied male population was either in the rebel army, or had been crippled or killed and the remaining part could not earn anything. There were no signs of agriculture of any account, no fields, no gardens, no domestic cattle, in fact nothing but pitch pine and where the poor people lived from [found a living] has ever been a riddle to me. It was a pity to see these half naked and starved people, especially the children emeciated, dried up so to speak, seemingly lost in apathy and ignorance of their miserable Existence. One felt more like giving than asking, or looking for anything.

On the 8th we had to cross the Lumber River. Originally it is but a good sized Creek, but presently it resembled a Lake more than a river. Exeptionally this bridge had not been destroyed. To guard against high water the bridge had been built very high and it afforded a funny sight to see the bridge just peeping out of the midle of a lake, as if swimming about, there beeing about half a mile of water at each End of it. The water was nearly stagnant that accounted for the bridge being not carried away. To further secure its stability, rocks had been piled on both edges of the bridge bed which served the double purpose of keeping the structure down and preventing passengers from walking of[f] into the water. After immense labor and trouble we finally got across, well pleased to have conquered one more serious obstacle.

On the 9th I was once more one of the fouragers and of course we got nothing, nor did we take trouble to persist in such useless undertaking. About noon we came at another smart creek with a funny name which I do not now remember; but I vividly remember the circumstances under which we crossed it. Allthough of good size and filled to the brim it had the good sense not to overflow its limits. The bridge allso was there. On the south bank were turpentine and rosin factories. Besides the refining building there were a number of long sheds filled with barrels of rosin and turpentine. Piles of rosin lay around like so many brick; barrels full of raw pitch, covered and uncovered stood round. We concluded to stop here to brew our noon Coffee. The soil about the Establishment and up to the bridge had, since years duration, been mixed up with pulverized and small pi[e]ces of rosin which could not be seen now.

Well. The fire was build. Some of the boys put pi[e]ces of rosin between the firewood to give the fire a good start. The scheme succeded bejond all Expectation. The rosin burned and melted. Very soon the very soil began to burn, no matter how wet. We tried to stamp out the fire, but had only the satisfaction to burn our footgear; we poured water onto the fire; that made it spread the more. It spread rapidly towards the sheds and then the grand Circus was fairly inaugurated. In an incredible short time after the fire reached the sheds, we had the best side show ever produced free of admittance. The rosin piles quickly caught fire, melted, and the burning fluid run down into the Creek, and floated on top of the water burning lustily. As the sheds stood up stream from the bridge the burning fluid soon set fire to the wood-work of the bridge. I called the men together in order to cross before it was to[o] late. From the opposite side we had chance and time to observe the proceeding. Not much fire or flame could be seen. An impenetrable thick, curling black smoke rolled upward and filled the air. Bill Ferguson[6] ven-tured the remark that if his satanic Majesty had any such Institution in his domains, we mortals need not wonder at the numerous volcanic eruptions and earthquakes so common on our globe. As to give force to his remarks, an explosion as from a thirty pounder set the air vibrating, and made us quiver all over; at the same time the air seemed all at once aflame. In quick succession one explosion followed the other, like a dozen batteries deliver-ing fire by file, profusely scattering splinters of sheds and factory in all di-rections.

At the first explosion, young Frank Extine, who had not crossed with us but stood just at the foot of the bridge ready to cross, was thrown of[f] his feet flat on the ground and did not stir a muscle. As the next explosions followed in quick succession, no one dared to cross and investigate what ailed him, but without further order every one was bent to increase the distance between the flying missiles and himself. It were the barrels, filled with turpentine which raised the racket. When the shooting stopped we went back to look after Extine. But the bridge was burning lustily and we dared not to cross. Presently Extine picked himself up and, seizing his rifle, loocked at the burning bridge. Then with a leap he started and dashed through the flames. He was not hurt at all. He was merely stunned and upset by the pressure of the air. He had not been insensible, but had thought it best to lay low as long as the racket should last. Nobody Else was hurt exept Bill Ferguson, who had his old defective hat knocked off and torn in a most careless manner. That, doubtless, was the rejoinder on his previous impious remark.

None of us thought any further of making Coffee for dinner but pur-sued our way towards the stipulated camping place. It was the first time that fouragers arrived at the camping ground ahead of the Corps. On the road we agreed not to say a word of what had happened, as we did not know how the accident would be regarded by the higher authorities. . . . At night in Camp the boys had a great deal to say about a fight which had come off somewhere, nobody knew Exectly, where. They had been making coffee for dinner when a tremenduous artillery firing was heard in the distance. (We were perhaps 3 miles ahead of them.) They were called to arms at once and hurried forward in a lively manner, as it was supposed Kilpatrick had run against the Johnnies and nee[d]ed help. Since that was not the case, speculation was great and different opinions were advanced as to the cause of the strange occurence. . . .

March 10th. Marched about 18. miles to day and camped about 10. miles south of Fayetteville.

March 11th. We took leave today of the god forsaken pine woods and swamps, and nobody felt sorry for it. Lieut. Cox[7] returned with two Johnny prisoners. The Lieutenant had been taken prisoner by the rebel Cavallery while out fouraging. The funny point of the affair was, that the Lieut. came home into camp, riding a horse purloined from his captors, and the two prisoners, his former guards walking meekley along. The latter admitted freely that they were caught by means of a genuine yanke trick; but they did not seem to be much worried about it. They were immediately paroled, but they went along with us to Fayetteville.

When we arrived within two miles of the City, rebel scirmishers undertook to arrest our progress. Genl. Hardee held the City with his Corps of Infantry and some Cavallery and Artillery. Of course we had to deploy scirmishers to take part in the game. Our Division was formed in line of battle to meet any Emergency. The Johnnies were unusually obstinate which made the impression as if they had a mind to fight it out right there. Another brigade was deployed in our scirmishline and step by Step the Johnnies were forced back on the town. When they were forced in the outscirts of the City, they were suddenly gone. We mistrusted their behavior at first, but when our scirmishers entered the city they found the Johnnies had gone; and when we entered the city from the south, the bridge over Cape Fear river on the north was burning. We camped in the outscirts of the City. . . .

March 12th. Marched through Fayetteville, crossed the Cape Fear river on the patched up bridge and wenth in camp half a mile north of the river.

Fayetteville is an extensive, but loose built City. The streets are broad and straight, but sidewalks are scarce. The buildings mostly of the cheap, common order and mostly unpainted. Shade trees seemed to be prohibited, judging by the scarcity of them. We remained hear until the 15th which short rest was wellcome for men and beast. On the afternoon of the 12th the U. S. tug boat "Davidson" and the gunboat "Eolus" reached Fayetteville from Wilmington which had been Captured by General Terry and Admiral David D. Porter in January. The 14th and 15th the first Regt. Michigan

Engeneers was ordered to destroy the arsenal and the Extensive machinery, which had formally belonged to the old U.S. armory at Harpers Ferry, and had been moved by the rebels to Fayetteville in April 1861. and used since that time in the manufacture and repair of arms for the Confederate armies. Every building was knocked down, and burned, and every piece of machinery utterly broken up and ruined. Much property of great use to an Enemy was here destroyed or cast in the river.[8] The 14th our hearts were made glad again by an all days rain.

March 15th. We were to move on again. Shortly after daybreak I set out with a party of fouragers. As we had left the dismal pitch pine woods behind us we Expected to do a rousing business to day. We followed the so called "Old Plankroad" for fuly three miles before we discovered any Clearings. Why the road bore that name was not very clear as no plank was visible nowhere. It was not even a decent land road. We were informed the Corps would camp the night at "Taylors Hole Creek." The road was terribly cut up, which prooved that rebel troops lately had passed here. . . . We hunted all day, but . . . found nothing. It was the last fouraging I attended to. During the night it rained again. Genl. Kilpatrick who was some 3. miles ahead of us, was much pressed by Wade Hampton. A brigade was forwarded to his support, which early next morning had a lively tussel with the Johnnies, but the latter were sent about their business.

March 16th. The 20th Corps took the lead to day. The passage of Taylors Hole creek made us much trouble, because of the low, marchy ground and much curduroying had to be done, which induced the men to call it: "Devils Hole Creek." Towards noon, General Wards Division developed the enemy behind light breastworks. Genl. Case's brigade, supported by a battery, made a resolute charge and broke Rhetts brigade, capturing 3. guns and 217. prisoners. It was found that this was merely an advance post, and the rebels retreated quickly behind a second line of substantial built breastworks. . . .

The battery captured was said to be the same one which inaugurated the war by firing the first shot at Fort Sumter in April 1861. The rebels, while retreating, to their main line left their dead and wounded on the field. Their wounded, 68 in number, were left in a neighboring house with a rebel Officer, 4. men and five days rations. The killed had to take care of themselfes. The two Corps, 20th and 14th were now brought in line as fast as they could be brought forward through the mud. The 15th and 17th. Corps were on an other road to our right and to[o] far away to be of any assistance. It was nearly night when we had pushed all of the rebels behind their works. It was an ugly night. Steady rain; every step made set the water splashing around. And in addition, the Johnnies being safe behind their works, kept popping away at us at random, which made it very unpleasant for us. I offered a wager to Captain B[o]rch[e]rdt that we would find the nest empty in the morning, but he declined the risk. Finally our batteries who, after immense labor, had come in position, treated them to a lively dose of shot and shell, which brought them to their senses, and after that they behaved like good boys. Next morning at day break investigation showed that the Johnnies had taken to their heels. This affair is called the battle of "Averysboro." Our casualties were twelve Officers and 65. men killed, and four hundred and seventy seven wounded, a total of 554. the greater part of which was of the 20th Corps as they came first in action.[9]

March 17th. We were quite early in motion. Thanks to the Johnnies retreat, we found the roads abominable. It must have been hard on the Johnnies to march in such a dark stormy night, on roads hardly passable by daylight. But after a few miles we turned to the right on the road to Goldsboro; whereas Hardee had kept the straight road towards Smithfield. The Goldsboro road, not so much cut up, enabled us to advance faster. But coming at the South river, a bridge had to be provided for, which delayed us an hour and a half. We marched about 15. miles, a good days work under the circumstances, and camped in a large field. . . .

March 19th. As our brigade had brought up the rear yesterday, we were at the head to day, and our Regt. at the head of the brigade; consequently the very first on the road. We started at about 7. A.M. As usual, fouragers had gone ahead. After having advanced about two miles we heard in the distance ahead of us faint reports of musket firing. That was nothing unusual with the fouragers, and we thought nothing more about it, exept that some of the rebel cavallery could not agree with our fouragers. But as we advanced, the firing became more distinct and animated, and seemed to be stationary; proof that the Cavallery this time was not willing to back out. Soon we drew near the scene of action. A number of our fouragers had taken position behind a large brick house, which stood to the left where the road enters an extensive swamp; the black swamp, I believe it was called; others had deployed as scirmishers in the woods. Colonel Fitch asked the men stationd behind the house, if they could not drive the Cavallery. The men replied there must be a lot of two legged Cavallery who needed some special inducements to quit the right of way. Fitch reported to Genl. Hobart, who commanded the brigade. Genl. Hobart at once deployed our Regt., as the first in line of march, as scirmishers in the woods to the right of the road; while the 33d Ohio which came next to us was deployed to the left of the road.

As soon as deployed the line advanced. The Johnnies gave slowly way now but keeping steady up musket firing. Soon we came in the swamp and were wallowing in the water. For about a mile that continued when we came on higher ground; at the same time the rebs refused to back an other step, and the increase in their fire indicated that reinforcements had been sent to them. Half our men were left in the scirmishline the other half set to work to built breastworks. A little while after, three guns ha[d] worked through the swamp. The Officer of the Artillery wanted to know where the rebel lines were, and, allthough not able to see any object to fire at in the woods, he threw shells at random, hoping the rebels would reply and thereby disclose their whereabouts. He had not long to wait. After firing a few shots the rebels replied, not with shells, but with solid shot, and with such precision that in a little while all the horses were down and the guns dismantled. A boy in my Comp. Herman Hasz was actually shot in two while bending to lift a little log to be put onto the breastworks.[10]

Meanwhile General Hobart; believing that we had to deal with Johnstons army, had formed the rest of the brigade, (perhaps 2200 men) in line and sent word to Genl. Carlin, Commanding division, requesting him to hurry forward the Division as we had developed the rebel army. But Carlin being not on the best of terms with Hobart, sent word back asking if the Genl. was afraid of a handfull of rebel Cavallery. This nettled Hobart and he immediately prepaired for a charge on the left side of the road where the swamp was more free of brush as on our side. At that moment, J.C. Davis, who comm[a]nded our Corps, who had been somewhat in the rear, came galopping up and at once took matters in hand. He took the two divisions (the 3d being behind [y]et with the train.) and formed them in line to the right of the road on high ground at the Edge of the swamp, the men setting to work to built some kind of protection. Shortly after, Genl. Williams, commanding 20th Corp, who marched on a road some miles to our left, having heard the noise, hurried forward with all possible speed to our assistance, forming the troops as fast as they arrived on our left. General Slocum, who commanded the left wing took charge of the whole. Genl. Kilpatrick came hurriedly from the left, dismounted his man, and extended the line to the left. The 15th and 17th Corps were on a road to[o] far to our right and could not be of any help to us during the day. Two of our Divisions being back with the train, could not be up before an hour or two.

Including Kilpatricks Cavallery we were about 28,000 men, while Johnston, without his Cavallery had fully 50,000. men.[11]

Meanwhile we in the scirmish line had an uncomfortable time of it. We wondered whether the Johnnies were waiting for our troops to charge, or they would undertake the job. Betwen us and the road on the left was only a short distance, but we could not see what happened there on account of the brush. Colonel Fitch was anxious to know about it, and told Maj. Walker to take care of the Regt. while he was going to see what happened there. He came yust in time seing Genl. Hobart leading our brigade in a charge on the rebel works, and seeing the rebel lines coming over the works in colums and making a countercharge, and driving back Hobart and his men. Colonel Fitch came running back, crying: "About face! Left oblike! double quick! March! March!" At the same time our Videttes who had been watching in our front, came running back, reporting the rebels were coming "en masse." Of course we double quicked to reach our lines, and the increasing whizzing of the bullets did not slacken our speed. A Lieutenant of Comp. F a former regular soldier and a brave man, was trotting along aside of me. We were Exchanging occasionally remarks, when he suddenly stopped, exclaimed: "Oh" and dropped on his face in the water. I stopped and found a bullet had entered his back just opposite the heart. He did not stir; help was out of the question and I hurried away to catch up with the Regt.[12]

The left oblike direction we had taken in the retreat brought us to the extreme right of our lines. That was held by a Regiment of New Jersey Zouaves, funny looking fellows as far as their Costume was concerned.[13] Very wide, crimson red pantaloons, enclosed from the knee downward in a sort of stocking called: "Comashes," blue blouse with dark red sash around the waist; a red, turkish "Fez" with long red tassel and no visor, instead of the regular army cap, or hat. They were mostly all Germans as their talking indicated. But in spite of their funny appearance the fellows understood their business as the Johnnies found out at their Cost. We jumped the little barrikade they had got up in short order, turned round and divided among them to wellcome the Johnnies. They were well pleased with the reinforcement. A fellow asked me whether the Johnnies were in line or Column. That was a question which puzzled me somewhat, and replied that pressing business had prevented me to investigate the matter in the swamp.

We soon found out however. Hardly had we made ourselfes comfortable among them when the Johnnies came in sight and a fearfull firing began. But it was soon seen that the Enemy, who came in two lines, overlapped our line on the right. Colonel Fitch instantly called the Regiment back and formed it on the right of the Zouaves with the right wing well refused so as to meet any attack on the flank. At the same time a battery came dashing through the woods and unlimbered just behind our Regt. We made room for them right and left and in a minute the Johnnies were served with double shotted Cannister. By this time the whole line, several miles in lenght, was in business to the teeth. We had 72. cannon at work besides Kilpatricks two light batteries. Thus, with the incessant rattle of musketry caused the very earth tremble. The brave Johnnies could not face such a storm of iron and led, and discharging their rifles, they turned back into the swamp.

In this manner we received six distinct assaults by the combined forces of Hooke [Hoke], Hardee and Cheatham under the imediate command of Genl. Johnston himself, without giving an inch of ground. A great advantage we had over the rebels was in Artillery, of which they had but little.[14] The three Cannon which we had to leave in the scirmish line, and which fell in their hands, were unfit for use as they themselves had disabled them.

It was allready dark when the last charge was made. The first quarter of the moon threw an uncertain light on the Scene. An hour previous, the two Divisions who had been with the trains, had come up. The men were eager to have a hand in the fray. If it had been an hour earlier and daylight, I am sure Genl. Slocum would have turned the tables on the Johnnies and charged them in turn, and I am sure we would have routed the whole outfit, as by this time they must have been entirely discouraged, But it was to[o] late for that and besides we had not broken the fast since early morning, and our wounded needed attention.

As no further charging was expected, a few videttes were posted and the men allowed to make their Coffee for supper. But how surprised we were when shortly after, two small rebel Regts. appeared directly in our rear and cooly requested us to surrender. And they meant business to[o], because they all held their guns ready to give fire. A bloody encounter seemed unavoidable. Colonel Fitch and others tried to explain to them that they were inside our lines, and better lay down their arms, or they would all be killed. But they maintained they were in front of our lines. Meantime the Commander of the battery had turned his guns around and the gunners stood, laneyard in hand, ready to fire in the rebel mass. The commander cried aloud: "Ground arms Johnnies, or we blow you to kingdom come"! They did ground arms and behaved afterward like good fellows. There were about 400. of them. They could not account for being in our rear. They had been separated from the main body they knew, but they could not see how they could circle round in the woods and land right in our rear. Moreover there were not many among them who felt sorry for the accident. . . .

March 20th. The first hour after daylight was spent in burrying our dead, which, luckily were not very many. Genl. Slocum prepared now to attack the Johnnies, who had withdrawn behind their works; but Genl. Sherman, who had arrived, had different views regarding Johnston and his army, and ordered Slocum not to attack Johnston, but to move up close to his works and merely keep him busy. Genl. Johnston had but one road to fall back on, the road through Smithfield to Raleigh, the Capital of North Carolina. This road in the rear of Johnston was crossed by mill creek, then a considerable stream, and spanned only by one bridge. Sherman directed Genl. Howard commanding 15th and 17th Corps, to direct his troops so that he got around Johnstons left in his rear so as to intercept his retreat to Smithfield and Raleigh. As Howard had to move his Corps some 20 miles across a swampy Country with hardley any road it took him untill shortley before the Evening on the 22d. when he found that Genl. Johnston had withdrawn his left wing in such a manner as to cover the bridge across Mill Creek. Genl. Logans 15th Corps had a smart fight with the Johnnies but night put a stop to further operations. The following morning, in spite of a lively rain Sherman ordered a general advance along the whole line, but it was found that Johnston had escaped during the night. We turned to the right to regain the Goldsboro road and marched to near the Neuse river where we encamped. . . .

March 24th. A trip of 18. miles brought us to Goldsboro. . . . If the reader had been in Goldsboro that 24th day of March 1865. and seen Shermans "bummers" passing through, he certainly would have taken them for a big lot of Vagabonds if nothing worse. No Officer or man wore a decent suit of clothing. For 10. weeks we had roughed it in the wood and swamps, and everything was tattered and torn, and worst of all the shoes. Good many wore, what they pompously called: "parlor mocassins," corsely drawn together of rawhide. Some wore a semblance of a hat, or cap; some had an old handkerchief or rag tied around their cranium; others did not care a snap about their scull and wore it as nature had made it. Others again wore the garb of the native, butternut colored, homespun, and were honeured with the title; "galvanized Johnnies"; others again had utilized their dogtent canvas for a new suit. But in one respect this motley crowd was perfect: Their ammunition and rifles were in exellent working order; General Johnston had found that out at his Cost. But now we were to have a little rest and trim up again before we started on the final "Round up." The camp

FACING NORTHWARD

of our Division was just south west of the City on high, dry ground, and the weather at once changed to spring and became plesant and stabile. General Sherman, apreciating the hardships we had endured, and the services performed, gave us entire rest exept such duties as are unavoidable in camp life. An occasional picket, or camp guard, procuring wood, etc. was all the duty required.

The first morning I took 12. men from the Compagny for a private fouraging Expedition for the benefit of the Comp. John with the mules went along of course. A three mile walk north brought us to a plantation where we found an abundance of the good things which we had missed so long. We pressed a cart into service to transport the stuff to camp.

On the second day the first train came in from Newbern. It brought us what we were so eagerly watching for; Letters and papers from home; the first since we had left Savannah. . . .

Goldsboro is a City much like Fayetteville, extensively laid out, but very little show for Enterprise. The few Citizens, besides women, children and darkies were mostly crippled and discharged rebel soldiers, quiet and inoffensive. They never had taken much stock in the rebellion and were glad the trouble was drawing to a Close.

By the 8th of April the army loked like itself again. We had received a new outfit of wearing apparel. The wagons were again replenished with rations and ammunition. Sherman issued an order to be ready to march on the 10th. After the battle of Bentonville Genl. Johnston had withdrawn behind Smithfield to cover Raleigh. That was west from Goldsboro and in that direction we now took our course.

April 10th. According to orders, shortly after sunrise the head of colum drew out of camp. During our stay at Goldsboro the weather had been Exellent. The roads, exept in marchy, or swampy spots, were dry. Woods and fields had donned their new spring dress; fruit trees and shrubs were in full bloom. About three or four miles out we met the rebel Cavallery Outpost who had built barricades across the road, but they did not wait for us to enter in conversation with them, but lit out without further Ceremony. We marched only about 10. miles when we went in Camp. It seemed as if the weather Clerk did not want us to enjoy a decent dry Campain, for at sundown all the gates of heaven seemed to open at once. For several houres it poured down untill the water stood inch high on level ground.

April 11th. The Johnnies had burned the bridge across the Neuse river and Pontoons had to be laid. At 10. A.M. we passed through Smithfield, which Johnston had left only the pr[e]vious afternoon. Shortly after we left

MEMOIRS OF A DUTCH MUDSILL

Smithfield we entered the low country again and curduroying here and there became the order of the day again. About noon we were gladened with the best news we had received during the war. By courier Genl. Sherman sent the good tidings that Genl. Lee had surrendered to Genl. Grant at Appomattox after 5. days of stubborn fighting.[15] The woods at once were ringing with cheers and jells as if possessed by an army of savages. One fellow of our Regt. felt so Elated that he smashed his rifle against a Cotton tree. Colonel Fitch, who happened to be near, laughingly reprimanded him for the rash deed saying: "That will cost you $14.00 my boy, and besides, we have not settled yet with General Johnston; you may have use for a gun [y]et."—"Colonel" the soldier replied, "I have carried that rifle for nigh three years. I do'nt know how many Johnnies it has hit, or knocked over. It has done its part. I will gladly pay Uncle Sam for the rifle, for the good news is worth that to me. As for Genl. Johnston and his men, Why, they will be glad if we will let them go home." A little while after the fellow was furnished with an other rifle and $14.00 were charged against his account.

April 12th. We had camped that night near the Raleigh and Newbern Railway 4. miles east of Raleigh. . . .

April 13th. Our brigade had the lead again and our Regt. at the head. At half past seven A.M. we entered the City. Our Regiment was marched into the Capitol grounds where it staked arms. The flag of the Regt. was immediately raisd over the Capitol. The rest of the brigade was encamped just outside the City. The passage of the troops through the City lasted all day. At first the people were rather shy but when they found the yanks would not hurt them, they began to fill the Avenues and streets and became very talkative. Raleigh is quite a big city, taking it from a southern point of view; Avenues and streets broad and straight, but common, cheap buildings most everywhere. The Capitol though is a fine structure, built on elevated ground in midle of a fine square. . . .

General Sherman had hurried forward the troops. He feared General Johnston might try to escape into Georgia. Again the 14th Corps was picked out to perform the flanking business, to head off Johnston, which required exessive marching. Our brigade had been kept at Raleigh doing provost duty untill 10. A.M. on the 15th when we started after the Corps, which was two days ahead of us. We traveled until midnight and, to make the thing more interesting, it rained more or less the whole day. But a few hours rest were allowed us and daylight, the 16th we started again The roads were muddy, but the weather was fine and we were not bothered with trains. We kept at it again till 10. P.M. I can assure you that rest and sleep was willcome that night.

April 17th. Again we were astir at daybreak. Marching about 12 miles we were halted near a big plantation about 9. A.M. After standing and sitting around for half an hour we were informed that we would remain here for the day. Selecting suitable campgrond we made ourselfes comfortable. While preparing dinner, the long roll was beaten by the drummers, a sign eather of great danger, or some important news. Of course, in a moment everybody was at arms. The brigade was formed in a hollow square as if to resist a Cavallery charge. But no Enemy was to be seen far or near. But instead of an enemy, General Hobart with his Aid came on horseback as if ready for a march, rode in the Centre of the square and the Aid read the following order from General Sherman: "The General commanding announces with pain and sorrow that on the evening of the 11th. instant, at the theater in Washington City his Exellency the President of the United States, Mr. Lincoln, was assassinated by one who uttered the State motto of Virginia. 'Sic semper tryannis.' (So all tyrants shall die.) At the same time the Secretaire of State, Mr. Seward, while suffering from a broken arm, was allso stabbed by an other murderer in his own house, but still survives, and his son was allso wounded, supposed fatally."[16]

It is impossible to describe the feelings of the men at the reading of this Order. They did make no demonstrations. They went quietly to their camping ground, uttering suppressed curses and maledictions on the assassins. It was well there was no prospect for an immediate battle in sight, for if that had been the case Johnstons army would have seriously felt the Effects and no Officer would have been able to subdue the wrath of the men. As it was the men committed some outrages, which they would not have done, but for this assassination. As I remarked before, we camped near a big plantation. The mansion was a princely structure and all the surroundings told of wealth, luxury and ease. But all the inhabitants had taken to flight; even the nigger village was deserted. Every eatable thing had been taken away or destroyed, but nothing of other things was disturbed. Furniture, pictures, carpets, lace curtains, screens, bedding and wearing apparel, etc. all in the best order. The men looked at it, but did not disturb anything. . . . Supper was made and enjoyed according to circumstances, and all settled down early, as we had been informed of an early start next morning. But about midnight the camp was suddenly illuminated as with a thousand electric lights. All the building of the plantation, the negro village included were burning brightly. It was a grand sight, and little was the pity lost at sight of the holocaust. It was not found out, nor was it asked for, who were the originators of the grand display untill after we were discharged at Washington. Then it was found that a few men of each Regt. of the brigade had secretly undertaken and finished the job thouroughly. . . .

April 18th. According to the warning given we were in motion at daylight. We passed by the burnt plantation and had to admit that the work had been thouroughly finished. . . . We had started not a whit to[o] early this morning, for the stars were twinkling when we arrived at "Martha's Vineyard," near Avons Ferry on the upper Cape Fear river, where our Corps was in position. In three days and a half we had marched full a hundred miles.

~

CHAPTER EIGHTEEN

Washington.
The Great Parade

~ Meanwhile Genl. Johnston having heard of Lees surrender, and Jeff Davis flight from Richmond, and seeing that he could not escape the clutches of Sherman, had, under flag of truce, sent a letter to Sherman asking for a personal interview with the view of final surrender. They met at Morrisville on the 18th, and a preparatory truce untill noon on the 24th was agreed upon.[1] Untill this time both armies were to remain in the position they now occupied. At the same time they agreed upon articles of surrender the same as General Grant had allowed to Genl. Lee and which had been approved by President Lincoln, with the exeption that Johnston proposed to sent the men home in Organizations of Regiments to the place where they had been organized, to prevent their breaking up in bands of guerillas, rowdies and robbers, plundering as they go along. Genl. Sherman saw no reason to object to the proposal and endorsed the same in the propositions for surrender to Washington to be adopted, or altered according to the views of the Government. . . . [2] The . . . agreement was immediately forwarded to Washington and General Grant for approoval, or correction, as they may deem advisable. What a fearfull dust this document raised will be seen hereafter.

April 19th. After Coffee we were marched into a large field on the east bank of Cape Fear river and told to put up tents as we would remain here untill further orders. The day was spent for the purpose of making the Camp as Comfortable as possible. The tents were all shaded with boughs, as it was becoming very hot during daytime. The following day strong details were made from the Regiments which were sent across the river, which was crossed by means of an old scow or flatboat. About a mile further on we came to the main road which comes from Richmond, Petersburg and Danville. A great part of Lees army, when they learned that Lee was going to surrender, were to[o] mad, and to[o] proud to lay down their arms before the yankees, and had run away to escape, what seemed to them a disgrace and dishonor. The greater part of them came up this road to South Carolina, Georgia and other southern States. The greater part of them carried still their rifles and accouterments. They all were taken up here. Their rifles and accoutrements taken away, and the men paroled. They had to give their names, as allso the Comp. Regt. brigade division, and Corps in which they served, place and State where they were enrolled, and the place they wished to go to. Then they had to sign their names to the parole papers, which very few were able to do. They were given from three to five days rations, according the distance they had to travel, and were dismissed. Most of them were well satisfied with the way the thing was done. Thousands were paroled on this road alone, which explains why General Lee surrendered so small an army at Appomattox. (About 38,000. men.) . . . [3]

On the 22d we received warning to be ready to move; that as soon as the armistice had expired, hostile movements would begin again. That was a great surprise, as we all expected that General Johnston would be glad to wind up the business. But it was not Genl. Johnstons fault. It came about in this way: The articles of agreement between Sherman and Johnston had reached Washington on the 21st. President Johnson immediately called a cabinet meeting at which Genl. Grant was present. It was thought that the articles were to[o] liberal regarding the rebel states, as for instance the deposition of the arms in the different State Capitols. There must have been a hidden enemity against Sherman in the Cabinet at Washington, because, instead of sending him instructions under what conditions Genl. Johnstons surrender would be accepted, they sent him an order to open hostilities as the armistice was ended. Then they ordered Genl. Grant to proceed to North Carolina, relieve Genl. Sherman of his command and bring the matter to a close. The secretaire of war Mr. Stanton aimed a dastardly kick at Genl. Sherman by publishing a lenghty article in the New York Tribune in which Sherman was called a traitor and political usurper. Genl. Halleck, who before Grant, had been commander in Chief of all the armies in the United States allso thought the time had come to vent his jealous spleen

WASHINGTON. THE GREAT PARADE

against Sherman. . . . Personally he could not do anything as he was merily [merely] in command of the military division of the James with Headquarters at Richmond, but, seeing that the Secretaire of war had acted so unfriendly towards Sherman, he sent a telegram to the war Department advising them that instruction be given to Genl. Shermans subordinate Officers to obey no orders given by him.

This telegram was immediately comunicated by the Secretaire of war to General Dix in New York and made public through the daily newspapers. Never has there been a more Cowardly attempt undertaken to destroy the unblemished character of one of the greatest patriots and soldier of the Country. It was well that Shermans army did not know anything of these Intrigues at the time, and that Hallecks was indignantly put under foot by General Grant. We first heard of it when we reached Richmond on the march homeward. The indignation of the army rose to such a pitch that it would have taken but a word and the army had marched to Washington and cleaned out the contemptible, cowardly brood. The army felt the insult more keenly than General Sherman himself, because the Copperhead papers were again loud in denouncing Shermans army as a horde of robbers and Cutthroats, commanded and led by a heartless brute, who would now scatter the army over the north to continue their lawles[s] outrages.

While all this was going on in Washington, Genl. Grant hastened to Raleigh to have a personal interview with Genl. Sherman. He arrived there on the 24th. He did not assume command of Shermans army, but having satisfied himself that Sherman had posted his troops in such a manner that Genl. Johnston and his army were actually prisoners, he instructed Sherman to conclude the surrender on the same terms granted to Genl. Lee, he went back to Washington. The surrender of Johnstons army was effected on the 26th of April 1865. at Greensboro North Carolina. With this act the Curtain fell and ended on[e] of the greatest, and bloodiest Rebellions recorded in history.

April 26th. We were to have an other scare before the sword should be put into the scabbard for good. About 11. P.M. we were suddenly aroused from slumber by a most lively firing of musketry and artillery about a mile to our right. Of course we were soon in fighting trim and stood waiting for orders and speculating as to the reason for the nights disturbance. Good many were of the Opinion that General Johnston was trying to breake the coil which entangled him and try to escape. Genl. Hobart sent Orderlies to assertain the cause of the exitement and soon we learned that Genl. Johnston had surrendered and the rebellion was crushed. As we were somewhat detached from the Corps, so to speak on outpost duty, we were the last to receive the wellcome news. No sooner was the news proclaimed, when the men began to blaze away with their rifles, and loaded again, and fired again partly as an endorsement of the surrender, partly as the last rites at the burial of the defunct Confederacy, and partly as the inauguration of peace and prosperity.—

April 27th. With light steps and proud bearing the men stepped of[f] this morning on the return march to Raleigh, where the army was to assemble for the march to Richmond. And well might they feel exalted and proud. After three years of untold hardships and privation, after many hard contested battles and scirmishes, victory perched on their banners, and unsullied, and unblemished should forthon wave the emblem of liberty over the land of the free. "Home, sweet home." was intonated by some one at the head of the Column and company after Comp. and Regiment after Regiment took it up, untill the air vibrated with the strains of the sweet melody. But there were allso many good reasons to temper the happy feelings. How many would inquire at home after father, husband, brother or sweetheart; how they died, and where they rested. One hundred strong healthy men the Company numbered when we left home, not a qua[r]ter of them were in the ranks now. But these reflections had to give way to speculations. Such who had no settled home would lay out elaborate plans and scheemes in what business they would engage, in what State or territory they would take up lands, etc. With such discussions time and distance passed unobserved and before we t[h]ought of it we went into Camp, having marched about thirty miles. . . .

May. 1st. At prompt 7 A.M. we started, homeward bound; drums beating, flags flying to the breeze, the men singing. Just a year ago we left Lookout Mountain for the Atlanta campain. What a difference. What immense amount of hard work had been done, what successes and tryumphs achieved, what hardships and privations endured, what immense territorry wrested from the enemy; and how many of the hundred thousand who shouldered the musket then were silent now forever. Then we went for strife and battle; to day we went in search of home, to once mor undertake the peacefull pursuit of life and happiness; to rest on our dearly earned laurels, proud in the fact that the Nation was saved from disgrace and ruin, that liberty and popular souvereignity henceforth be the ruling power in the coming great Nation. (How much the honest veterans were mistaken in the latter proposition, every observing citizen, and especially the veterans have found out by this time.)

WASHINGTON. THE GREAT PARADE

It seems our Commanders had not noticed, or did not care about Genl. Shermans Order that the marches should be easy, about 15. miles a day. Sherman himself was not with us. It certainly was nearer 30. than 15. miles we had marched to day. Exhausted and hungry we halted long after dark.

May 2d. At dawn we were astir again. During the day we passed through Oxford, which was considered by the good North Carolina people quite a big City. In one respect they were right; if broad and long streets with plenty of building room for coming generations to apropriate, constitutes a City. It seems to have been a principle with the early settlers in the southern States, that, whenever they platted a village, to allot room enough for a million of inhabitants. As the peculiar social arraingement in the southern states was not favorable for investment in City property, or for settling permanently in the city; the result usually was, that a few poor looking buildings were scattered over a large territorry, the streets grown over with rank grass and weeds, no sidewalks were known, and the large commons who in vain waited for purchasers, were taken care of by pigs, goats, chickens, and so forth. While we passed through, quite a number of returned rebel soldiers were gathered in the streets. Some of them would shake hands and wish us good speed and happy voyage, while others would frown and add all sorts of unsavory Expressions according to inclination. Of course we felt to[o] happy to resent such outburst of personal feeling, which, after all, were but natural, and replying now and then in a jocular way, went right along.

It was again an exessive long march to day, and late in the afternoon the stragling became general. If rebel cavalry had been in our rear today as [formerly] they could have made a rich harvest. I allso was oblidged to fall behind because the "break bone fever," as it was called by the men, which had bothered me much since we left Savannah returned with renewed force. It was 10. P.M. when I finally arrived in camp, but I was not the last one. Untill midnight the tired came slowly limping on in small groups.

May 3d. Expecting the same treatment to day, I held a council of war with John, which resulted in a sort of rig, or sadle on the mules which enabled us to put half the rifles of the Comp. on the mules. Reliefs were made from time to time in order that all had the same benefit. To be relieved of 13. pounds weight during a days [march] makes a great difference in endurance. The men went in the woods and cut wa[l]king-stick[s], which they designated as their reserve legs. The result was that, allthough the march was fully as long as the previous days, but two men had dropped behind from the Compagny.

On the 4th we crossed the Nottaway river and late in the night encamped in the neighborhood of Nottaway Courthouse.

On the 5th about noon we arrived at the Appomattox river where we were detained for an hour because of laying pontoons for a passage. . . .

May 6th. We were now on historic ground. Here in the vicinity it was where the final strugles between Grants and Lees armies took place. Everywhere, since we had crossed the Appomattox, we found signs of the fearfull strugle which had taken place. Scattered breastworks, trees and limbs broken and splintered by the artillery, fences down; broken, or burned wagons and ambulances dismounted cannon and cassons, and above all the number of new made graves, some with, the most withouth little head boards giving name, Comp. and Regt. were the silent witnesses of the last agonies of the dieing Confederacy. And up to the James river, to the very gates of Richmond the roads were strewn with household articles of evry description; the panic stricken people had tried to save from the supposed barbarous victors, but had abanonded them in their haste to get away. Poor, deluded people. They might have safely remained at home, for not a hair on their head would have been disturbed.

About 6. P.M. we arrived at the south banks of the James river, opposite Belle Island and a mile above Manchester, a small city opposite Richmond on the south banks of the river. We went in camp in a large pine grove which, in years gone by must have been a cottonfield, as the still traceable high drills, or ridges between the trees clearly indicated. Here we learned that the exessessive marching we had been treated to, was merely a race between the 14th and 20th Corps; instigated by the respective Corps Commanders, Genls Jeff C. Davis and Williams, to settle a dispute between them, which Corps could march the faster, and arrive first at the James river. We had the satisfaction of having beaten the 20th Corps by arriving 4. hour ahead of them. It was an unwarranted and cruel practice at best and the soldiers felt not much elated about it. We had traveled 180. mils in 6. days.

May 7th. We were informed that the Corps would remain until further orders. The 15th and 17th Corps had not arrived yet, owing to the more sensible view of their General Officers, who took easy marches according to Shermans orders. Anxious as we were to reach home, a rest was very wellcome. Any one of the man who wished to explore Manchester; or see the sights of Richmond was furnished a pass for the day, good untill 8. P.M. when they had to be back for roll call. But very few made use of the privilege th[at] day, but went bathing in the river.

WASHINGTON. THE GREAT PARADE

Being refreshed by a days rest and a good sleep I started by times on a tour of inspection, or rather investigation. Manchester is a quiet little City, but now, of course, it looked deserted and forlorn. There were plenty of stores and business places but no business was done. Why? Because, when the Confederacy Colapsed, their paper money colapsed along with it, and that was all they had. Nobody would give a dime for a ten dollar note of that stuff, exept perhaps, to keep it as a Curiosity. Besides, all trade and commerce with the northern States and the outside world had stopped years ago. Nothing but the product of the southern States was on sale, and that was very limited, as all provisions raised in the Atlantic rebel states was hardly sufficient to keep their armies from starvation. Woolen goods, calicos, silks, etc. were out of the question; Boots and shoes cost an enormous price. The people, as everywhere in the southern States, were Clad in coarse homespun. Not even a sheet of writing paper could be procured. The printing paper used was a sort of wall paper and could be printed only on one side; pencils were even more scarce than paper. At present most of the people were drawing rations from the government, the same which they so persistently sought to destroy. The people, that is the whites, were sullen and remorse, and would avoid to enter into any Conversation. After several futile attempts to make some one speak, I gave up and gathered my information from the darkies, who were talkative to the fullest extent, and whom it was difficult to stop, when once set agoing.

"On to Richmond." used to be the war cry of the grand Army of the Potomac. They went near there several times, took a look at it, and then left it alone. They finally got hold of it by taking Petersburg. It was not so difficult now. Only crossing the canal and river and the first step from of[f] the bridge landed me in the famous city. The first building I met with was the renowned "Libby Prison," a long, plain, two storied brick building, close to the bridge and river. It was just as the prisoners had left it, a month ago; filthy and dirty bejond description. There was not a single article of furniture to be seen. no chair, no table, no bedstead, or bunk. The prisoners had to sleep in the dirt on the bare floor. Even the mine, which was dug by a number of Officers during the winter 63. to 64. and through which about 150. prisoners escaped, was undisturbed. Before the war the building had been a tobacco warehouse, owned by a Mr. Libby. Across the street and half a block west, was Castle Thunder, another brick prison pen, not quite as big, but in other respects a true Copy of Libby. In these pens tens of thousands true union men had suffered untold miseries, and thousands had died without the slightest attention usually afforded to human beings. A fine example of southern chivallry and hospitality.

Disgusted with the sights, and reflections consequent, I left the pens to see some of the real City, since four years the Capital of the Confederacy. Going one block north, and looking west, a large area of burned ruins surprised me. A strip, severall block wide and extending from east to west along the south Side of the City was nothing but a heap of ashes and a lot of desolate looking ruins of stone and brick walls. The enraged rebels, when they saw the yankees could not be longer kept at bay, set the City on fire at several places and took to their heels like a pack of cowardly curs, leaving the poorer Class of people and negroes to their fate. If not General Weitzel and his division had arrived in time, the whole City probably would have been consumed. But the soldiers set to work manfully and saved all what could be saved. A darkey of whom I inquired about the origin of the fire, said he did not know as to the first origin, but he knew that, while Genl. Weitzels troops were fighting the fire, two fellows were caught in other parts of the City trying to start more fires. General Weitzel ordered them fellows to be hanged immediately, and their bodies to hang for 24. hours as a warning to others. The fellows, before they were hoisted had said that they acted under orders of Jeff Davis and the Secrataire of War, given to them just before they fled the City, but they should wait untill the yanks were in the City that it might be charged to them. Whether that is true or not, is hard to tell, anyway it did not save the fellows.

I left the burned district and went towards the heart of the City. The people seemed to be well satisfied with the new order of things. The rank rebels had most all left and only shopkeepers with empty shops and poor people were left. Among the latter were many who before the war had been well to do, but the confederacy had swallowed everything. They now cursed the bankrupt scheme and everything connected with it, but it was to[o] late now. It was indeed a bitter lesson for them.

The Capitol is a fine structure, allmost in the heart of the City. It is built on a sort of hill, overlooking nearly the whole City. A fine park with shade trees and statues surrounded it. A few streets west of the Capitol is the former headquarters of Jeff Davis. Guards were posted there to see that nothing was disturbed, or taken away. Everything was just as Jeff had left it, and everything indicated that he had left in a great hurry. Desks, drawers and doors stood open. papers, maps and books were strewn about, wearing apparel of all kind and sizes was laying around, a Major Generals uniform coat lay on the stairway. Big maps and pictures Covered the walls. I longed to take something along as a keepsake, a relique, but the Officer, who acted as cicerone was immoveable in that respect. Finally I grabbed a newspaper and told him I would keep that, if he did arrest me for it. He made no opposition and I left, sat down in the shade to investigate the price [prize]. It happened to be the Richmond Whig of April 8th 1865. the last one printed under Jeffs rule. It contained the dispatch of Genl. Lee to Jeff of April 6th notifying him that Petersburg had been taken by the Yankees, and that he (Jeff.) had now to look out for himself as Richmond was no longer a safe place for him; together with a whining article of the sad fate of the defun[c]t Confederacy, but it had the good sense to advise the people to bow peacefully under the yoke of the oppressors. I took the paper home and took good care of it, but after a few years some good friend found a chance to confiscate the same. That shabby trick I have not forgiven [y]et and do not think I ever will. It contained very interesting reading and meditations about the last agonies of the expiring Confederacy. It still cherished the hope that Lee. might be able to join Johnstons Army in North Carolina with his scattered forces, but it was more in a way of an "easy letting down" than anything Else.

From here I went to "Belle Island" the famous spot were so many thousands of union prisoners were [k]ept and starved during the war. It is situated in the midle of the James river, a short distance above, and west of the City. Whoever christened that spot "Belle Island" must have seen a mirage, or else he was an incurable crank, for it is the most desolate looking spot of barren sand and shapeless boulders I ever met with. No shed, or building, or shade of any kind. And here the poor, starved prisoners had to face the glaring sun of the summer as well, as the rain, and sleet, and incclemency of the winter. It is enough to curse and damn the entire rebel brood if one thinks of it.

May 10th. At 6. A.M. we formed in line for the trip to Washington. Before we started, Colonel Fitch called me to the front of the Regt. and handed me the comm[i]ssion as Captain. "You must not blame me," he said, "you would have had that long ago, if you had been willing to quit your Compagny." The boys gave a hearty cheer, so much so that I felt somewhat embarrassed. Our route led us through Richmond. Genl. Halleck expected, as is customary, that Shermans army should pass in Review before him. To that end he, with his staff had taken position on the balcony of the Capitol, where the army had to pass by. But Sherman, smarting [y]et under the contemptible assault, Halleck had played on him just before Johnstons surrender, ordered the Corps commanders not to pay any attention to Genl. Halleck, but march by, arms at shoulder shift and route step. Genl. Sherman himself, at the head of the army, did not even salute Genl Halleck. When the latter saw how matters stood, he quickly withdrew. . . . [4]

The march to Washington was a severe one. Again it was conducted on the race plan. During four years both armies had repeatedly crossed and recrossed the State, and had left desolation and ruin in their wake, but many of their people were defiant [y]et. One day we stopped at the roadside to make Coffee. Near by was a fine looking building. A pump stood in sight and many of the men went there to get a cool drink of water. Among them was Lieut. Col. Walker. Two midle aged ladies stood on the floor of the Veranda. Walker, waiting his turn to be helped to a drink, inquired of the woman if they were not glad the war was ended and we could be friends again. "What! friends?" one of them replied. "No never! We never can be friends with the yankees. You have beaten us now but you can not subdue us; never."—"Oh, come, come, now" Walker replied laughing. "we did not want to subdue you, we only wanted you to stick to your contract." That rattled the woman still more and she began to wind of[f] a long string of ugly names and abuses on the yankees to the great delight of the men. Finally, the woman having exhausted herself, Walker said: "Nay, my dear ladies, you cannot deceive me. I am sure if you were yet in your rosy days, you would not hesitate to take one of those fine boys to your bosom." That was to[o] much. The allusion to their doubtfull age was more than their temper could stand, and amidts the laughter and shouts of the soldiers they ran into the house, slamming the door behind them.

Our route brought us in the neighborhood of the former battlefield of the wilderness. Good many of the Officers and soldiers wished to see the grounds and the lay of the memorable battleground where Grant and Lee's armies fought so desperate without any decisive result, and of which so much has been talked and written about. One day was set apart for that purpose and any one who wished to go could do so. The great majority remained in camp to nurse their tired limbs. I went along to the bloody field. The traces of the contest of a year ago Could easy be found. Trees broken or splintered; the places where batteries had been in position, here and there an attempt to build breastworks; and above all, the numerous ridges and hills where the fallen heroes were bedded for their Eternal rest. Everything denoted that a fearfull struggle had taken place here. But in

WASHINGTON. THE GREAT PARADE

general we found the battlefield no more of a wilderness than we had found them in numbers of battles out west and south. I for my part would rather fight on the wilderness battlefield, than in the Cedarswamps at Stone river, or in the swamps and briars below Kenesaw Mountain, Georgia, or in the swamps of the Pocotaligo and Tullafinny rivers in South Carolina. Battlefields seldom are, or never can be made for convenience sake. On the field of the first Bull Run battle we allso stopped half a day to look over the situations. It is no wonder our new, three months soldiers met with such a severe repulse here, because, the high, craggy, brush covered banks of the crooked Bull Run furnished an exellent natural line of defense, which our troops were ordered to carry from open, unsheltered fields. Veterans might have made short work and a brilliant success of it, but for new troops, Officers and men alike, it was a severe task.

On the 18th of May our Corps arrived at the south bank of the Potomac, two miles below Alexandria where we went in Camp, the 15th 17th and 20th Corps arriving the next day. Here, a long lost soldier, whom I never had seen, but whose name had been borne on the rolls of the Comp, appeared hale and hearty, and reported for duty. His name was George Demuth [Demouth].[5] He with a lot of others had been drafted in the spring of 1864. and assigned to the first Wis. Ift. Rgt. During a scirmish near Kenesaw Mountain in June he suddenly had left the lines, saying that he was wounded. Since that time nothing was heard of him. When in Sept. the recruits of the first Wisconsin Regt. were transferred to our Regt. he was assigned to my Comp. In the remarks of his descriptive roll it read: "Absent without leave since June 16th 1864." His comrades who had been in line with him would not believe that he had been wounded. I asked him where and in what hospital he had been. He said he had been in no hospital; that the surgeon had given him leave to go home. That was simply a made up story, because Every surgeon had to report to the proper Comp. Commander the names of all soldiers in hospitals, on leave, transferred or discharged. As he was carried on the rolls now as a deserter, I was obliged to put him under arrest and prefer charges against him. If he could clear himself then before a Court martial he would be all right. That my suspicion was correct was prooved by him a fortnight later. While we were in Camp near Georgetown a number of men went to a creek a half a mile off to do some washing. Demouth asked for leave to go along with them. I appointed two men to keep watch of him and bring him back. But they returned without him. He had given them the slip while washing. I suspected they did not care much about him, neither did I. It saved me a lot of trouble and prevented him from ever drawing a cent of pay or pension.

On the 20th severall of us made a visit to Alexandria which is conspicuous for the figure it cut at the beginning of the Rebellion. From the start it was a rabiate [rabid] secesh nest. Since the rebels had fired the first gun at Fort Sumter, a rebel flag had proudly waved over the City from the top of the Ebbit house, allmost in sight of Washington [until] Early in May 1861. . . . Since that time Alexandria was held and occupied by the yankees who, it can easyly be immagined, kept close watch of the turbulant Element and several of the most unruly were arrested and confined in the old Capitol prison at Washington, or at Fort Hamilton in New York harbour. The rebels, not liking these proceedings, had left one by one untill there was nothing left but the poorer Class who were unable to get away. So it came about that in the Course of four years, the City had been converted in a military Post and supply depot; the buildings being used for hospitals, barracks, offices and store rooms. The inhabitants, besides the garrison, were mostly negroes and poor whites who were employed by the government. Having looked over the little City we arrived at the wharfs, where several steamers were ready to leave for Washington. As that was only 6. miles distant, and being the hub about which the complicated machiniry of the United States turned, we concluded to take a look at the Elephant and went abord one of the Steamers.

On inquiry we were informed that the boat would stay only an hour at Washington and return. That suited us exactly and half an hour later we were landed near the Navy yard, East of Washington. That is a big institution where thousands of men were as busy as bees in a hive. As soon as we set foot on land we noticed that all shops and buildings were draped in mourning; all flags were at half mast in memory of the martyr president Lincoln. Our calculation to see Washington was a total failure, for we were not half through with the sights in the navy yard when the bell of the steamer reminded us it was time to return. We did not dare to stay over night in Washington, because we had no leave, and worse, no money. We cast a longing look at the immense dome of the Capitol, which rose on a hill half a mile to the west, and went abord.

May 23d. Successively the different Corps of Shermans Army had Arrived and were encamped on the south bank of the Potomac from below Alexandria to the Arlington hights opposite and south of Washington. Today we received orders to be ready by to morrow morning for the final grand

WASHINGTON. THE GREAT PARADE

parade through Washington. We were to go in the same manner as we had gone through Georgia and the Carolinas; Packmules and all included. That pleased the soldiers immensely and our only regret was, that we did not look quite so ragged now, as we did when we emerged from the Carolina swamps and briars at Goldsboro, North Carolina, two Months ago.

May 24th. At 5. A.M. we started for the grand parade, which was to be our last march. It was 8. miles to the long bridge, which leads across the Potomac river and flats, and is a mile and a half long. As our Corps was the last in line of march, we had to wait here over an hour untill the other three Corps had passed. Finally at 10. A.M. we were on the move again. We passed by Capitol hill on the west side of which Pensilvania Avenue begins. The Avenue is very broad, perhaps the broadest in the United States, and stretches in a straight line from the Capitol to, and past, the White House. I do not know how long it is, but it seemed to me to be several miles. Its width enabled us to march in full Comp. front. The avenue was filled with people from one end to the other, and from the broad sidewalks to the top of the roofs. The news, that the two grand armies of Grant and Sherman would pass in Review through Washington was spread through the papers, and had drawn people from afar and near, anxious to have a look at the old war worn veterans. The army of the Potomac had passed through the day before; but the people wanted to see Shermans army, Shermans "Bummers," who had tramped and fought their way from the Ohio to the gulf and from there to Washington and never turning their back to the foe. The people would not stop cheering, and flowers and greens were thrown so profusely on the veterans as to cover the avenue hand high with them. The pack mules especially were of uncommon interest. No other army had ever used them; nor did they have any use for them, as they allways could use wagons for transportation.

At the white house, a large, terrace like platform, or revieewing stand, had been erected where President Johnson and his Cabinet, the foureign Ambassadors, the members of the supreeme Court, many Genls of the army, Senators and Gouverneurs of States and other persons of high rank and qualification (?) were seated, well intermixed with ladies and even— Babies. Here, Genl. Sherman disclosed a marked trait of his character. Riding at the head of the army and arriving opposite the Presidents seat, he saluted, dismounted, left his horse in the care of an aid and mounted the steps to the platform. The President and all the people on the platform had risen from their seats as a mark of respect. The President advanced a

step and shock hands with Sherman; thee members of the Cabinet and the
Genls. following one by one did the same. Secretaire of war Stanton, who
was allso present, advanced and offered his hand. But Sherman feigned not
to see him, but turned and took the seat next to the President, which had
been reserved for him. At first sight this may seem a small, spitefull revenge, but when one considers the mean, contemptible tricks Stanton had
played on Sherman, the matter appears in a different light.[6]

So far everything was bright and lovely; but a silent, irrepressible gloom
seemed to be cast over, and pervade through the Ceremony. Why? Through
all the decorations, tryumphal arches, wreaths and guirlands, the sombre,
dark draperies in memory of the assassinated Lincoln, was, like the sceleton
in the cupboad, visible everywhere. It would and could not be surpr[e]ssed.
That hero, with unswerving patriotism and steady hand, had guided the
ship of the nation safe through the wild waves and treacherous breakers of
treason and rebellion, was like John Brown, "mouldering in the grave," but
his soul will march along for ever and ever.—

It takes quiet a little time to pass 72,000. men by a given point, the
platoons at 12. steps distance, Cavallery and Artillery included. It is therefore no wonder that it was past 4. P.M. when the last platoon marched past
the reviewing stand. The day had been very hot. Since 5. in the morning we
had been on our legs; it was no wonder that we felt considerable played out.
It was therefore that, with a sense of great relief and satisfaction, we heard
the wellcome order; "Halt! Right dress! Stake arms!" That was about 2.
miles west of Washington near Georgetown. It had been our last march;
the last time we staked arms in the service of a new born nation.

The next morning at roll call Orders were read for the guidance of the
troops while here. Half of the troops might obtain passes alternately every
day to go to Washington, but were warned to keep straight or they might
get into trouble, which some of them did nevertheless. It was well that
money was scarce among the men or good many of them would have overtaxed their normal powers of endurance in celebrating the successfull termination of the war. . . .

The following day I went to Washington to look round a little. Of course
the City was full to overflowing with sightseeing soldiers. I soon found that
one day would be like a drop in an Empty bucket. The white house, the
State and Treasure departments and the world renowned Smithsonian Institute could be merely looked over the first day. Arriving in camp at night
I found an order that on the next day all arms, ammunition, accourtrements,

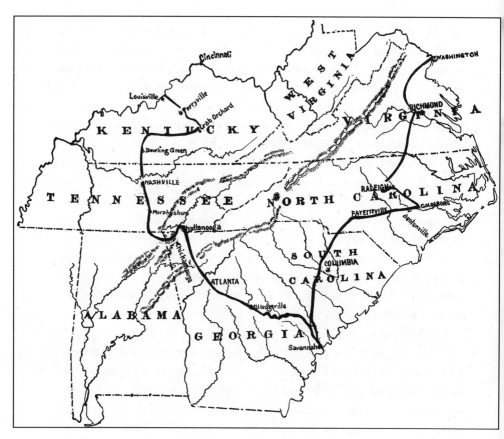

"March of the Twenty-first Wisconsin Infantry." From Fitch, *Echoes of the Civil War*. (Courtesy State Historical Society of Wisconsin)

Camp and garrison Equippage, horses, mules etc. had to be turned over to the Ordnance and Quartermaster Departments. That was a wellcome Order but I felt sorry for my gray mule. I had been in hopes to be allowed to take it home with me but that was no go; "the mule had done its duty, the mule must go." . . .

Preparing the final muster out rolls and discharges was now the next step. Not all men were discharged; only veterans and such whoose term of service [would] expire during the next three months. In our Regt. that meant only such men who had enlisted in the original organisation in Aug. 1862. Recruits and drafted men were transferred to the 3d. Wisconsin Regt. and sent to Louisville to await further orders. Of the original Volunteers there were not many left in the Regt. Of my Comp. only 18. were left from the one hundred who left Camp Bragg in 1862. for Dixie land to add their mite to suppress the rebellion. Only 7. of the 18. had never been absent from the

Comp. during the three years. They certainly deserve to be mentioned here.
They were: Lieut. L. C. Waite, Orderly Sergt. Joseph D. Holden, Sergt
Sylvester Greeley. Sergt. Chs. Lymer. Corp. James P. Walker, Drummer
Harold Galpin and Priv. Spencer Orlup. and finally myself. Of the balance
of the 100. 27. found their resting place in southern soil; 37. were discharged
on account of wounds or other disability, 16. were transferred to the Invalid
Corps on account of disability for field duty, and 2 were transferred to the
Engeneur Corps. Recruits and drafted men transferred to the 3d Regt. num-
bered 45.[7]

June 8th was an all important day for us. It restored us to citizenship and
liberty. At 8. A.M. we received our discharge documents black on white.
The government had no further military claim on us. All what remained to
do now was the transportation home and the final pay and muster out. Pay
was due us from the 1st of Nov. 1864. We were informed that on the next
day we were to start by rail for Milwaukee. The men nearly ran wild with
joy and the cheering and dancing did not stop untill they were exhausted.

Notes

∾

INTRODUCTION

1. "Claimant's Statement: Case of John H. Otto, no. 419905," dated July 30, 1884; Soldier's Certificate no. 288806: Can no. 5793, Bundle no. 29. Records of the Adjutant General's Office, 1780s–1917 (Record Group [hereafter RG] 94): Records of the Record and Pension Office, National Archives, Washington, D.C.

2. Soldier's Certificate no. 288806: Can no. 5793, Bundle no. 29. Records of the Adjutant General's Office, 1780s–1917 (RG 94): Records of the Record and Pension Office, National Archives, Washington, D.C.

3. Copy of Death Record: John Henry Otto, Wood County Register of Deeds, State of Wisconsin Department of Health—Bureau of Vital Statistics.

4. Michael H. Fitch, *Echoes of the Civil War as I Hear Them* (New York: R. F. Reno, 1905), 96.

5. Mitford M. Matthews, ed. *A Dictionary of Americanisms on Historical Principles* (Chicago: Univ. of Chicago Press, 1951), 2: 1097.

I. THE ORGANIZATION OF COMPANY D, 21ST REGIMENT OF WISCONSIN VOLUNTEER INFANTRY

1. Maj. Frederick Schumacher of Milwaukee, Wisconsin, enlisted July 16, 1862. He had served as a captain in Company F of the 6th Infantry Regiment prior to his commission in the 21st Infantry. He was killed in action on October 8, 1862, at the battle of Chaplin Hills (Perryville), in Kentucky. Wisconsin Adjutant General's Office, *Regimental Muster and Descriptive Roll (Blue Books), 1861–1865*, 59 vols., ca. 1885 (ser. 1142); and *Regimental Muster and Descriptive Roll (Red Books), 1861–1865*, 57 vols., 1866 (ser. 1144), Records of the 6th and 21st Infantry; Archives Division, State Historical Society of Wisconsin, Madison, Wisconsin. Series 1144 (Red Books)

was compiled during the war and shows the name, rank, birth place, age, occupation, marital status, date, place, and by whom enlisted, term of service, physical description, date and place of mustering in, name of mustering officer, town or ward and county of residence, town or ward and congressional district to which credited, and remarks. Series 1142 (Blue Books) is a revised and corrected version of Series 1144, compiled by the Adjutant General ca. 1886, from sources then available, many of which no longer exist. Soldiers' identities were taken from their respective Regimental Muster Rolls; henceforth both red and blue books are cited as RMR, followed by the regiment or regiments in which the soldiers served.

2. Capt. John Jewett Jr. of Appleton, Wisconsin, received his commission August 26, 1862. He died of disease November 21, 1862, near Mitchellsville, Tennessee. RMR, 21st Infantry.

3. The 26th Wisconsin Infantry was organized under the command of Col. William H. Jacobs at Camp Sigel, Milwaukee, Wisconsin. The camp was named in honor of Franz Sigel, who was instrumental in rallying Germans to fight on the Union side. "I fights mit Sigel" was its slogan. The 26th Infantry was just over a thousand strong when it was officially mustered into U.S. service on September 17, 1862, and almost 90 percent of the regiment's members were of German heritage. E. B. Quiner, *The Military History of Wisconsin: A Record of the Civil and Military Patriotism of the State, In the War For the Union* (Chicago, 1866), 765. For further information on Sigel and the 26th Wisconsin, see James S. Pula, *The Sigel Regiment: A History of the 26th Wisconsin Volunteer Infantry, 1862–1865* (Campbell, Calif.: Savas, 1998), and Stephen D. Engle, *Yankee Dutchman: The Life of Franz Sigel* (Baton Rouge: Univ. of Louisiana Press), 1999.

4. Capt. Henry Turner of Appleton, Wisconsin, enlisted August 7, 1862. He was severely wounded during the Atlanta campaign and resigned his commission March 19, 1865. RMR, 21st Infantry.

5. Capt. John Henry Otto enlisted August 12, 1862, at Appleton, Wisconsin. He progressed through the enlisted ranks from third sergeant to first sergeant. He was officially commissioned as a second lieutenant on November 22, 1862, and received his promotion to first lieutenant November 21, 1864. He received a promotion to the rank of captain on April 27, 1865, but was not mustered in as such. Ibid. Twenty-two years after the war, on December 14, 1887, Captain Otto's service record was amended by the secretary of war. He was officially mustered into service at the rank of captain from April 27, 1865, and mustered out and honorably dismissed as a captain as of June 8, 1865. *Special Orders no. 290*, Wisconsin Adjutant General's Office, *Records of Civil War Regiments, 1861–1900* (ser. 1200), 259 archives boxes, State Historical Society of Wisconsin, Archives Division, Madison, Wisconsin, box 109, folder 6. (These records will be cited hereafter as WAGR, ser. 1200, followed by the box and folder number.)

6. Cpl. Amos Lawrence of Appleton, Wisconsin, enlisted August 8, 1862. He was absent from the company when it was mustered out of active military service. RMR, 21st Infantry.

7. Cpl. William H. Wood of Appleton, Wisconsin, enlisted August 11, 1862. He transferred to the 3d Wisconsin Infantry, June 8, 1865. Sgt. John Dey of Greenville, Wisconsin, enlisted August 11, 1862. He was taken prisoner at Chaplin Hills and was wounded at Atlanta. He mustered out of service May 19, 1865. Ibid.

8. Col. Benjamin J. Sweet of Chilton, Wisconsin, received his commission July 12, 1862. He had served as a lieutenant colonel in the 6th Wisconsin prior to receiving his commission in the 21st. He was severely wounded at the battle of Chaplin Hills and resigned his commission on September 8, 1863. Maj. Michael H. Fitch of Prescott, Wisconsin, received his commission as a major on December 19, 1862. He later became the colonel of the 21st. Quartermaster Henry C. Hamilton of Two Rivers, Wisconsin, enlisted July 22, 1862. He resigned his commission May 23, 1863. *RMR*, 6th and 21st Infantry.

9. These "Belgian rifles" are very likely the same "European muskets of uncouth pattern, which the volunteers will not touch" described by General Sherman in his *Memoirs*, as having been furnished to his troops, and refused, nearly a year earlier: "We had received only about twelve thousand Belgian muskets, which the Governor of Pennsylvania had refused, as had also the Governor of Ohio, but which had been adjudged good enough for Kentucky." William Tecumseh Sherman, *Memoirs of General W. T. Sherman* (New York: Library of America, 1990), 219, 222.

10. Capt. Fred W. Borcherdt of Manitowoc, Wisconsin, was commissioned to first lieutenant in Company D on November 22, 1862. He became the acting adjutant on October 1, 1863, and attained the rank of captain in Company E on November 21, 1864. *RMR*, 21st Infantry. Additional information on Borcherdt and other soldiers from Manitowoc can be found in Kerry A. Trask, *Fire Within: A Civil War Narrative from Wisconsin* (Kent, Ohio: Kent State Univ. Press, 1995).

11. First Sgt. Charles L. Fay of Appleton, Wisconsin, enlisted August 11, 1862. He was severely wounded October 8, 1862, at the battle of Chaplin Hills and was discharged on November 1, 1862, due to wounds received in action. Sgt. Hamlin B. Williams of Appleton, Wisconsin, enlisted August 15, 1862. He was wounded in the battle of Chaplin Hills and was discharged on December 14, 1862, due to wounds received in action. Sgt. Theodore Clark of Ellington, Wisconsin, enlisted August 8, 1862. He died of disease March 4, 1863, at Murfreesboro, Tennessee. *RMR*, 21st Infantry.

2. PREPARING FOR ACTUAL WARFARE

1. In late August and early September Bragg left the Chattanooga area and moved toward middle Kentucky. Crossing the Tennessee River with approximately fifty thousand troops, he moved toward Waldon's Ridge. Buell waited near McMinnville with approximately thirty thousand troops ready for deployment and an additional fifteen thousand men on garrison and guard duty. Bragg's progress toward Louisville and Cincinnati, coupled with Buell's timid policy of "watch and wait," created alarm in both cities. Stephen D. Engle, *Don Carlos Buell: Most Promising of All* (Chapel Hill: Univ. of North Carolina Press, 1999), 276–83.

2. Pvt. Phillip Rose of Ellington, Wisconsin, enlisted August 14, 1862, and was discharged August 28, 1863. *RMR*, 21st Infantry.

3. Pvt. Antoine H. Van Stratum of Appleton, Wisconsin, enlisted August 15, 1862, and was transferred to the Veterans Reserve Corps on September 30, 1863. Ibid.

4. Pvt. Walker J. Fish of Appleton, Wisconsin, enlisted August 15, 1862, and was discharged from military service September 24, 1863. Ibid.

5. Pvt. James H. Orr of Appleton, Wisconsin, enlisted August 14, 1862, and was hospitalized for what was believed to be insanity on May 8, 1863. Ibid.

6. Cpl. George R. Nye of Hortonia, Wisconsin, enlisted August 14, 1862, and died December 31, 1862, at Covington, Kentucky, due to disease. Pvt. William B. Nye of Greenville, Wisconsin, enlisted August 14, 1862, and died February 4, 1863, at Murfreesboro, Tennessee, due to disease. Ibid.

7. The 24th Illinois records list 1st Lt. August Steffens of Appleton, Wisconsin, who enlisted in June 1861 and was promoted to the rank of captain in Company I. *Illinois Adjutant-General's Office: Report of the Adjutant General's Office, State of Illinois, Containing Reports for the Years 1861–1866*, revised by Brig. General J. W. Vance, 9 vols. (Springfield, Ill.: H. W. Rokker, 1886), 2: 318. (Illinois soldiers have been identified from the above source, where they can be found listed under their respective regiments. Cited hereafter as *RAGO, Illinois*.)

8. Pvt. Frank Stowe was accidentally wounded at Louisville, Kentucky, and was granted a surgeon's certificate of disability and discharged from active military service on July 22, 1864. Sgt. Curtis Mitchell of Bovina, Wisconsin, enlisted August 12, 1862. *RMR*, 21st Infantry.

9. Col. Henry A. Hambright of Lancaster, Pennsylvania, was authorized to recruit a regiment of infantry in August 1861. He mustered into the U.S. service as colonel of the 79th Pennsylvania on October 18, 1861, and mustered out on July 12, 1865. Samuel Bates, *History of the Pennsylvania Volunteers, 1861–1865*, 25 vols. (Wilmington, N.C.: Broadfoot, 1993), 4: 1075, 1083.

10. In an attempt to escape political oppression, German refugees flocked to the United States after the unsuccessful revolution of 1848. They fervently believed in a philosophy of political idealism and social radicalism, based on a violent aversion to tyranny. Along with their political philosophy came their Old World customs and social traditions. One of these traditions was that of the fifty-year-old "Turner Society." The Turner Society fostered nationalism and patriotism through a program of disciplined physical training and gymnastics. The German word *turnen* means "to perform gymnastics" and is believed to have evolved into the name "Turner." When the immigrants landed in America, they quickly reformed their society and became involved in the country's politics, evincing a strong antislavery sentiment. The German Turner Society of Wisconsin recruited thousands of German immigrants during the war. The predominately German 9th and 26th Infantry Regiments were recruited from the German immigrant population of eastern Wisconsin. Richard N. Current, *The History of Wisconsin: The Civil War Era, 1848–1873*, 2 vols. (Madison: State Historical Society of Wisconsin, 1976), 2: 306–8.

11. "Genl. Buel" is actually Gen. Don Carlos Buell, born in Lowell, Ohio, and a member of the West Point class of 1841. General Buell was removed from command on two separate occasions. The first was a temporary penalty for not attacking Bragg at Munfordville, Kentucky. The second was permanent, on October 30, 1862, for his disastrous handling of the battle of Perryville. Engle, *Don Carlos Buell*, 280–83.

12. On the first of October, Bragg's army was at Bardstown, and Kirby Smith's army at Frankfort. Bragg was not retreating toward the Cumberland Gap but was at Lexington with Smith, occupied with preparations to install a Confederate government over Kentucky. The inauguration took place October 4 at Danville. Bragg's and Smith's armies were not united before the battle of Perryville; it was only on

October 11, 1862, after Bragg's retreat from Perryville, that they joined, at Camp Dick Robinson near Bryantsville. On October 12 Bragg decided to retreat his forces through the Cumberland Gap. Kenneth W. Noe, *Perryville: This Grand Havoc of Battle* (Lexington: Univ. Press of Kentucky, 2001), 100–106.

3. PROGRESS AND INCIDENTS OF OUR FIRST CAMPAIGN

1. Pvt. Richard Baker of Grand Chute, Wisconsin, enlisted August 8, 1862, and was killed in action at the battle of Chaplin Hills on October 8, 1862. Pvt. Walton Baker, the son of Richard Baker, enlisted August 12, 1862, and died of disease on December 11, 1862, at Mitchellsville, Tennessee. Pvt. Ephraim Walker of Greenville, Wisconsin, enlisted August 11, 1862. His brother Cpl. James P. Walker, also of Greenville, enlisted August 15, 1862. Both mustered out of military service June 8, 1865. *RMR*, 21st Infantry.

2. Maj. Gen. Lovell Harrison Rousseau was born near Stanford, Lincoln County, Kentucky, on August 4, 1818. He studied law at Lexington and moved to Indiana, where he was elected to the state legislature. In 1860 he moved back to Kentucky, where he was elected senator. He became a major general on October 22, 1862, and served the Union throughout the war. Ezra J. Warner, *Generals in Blue: Lives of the Union Commanders* (Baton Rouge: Louisiana State Univ. Press, 1964), 412–13.

3. Pvt. Braton Newell of Freedom, Wisconsin, enlisted August 12, 1862. He died of disease November 19, 1862, near Mitchellsville, Tennessee. Pvt. Foster Pearson of Appleton, Wisconsin, enlisted August 11, 1862. He died of disease March 13, 1863, at Murfreesboro, Tennessee. *RMR*, 21st Infantry.

4. A slightly different account of this incident is given by Col. (then Lt. Col.) Michael H. Fitch in *Echoes of the Civil War as I Hear Them*, 55–56.

5. Cpl. August Pierrelee of Appleton, Wisconsin, enlisted August 12, 1862. He was wounded May 14, 1864, at the battle of Resaca, Georgia. *RMR*, 21st Infantry.

4. THE BATTLE OF PERRYVILLE, OR CHAPLIN HILLS

1. Sgt. Charles Lymer of Appleton, Wisconsin, enlisted August 14, 1862, and mustered out of military service June 8, 1865. *RMR*, 21st Infantry.

2. A description of the cornfield battle is given in Fitch, *Echoes of the Civil War*, 53–64.

3. Capt. David Stone did not serve with the 4th Kentucky Battery. He was actually in command of the 1st Kentucky Light Artillery, Battery A, during the battle of Perryville. Capt. Asahel K. Bush, whose battery was posted alongside Stone, commanded the Fourth Battery of the Indiana Light Artillery. Kenneth A. Hafendorfer, *Perryville: The Battle for Kentucky*, 2d ed. (Utica, Ky.: McDowell, 1991), 445.

4. Capt. Asahel K. Bush, Indiana Light Artillery, Fourth Battery, lost three killed and eight wounded at Perryville; Capt. David Stone, 1st Kentucky Light Artillery, Battery A, lost three killed, nine wounded, and one missing. Ibid.

5. In January of 1863 Capt. D. C. Stone of the 1st Kentucky Artillery, Battery A, was brought before a court-martial on four charges. The first charge, "Violation of

the 52d Article of War," had to do with his conduct at Perryville. The specification read: "The said Capt. D. C. Stone did during the battle of Chaplin Hills on the 8th day of October 1862 and whilst his battery was hotly engaged with the enemy, go to the rear, between the lines of limbers and caissons of his battery, a position sheltered from the fire of the enemy, and did there, through fear, lie down upon the ground, and did remain in that attitude for some minutes, that is to say, twenty minutes more or less." Captain Stone was found not guilty of this charge but guilty of three other charges not related to his conduct at Perryville and was dishonorably dismissed from the service. On May 18, 1863, President Lincoln removed the disability laid on Captain Stone by his court-martial, but Stone was unsuccessful in his attempt to be restored to the command of his battery. He accepted a commission in the 5th U.S. Cavalry and served through the end of the war, mustering out in the spring of 1866. Court-martial file for Capt. David Stone 1st Bat. of Kent. Light Arty. (File LL-204), General Court Martial Files, Judge Advocate General (Army), RG 153, National Archives, Washington, D.C.

6. *RMR*, 21st Infantry, and *WAGR*, ser. 1200 have no listing for this soldier.

7. Col. John C. Starkweather described this phase of the battle in his after-action report to Gen. William S. Rosecrans: "I immediately advanced 1st Wisconsin to front supported by oblique fire from 79th Penn and with cannister from my artillery held such position until many of the artillery horses were killed and [the] balance became unmanageable creating such confusion that proper discharges could not be continued. Other regts on my right were at this time retiring and being unable to obtain any support for them I ordered the 79th Penn, 24th Ill. & 1st Wis. to hold their positions while Stone's Battery of four guns & Bush's Battery of two guns (all that was manageable) were retired to a new and safer position. The retirement was made in good order & the fire from the artillery again opened. A part of the 1st Wis. then charged to the front capturing the colors of the 1st Tenn the fire from the 79th & 24th Ill held the enemy in check while the balance of the 1st Wis took by hand every remaining gun and caisson from the field." After Action Report of Colonel John C. Starkweather, October 11, 1862, from the headquarters of the Twenty-eighth Brigade, Third Division. Directed to Gen. W. S. Rosecrans. *WAGR*, ser. 1200. Records of the 1st Wisconsin Infantry, box 3, folder 1, Reports. The guns that were removed from the field by the 1st Wisconsin were from the 4th Indiana Light Artillery, commanded by A. K. Bush. Hafendorfer, *Perryville*, 312.

8. The regimental records do not list an H. A. Bennett. They do list a James H. Bennett, who enlisted August 14, 1862, and was transferred to the Veterans Reserve Corps, November 1, 1863. Pvt. Dorset S. Smith of Appleton, Wisconsin, enlisted August 15, 1862. He was transferred to the Veterans Reserve Corps on May 1, 1864, and mustered out June 8, 1865. Pvt. Remick Knowles of Freedom, Wisconsin, enlisted August 11, 1862. He was taken prisoner of war on December 30, 1862, on the Jefferson Pike. He was transferred to the 155th Company, Second Battalion, Veterans Reserve Corps, June 30, 1865, at Nashville, Tennessee, under General Order 116. *RMR*, 21st Infantry.

9. Maj. Gen. Alexander McCook commanded the First Army Corps of which Brigadier General Rousseau's Third Division was a part at the battle of Perryville. Hafendorfer, *Perryville*, 444.

10. Pvt. Charles Herb of Black Creek, Wisconsin, enlisted August 13, 1862, and mustered out May 15, 1865. Ibid.

11. Pvt. Charles Buck of Dale, Wisconsin, enlisted August 15, 1862, and mustered out June 8, 1865. Sgt. Sylvester Greeley of Ellington, Wisconsin, enlisted August 9, 1862, and mustered out June 8, 1865. Pvt. John Buboltz of Maple Creek, Wisconsin, enlisted August 14, 1862. He was wounded at the battle of Chaplin Hills and taken prisoner of war at the battle of Stone's River, Tennessee. Ibid.

12. The OR gives the following casualty figures for the 21st Wisconsin at Perryville: killed, 38; wounded, 103; missing, 56; total, 197. Hafendorfer, *Perryville*, 445. An anonymous history of the 21st Wisconsin found in the WAGR, ser. 1200, box 106, folder 1 (cited hereafter as "History of 21st Wisconsin"), gives the 21st's losses at Perryville as 42 killed, 101 wounded, 36 missing, total 179. Colonel Starkweather's report (cited in note 6 above) gives figures of 41 killed, 101 wounded, 15 missing, and 21 prisoners, a total of 178 out of 663 engaged.

13. Cpl. Sanford W. Rexford of Ellington, Wisconsin, enlisted August 13, 1862. He was wounded in action at the battle of Chaplin Hills. He mustered out June 8, 1865. RMR, 21st Infantry.

5. IN WHICH WE CHASE BRAGG AGAIN, WHICH AMOUNTS TO NOTHING

1. Brig. Gen. Felix Kirk Zollicoffer, C.S.A., was killed under unusual circumstances on January 19, 1862, by Brig. Gen. Speed Smith Fry, U.S.A., during the battle of Logan's Cross Roads (Mill Springs, Kentucky). Fry positioned his men near a woodlot containing a fence adjoining the Mill Springs Road. To his front was an open field, over which the Confederate attack pushed a portion of the Union troops. Because Fry could not properly observe the Confederate lines due to battlefield conditions, he moved slightly forward of the stone fence. He was approached by a mounted rider. Dense smoke obscured the rider's identity until he exchanged several shots with Fry and several nearby soldiers. The rider was fatally shot and soon identified as Zollicoffer. Robert Underwood Johnson and Clarence Clough Buel, eds., *Battles and Leaders of the Civil War*, 4 vols. (Secaucus, N.J.: Book Sales, 1985), 1: 387–92.

2. Cpl. George J. Rawson of Hortonville, Wisconsin, enlisted August 9, 1862. He was wounded May 14, 1864, at the battle of Resaca, Georgia, and was sent to Madison, Wisconsin, where he died of his wounds on March 8, 1865. Pvt. Henry Knowles of Freedom, Wisconsin, enlisted August 8, 1862. He was taken prisoner at the battle of Chickamauga and sent to Andersonville Prison, where he died on October 11, 1864. RMR, 21st Infantry.

3. Pvt. Eleanor H. Gilbert of Appleton, Wisconsin, enlisted August 15, 1862, and was captured during the battle of Chickamauga on September 20, 1863. He was absent from the regiment when it mustered out of service. Ibid.

4. Gen. John Hunt Morgan, C.S.A., was in command of the new 2d Kentucky Cavalry during the first of his raids. It included Kentuckians, Georgia partisans, Texas Rangers, and Tennessee partisans. Morgan left Knoxville, Kentucky, on July 4, 1862, and entered the area of Tomkinsville, Kentucky, around July 9. Having cap-

tured several companies of Union cavalry at Tompkinsville, he continued his raid, capturing Glasgow on the 10th and Lebanon on the 11th, and traveling as far north as Cynthiana. The political fallout was immediate. The Lincoln administration called General Halleck to Washington and admonished him; General Buell was also rebuked for his role in the Union defense. General Morgan would lead two other Kentucky raids, as well as his famous raid of July 1863 into Ohio. The culmination of the Ohio and Indiana raid was the capture of Morgan and his cavalry by Union troops on July 26, 1863, near West Point, Ohio. Morgan was sent to the Ohio Penitentiary, from which he escaped on November 26. He rejoined the Confederacy and was subsequently tracked down and killed in action on September 4, 1864, at Greenville, Tennessee. James A. Ramage, *Rebel Raider: The Life of General John Hunt Morgan* (Lexington: Univ. Press of Kentucky, 1986), 91–106, 170–82, 226–44.

5. Pvt. John Molitor of Appleton, Wisconsin, enlisted August 14, 1862. He received a surgeon's certificate of disability and was discharged December 31, 1862. Cpl. Maurice F. Grunert of Ellington, Wisconsin, enlisted August 13, 1862, and mustered out of service May 16, 1865. RMR, 21st Infantry.

6. Lt. Col. Harrison C. Hobart of Chilton, Wisconsin, was commissioned on July 22, 1862. He served as a lieutenant colonel and colonel in the field and staff unit of the Twenty-first Infantry. He was breveted to brigadier general of volunteers on January 12, 1865, and mustered out of service on June 8, 1865. Capt. John C. Goodrich, Company A, 1st Wisconsin, was commissioned as a first lieutenant August 28, 1861, and was promoted to captain on September 13, 1861. He was assigned to temporary duty commanding the 21st Infantry on October 10, 1862, by order of Gen. John C. Starkweather of the 1st Infantry. Goodrich returned to the 1st Infantry in December 1862 and was assigned to the regimental field and staff. Ibid., 21st and 1st Infantry.

7. In the 1859 Wisconsin gubernatorial election Republican candidate Alexander W. Randall defeated Democrat Harrison C. Hobart with approximately 52 percent of the total votes cast. Richard Nelson Current, *The History of Wisconsin: The Civil War Era, 1848–1873* (Stevens Point, Wis.: Worzalla, 1976), 2: 272–75.

8. Pvt. Amazie Pollock of Freedom, Wisconsin, enlisted August 11, 1862. He was granted a surgeon's certificate of disability and discharged on March 18, 1863. Pvt. John W. Knowles, also of Freedom, enlisted August 12, 1862, and was discharged February 13, 1863, due to a disability. He was a brother of Henry and Remick Knowles. Pvt. David W. Peebles of Ellington, Wisconsin, enlisted August 9, 1862, and died of disease January 6, 1863, at Nashville. Pvt. Thomas Simpson of Grand Chute, Wisconsin, enlisted August 12, 1862, and died of disease January 19, 1863, at Nashville. RMR, 21st Infantry.

9. Surgeon Samuel J. Carolin of Fond du Lac, Wisconsin, enlisted July 17, 1862, and died of heart disease November 4, 1862, near Bowling Green, Kentucky. Second Asst. Surgeon Sidney S. Fuller of Appleton, Wisconsin, served in the Field and Staff Unit and mustered out of service March 7, 1864. The Field and Staff Unit comprised the commissioned and non-commissioned officers essential to manage the daily affairs of the regiment, including a Regimental Surgeon and one or two Assistant Surgeons, as well as Hospital Stewards. Ibid.

10. Buell was relieved from command on October 24, 1862; Gen. W. S. Rosecrans took over on the 30th. The reason given for Buell's dismissal was his failure to

follow up General Bragg quickly after the battle of Perryville. An inquiry followed in November, wherein a military commission looked into what it believed had been dilatory tactics, but no recommendation was ever given. Buell awaited orders for more than a year before he resigned his commission on June 1, 1864. Warner, *Generals in Blue,* 51–52.

11. Surgeon James Theodore Reeve of Green Bay, Wisconsin, was the assistant surgeon of the 10th Wisconsin Infantry and later the surgeon of the 21st Infantry. He joined the regiment as first assistant surgeon on August 11, 1862, and was appointed as surgeon on November 10, 1862, after the death of Surgeon Samuel J. Carolin. *RMR,* 10th and 21st Infantry.

12. In early November 1862 Gen. John C. Breckinridge commanded the Confederate Army of Middle Tennessee. He was determined to mark his presence in the region and contrived several raids in and around Gallatin. Beginning on November 5 General Morgan's cavalry launched a raid with the intention of destroying several hundred railroad cars near Nashville. The raid failed but clearly demonstrated the Confederate presence. On November 8 Morgan's troops marched out of Gallatin with the express aim of ambushing General Rosecrans's Army of the Cumberland, which was marching south on the Louisville and Nashville Pike. Morgan's men numbered only around two hundred and on the morning of the 8th found Rosecrans's army just north of Nashville. The raid was a success, with the reported loss of only one raider. The Union infantry belatedly managed to drive off the attackers, only to be ambushed a second time in its rear. Morgan and his men made good their escape and returned to the Confederate lines. On November 9 Morgan left his command to resume his courtship of his future wife, Mattie, and plan for their marriage on December 14. There was no reported fighting between Rosecrans's army and Morgan's troops on November 11, 1862. Ramage, *Rebel Raider,* 125–27.

13. Pvt. Miles H. Fenno of Appleton, Wisconsin, enlisted August 15, 1862. He transferred to the 62d Regiment of U.S. Colored Troops June 3, 1864, under Special Order Number 97 from the War Department. *RMR,* 21st Infantry. Regimental records cite vol. 8, page 151, of War Department Promotions, which lists a commission to second lieutenant, 4th Regiment, U.S. Colored Infantry Troops, on November 5, 1864. *WAGR,* ser. 1200.

14. Pvt. Richard A. Pearse of Appleton, Wisconsin, enlisted August 11, 1862. He died of disease November 23, 1862, at Mitchellsville, Tennessee. *RMR,* 21st Infantry.

15. Pvt. Henry Vandebogart of Grand Chute, Wisconsin, enlisted August 11, 1862, and died of disease June 21, 1863, at Murfreesboro. Ibid.

16. Capt. John Jewett Jr. died November 21, 1862, near Mitchellsville, Tennessee. Ibid. The Outagamie County Veterans' Service cemetery records show that Capt. John D. Jewett Jr. is buried in the Grand Army of the Republic section, Riverside Cemetery of Appleton, Wisconsin. *Alphabetical Grave Registration: Outagamie County* (Appleton, Wisconsin, 1995). Wisconsin Veterans' Administration Veterans' Service Office.

17. Pvt. Joseph Woodland of Grand Chute, Wisconsin, enlisted August 14, 1862, and was discharged for disability March 18, 1863. *RMR,* 21st Infantry.

18. Regimental records show the following: Pvt. William Gerry of Appleton, Wisconsin, was discharged February 23, 1863; Pvt. Anson Tollman of Appleton, Wisconsin, was discharged February 27, 1863; Pvt. Nelson B. Draper of Ellington, Wisconsin,

mustered out June 8, 1865; Pvt. Ephraim Walker of Greenville, Wisconsin, mustered out June 8, 1865; Pvt. Allen W. Ballard of Appleton, Wisconsin, was discharged May 20, 1863; Pvt. Daniel B. Cushman of Grand Chute, Wisconsin, was transferred to the Veterans Reserve Corps and mustered out June 30, 1865; Pvt. Levant Vandebogart of Grand Chute, Wisconsin, mustered out May 22, 1865; Pvt. George Herrick of Center, Wisconsin, was transferred to the Veterans Reserve Corps and mustered out July 17, 1865; and Pvt. Thomas (Henry) Simpson of Grand Chute, Wisconsin, died of disease January 19, 1863, at Nashville, Tennessee. Ibid.

19. Capt. Rudolph J. Weisbrod of Oshkosh, Wisconsin, enlisted August 22, 1862. He served in Company E and was commissioned as a second lieutenant on August 22, 1862, a first lieutenant on October 16, 1862, and a captain on February 20, 1863. He was granted a surgeon's certificate of disability and discharged from the service December 29, 1864. Capt. Joseph La Count of Manitowoc Rapids, Wisconsin, was commissioned as a second lieutenant August 9, 1862, as a first lieutenant March 19, 1864, and as a captain October 19, 1864. He mustered out with the regiment on June 8, 1865. Ibid.

20. Regimental records show the deaths or discharges of the following men: Dor A. Gurnee of Ellington, Wisconsin, discharged February 14, 1863; Governeur M. Davis of Ellington, Wisconsin, discharged April 16, 1863; Edwin H. Bowen of Appleton, Wisconsin, discharged February 1863; Walker J. Fish of Appleton, Wisconsin, discharged September 24, 1863; Seymour M. Dickerson of Liberty, Wisconsin, discharged February 18, 1863; Robert W. Logan of Hortonville, Wisconsin, discharged February 13, 1863; Thomas Logan of Appleton, Wisconsin, discharged July 29, 1863; William H. Priest of Appleton, Wisconsin, discharged February 27, 1863; Andrew T. Sherwood of Appleton, Wisconsin, discharged November 23, 1862; William Smith of Grand Chute, Wisconsin, discharged February 16, 1863; John F. Tupper of Appleton, Wisconsin, discharged September 19, 1863; Thomas Simpson of Grand Chute, Wisconsin, died January 19, 1863; and David W. Peebles of Ellington, Wisconsin, died January 6, 1863. Ibid.

6. THE BATTLE OF STONE RIVER, OR MURFREESBORO

1. Pvt. Miles Hoskins of Shiocton, Wisconsin, enlisted August 12, 1862. He was severely wounded on August 7, 1864, at the battle of Ezra Church and died from his wounds August 8, 1864. *RMR*, 21st Infantry.

2. Pvt. Nelson B. Draper of Ellington, Wisconsin, enlisted August 12, 1862. He mustered out June 8, 1865. Ibid.

3. The official records differ from Otto's account. In his report Colonel Starkweather states he ordered the advance of the regiment, saving the regimental train. Report from Colonel Starkweather, *War of the Rebellion: A Compilation of the Official Records of the Union and Confederate Armies*, 128 vols. (Washington, D.C.: GPO, 1880–1901), part 1, 20: 391–93. Cited hereafter as *OR*. Maj. Michael J. Fitch states he actually ordered the initial advance of the 21st by ordering them to fall in and advance on the pike toward the attacking cavalry forces of General Wheeler. *Echoes of the Civil War*, 97. Sgt. Mead Holmes Jr. appears to substantiate Captain Otto's and Major Fitch's account. *A Soldier of the Cumberland: Memoir of Mead Holmes, Jr.*,

388 *Sergeant of Company K, 21st Regiment Wisconsin Volunteers.* (Boston: American Tract Society, 1864), 134.

4. Pvt. Charles H. Warner of Appleton, Wisconsin, enlisted August 15, 1862. A company muster roll dated January 1863 shows he was taken prisoner on December 30, 1862, at Stone's River, and paroled. A company casualty report shows that he returned to duty October 30, 1863. *RMR,* 21st Infantry.

5. Pvt. Benjamin S. Turney of Liberty, Wisconsin, enlisted August 15, 1862. He died of wounds at Jefferson, Tennessee, December 30, 1862. Ibid.

6. An unsigned report of this engagement in *WAGR,* ser. 1200, reads as follows: "A rebel officer who was injured in the engagement reported that Wheeler lost 80 men killed & wounded." Box 107, folder 3, Reports.

7. Capt. Simeon B. Nelson of Menasha, Wisconsin, was commissioned August 26, 1862. He was taken prisoner on the Jefferson Pike. He resigned his commission on April 25, 1863. *RMR,* 21st Infantry.

8. Pvt. Robert Hutchinson of Maple Creek, Wisconsin, enlisted August 14, 1862. He transferred to the U.S. Veteran Volunteer Engineers on July 4, 1864, as an artificer. He mustered out of service on June 27, 1865. Ibid.

9. Lt. John Yaryan of General Wood's staff gives an account of the flight of General Crittenden's corps: "Soon fugitives and stragglers emerged from the cedars in full view, and came toward us on the run, followed by confused masses of panic-stricken troops firing their muskets in the air, or back in the faces of their comrades, following them." Peter Cozzens, *No Better Place to Die: The Battle of Stones River* (Urbana: Univ. of Illinois Press, 1990), 130.

10. Pvt. (Principal Musician) Harold Galpin of Appleton, Wisconsin, enlisted August 15, 1862, and mustered out June 8, 1865. Private Galpin, fourteen, was the company drummer. *RMR,* 21st Infantry.

11. Mr. B. Gould of Fond du Lac (author's note). Hospital Steward Edward H. Gould of Fond du Lac, Wisconsin, enlisted August 14, 1862. He was originally assigned to Company F and transferred to the Field and Staff September 5, 1862, where he assumed the duties of the regimental hospital steward. Gould's records do not indicate that he was wounded. Ibid.

12. The Russian Imperial Navy's Atlantic Fleet entered U.S. waters on September 23, 1863. The first of two ships arrived at New York Harbor on Thursday the 23d, with four additional ships arriving several days later. By October 12, 1863, six additional warships had entered San Francisco Bay. The reported purpose of the fleet's arrival was to escape the harsh Russian winter and avoid a European war after Russia's suppression of a Polish revolt. E. B. and Barbara Long, *The Civil War Day by Day: An Almanac 1861–1865* (New York: Da Capo, 1971).

13. E. B. Quiner relates this incident in *The Military History of Wisconsin:* "The horse of Lieutenant Starkweather was killed by a cannon ball on the 1st of January, and being in good condition, was cut up, and partaken of by many of the soldiers" (431).

14. Pvt. John W. Sweetser of Greenville, Wisconsin, enlisted August 14, 1862, and died of disease on January 23, 1863, at Nashville. The records of Company D do not list a William "Sweetzer." *RMR,* 21st Infantry.

15. The quotation is from Schiller, *Die Vershwörung de Fiesco zu Genua,* act 3, scene 4.

16. Gen. August Von Willich was born in Russia on November 10, 1810. He joined the U.S. Army in 1861 and became one of its premier officers. He was well known for his ability to raise German recruits and for his innovation of commanding his troops with the use of bugle calls. He distinguished himself at the battles of Shiloh and Perryville. Warner, *Generals in Blue* 565–66.

17. Gen. James Scott Negley was a native of Pennsylvania, born December 22, 1826. He commanded a division under General Thomas and was promoted to major general for his leadership at Stone's River. At the battle of Chickamauga, General Negley became embroiled in a controversy over his command of the Second Division, 14th Corps, under Thomas. He was never placed in command of troops in the field again and resigned in January 1865. Ibid., 341–42.

18. Rosecrans reported his losses at Stone's River as 1,553 killed, 7,245 wounded, and 2,800 captured, for a total of 11,598; Bragg reported 10,125 killed, wounded, and missing. Henry M. Cist, *The Army of the Cumberland* (New York: Scribner's, 1882), 127.

7. ABOUT OUR "COOZIE" WINTER QUARTERS, LIGHT DUTY, AND OUR BULLY PICNIC IN GENERAL

1. Pvt. Alfred Abbott of Freedom, Wisconsin, was taken prisoner at the battle of Chickamauga. He was sent to the Andersonville prison camp and died there of disease on August 9, 1864. *RMR*, 21st Infantry.

2. Pvt. Henry S. Spaulding of Appleton, Wisconsin, was transferred to the Invalid Corps (Veterans Reserve Corps), July 27, 1863, and mustered out of service on July 15, 1865. Ibid.

3. Pvt. George Mansur of Ellington, Wisconsin, enlisted August 7, 1862, and died of disease on February 18, 1863, at Murfreesboro, Tennessee. Ibid.

4. Although Otto makes no mention in his entry for October 8, 1862, of a "snub" by Assistant Surgeon Fuller, a deposition by James P. Walker in support of Otto's pension claim dated February 28, 1884, found in the National Archives, mentions the incident:

> I do not know of his being treated atall while in the service the only time I now remember of him reporting to a Doctor was on the morning of the 8th of October 1862 just before the battle of pereevill [Perryville] he was suffering with a diorcale [*sic*] the Doctor insulted him and he told him to go to h———ll and that he would die before he would aske a jackass of a Doctor for any assistance and as far as I know he never called on them again.

"Proof of Disability": deposition of James P. Walker, February 28, 1884; Soldier's Certificate no. 288806, Can no. 5793, Bundle no. 29; Records of the Adjutant General's Office, 1780s–1917 (RG 94): Records of the Record and Pension Office, National Archives, Washington, D.C.

5. Sgt. Theodore Clark of Ellington, Wisconsin, died of disease on March 4, 1863, at Murfreesboro, Tennessee. *RMR*, 21st Infantry.

6. Pvt. Anson Tollman of Appleton, Wisconsin, was discharged due to a disability February 27, 1863. Pvt. Daniel B. Cushman of Grand Chute, Wisconsin, was transferred to the Invalid Corps August 1, 1863. He mustered out on June 30, 1865. Ibid.

7. Pvt. George Herrick of Center, Wisconsin, enlisted August 14, 1862. He was taken prisoner at Nolansville. He was transferred to the Veterans Reserve Corps on September 27, 1864, and mustered out July 17, 1865. Pvt. James A. Woolcott of Grand Chute, Wisconsin, enlisted August 14, 1862. He was taken prisoner at Nolansville. He was transferred to the Veterans Reserve Corps on September 1, 1863, and mustered out July 14, 1865. Ibid.

8. Chaplain Orson P. Clinton returned to his home of Neenah, Wisconsin, with approximately twenty-seven thousand dollars in military greenback currency. Upon his arrival he sent each family named on the company commanders' list the allotted amount. He carried this amount of currency in his personal blanket, keeping it with him the entire time. Fitch, *Echoes of the Civil War,* 230.

9. Col. Benjamin J. Sweet resigned his commission September 8, 1863. He later served as commander of the Eighth Regiment of the Invalid Corps and on September 26, 1863, took command of Camp Douglas, Chicago, Illinois. His efforts to improve the camp conditions were beneficial to all parties. For a further study of life in Camp Douglas and Colonel Sweet's efforts, see George Levy, *To Die in Chicago: Confederate Prisoners at Camp Douglas, 1862–1865* (Evanston, Ill.: Evanston, 1994).

10. Colonel Fitch gives an explanation of his promotion over seven other line officers in the 21st in his memoirs. *Echoes of the Civil War,* 118.

11. Capt. Alphonso S. Godfrey of Oshkosh, Wisconsin, resigned his commission on February 20, 1863, due to a disability. *RMR,* 21st Infantry.

8. EXPEDITION INTO EAST TENNESSEE

1. Second Lt. James H. Jenkins of Oshkosh, Wisconsin, was commissioned August 2, 1862, and assigned as adjutant on February 4, 1863. *RMR,* 21st Infantry.

2. First Sgt. Egbert J. Scott of Appleton, Wisconsin, enlisted August 15, 1862. He was taken prisoner at Chickamauga and sent to Andersonville, where he died of disease on August 4, 1864. Ibid.

3. Sgt. Joseph D. Holden of Appleton, Wisconsin, enlisted August 7, 1862, and mustered out June 8, 1865. Cpl. McKendry Rawson of Hortonville, Wisconsin, enlisted August 13, 1862, and mustered out May 15, 1865. Second Lt. Lyman C. Waite of Appleton, Wisconsin, enlisted August 15, 1862, and was commissioned a second lieutenant on April 27, 1865. He mustered out June 8, 1865. Ibid.

4. An account of this incident, based on a story in a Nashville newspaper, is given in Rossiter Johnson, *Campfires and Battlefields: A Pictorial Narrative of the Civil War* (New York: The Blue and the Grey Press, 1958), 503. Another account of what seems to be the same incident is given in Thomas B. Van Horne, *The Army of the Cumberland* (1875; rpt., New York: Smithmark, 1996), 219–20. According to Van Horne's account, the incident took place in June not April; the spies were Col.

Lawrence A. Williams and Lieutenant Dunlap, the former having served in the U.S. Army. They were tried by drumhead court-martial and hanged June 9, 1863, by order of General Rosecrans.

5. The report of Col. Robert H. G. Minty indicates that he was in command of the First Cavalry Brigade and of the batteries of artillery that went along on the expedition. Colonel Minty was originally from the 4th Michigan Cavalry and took along the following artillery pieces: two brass pieces, one rifled, one howitzer, and two small mountain howitzers. The cavalry units assigned to this task were under the command of Brig. Gen. David S. Stanley, attached to the 14th Corps, Cavalry Division, First Brigade: 2d Indiana Cavalry, 3d Kentucky Cavalry, 7th Pennsylvania Cavalry, and 4th Michigan Cavalry. Report 6, by Col. Robert H. J. Minty, 4th Michigan Cavalry, OR, ser. 1, vol. 23, 156–58.

6. An account of the capture of Dick McCann is given in *A History of Morgan's Cavalry*, first published in 1867: "Exchanging a few shots with the cavalry, this party retreated upon the Sparta Road—McCann's horse was shot in the melee and fell, bringing him to the ground. He sprang to his feet and standing in front of the charging column, shouted, 'You have got the old chief at last,' seeking to produce the impression that he was General Morgan and so favor the latter's escape. McCann was ridden over, severely sabred, and captured." Basil W. Duke, *A History of Morgan's Cavalry*, ed. Cecil Fletcher Holland (Bloomington: Indiana Univ. Press, 1960), 389–90.

7. In March 1863 Gen. Ambrose Burnside entered Kentucky with several divisions of the 9th Corps and took command of the Department of the Ohio. By May, the 9th and 23d Corps were concentrated together near the upper Cumberland. Burnside, and a portion of the 23d Corps, occupied Knoxville on September 2, 1863. William Marvel, *Burnside* (Chapel Hill: Univ. of North Carolina Press, 1991), 314–31.

8. The court-martial proceedings and trial of William A. Selkirk took place under General Orders No. 123, on May 5, 1863. The trial was commissioned by Major General Rosecrans. Col. J. W. Burke, 10th Ohio Volunteer Infantry, was appointed president of the court. The two other parties to the crime of murder, and the traveling companions of William Selkirk, were George Williams and George Lyles, both from Wilson County, Tennessee. All parties were found guilty of the crime of murder and executed. The execution by hanging of William Selkirk was carried out on Friday, June 5, 1863. George Williams and George Lyles were executed several days later. Entry for William A. Selkirk: Civilian, State of Tennessee, Wilson County, Electrostatic Copy NARA of Court-Martial file MM-521; 6w4/6/3/c, box 934, Civil War 1861–1865; *Proceedings of the U.S. Army Court-Martial and Military Commissions*, RG 153, National Archives, Washington, D.C.

9. Col. Michael H. Fitch corroborates the presence of Annie Weaver at William Selkirk's execution. He reveals that when prisoner Selkirk dropped through the gallows trap door, Annie Weaver clapped her hands. *Echoes of the Civil War*, 123.

10. The *Adjutant General's Report for the State of Indiana*, vol. 7 (1861–1865), shows a Pvt. David Blaser, who enlisted February 18, 1863, in the 4th Indiana Light Artillery Battery. He was court-martialed on June 20, 1863, and was sentenced to be shot for desertion to the enemy. *Report of the Adjutant General, State of Indiana:*

Volume 7, 1861–1865, Containing Rosters of enlisted men of Indiana regiments numbered from the one hundred and eleventh to the one hundred and fifty-sixth, inclusive; colored troops; and batteries light artillery, numbered from the first to the twenty-sixth, inclusive (Indianapolis: Samuel M. Douglas, State Printer, 1867). The sentence of execution by firing party was carried out June 20, 1863. The trial proceedings show that three Wisconsin officers served on the court. Capt. Charles H. Walker, Company K, 21st Infantry, served as Judge Advocate of the trial board, and Capt. William S. Mitchell, 1st Wisconsin Infantry, and Capt. Robert Harkney, 10th Wisconsin Infantry, as board members. Entry for Private David Blazer, 4th Indiana Light Artillery Battery; Court-Martial File (LL-643), National Archives microfilm publication (M-1523); Civil War 1861–1865; *Proceedings of the U.S. Courts-Martial and Military Commissions of Union Soldiers Executed by U.S. Military Authorities, 1861–1866;* RG 94, National Archives, Washington, D.C. Private Alfred Galpin, Company H, 1st Wisconsin Infantry Regiment, was on detached service with the 1st Indiana Light Artillery Battery, and was a witness to the execution of Blaser:

> After wards orders came to fall in at 10.30 to see Blazer & the Regular executed. Went out in field near pike. Division in 3 sides of hollow square formation for the shooting of the regular but we of the Baty. were so distant we could see nothing. Then part of our Brig. (or all?) over near 21st Wis. camp to see Blazer get his [quittance]. We were placed close behind & to R. of firing squad. Blazer was game. 7 bullets struck him yet he squirmed & writhed a long time.

Alfred M. Galpin, *Galpin Family Papers: MSS-182 Letters and papers of Private Alfred Galpin II. Company H, 1st Wisconsin Infantry Regiment.* Entry for Saturday, June 20, 1863; Diary for 1863, 84. Archives Division, State Historical Society of Wisconsin, Madison. Another account of the execution is given by Col. Michael H. Fitch, *Echoes of the Civil War,* 123.

9. THE TULLAHOMA CAMPAIGN

1. The spy referred to is believed to be Samuel Davis, who worked for the notorious Confederate spymaster Col. S. Shaw, who went by the name of "Captain Coleman." When Davis was caught he had some very incriminating evidence in his saddlebags. A letter from Brig. Gen. G. M. Dodge to Maj. R. M. Sawyer, dated Pulaski, Tennessee, November 20, 1863, containing the news of Davis's capture, and letters found in his possession, including one from Captain Coleman to Col. A. McKinstry, Provost Marshal General of Bragg's Army of Tennessee, containing details of the strength and location of Federal troops in middle Tennessee, and gifts to General Bragg from Shaw or "Coleman," can be found in the OR, ser. 1, vol. 31, part 3, 208–11. Davis, who was wearing a Federal soldier's coat when captured, was tried and convicted of being a Confederate spy on November 23, 1863. He was executed November 27, 1863, after refusing a pardon offered him to reveal the identity of Coleman, whom Dodge unwittingly had in his custody at the same time as Davis.

Dodge's version of the incident can be found in Grenville M. Dodge, *The Battle of*
Atlanta and Other Campaigns (1911; rpt., Earlysville, Va.: Old Books, 1996), 165–70.

2. We have been unable to locate any reference to this engagement in the official record. Colonel Baird, as commander of the division, should have filed a report but was not present at the engagement, according to Otto. The record at the regimental level is less than complete—Colonel Fitch notes in his book that no regimental report for the 21st was filed as long as General Starkweather was brigade commander (*Echoes of the Civil War*, 96). So Otto may be correct, and the engagement one "not mentioned in history." On the other hand, since no precise date is given, it may also be that the record exists but has not been located.

3. Pvt. Levant Vandebogart was absent from Company D starting May 23, 1863, when he was sent to the convalescent camp at Murfreesboro, Tennessee. He was sent to the Invalid Corps (Veterans Reserve Corps) in July 1863. *RMR*, 21st Infantry.

4. William M. Lamars in his biography of Rosecrans gives the following account of the forces of the opposing armies: "On the eve of Rosecrans' advance, the striking forces of the two armies were approximately equal. Bragg's effective strength was 46,665: 30,449 infantry, 13,962 cavalry, and 2,254 artillery; Rosecrans' was 50,017: 40,146 infantry, 6,806 cavalry, and 3,065 artillery. Behind Rosecrans' force stood a reserve corps of 12,575, and garrisons at Nashville and elsewhere." William M. Lamars, *The Edge of Glory: A Biography of General William S. Rosecrans, USA* (Baton Rouge: Louisiana State Univ. Press, 1999), 275.

5. Minty's brigade and Mitchell's division captured Shelbyville on June 27, 1863, capturing about five hundred prisoners; about two hundred Rebel soldiers drowned trying to swim the Duck River. Van Horne, *The Army of the Cumberland*, 227.

6. General Rousseau gave losses in his division at Hoover's Gap as First Brigade, one killed, ten wounded; Second Brigade, twelve wounded; Third Brigade, three killed, twenty wounded. Fitch, *Echoes of the Civil War*, 124.

7. Capt. James M. Randall of Weyauwega, Wisconsin, was commissioned on March 29, 1863. He had served as a first sergeant and second lieutenant in Company B of the 14th Infantry prior to his commission in the 21st. *RMR*, 21st Infantry.

8. Lamers confirms that Rosecrans knew of the defeat of Lee at Gettysburg on July 4: "From June 30 until the morning of July 4 anxious questions were asked in Middle Tennessee concerning the fate of the Army of the Potomac. Then Stanton's dispatch announcing the victory at Gettysburg reached Rosecrans." *The Edge of Glory*, 288.

9. Pvt. James H. Bennett was recorded as absent without leave on October 6, 1862. He returned to the company May 30, 1863, and the charge of desertion was dropped April 1, 1863. The company records do not list a charge of desertion for Sgt. John Dey. Sergeant Dey transferred to the Veterans Reserve Corps under Circular 9. Cpl. Amos Lawrence deserted the regiment at Camp Chase, Ohio, in September 1864. The charge of desertion was dropped March 31, 1865, and he was reduced to the ranks. "To reduce (a noncommissioned officer) to the ranks" means to degrade him to the rank of private. Pvt. Joel Prince deserted the regiment on October 8, 1862, at Louisville, Kentucky. The charge of desertion was dropped on July 20, 1886. The charges were dropped by the Adjutant General's Office and were listed under the regimental records as an official notice, dated 1886. No charge of

desertion is listed in the records for Pvt. Charles H. Warner. He was taken prisoner on December 30, 1862, and then sent to the hospital at Murfreesboro, Tennessee. He returned to the company on October 30, 1863, and mustered out with the company on June 8, 1865. Cpl. William H. Wood deserted the regiment October 10, 1862, at Clarksville, Kentucky. He was charged with desertion and held in arrest at division headquarters in July 1863. He returned to the company August 17, 1863, and was found guilty of desertion by general court-martial. He was sentenced on August 31, 1863, at Camp Lawson, Alabama, to one year's confiscation of pay and allowances, sixty days' confinement at hard labor, and thirty days with ball and chain. He returned to the company on November 1, 1863. He was also to make good his absence from October 10, 1862, to August 16, 1863. *RMR*, 21st Infantry.

10. A total of 31,600 prisoners were surrendered at Vicksburg along with 172 cannon, about 60,000 muskets, and a large amount of ammunition. Ulysses Simpson Grant, *Memoirs and Selected Letters: Personal Memoirs of U.S. Grant; Selected Letters 1839–1865* (New York: Library of America, 1990), 384.

11. Pvt. Alverson B. Everetts of Appleton, Wisconsin, enlisted September 11, 1862. He served in Company B of the 1st Cavalry and mustered out July 19, 1865. *RMR*, 1st Cavalry.

12. Pvt. Jacob W. Rexford of Richmond, Wisconsin, enlisted August 9, 1862. He was taken prisoner at Murfreesboro. He mustered out June 8, 1865. Ibid., 21st Infantry.

10. THE CHICKAMAUGA CAMPAIGN

1. First Lt. Charles H. Morgan of Blackwolf, Wisconsin, was commissioned August 12, 1862. He was taken prisoner at the battle of Chaplin Hills (Perryville), Kentucky, on October 8, 1865. He was also captured at the battle of Chickamauga on September 20, 1863, and was sent to Libby Prison from where he was able to escape and return to the regiment on February 22, 1865. *RMR*, 21st Infantry.

2. Crittenden's demonstration before Chattanooga, including the shelling of the city, actually took place August 21, not September 11. Bragg was no longer in Chattanooga on the 11th, having abandoned the city on the 7th. Cist 178; Peter Cozzens, *This Terrible Sound: The Battle of Chickamauga* (Urbana: Univ. of Illinois Press, 1992), 35–37, 56–57.

3. Starkweather's aide de camp was 1st Lt. Robert J. Nickles of Milwaukee, Wisconsin. He joined Company C of the 1st Infantry August 6, 1862, rose from sergeant major to first lieutenant, and was killed in action September 11, 1863, at the battle of Dug's Gap. Quiner, *Military History of Wisconsin*, 432. He joined Starkweather's staff on May 13, 1863. An official notice from the Adjutant General's Office, Washington, D.C., dated November 3, 1863, notifies the governor of Wisconsin of this officer's death. Regimental records cite the *Roll of Honor*, vol. 2, 193, which indicates that he is buried in the Chattanooga Cemetery, Section C, Grave G. *RMR*, 1st and 21st Infantry.

4. Principal Musician Hosea B. Paine of Oshkosh, Wisconsin, enlisted August 21, 1862. He was listed as a drummer. Principal Musician Albert H. Owen of Menasha, Wisconsin, enlisted August 19, 1862. He was listed as a fifer. *RMR*, 21st Infantry.

1. The death of Adj. Charles Searles is described in an official combat report dated September 23, 1863, by the brigade commander, Brig. Gen. John Starkweather, at Chattanooga, Tennessee. Starkweather states that Searles was shot from his horse during the attack of Col. Daniel Govan's Arkansans. *WAGR,* ser. 1200, 1st Infantry Records, box 3, folder 1, Reports.

2. The 11th Kentucky Infantry was not on the field at Chickamauga. The 10th Kentucky Infantry, commanded by Col. William Hays, was part of the counterattack directed at Col. Daniel Govan's Arkansans, an attack that carried through the area of battle fought over by Starkweather's brigade. Cozzens, *This Terrible Sound,* 150.

3. The two-gun battery referred to was the remnant of Lt. George Van Pelt's 1st Michigan Light Artillery, Battery A, and of Lt. D. Flansburg's, 4th Indiana Light Artillery. The guns had been captured by the Arkansans of Colonel Govan and returned to Union hands in the counterattack of Col. John T. Croxton. Cozzens, *This Terrible Sound,* 150. Pvt. Alfred Galpin, Company H, 1st Wisconsin Infantry, was on detached service with the 4th Indiana Light Artillery at the battle of Chickamauga. He described the capture of the guns: "Our entire Battery was Captured but was in the enemy's possession only about ten minutes—when the 10th Kentucky, et. al. recaptured it." Galpin Family Papers, entry for Saturday, September 19, 1863, Diary for 1863, 96.

4. Brig. Gen. August Willich's Brigade, 20th Army Corps, Second Division, First Brigade, consisted of the 32d and 39th Indiana (the 39th was mounted and detached from the brigade) and the 15th and 49th Ohio. All of these regiments are believed to have been armed with the standard Enfield or Springfield rifle-musket. Col. John T. Wilder's brigade of the 14th Army Corps, Fourth Division, First Brigade, consisted of the 17th and 72d Indiana and the 92d and 98th Illinois. The 17th Indiana, Colonel Wilder's original regiment, fought near Starkweather's brigade of which the 21st Wisconsin was part. Wilder's regiment was armed with the Spencer repeating rifle, a .52 caliber weapon that held seven cartridges in a tubular magazine within the butt stock. Operation of a lever at the bottom of the rifle fed rim-fire cartridges into the chamber, one at a time. The men of Colonel Wilder's brigade had armed themselves with the repeating rifles by purchasing them with a bank loan obtained in Wilder's home town. Cozzens, *This Terrible Sound,* 15.

5. There is no record of a Confederate general by the name of Pope. The reinforcements Bragg received at Chickamauga consisted of Longstreet's corps from the Army of Northern Virginia and two divisions sent from Mississippi by Gen. Joseph E. Johnston. Some of these reinforcements arrived as early as August 27; others (and Longstreet himself) did not arrive at the front until late on the night of September 19. After the arrival of his reinforcements on September 19, Bragg's forces numbered between sixty-eight and seventy-two thousand, minus the day's losses, while Rosecrans's forces numbered about fifty-seven thousand, minus the day's losses. Cozzens, *This Terrible Sound,* 38, 294, 301, 350.

6. A report by Brig. Gen. John C. Starkweather dated September 23, 1863, at the headquarters of the Second Brigade, First Division, 14th Army Corps, Chattanooga, Tennessee, and directed to Capt. Russ H. Polk, assistant adjutant general,

396

clarifies the defensive positions of the respective regiments. By 9:30 A.M. on September 20, the Federal positions had been formed; in appearance they resembled a large horseshoe. General Dodge formed the north or left wing, while General Starkweather, holding the center, was flanked on the south or right wing by General Hazen. The center, part of the two-tiered line of defense, was held by the 1st Wisconsin and the 24th Illinois on the first line, and the 79th Pennsylvania and 21st Wisconsin on the second line. *WAGR*, ser. 1200, 1st Infantry Records, box 3, folder 1, Reports.

7. Gen. James Longstreet arrived at Catoosa Station, near Ringold, at approximately 2:00 P.M. September 19. He arrived at the front near the break of day, September 20. Cozzens, *This Terrible Sound*, 299, 315.

8. The Second Brigade, First Division, 14th Army Corps had the following artillery units attached at the battle of Chickamauga: the 4th Indiana Light Artillery; Battery A of the 1st Michigan Light Artillery; and Battery H of the 5th U.S. Artillery. Cozzens, *This Terrible Sound*, 538. Capt. Cyrus O. Loomis served with Battery A, 1st Michigan Light Artillery. *Record of Service of Michigan Volunteers in the Civil War, 1861–1865*, 46 vols. (Kalamazoo, Mich.: Ihling Bros. and Everard, 1905), 42: 1.

9. Pvt. Spencer Orlup of Appleton, Wisconsin, enlisted August 14, 1862. He mustered out June 8, 1865. Pvt. Carl Buchholz of Greenville, Wisconsin, enlisted August 16, 1862. The enrollment clerk recorded his age as fifty-four. *RMR*, 21st Infantry.

10. Pvt. Charles Buck was wounded at Chickamauga, Georgia, September 20, 1863. Ibid.

11. Capt. August Mauff, Company E, 24th Illinois, was not killed in action at Chickamauga. He survived the battle and mustered out August 6, 1864. *RAGO, Illinois*, 2: 310.

12. E. B. Quiner in *The Military History of Wisconsin* indicates that Starkweather was "wounded in the leg by a piece of shell" (434). General Starkweather's 1st Infantry records do not show that he was wounded during the battle of Chickamauga. *RMR*, 1st Infantry.

13. Pvt. John G. Shockley of Appleton, Wisconsin, served in Company D. He was wounded September 19, 1863, at the battle of Chickamauga, and sent to the hospital at Nashville, Tennessee. He returned to duty June 6, 1864, and was promoted to commissary sergeant. *RMR*, 21st Infantry.

14. Capt. William Wall of Oshkosh, Wisconsin, enlisted August 11, 1862, was commissioned as a first lieutenant on August 26, 1862, and as captain February 20, 1863. He was detailed as Colonel Starkweather's aide de camp and ordnance officer, Third Brigade, from January 20, 1863, under Special Field Order 62 from the Military Division of Mississippi, dated May 27, 1863. He was discharged January 18, 1865. Ibid.

15. The "fatal order" was from Maj. Gen. William S. Rosecrans to Brig. Gen. Thomas A. Wood, drafted by Maj. Frank S. Bond, aide de camp. It directed Wood to "close up on Reynolds as fast as possible, and support him." The withdrawal of General Wood's troops opened a wide gap in the Union defenses, allowed the Confederates to press their attack, and caused the retreat of the Union forces. For a

closer examination of the "fatal order" refer to Cozzens, *This Terrible Sound*, 357–67, and *OR*, vol. 30, 625–42.

16. Maj. Gen. Gordon Granger reported to Thomas with two brigades of his Reserve Corps at about 1:45 P.M. Cozzens, *This Terrible Sound*, 443.

17. Col. Harrison C. Hobart was taken prisoner September 20, 1863, at Chickamauga. He survived his captivity and escaped from Libby Prison on February 9, 1864, returning to duty with the 21st Infantry April 1, 1864. He was promoted to the rank of brigadier general, U.S. Volunteers, on January 12, 1865. *RMR*, 21st Infantry.

12. CHATTANOOGA: BATTLES OF LOOKOUT MOUNTAIN AND MISSIONARY RIDGE

1. The following men of Otto's company were wounded at Chickamauga: Charles Buck, Sylvester Greeley, Michael Hammond, Charles Herb, McKendry Rawson, Sanford Rexford, and John Shockley. Pvt. Miles Hoskins's record shows that he was still absent from the company, recovering from wounds received during the battle of Chaplin Hills. He returned to the company on October 3, 1863. *RMR*, 21st Infantry.

2. The following were taken prisoner at Chickamauga: Col. Harrison Hobart, Alfred Abbott, Eleanor H. Gilbert, Charles Herb, Almiran Kling, Henry Knowles, Curtis Mitchell, Mead Seaman, E. B. Scott, and Samuel W. Turney. Ibid.

3. The following men died at Andersonville Prison: Alfred Abbott, Henry Knowles, Mead Seaman, Samuel W. Turney, and Egbert Scott. Sgt. Egbert J. Scott was listed by Captain Otto as having died in Belle Island Prison, but regimental records indicate he died August 4, 1864, at Andersonville. A total of eighty-three men from the 21st were taken prisoner at Chickamauga. Of those, forty-four survived their incarceration. Twenty-eight died at Andersonville, six at Danville, one at Richmond, and one at Charleston, South Carolina. Ibid. Andersonville National Military Park burial records show there were thirty-seven 21st Infantry soldiers who died at the prison and are buried in the park's cemetery. Five of those soldiers were from Company D. A total of 641 Wisconsin soldiers perished at Andersonville. Tabular printout of selected portion of the prisoner of war database, U.S. Department of Interior, National Park Service, Andersonville Historic Site, Andersonville, Georgia. The printout was provided by Sue Fuller, National Park Service. For a complete study of the prison at Andersonville, see William Marvel, *Andersonville: The Last Depot* (Chapel Hill: Univ. of North Carolina Press, 1994).

4. A careful examination of Company D muster rolls shows fourteen men lost at Chickamauga, but no accurate number of men available for duty can be determined. Regimental muster rolls recorded nine killed, twenty-three wounded, eighty-three prisoners (a total of one colonel, twelve other line officers, and seventy enlisted men), and an unknown number of missing, for a total of 115. Brig. Gen. John C. Starkweather, commanding the Second Brigade, First Division, 14th Corps, reported the 21st's losses as two enlisted men killed; four commissioned officers and thirty-two enlisted men wounded; and nine commissioned officers and sixty-seven enlisted men missing—for a total of 114. Captain Otto's assessment that other regiments

and companies suffered greater losses is borne out by Starkweather's report of September 23, which gives losses for the other regiments in the brigade as follows: 1st Wisconsin 200, 79th Pennsylvania 137, and 24th Illinois 157. *RMR,* 21st Infantry; *WAGR,* ser. 1200, 1st Infantry Records, box 7, folder 5, Reports.

5. Cpl. William Murphy of Blackwolf, Wisconsin, enlisted August 21, 1862, and was reduced in rank September 24, 1863 (reason not indicated). *RMR,* 21st Infantry.

6. Sgt. John Dey was reduced to the ranks June 30, 1863 (reason not given). Ibid.

7. By one account, General Bragg, after the battle of Chickamauga, accepted an exchange of wounded prisoners but denied permission to bury the dead. Union dead on that part of the field occupied by General Longstreet's forces were buried, but many of those on the right, where General Polk commanded, were left unburied. They were buried by General Cruft some two months later. Van Horne, *The Army of the Cumberland,* 341–42. However, reports and correspondence in the OR indicate that for the first five days after Chickamauga, neither Rosecrans nor any of his senior subordinates had any contact with Bragg over the burial of Federal dead or the care of Federal wounded in Confederate hands. On September 26, Rosecrans sent Bragg a proposal for supplying food and medical supplies for the Federal wounded in his hands; Bragg accepted the next day. On September 28, Bragg gave permission to remove the bodies of general officers along with the wounded on the field but withheld permission for removal of the bodies of others until "a more opportune time." ser. 1, vol. 30, part 3, 872, 893, 911, 927.

8. Additional details of the near starvation among Federal troops in Chattanooga during the siege and of the desperate measures to which they resorted can be found in Peter Cozzens, *The Shipwreck of Their Hopes: The Battles for Chattanooga* (Urbana: Univ. of Illinois Press, 1994), 7–11, 22.

9. Maj. Gen. William Starke Rosecrans was relieved of command of the Army of the Cumberland on October 19, 1863. The decision to relieve Rosecrans was ultimately made by General Grant; Secretary of War Stanton recommended replacing Rosecrans with Thomas, but President Lincoln decided to leave the decision to Grant, who was provided with two sets of orders, one relieving Rosecrans and the other leaving him in command. Grant chose the former. Cozzens, *This Terrible Sound,* 527.

10. Second Lt. Julius P. Bissel of Oshkosh, Wisconsin, enlisted August 12, 1862, as a sergeant in Company C; he resigned his commission as a second lieutenant November 16, 1863. *RMR,* 21st Infantry.

11. Captain Otto filed two company muster-roll reports on February 10, 1864. The reports are monthly compilations of the status of the men in both Company C and Company D and indicate that he was in charge of both companies on that date. *WAGR,* ser. 1200, 21st Infantry Records, box 106, folders 3–13. Second Lt. Gustavus Jaeger of Neenah, Wisconsin, enlisted August 13, 1862. A muster roll dated September 1863 indicates he was in command of Company C in March and April 1864. He mustered out of service June 8, 1865, at Washington, D.C. *RMR,* 21st Infantry.

12. The 2d, 3d, 5th, 6th, 8th, and 12th Wisconsin Light Artillery Batteries, plus Battery C of the 1st Wisconsin Heavy Artillery, were in action or held in reserve at the battle of Chattanooga. The regimental roster and the *Index to the Wisconsin Volunteers, 1861–1865,* do not list a Captain Truesdell as commanding any of the batteries. Ibid.; *WAGR: Index to Wisconsin Volunteers 1861–1865,* ser. 1143, 3 vols. (origi-

nal alphabetical index). The artillery batteries that were located on Mocassin Point were the 10th Indiana Light Artillery Battery and the 18th Ohio Light Artillery Battery. Cozzens, *The Shipwreck of Their Hopes*, 162.

13. Capt. William A. Fargo of Fond du Lac, Wisconsin, enlisted August 12, 1862. He was a sergeant, second and first lieutenant, and captain in Company H. He resigned his commission January 7, 1865. *RMR*, 21st Infantry.

14. Capt. August Steffens was "dismissed" January 13, 1864. *RAGO, Illinois*, 1: 318.

15. Confederate forces on Missionary Ridge actually numbered about sixteen thousand, with nine batteries of artillery. Cozzens, *The Shipwreck of Their Hopes*, 248.

16. The headquarters of General Bragg was the home of Lt. Col. B. F. Moore, 19th Tennessee Infantry. James Lee McDonough, *Chattanooga: A Death Grip on the Confederacy* (Knoxville: Univ. of Tennessee Press, 1991), 204.

17. The positions held by the Confederates in and around the home of Colonel Moore were driven in by strong Federal forces. Bragg's headquarters were attacked and carried by parts of Col. Francis T. Sherman's and Col. Nathan H. Walworth's brigades, plus the 64th and 125th Ohio and the 79th Illinois. The Union forces captured several artillery pieces and nearly captured General Bragg in the process, but Bragg escaped on horseback among the retreating Confederate forces. Cozzens, *The Shipwreck of Their Hopes*, 306–7.

18. Sherman notes that on November 14 Grant told him that "the men of Thomas's army had been so demoralized by the battle of Chickamauga that he feared they could not be got out of their trenches to assume the offensive," but that if Sherman's troops were to attack first, "he had no doubt the Cumberland Army would fight well." *Memoirs*, 387.

19. The official record gives Grant's losses as 684 killed; 4,329 wounded; and 322 captured or missing. The Army of Tennessee reported losses of 361 killed; 2,180 wounded; and 4,146 missing; General Grant, however, reported 6,142 prisoners taken. Cozzens, *The Shipwreck of Their Hopes*, 389.

20. After his replacement by Johnston, Bragg served as a military adviser to Jefferson Davis. Called the Confederacy's "general in chief," Bragg supervised all Confederate military operations. Grady McWhiney, *Braxton Bragg and Confederate Defeat*, vol. 1: *Field Command* (New York: Columbia Univ. Press, 1969), x.

21. The "open letter to the powers at Washington" referred to here has not been identified. Sherman's views on the consolidation of veteran regiments are detailed in several letters in Brooks D. Simpson and Jean V. Berlin, eds., *Sherman's Civil War: Selected Correspondence of William T. Sherman, 1861–1865* (Chapel Hill: Univ. of North Carolina Press, 1999): to Ellen Ewing Sherman, April 23, 1863 (455–56); to John Sherman, April 23, 1863 (458–59); to John Sherman, April 26, 1863 (462–63); to Ulysses S. Grant, June 2, 1863 (474–76).

22. Sgt. (later Lt.) Lyman C. Waite was detailed to recruiting duty in Wisconsin starting November 21, 1863, and ending in February 1864. Capt. Henry Turner was detailed to recruiting service in Wisconsin starting December 6, 1863, until November 1864. *RMR*, 21st Infantry.

23. Lt. Col. Archibald Blakeley of Butler County, Pennsylvania, was mustered into military service October 18, 1861, and resigned his commission on April 8, 1864. J. T. Gibson, ed., *History of the 78th Pennsylvania Volunteer Infantry* (Mount Vernon, Ind.: Windmill, 1992), 19–21, 195.

24. The soldier-photographer is believed to be Pvt. William B. Roper, Company C of the 78th Pennsylvania Volunteer Infantry. Company C was raised in Clarion County, Pennsylvania, in 1861, and Private Roper enlisted on September 16. Gibson, *History of the 78th Pennsylvania Volunteer Infantry*, 204–8. The 1860 census report listed Roper's civilian occupation as artist. U.S. Bureau of the Census, *Eighth Census of the United States. 1860. Population Schedule. Clarion County, Pennsylvania*, RG 653, reel 1095. The U.S. Park Service historian indicates the date of Roper's death as March 11, 1864. U.S. Department of Interior, National Park Service, Chickamauga and Chattanooga National Military Park History Center, Fort Oglethorpe, Georgia.

13. PREPARATION FOR THE ATLANTA CAMPAIGN

1. "Colonel Straight" was Col. Abel D. Streight, who was not, however, the real leader of the Libby tunnel escape. Col. Thomas E. Rose engineered the escape but was recaptured, along with forty-seven other fugitives. Colonel Streight, along with sixty-one others, eluded capture through the help of a group of Unionist Richmond women and went on to become a highly vocal critic of conditions in Libby Prison. Frank L. Byrne, "Libby Prison: A Study in Emotions," *Journal of Southern History* 24 (Nov. 1958): 430–44. In an account of the escape read before the commandery of the state of Wisconsin, Military Order of the Loyal Legion of the United States, in 1891, Bvt. Brig. Gen. Harrison C. Hobart claims to have been in command of the escape. "Libby Prison: The Escape," *MOLLUS Wisconsin War Papers* (Milwaukee, 1891; rpt., Wilmington, N.C.: Broadfoot, 1993), 1: 400.

2. Pvt. Michael Hammond of Appleton, Wisconsin, enlisted August 13, 1862, and was severely wounded at Chickamauga. He mustered out with the regiment on June 8, 1865. Hospital Steward Peter E. Dane of Appleton, Wisconsin, enlisted August 11, 1862, and transferred to the U.S. Veteran Volunteer Engineers on July 18, 1864. *RMR*, 21st Infantry. Col. Geza Mihalotzy was in command of the 24th Illinois during a skirmish near Dalton, Georgia, on February 24, 1864, and was shot through the left side while making an inspection of the regiment's picket line. He died of his wounds on March 11, 1864, and was buried at the national cemetery near Dalton. *RAGO, Illinois*, 2: 327.

3. Pvt. Charles Russell of Appleton, Wisconsin, enlisted August 14, 1862. He was taken prisoner of war March 10, 1865, and was absent from his company when the regiment mustered out. *RMR*, 21st Infantry.

4. See note 11, chapter 12. Lieutenant Jaeger was absent from the regiment during the winter of 1863–64 due to the wounds he received in action at Chickamauga, September 20, 1863. He was granted a leave of absence and sent to his family's home in Ohio. Returning to the regiment he was placed in command of Company C during March and April 1864 and was in command of Company K from November 1864 until February 1865. Ibid.

5. Sherman's "Negro letter," to which Otto refers here, was written not to the president but to John A. Spooner, a recruiting officer appointed by the commonwealth of Massachusetts; it can be found in Simpson and Berlin, *Sherman's Civil*

War, 677–78. Another letter on the same subject to Adjutant General Thomas, in charge of raising colored troops in the West and Southwest, is given in S. M. Bowman and R. B. Irwin, *Sherman and His Campaigns: A Military Biography* (New York: C. B. Richardson; Cincinnati: C. F. Vent; Springfield, Ill.: W. J. Holland, 1865), 238–39. The letter to Spooner was reprinted in the *Chicago Tribune,* August 18, 1864. The *OR,* ser. 1, vol. 38, part 5, 136–37, 169, 210, contains two telegrams from Sherman to Halleck protesting the law allowing state recruiting agents in the Rebel states, a telegram from Lincoln to Sherman in support of the law, and Sherman's reply to Lincoln in which he promises to respect the law. John F. Marzalek, *Sherman's Other War: The General and the Civil War Press* (Kent, Ohio: Kent State Univ. Press, 1999), 181–85.

6. The left wing was informally called the "Army of Georgia" during the march through Georgia and the Carolinas, but the 14th and 20th Corps officially took the title only after the battle of Bentonville. Van Horne, *The Army of the Cumberland,* 543.

7. Sherman's army numbered 98,797 men—60,733 in the Army of the Cumberland, 24,465 in the Army of the Tennessee, and 13,559 in the Army of the Ohio. Johnston's army numbered 44,900. Sherman, *Memoirs,* 487; Van Horne, *The Army of the Cumberland,* 371.

8. Gen. William Passmore Carlin had received a colonel's commission on August 15, 1861. He distinguished himself at Perryville and was promoted to brigadier general in November 1862. He commanded the First Division, 14th Corps in the Carolina campaigns and was breveted to major general in both the regulars and volunteers. Warner, *Generals in Blue,* 69–70.

9. Pvt. Jacob Schneider of Menasha, Wisconsin, enlisted January 4, 1864. He was not one of the original volunteers but a new recruit. He transferred to the 3d Wisconsin Infantry on June 8, 1865. *RMR,* 21st Infantry.

10. Pvt. Jacob Rheiner of Menasha, Wisconsin, enlisted January 4, 1864. He was not an original volunteer but a new recruit. Ibid.

11. Maj. Gen. James Birdseye McPherson, an 1853 West Point graduate, was serving as a first lieutenant of engineers when the war broke out. By October 1862 he had been promoted to major general of volunteers. He took command of Sherman's old Army of the Tennessee on March 26, 1864, and led them through the subsequent campaign in northern Georgia. He was killed in action July 22, 1864, near Atlanta. Warner, *Generals in Blue,* 306–8.

14. THE BATTLE OF RESACA: TEDIOUS SKIRMISHING AND FINAL ADVANCE

1. Richard M. McMurry calls Johnston's failure to guard Snake Creek Gap "one of the great mistakes of the war" and doubts that he even knew of its existence, in spite of earlier claims to the contrary. Richard M. McMurry, *Atlanta 1864: Last Chance for the Confederacy* (Lincoln: Univ. of Nebraska Press, 2000), 48, 66, 213.

2. Maj. Gen. John McAllister Schofield commanded the Army of the Ohio (23d Corps) during the Atlanta campaign, and later the Department of North Carolina. Maj. Gen. Oliver Otis Howard commanded the 4th Corps in the Atlanta

campaign, and after the death of General McPherson, Sherman assigned him to the command of the Army of the Tennessee. Maj. Gen. Joseph Hooker, commander of the 20th Corps, resigned his command after the promotion of Howard, his subordinate. Warner, *Generals in Blue*, 233–35, 237–39, and 425–26.

3. Pvt. Frank Extine of Appleton, Wisconsin, enlisted January 25, 1864, and transferred to the 3d Infantry June 8, 1865. *RMR*, 21st Infantry.

4. Maj. Gen. James Birdseye McPherson commanded the Army of the Tennessee. He was killed in action near Atlanta, Georgia, July 22, 1864. Albert Castel, *Decision in the West: The Atlanta Campaign of 1864* (Lawrence: Univ. Press of Kansas, 1992), 398–99.

5. Pvt. Peter Green of Menasha, Wisconsin, enlisted December 21, 1863, and transferred to the 3d Infantry June 8, 1865. *RMR*, 21st Infantry.

6. Pvt. Lewis H. Sykes of Freedom, Wisconsin, enlisted August 14, 1862. He served on detached duty with the 4th Indiana Light Artillery battery from March 3, 1863, to November 24, 1863. He was killed in action at the battle of Resaca on May 14, 1864. Ibid.

7. The "History of the 21st Wisconsin" gives the regiment's casualties at Resaca as nine killed and thirty-eight wounded. *WAGR*, ser. 1200, box 106, folder 1.

8. Surgeon Benjamin C. Brett's casualty report for the battle of Resaca, dated May 16, 1864, indicates that Corporal Rawson was "shot through the right lung" and that Corporal Pierrelee was "shot through the left foot." The company descriptive list, which was filled out for soldiers separated from their regiments due to illness, desertion, or long-term detached service, does not show a casualty record for Private Jenkins, nor does Surgeon Brett's casualty report list Jenkins. Ibid., box 107, folder 3, Reports.

9. Brig. Gen. Peter J. Osterhaus commanded the First Division of Maj. Gen. John A. Logan's 15th Corps during the battle of Resaca. His report on the battle can be found in *OR*, ser. 1, vol. 38, part 3, 124–28; Gen Logan's report is in the same volume, 90–112. Both reports substantially agree with Otto's account of Osterhaus's assault of Bald Hill (not so named in the reports), except that the action seems to have taken place on May 13, not May 15.

10. Maj. Gen. Jefferson C. Davis commanded the Second Division of the 14th Corps. His report of operations between May 1 and August 22, 1864, describes the capture of Rome, Georgia, on May 18: "Three field pieces, five 32-pounder garrison guns, and two 8-inch howitzers were abandoned, and fell into our hands. The large iron-works and machine-shops of Noble and Company, upon which the enemy relied for a large part of his ordnance supplies and repairs, were captured in good condition." *OR*, ser. 1, vol. 38, part 1, 630.

11. The Know-Nothing Society, or American Party, was formed in New York in 1849 and enjoyed a brief but spectacular success. Its anti-immigrant platform called for restrictions on the immigration of paupers and criminals, strict voter-registration laws, and a twenty-one-year probationary period for naturalized citizens. Richard H. Sewell, *A House Divided: Sectionalism and the Civil War, 1848–1865* (Baltimore: Johns Hopkins Univ. Press, 1988), 41.

12. Pvt. Albert C. Bartlett of Rosendale, Wisconsin, enlisted March 24, 1864, and mustered out on June 8, 1865. Company records indicate that he was thirty-three at the time of his enlistment. *RMR*, 21st Infantry.

13. Maj. Gen. Richard W. Johnson commanded the First Division of the 14th Corps during the Atlanta campaign. He was badly wounded during the battle of New Hope Church, May 28, 1864, and upon his recovery became chief of cavalry of the Military Division of the Mississippi. Maj. Gen. John White Geary commanded the Second Division of the 20th Corps in the "March to the Sea" and then served as military governor of Savannah. Warner, *Generals in Blue*, 169–70, 253–54.

14. These were actually two separate engagements, though close together. See Castel, *Decision in the West*, 221–41.

15. Pvt. John Sutschutz of Menasha, Wisconsin, enlisted January 4, 1864, and was transferred to the 3d Infantry on June 8, 1865. Pvt. John Derby of Menasha, Wisconsin, enlisted January 4, 1864, and was transferred to the 3d Infantry on June 8, 1865. *RMR*, 21st Infantry.

16. The hospital registers indicate that Pvt. James Orr was "sent to G.[eneral] H.[ospital] 05–08–63, insanity, returned to duty 06-02-63; sent to same 11-21-63, retd. 12–16–63, insanity." He mustered out with his company on June 8, 1865. Ibid.

17. Cpl. Charles H. Hilfert of Menasha, Wisconsin, enlisted January 4, 1864, and transferred to the 3d Infantry on June 8, 1865. Ibid.

18. Lt. James E. Stuart of Oshkosh, Wisconsin, enlisted August 4, 1862. He was commissioned as a second lieutenant on February 4, 1863, and was promoted to first lieutenant on December 23, 1863. He mustered out of service on June 8, 1865. Ibid.

19. Pvt. Julius Weinert of Menasha, Wisconsin, enlisted January 4, 1864, and transferred to the 3d Infantry on June 8, 1865. Ibid.

20. Pvt. John Robinson of Neenah, Wisconsin, enlisted August 14, 1862. He was killed in action on May 31, 1864, at the battle of Dallas, Georgia. Ibid.

21. Pvt. Simon Shelley of Brothertown, Wisconsin, enlisted August 13, 1862, and was severely wounded on May 28, 1864, at Dallas, Georgia. Hospital records from the Harvey General Military Hospital in Madison, Wisconsin, show that Private Shelley received a severe gunshot wound to the lower jaw and left shoulder. Entry for Private Simon Shelley, Company E, 21st Wisconsin Infantry Regiment, Wisconsin Hospital Register 71, Harvey General Hospital, National Archives microfilm publication (9W3/11/10/D); Records of the Record and Pension Office, 1784–1917; RG 94, Adjutant General's Office, National Archives, Washington, D.C.

22. Second Lt. Hiram K. Edwards of Clayton, Wisconsin, was commissioned May 8, 1863. He had served in company G of the 3d Wisconsin Volunteer Infantry as a sergeant and second lieutenant before joining Company A of the 21st Infantry. He attained the rank of captain in Company A and mustered out on June 8, 1865. Capt. Albert Bradish of Neenah, Wisconsin, was commissioned November 21, 1864. He served in Company I and mustered out on June 8, 1865. *RMR*, 21st Infantry.

23. The officer known as "Buckskin" or "Old Leather Breeches" was Capt. Hubert Dilger, who served with the 2d Ohio Light Artillery Regiment. A description of the battle of Chancellorsville and the participation by Captain Dilger is given by Maj. Gen. Oliver O. Howard in Johnson and Buel, *Battles and Leaders of the Civil War*, 1: 197–201. A biography by Dilger's grandson, Carl A. Keyser, *Leatherbreeches: Hero of Chancellorsville* (Amherst, N.H.: Amherst Press, 1989), like Otto's memoir, gives a German immigrant's perspective on the war.

1. The action at Big Shanty (now known as Kennesaw), Georgia, also referred to as the Andrews Raid, took place on April 12, 1862. The raid was commanded by the Union spy James J. Andrews and was made up of twenty-four Union army volunteers. Plans were laid to capture a Southern train and travel the northern parts of the Georgia State Railroad, causing as much destruction as possible by burning the northern sections of bridges. Andrews and his men captured a locomotive named "The General" at Big Shanty and began their ill-fated journey. The raid ended in total failure; Andrews and seven other members were hanged as spies. The other members of the raid were held as prisoners or escaped confinement. William Pittenger, "The Locomotive Chase in Georgia," in Johnson and Buel, *Battles and Leaders of the Civil War,* 2: 709–16. Pittenger was one of the soldiers involved in the raid. His 1887 book on it has recently been reissued: William Pittenger, *The History of the Andrews Railroad Raid in Georgia in 1862* (Scituate, Mass.: Digital Scanning, 2001).

2. Sgt. Julius Hesse of Neenah, Wisconsin, enlisted August 13, 1862, and was wounded in the engagement at Kennesaw Mountain, Georgia, on July 2, 1864. He was reduced to the ranks on November 1, 1864, while absent from the company. He was absent, sick, or wounded, in March 1865 and mustered out of the regiment June 6, 1865, by orders from Washington, D.C. RMR, 21st Infantry.

3. Lt. Gen. Leonidas Polk, C.S.A., was killed on June 14, 1864, atop Pine Mountain while reconnoitering Union positions. Castel, *Decision in the West,* 275–77.

4. Sherman gives his losses at Kennesaw Mountain as 2,500 killed and wounded, and he quotes Johnston's "Narrative," which gives the Confederate losses in killed and wounded at 808. *Memoirs,* 531. Castel calculates Sherman's losses as a total of 2,638 killed, wounded, and missing, and Johnston's losses as "about 700." *Decision in the West,* 319–20.

5. Pvt. Levant Vandebogart was absent from Company D starting May 23, 1863, when he was sent to the Convalescent Camp at Murfreesboro, Tennessee. He was sent to the Invalid Corps (Veterans Reserve Corps) in July 1863. RMR, 21st Infantry.

6. Pvt. Samuel C. Sargent of Oshkosh, Wisconsin, enlisted August 12, 1862, giving his occupation as machinist. Regimental records cite the *Roll of Honor,* vol. 18, 355, which lists Private Sargent as having died February 23, 1866, and having been buried in a "private lot." Ibid.

7. Cpl. Norman W. Northam of Oshkosh, Wisconsin, enlisted August 13, 1862, and served in Company C. A bimonthly muster roll indicates that Northam was in the hospital in February 1865 but does not list the reason. Ibid.

8. Brig. Gen. Kenner Garrard commanded the Second Cavalry Division of the Army of the Cumberland during the Atlanta campaign. Warner, *Generals in Blue,* 167–68.

9. Brig. Gen. Winfield Scott Featherston, C.S.A., was not killed, but served the Confederacy until the end of the war, when he surrendered in North Carolina. After the war he returned to his law firm in Mississippi and entered the state legislature. Brig. Gen. Edmund Winston Pettus, C.S.A., was wounded during the Carolina campaign but survived the war and established a legal practice in Selma, Alabama; he would serve in the U.S. Senate until his death in 1907. Brig. Gen. Clement Hoffman Stevens was severely wounded on July 20, 1864; he was removed

from the battlefield and taken to Atlanta, where he died July 25, 1864. No record
can be found of a Confederate general by the name of Long killed in the Atlanta
area during 1864. Maj. Gen. William Henry Talbot Walker was killed in action
July 22, 1864, during Hardee's attack on the Federal left. Ezra J. Warner, *Generals in
Gray: The Lives of the Confederate Commanders* (Baton Rouge: Louisiana State Univ.
Press, 1959), 86–87, 238–39, 291–92, 323–24.

10. Maj. Gen. Grenville Mellen Dodge commanded the 16th Corps during the
Atlanta campaign. He went on to command the Department of Missouri and later
the Department of Kansas. After the war he built the Union Pacific Railroad. Maj.
Gen. Francis Preston Blair commanded the 17th Corps during the Atlanta campaign. He resigned his commission in November 1864. Warner, *Generals in Blue*,
35–37, 127–28.

11. No record can be found for a General Greathouse, on the Northern side,
killed in action during the Atlanta campaign. Sherman in his report on the battle
of Atlanta estimated Confederate casualties at eight thousand; Castel believes this
estimate is too high and that Confederate casualties were about 5,500. *Decision in
the West*, 412.

12. Maj. Gen. Henry Warner Slocum was assigned command of the 20th Corps
after the death of General McPherson. Maj. Gen. John McCauley Palmer commanded the 14th Corps at Chattanooga and during the Atlanta campaign. In August 1864 he requested that Sherman relieve him of command because of an argument over relative rank. He ended the war in command of the Department of
Kentucky. Warner, *Generals in Blue*, 358–59, 451–53.

13. The 21st Infantry records lack casualty reports for the officers of Companies
F and H during the battle of Peachtree Creek. Surgeons Reeve, Fuller, and Brett
do not mention any officers wounded in either company at Peachtree Creek. *RMR*,
21st Infantry; *WAGR*, ser. 1200, 21st Infantry records, box 107, folder 3, Reports.

14. General Logan's report on the battle of Ezra Church is given in Sherman's
Memoirs. Logan gives casualty figures as follows: 50 killed, 449 wounded, and 73
missing, for a total of 572. Confederate prisoners were 106, exclusive of wounded,
of whom 73 were captured; Confederate killed were about 765. Logan estimates
the total Rebel loss at between six and seven thousand. Sherman, *Memoirs*, 563–64.
Castel gives Union losses at Ezra Church at 632 killed, wounded, and missing; he
estimates Confederate losses at "close to 3,000." *Decision in the West*, 434.

15. In a letter to his wife written August 9, 1864, in the field near Atlanta, Sherman
states, "I am capturing & sending north hundreds of prisoners daily and have not
intercourse with the Enemy. I have not exchanged a single message, not even a flag
of truce." Simpson and Berlin, *Sherman's Civil War*, 685. The correspondence between Sherman and Hood to which Otto refers may be the later exchange of
letters after the fall of Atlanta, when Sherman ordered the civilian population to
leave the city. See ibid., 704–7.

16. Capt. Henry Turner of Appleton, Wisconsin, was severely wounded on
August 7, 1864, at Atlanta. The officers casualty list indicates that he was shot through
the neck. Sgt. John Dey of Greenville, Wisconsin, was slightly wounded August 7,
1864, at Atlanta. The casualty list indicates that Dey received a slight flesh wound,
having been shot through the left thigh. Pvt. Miles Hoskins of Shiocton, Wisconsin, was wounded on August 7, 1864, at Atlanta. The casualty list indicates that

Private Hoskins was shot through the bowels ("Mortal") and died August 8, 1864, at the field hospital near Atlanta. *WAGR*, ser. 1200, 21st Infantry records, box 107, folder 3, Reports.

17. Pvt. Henry Fink of Oshkosh, Wisconsin, enlisted August 15, 1862. He was killed in action on August 23, 1864, at Atlanta. *RMR*, 21st Infantry.

18. Lt. Gen. William Joseph Hardee (1815–1873) fought at Shiloh, Perryville, and Stone's River, and after Missionary Ridge he temporarily commanded the Army of Tennessee. He was offered permanent command but declined, and the command was given to Joseph E. Johnston. After Johnston was replaced by Hood, Hardee asked for a transfer and was given command of the defenses of coastal Georgia and the Carolinas. His *Rifle and Light Infantry Tactics* was the standard manual for officers on both sides of the Civil War. John A. Garraty and Mark C. Carnes, eds., *American National Biography* (New York: Oxford Univ. Press, 1999). A scholarly biography of Hardee is Nathaniel Cheairs Hughes Jr., *General William J. Hardee: Old Reliable* (Baton Rouge: Louisiana State Univ. Press, 1992).

19. Second Lt. William C. Hubbard of Oshkosh, Wisconsin, enlisted as a sergeant on August 21, 1861. He was commissioned as a second lieutenant on January 1, 1865, and served in Company C. He mustered out on June 8, 1865. First Lt. Edgar Vredenburg of Winneconne, Wisconsin, enlisted August 14, 1862, as a sergeant, and was commissioned as a first lieutenant on August 31, 1864. *RMR*, 21st Infantry.

20. Pvt. Cornelius Endone of Menasha, Wisconsin, enlisted December 19, 1863, giving his residence as the Oneida Indian Reservation, Brown County, and his place of birth as New York. He was officially listed as missing in action on September 6, 1864. Ibid.

21. Correspondence on the removal of the citizens from Atlanta is given in Sherman's *Memoirs*, 593–602; the official account of the people sent south is also given on pages 1012–26.

22. A request for a twenty-day leave of absence was filed by John Henry Otto on August 22, 1864, from the regiment's camp near Atlanta; the reasons given were to return to his hometown and rebuild his family dwelling, which had been consumed by fire on August 10. The original request is located in the *WAGR*, ser. 1200, 21st Infantry records, box 110, folder 6.

16. THE ARMY FOUND AGAIN. SAVANNAH.
A VALUABLE CHRISTMAS PRESENT

1. Quartermaster Bartholomew J. Van Valkenburg of Two Rivers, Wisconsin, enlisted August 14, 1862, and was promoted to sergeant major on September 5, 1862. He was commissioned as a captain on May 21, 1863, and was made an acting quartermaster of volunteers on May 18, 1864. *RMR*, 21st Infantry.

2. The records for Company D show the following 10th Infantry replacements: Charles F. Adams, Company H; Leland M. Amandon, Company G; Michael Baker, Company H; Or-ville S. Coddington, Company K; Gale Cram, Company K; Gilbert Gilsen, Company K; Eli Gray, Company D; Herman Hermanson, Company K; Horace J. Knox, Company K; and Peleg B. Ross, Company K. Ibid.

3. Sherman's strength at the beginning of his march to the sea was approximately 60,000 infantry and 5,500 cavalry, with one piece of artillery for each thousand men. Van Horne, *The Army of the Cumberland,* 515.

4. Joseph Emerson Brown (1821–94) was elected governor of Georgia in 1857 and reelected in 1859, 1861, and 1863; he remained in office until June 25, 1865. After Lincoln's election he strongly supported secession but consistently opposed the Confederate government's authority over the states. After the fall of Atlanta Sherman unsuccessfully tried to arrange peace negotiations with him in a bid to separate Georgia from the Confederacy. Garraty and Caracs, *American National Biography.* A standard biography is Joseph H. Parks, *Joseph E. Brown of Georgia* (Baton Rouge: Louisiana State Univ. Press, 1977).

5. The 12th Georgia Infantry did not fight at the battle of Stone's River, nor did it have a colonel named Hector Burton. *Confederate Military History,* vol. 7: *Georgia.* (Wilmington, N.C.: Broadfoot, 1987), 34–35.

6. It was Gen. Jeff. C. Davis at Ebenezer Creek who actually took up the pontoon bridge before the black camp followers could cross. Joseph T. Glatthaar, *The March to the Sea and Beyond: Sherman's Troops in the Savannah and Carolinas Campaigns* (1985; rpt., Louisiana State Univ. Press, 1995), 64. Sherman mentions the incident and includes a letter from General Halleck, dated December 30, 1864, in which Halleck repeats the accusation against Sherman as current among certain of the president's advisers. *Memoirs,* 724, 728.

7. Sherman relates a similar incident with a "torpedo" (land mine) as having happened to an officer of the 17th Corps on December 8, and he reports having ordered Rebel prisoners to march in front, with picks and spades, to explode their own torpedoes or dig them up. *Memoirs,* 670.

8. The preceding two sentences, as well as the last two sentences in the previous paragraph, are paraphrased from Bowman and Irwin, *Sherman and His Campaigns,* 292–93.

9. This sentence is paraphrased from ibid., 312.

10. A letter from General Sherman to President Lincoln, dated December 22, 1864. Sherman, *Memoirs,* 711.

11. Special Field Order No. 15, from the Headquarters Military Division of the Mississippi, in the Field, Savannah, Georgia, [dated] January 16, 1865. Issued by Maj. Gen. W. T. Sherman. Sherman, *Memoirs,* 730.

12. Sherman's Field Order No. 15 was contrived to solve the desperate problem of destitution among the Negroes who had fled the South's plantations. Sherman followed a plan of wholesale redistribution of lands formerly held by prominent citizens in several areas of the deep South. He granted ownership of the confiscated South Carolina and Georgia sea islands and many miles of the abandoned rice fields along the adjacent rivers to the Negroes. The lands were divided into farms of forty acres, and Negro families were granted "possessory titles" until such time as the Congress could act upon their final disposition. Gen. Rufus Saxton was appointed Inspector of Settlements and Plantations. He settled forty thousand Negroes in these areas and testified to the program's success. But early in the era of Reconstruction, President Andrew Johnson saw to it that the lands were eventually returned to the original owners and their heirs, citing as justification Article 3,

Section 3, Part 2 of the Constitution of the United States, which states that "The Congress shall have power to declare the punishment of treason, but no attainder of treason shall work corruption of blood, or forfeiture except during the life of the person attained." Thus Sherman's radical Field Order No. 15, and early compliance with the Thirteenth Amendment, fell far short of their intended aims. James M. McPerson, *Battle Cry of Freedom: The Civil War Era* (New York: Ballantine, 1989), 840–44; Kenneth M. Stampp, *The Era of Reconstruction 1865–1877* (New York: Vintage, 1965), 124–27.

13. Pvt. Eli Gray of Big Springs, Wisconsin, originally enlisted in Company D of the 10th Wisconsin Infantry. He was transferred to the 3d Infantry on June 8, 1865. No record can be found for an Eli Gray in the 3d Infantry Regiment. Pvt. Gale Cram of Iola, Wisconsin, originally enlisted in Company K of the 10th Infantry. He received a surgeon's certificate of disability and was discharged on May 26, 1865. Pvt. Orvil L. Coddington of Waupun, Wisconsin, originally enlisted in Company K of the 10th Wisconsin Infantry. He was transferred to the 3d Wisconsin Infantry on June 8, 1865, and mustered out June 26, 1865. He is listed in the 3d Infantry records under the name of Caddington. *RMR*, 21st Infantry.

17. FACING NORTHWARD: AVERYSBORO.
THE BATTLE AT BENTONVILLE

1. Pvt. Henry Krafft of Cascade, Wisconsin, enlisted August 18, 1862. He transferred into the 21st Infantry from Company H of the 1st Wisconsin Infantry and mustered out June 8, 1865. *RMR*, 21st Infantry.

2. We have been unable to identify this soldier. Of the sixty-one soldiers named Whitcomb in the Union cavalry listed on the National Park Service's Web site, "Civil War Soldiers and Sailors System," at http://www.itd.nps.gov/cwss/, only one is listed as a captain, and his unit apparently was stationed in Minnesota throughout the war.

3. The 21st Infantry regimental records list the following officers: 2d Lt. James H. Jenkins, adjutant, of Oshkosh, Wisconsin, originally with Company B; Capt. James M. Randall of Weyauwega, Wisconsin, originally a sergeant in Company B of the 14th Infantry, and then a second lieutenant; Capt. William L. Watson of St. Lawrence, Wisconsin, Company G, then a first lieutenant; and 1st Lt. Charles H. Morgan of Black Wolf, Wisconsin, then a second lieutenant, Company F. These officers were all taken prisoner on September 20, 1863, during the battle of Chickamauga. *RMR*, 21st Infantry.

4. These orders are included in General Orders No. 26, dated February 16, 1865, dealing with the prescribed elements of the march toward Fayetteville, North Carolina. Sherman, *Memoirs*, 758–59.

5. Otto has taken the preceding two paragraphs almost verbatim from Bowman and Irwin, *Sherman and His Campaigns*, 343. Otto twice cites this book and appears to have borrowed from it several times for descriptions of the movements of the army. An in-depth study of the controversy surrounding the burning of Columbia can be found in Marion Brunson Lucas, *Sherman and the Burning of Columbia* (College Station: Texas A&M Univ. Press, 1976).

6. The 21st Infantry regimental records do not show a Bill or William Ferguson. They do list a Pvt. George Ferguson of Davenport, Wisconsin, who served in Company D. He originally enlisted in Company C of the 1st Infantry and transferred to the 21st on November 27, 1863. He transferred to the 3d Infantry on June 8, 1865, when the 21st mustered out of service. *RMR,* 21st Infantry.

7. The 21st Infantry records show a listing for a sergeant John W. Cox of Oshkosh, Wisconsin, who enlisted August 14, 1862, and mustered out June 8, 1865, at Washington, D.C. The regimental records do not show a promotion to the rank of lieutenant for this soldier. Ibid.

8. Parts of this paragraph are taken almost verbatim from Bowman and Irwin, *Sherman and His Campaigns,* 353, 367.

9. Sherman notes the capture of Rhett's brigade with three guns and 217 prisoners, Rhett's casualties of 108 killed and 68 wounded (left in a house in care of an officer and four men of the Rebel prisoners), as well as Union losses of 12 officers and 65 men killed, and 477 wounded. *Memoirs,* 783–84.

10. Pvt. Herman Hasz of Prairie du Chien, Wisconsin, served in Company D, having transferred from Company H of the 1st Wisconsin Infantry. He was killed in action on March 19, 1865, at Bentonville, North Carolina. *RMR,* 21st Infantry.

11. At noon on the nineteenth, the Confederates had about 10,000 troops on the battlefield, against about 2,000 Union troops; by late afternoon, the Confederates had about 16,000 troops against about 20,000 Union troops. By the next day, Johnston had managed to gather about 20,000 men, while Sherman had about 55,000. Mark L. Bradley, *Last Stand in the Carolinas: The Battle of Bentonville* (Campbell, Calif.: Savas Woodbury, 1996), 178, 309, 347.

12. The 21st Infantry records show that only one officer was killed during the battle of Bentonville on March 19, 1865. The officer was 1st Lt. Edward S. Midgley of Fond du Lac, Wisconsin. Lt. Midgley had been a sergeant in Company H before being promoted to the rank of first lieutenant. This man is probably the officer to whom Captain Otto refers. In a casualty report and list of burial locations dated June 5, 1865, sent to Lt. Col. Michael H. Fitch by Chaplain Orson P. Clinton, is a description of the death of Midgley: "1st Lieutenant, Mortally wounded in action, Bentonville, N.C., March 19, 1865 and died on the field. Buried on the field in the woods, name cut on a tree near." *WAGR,* ser. 1200, 21st Infantry, box 107, folder 3, Reports. See also *Quarterly Returns of Deceased Soldiers,* box 108, folder 1.

13. The regiment of New Jersey Zouaves to which Captain Otto refers may have been the 35th New Jersey Infantry, which was at the battle of Bentonville. Company G was known as the "Cladek Zouaves," in honor of its commander Col. John J. Cladek. Company H was also a veteran Zouave unit. Donald A. Sinclair, *A Bibliography of the Civil War and New Jersey* (New Brunswick, N.J.: Rutgers Univ. Library, 1961), 66. Other New Jersey troops at Bentonville were the 13th New Jersey and the 33d New Jersey. The 17th New York was also a Zouave regiment and could have been the regiment Otto mentions. Nathaniel Cheairs Hughes Jr., *Bentonville: The Final Battle of Sherman and Johnston* (Chapel Hill: Univ. of North Carolina Press, 1996), 239, 248n42.

14. The preceding two sentences are taken almost verbatim from Bowman and Irwin, *Sherman and His Campaigns,* 372. Although major Confederate assaults on the nineteenth lacked effective artillery support, Major A. Burnet Rhett's artillery

battalion remained parked in the rear of the battlefield and was never brought up. Bradley, *Last Stand in the Carolinas,* 304.

15. General Sherman's order informing his troops of the defeat of Lee at Appomattox is dated April 12, 1865, not April 11. Sherman, *Memoirs,* 832.

16. Special Field Orders No. 56. Sherman, *Memoirs,* 839.

18. WASHINGTON. THE GREAT PARADE

1. Sherman and Johnston actually met at the house of a Mr. Bennett, near Durham Station, on April 17 and 18. Sherman, *Memoirs,* 837–42.

2. A copy of the agreement between Johnston and Sherman is given ibid., 844–45.

3. General Lee actually surrendered only 28,356 officers and men to General Grant. Grant had also captured between March 29 and the date of surrender (April 9, 1865) 19,132 men, in addition to those killed, wounded, and missing during that time. Grant, *Memoirs and Selected Letters,* 441.

4. Sherman states that he sent Halleck an enciphered dispatch indicating that he preferred not to meet with him as he passed through Richmond, and says that Halleck had ordered a review of the 14th Corps by himself, which Sherman forbade. *Memoirs,* 863. Sherman's run-in with Halleck is described in detail in John F. Marszalek, *Sherman: A Soldier's Passion for Order* (New York: Vintage, 1994), 350–53.

5. Pvt. George Demouth of Milwaukee, Wisconsin, was drafted November 10, 1863, into Company H of the 1st Wisconsin Infantry. He was thereafter transferred to the 21st Infantry and then to the 3d Infantry. RMR, 21st Infantry.

6. The incident between General Sherman and Secretary of War Stanton is recounted by Sherman in his memoirs: "I shook hands with the President, General Grant, and each member of the cabinet. As I approached Mr. Stanton, he offered me his hand, but I declined it publicly, and the fact was universally noticed." Sherman, *Memoirs,* 866.

7. Regimental records indicate 105 original enlistments in Company D. Of those men enlisted in August 1862, five were killed in action, eighteen died of disease or wounds, and eighteen were wounded but survived. Twenty-five men were discharged from active military service due to disease or wounds received in action, and ten were transferred to the Invalid Corps for similar reasons. Three men were listed as missing when the regiment answered the last roll call in 1865. RMR, 21st Infantry.

Bibliography

~

STATE HISTORICAL SOCIETY OF WISCONSIN
ARCHIVES RECORDS

Civil War Records

Adjutant General's Records. County Draft Books, 1862–1863. Ser. 1145. 2 vols.
———. District Enrollment Board Rolls of Draftees and Substitutes, 1863–1865. Ser. 1148. 5 boxes.
———. Index to Wisconsin Volunteers 1861–1865. Ser. 1143. 3 vols. (Original alphabetical index).
———. Regimental Muster and Descriptive Rolls (Blue books), 1861–1865, ca. 1885. Ser. 1142. 59 vols.
———. Regimental Muster and Descriptive Rolls (Red books), 1861–1865. Ser. 1144. 57 vols.
———. Records of Civil War Regiments 1861–1893. Ser. 1200, 1st–53d Infantry, 1st–4th Cavalry, 1st–13th Light Artillery, 1st Heavy Artillery, U.S. Engineers, U.S. Sharpshooters, and U.S. Colored Troops. 172 boxes.
———. State Military Agents' Correspondence, 1862–1865. Ser. 1147. 1 box.
———. State Military Agents Hospital Reports, 1862–1865. Ser. 1146. 5 boxes.
———. Officer Records of Volunteer Regiments, 1861–1890. Ser. 1201. 12 boxes.
Office of the Executive Records. (Governor's Records.) Records of Disposition of Personal Effects of Dead Wisconsin Soldiers, 1863. Ser. 56. 1 vol.
———. (Governor's Records.) Applications for Commissions, 1861–1865. Ser. 65. 9 boxes.
Quiner, Edwin Bentley. *Correspondence of the Wisconsin Volunteers, 1861–1865.* MSS 600 [newspaper clippings collected during the Civil War by E. B. Quiner]. 18 vols.
———. Desertion Records—Civil War, 1861–1867. Ser. 293. 1 vol.

412 ———. Lists of Deserters and Deserters Excused, 1866, 1868. Ser. 298. 1 box.
———. Veterans Reserve Corps (Volunteers Aid), 1864–1865. Ser. 250. 1 vol.
United States. Army. Wisconsin Infantry Regiment, 21st (1862–1865). Company G. 21st Regiment, Company G, descriptive book, 1862–1865. Ser. 1229 (1 vol.).
United States. Army. Wisconsin Infantry Regiment, 21st (1862–1865). 21st Infantry Hospital Records, 1863–1865. Ser. 1230.

Manuscripts

Clinton, Orson P. 1808–1890. Papers and Letters, 1862–1864. [Microform], Microfilm 60. Chaplain 21st Wisconsin Infantry Regiment. 1 reel of microfilm (35 mm).
Galpin, Alfred Maurice, 1901–1983. Galpin Family Papers: MSS–182. Letters and papers of Pvt. Alfred Galpin II. Company H, 1st Wisconsin Infantry Regiment.
Knapp, Charles Webster. Civil War Letters, 1864–1865: SC 538. Company K, 21st Wisconsin Infantry Regiment.
Reeve, James T. (James Theodore), 1834–1906. Papers, Letters, and Diarys of Surgeon James T. Reeve: WIS-MSS-3P. Regimental Surgeon, 21st Wisconsin Infantry Regiment.

NATIONAL ARCHIVES RECORDS, WASHINGTON, D.C.

Records of the Adjutant General's Office, 1780s–1917. Record Group 94: Records of the Record and Pension Office, 1784–1917.
Records of the Adjutant General's Office, 1780s–1917. Record Group 94: Proceedings of the U.S. Courts-Martial and Military Commissions of Union Soldiers Executed by U.S. Military Authorities, 1861–1866.
Records of the Office of the Judge Advocate General (Army). Record Group 153: Court-Martial Records, 1805–1939.
Records of the Provost Marshal General's Bureau (Civil War). Record Group 110. Records of the Central Office, 1862–1889.
Records of the Veterans Administration. Record Group 15: Civil War Pension Files, 1861–1934.
United States. Census Office. 8th Census, 1860. Population schedules of the 8th census of the United States. Record Group 653.

OFFICIAL GOVERNMENT PUBLICATIONS

State of Illinois

Adjutant General's Office: Report of the Adjutant General's Office, State of Illinois, containing reports for the years 1861–1865. 9 vols. Vol. 2, revised by Brig. Gen. J. W. Vance. Springfield, Ill.: H. W. Rokker, State Publisher, 1886. 24th Infantry regimental records.

State of Indiana

Report of the Adjutant General, State of Indiana: vol. 7, 1861–1865; 9 vols., Containing rosters of enlisted men of Indiana regiments numbered from the one hundred and eleventh to the one hundred and fifty-sixth, inclusive; colored troops; and batteries light artillery, numbered from the first to the twenty-sixth, inclusive. Indianapolis: Samuel M. Douglas, State Printer, 1867.

State of Michigan

Adjutant General's Office: Record of Service of Michigan Volunteers in the Civil War, 1861–1865. Published by Authority of the Senate and House of Representatives of Michigan Legislature, under the direction of Brig. Gen. George H. Brown, Adjutant General. 46 vols. Kalamazoo, Mich.: Ihling Bros. and Everard, 1905.

State of Wisconsin

Roster of the Wisconsin Volunteers: War of the Rebellion, 1861–1865. Jeremiah M. Rusk, Governor, Democrat Printing Company, State Printer, 1886. Madison, Wis. 2 vols.

Wisconsin Volunteers: War of the Rebellion, 1861–1865. Madison, Wis., 1914 (published index).

United States

National Park Service. "Civil War Soldiers and Sailors System." http://www.itd.nps.gov/cwss/.

U.S. Bureau of the Census; *Eighth Census of the United States. 1860. Population Schedule. Clarion County, Pennsylvania.* Record Group 653, reel 1095.

War of the Rebellion: A Compilation of the Official Records of the Union and Confederate Armies. Washington, D.C.: U.S. Government Printing Office, 1880–1901.

Other Published Sources

Bates, Samuel P. *History of the 79th Pennsylvania Infantry Regiment, 1861–1865.* 25 vols. Wilmington, N.C.: Broadfoot, 1993.

Beers, J. H. *Commemorative Biographical Record of Fox River Valley.* Chicago, 1895.

Boatner, Mark M., III. *The Civil War Dictionary.* New York: Vintage, 1991.

Bowman, S. M., and R. B. Irwin. *Sherman and His Campaigns: A Military Biography.* New York: C. B. Richardson; Cincinnati: C. F. Vent; Springfield, Ill.: W. J. Holland, 1865.

Bradley, Mark L. *Last Stand in the Carolinas: The Battle of Bentonville.* Campbell, California: Savas Woodbury, 1996.

Byrne, Frank L. "Libby Prison: A Study in Emotions." *Journal of Southern History* 24 (Nov. 1958): 430–44.

414   Castel, Albert. *Decision in the West: The Atlanta Campaign of 1864.* Lawrence: Univ. Press of Kansas, 1992.

———. "The Fort Pillow Massacre: A Fresh Examination of the Evidence." *Civil War History* 4, no. 1 (March 1958).

———. *William Clarke Quantrill: His Life and Times.* New York: Frederick Fell, 1962.

Cist, Henry M. *The Army of the Cumberland.* New York: Scribner's, 1882.

Confederate Military History. Extended ed. Vol. 7: *Georgia.* Wilmington, N.C.: Broadfoot, 1987.

Cozzens, Peter. *No Better Place to Die: The Battle of Stones River.* Urbana: Univ. of Illinois Press, 1990.

———. *The Shipwreck of their Hopes: The Battle for Chattanooga.* Urbana: Univ. of Illinois Press, 1994.

———. *This Terrible Sound: The Battle of Chickamauga.* Urbana: Univ. of Illinois Press, 1992.

Current, Richard N. *The History of Wisconsin: The Civil War Era, 1848–1873.* 2 vols. Madison: State Historical Society of Wisconsin, 1976.

Davis, George B., et al. *Atlas to Accompany the Official Records of the Union and Confederate Armies.* Washington, D.C.: Government Printing Office, 1891–95.

Dodge, Grenville M. *The Battle of Atlanta and Other Campaigns.* 1911; Earlysville, Va.: Old Books, 1996.

Duke, Basil W. *A History of Morgan's Cavalry.* 1867. Ed. Cecil Fletcher Holland. Civil War Centennial Series. Bloomington: Indiana Univ. Press, 1960.

Engle, Stephen D. *Don Carlos Buell: Most Promising of All.* Chapel Hill: Univ. of North Carolina Press, 1999.

———. *Yankee Dutchman: The Life of Franz Sigel.* Baton Rouge: Univ. of Louisiana Press, 1999.

Faust, Patricia. Historical Times *Illustrated Encyclopedia of the Civil War.* New York: Historical Times, 1986.

Fitch, Michael H. *Echoes of the Civil War as I Hear Them.* New York: R. F. Reno, 1905.

———. *The Chattanooga Campaign, with Reference to Wisconsin's Participation Therein.* Madison: Wisconsin History Commission, 1911.

Garraty, John A., and Mark C. Carnes, eds. *American National Biography.* New York: Oxford Univ. Press, 1999.

Gibson, J. T., ed. *History of the 78th Pennsylvania Infantry Regiment.* Mount Vernon, Ind.: Windmill, 1992.

Glatthaar, Joseph T. *Forged in Battle: The Civil War Alliance of Black Soldiers and White Officers.* 1990; rpt. New York: Meridian, 1991.

———. *The March to the Sea and Beyond: Sherman's Troops in the Savannah and Carolinas Campaigns.* 1985; rpt. Baton Rouge: Louisiana State Univ. Press, 1995.

Grant, Ulysses Simpson. *Memoirs and Selected Letters: Personal Memoirs of U.S. Grant; Selected Letters 1839–1865.* New York: Library of America, 1990.

Hafendorfer, Kenneth A. *Perryville: The Battle for Kentucky.* 2nd ed. Utica, Ky.: McDowell, 1991.

Hobart, Harrison H. "Libby Prison: The Escape." In *War Papers: Being Papers Read before the Commandery of the State of Wisconsin, Military Order of the Loyal Legion of the United States.* 1: 394–409. Milwaukee, 1891; rpt. Wilmington, N.C.: Broadfoot, 1993.

Holmes, Mead. *A Soldier of the Cumberland: Memoir of Mead Holmes Jr., Sergeant of*
Company K, 21st Regiment Wisconsin Volunteers. Boston: American Tract Society,
[1864].

Hughes, Nathaniel Cheairs, Jr. *Bentonville: The Final Battle of Sherman and Johnston.*
Chapel Hill: Univ. of North Carolina Press, 1996

———. *General William J. Hardee: Old Reliable.* Baton Rouge: Louisiana State Univ.
Press, 1992.

Johnson, Robert Underwood, and Clarence Clough Buel, eds. *Battles and Leaders*
of the Civil War. 4 vols. Secaucus, N.J.: Book Sales, 1985.

Johnson, Rossiter. *Campfires and Battlefields: A Pictorial Narrative of the Civil War.*
New York: The Blue and the Grey Press, 1958.

Keyser, Carl A. *Leatherbreeches: Hero of Chancellorsville.* Amherst, N.H.: Amherst
Press, 1989.

Lamars, William M. *The Edge of Glory: A Biography of General William S. Rosecrans,*
USA. Baton Rouge: Louisiana State Univ. Press, 1999.

Levy, George. *To Die In Chicago: Confederate Prisoners at Camp Douglas, 1862–1865.*
Evanston, Ill.: Evanston, 1994.

Long, E. B., and Barbara Long. *The Civil War Day by Day: An Almanac 1861–1865.*
New York: Da Capo, 1971.

Lucas, Marion Brunson. *Sherman and the Burning of Columbia.* College Station:
Texas A&M Univ. Press, 1976.

Markle, Donald E. *Spies and Spymasters of the Civil War.* New York: Hippocrene,
1994.

Marvel, William. *Andersonville: The Last Depot.* Chapel Hill: Univ. of North Carolina Press, 1994.

———. *Burnside.* Chapel Hill: Univ. of North Carolina Press, 1991.

Marzalek, John F. *Sherman's Other War: The General and the Civil War Press.* Kent,
Ohio: Kent State Univ. Press, 1999.

———. *Sherman: A Soldier's Passion for Order.* New York: Vintage, 1994.

Matthews, Mitford M., ed. *A Dictionary of Americanisms on Historical Principles.*
Chicago: Univ. of Chicago Press, 1951.

McDonough, James Lee. *Chattanooga: A Death Grip on the Confederacy.* Knoxville:
Univ. of Tennessee Press, 1991.

McMurry, Richard M. *Atlanta 1864: Last Chance for the Confederacy.* Lincoln: Univ.
of Nebraska Press, 2000.

McPerson, James M. *Battle Cry of Freedom: The Civil War Era.* New York: Ballantine,
1989.

McWhiney, Grady. *Braxton Bragg and Confederate Defeat.* Vol. 1: *Field Command.*
New York: Columbia Univ. Press, 1969

Miles, Jim. *Fields of Glory. A History and Tour Guide of the Atlanta Campaign.* Nashville, Tenn.: Rutledge Hill, 1989.

———. *Stones River: Bloody Winter In Tennessee.* Knoxville: Univ. of Tennessee
Press, 1980.

Noe, Kenneth W. *Perryville: This Grand Havoc of Battle.* Lexington: Univ. Press of
Kentucky, 2001.

Parks, Joseph H. *Joseph E. Brown of Georgia.* Baton Rouge: Louisiana State Univ.
Press, 1977.

416 Pittenger, William. *The History of the Andrews Railroad Raid in Georgia in 1862.* Scituate, Mass.: Digital Scanning, 2001.

Pula, James S. *The Sigel Regiment: A History of the 26th Wisconsin Volunteer Infantry, 1862–1865.* Campbell, Calif.: Savas, 1998.

Quiner, E. B. *The Military History of Wisconsin: A Record of the Civil and Military Patriotism of the State, in the War for the Union, 1861–1865.* Chicago: 1866.

Ramage, James A. *Rebel Raider: The Life of General John Hunt Morgan.* Lexington: Univ. Press of Kentucky, 1986.

Reid, Richard J. *They Met at Perryville.* Fordsville, Ky.: Sandefur, 1987.

Sewell, Richard H. *A House Divided: Sectionalism and the Civil War, 1848–1865.* Baltimore. Md.: John Hopkins Univ. Press, 1988.

Sherman, William Tecumseh. *Memoirs of General W. T. Sherman.* New York: Library of America, 1990.

Simpson, Brooks D., and Jean V. Berlin, eds. *Sherman's Civil War: Selected Correspondence of William T. Sherman.* Chapel Hill: Univ. of North Carolina Press, 1999.

Sinclair, Donald A. *The Civil War and New Jersey.* New Brunswick: Friends of the Rutgers Univ. Library for New Jersey, Civil War Centennial Commission, 1961–1965.

Stampp, Kenneth M. *The Era of Reconstruction.* New York: Vintage, 1965.

Trask, Kerry A. *Fire Within: A Civil War Narrative from Wisconsin.* Kent, Ohio: Kent State Univ. Press, 1995.

Van Horne, Thomas B. *The Army of the Cumberland.* 1875; rpt. New York: Smithmark, 1996.

Warner, Ezra J. *Generals in Blue: Lives of the Union Commanders.* Baton Rouge: Louisiana State Univ. Press, 1964.

————. *Generals in Gray: The Lives of the Confederate Commanders.* Baton Rouge: Louisiana State Univ. Press, 1959.

Wyeth, John Allen. *That Devil Forrest: The Life of General Nathan Bedford Forrest.* Baton Rouge: Louisiana State Univ. Press, 1989.

Yandoh, Judith. "Mutiny at the Front." *Civil War Times Illustrated* 34, no. 2 (May–June 1995): 32–36, 68–70.

ADDITIONAL MISCELLANEOUS SOURCES

The Filson Club Historical Society. Louisville, Kentucky.

George Eastman House. International Museum of Photography and Film. Rochester, New York.

Lawrence University Library. Appleton, Wisconsin

Schumacher Library. Olbrich Botanical Gardens, Madison, Wisconsin.

United States Department of Interior, National Park Service. Andersonville Historic Site, Andersonville, Georgia.

United States Department of Interior, National Park Service. Chickamauga and Chattanooga, National Military Park, Fort Oglethorpe, Georgia.

Veterans Administration. State of Wisconsin. Outagamie County, Veterans' Service Office, Administration Bldg. Appleton, Wisconsin.

Wood County Register of Deeds. State of Wisconsin Department of Health—Bureau of Vital Statistics.

Index

Abbott, Alfred, 102, 192
Ackworth Station, 259
Alexandria (Va.), 373
Allatoona Pass, 248, 259, 290
Amandon, Leland, 298
Andersonville (Ga.), 192
Appleton (Wis.), 285–86
Appomattox (Va.), 359, 363, 367
Argyle Island, 312
Army of the Cumberland, 62, 199, 206, 209, 211–12; consolidated into Army of Georgia, 232
Army of Georgia, 232
Army of the Ohio, 27, 62, 206
Army of the Potomac, 16, 197–98, 368, 374
Army of the Tennessee, 198, 206, 245, 272
Atlanta, Battle of, 272
Atlanta, bombardment of, 271–72, 274, 282–83
Atlanta campaign, 232–83, 239
Atlanta (Ga.), 278, 283, 291; destruction of, 290
Averysboro, Battle of, 352–53

Baird, Absalom, 137–38; at Chickamauga, 177, 183, 187; at Dug Gap, 162; replaces General Rousseau, 139
Baker, Richard, 33, 45; death of, 52
Baker, Walton, 33, 66, 70
Bald Hill, 245–46
Ballard, Allen W., 71

Banks, Nathaniel, 225
Bardstown (Ky.), 31
Barnwell (S.C.), 338
Bartlett, Albert C., 250
Beauregard, Pierre G. T., 344
Belle Isle (Va.), 192, 367, 370
Bennett, James H.: desertion at Perryville, 48, 151
Bentonville, Battle of, 353–57
Big Shanty, 261, 263, 290
Bissel, Julius P., 200–201, 204
Blackstock (S.C.), 344
Blackville (S.C.), 339
Blair, Francis Preston, 271
Blakeley, Archibald, 215, 220
Blaser, David, 131, 133
bloodhounds, 299, 304, 329
Borcherdt, Fred, 223; adjutant of 21st Wisconsin, 200; at Averysboro, 353; character of, 11, 110; detailed to brigade headquarters, 152; mentioned, 39, 159, 200, 227, 279–80, 296–97; promoted to first lieutenant, 110
bounties, 10, 214
Bowen, Edwin H., 74
Bowling Green (Ky.), 61, 64, 71, 204
Bradish, Albert, 223, 217, 260, 279–82
Bragg, Braxton: appointed general-in-chief, 213; at Chickamauga, 165–66, 171, 179, 185–86; besieges Chattanooga, 194; character, 195–96; dismissal, 212;

Bragg, Braxton (*cont.*)
at Dug Gap, 162; in Kentucky, 16–17, 23–24, 41; at Lookout Mountain and Missionary Ridge, 206–8, 211–12; mentioned, 135, 137, 164–65, 191; at Perryville, 49; retreat from Murfreesboro, 104; retreat from Perryville, 53, 55; retreats from Chattanooga, 162; retreats to Chattanooga, 145; at Stone's River, 82, 83, 93, 96; at Tullahoma, 139–40, 144
Brannan, John M., 177, 182
Bridgeport (Ala.), 158, 194–95, 197
Brown, Joseph Emerson, 298
Brown's Ferry (Tenn.), 206
Buboltz, John, *222;* as cook, 77, 200, 216, 217–18, 227–28, 283, 292–94, 295, 296–97; as forager, 301, 305, 358, illness, 234, 248; mentioned, 366; on retreat from Chickamauga, 189; returns from hospital, 358; taken prisoner on Jefferson Pike, 78–80; as wine merchant, 218–20; witness to Sergeant Dey's desertion, 51–52
Buchholz, Charles, *222,* 179, 192, 240
Buck, Charles, *222;* at Chickamauga, 180, 191; at Pumpkin Vine Creek, 256–57; at Stone's River, 78, 81, 92; witness to Sergeant Dey's desertion, 51–52
Buell, Don Carlos: in Kentucky, 16, 24, 27, 54; relieved of command, 62
Buell, George P., 310, 313
Bull Run, Battle of, 372
Burnside, Ambrose, 124, 197
Butler, Matthew C., 326, 346–47
Buzzard Roost. *See* Rocky-face Ridge
Buzzard Roost Gap, 225, 236–37, 240

Camp Andrew Johnson, 72
Camp Bragg, 4, 8–13
Camp Creek, 241
Camp Douglas, 112
Captain Buckskin. *See* Dilger, Hubert
Carlin, William Passmore: as brigade commander, 233; at Bentonville, 354; as division commander, 291; mentioned, 300, 347; at Resaca 242, 254–55, 256, 260
Carolin, Samuel J., *61,* 40; death, 61–62
Case, Henry, 352
Cassville (Ga.), 247, 265, 286
Cave City, 282
Chancellorsville, Battle of, 260
Chaplin Hills, Battle of. *See* Perryville, Battle of

Charleston Courier and Mercury, 263, 265, 327, 342, 344
Charleston (S.C.), 326, 344
Chattanooga (Tenn.), 140, 158, 162, 190, 191; siege of, 193–206; as supply depot, 230
Chattanooga road: strategic importance of, 165–67, 171–72
Cheatham, Benjamin Franklin, 326, 356
Chickamauga, Battle of, 168–87
Cincinnati: defense of, 16–17
Clark, Theodore: appointed fifth sergeant, 11; death, 103; goes on picket for Otto, 38–39; illness, 85, 102; mentioned, 54; at Perryville, 50; resigns as orderly, 65
Clinton, Orson P.: 111, 174, 220, 252; papers of, xiv
Coddington, Orville, 321
Columbia (S.C.), 326, 340, 342, 344; burning of, 341
Company C (21st Wisconsin), 200–201, 202, 230
Company D (21st Wisconsin): casualties at Chattanooga, 196–97, 210, 212; casualties at Chickamauga, 180, 181, 191–92; casualties at Perryville, 52; casualties at Resaca, 243; deserters from, 48, 51–52, 151, 155–56, 193–94; disabled soldiers at Bowling Green, 71; disabled soldiers at Camp Andrew Johnson, 74; disabled soldiers at Murfreesboro, 102–3; disabled soldiers at Savannah, 321; disabled soldiers on Tullahoma campaign, 139; officers, 11; Oneida Indians in, 214; original recruits at muster-out, 377; Otto in command, 152; promotions, 119; ration savings funds, 202–3; receives recruits, 230; at Pumpkin Vine Creek, 255–59; receives transfers from 1st Wisconsin, 283; receives transfers from 10th Wisconsin, 290; recruitment of, 2–4; soldiers, died in prison, 192; soldiers, taken prisoner at Chickamauga, 192
Company ration savings funds, 66–67, 202–3
consolidation of regiments, 213–14
Copperheads: mentioned, 269, 285, 325; newspapers of, 198, 211, 265, 319–20, 327, 364; and postwar treatment of veterans, 59, 109, 111; in Union army, 45, 151, 262
Corse, John M., 289
Covington (Ga.), 293
Covington (Ky.), 17, 22–24

Cowan Station (Tenn.), 152
Cox, John W., 351
Crab Orchard (Ky.), 54
Cram, Gale, 321
Craven House, 207
Crittenden, Thomas: at Chickamauga, 177;
    at Chattanooga, 207, 209; on Chicka-
    mauga campaign, 158, 162, 165–66; com-
    mands Twenty-first Corps, 62; Cumber-
    land Gap, 27; at Stone's River, 82, 91, 93;
    on Tullahoma campaign, 139–40
Cushman, Daniel B., 71, 103

Dahlgren, John, 313
Dalton (Ga.), 225, 237, 240
Dane, Peter E., 225
Danville (Ky.), 54
Davis, Governeur M., 74
Davis, Jefferson (C.S.A.), 212, 268, 344,
    362, 369–70
Davis, Jefferson C. (U.S.), 206, 248, 253,
    311, 367; at Bentonville, 354; replaces
    Palmer, 272
Democrats, northern. See Copperheads
Demouth, George, 372–73
Dennison (Ohio), 193
Department of the Mississippi, 206
Derby, John, 255
Destroying Brigade, 294–95, 327
Dey, John, 222; as candidate for first
    lieutenant, 6; appointed second
    sergeant, 11; reports sick, 39; desertion at
    Perryville, 50–52, 151; reduced to the
    ranks, 193–94; wounded at Atlanta, 194,
    275; mentioned, 49
Dickinson, Seymour M., 74
Dilger, Hubert, 260, 271–72
Dodge, Grenville Mellon, 271
Draper, Nelson, 222, 71, 78–79, 139, 242, 244
Dug Gap, 162
"Dutch squad," xiii, 5, 8, 33, 58

Eatonton (Ga.), 295
Edgefield (Tenn.), 72
Edwards, Hiram K., 190, 203, 260, 279–82
88th Indiana Infantry, 233
86th Illinois Infantry, 270
Eleventh Corps, 206, 260; consolidated
    into Twentieth Corps, 212
Emancipation Proclamation, 34, 88
Endone, Cornelius, 282
Engineer Corps, 313

Evarts, Alverson B., 151
Extine, Frank, 240, 350
Ezra Church, Battle of, 273

Fargo, William A., 203, 281
"Fatal order," at Chickamauga, 183
Fay, Charles, 11, 33
Fayetteville (N.C.), 351–52
Featherston, Winfield Scott, 270
Fenno, Miles, 222, 65, 248
Ferguson, George (Bill), 350
Fernandez, Sam H., 223
Fifteenth Corps: in Atlanta campaign,
    237, 246, 249, 271, 272, 278; at Benton-
    ville, 354, 357; at Chattanooga, 206; in
    Carolinas campaign, 326, 340–41, 346,
    348, 352; in Savannah campaign, 290,
    312, 313, 315, 316. See also Logan, John A.;
    McPherson, James Birdseye; Dodge,
    Grenville Mellen
15th Kentucky Infantry, 233
58th Indiana Infantry, 313 See also Buell,
    George P.
Fink, Henry, 276–77
Firebugs. See Destroying Brigade
1st Wisconsin Infantry: at Chickamauga,
    168; disbanded, 283; at Dug Gap, 162;
    mentioned 26, 35–36, 71, 129, 372; at
    Perryville, 46–47, 48; at Pumpkin Vine
    Creek, 255–56
1st Wisconsin Cavalry, 151
Fish, Walker: discharged, 74; humorous
    remarks of, 20, 21, 38, 42, 74; mentioned,
    58; as provision guard, 55
Fitch, Michael, 9; adjutant of 21st
    Wisconsin, 8; at Atlanta, 274–75; at
    Bentonville, 353, 354, 356; Civil War
    memoir of, xiv; disciplined by Colonel
    Sweet, 32–33; as drill instructor, 72; at
    Jefferson Pike, 79; on Liberty Pike, 121;
    on Lookout Mountain, 215, 218;
    mentioned, 227–28, 280–82, 370;
    promoted to major, 112; at Pumpkin
    Vine Creek, 257–58; in Savannah
    campaign, 309, 316, 320
Forrest, Nathan Bedford, 149–50
Fort McAllister, 313
44th Georgia Infantry, 270
42d Indiana Infantry, 233, 255, 262, 270
Fourteenth Corps: at Allatoona Pass, 249;
    at Atlanta, 271, 272, 278; at Buzzard
    Roost Gap, 225; in Carolinas campaign,

Fourteenth Corps (*cont.*)
326, 346, 348, 352, 359; at Chickamauga, 177, 187; at Chattanooga, 207, 209, 212; in Chickamauga campaign, 158, 165, 171; on march to Washington, 367; mentioned, 62; at Peach Tree Creek, 269; in Savannah campaign, 311–312; at Snake Creek Gap, 237; at Stone's River, 82, 89; in Tullahoma Campaign, 104, 139, 150, 151. *See also* Rosecrans, William S.; Thomas, George H.; Davis, Jefferson C.

Fourth Corps, 212, 236–37, 240, 271, 278. *See also* Granger, Gordon

4th Indiana Battery, 131, 178

Franklin (Tenn.), 120

Fry, Speed Smith, 54

Fuller, Sidney S., *61*, 62, 102

Gallatin (Tenn.), 71

Galpin, Harold, *222*, 82, 377

Garrard, Kenner, 269

Geary, John White, 253

Germans: in Union army, xiii, xvi, 3, 5, 26–27, 48, 173, 245, 260, 355; prejudice against, xiii, xvi, 5, 33; 228, 248, 263. *See also* "Dutch squad"

Gerry, William, 71

Gettysburg, Battle of, 150, 197

Gilbert, Eleanor, 55, 69–70, 166,192, 199

Glasgow (Ky.), 57

Godfrey, Alphonso S., *113*, 112–13, 200

Goldsboro (N.C.), 357–58

Goodrich, John C., 49, 60

Gould, Edward H., 84

Govan, Daniel, 278

Granger, Gordon, 183–84, 187. *See also* Fourth Corps

Grant, Ulysses S.: at Appomattox, 359; at Chattanooga, 206, 209–10; distrusts Army of Cumberland, 211–12; and terms of Johnston's surrender, 362–64; at Vicksburg, 151

Gray, Eli, 321

Greeley, Sylvester, *222*; at Chickamauga, 176, 191; mentioned, 330, 337–38, 377; promoted to sergeant, 119; at Pumpkin Vine Creek, 257; at Savannah, 316; witness to Sergeant Dey's desertion, 51–52

Green, Peter, 241

Greensboro (N.C.), 364

Grunert, Maurice F., *222;* appetite of, 89, 206; at Chickamauga, 169–71;

demoralized, 58; sent to hospital, 231; at Stone's River, 92, 99

Gurnee, Dor A., 74

Halleck, Henry W., 118, 197–99, 363–64, 370–71

Hambright, Henry A., 27, 114–16, 141, 208

Hamilton, Henry C., *9*, 8

Hammond, Michael, 191, 225

Hampton, Wade, 326, 341, 343, 346–47, 352

Hardee, William Joseph, 278, 279, 311, 315; at Averysboro, 353; at Bentonville, 356; at Charleston, 326, 344; evacuates Savannah, 316–17; at Fayetteville, 351

Harding, Alfred H., *223*

Hasz, Herman, 354

Hazen, William Babcock, 313, 341

Herb, Charles: as cook, 77; demoralized, 58; as forager, 77, 107; mentioned, 56; at Perryville, 50; at Stone's River, 92; taken prisoner at Chickamauga, 192; wounded at Chickamauga, 191

Herrick, George, 71, 103

Hesse, Julius, 262

Hilfert, Charles Henry, 257, 275, 279

Hill, Daniel Harvey, 172

Hobart, Harrison, *59;* absent on leave, 42; appoints Otto to drill officers, 67–68; at Bentonville, 353–55; at Chickamauga, 174, 184, 186–87, 239, 192; escapes from Libby Prison, 224–225; on Liberty Pike, 121–22; mentioned, 103, 127, 360, 364; at Peach Tree Creek, 272; at Pumpkin Vine Creek, 255–56, 257–58, 259; at Resaca, 240; in Savannah campaign, 291, 293, 297, 309, 316; on Salem Pike, 114–15; succeeds Sweet, 112; takes command of 21st Wisconsin, 60. *See also* 21st Wisconsin Infantry

Hoke, Robert F., 356

Holden, Joseph, *222*, 119, 255, 284–86, 323, 377

Holmes, Mead Jr.: memoir, xiv

Hood, John Bell, 253; abandons Atlanta, 278–79, 283; at Battle of Atlanta, 272; at Battle of Ezra Church, 273; at Nashville, 317–18; at Peach Tree Creek, 269–71; replaces Johnston, 268; at siege of Atlanta, 273, 277, 278

Hooker, Joseph: in Atlanta campaign, 237, 240, 249, 263, 271; at Chattanooga, 205–6, 209–10, 212; at New Hope Church, 253; resigns, 272. *See also* Twentieth Corps

Hoover's Gap, 142
Hoskins, Miles, *222*, 77, 137, 191; death of, 275
Howard, O. O., 236–37, 240, 271, 278; at Bentonville, 357; in Carolinas campaign, 341; succeeds McPherson, 272. *See also* Fourth Corps
Hubbard, William C., 230, 281
Hutchinson, Robert, 81

Indians (Oneida), 214, 232–33, 241, 243, 256, 282
Invalid Corps, 71, 102, 103, 152, 266

Jackson, Andrew, *222*, 242, 243
Jaeger, Gustavus, 201, 230
Jefferson Pike: skirmish on, 79–81
Jenkins, Henry, 243, 257
Jenkins, James Howard, *118*, 118, 150, 153, 340
Jewett, John, Jr., *2;* agrees to raise company, 2; feud with Otto, 11, 25–26, 34, 39–40, 43, 50, 65–66; political opinions of, 45; illness of, 61, 64, 66, 67; death of, 69; mentioned, 4, 5, 21, 31, 32, 33–34, 38, 62; profession, xiii, 2; recruitment of Company D, 3. *See also* Company D (21st Wisconsin)
Johnson, Andrew, 363, 374
Johnson, Richard W., 165, 253
Johnston, Joseph E.: at Allatoona Pass, 248–49, 259; at Bentonville, 356–57; in Georgia, 232, 236, 264; 246; at Kennesaw Mountain, 261, 263; at Resaca, 240, retreats from Resaca, 247; retreats to Atlanta, 266; reinstated, 344; relieved of command, 268; retreats from Bentonville, 358–59; succeeds Bragg, 212, 225; surrender of, 362–64
Jonesboro (Ga.), 278, 279

Kennesaw Mountain, 259, 261, 263
Kilpatrick, Hugh Judson: in Atlanta campaign, 264–65; in Carolinas campaign, 326, 327, 343, 346, 352, 354, 356; in Savannah campaign, 290, 298
Kingston (Ga.), 246, 247, 286, 290
Kling, Almiran, 192
Know-nothings, 248
Knowles, Henry, 55, 192
Knowles, Remick: desertion at Perryville, 48; malingering of, 233–34, 266; at Pumpkin Vine Creek, 255; at Resaca,

240, 242, 244; sent to hospital, 152; taken prisoner on Jefferson Pike, 80
Knowles, William, 61, 70
Knoxville (Tenn.), 197
Krafft, Henry, 329, 336–37

La Count, Joseph, *74,* 72
Lawrence, Amos, 3, 6, 11, 28, 48, 151
Lee, Robert E., 150, 359, 363
Lee, Stephen D., 278
Lexington (S.C.), 339
Libby Prison, 80, 224–25, 368–69
Lincoln, Abraham, 198, 230, 286, 318, 362; assassination, 360
Logan, John A., 272, 341, 357. *See also* Fifteenth Corps
Logan, Robert, 74
Logan, Thomas, 74
Longstreet, James, 176, 178, 184–85
Lookout Mountain, 158, 161, 194, 201, 205–6, 232; occupation by Union army, 214–20
Lookout Mountain, Battle of, 207–9
Loomis, Cyrus O., 178, 179, 180, 184–86
Loomis's Battery (Battery A, 1st Michigan Light Artillery): at Chickamauga, 178, 179, 180–81, 184–86; at Stone's River, 89, 90. *See also* Loomis, Cyrus O.
Lost Mountain, 261, 263
Louisville (Ga.), 300
Louisville (Ky.), 16, 23–24
Lymer, Charles, *222;* at Chickamauga, 180; as cook, 77, 248, 266; demoralized, 58; mentioned, 32, 39, 44, 70, 234, 275, 323, 377; at Resaca, 242; at Stone's River, 90–91, 92; witness to Sergeant Dey's desertion, 51–52

Manchester (Tenn.), 145
Manchester (Va.), 367–68
Mansur, George, 102–3
Marietta (Ga.), 259, 261, 264–65, 290
Mauff, August, 180, 203
Maxville (Ky.), 44
McCann, Dick, 122–23
McClellan, George B., 285
McCook, D. M.: at Chattanooga, 207, 209; at Chickamauga, 168, 173, 177; on Chickamauga campaign, 158, 162, 165, 167; commands Twentieth Corps, 62; mentioned, 27, 117; at Perryville, 49; at Stone's River, 82; on Tullahoma campaign, 139–140. *See also* Twentieth Corps

McMinnville (Tenn.), 122, 123, 139
McPherson, James Birdseye, 237, 240, 245, 246, 247, 266, 271; death, 272
Mihalotzy, Geza: at Chickamauga, 169; death of, 225–26; mentioned, 41, 58, 204–5; on Salem Pike, 116; at Stone's River, 84. *See also* Twenty-fourth Illinois Infantry
Milledgeville (Ga.), 298
Mill Springs, Battle of, 54
Minty, Robert H. G., 122, 123, 140
Missionary Ridge, 158, 161, 165, 177, 190, 194, 201, 206
Missionary Ridge, Battle of, 209–12
Mitchell, Curtis, 26, 41, 119, 192
Mitchelville (Ky.), 64
Mocassin Point, 201, 205
Moliter, John: 58, 70
Monticello (S.C.), 343
Morgan, Charles H., 157–58, 340, 341–43
Morgan, John Hunt: in East Tennessee, 123–28; at Glasgow, 57; near Bowling Green, 64, 70; on Liberty Pike, 121–23.
mounted infantry, 117, 140
Murfreesboro (Tenn.), 103–4, 134
Murfreesboro, Battle of. *See* Stone's River, Battle of
Murphy, William, 192

Nashville (Tenn.), 317
Negley, James Scott: at Chickamauga, 177, 183; at Dug Gap, 162–63; at Stone's River, 96
Negroes: as camp followers, 149, 293, 300, 306, 318; in Confederate service, 232; contrabands, 34; granted land by Sherman, 318–19; sale of, 72, 157, 299; in Union army, 230–31, 319, 321
Nelson, Simeon B., *80*, 80
Newell, Braton, 36, 66, 67, 68–69
New Hope Church, Battle of, 253–54
94th Ohio Infantry, 233
Ninth Corps, 321
Nolansville (Tenn.), 77, 78, 107
Northam, Norman W., 267
Nye, George, 24, 102
Nye, William B., 24, 102

104th Illinois Infantry, 233, 241, 250, 270
Orchard Knob, 209
Orlup, Spencer, *222,* 178, 377
Orr, James: desertion at Perryville, 44, 48; malingering of, 27–8; mentioned, 23, 275; shoots at Otto, 256–57, 259

Osterhaus, Peter, 206, 245–46, 313
Otto, John Henry, *221, 222, 223;* accuracy of account, xiv-xv; appointed orderly sergeant, 66; appointed third sergeant, 11; captures scow, 308–10; at Chickamauga, 174–75, 186–87; in command of Company A, 190; in command of Company C, 200–201; in command of Company D, 152; commissioned as captain, 370; commissioned as first lieutenant, 320; commissioned as second lieutenant, 135; death, xi; desertion from Prussian army, ix, 3; as drill instructor, 67–68, 72, emigration to America, ix, 3; enlistment in Union army, ix-x, 3; family, ix-x; feud with Captain Jewett, 11, 25–26, 34, 39–40, 43, 50, 65; invents remanufactured tobacco, 202; leave of absences, 276, 284–86; on Lookout Mountain, 215–20; at muster out, 377; near drowning, 147–48; obtains ration savings funds, 202–3; placed in command of Companies F and H, 272; postwar life; x-xi; as provision guard, 55; Prussian army career, ix, 1–3; recruits Germans, 2–4; refuses picket duty, 279–82; relieved of command of Company C, 230; resumes command of Company D, 275; at Savannah, 315–16; scavenges boots at Stone's River, 97–98; wounded at Perryville, 46; wounded on retreat from Chickamauga, 190–91. *See also* Company D (21st Wisconsin)
Owen, Albert B., 164
Oxford (Ga.), 294
Oxford (N.C.), 366

Paine, Hosea B., 164
Palmer, John McCauley, 207, 225, 249; resignation, 272
Peach Tree Creek, Battle of, 269–71, 272
Pearse, Richard A., 66, 67, 69
Pearson, Foster, 36, 102
Peebles, David, 61, 74
Perryville, Battle of: "cornfield battle," 46–48; description of battlefield, 53; field hospital at, 49–50; Otto's account of, 45–52; retreat of 21st Wisconsin, 47–48
Pettus, Edmund Winston, 270
Picket Mills, Battle of, 253–54
Pierrelee, August, *222;* at Chattanooga, 196–97; at Chickamauga, 178, demoralized, 58; as forager, 41, 77, 107; indisposi-

tion of, 89–90, 103; promoted to
corporal, 119; wounded, 197, 243
Pine Mountain, 261, 263
Poe, Orlando M., 290
Polk, Leonidas, 263
Pollock, Amazie, 61, 103
Port Royal (S.C.), 315
Priest, William H., 74
Prince, Joel, 151
Pumpkin Vine Creek, 253

Raleigh (N.C.), 359, 365
Randall, Alexander W., 60
Randall, James M., *148*, 148, 157, 163, 340,
   341–43
Rawson, George, *222*, 55, 86, 119, 145, 159,
   164, 243
Rawson, McKendry, 119, 178, 181, 191
Red River campaign, 225
Resaca, Battle of, 240–47
Resaca (Ga.), 225, 237, 240
Reeve, James T., *63;* appointed surgeon of
   21st Wisconsin, 62; mentioned, 152, 277;
   papers of, xiv
Rexford, Jacob, *222*, 152, 248, 249
Rexford, Sanford, 52, 152, 191
Reynolds, Joseph J., 122, 165; at
   Chickamauga, 177, 186
Rheiner, Jacob, 235–36, 258, 303–4
Rhett's Brigade, 352
Richmond (Va.), 365, 367–70
rifles: Austrian, 18, 117; Belgian, 10;
   breechloading, 117, 173, 331; Enfield, 117;
   sharps, 117, 331
Ringgold (Ga.), 233, 234
Ringgold Gap, 212, 234
Robinson, John, 258–59
Rocky-face Ridge, 225, 236–37
Rome (Ga.), 158, 248, 289
Roper, William B., 220
Rose, Philip: bragging of, 17, 21, 22, 29, 41;
   desertion at Perryville, 44, 48
Rosecrans, William Starke: at Chicka-
   mauga, 176, 183; in Chickamauga cam-
   paign, 162, 165–66, inspects Fourteenth
   Corps, 151; mentioned, 120, 133, 141–42,
   151, 193; military successes, 64; at
   Murfreesboro, 103–4, 134; relieved from
   command of Army of Cumberland, 198;
   reorganizes army, 117–18, 197; retreat to
   Chattanooga, 183, 198; service in Department of Missouri, 198–99; at Stone's
   River, 83, 91, 96; succeeds Buell, 62

Rossville Gap, 190, 199, 207, 209, 232
Rosswell (Ga.), 269
Rough and Ready (Ga.), 282
Rousseau, Lovel H., 27, 35–37, 132, 134,
   resignation, 139
Russell, Charles, 226–27

Salisbury (N.C.), 342
Sandersville (Ga.), 299
Sargent, Samuel C., 267
Savannah (Ga.), 311, 312, 315, 317, 318;
   capture of, 318
Schneider, Jacob, 235
Schofield, John McAllister, 237, 240, 249,
   266, 271. *See also* Twenty-third Corps
Schumacher, Frederick, *2;* character of, 10–
   11; commands 21st Wisconsin, 42; death,
   49, 52; mentioned, 4, 8, 40; organizes 21st
   Wisconsin, 1–2; at Perryville, 46, 49;
   presented with horse, 27; Prussian army
   career, 1–2; sense of humor, 12, 18, 21–22
Scott, Egbert J., 119, 192
scurvy, 267–68
Seaman, Mead H., 66, 192
Searles, Charles, 168–69
Selkirk, William A., 130, 132
Seventeenth Corps: in Atlanta campaign,
   237, 246, 249, 271, 272, 278; at Bentonville, 354, 357; in Carolinas campaign,
   326, 341, 346, 348, 352; at Chattanooga,
   206; in Savannah campaign, 290, 312,
   315, 316. *See also* Blair, Francis P.
78th Pennsylvania Infantry, 215, 229
79th Pennsylvania Infantry: at Chickamauga, 168, 185; at Dug Gap, 162; in
   East Tennessee, 124, 130; mentioned, 26,
   35–36, 71, 105; at Perryville, 46–47, 48; at
   Stone's River, 90
Seward, William Henry, 360
Shelbyville (Tenn.), 104, 139–40
Sheridan, Philip, 134–35, 170, 183, 185–86
Sherman, William T.: in Atlanta campaign, 247, 248, 259, 263–69, 272, 273–74,
   277; at Bentonville, 357, 358–59; at
   Buzzard Roost Gap, 236–37; in
   Carolinas campaign, 326, 327, 328, 341,
   343, 358, 360; at Chattanooga, 206, 209–
   10; grants land to Negroes, 318–19; at
   Kennesaw Mountain, 264; letters of, 213,
   230–31, 318; mentioned, 366; Meridian
   raid, 225; refuses to salute Halleck, 370–
   71; refuses to shake Stanton's hand, 375;
   in Savannah campaign, 289, 290–92, 293,

Sherman, William T. (*cont.*)
298, 313, 315, 318, 319; sends citizens out
of Atlanta, 283; and terms of Johnston's
surrender, 362–64; ties rebel civilians to
locomotives, 265; at Vicksburg, 151
Sherwood, Andrew T., 74
Shockley, John, 181, 191
Sigel's Regiment (26th Wisconsin
Infantry), 3
Simpson, Thomas (Henry), 61, 66, 71, 74
Sixteenth Corps, 271, 272, 278, 346, 348
Slocum, Henry Warner, 272, 277, 278,
316–17, 357
Smith, Dorset, 48, 144, 152
Smithfield (N.C.), 358
Smith, Kirby: joins with Bragg, 27
Smith, William, 74
Smyrna (Ky.), 72
Smyrna Camp Grounds, 265, 290
Snake Creek Gap, 237, 240
Spaulding, Henry, 102
spies, Confederate, 120, 134–35, 137
Stanton, Edwin M., 198, 213, 363, 375
Starkweather, John C.: at Chickamauga,
168–69, 172–73, 175–76, 181–82, 184–85;
commander of Twenty-eighth Brigade,
26; death of aide de camp at Chicka-
mauga, 168–69; death of aide de camp
at Dug Gap, 163; at Dug Gap, 163–64;
in East Tennessee, 122–30; on Manches-
ter Pike, 137–38; at Perryville, 45, 48, 49;
resignation, 233; on retreat from
Chickamauga, 189–90; at Stone's River,
79, 81, 83, 90, 92–93, 95, 96; on Tulla-
homa campaign, 144–45; wounded, 208
Starkweather, William, 203
Steedman, James Blair, 187, 289
Steffens, August: at Chickamauga, 175;
dismissal, 203–5; enlistment, 205; meets
Otto in Covington, 24–5; mentioned,
41, 56, 57, 77; wounded at Perryville, 75
Stevens, Clement Hoffman, 270
Steven's Gap. *See* Dug Gap
Stevenson (Ala.), 158, 193, 194
Stewart, Alexander P., 253, 278
Stone Mountain (Ga.), 290
Stone's Battery (1st Kentucky Light
Artillery, Battery A), 36, 46, 47,
Stone's River, Battle of, 81–96; night
skirmishes during, 95
Stowe, Frank, 26
Streight, Abel D., 224
Stuart, James E., *223*, 257–58

Sumter, Fort, 373
Sutschutz, John, 255, 298
Sweet, Benjamin J., *7*; appointed
commander of Camp Douglas, 112; at
Camp Bragg, 8; character, 11; disciplines
Adjutant Fitch, 33; illness at Perryville,
42, 45; mentioned, 21, 40; opposes slave-
catchers, 34–35; wounded at Perryville, 49
Sweetser, John W., 94
Sykes, Lewis, *222*, 242, 243

Taylor's Gap. *See* Dug Gap
Tilton (Ga.), 237, 240
10th Wisconsin Infantry, 233, 290
33d Ohio Infantry, 233, 241, 270, 276, 296,
353
Thomas, George H.: at Buzzard Roost
Gap, 236; at Chattanooga, 206–7, 209,
211; at Chickamauga, 165–66, 175, 183–
84, 186, 187; commands Fourteenth
Corps, 62; mentioned, 213, 225; at Mill
Springs, 54; at Nashville, 317; at Peach
Tree Creek, 270; at Resaca, 247; at
Stone's River, 82; succeeds Rosecrans,
198; on Tullahoma campaign, 139, 141–
43. *See also* Fourteenth Corps
Tollman, Anson, 71, 103
Tullahoma (Tenn.), 104, 139
Tunnel Hill, 212, 234
Tupper, John F., 74
Turchin, John B., 186
Turner, Henry: absent from company, 214;
as acting major, 152; in Chickamauga
campaign, 153, 159, 164; demoralized,
109; elected first lieutenant, 6; enlists in
Union army, 3; intercedes for Otto,
65–66; mentioned, 32, 33, 38, 43, 56, 97,
101, 107, 108, 135–36, 145, 193; offers to
promote Otto, 109–10; at Perryville, 49,
50; placed in command of Company D,
272; returns to company, 268; resignation, 322; wounded at Atlanta, 275, 322
Turners, 27, 37, 103
Turney, Benjamin S., 79
Turney, Samuel W., 192
Twelfth Corps, 206; consolidated into
Twentieth Corps, 212
Twentieth Corps: at Atlanta, 271, 272, 277,
290; at Bentonville, 354; in Carolinas
campaign, 326, 346, 347, 348, 352–53; at
Chattanooga, 207, 209; at Chickamauga,
177; on Chickamauga campaign, 158, 162;
consolidated into Fourth Corps, 212; on

march to Washington, 367; mentioned, 62; new organization formed from Eleventh and Twelfth Corps, 212, 237, 249; at Peach Tree Creek, 269–70; in Savannah campaign, 298, 310, 311–12, 316–17, 320; at Stone's River, 76, 82; on Tullahoma Campaign, 104, 139. *See also* McCook, D. M.; Williams, Alpheus S.

Twenty-first Corps: at Chattanooga, 207, 209; at Chickamauga, 177; on Chickamauga campaign, 158, 162; consolidated into Fourth Corps, 212; mentioned, 62; at Stone's River, 81, 82, 89, 91, 93; on Tullahoma Campaign, 104, 139. *See also* Crittenden, Thomas

21st Wisconsin Infantry: assigned to First Brigade, First Division, 232, 233; assigned to Twenty-eighth Brigade, 26; at Atlanta, 274–75; at Bentonville, 353–57; casualties at Chickamauga, 192; casualties at Ezra Church, 273; casualties at Hoover's Gap, 144; casualties at Missionary Ridge, 212; casualties at Perryville, 52; casualties at Resaca, 243; at Chickamauga, 168–69, 185, 186–87; at Dug Gap, 162–63; election of first lieutenant, 5–6; first battle of, 42–52; first to enter Raleigh, 359; hides runaway slaves, 35–38; on Lookout Mountain, 214–20; mustering in, 10; officers, 8; outfitting, 10, 18; at Peach Tree Creek, 270–71; promotions, 109–10, 112, 118–19; at Resaca, 241–47; receives transfers from 10th Wisconsin, 290; recruitment, xiii, 1–4

Twenty-eighth Brigade, 26

24th Illinois Infantry: band of, 37, 58, 149; at Chickamauga, 168, 181; death of Colonel Mihalotzi, 225–26; at Dug Gap, 163; in East Tennessee, 124, 130; mentioned, 25, 26, 35–36, 71, 103; at Perryville, 46–47; as provision guards, 56; at Stone's River, 90

26th Wisconsin Infantry, 2

Twenty-third Corps, 237, 240, 249, 271, 278

Tyree Springs (Ky.), 71–72

Vandebogart, Henry, 67, 86, 90, 135–36

Vandebogart, Levant, 71, 139, 266

Van Stratum, Antoine H., 18, 32, 35, 39; illness of, 56, 139

Van Valkenburg, Bartholomew, *223*, 286–89

Veterens' Reserve Corps. *See* Invalid Corps

Vicksburg, capture of, 151, 198

Vredenburg, Edgar, 281

Waite, Lyman C., *222*, 119, 154, 214, 248, 377

Walker, Charles H., *113*; at Bentonville, 354; commands 21st Wisconsin, 190, 192–93, 200, 218, 227–28, 309; mentioned, 112–13, 157, 371

Walker, Ephraim, *222*; at Chattanooga, 196–97; humorous remarks of, 41, 42; illnesses of, 71, 102, 158; mentioned, 33, 44; at Savannah, 321; at Stone's River, 86

Walker, James P., *222*, 33, 44, 119, 144, 179, 232–33, 377

Wall, William, *182*, 131–32, 181–82, 190

Ward, William T., 352

Warner, Charles, 79, 151, 193, 195

Washington (D.C.), 370; grand parade in, 373–75

Watson, William L., 340, 341–43

Weaver, Annie, 130–32

Weinert, Julius, 258

Weisbrod, Rudolph J., *73*, *223*; at Chattanooga, 210; at Chickamauga, 186–87; as drill instructor, 72, mentioned, 203; at Pumpkin Vine Creek, 255; on Salem Pike, 114; at Savannah, 315–16

Western troops: success of, 16; 178

Wheeler, Joseph: in Carolinas, 326, 343; in defense of Savannah, 290, 300; at Stone's River, 82, 193

Wilderness, Battle of, 371

Williams, Alpheus S., 354, 367

Williams, Hamlin B., 11, 25, 46, 47

Willich, August von: character of, 173–74; at Chickamauga, 171–74, 176; at Mill Springs, 54; at Stone's River, 95

Winchester, Alabama, 150

Winnsboro (S.C.), 344

Wood, Thomas J., 183, 341

Wood, William H., *222*; appointed eighth corporal, 11; as candidate for first lieutenant, 6; court-martialed, 156, 229–30; desertion of, 48, 151, 155–56

Woodland, Joseph, 69–70

Woolcott, James A., 103

Zouaves, 355

Zollicoffer, Felix Kirk, 54

425

~

Memoirs of a Dutch Mudsill
was designed and composed by Saul Flanner
in 10.7/14.2 Adobe Caslon on
a Macintosh G4 using PageMaker 7.0;
printed by sheet-fed offset lithography on
50-pound Glatfelter Offset Natural stock, and
Smyth sewn and bound over binder's boards in
Arrestox B cloth by Thomson-Shore, Inc.;
and published by
The Kent State University Press
KENT, OHIO 44242